Unipolar Politics

SOCIAL & BEHAVIORAL SCIENCES   *Political Science*   *International Relations*

37-6521   JZ6005   98-36783 CIP

Unipolar politics: realism and state strategies after the Cold War, ed.
by Ethan B. Kapstein and Michael Mastanduno. Columbia, 1999. 525p bibl
index afp ISBN 0-231-11308-0, $47.50; ISBN 0-231-11309-9 pbk, $18.50

A product of the "Changing Security Environment" project at Harvard University's
John M. Olin Institute for Strategic Studies, this volume presents a dozen original theoretical essays that explain the direction of world politics now that the bipolar structure of the
Cold War has dissipated. The range of approaches is sufficiently broad to provide stimuli
for a variety of interests. Several essays focus on economic issues; one assesses state
behavior under conditions of resource deprivation and scarcity, the political economy of a
"realist's" world, and the role of economics in Japanese national strategy. An intriguing
essay examines how Chinese political elites define their external environment as the basis
of foreign policy. American foreign policy is examined on the basis of threats that are subjected and projected according to some element of balance. A sophisticated path analysis
examines the power and interests of Russia, Germany, France, and Japan. The book is a
valuable research-oriented guide to case studies in areas already covered and theoretical
approaches to other regions. Recommended for upper-division undergraduates, graduate
students, and faculty interested in international relations theory.—*S. R. Silverburg,
Catawba College*

D1262429

Unipolar Politics

Realism and State Strategies After the Cold War

Ethan B. Kapstein and Michael Mastanduno,
Editors

COLUMBIA UNIVERSITY PRESS   NEW YORK

COLUMBIA UNIVERSITY PRESS
Publishers Since 1893
New York, Chichester, West Sussex
Copyright © 1999 Columbia University Press
All rights reserved
Library of Congress Cataloging-in-Publication Data
Unipolar politics : realism and state strategies after the Cold War /
    Ethan B. Kapstein and Michael Mastanduno, editors.
        p.   cm.
    Includes bibliographical references and index.
    ISBN 0-231-11308-0 (cloth). — ISBN 0-231-11309-9 (pbk.)
    1. International relations.   2. World politics—1989–
I. Kapstein, Ethan B.   II. Mastanduno, Michael.
JZ6005.U55   1999
327.1'09'049—dc21   98-36783
                                                      CIP
Casebound editions of Columbia University Press books are printed on permanent
and durable acid-free paper.
Printed in the United States of America
c 10 9 8 7 6 5 4 3 2 1
p 10 9 8 7 6 5 4 3 2 1

Contents

List of Contributors

ETHAN KAPSTEIN is the Stassen Professor of International Peace in the Humphrey Institute of Public Affairs and Department of Political Science at the University of Minnesota.

MICHAEL MASTANDUNO is Professor of Government and Director of the Dickey Center for International Understanding at Dartmouth College.

RANDALL SCHWELLER is Assistant Professor of Political Science at Ohio State University.

JONATHAN KIRSHNER is Associate Professor of Government at Cornell University.

DANIEL DEUDNEY is Associate Professor of Political Science at Johns Hopkins University.

JOHN IKENBERRY is Associate Professor of Political Science at the University of Pennsylvania.

RICHARD SAMUELS is Ford International Professor of Political Science at the Massachusetts Institute of Technology.

ERIC HEGINBOTHAM is a Ph.D. candidate in the Department of Political Science at the Massachusetts Institute of Technology.

NEIL MACFARLANE is the Lester B. Pearson Professor of International Relations at the University of Oxford.

IAIN JOHNSTON is Associate Professor of Government at Harvard University.

JOSEPH GRIECO is Professor of Poltical Science at Duke University.

MICHAEL LORIAUX is Associate Professor of Political Science at Northwestern University.

MARK KRAMER is a Research Associate at the Shelby Cullom Davis Russian Research Center at Harvard University.

Preface

For the past decade, policymakers and scholars who focus on international affairs have found themselves adrift without chart or compass. The end of the Cold War surely meant profound changes in the international system, but what form did the "new world order" take? Were we on the road toward a world of liberal, peace-loving democracies, as Francis Fukuyama proposed in "The End of History?" Or were we facing instead, as Samuel Huntington asked, "The Clash of Civilizations?" Wherever one looked, scholars and policymakers seemed to be presenting conflicting visions of world politics, and in most cases they failed to provide the sort of testable propositions that would help us discover whether or not their assertions were correct.

At the level of foreign policy, authors were also asking about the future direction that countries would take around the world. Would the Western alliance survive the end of the Cold War, or was it doomed to collapse? Would Japan and/or China challenge American leadership, or would they "bandwagon" with the United States? Was the European Union likely to develop a single foreign and defense policy, or would it continue to "free-ride" on Washington? Again, we have faced a barrage of questions and answers without a filter to help us separate out the serious ideas from those that were frivolous.

The authors of this volume came together to bring some analytical clarity to the increasingly contested realm of world politics. Specifically, we wanted to know whether the dominant research program in international relations, realism, could help us to understand both changes in the systemic environment and in the grand strategies of nation-states. Overall, our answer is "yes."

At the systemic level, we took the concept of polarity seriously, and focused on what the world was like now that one country, the United States, dominated other states in economic, security, and even cultural terms. What was the meaning of international politics in a unipolar system, and how stable was that order? Not surprisingly, most authors feel that unipolarity is fundamentally an unstable system, and that the United States should expect an array of challenges. Some of these would naturally come from other emerging powers, while others, and perhaps the most significant among them, would come from inside the American polity itself, blocking Washington's leadership activities.

This book was written in the context of the *Changing Security Environment* project at Harvard University's John M. Olin Institute for Strategic Studies. We would like to express our gratitude to Professor Samuel Huntington, director of the Olin Institute, not only for his support of this work, but more broadly for his unwavering commitment to academic research in the field of national security. More than any other individual, Sam has animated contemporary security studies, and all of us who seek to pursue scholarship in that area owe him a considerable debt.

We also wish to thank Ms. Inga Peterson of the Olin Institute for her administrative assistance, and Mr. Keith Vargo of the Stassen Center at the Humphrey Institute for Public Affairs, University of Minnesota, for turning twelve different word processing programs into a book! Finally, we want to express our appreciation to each of our authors for their hard work, as well as to Ms. Kate Wittenberg, editor-in-chief of Columbia University Press, who supported this project from its early stages, and whose anonymous referees provided us with a superb set of constructive comments on an earlier draft.

Ethan B. Kapstein
Michael Mastanduno
February 23, 1998

Unipolar Politics

1   Realism and State Strategies
After the Cold War

Michael Mastanduno and Ethan B. Kapstein

Since 1989, the world's great powers have been struggling to chart a course through the changed political landscape. That landscape is shaped by two prominent features. On the one hand, the United States dominates the terrain as the only superpower, in possession of superior capabilities and able to advance its particular interests across a wide range of political, military, and economic issues. On the other hand, a new set of challenges and challengers has forced scholars and policymakers in every country to raise uncomfortable questions about the national interest and the direction of international policy. The emergence of China as a great Asian power, for example, must be of concern to its neighbors, just as an erratic Russia remains a global worry. Since no foreign government can rely on Washington to respond to every crisis, and since the United States will not be the world's leader forever, states must retain some independent capacity for action. There will likely be any number of regional issues in which the United States will choose not to exercise its power, and in some cases a group of countries might even seek to balance against the United States. The end of the Cold War has brought with it the emergence of new strategic dilemmas for nation-states; governments have no choice but to calculate their national interests in this international environment and muster the resources needed to advance them.

This volume was written as an initial effort to understand how states are actually navigating the end of the Cold War. In that sense its purpose is largely empirical: to analyze and explain the "grand strategies" of important actors in the contemporary international system. We seek to answer such questions as: What are the likely patterns of conflict and cooperation in relations among the major nation-states? How have these major powers— the United States, Russia, Japan, Germany, China, France—defined and pursued their national interests in the absence of the overwhelming yet somehow reassuring constraint of the Cold War? And how are smaller powers—especially those of central and eastern Europe, which have so often been in the crucible of world politics—responding? The book addresses these questions through chapters that focus both on the contemporary international system and on case studies of particular nation-states.

The second purpose of this book is theoretical: to see whether we can make any general statements about the state behavior we have observed, or at least develop arguments for future testing drawn from our current understanding of foreign policymaking. In particular, we explore the question of the extent to which the intellectual construct known as "realism," with its emphasis on international anarchy, insecurity, and the state, helps to illuminate contemporary world politics. We focus on realism not only because it remains the dominant paradigm in the study of international relations, but also because it has come under increasing attack by a battery of scholars.[1] Realism's critics believe that it is particularly ill-equipped to account for international politics in a new world characterized by the improbability of war among great powers, the declining significance of territorial acquisition, the spread of liberal democracy and interdependent market economies, and the growing importance of non-state actors.[2] Still, no alternative paradigm now stands ready to take realism's place.[3]

To date, several volumes have appeared that use the end of the Cold War primarily as a vehicle for engaging in "paradigm wars"—conceptual debates over the relative merits of realist versus other explanatory frameworks.[4] Although we draw on those debates, it is not our purpose to recapitulate them. Rather, our emphasis is on the fit between theoretical propositions drawn from the realist framework and the preliminary empirical evidence offered by the post-Cold War world.[5]

The end of the Cold War, of course, has provided students of international relations with a unique opportunity to engage in the testing and refinement of various theories. It is not often that a global "systemic shock" occurs which affects nearly all the actors on the world stage at the same time.[6] Realist theories rely heavily on the structure of the international system—the distribution of power—as the key factor in accounting for foreign policies and international outcomes. The collapse of the Soviet Union represented a major change in the international structure, and almost every government has had to reconsider if not change its foreign policies as a result. If realism provides a worthwhile explanatory framework, then propositions derived from it should yield insights about state strategies and behavior in light of this shift in the global distribution of power.

The overall assessment of the chapters below is that the much-anticipated death of realism is premature. Realism remains a powerful and valuable explanatory framework, the end of the Cold War notwithstanding. Most of the contributors find some variant of realism helpful in understanding the foreign policy predicaments of particular states. This holds for the advanced states of the capitalist world, as well as for the states of the former communist world. And, it applies in the arena of foreign economic policy as well as in what is usually considered realism's traditional preserve—national security policy.

Randall Schweller, for example, draws on classical realism to advance an argument about positional competition among states under conditions of scarcity. Jonathan Kirshner looks to the tradition of both liberal and mercantilist writings to generate "the political economy of realism," i.e., a set of core realist propositions that may be tested against developments in the post-Cold War world economy. Daniel Deudney and John Ikenberry, in a more critical vein, offer what they term structural liberalism as an alternative to realism to account for peace among major powers after the Cold War. Eric Heginbotham and Richard Samuels propose the idea of "mercantile realism"—a variant of realism that focuses mainly on the role of economic policy in national strategy—to explain Japanese behavior, while Iain Johnston looks to "identity realism," or the way in which elites define or construct the external environment, to explain Chinese behavior. Michael Mastanduno draws on classical and structural realist arguments to develop a "balance-of-threat" explanation of U.S. security strategy after the Cold War. For Neil MacFarlane, Joseph Grieco, and Michael Loriaux, state calculations of power and interest in Russia, Germany, Japan, and France have evolved and in particular historical and geopolitical contexts, shaping "path-dependent" strategies that have been influenced but not overwhelmed by the end of the Cold War. For Mark Kramer, the end of the Cold War has meant a whole new set of strategic dilemmas for governments in central and eastern Europe and efforts to resolve them through the development of alliance relationships with the West. Finally, in his effort to explain post-Cold War outcomes in the international political economy, Ethan Kapstein draws on the arguments of hegemonic stability theory as articulated by realist thinkers such as Robert Gilpin and Stephen Krasner.[7]

Collectively, these chapters remind us that realism is a research program, bound by a core set of shared assumptions, rather than a single theory. Our authors focus primarily on the distribution of power, relative position, and the role of the state and state calculations of power and interest in deriving explanations of foreign policy behavior. They are less concerned with regime type, shared values, international institutions, or interest group politics as independent sources of state strategies and international outcomes.[8] However, several authors do move beyond an exclusive emphasis on material capabilities and take seriously the contribution of nonmaterial factors in shaping foreign policy. Johnston's emphasis on cultural identity, Loriaux's reliance on the emergence of shared norms, and Mastanduno's concern with threat perception and response constitute salient examples. The authors in this volume find the realist framework valuable but also prove willing to broaden or look beyond it, drawing on the insights of other research programs in their efforts to develop better explanations for state behavior.

Existing realist arguments, however, do not all fare equally well. Indeed, the realist theory that receives the least empirical support is currently the most prominent one in the international relations literature—the neorealist balance-of-power theory associated with the work of Kenneth Waltz and his followers.[9] Specifically, we find little evidence of military balancing by the major powers of Europe and Asia against the world's only superpower. The chapters below demonstrate unequivocally that the predictions and behavioral expectations plausibly derived from Waltz's theory do not square, thus far, with the behavior of the major powers after the Cold War.

But this critical questioning of Waltz's version of balance-of-power theory is not tantamount to a rejection of the realist tradition. Neorealism does not define the entire paradigm, even though critics and proponents sometimes treat it that way. The contributors to this volume draw largely on the richness of classical realism, with its focus on the factors shaping foreign policy as opposed to those that determine international outcomes, and most of them have combined classical realism's insights *with* a systemic perspective in an effort to construct effective explanations of state behavior. Indeed, this volume could be viewed as part of the ongoing effort to elaborate an alternative realist vision, one that goes inside the "black box" of state decisionmaking to explore how foreign policy officials conceive of the international environment and their place within it in order to calculate and pursue national interests.[10]

Not surprisingly, no single theory or explanation emerges from this volume as a clear alternative to Waltz's seminal contribution. Instead, the chapters cluster around two realist arguments that emphasize different aspects of the post-Cold War international order. Together, they provide a compelling picture of the forces influencing foreign policymaking today.

The first argument centers on what might be called *unipolar politics*. Neorealist balance-of-power theory typically underemphasizes unipolarity, treating it as an inevitably brief transition to yet another era of multipolar balancing.[11] Yet the chapters demonstrate that a principal foreign policy challenge for each of the states analyzed, including the United States, is to adjust their strategies to the emergence and possible endurance of a unipolar distribution of power. Some states have been determined to "bandwagon" with the United States and rely on American power for their security into the foreseeable future. Others, such as China and Russia, want to hedge their bets; nonetheless, they have been more inclined since 1990 to seek integration into the political and economic institutions of the U.S.-dominated international order rather than try to weaken or undermine that order. What is most striking, in the context of neorealist balance-of-power theory, is the reluctance of other major powers to engage in an individual or collective strategy of balancing against the preponderant power of the United States in an effort to create an alternative international order.

The absence of balancing at the core of the international system does not imply the absence of conflict among major powers. Our second realist argument emphasizes the importance of *positional competition* among states beyond the realm of military security. For realists, positional competition is an enduring consequence of an anarchical international system. Although major powers currently may not be competing militarily, positional conflicts over resources, markets, prestige, and political influence are prevalent and will persist. Several of the chapters analyze the strategies that different states have devised in an effort to improve their standing in international economic competition, influence weaker neighbors, or compete for international respect and prestige.

At first glance, these two arguments offer clashing visions of the contemporary international system. The image depicted by unipolar politics is one of cooperation among the major powers, as others accept the reality of American hegemony, recognize the high costs of challenging that hegemony, and adapt their strategies to make the most of their position in the new structure. This image portrays the United States, for its part, as acting to preserve its dominant position by reassuring and integrating potential challengers.

In contrast, the vision offered by positional competition is of an ongoing struggle for power and international influence that could eventually spill over from the relatively benign forms it is taking at present to the more traditional forms of military and territorial competition among major powers. This is world politics of the bare knuckles variety, in which each state seeks to maintain if not improve its position in the hierarchy.

Yet these images need not be mutually exclusive. Cooperation and competition among major powers may coexist uneasily. As stated at the outset, there is no guarantee that the present dominant position the United States enjoys will last forever. Prudent governments will seek to bandwagon with the United States while still maintaining some independent capacity for action, either through the mustering of internal resources or through the cultivation of regional or global relationships. This is the very tightrope that states must now walk, as they seek to avoid alienating Washington while pursuing their particular interests. Washington, in turn, faces the ongoing problem of pursuing its own interests without triggering the formation of a balancing coalition against it.

Can the major powers cross these tightropes without falling? The analyses contained in this volume suggest that the contemporary order may be stable for the time being, but that the walk will continue to be a delicate one. Russia's leaders, for example, are somehow seeking both accommodation with the West *and* the restoration of Russian hegemony in the former Soviet area. This latter effort, however, could prove threatening to the West or at least contentious in terms of Western interests and values. Similarly, China is striving for deeper integration into the world economy, but at the same time its leaders gain political benefits from depicting the country's security environment as threatening and hostile. Their willingness to act on that image, for example against Taiwan or in the south China Sea, generates regional insecurity and prompts confrontation with the United States. Germany and France are struggling to maintain the prudent cooperation that served them so well during the Cold War, but now without the glue of the external security threat and in the face of significant economic and social pressures at home as the costs of European integration seem to mount.

Japan's leaders have been anxious to preserve the positive aspects of the Cold War status quo, but they face economic stagnation, trading partners who are less willing to accept asymmetrical market arrangements, and a United States whose security guarantee necessarily seems less certain without the Cold War. Finally, the United States, the most important player in the system, is trying to preserve its unipolar position through a global engagement strategy. U.S. officials, however, face a public and Congress that have proven reluctant to support military intervention, skeptical of foreign assistance, and anxious about America's role in the global economy.

The rest of this chapter expands on the themes introduced above. The next section reviews the realist research program and criticisms of neorealism raised in the volume's chapters. The following two sections elaborate the arguments of positional competition and unipolar politics.

The Realist Research Program and Neorealist Theory After the Cold War

Realism contains a set of core assumptions from which a variety of hypotheses and explanations can be generated. As the chapters in this volume demonstrate, there is no single "theory of realism," and realism *per se* cannot be tested, confirmed, or refuted. A recent and serious scholarly attempt to test "realism" as opposed to particular realist theories found that the "scientific study of realism is difficult because it is not often specific enough to be falsifiable."[12] Particular realist theories, however, can and should be constructed specifically enough to be falsifiable.[13]

The following set of assumptions are generally accepted in the chapters below as providing the foundation for the realist research program in international relations. First, the most important actors in international politics are "territorially organized entities"—city-states in antiquity, and nation-states in the contemporary era.[14] Nation-states are not the only actors on the current world scene, but realists assume that more can be understood about world politics by focusing on the behavior of and interaction among nation-states rather than by analyzing the behavior of individuals, classes, transnational firms, or international organizations.

Second, realists assume that state behavior can be explained as the product of rational decisionmaking. As Robert Keohane puts it, for the realist "world politics can be analyzed *as if* states were unitary rational actors, carefully calculating the costs of alternative courses of action and seeking to maximize their expected utility, although doing so under conditions of uncertainty."[15] States act strategically and instrumentally, in an arena in which the "noise level" is high. The problem of incomplete information is compounded because states have incentives to conceal or misrepresent information to gain strategic advantage. Consequently states may miscalculate, but not so frequently that they call into question the rationality assumption.[16]

Third, realists emphasize the close connection between state power and interests. States seek power (defined both as relative material capabilities and relative influence over outcomes) in order to achieve their interests, and they calculate their interests in the context of the international environment they confront. While all states seek power, it is not necessary to assume that states seek to *maximize* power. Not every state needs or wants nuclear weapons, for example. Similarly, although security and survival are the highest priority in terms of state interest, there is no need to assume that states always strive to *maximize* security at the expense of other goals. States pursue an array of interests; the key point for realists is that in defining the so-called national interest, state officials look "outward," and respond to the opportunities and constraints of the international environment.

Fourth, realists believe that relations among states are inherently competitive. While states compete most intensely in the realm of military security, they compete in other realms as well, particularly in economic relations. To say that states "compete" means that states care deeply about their status or power position relative to other states, and that this concern guides state behavior. Competition is a consequence of anarchy, which forces states ultimately to rely on themselves to ensure their survival and autonomy. This does not imply cooperation is impossible, only that states will approach cooperative ventures with a concern for the impact of those ventures on their relative power positions.[17]

Waltz's balance-of-power theory, often labeled neorealism, remains the most prominent realist theory of international relations. As such, it provides the starting point for analysis in most of our chapters. At its core is an argument about international interactions and their outcomes; it is not explicitly a theory of foreign policy, or why states act the way they do. Waltz's approach is systemic and his model is parsimonious. He posits that international systems are anarchic as opposed to hierarchic and that states are functionally similar rather than differentiated. The key independent variable is international structure, or the distribution of capabilities across states.

From this, Waltz derives the hypotheses that (1) states will balance against a preponderant power, (2) balances of power will inevitably form and recur, and (3) bipolar or two-power systems will be less war-prone and more stable than multipolar ones.[18]

Waltz's contribution has been extraordinarily influential, shaping the realist research agenda for almost two decades and inspiring scholarship and debate on an array of fundamental issues including the stability of international systems, the causes of alliances, and the nature of international theory itself. As is the case for any major social science contribution, the theory has also attracted considerable criticism. Some fault the theory for positing an overly narrow conception of international structure, and for being incapable of explaining the all-important problem of international system change.[19] Others point out that Waltz provides little systematic evidence for his central claim of the recurrence of balancing, and relies instead on selected illustrations that tend to confirm his expectations.[20] Paul Schroeder's recent survey of European diplomatic history, for example, casts doubt on the empirical validity of Waltz's claims.[21]

Given the centrality of Waltz's argument, and the obvious temptation of testing it in the setting of a unipolar system, virtually all of the chapters do so against the available evidence compiled since the end of the Cold War. The result is a strong consensus that neorealist balance-of-power theory does not provide an effective explanation either for the behavior of particular states or for their interactions regionally or globally. For example, Johnston's chapter finds no evidence that China is developing forces to balance the United States, or that it is seeking to coordinate its diplomacy with possible U.S. adversaries in the same way that it sought coordination against the Soviet Union during the 1970s and 1980s. Rather than reducing its economic dependence on the United States, China is increasing it, and Chinese behavior in Asia has hardly prompted other states to weaken their security ties to the United States. MacFarlane argues that the most developed parts of Russian cooperation with the West lie in the realm of security, notwithstanding the provocative prospect of NATO expansion. Rather than pursue balancing against the United States, Russia's leaders have emphasized a "strategic partnership" with America in which Russia is *de facto* the subordinate partner. Russia has even sought assistance from the United States in dismantling its nuclear weapons—hardly the stuff of balance-of-power theory.

In their chapter, Heginbotham and Samuels argue that Japan has embarked on a long-term path of downsizing its military forces, even though defense budgets and military capabilities elsewhere in East Asia have been growing rapidly. Faced with the prospect of an increasingly powerful China, Japan seems inclined neither to seek regional allies who will balance against China nor to develop an independent nuclear capability. Instead, it continues to rely heavily on its bilateral security treaty with the United States.

In the context of Europe, Michael Loriaux finds the striking absence of balancing by France against the power of a resurgent and reunified Germany. Mark Kramer shows that, contrary to the expectations and explicit predictions of some neorealists at the end of the Cold War, the states of central Europe and especially Ukraine have foresworn reliance on nuclear weapons, the most potent capabilities available to them to balance Russian power. And, in accounting for German and Japanese regional strategies, Joseph Grieco demonstrates that changes in polarity—the key variable in neorealist theory—do not correlate with changes in state behavior.

Proponents of neorealist balance-of-power theory might counter that Waltz's intention was to explain international outcomes, not the foreign policies of particular states. Waltz, in fact, makes that point explicitly.[22] Yet, if balancing behavior is to be a systemic outcome, at least some, if not all, major powers need to be engaged in it. Or, as Johnston notes, "while *one* single-country test of neorealist propositions is not sufficient to confirm or undermine neorealist claims, neorealists ought to be concerned about the cumulative implications of *many* single-country tests."[23] The post-Cold War evidence to date is fairly clear at both the national and the systemic levels— other states are not balancing the preponderant power of the United States.

Neorealists might respond that it is too soon to tell, and that balancing behavior will emerge eventually. For example, the European Union's effort to create a common currency, the "euro," arguably could be conceived as an attempt to create a balance against U.S. financial hegemony. The revival of bilateral diplomacy between Russia and Japan, or Russia and China, could develop into closer relationships based on a shared anxiety about U.S. preponderance. Leaving aside the fact that the most prominent neorealists have predicted a fairly rapid transition to multipolar balancing, the "too soon to tell" point is a fair one. The evidence from the post-Cold War world can only be preliminary at this stage, and therefore it would be highly imprudent to abandon or discard Waltz's theory.[24] The initial experience of the post-Cold War system, however, does suggest that it is sensible to develop and explore additional hypotheses and propositions. This volume's contributors take up that challenge and in so doing they elaborate two realist images of the contemporary international system that are not centered around military balancing among the great powers.

Positional Competition After the Cold War

The traditional realist image of the international system emphasizes security competition among greater and lesser powers under the ever-present threat of war. States engage in internal and external balancing to ensure survival and protect their autonomy. Wars occur because there is no higher authority to prevent them, and because powerful states at times view the use of force as a viable instrument to gain territory, extend political influence, or establish hegemony over other states in the system.

Relations among the great powers after the Cold War may offer a very different picture. Nuclear weapons and highly destructive conventional ones have made the costs of war among them almost prohibitive. Great powers, even in circumstances of intense conflict such as the Cold War, have sought to avoid direct military confrontation. The acquisition of territory by force is no longer considered a legitimate "right" of great powers, and in any event territorial acquisition is arguably less valuable as advanced economies have become more knowledge- and technology-based than natural-resource-based.[25] Ideological competition among great powers has also waned, notwithstanding the "clash of civilizations" hypothesis.[26] In sum, even if the probability of war has not dropped to zero, the present-day international environment is one in which fundamental threats to state survival and the prospects of "hegemonic war" among great powers appear exceedingly remote.

Is realism still relevant in a world that lacks the proximate threat of a great power military conflict? Contributors to this volume answer in the affirmative by returning to a core realist premise—the persistence of positional competition among states in an anarchic environment. If military competition is de-emphasized, states will compete for power and influence in other realms and over other values.

The clearest depiction of present-day politics as positional competition among great powers is offered by Schweller. He argues that the key concept for understanding international competition is scarcity rather than security. The great game of world politics is a struggle for control over scarce prizes, such as political prestige, technological primacy, or influence over neighboring states. In some international environments "security" may be a scarce commodity, but in others it may not be. Schweller argues that neorealism's overriding emphasis on security as the driving force of state behavior is misleading, and he questions the explanatory power of neorealism when survival is not at stake. He finds that the real struggle among great powers today is in the economic arena, and that differences in national economic growth rates, instead of dampening positional competition, actually exacerbate it.[27]

Heginbotham and Samuels offer a version of this general argument in devising their explanation for Japanese strategy. Their model of mercantile realism expects policymakers to routinely assign primacy to economic and technological power in calculations of state security. They expect state officials over the long-term to pursue economic primacy even in the absence of military security concerns, and in some cases even at the expense of military security. Japan is the paradigmatic case of the mercantile realist state. Heginbotham and Samuels argue that Japanese mercantile strategy has its origins in the international environment of the nineteenth century, and has taken on the attributes of a "strategic culture" which has evolved and continues to inform national strategy in the post-Cold War environment.

The theme of positional competition outside the military realm runs through other chapters as well. Kirshner's realist theory of political economy predicts that multilateral economic cooperation will falter and that the world economy will become increasingly regional. Regionalism allows great powers to take advantage of interdependence while retaining autonomy and exploiting asymmetries in size and power. MacFarlane sees Russia's determination to regain control over the former Soviet Union as driven in part by a need to reestablish a sphere of political influence befitting of great power status. Similarly, Johnston argues that China's regional ambitions reflect a desire for respect and recognition as a great power. Mastanduno argues that America's shifting position in the international security and economic structures led it during the early 1990s to be more sensitive to positional competition in its economic relations with other advanced industrial states.

An emphasis on positional competition broadens the realist research agenda at the level of both foreign-policy analysis and international systemic outcomes. Since states must engage in multiple arenas (political, economic, military) simultaneously, positional competition highlights the complexity of state objectives and the tradeoffs state officials face as they seek to attain them.[28] Japan's leaders confront the problem of retaining a stable security environment after the Cold War (in effect, of dampening positional security competition), so that Japan can once again compete effectively in the economic arena. For the United States, the challenge is to maintain or improve its position in international economic competition without jeopardizing its legitimacy as the world's political and military leader. The tradeoff for Russia is how far to expand its regional influence without compromising its global economic and security strategy of extracting benefits through integration into the U.S.-led economic and security institutions. How states conceive of and manage these and similar tradeoffs across objectives is an important aspect of statecraft and one that has been understudied by realists as well as international relations scholars more generally.

Similarly, the sources or motives underlying state behavior in positional competition are a rich area for exploration. The mercantile realism put forth by Heginbotham and Samuels may provide a good model for Japan's behavior, but an important next step would be to formulate a more general argument that could be tested against other cases. Why do some states fit the mercantile realist profile while others do not? Schweller depicts positional competition as the norm in international relations, but why do different states choose to focus their efforts in one arena of positional competition as opposed to another? Nuclear weapons, for example, bring power and prestige in the international system, yet as Kramer and others have shown, many states within reach of that capability have chosen to forego it.[29]

Questions of why and where states compete are complemented by those of how they compete: which instruments of policy are most useful, and in which arenas? Are sources of power fungible across issue-areas?[30] To take a seemingly nonrealist example, several authors in this volume highlight the importance of international institutions as instruments of statecraft. Loriaux, for example, shows that both Germany and France have manipulated the institutions of the European Union to pursue economic and security goals. Grieco explains the variation in the extent to which Germany and Japan rely on institutions, and Mastanduno points to the use of institutions by the United States to dampen the incentives for other states to balance its preponderant power. As a self-conscious realist, John Mearsheimer has recently argued that international institutions have only a marginal impact on systemic outcomes.[31] If this is so, why then do so many states use institutions as instruments of foreign policy?

At the systemic level, the image of positional competition directs attention to the international economy and to the links between the economic and security systems. Under what circumstances does international economic competition seriously damage multilateral economic cooperation? This is an important question that has taken on new life in recent years. Deudney and Ikenberry see multilateral economic cooperation as institutionalized and robust; positional competition can take place without harming the overall economic system. Most realists tend to be more pessimistic, especially if institutions are malleable and prone to manipulation by states. To the extent that economic cooperation is a function of international security commitments, the future is even more in doubt.[32] As Kirshner argues, the post-Cold War setting offers an ideal environment for testing these and other competing claims.

An important related question is, under what circumstances does economic conflict spill over into international security conflict? Contemporary realists have only begun to address this question systematically, drawing on the rich experience of the 1930s, the pre-World War I environment, and earlier periods in the history of the state system.[33] The answers developed will prove crucial to our understanding of the prospects for great-power peace over the coming decades.

Finally, realists have devoted hardly any attention to whether the concepts familiar in the study of positional competition in the military realm are useful in understanding positional competition in the economic realm. Do states balance economic power, as they do military power? Are there economic security dilemmas, and the technological equivalent of arms races? Heginbotham and Samuels introduce these possibilities; a rich opportunity for realist political economy awaits.

THE POLITICS OF UNIPOLARITY

The structure of the contemporary international system is unipolar.[34] The United States leads its competitors by a wide margin in overall military capabilities and the ability to project its forces globally. Its defense spending is greater than that of all the other great powers combined. It also remains the world's dominant power economically, even if by a lesser margin than during the first two decades of the cold war. Its corporations remain at the cutting edge of nearly every military and consumer technology. The large size of its domestic market, its generous resources endowments, and its "soft" power attributes, such as its ideological and cultural appeal and language, assure that no other power is currently in a position to rival the United States.

The more contentious question is, how much does unipolarity matter? Neorealists and a variety of nonrealists may find common ground in answering "not very much." Neorealists expect unipolarity to give way quickly to multipolarity as other powers move individually and collectively to balance the preponderant power of the United States. For liberals, the distribution of power is far less important than the degree of institutionalization and the domestic identity of states in accounting for foreign policy behavior and international outcomes. Unipolarity is similarly a less salient explanatory factor for those who hold the more pessimistic belief that the future of international relations portends a clash of civilizations or the widespread disintegration of the nation-state.

In contrast, many of the contributors to this volume hold that the distribution of power in general, and unipolarity in particular, matter a great deal. The unipolar distribution of power shapes state behavior, and in ways not anticipated by Waltz's balance-of-power theory. Instead of responding by balancing, states are adjusting in various ways to the reality of a U.S.-centered international system.

Grieco's chapter provides a strong example. He shows that American hegemony has been decisive in shaping Japanese and German preferences for regional institutionalization during the Cold War and after. U.S. power, he argues, set these two major states on highly different trajectories regarding their interest in regionalism. These trajectories are still in evidence today and are being reshaped by U.S. power after the Cold War. America's strong preference for "open regionalism" in East Asia, for example, has done much to discourage Japan from crafting or cooperating in exclusionary political and economic arrangements.

Kramer demonstrates that Poland, Hungary, and the Czech Republic have been so determined to bandwagon with the U.S.-led NATO alliance that they have shaped their foreign and defense policies in pursuit of this priority goal. Each state has renounced an independent nuclear capability, yet has also expressed a willingness to have U.S. nuclear weapons placed on their soil if that would facilitate entry into the alliance.

Even Deudney and Ikenberry's chapter, which self-consciously puts forth a nonrealist argument, tends to concede the importance of the unipolar distribution of power. The authors argue that the absence of serious political or economic conflict among Western states is a function of what they label structural liberalism, or the institutionalization of a system of consensual and reciprocal relations among participating states. Yet they find that this system remains remarkably Washington-centered. American hegemony is so essential to the maintenance of the system that it is built into their definition of its essential features. For example, they argue that the "penetrated" character of U.S. hegemony facilitates cooperative relations by giving other states a say in how policies are developed at the core of the system.

Other examples abound. France, after failing to gain European support for more independent West European defense initiatives, has deepened its participation in the American-led NATO structure.[35] Germany and Japan have crafted long-term security strategies around an American military presence on their soil and in their regions. Russia abandoned its traditional ally, Iraq, and followed the American-led coalition during the Gulf War, and subsequently accepted an arrangement whereby Russian forces served under U.S. command in the implementation of the Bosnian peace accords. In the "near abroad," where Russian foreign policy generally has been assertive, Russian leaders have proceeded cautiously in relations with countries of particular strategic or political interest to the United States, such as the Baltic states.

Unipolarity is shaping the behavior of all the major players in the system, including the United States. Mastanduno's chapter shows that U.S. officials have responded to the new distribution of power by devising strategies to preserve America's dominant position. These include efforts to engage status quo-oriented states, confront revisionist states, and use multilateral institutions to reinforce the perception that America's preponderant power is not being exercised arbitrarily or in a threatening manner. In the concluding chapter, Kapstein argues that outcomes in the international political economy continue to reflect Washington's preferences in the trade and financial issue-areas, and he notes that an increasing number of states are seeking to join existing regimes that still reflect U.S. power and purpose.

A unipolar distribution of power thus offers the prospect of cooperative relations among major powers, as other states, some eagerly and some more grudgingly, recognize the high costs of challenging U.S. hegemony and the potentially considerable benefits of going along in the U.S.-dominated system. But will this unipolar system persist, and for how long? At this stage there can be no definitive answer to that question.

Still, it is possible to sketch the types of challenges that must be addressed by the American state if the unipolar "moment" is to endure. Here we focus on two obvious suspects. The first set of challenges emerges from the stresses and strains associated with American domestic politics. The second set results from strategic choices made by other states—choices that may be influenced by U.S. behavior. The preservation of unipolarity requires U.S. officials to manage these twin challenges simultaneously.

Managing Domestic Constraints

It could be argued that one's vision of contemporary international politics must be directly tied to one's vision of American politics. To be sure, the United States has been affected by international politics. The Japanese attack on Pearl Harbor brought the nation into the Second World War, while Soviet actions in postwar Europe forced the creation of the Marshall Plan and the North Atlantic Treaty Organization. But, to a remarkable degree over the past half-century, U.S. officials have been able to shape international politics to their liking. For example, as Deudney and Ikenberry discuss, the development of free trade and monetary regimes reflected American preferences for a liberal economic order, one in which prosperity, stability, and peace among advanced industrial states formed a virtuous triangle.

Why did the United States pursue an "open" as opposed to "closed" economic policy after World War II? A variety of interest groups were in favor of a return to protectionism, but U.S. officials moved policy in a different direction. The realization of America's dominant economic position, coupled with the need to create an anti-Soviet coalition, created strong incentives within the state and society for a liberal trade policy.[36] Both state and internationalist business elites came to appreciate the role that exports might play in the American economy and in cementing U.S. alliance systems. These internationalist interests prevailed, and over the ensuing decades Washington led the world in the creation of regimes that progressively liberalized trade so that it could serve as an important source of global economic growth. Domestic opposition to free trade was bought off by side-deals with powerful interests (e.g. the international textile agreement), through direct worker compensation, and by a system of administrative remedies that channeled demands for protection away from the political arena.[37] Indeed, the trade regime even endured the shift from an American economy that once generated trade surpluses to one that has had chronic deficits, and has been strengthened by the completion of the transformation of the GATT into the potentially more powerful WTO.

Yet, the past two decades have also witnessed the emergence of new challenges to America's liberal consensus from several different quarters.[38]

During the 1970s, traditional manufacturing industries harmed by international competition (e.g., steel and autos) led the charge in lobbying for trade protection. During the 1980s, there were those who believed that America's liberal trade policy toward Asian developmental states was inappropriate and unfair to American industry, and that the U.S. manufacturing base was being "hollowed out" by mercantile competitors who relied on business-government partnerships. Samuel Huntington, for example, wrote that "America and Japan are engaged in an economic cold war . . . [and] Japan has been doing better than we in that war."[39] During the 1990s, the populist concern has emerged that trade with less developed countries subjects American workers to a different form of unfair competition—that of cheap labor, poor working conditions, and lax environmental standards. The intense U.S. debate over NAFTA, lingering concern over the threat of the WTO to U.S. "sovereignty," and the failure of the Clinton administration to obtain "fast track" trade negotiating authority in 1997 reflect this sentiment.

To date, these challenges have been weathered and a winning coalition in favor of a more explicitly nationalist or protectionist trade policy has not been formed. Over the long term, however, the threat will be kept alive by large merchandise trade deficits and the persistence and, it would appear, worsening of economic inequality in the United States. As the gap between have and have-nots increases, political pressure will continue to be directed outward at an international economy that seems to many to be responsible for perpetuating and exacerbating domestic economic problems.[40]

American officials must withstand or deflect these pressures if they seek to preserve America's dominant global position. If instead they succumb and turn the U.S. economy inward, other governments facing similar pressures will be tempted to do the same. The ensuing economic conflicts would make it difficult for U.S. officials to induce other states to participate in an American-centered system, and could lead to a resurgence of great power economic and geopolitical competition. In their efforts to counter these domestic pressures, U.S. officials have the advantage of being able to mobilize those societal interests, such as multinational corporations, that benefit most from openness and interdependence.[41] But, compared to their Cold War predecessors, they will find it more difficult to invoke external security threats to build political support at home for economic openness and a U.S. leadership role in the liberal world economy.

We should expect sustained domestic pressure on America's strategy of international *political* leadership as well. Robert Tucker has recently observed that the "great issue" of current U.S. foreign policy is "the contradiction between the persisting desire to remain the premier global power and an ever deepening aversion to bear the costs of this position."[42] Although risking American lives in faraway places for the purpose not of meeting an identifiable threat but of maintaining "stability" around the world may make sense to U.S. foreign policy officials, the American public has become increasingly reluctant to bear the economic-political costs of a global engagement strategy after the Cold War. In the face of domestic and congressional pressure, administration officials have struggled to maintain the defense and foreign assistance budgets and to protect funds for the day-to-day operations of overseas U.S. embassies. More ambitious initiatives, such as the equivalent of a "Marshall Plan" for Russia and Eastern Europe, are simply out of the question. On the political side, the lingering of the so-called Vietnam syndrome has combined with a sense of security and relief prompted by the collapse of the Soviet threat to produce an extreme unwillingness on the part of the U.S. public to tolerate even minor casualties in armed conflicts.

One response by American officials to these constraints has been to emphasize economic burden-sharing in foreign policy commitments. The Bush administration set the standard: during the Persian Gulf war, it extracted contributions from other coalition members with a zeal and effectiveness that led some to speculate that America made a net profit on the intervention, and others to characterize U.S. forces as mercenaries.[43] The Clinton administration's 1994 deal on nonproliferation with North Korea obliges Japan and South Korea to pick up a significant part of the cost of providing alternative energy sources to North Korea. Clinton officials have also made clear that they expect European states to bear the burden of Bosnian reconstruction.[44]

A second response has been to emphasize "pragmatism" in military interventions. Foreign policy officials have been most concerned to avoid excessive commitments, minimize costs and casualties, and develop "exit strategies" even at the risk of leaving unfinished business. In Somalia, for example, the Clinton administration moved quickly from a humanitarian mission to a more ambitious nation-building exercise, but abruptly ended its efforts after taking relatively light casualties in a firefight. In Bosnia, the Bush and Clinton administrations delayed direct intervention until 1995. Since intervention, Clinton officials have responded to domestic pressure by setting deadlines for withdrawal, but have extended those deadlines in the face of evidence that the Bosnian situation is far from stabilized.

Thus far, American officials have managed to maintain adequate public support for international leadership after the Cold War. But, as Mastanduno's chapter argues, in the absence of a central strategic threat this domestic challenge is likely to persist. The current intervention in Bosnia can still sour, and future interventions are inevitable if the United States continues to pursue global engagement and take primary responsibility for regional stability. Yet, it is hard to imagine that the domestically acceptable Persian Gulf formula—clear threat, low casualties, quick settlement, ample external support, and financing—can be replicated across a series of regional crises. Domestic political support could quickly evaporate should a regional crisis turn bloody, leading perhaps to an "agonizing reappraisal" of America's extensive post-Cold War international commitments.

GLOBAL CHALLENGES

U.S. officials seeking to preserve their unipolar advantage must look outward as well as inward. Is any serious challenger to U.S. hegemony with the necessary combination of formidable capabilities and global ambitions likely to arise?

There is little evidence to date of a single power or group of powers rising in the near future.[45] Take the case of Japan, widely feared during the 1980s as a pretender to economic and eventual political hegemony. But during most of the 1990s Japan's economy has been unable to rebound from a deep recession, and it has yet to develop the kind of military power needed to defend its own much less other Asian sea (and air) lines of communication. Japan also faces some potentially serious security concerns of its own in East Asia. As Heginbotham and Samuels argue, these have led it to reemphasize the importance of its bilateral alliance with the United States rather than pursue an independent much less a globally ambitious foreign policy. U.S. officials, for their part, have reinforced this direction in Japanese policy by reaffirming and strengthening the bilateral security alliance.

With the Japanese challenge suspended at least for now, the rise of China has loomed especially large. But foreign policy analysts in the United States and abroad may have exaggerated the Chinese "threat" to the international order. China's expected, rapid rise to economic dominance is based on questionable assumptions regarding the current size of its economy and, even more problematic, its ability to retain political stability and domestic cohesion over an extended period of time.[46] China is becoming increasingly dependent on the international system, and especially the United States, for food, fuel, capital, technology, and export markets. To the extent that it continues to pursue a policy aimed above all at economic growth, its foreign policy options will be constrained. China's leaders would act more aggressively in international politics at their peril, for it would threaten the country's continued access to needed economic and technological inputs. U.S. officials have sought to reinforce this point more positively, by downplaying human rights concerns and by promising China economic and political benefits in exchange for what the United States judges to be responsible foreign policy behavior.

What about Russia? In contrast to China, it is quite possible that western analysts have understated its power potential. Russia continues to possess the largest army in Europe (even if its performance is questionable), has a still oversized defense industrial base, and an economy rich in human capital. Russia has significant disputes with the United States and Western Europe over such issues as NATO expansion and the containment of Iraq, leading to domestic pressures for an independent and sometimes conflictual foreign policy. Could Russia reemerge as a global challenger?

Again, the answer for the foreseeable future would appear to be in the negative. As MacFarlane's chapter shows, Russia seems to have accepted a subordinate role globally while it pursues regional hegemony. Russia's requirements for IMF assistance, and for Western capital and technology, have led it to seek compromises with the United States over many issues of mutual concern. During 1996 and 1997, for example, despite all of their public protests, Russia's leaders managed to find a face-saving formula for accepting NATO's eastward expansion. They also settled for a subordinate role under U.S. command in the Bosnian peacekeeping effort, and have tried to walk a delicate line between improving relations with Iraq and cooperating with the U.S.-led effort to repress Iraq.

Finally, one could conceivably view the European Union as a challenger to the American-dominated international system. Its population, technological potential, and gross national product could provide the basis for a strong military and economic power, were it truly united. As noted above, the European monetary union, with its creation of the "euro" as a common currency, could be viewed in part as a continental effort to balance against America's financial hegemony.

But the EU is far from playing the role of a superpower. Most obviously, it continues to lack a unified foreign and defense policy, making it incapable of defending itself, much less projecting power overseas. Europe's most powerful state, Germany, has defined its post-Cold War security in terms of continued dependence on the military power and presence of the United States. Further, years of economic recession are taking their toll, sapping a great deal of public support for the European project. For its part, U.S. policy continues to support European integration, on the condition that it does not compromise the lead role of NATO and the United States in European security affairs.

What about a collective response to American hegemony? Here, too, possibilities exist but near-term prospects are remote. The relationship between China and Japan is constrained by historical resentments and the potential for economic and territorial disputes. Each state seems to rely on the United States to keep the other at bay. Japan and Russia have economic complementarity but long-standing territorial disputes, and both would be wary of alienating the United States. Talk of a Russian-Chinese alliance surfaces from time to time, but most analyses see little possibility given the current configuration of power and interests.

Overall, then, it would seem that for some time the United States will face a world without any significant challenge to its hegemonic position. As Mastanduno's chapter argues, hegemonic challengers could emerge more quickly if U.S. officials fail to manage domestic constraints or succumb to the tendency to exercise foreign policy power arbitrarily or unilaterally. And, one could conceive of an entirely different array of global problems that would test Washington, ranging from the "clash of civilizations" to ozone layer depletion. But presumably such problems would test other countries as much if not more than the United States. For example, the further spread of Islamic fundamentalism would be of particular concern to Western Europe, and a renewed energy crisis would jeopardize European and east Asian economies more than that of the United States. Indeed, a world of "nontraditional" threats might even play to the United States, further increasing its "lead" over potential challengers.

CONCLUSION

The authors contributing to this volume all accept the profound changes that have occurred in the international system, including globalization, democratization, the receding prospect of great power war, and the emergence of the United States as the sole superpower. In light of these changes, many scholars argue that world politics are experiencing a seismic shift, and that paradigms other than realism are needed to understand contemporary international relations. However, the chapters that follow show that the traditional language of politics and the factors of direct relevance to realism—anarchy, the power and interests of states, and positional competition—still provide a powerful conceptual framework for analyzing state behavior.

This is not to dismiss the insights of other perspectives. On the contrary, several authors combine traditional realist arguments with an emphasis on nonmaterial factors such as state identity and threat perception in accounting for state behavior after the Cold War. By doing so, they sacrifice the parsimony of neorealism, but regain the richness of a classical realism that was all but forgotten in a simpler world with its narrow focus on the military capabilities of the superpowers.[47] More important, they open the door to a better understanding of the international political environment in which states are making their strategic choices, for good or for ill.

NOTES

1. See, for example, John A. Vasquez, "The Realist Paradigm and Degenerative versus Progressive Research Programs: An Appraisal of Neotraditional Research on Waltz' Balancing Proposition," *American Political Science Review* 91 (4) (December 1997): 899–912; Charles W. Kegley, Jr., "The Neoidealist Moment in International Studies? Realist Myths and the New International Realities," *International Studies Quarterly* 37 (2) (June 1993): 131–46; Richard Ned Lebow, "The Long Peace, the End of the Cold War, and the Failure of Realism," *International Organization* 48 (Spring 1994): 249–78; and John Lewis Gaddis, "International Relations Theory and the End of the Cold War," in Sean Lynn-Jones and Steven Miller, eds., *The Cold War and After: Prospects for Peace* (Cambridge: MIT Press, 1993): 323–88. For one reaction, see Robert G. Gilpin, "No One Loves a Political Realist," *Security Studies* 5 (1996): 3–28.

2. Ole Holsti argues that realism's "deficiencies are likely to become more rather than less apparent in the post-cold war world." See Holsti, "Theories of International Relations and Foreign Policy: Realism and Its Challengers," in Charles W. Kegley, ed., *Controversies in International Relations Theory: Realism and the Neoliberal Challenge* (New York: St. Martin's, 1995), 35–65, quote at p. 57.

3. Ethan Kapstein, "Is Realism Dead? The Domestic Sources of International Politics," *International Organization* 49 (4) (Fall 1995): 751–74.

4. David Baldwin, ed., *Neorealism and Neoliberalism: The Contemporary Debate* (New York: Columbia University Press, 1993); Kegley, ed., *Controversies in International Relations Theory*; and earlier, Robert O. Keohane, ed., *Neorealism and Its Critics* (New York: Columbia University Press, 1986).

5. Previous efforts to assess the empirical utility of realism include John A. Vas-

quez, *The Power of Power Politics: A Critique* (New Brunswick: Rutgers University Press, 1983), and Frank W. Wayman and Paul F. Diehl, eds., *Reconstructing Realpolitik* (Ann Arbor: University of Michigan Press, 1994). See also Benjamin Frankel, "Restating the Realist Case: An Introduction," *Security Studies* 5 (1996): ix-xx, and the other essays contained in the special issue of that journal devoted to an analysis of realism.

6. We acknowledge our intellectual debt to Peter Katzenstein, ed., *Between Power and Plenty: Foreign Economic Policies of Advanced Industrial States* (Madison: University of Wisconsin Press, 1978), which similarly examined the impact of a systemic shock—the energy crisis of 1973–74—on the foreign policies of various states.

7. Robert Gilpin, *War and Change in World Politics* (Cambridge: Cambridge University Press, 1981), and Stephen D. Krasner, "State Power and the Structure of International Trade," *World Politics* 28 (Fall 1976): 317–47.

8. The clearest exception is the chapter by Deudney and Ikenberry, which focuses on regime type and shared values as primary explanatory factors.

9. Kenneth Waltz, *Theory of International Politics* (Reading, MA: Addison-Wesley, 1979), and, as applied to the post-Cold War era, "The Emerging Structure of International Politics," *International Security* 18 (2) (Fall 1993): 44–79. See also Christopher Layne, "The Unipolar Illusion: Why New Great Powers Will Rise," *International Security* 17 (4) (Spring 1993): 5–49.

10. For example, Jack Snyder, *Myths of Empire: Domestic Politics and International Ambition* (Ithaca: Cornell University Press, 1991). For a review essay of representative works, see Gideon Rose, "Soft Realism: A Review Essay," (unpub., April 7, 1996). A strong argument that neorealism needs to develop theories of foreign policy is Colin Elman, "Horses for Courses: Why *Not* Neorealist Theories of Foreign Policy?" *Security Studies* 6 (1996): 7–53.

11. Layne, "The Unipolar Illusion," and Waltz, "The Emerging Structure of International Politics."

12. Wayman and Diehl, *Reconstructing Realpolitik*, p. 26.

13. As Patrick James reminds us, two theories from within the same research program may compete with each other, and the evidence at some point may lead to one theory surviving while the other is falsified. See James, "Neorealism as a Research Enterprise: Toward Elaborated Structural Realism," *International Political Science Review* 14 (2) (1993): 127. See also Stephen G. Brooks, "Dueling Realisms," *International Organization* 51 (3) (Summer 1997): 445–477, for a useful effort to differentiate among strands of realist theory.

14. Robert O. Keohane, "Theory of World Politics: Structural Realism and Beyond," in Keohane, ed., *Neorealism and Its Critics*, and Gilpin, "Richness of the Tradition," 304–5.

15. Keohane, "Theory of World Politics," 165.

16. John Mearsheimer, "The False Promise of International Institutions," *International Security* 19 (3) (Winter 1994–95): 9.

17. Joseph Grieco, *Cooperation Among Nations: Europe, America, and Non-Tariff Barriers to Trade* (Ithaca: Cornell University Press, 1990).

18. Waltz, *Theory of International Politics*.

19. See Barry Buzan, Charles Jones, and Richard Little, *The Logic of Anarchy: Neorealism to Structural Realism* (New York: Columbia University Press, 1993); Steven Forde, "International Realism and the Science of Politics: Thucydides, Machiavelli, and Neorealism," *International Studies Quarterly* 39 (2) (June 1995): 141–60; Alexander Wendt, "Constructing International Politics," *International Security* 20 (1) (Summer 1995): 71–80; John G. Ruggie, "The False Promise of Realism," *International Security* 20 (1) (Summer 1995): 62–70; and Robert W. Cox, "Social Forces, States, and World Orders: Beyond International Relations Theory," in Keohane, ed., *Neorealism and Its Critics*, 204–54.

20. Keohane, "Theory of World Politics," 172.

21. Paul W. Schroeder, "Historical Reality vs. Neorealist Theory," *International Security* 19 (1) (Summer 1994), 108–148.

22. Waltz, *Theory of International Politics*.

23. Iain Johnston, "Realism(s) and Chinese Security Policy in the Post-Cold War Period," this volume.

24. Of the contributions below, only Schweller's argues explicitly that neorealist theory should be abandoned. Other contributors are more circumspect, and some find at least some empirical support for the theory. Mastanduno, for example, finds Waltz's framework helpful in understanding U.S. intervention and international economic strategies after the Cold War, even though it is less helpful in explaining the broader U.S. security strategy. Nonrealist critics of Waltz, of course, have been more certain that the theory should be discarded.

25. Though, for a contending view, see Peter Lieberman, *Does Conquest Pay? The Exploitation of Occupied Industrial Societies* (Princeton: Princeton University Press, 1996).

26. Samuel P. Huntington, *The Clash of Civilizations and the Remaking of World Order* (New York: Simon and Schuster, 1996).

27. Schweller's argument echoes that of V. I. Lenin, *Imperialism: The Highest Stage of Capitalism*, and Gilpin, *War and Change in World Politics* (Cambridge: Cambridge University Press, 1981).

28. A classic effort is William Domke, Richard Eichenberg, and Catherine Kelleher, "The Illusion of Choice: Defense and Welfare in Advanced Industrial Democracies, 1948–1978," *American Political Science Review* 77 (1) (March 1983): 19–35.

29. See, for example, Mitchell Reiss, *Without the Bomb* (New York: Columbia University Press, 1988).

30. David Baldwin, "Power Analysis and World Politics: New Trends vs. Old Ten-
    dencies," *World Politics* 31 (January 1979): 161–94, and Robert J. Art, "Amer-
    ican Foreign Policy and the Fungibility of Force," *Security Studies* 5 (Summer
    1996): 1–36.
31. Mearsheimer, "The False Promise of International Institutions."
32. Joanne Gowa, *Allies, Adversaries and International Trade* (Princeton: Princeton
    University Press, 1994).
33. See, for example, Dale Copeland, "Economic Interdependence and War," *In-
    ternational Security* 20 (1996): 5–41.
34. See Joseph Nye, *Bound to Lead: The Changing Nature of American Power* (New
    York: Basic Books, 1990); Charles Krauthammer, "The Unipolar Moment,"
    Foreign Affairs 70 (1) (1990–91); and Layne, "The Unipolar Illusion."
35. Robert J. Art, "Why Western Europe Needs the United States and NATO,"
    Political Science Quarterly 111 (1) (Spring 1996): 1–39.
36. See, for example, Robert Gilpin, *U.S. Power and the Multinational Corporation*
    (New York: Basic Books, 1975); Robert Pollard, *Economic Security and the
    Origins of the Cold War, 1945–1950* (New York: Columbia University Press,
    1985; and Melvyn Leffler, *A Preponderance of Power: National Security, the
    Truman Administration, and the Cold War* (Stanford: Stanford University Press,
    1992).
37. I. M. Destler, *American Trade Politics: System Under Stress* (Washington: In-
    stitute for International Economics, 2nd. ed., 1992).
38. Robert Lawrence and Charles Schultze, eds., *American Trade Strategy: Options
    for the 1990s* (Washington, DC: The Brookings Institution, 1990); Jagdish
    Bhagwati and Hugh T. Patrick, *Aggressive Unilateralism: America's 301 Trade
    Policy and the World Trading System* (Ann Arbor: University of Michigan Press,
    1990); Paul Lewis, "Is the U.S. Souring on Free Trade?" *New York Times*, June
    25, 1996, D1.
39. Samuel Huntington, "Economic Power in International Relations," (Princeton
    University: Center for International Studies, Research Program in International
    Security, Monograph Series #1, 1993), 12. See also Huntington, "Why Inter-
    national Primacy Matters," *International Security* 17 (4) (Spring 1993): 68–83.
40. Ethan B. Kapstein, "Workers and the World Economy," *Foreign Affairs* 75 (3)
    (May–June 1996).
41. Helen Milner, *Resisting the Protectionist Temptation* (Princeton: Princeton
    University Press,).
42. Robert W. Tucker, "The Future of a Contradiction," *The National Interest* (43)
    (Spring 1996): 20.
43. U.S. Congress, House, Committee on Ways and Means, *Foreign Contributions
    to the Costs of the Gulf War*, hearings, 102nd Congress, 1st session, July 31,
    1995.

44. Christopher Wren, "The G.I.s Don't Carry a Marshall Plan," *New York Times*, Dec. 17, 1995, 14.
45. For further elaboration of this argument, see the chapter by Kapstein.
46. "How Poor is China?," *The Economist*, October 12, 1996, 35–36.
47. Robert G. Gilpin, "The Richness of the Tradition of Political Realism," *International Organization* 38 (1984): 287–304.

2   Realism and the Present Great Power System: Growth and Positional Conflict Over Scarce Resources

Randall L. Schweller

There is no "theory" of political realism; instead there are many competing and complementary realist theories derived from the same first principles and basic set of assumptions. Though richly diverse in their theoretical and empirical concerns, all self-described realists share a political philosophy or worldview that is profoundly pessimistic about the human condition, moral progress, and the capacity of human reason to create a world of peace and harmony. This pessimism derives from the realist view of international politics as a perpetual struggle among groups for security, prestige, and power and influence, *viz.*, control over territory, scarce resources and the distribution of those resources, the behavior of other groups, and the world economy. In more technical terms, realists see a world of constant positional competition among groups under conditions of scarcity. By positional I mean that what counts is not the players' absolute skills or capabilities but how they perform relative to their opponents. A change in the absolute capability of any actor (holding constant the remaining actors' capabilities) has important consequences not only for that player but also for the other players.[1] By competition I mean that the primary goal of the players is to win or, at a minimum, to avoid relative losses.[2]

Neorealism's assumption that states seek to maximize their security (not power or influence) transforms classical realism from a game of pure positional competition to one of collaboration with mixed motives. This is because, among security-seeking states, there is no inherent competition—no state seeks to win at the others' expense.[3] This is not to suggest that security is never a positional good. The familiar concept of the security dilemma explains how one state's gain in security necessarily makes others less secure. But the security dilemma operates only under very specific conditions: (1) when security is scarce (offense has the advantage over defense), (2) states cannot signal their true intentions (offensive weapons and doctrines are indistinguishable from defensive ones), and (3) there is no true aggressor (otherwise, states are arming to defend themselves against a real threat). In theory and under most real-world conditions, security is a positive-sum value; it can be both commonly desired and commonly shared without diminishing its enjoyment for any individual actor.[4] The same cannot be said for positional goods, such as prestige, status, political influence, leadership, political leverage, or market shares.[5] All states cannot simultaneously enjoy a positive trade balance; and if everyone has status, then no one does. Indeed scarcity confers status.[6] Positional competition is therefore zero-sum, in that a gain (loss) for one player becomes a corresponding loss (gain) for the opponent(s).

Positional conflict is an especially virulent subset of positional competition, in which at least one of the parties, and usually both, seeks the total destruction or subjugation of the other: for example, civil wars and many ethnic and religious conflicts. In these "winner takes all" struggles, bargaining is impossible; there is no cooperative solution. In Waltz's words, "the parties contend not simply over the difficult issue of who shall gain or lose. They struggle instead with the calamitous question: Who shall dominate whom? The answer to that question can satisfy only one of the parties."[7] Likewise, Richard Betts points out that the root issue of all wars is always the same: "Who rules when the fighting stops."[8] This is the essence of positional conflict.

All realists share the conviction that anarchy is a persistent condition that cannot be transcended, and so states will continue to struggle, as they always have, for scarce resources, whether material or social in nature. Seen in this light, political realism supports a set of theories about the competitive state: how it can best advance its national interests (economic, territorial, security, diplomatic, etc.) in a self-help competition against other states. To generate prudent policy prescriptions, realists have been preoccupied with causal theorizing about the timeless "is" and "was" of external conduct; about the primacy of "state necessity" over moral obligation. Where traditional liberalism conceives of politics in terms of ideas, history as progress, universal ethics, and the voice of reason, classical realism views the political process as a succession of phenomena governed by mechanical laws of causation. Nowhere is this scientific, moral relativist conception of history and international relations more apparent than in E. H. Carr's three tenets of realism: (1) the course of history can be understood as a cause-and-effect sequence; (2) theory does not create practice, but practice theory; and (3) politics are not a function of ethics; morality is the product of power.[9] Carr might have added two more realist foundations: (4) humankind's "tribal nature" ineluctably leads to group conflict and competition; and so (5) humankind cannot transcend conflict through the progressive power of reason to discover a science of peace.[10]

This contrast between, on the one hand, realism's cyclical and generally pessimistic view of history and its emphasis on the imperative of *raison d'état* and, on the other, traditional liberalism's conviction that ideas shape history, that history is progress, and that states are relatively free to make ethical and moral choices stems partly from geography: the great Continental realist thinkers experienced constant insecurity and war, while their liberal counterparts in the English-speaking world enjoyed insular security.[11] This has led to the common, but I believe incorrect, view that political realism best explains state behavior when security is scarce, conquest pays, and global economic growth is stagnant or declining; conversely, the liberal paradigm works best under conditions of global economic prosperity and interdependence, which both drive up the costs and reduce the benefits of wars fought for territorial expansion. Thus, James Goldgeier and Michael McFaul assert: "In the core, economic interdependence, political democracy, and nuclear weapons lessen the security dilemma; the major powers have no pressures for expansion. The result is a relationship consistent with a liberal model of international politics."[12]

In this chapter, I argue precisely the opposite: because positional goods are subject to absolute limitations in supply, economic growth and prosperity, far from ameliorating intergroup conflict, tend to exacerbate it.[13] Specifically, growth creates social scarcity either indirectly through congestion and crowding out or directly by decreasing the satisfaction one derives from scarcity itself (e.g., it is more difficult to find status symbols, to stay in front, or to be a snob). These dynamics, in turn, intensify positional competition. Simply put, as societies grow more affluent, everyone must run faster simply to stay in place and to "keep up with the Joneses." The is also true for states in the international system in times of rapid global growth and expansion. Neorealists call this keeping up with the Joneses behavior "the sameness effect," whereby states imitate the successful practices of their rivals or risk falling behind.[14] More generally, realists from Thucydides to Robert Gilpin have viewed uneven rates of economic growth, which continually redistribute power in the system and thereby undermine the international status quo, as a primary cause of interstate conflict and competition.[15]

Given the logic of positional competition under conditions of scarcity and the law of uneven growth of power among states, even status-quo states, those satisfied with the existing international order, and their place in that order, must be concerned about relative gains and losses simply to preserve their current relative-power position and, by extension, their level of security, prestige, and influence in the system. The key point is: even when security is plentiful and there is no aggressor on the horizon, rapid growth will intensify a relative-gains orientation among essentially satisfied states, and so the realist perspective will continue to offer the best explanations of international politics.

THE LIBERAL CHALLENGE

Inasmuch as liberal thought tends to flourish in times of peace and prosperity, however, we should soon see the demise of realism's appeal as the dominant perspective in international politics, particularly as a theory of foreign relations among the developed countries. Leading the anti-realism attack, Richard Ned Lebow bluntly asserts:

> Today, structural realism is largely discredited, and traditional realism is on the defensive. The peaceful end to the Cold War and the ensuing transformation from a world dominated by two superpowers to a more complex and diverse international order stand in sharp contrast to the predictions of most realists. Many scholars find extraordinarily pessimistic realism's insistence that, in conditions of anarchy, states can never create enduring cooperative relations. They believe that it is directly contradicted by the achievements of the European Union and the dense network of political and economic arrangements with North America and the Pacific Rim.[16]

This was also the theme of Charles Kegley's presidential address to the International Studies Association in 1993: "[A]s the Cold War has ended, the emergent conditions in this 'defining moment' transcend the realpolitik that has dominated discussion of international affairs for the past five decades and invite a reconstructed paradigm, perhaps one inspired by the idealist ideas associated with the Wilsonian vision."[17] Kegley advocates reconstructing or abandoning realism because, in contrast with "the conflict-ridden fifty-year system between 1939 and 1989 when lust for power, appetite for imperial expansion, struggle for hegemony, a superpower arms race, and obsession with national security were in strong evidence," the post-Cold War system finds, among other things, "the economic underpinnings of world politics . . . receiving increasing emphasis," which "conforms to Wilson's vision, not to realpolitik."[18]

Realists are far less sanguine about the future of world politics: free of the common Soviet threat, the winning Western alliance will break apart; former friends will become rivals; and concern over relative shifts in power will intensify. Liberal predictions of a harmonious, borderless world,[19] they claim, confuse causes with their consequences. The rise of economic interdependence, international institutions, and democratic values did not cause international cooperation nor did they end the Cold War; they were the effects of strategic bipolarity, nuclear deterrence, and American hegemony in the capitalist alliance. The question remains, however: Is realism still a useful perspective for explaining contemporary world politics?

I believe that it is, but realists must reconsider their theories in the context of the current international climate. This can be done without abandoning realism's core principles, but by recapturing the theory's traditional paradigmatic axioms, which have been sacrificed over the past several decades in a futile endeavor to construct an ultra-parsimonious but still useful theory. The problem of realism's perceived limitations was exacerbated when Waltz and subsequent structural realists jettisoned the theory's traditional concern for power as influence and began focusing solely on international security and stability. This switch made the theory somewhat logically inconsistent and apolitical; in so doing, it needlessly exposed realism to various assaults that could not have been leveled against the theory in its more traditional form. To remedy these theoretical problems and to remain relevant, realism must reemphasize competition for scarce resources and primacy in goods that are inherently positional (e.g., prestige, leadership, or market share). Such competition has been and will remain the driving force of international politics.

The rest of this chapter unfolds as follows: the first section lays out the basic argument that, according to classical realism, positional competition and scarcity rather than security are the root causes of conflict. The second section addresses two questions: Is structural realism still relevant? What is the polarity of the current system? Concluding that the concept of polarity no longer captures the essential nature of today's system, the third section offers stratification and status as an alternative way of conceptualizing the more variegated positional aspects of international structure. The fourth section articulates the relationship between positional goods and social and physical scarcity. The fifth section extends the prior analysis to explain how growth causes positional competition and conflict. Finally, I argue that realism can remain a relevant and useful theory of international relations and foreign policy by returning to its traditional concerns—that is, by emphasizing scarcity and the struggle for primacy as the root causes of ethnic and international conflict, and recognizing that states seek, in addition to security, to enhance their political influence and autonomy.

HOBBES'S THREE CAUSES OF CONFLICT UNDER ANARCHY

For structural (or neo-) realists, anarchy and its consequences are *the* timeless factors defining the study of international relations. Operating in a competitive, self-help realm, states, according to Waltz, "cannot let power, a possibly useful means, become the end they pursue. The goal the system encourages them to seek is security. Increased power may or may not serve that end. . . . The first concern of states is not to maximize power but to maintain their position in the system."[20] Positing security as the highest end of states, Waltz maintains that great powers balance against, rather than bandwagon with, the most likely winner in a competition for leadership: "Nobody wants anyone else to win; none of the great powers wants one of their number to emerge as leader."[21] The compelling impact of external structural forces—beyond the control of individual leaders—"stimulates states to behave in ways that tend toward the creation of balances of power."[22] In addition to the prevalence of balancing over bandwagoning behavior, neorealists claim that structural constraints explain the abovementioned "sameness effect": states either imitate the successful practices of their competitors or they fall by the wayside.[23]

In balancing behavior and the sameness effect, the essential point is that, for neorealists, the competition for leadership is framed in terms of self-preservation, namely, states fear "being dominated or even destroyed by others."[24] As a result, neorealists are relatively silent about other important state goals, such as "tranquility, profit, and power," which Waltz views as secondary interests that can only be safely sought "if survival is assured."[25] Recognizing that survival is indeed, as Waltz claims, the sine qua non for the pursuit of other goals, the question arises: "When survival is assured, what does neorealism explain?"

Likening international politics to a Hobbesian state of nature, structural realists usually explain conflict in tragic terms: even when all states seek nothing more than survival, they may be continually disposed to fighting one another as a result of their craving for security. This security-based interpretation of Hobbes, however, is misleading. True, Hobbes claimed that, "even if a *majority* of men were seeking only security" [by implication, a considerable number still desire power for gain and prestige], they too, being unable to distinguish the "wicked" from the "righteous, would have to use "force and wiles," suspecting all others of aggressive motives. But, for Hobbes, distrust is not the only, or even the primary, reason for conflict:

> All men in the state of nature have a desire and will to hurt, but not preceeding from the same cause, neither equally to be condemned. . . . So that in the nature of man, we find three principal causes of quarrel. First, competition; secondly, diffidence; thirdly, glory. The first maketh men invade for gain; the second, for safety; and the third for reputation.[26]

Similarly, Thucydides explains Athenian imperialism not in terms of security and fear, that is, as a response to anarchy and the security dilemma (which was the motivation for Sparta's initiation of the war), but rather in terms of the natural human desire for profit and glory.[27] Noting this, Steven Forde concludes: "Honor, and profit (i.e., self-interest understood as aggrandizement rather than bare preservation) are necessary to account for [Athenian expansionism]. And these are impulses rooted in human nature, independent of the structural imperatives of international politics."[28]

Of the three human motivations causing conflict, Hobbes claimed that "the most frequent reason why men desire to hurt each other" is not security or glory but rather "that many men at the same time have an appetite to the same thing; which yet very often they can neither enjoy in common, nor yet divide it; whence it follows that the strongest must have it, and who is strongest must be decided by the sword."[29] Likewise, the modern-day father of realism, Hans Morgenthau, viewed struggle and competition among individuals as inevitable, since: "What one wants for himself, the other already possesses or wants, too."[30]

Of course, security may, at times, be a scarce resource, particularly when strong, predatory states use their power to make others feel less secure; and power, when it is not recklessly pursued, tends to promote the goal of self-preservation. But security can be commonly enjoyed; and indeed it is most robust when it is universally shared. Among security-seekers, there is no conflict between individual and aggregate benefits. Everyone is made more secure by installing sturdy locks on their doors. Individual benefits of this type add up—the sum of individual actions taken together is positive. This is precisely what is not true for positional goods. What each of us can attain, all cannot. Most individuals, for example, want to occupy "upper echelon jobs;" but if everyone advances, no one does. The value of a college degree as a means to a superior job declines as more people achieve that level of education. If everyone stands on tiptoe, no one sees better.[31] Likewise, the desire for political power and influence, as Morgenthau suggests, is positional in nature and may be limitless in scope:

> [T]he desire for power is closely related to [selfishness] but is not identical with it. For the typical goals of selfishness, such as food, shelter, security . . . have an objective relation to the vital needs of the individual[.] . . . The desire for power, on the other hand, concerns itself not with the individual's survival but with his position among his fellows once his survival has been secured. Consequently, the selfishness of man has limits; his will to power has none. For while man's vital needs are capable of satisfaction, his lust for power would be satisfied only if the last man became an object of his domination, there being nobody above or beside him, that is, if he became like God.[32]

Driven by a natural, animal-like instinct to acquire power—an animus dominandi—and compelled by his environment to compete for scarce resources, "[m]an cannot hope to be good but must be content with being not too evil."[33]

Neorealists would, no doubt, charge that my claim that security is a positive-sum good overlooks the crucial role of uncertainty and incomplete information in explaining state behavior under anarchy; that I am too confident in the ability of status-quo states to recognize one another's benign intentions. In response, I do not deny that anarchy creates uncertainty, particularly, as Waltz suggests, under multipolarity. For example, Chamberlain and others misperceived Hitler as a "normal" German statesman with legitimate and limited pan-German revisionist goals; Stalin refused to believe that Germany would attack the Soviet Union in 1941; and the Kaiser believed that Germany was being encircled. These well-known cases of misperception, however, all involved a true aggressor state. To disprove the claim that, among status-quo states, security is a positive-sum game and therefore relatively easy to achieve, one has to show examples of wars that resulted from uncertainty when all states sought nothing more than security.

To be sure, uncertainty matters under anarchy, but it is not fatal and does not lead to war in the absence of a true aggressor.[34] Uncertainty may explain why a war unfolded the way it did, or why an aggressor went undeterred or underbalanced, but it alone cannot explain the outbreak of war. And indeed, the empirical record strongly supports this position. As Dan Reiter has recently shown, the powder-keg explanation of war is more myth than reality: he finds "only three examples of preemption among the 67 interstate wars between 1816 and 1980," and in each of these three cases, "non-preemptive motivations for war were also present."[35] In *Man, the State, and War*, Waltz, too, argued that, in a world consisting only of security-seekers, there would be no balancing and military competition: "If all states wanted simply to survive, then none would need to maintain military forces for use in either defensive or offensive action."[36] But even in such a world, and we may have entered one, primacy and the power to influence others still matter; for as long as there is politics, there will be a struggle over who gets what, when, and how.[37] As Samuel Huntington suggests: "If power and primacy did not matter, political scientists would have to look for other work."[38]

In summary, realism has traditionally emphasized scarcity over security as the primary cause of conflict under anarchy. As long as things commonly desired cannot be commonly enjoyed, whether prestige, leadership, status, market shares, investment opportunities, control over others or the environment, states will struggle to maintain and extend their power and influence and international politics will be consistent with the realist perspective. Nicholas Spykman's words, written more than fifty years ago, still ring true: "Strife is one of the basic aspects of life and, as such, an element of all relations between individuals, groups, and states. A world without struggle would be a world in which life had ceased to exist"[39]

IS STRUCTURAL REALISM STILL RELEVANT?

While all this appears to be common sense and substantially sound, many contemporary observers claim that political realism no longer explains great power behavior. The nuclear revolution, the spread of democracy, and the end of the Cold War, among other factors, they claim, have fundamentally changed relations among the developed countries.[40] For Waltzian structural realists, the most ominous development is the emergence of unipolarity. To the faithful, of course, this is but a passing phase: new great powers will quickly emerge because states balance against threatening accumulations of power, regardless of the hegemon's intentions.[41] The recurrent formation of balances of power is crucial to Waltz's theory and, to a lesser extent, to traditional realism. If this is called in question, the theory's predictions will be off the mark, and its prescriptions (e.g., in support of managed nuclear proliferation)[42] may prove disastrous. For structural realists, the question arises as to whether there is a balance of power at the core. If so, how and in what areas are the great powers balancing each other? Is global polarity—the theory's lone causal variable—still a useful concept? If not, can the theory's deductions about polarity's effects on system stability and state behavior be usefully applied to regional subsystems instead?

What Is the Polarity of the System?

At first glance, the problem of determining the polarity of the current international system seems as easy as subtracting one from two: when one of two superpowers collapses, the system goes from bipolarity to unipolarity. Unfortunately, the problem is not that simple. While the United States has gained relative to the former Soviet Union, as has everyone else, it has lost ground since the 1950s vis-à-vis its allies, especially Germany and Japan. America remains the most formidable military power in the world, but its relative strength has declined in other areas, such as monetary reserves, trade, and technology.[43] As a result, the distribution of power is both more unipolar and less concentrated than it was at the height of the Cold War; it is, in the words of Stephen Krasner, "at the same time, both flatter and more single peaked."[44] Moreover, in the absence of a discernible, "unified" security threat, America as a unipolar power may paradoxically exert less global political influence than it did under bipolarity.[45] Indeed, the effects of international structure may be far less important today than in the past, such that unipolarity now coexists with regional multipolarity. To account for these somewhat contradictory trends, Samuel Huntington coined the term "uni-multipolarity" to describe the system's structure, and several security experts have adopted this view.[46]

Alas, there is no orthodoxy regarding the polarity of the current system: descriptions of the system's structure run the gamut, from unipolarity to multi-multipolarity. This is nothing new. In 1975, Joseph Nogee observed: "Some of the terms used to designate the current international structure are: bimodel, bipolar, loose bipolar, very loose bipolar, tight bipolar, bi-multipolar, bipolycentric, complex conglomerate, détente system, diffuse bloc, discontinuity model, hetero-symmetrical bipolarity, multipolar, multihierarchical, multibloc, pentapolar, polycentric, oligopolistic, tripolar, and three tiered multidimensional system within a bipolar setting."[47] Two things are clear: the confusion surrounding the concept of polarity predates the current era and this problem will persist until scholars form a consensus on the question: What distinguishes a pole from other actors in the system?

Some analysts identify polar status with economic capabilities, usually gross national product (GNP).[48] Measured by GNP, the structure of the present system is tripolar, with the United States as the strongest pole and Japan and Germany (or a German-led European Community) as lesser poles.[49] Thus, President Clinton, at the Tokyo summit in July 1993, spoke of "a tripolar world, driven by the Americas, by Europe, and by Asia."[50] Adherents of the tripolar view predict the emergence of regional trading blocs, each headed by one of the Big Three capitalist states. In this vein, the Japanese Foreign Minister Yohei Kono suggested in January 1995 that "[t]here is a growing view that we have entered an era when nations pit their economic interests and those of their region in competition against one another";[51] and Jacques Attali, in his *Lignes d'Horizon*, predicted that the United States will ally with Japan against a European bloc that will eventually include Russia.[52]

Others studies rely exclusively on military power to determine polar status. Members of this school disagree, however, over what capabilities should be counted and precisely how much military power is required to qualify for polar status. John Mearsheimer, for example, claims that a polar power is one that has "a reasonable prospect of defending itself against the leading state in the system by its own efforts."[53] Using this definition, the current system remains bipolar, since Russia, though shorn of two layers of empire, can still reasonably expect to defend itself against an American attack. Indeed, by this definition, China might also qualify as a pole. Others in this school equate polarity in the nuclear age with nuclear power; still others with superpower status, and superpower status with possession of a second-strike capability. Among the former, the international structure is pentapolar (India claims not to possess nuclear weapons); the latter would identify the current system as still bipolar.

Yet another school defines polarity in ideational or attitudinal terms. In *Action and Reaction in World Politics*, for example, Richard Rosecrance emphasized the ideological bases of polarity. This led him to categorize the 1822–1848 period as a bipolar split between liberalism and conservatism; the 1918–1945 system as a bipolar struggle between fascism and democracy (why not tripolar with the inclusion of communism?); and the 1945–1960 period as a tripolar contest among communist, Western, and neutralist forces.[54] If ideational divisions are used to measure polarity, then the current system could be described as either unipolar, bipolar, or multipolar. According to Fukuyama's "end of history" argument, which posits the triumph of liberal-democratic ideology, the world is unipolar.[55] By contrast, those who see, in Kishore Mahbubani's phrase, "the West against the Rest" as the main axis of world politics in the future would characterize the current system as bipolar.[56] While those who share Samuel Huntington's vision of a coming "clash of civilizations" predict a multipolar struggle among Western, Buddhist, Confucian, Japanese, Slavic-Orthodox, Latin American, Hindu, and Islamic cultures.[57]

One possible way to gain a consensus on system structure is to combine the various elements commonly viewed as important bases of power. In fact, those most actively engaged in the measurement of polarity and state power, as opposed to the vast majority who simply proclaim the system's structure, overwhelmingly agree that states should be ranked according to how they score on several dimensions of power capabilities. Studies of this type usually include three general categories of capability measures: population and territory or critical mass, economic strength, and military capabilities.[58] Using this multidimensional measure of polarity, the current international system is unipolar because, while some states possess formidable economic power (Japan and Germany), others, great military power and critical mass (Russia and China), only the United States possesses imposing strength on all three dimensions of power.

The problem with this method of measuring polarity, however, is that it was designed to measure conventional war-fighting capability among states: critical mass is a measure of staying power; the economic indicators are proxy measures for war potential; and the military indicators measure the balance of forces-in-being. In estimating the relative war-fighting capability of nations, it is reasonable to assume, as this method does, that different types of resources are linked in a meaningful way. But if power is conceptualized as political influence, this type of calculus is often misleading, especially

when economic, military, and diplomatic resources are not integrally related—when a state can achieve military power without economic power,
or economic and political power without military power, and so on.

For the sake of argument, however, let us assume that neorealists are
correct in describing the present system as unipolar. Since, by definition,
great power balancing cannot occur in such a system, unipolarity poses a
serious problem for neorealist theory: it eliminates the central dynamic—
recurrent balances of power at the center of international politics—that Waltzian realism purports to explain. In the current unipolar system, the only
states with any hope of pooling their resources to balance the United States
are secondary powers: Britain, France, Germany, Russia, Japan, and China.
But Waltz's theory only covers the great powers, not eligible ones, and so it
has nothing directly to say about secondary states balancing against a pole.
Moreover, contrary to Layne's assertion of prior unipolar moments in history
that drove eligible states to become polar powers, a central point of Waltz's
theory is that the system's polarity has changed only once, moving from
multipolarity to bipolarity after 1945. Worse still for neorealists, there is no
hint of military rivalry between the United States and the other potential
great powers, with the possible exception of China—and even this seems
unlikely given the prevailing view among Chinese strategists that China
"cannot counterbalance US power but should try to improve relations with
it."[59]

Even if, as Layne and Krauthammer claim, unipolarity is only a geopolitical interlude that will soon give way to multipolarity, it is unlikely that
security vis-à-vis the United States will be the driving force behind the predicted structural change. The advent of the nuclear revolution has dramatically increased the costs of war, while economic interdependence has low-
ered the possible gains from territorial conquest. Moreover, the two most
eligible candidates for polar status, Japan and Germany, share America's
liberal democratic values. In contrast with the recent past, today's generation
sees peace rather than war as the natural state of affairs among the developed
countries. The current industrialized powers simply do not feel threatened
by each other. Indeed, the Cold War ended peacefully precisely because the
Soviet Union did not face the same incentives to use force as did past declining states: armed with an overwhelming nuclear deterrent, Gorbachev
could safely relinquish two layers of empire.[60] The collapsing Soviet regime
hardly feared a predatory response from the triumphant rival superpower or
the newly created German hegemon in Europe; instead, it expected huge

amounts of American and German aid. In short, with regard to great power security, the present does not appear to resemble the past.[61] This is not to suggest that great power war is impossible. Indeed, the situation could change dramatically if either Vladimir Zhirinovksky or General Aleksandr Lebed, both nationalists, or Gennadi Zyuganov, a Communist, came to power in Russia. But no matter who is running the country, it is unlikely that Russia will be able to reclaim its superpower status.

If a global view of polarity is no longer useful, one way to salvage structural realism might be to apply it to regional subsystems, in which a group of states interact mainly with one another. Several recent realist works have explicitly adopted this regional perspective: John Mearsheimer employs structural-realist logic to forecast the future of the new multipolar Europe; Aaron Friedberg and Richard Betts work within a more traditional realist framework to generate predictions on the future of Asia under multipolarity.[62] The term "multi-multipolarity," coined by Friedberg,[63] implies that the distribution of capabilities at the regional level is now driving state behavior, particularly with respect to military competition, more than the global balance of power. Why should this be so?

The term "system" means a set of elements so interrelated as to form a whole. At its birth, the modern state system consisted solely of the contiguous cluster of European states, and so its "systemness" could scarcely be questioned. When, in the aftermath of World War I, extra-European great powers emerged, the battle among three universalist ideologies—fascism, communism, and liberal capitalism—connected the globe in such a way that it still made sense to talk of an international system. The end of the Cold War has, at least temporarily, eliminated global military competition, and so security has become more of a regional issue. Only the United States has the capability to engage in balancing behavior on a global scale, but against whom? Fantasies aside, the United States is too weak to impose a Pax Americana on the world and too powerful to return to the womb.[64] The only realistic options available are to assume the role of an offshore balancer à la nineteenth-century Britain or try to become the center of a global system of alliances à la Bismarck's Germany.[65] In either event, the polarity of the present international system will prove to be less important in determining the behavior of states than it was in past systems. Lacking a global military competition, the current system may be described as a chandelier-type structure composed of loosely coupled, regional constellations. In this view, the structure of international politics is now "subsystem dominant," in that the behaviors of regional subsystems determine the properties exhibited by the larger global system of which they are a part.[66]

Yet, this regional formulation, too, suffers from a military, brute-force bias, which appears far less relevant for characterizing relations among today's developed powers than it has in the past. With no aspirant to forceful global domination on the horizon, we seem to have entered a period of world politics when all of the most powerful states are "freed of critical threats to their physical security."[67] As security issues have receded in importance, other issues of great power competition (e.g., for political influence within regions and institutions, technological leadership and global market share of home-based firms) have risen to prominence. The point is that the concept of polarity assumes that a single faultline can be constructed for the purpose of distinguishing one class of states from another; that one and only one important hierarchy exists in the international system. This has never been the case, and it is even less so today. If we relax this assumption, status and prestige in the international system more resemble the highly variegated nature of stratification in most domestic societies. Let us, therefore, consider yet another way to conceptualize the structure of the present global system: as a system of diverse stratification in terms of the types of prestige and status, over which the great powers compete and define their identities.

System Stratification: The Hierarchy of Prestige and Status

Just as individuals in domestic societies are stratified into privileged and underprivileged groups, states in international systems are hierarchically arranged by status or prestige. Stratification in both domestic and international systems can be measured along two dimensions: degree (amount of inequality) and type (measures of inequality or the means of status). In terms of the degree of stratification, the inequality of nations is, in many ways, far greater than it is among individuals in domestic society. As Robert Tucker observes: "In their physical extent, population, natural resources, and geographic position, states are, as it were, born unequal; so much so, indeed, that by comparison the natural inequalities among individuals appear almost marginal."[68] The international system is oligarchical (or hierarchic) precisely because it is an anarchic one, wherein might makes right and differences in power and wealth serve to perpetuate inequality rather than alleviate it.[69] Polarity is one way to capture this inequality in power and status, but there are others. David Strang, for instance, defines status in terms of recognition by members of the Western state society; this formulation yields three statuses: sovereign, dependent, and unrecognized.[70]

As for the types of stratification in domestic and international systems, status has been defined and won by many different means throughout the ages. Sociologists commonly recognize that status in domestic societies is achieved in various ways (e.g., birth, class, commerce, authority, education) and that the criteria of status changes over time and across societies, (e.g., the amount of land owned, the number of cattle owned, the number of slaves owned, occupation, wealth, or the reputation of schools attended). Less appreciated by international relations theorists is that status in the international system also varies across time and space.[71] To gain recognition as top dog, states have engaged in all sorts of competitions: competitive acquisitions of sacred relics in Ancient Greece, competitive palace-building in the eighteenth century, competitive colonialism and railway building in the nineteenth, and competitive space programs in the twentieth.[72]

Military success has always been the chief mark of status and prestige. Thus, following R. G. Hawtrey, Robert Gilpin defines prestige as the reputation for power, that is, other countries' subjective calculation of a state's military strength and its willingness to exercise its power.[73] Prestige is the everyday currency of international relations that decides all diplomatic conflicts short of war. For Gilpin especially, the hierarchy of prestige is a "sticky" social construct that most accurately represents the actual power distribution among the great powers after a hegemonic war, when the system is said to be in equilibrium.[74]

In most historical eras, however, prestige and status have not been derived from military strength alone. In the ancient Chinese multistate system (771– 680 B.C.), for instance, the position of a state in the hierarchy was determined by both its military power and the rank of its ruler: duke, marquis, earl, viscount, or baron.[75] In the Greek city-state system (600–338 B.C.), the preeminent status of Sparta and Athens was partly a result of their acknowledged leadership of the oligarchic and democratic forces. Similarly, the prestige of the Soviet Union and the United States during the Cold War partially derived from their leadership of the two rival ideological camps.

In contrast, status and prestige in Europe from the fourteenth to the sixteenth centuries depended above all on dynastic glory, which was variously measured by the amount of territory and population ruled, the extravagance of royal display, the size of palaces and style of entertainment, and the dynasty's success in arms, in securing order and centralizing power, and, especially, in the marriage stakes. Indeed, the dynastic principle, by conferring status according to the whims of the marriage market, engendered a highly unstable class structure, in which the meekest of states could suddenly attain an exalted status.

From 1559 to 1598, Europe divided along religious lines between Protestants (Calvinists) and Catholics; Geneva and Rome; the reformation and the counter-reformation. In this Manichean world of believers and heretics, the prestige of Spain and Sweden rested not only on their military power (and depended heavily on it) but also on their reputations as the most zealous champions of their respective faiths. To conceive of international hierarchy during these times simply in terms of state power would be to ignore the depth of confessional strife that had virtually halted normal diplomatic discourse and snapped the traditional links among states. In J. H. Elliott's words, "those who fought in the Protestant ranks all subscribed . . . to a common vision of the world. It was a world in which the Christian was engaged in ceaseless struggle against the power of Satan; in which the pope himself— the child of Satan—was the anti-Christ, and his works were the works of idolatry, of darkness and superstition. The forces of darkness wrestled with the forces of light."[76] In this new system of stratification, respect was increasingly accorded not to the dynasty but to the regime, and the conventional stratification along the lines of size and power was supplemented by a new classification in terms of religion.[77]

After the Peace of Westphalia, the concept of sovereign widened beyond that of the ruler to include the state. Rulers no longer simply subordinated the nation to their own power; they attempted to advance the glory of the state, whose greatness they personified. This led to a perpetual competition for glory among sovereigns and their states that manifested itself in a series of diplomatic disputes over status, for example, the precedence to be accorded to ambassadors; frequent armed clashes at sea over the demands of one fleet for a naval salute from another; at least two wars, the Anglo-Dutch War and the War of Jenkin's Ear; and new territorial ambitions, which every ruler in Europe harbored.[78]

In addition to diplomatic and territorial ambitions, status and pride became increasingly associated with a society's culture and civilization, and prestige was conferred accordingly:

France won status as much through her artistic achievements, her great writers and thinkers, and the finery of her court and palaces, as through military conquests. The political system and political philosophers of Britain won her as much prestige as her overseas possessions. The governmental and cultural reforms of Peter the Great and Catherine, as much as their military successes, won Russia's acceptance as a member of the European family. Prussian administrative advances added almost as greatly to her reputation and success as the conquest of territory. Conversely, Spain sank almost as much because of the decline in her cultural achievement as of her military power. Turkey, even though she remained a significant military power, was not a member of European society in the eyes of most contemporaries because she lacked the marks of "civilization."[79]

In the succeeding age of nationalism (1789–1914), the superior status of five powers—Britain, Russia, Austria, Prussia, and later France—was codified in the Treaty of Chaumont of 1814, which established the Concert of Europe. The Concert system was designed as a great power club that exercised tutelage over the rest of Europe, for, it was believed, "only the great powers possessed the resources, the prestige, and the vision to contend with the transcendent concerns of peace and war, of stability and disorder."[80] In this way, "concert diplomacy actively cultivated the conception of the great powers as a unique and special peer group."[81] The concept of prestige had as much to do with the Concert's downfall as with its birth: because the Concert's decisions were voluntary, unanimity rather than majority rule prevailed, and so issues "that entailed a possible challenge to the interests or an affront to the prestige of a great power could not be feasibly discussed or resolved."[82] As a result, many of the most urgent problems did not receive attention or treatment, and the system eventually collapsed.

By the late nineteenth century, possession of colonies became the mark of status and a source of both pride and envy. France's decision to occupy Tunisia in 1881, for instance, was motivated less by the material interests at stake than by a sense of injured national self-esteem and the belief that failure to take action would result in insufferable humiliation. "Europe is watching us, is making up its mind whether we amount to anything or not; a single act of firmness, of will and determination . . . and we shall regain our rightful place in the eyes of other nations; but one more proof of our weakness, and we shall end up by letting ourselves sink to the level of Spain."[83] Similarly, France's determination to force Britain to abandon its unilateral occupation of Egypt, climaxing in the Fashoda crisis of 1898, was driven more by injured self-esteem and prestige considerations than by the "Mediterranean balance."

France was by no means the only power that viewed colonies as a source of prestige. Nations that had grown to power too late to hold a colonial share commensurate with their actual power, such as Germany, Japan, and Italy, "felt deprived and aggrieved, and so sought to make up for lost ground. Germany's call for a place in the sun was a demand for prestige, rather than the territory or resources, derived from colonialism."[84]

From the end of World War I to the end of the Cold War, ideology once again emerged as an important source of international status and prestige. In the period between the world wars, the great powers were divided into three ideological camps: fascism, communism, and liberal democracy. Other faultlines existed depending on one's perspective. States dissatisfied with the Versailles settlement saw a world divided between "haves" and "have-nots"; satisfied countries saw it divided between "peace-loving" and "bandit" nations. However one drew the lines, ideology played an important role in determining how states chose sides, particularly at the outset of the war.

During the Cold War, status was gained in various ways: the United States became the unquestioned leader of the "West," while the Soviets and Chinese competed for leadership of the Communist International. In response, Nehru's India, Tito's Yugoslavia, Sukarno's Indonesia, and Nasser's Egypt achieved status as co-leaders of the nonaligned movement to promote a third path between capitalism and communism. Egypt's stature was further enhanced when Nasser—having successfully defied Britain and France in 1956, and having thwarted Iraq's bid for regional hegemony in 1957— emerged as the leading apostle of Pan-Arabism. Since Nasser, Egypt's status has been defined by its involvement in the Arab-Israeli peace process. In contrast, revolutionary Iran has established its credentials among Muslim fundamentalists throughout the world by asserting Islamic principles and waging war against both Soviet and Western influences. Permanent membership in the United Nations Security Council has also become a source of status and prestige. And, somewhat paradoxically, while the distribution of capabilities in the bipolar system was highly concentrated at the top, the zero-sum nature of the Soviet-American rivalry temporarily elevated the status of many weak states such as Cuba, El Salvador, Nicaragua, Afghanistan, North and South Vietnam, Angola, and Grenada.

Today, many other factors aside from military strength and ideological appeal have become the means of achieving international status and winning respect: political development, technological and scientific achievement, cultural level, environmental responsibility and leadership, market shares of national firms, amount of foreign direct investment, generousness of foreign aid, strength and dominance of the national currency and financial institutions, competitiveness of the global high-tech sector, etc. Status is also being defined more on a regional than a global basis. Germany, Japan, and the United States, for instance, see themselves as "captains" of their respective superblocs, particularly in terms of the regional dominance of their currencies.

Among the present great powers, the rivalry for status is no longer being fought on battlefields for the purpose of establishing a preferred political, religious, or ideological order. These kinds of conflicts have been replaced by a far less dangerous but equally brutal global competition among the developed countries to attract investment, to strengthen the global competitiveness of their national firms and workers in key high-tech sectors,[85] and, most noticeably, to assist (by any means necessary) domestic firms competing for a share of the more than one trillion dollars in infrastructure megaprojects (e.g., power plants, airports, and telecommunications systems) in Asia, Latin America, and the Middle East.[86] While economic might has supplanted military strength as the primary currency of national power and prestige, trade talks have replaced arms control as the most contentious form of diplomacy, and economic espionage—which aims to obtain high-tech secrets with commercial applications—has replaced military spying as the top priority of intelligence services.[87]

Status, however, is by no means limited to economic and technological prowess. The majority of German experts and policymakers, for instance, view their country as a model of international "civility" and responsibility in its dedication to multilateral cooperation and peaceful solutions to international conflicts.[88] Some go so far as to suggest that Germany should be "aiming at a national policy in the international interest" and that "in this regard the values of peace-maintenance, safeguarding of nature, human rights, and the elimination of poverty have priority."[89] Former foreign minister Hans Genscher writes:

> Germany's power has certainly increased since unification because the country has shed the limitations on its sovereignty and room for maneuver that accompanied the division of Germany. Still, the increased responsibility for our foreign policy is not so much the result of German unification as it is the consequence of the changes in Europe and the world; the understanding of German foreign policy as policy

based on responsibility ("Verantwortungspolitick") rather than policy based on power ("Machpolitik") has remained unaffected by unification. It is only through the continued adherence to these principles that a European Germany can secure the kind of influence in the future that it had acquired in the years up to 1989.[90]

To be sure, it is a decidedly anti-realist, "seraphic vision of a Germany diligently exercising its new found responsibilities in pursuit of universal brotherhood."[91] It is consistent, however, with the notion of different types of stratification among states as opposed to a single hierarchical structure — poles and nonpoles.

Germany's image of itself suggests that prestige need not always be a positional good: *if everyone defines prestige differently, it can be commonly enjoyed; actors can feel "good about themselves" without bringing others down in the process.* In theory, it is possible to imagine a world in which states create unique roles and images for themselves without harming others' sense of self. In practice, however, it is extremely unlikely that such a highly specialized world will emerge. As Waltz points out, the pressures and dynamics of a competitive self-help system produce a tendency toward the sameness of competitors.[92] Returning to the case of Germany, it seeks respect as *the* model of a responsible civilian state; but without traditional military and political power to back up that role, it will continue to be a political dwarf, e.g., relying on the United States to clean up the mess it caused in Bosnia.

POSITIONAL GOODS AND SOCIAL SCARCITY

Positional goods "are either (1) scarce in some absolute or socially imposed sense or (2) subject to congestion or crowding through more extensive use."[93] Scarcities, in terms of absolute limitations on consumption opportunities, may arise for three different reasons. First and most familiar is physical scarcity (e.g., Rembrandts, antiques, colonies, or certain raw materials). The causal connection between scarce physical resources and interstate conflict is perhaps the oldest theme in international relations theory, especially among realist works. In this tradition, Gilpin writes: "With the aging of an international system and the expansion of states, the distance between states decreases, thereby causing them increasingly to come into conflict with one another. The once-empty space around the centers of power in the system is appropriated. The exploitable resources begin to be used up, and opportunities for economic growth decline. . . . Interstate relations become more and more a zero-sum game in which one state's gain is another's loss."[94] More recently, the environment-qua-security literature finds, to no one's surprise, "significant causal links between scarcities of renewable resources and violence."[95]

The other two types of scarcity arise not from physical but social limits on the absolute supply of particular goods. "Such social limits exist," Hirsch notes, "in the sense that an increase in physical availability of these goods or facilities, either in absolute terms or in relation to dimensions such as population or physical space, changes their characteristics in such a way that a given amount of use yields less satisfaction."[96]

Satisfaction that derives from scarcity itself is called *direct social scarcity*. This common phenomenon is rooted in various psychological motivations, such as envy, pride, snobbishness. Another form of social scarcity emerges as a byproduct of consumption. Hirsch calls this phenomenon *incidental social scarcity* to refer to social limitations that arise among goods valued for their intrinsic qualities independent of the satisfaction or position enjoyed by others that are nonetheless influenced by the consumption or activity of others. The typical manifestation of this type of social scarcity is congestion (or crowding out) in both its physical (traffic, overpopulation) and social (leadership, superior jobs, prestige, title, privilege) forms. An example of incidental social scarcity in global affairs is the increased demand for oil due to the emergence of newly industrialized states; or, more generally, the destruction of the global commons due to overutilization of dwindling resources or the dumping of industrial waste products into common water supplies. Both cases are examples of how growth can produce scarcity and conflict.

GROWTH AND POSITIONAL COMPETITION AND CONFLICT

This section briefly discusses three generic ways (the Jones effect, relative deprivation, and status inconsistency) that growth heightens positional concerns with respect to ethnic conflict and international economic and military rivalries. The three hypotheses are used to suggest possible explanations for various types of ethnic conflict and international economic and military rivalries.

The Jones Effect

"Status or position," Martin Shubik observed, "is often more important than wealth or other physical goods."[97] Under positional competition, knowledge of an improvement in B's welfare often causes A's welfare to decline. In common parlance, this form of envy, which is especially prevalent in affluent societies, is described by the phrase "keeping up with the Joneses." Economists refer to this Jones Effect as the "relative income hypothesis":

> Formally this hypothesis states that what matters to a person in a high consumption society is not only his absolute real income, or his command over market goods, but his position in the income structure of society. In an extreme case, the citizen would choose, for example, a 10 per cent increase in his real income provided that the average real income of society remained unchanged rather than a 50 per cent increase in his real income accompanied by a 50 per cent increase in the real income of every one else in society. . . . [I]n its more general form—the view that in the affluent society a person's relative income also affects his welfare—it is hardly to be controverted. After all, the satisfaction we derive from many objects depends, in varying degrees, both on the extent of their scarcity and on the prestige associated with our ownership of them. . . . [T]his Jones Effect . . . can only grow with the general rise in living standards.[98]

States, as well as individuals, are susceptible to the Jones Effect. Diplomatic history is replete with examples of conflict and sometimes war driven by envy and snobbishness. The failed Italian campaign in Northern Abyssinia in 1896, for example, was motivated by Crispi's jealousy of the other powers' imperial prestige and his determination not to allow Italy to lag too far behind in the race: "We cannot remain inactive and allow other powers to occupy all the unexplored parts of the world." Reflecting on the Adua disaster, the Marchese di Rudini "confessed that the Italians had . . . simply gone in order to keep up with the expansion of the other powers, 'in the spirit of imitation, a desire for sport, and for pure snobism.' "[99] In the eighteenth century, snobbism prevented Turkey, a significant military power deemed uncivilized by the Western powers, from membership in European society. More recently, "Egypt's initiation of war with Israel in 1973 and Argentina's occupation of the Falkland Islands in 1982 were both motivated by considerations of prestige," Aaron Friedberg suggests, "rather than any expectation of direct material benefit."[100] Today, some experts see status-seeking as a partial explanation for the proliferation of indigenous arms industries in the Third World and the bias in favor of modern weaponry: "Advanced weapons—and their capacity to produce them—are coveted not only for their destructive efficiency, but also for their 'symbolic throw weight.'"[101]

Turning to the international political economy, we see that the main objective of mercantilism is to maximize the state's wealth relative to that of other states—at the very least, the state must keep up with the Joneses. Viewing the pursuit of wealth as a zero-sum game, mercantilists are more interested in their state's position within the international pecking order than they are in maximizing the state's absolute gains from trade. Thus, the German mercantilist P. W. von Hörnigk observed in 1684: "Whether a nation be to-day mighty and rich or not depends not on the abundance or scarcity of its powers or riches, but principally on whether its neighbours possess more or less than it. For power and riches have become a relative matter, dependent on being weaker and poorer than others."[102] National power maximization, according to mercantilists, can be achieved "as well, if not better, by weakening the economic power of other countries instead of strengthening one's own. If wealth is considered the aim, this is the height of absurdity, but from the point of view of political power it is quite logical. . . . Any attempt at economic advance by one's own efforts in one country must have appeared pointless, unless it consisted in robbing other countries of part of their possessions. Scarcely any other element in mercantilist philosophy contributed more to the shaping of economic policy, and even of foreign policy as a whole."[103]

Using similar logic in 1985, a clear majority (60%) of Americans, most of whom had been free traders during the 1950s and 1960s, when the United States was at the apex of its economic power, supported the idea of limiting imports even if it meant less choice for Americans.[104] Five years later, in July 1990, a Wall Street Journal/NBC News poll "found that an overwhelming majority (86%) of Americans would prefer a policy of slower growth in both Japan and the United States, over one in which both grew faster, if the latter meant allowing Japan to take the lead economically."[105] To the horror of mainstream economists, it appears that ordinary citizens tend to agree with the words of the English mercantilist Roger Coke (1675): "[I]f our Treasure were more than our Neighbouring Nations, I did not care whether we had one-fifth part of the Treasure we now have."[106]

Today's mercantilists recognize mutual gains from trade, but they continue to emphasize the distribution of those gains. In a competitive, self-help system, states must be concerned with maintaining and improving their position within the international division of labor or else face the consequences of deindustrialization and a declining standard of living for their citizens. When long-term economic growth is considered, how well or poorly a country performs will significantly affect the lives of its citizens. As Michael Boskin, a Stanford economist, avers: "Modest variations in growth rates compounded over, say, a generation or two, can drastically alter the nature of an economy and a society."[107] In fact, if we "compound real per capita income over two generations in two hypothetical, initially identical economies at 1.5 percent and at 2 percent, respectively," the "more rapidly growing economy becomes one-third as wealthy as the less rapidly growing economy."[108] The power of compounding growth rates explains how the United States—largely rural in 1850—shortly thereafter became the greatest industrial power in the world, while Great Britain sank to a position of relative economic inferiority even in Europe.

Sometimes, particularly under conditions of anarchy, positional competition à la the Jones Effect is driven not just by snobbism or the need to maintain a positive trade balance or social identity but also, as Grieco maintains, by the fear of being dominated or even destroyed by others.[109] As long as sovereign entities exist under anarchy, security concerns will never entirely disappear and military power will continue to buy political influence. While a great-power war currently seems remote, only the most superficial observer would conclude that states' greed and glory-seeking, their search for prestige, status, and wealth, will always be kept nonviolent.[110] Thus, as Josef Joffe declares: "Hard power—men and missiles, guns and ships—still counts. It is the ultimate, because existential, currency of power."[111] Because unequal gains can make even friends more domineering or potentially more powerful rivals, realists claim that international cooperation is difficult to achieve and even harder to maintain.

Fear of domination is also at the root of ethnic group conflict in severely divided societies. The issues center on which group will govern, how resources will be distributed, how the country should be divided. Ethnic groups engaged in these particularly bitter, zero-sum struggles want, above all, to make relative gains at the expense of their rivals and not just to improve their lot in absolute terms. On this crucial point, Donald Horowitz writes:

> Group claims are not necessarily equal. Some groups seek domination, not the mere avoidance of it. Some seek to exclude others from

the polity altogether, and some seek merely to be included on equal terms. If all groups merely wanted inclusion, distrust and anxiety would still make ethnic conflict serious, but more tractable than it is. What makes it intractable is that claims to political inclusion and exclusion have an area of mutual incompatibility. . . . What is sought is not necessarily some absolute value but a value determined by the extent to which it reduces another group's share. Demands are often cast in relative terms, and conflict-reducing proposals that involve expanding the pool of goods available to all groups typically have little appeal. Not 'how many?' but 'what fraction?'—that is the key question. . . . Just as relative group worth is at issue, so is relative power. . . . Ethnic conflict is, at bottom, a matter of comparison.[112]

Precisely because it is a positional competition, ethnic conflict often intensifies, rather than subsides, as the economic pie expands.

Sometimes the question is not simply "who gains more?" but rather "who will dominate whom?" Conflicts of this type are examples of positional conflict *par excellence*: "Either these conflicts end definitely and abruptly as a result of military action, or they continue in crisis as long as the goal of destruction remains part of the policy of one of the parties."[113] Given the all or nothing nature of these struggles, economic growth, rather than solving the problem, fuels the fighting by replenishing the combatants' war chests.

Relative Deprivation: The Appetite for Power and Prestige Grows with the Eating

Another way that economic growth exacerbates conflict is by shifting aspiration levels from comparisons of current performance with past experience to comparisons with groups that have greater social, economic, and occupational status. Social psychologists use the concept of relative deprivation to explain this phenomenon. "People who once acquiesced in deprived economic conditions because they could visualize no practical alternative now begin to reassess their prospects and possibilities. . . . They now compare their present conditions and opportunities with those of other groups who are materially better off than they and ask by what right the others should be so privileged. Perversely, then, as their objective conditions improve, they become more dissatisfied because their aspirations outdistance their achievements."[114] For this reason, it is argued, social mobilization, often seen as a benefit of modernization, tends to foster ethnic strife, particularly when the benefits of modernity, such as economic and educational opportunities, are unevenly distributed among ethnic groups:[115]

> People's aspirations and expectations change as they are mobilized into the modernizing economy and polity. They come to want, and to demand, more—more goods, more recognition, more power. Significantly, too, the orientation of the mobilized to a common set of rewards and paths to rewards means, in effect, that many people come to desire precisely the same things. Men enter into conflict not because they are different but because they are essentially the same. It is by making men 'more alike,' in the sense of possessing the same wants, that modernization tends to promote conflict.[116]

This same "appetite-for-power-grows-with-the-eating" argument applies to rising states in the international system.[117] It is the basic logic behind lateral pressure theory developed by Nazli Choucri and Robert North.[118] Their analysis of great power behavior between 1870 and 1914 revealed that "expansionist activities are most likely to be associated with relatively high-capability countries, and to be closely linked with growth in population and advances in technology; and that growth tends to be associated with intense competition among countries for resources and markets, military power, political influence, and prestige."[119] Here, physical and social scarcity arise through crowding out and congestion.

Growth, Status Inconsistency, and Conflict

Status inconsistency as a result of growth is also strongly correlated with both domestic and foreign conflict.[120] In the domestic context, this means that the patterns of social mobility in modernizing societies often determine whether growth alleviates or exacerbates ethnic strife. As Jack Goldstone points out: "When social mobility is low and the composition and size of elites are stable, there is generally little conflict. However, when social mobility rises, as new groups acquire skills, gain middle-class and professional positions, while social and political institutions still deny them greater status and full political participation, conflicts generally arise."[121] In Marxist theory, a similar process explains revolutions: the means of economic production outgrow the social and political superstructure (e.g., law and class structure), thereby engendering a contradiction between the forces of production and the relations of production. Applying this logic to international politics, Gilpin argues that hegemonic wars are the result of a disjuncture between the system's superstructure—its governance, hierarchy of prestige, rules, and division of territory—and the underlying distribution of power. Status inconsistency therefore drives both war and change in the international system.[122]

Today's China provides a clear example of rapid economic growth producing dissatisfaction and belligerence over perceived status inconsistency. Lucian Pye observes:

> The economic successes of Deng's reforms should have warmed up relations [with the U.S.], making the Chinese more self-confident and at ease with the outside world, less touchy about slights to their sovereignty or perceived meddling in their internal affairs. However, this success has only generated greater tensions and frustrations. The Chinese take seriously the forecast that they will soon have the world's largest economy. They therefore feel that they deserve recognition and respect as a superpower-in-waiting. It is not enough that they are already a permanent member of the United Nations Security Council and one of the five nuclear powers. Somehow all of their accomplishments of the last two decades have not produced as dramatic a change in their international status as they had expected or believe is their due.[123]

It is significant that status-maximizing behavior of this sort is driven more by an opportunity for gain than it is by fear. The correct analogy is not Wolfers's "house on fire" but rather his lesser-known "race track" analogy: when an opening in the crowd appears in front of a group of people, they rush forward to fill the gap.[124] Likewise, a strong country will feel compelled by opportunity to fill a power vacuum. China's recent military buildup, if motivated by the desire for greater status, may thus not be related to others' defense spending. If a correlation does exist, it will be in the opposite direction of that predicted by balance-of-power or threat theory: as others spend less, China, seeking to make relative gains and increase its international status, will seize the opportunity to spend more.

In summary, economic growth and social mobility are often a direct cause of conflict and competition. This is because our satisfaction with many objects often "depends upon their publicly recognized scarcity irrespective of their utility to us."[125] Economic growth increases both the demand for and scarcity of such positional goods. Because economic expansion causes aspiration levels to rise and converge, it becomes impossible for most people to achieve their goals of greater prestige and status. As a result, they become more dissatisfied with their condition even though their absolute welfare has improved. Thus, the economist E. J. Mishan pessimistically concludes, "the more truth there is in this relative income hypothesis—and one can hardly deny the increasing emphasis on status and income-position in the affluent society—the more futile as a means of increasing social welfare is the official policy of economic growth."[126]

CONCLUSION: REALISTS MUST REEMPHASIZE POWER POLITICS

To the extent that scholars and practitioners have been getting off the realist train at various stops over the past decade or so, this has been more a response to the shortcomings of neorealism than to the explanatory pull of the neoliberal or other alternatives. By sacrificing richness for rigor and replacing power with security as the primary goal of states, structural realists have constructed a theory that caricatures more than it models classical realism. At its core, classical realism is a theory of the state and international competition, and it is written in terms of power politics. It is not, primarily, a theory about how states acquire security or about strictly defense issues. Indeed, the best treatments of realism's intellectual roots may be found not on its security side (e.g., the literature on balance of power, the security dilemma, or deterrence theory), but rather in its related economic philosophy of mercantilism.[127]

As truly positional concepts, primacy, prestige, leadership, and status accurately reflect realism's emphasis on perpetual competition, relative-gains, and real conflicts of interests—not the imagined ones associated with the security dilemma/spiral model of conflict that has become the theory of choice among Waltzian structural realists.[128] Many important theories emphasize physical scarcity (e.g., raw materials, colonies, territory)[129] and social scarcity (e.g., prestige, influence, global leadership).[130] While some fall outside the realist perspective, all of them support the traditional realist notion that the desire for power and influence intensifies as nations become more powerful. In contrast to Waltzian "defensive" realists, traditional realists shared Frederick the Great's belief that "at all times it was the principle of great states to subjugate all whom they could and to extend their power continuously."[131] Subjugation is perhaps too harsh a word even for the most hard-boiled of today's realists; but the basic point holds: realism is about power politics. Contemporary realism has been drained of politics; it needs a reinjection.

This can be done by broadening neorealism's rather narrow assumption of state interest as security-maximization to include autonomy- and influence-maximization to promote the state's welfare, values, prestige, status, and diplomatic aims. There are tradeoffs among these three perennial foreign policy objectives: alliances may increase the state's security but decrease its autonomy; power-maximization, if pursued recklessly, may decrease the state's security and usually risks its autonomy (e.g., Fascist Italy accepted satellite status within the Nazi orbit to enhance its global power and prestige; Hitler's reckless pursuit of power cost Germany its autonomy); autonomy often comes at the expense of security and sometimes influence in terms of voice opportunities (which France, by sacrificing its monetary autonomy, hopes to gain vis-à-vis Germany within the European Monetary System). Theories of foreign policy should attempt to identify the optimum combination of all three objectives for any given state. At a time when none of the great powers harbors aggressive intent, this is a particularly urgent task for realists, whose current fixation on security leaves their theories with little explanatory and prescriptive power regarding the system's core states.

Acknowledgments

An earlier version of this paper was presented at the Olin Institute Conference on "Realism and International Relations After the Cold War," Harvard University, Cambridge, MA (December 1995). I am grateful to John Champlin, Daniel Deudney, Joseph Grieco, Richard Herrmann, Judith Kullberg, Richard Ned Lebow, Michael Mastanduno, Richard Meltz, Kevin Murrin, Richard Samuels, Jack Snyder, and Kim Zisk for their helpful comments.

NOTES

1. See Robert H. Frank, "Positional Externalities," in Richard J. Zeckhauser, ed., *Strategy and Choice* (Cambridge: MIT Press, 1991), 25–47; and Thomas Schelling, "Hockey Helmets, Daylight Saving, and Other Binary Choices," in Schelling, *Micromotives and Macrobehavior* (New York: Norton, 1978), chap. 7.
2. See Samuel P. Huntington, "Why International Primacy Matters," *International Security* 17(4) (Spring 1993): 68–83.

3. See Randall L. Schweller, "Neorealism's Status-Quo Bias: What Security Dilemma?" *Security Studies* 5(3) (Spring 1996), esp. pp. 103–4, 116–19. See also the discussion of predation as a cause of competitive, self-interested security strategies, in Alexander Wendt, "Anarchy Is What States Make of It: The Social Construction of Power Politics," *International Organization* 46(2) (Spring 1992): 407–10.

4. For the view that realism predicts cooperative security strategies under many conditions, see Charles L. Glaser, "Realists As Optimists: Cooperation As Self-Help," *International Security* 19 (3) (Winter 1994–95): 50–90.

5. For positional goods and social scarcity, see Fred Hirsch, *The Social Limits to Growth* (Cambridge: Harvard University Press, 1976); see also Robert Jervis, "International Primacy: Is the Game Worth the Candle?" *International Security* 17(4) (Spring 1993): 58–59.

6. I am indebted to Philip Tetlock for this phrase. For formulations of status-maximizing behavior, see Martin Shubik, "Games of Status," *Behavioral Science* 16(3) (March 1971): 117–29; and E. J. Mishan, *What Political Economy Is All About* (Cambridge: Cambridge University Press, 1982), chap. 17. For an excellent discussion of the status–prestige motivations behind China's power-maximizing behavior, see Alastair Iain Johnston, "Realism(s) and Chinese Security Policy in the Post-Cold War Period," in this volume.

7. Kenneth N. Waltz, "Conflict in World Politics," in Steven L. Speigel and Kenneth N. Waltz, eds., *Conflict in World Politics* (Cambridge, MA: Winthrop, 1971), 463.

8. Richard K. Betts, "The Delusion of Impartial Intervention," *Foreign Affairs* 73(6) (November–December 1994): 21.

9. Edward Hallett Carr, *The Twenty Years' Crisis, 1919–1939: An Introduction to the Study of International Relations* (New York: Harper [1946], 1964), 63–64. Carr claims to have derived these three foundation-stones of realism from Machiavelli. Spykman expresses the realist position on the relationship between morality and power politics thusly: "The statesman who conducts foreign policy can concern himself with values of justice, fairness, and tolerance only to the extent that they contribute to or do not interfere with the power objective. They can be used instrumentally as moral justification for the power quest, but they must be discarded the moment their application brings weakness. The search for power is not made for the achievement of moral values; moral values are used to facilitate the attainment of power." Nicholas John Spykman, *America's Strategy in World Politics: The United States and the Balance of Power* (New York: Harcourt, 1942), 18.

10. For the realist view of tribalism as a structural constraint on moral political action, see Reinhold Niebuhr, *Moral Man and Immoral Society* (New York: Scribner's, 1932); Carr, *The Twenty Years' Crisis*, 157–59; Spykman, *America's*

Strategy in World Politics, 12–19; and Robert Gilpin, "The Richness of the Tradition of Political Realism," in Robert O. Keohane, ed., *Neorealism and Its Critics* (New York: Columbia University Press, 1986), 305. For the classic realist critique of liberal rationalism and its notion that human reason can overcome politics, conflict, and evil, see Hans J. Morgenthau, *Scientific Man vs. Power Politics* (Chicago: The University of Chicago Press, 1946), esp. pp. 90–95 and chap. 8.

11. For this argument, see the introduction to Arnold Wolfers and Laurence W. Martin, *The Anglo-American Tradition in Foreign Affairs: Readings From Thomas More to Woodrow Wilson* (New Haven: Yale University Press, 1956).

12. James M. Goldgeier and Michael McFaul, "A Tale of Two Worlds: Core and Periphery in the Post-Cold War Era," *International Organization* 46(2) (Spring 1992): 469. Robert Jervis makes a similar argument in his "The Future of World Politics: Will It Resemble the Past?" *International Security* 16(3) (Winter 1991–92), especially pp. 46–55.

13. My claim that economic issues are inherently more positional than are security concerns under most conditions partly explains, I believe, why the U.S. is, as Mastanduno suggests, currently playing security "softball" and economic "hardball" in its relations with other major powers. See Michael Mastanduno, "Preserving the Unipolar Moment: Realist Theories and U.S. Grand Strategy After the Cold War," *International Security* 21(4) (Spring 1997): 49–88; and Mastanduno's chapter in this volume.

14. As Waltz points out, in self-help systems, "competition produces a tendency toward sameness of the competitors." Kenneth N. Waltz, *Theory of International Politics* (Reading, MA: Addison-Wesley, 1979), 127.

15. Similarly, Paul Kennedy observes: "An economically expanding Power—Britain in the 1860s, the United States in the 1890s, Japan today—may well prefer to become rich rather than to spend heavily on armaments. A half-century later, priorities may well have altered. The earlier economic expansion has brought with it overseas obligations (dependence upon foreign markets and raw materials, military alliances, perhaps bases and colonies). Other rival Powers are now economically expanding at a faster rate, and wish in turn to extend their influence abroad. The world has become a more competitive place, and market shares are being eroded." Paul Kennedy, *The Rise and Fall of the Great Powers: Economic Change and Military Conflict From 1500–2000* (New York: Random House, 1987), xxiii.

16. Richard Ned Lebow, "Cold War Lessons for Political Theorists," *The Chronicle of Higher Education* 42 (20) (January 26, 1996): B2.

17. Charles W. Kegley, Jr., "The Neoidealist Moment in International Studies? Realist Myths and the New International Realities," *International Studies Quarterly* 37(2) (June 1993): 131–32. Kegley continues: "The long-term trajectories

6o   REALISM AND THE PRESENT GREAT POWER SYSTEM

6o

in world affairs appear to have converged to create a profoundly altered international system in which [Wilson's] ideas and ideals now appear less unrealistic
and more compelling." Ibid., 134.

6o

18. Ibid., 133, 135.

19. See, for example, Stephen R. Graubard, ed., What Future for the State?, special
issue, Daedalus 124(2) (Spring 1995); James N. Rosenau, Turbulence in World
Politics: A Theory of Change and Continuity (Princeton, N.J.: Princeton Uni-
versity Press, 1990); John G. Ruggie, "Territoriality and Beyond: Problematizing
Modernity in International Relations," International Organization 47(1) (Win-
ter 1993): 139–74; James N. Rosenau and Ernst-Otto Czempiel, eds., Gover-
nance Without Government: Change and Order in World Politics (New York:
Cambridge University Press, 1992); and Ernst-Otto Czempiel and James N.
Rosenau, eds., Global Changes and Theoretical Challenges: Approaches to
World Politics for the 1990s (Lexington, MA: Lexington Books, 1989).

20. Waltz, Theory of International Politics, 126.

21. Ibid.

22. Ibid., 118.

23. Ibid., 77, 128; Christopher Layne, "The Unipolar Illusion: Why New Great
Powers Will Rise," International Security 17(4) (Spring 1993): 11, 15–16.

24. Joseph M. Grieco, "Understanding the Problem of International Cooperation:
The Limits of Neoliberal Institutionalism and the Future of Realist Theory,"
in David A. Baldwin, ed., Neorealism and Neoliberalism: The Contemporary
Debate (New York: Columbia University Press, 1934), 303.

25. Waltz, Theory of International Politics, 126.

26. Quoted in Wolfers, The Anglo-American Tradition, 28–29.

27. Thucydides, The Peloponnesian War, translated by R. Crawley (New York: Random House, 1982), 1.75, 1.76

28. Steven Forde, "International Realism and the Science of Politics: Thucydides,
Machiavelli, and Neorealism," International Studies Quarterly 39(2) (June
1995): 146, 148.

29. Wolfers, The Anglo-American Tradition, 28.

30. Morgenthau, Scientific Man vs. Power Politics, 192

31. These examples are borrowed from Hirsch, Social Limits to Growth, 3–7.

32. Morgenthau, Scientific Man vs Power Politics, 192–93 (emphasis added).

33. Ibid., 192.

34. Schweller, "Neorealism's Status-Quo Bias."

35. Dan Reiter, "Exploding the Powder Keg Myth: Preemptive Wars Almost Never
Happen," International Security 20(2) (Fall 1995): 32–33.

36. Kenneth N. Waltz, Man, the State and War: A Theoretical Analysis (New York:
Columbia University Press, 1959), 203–4. Similarly, Waltz said: "An understanding of the third image makes it clear that the expectation [of perpetual
peace] would be justified only if the minimum interest of states in preserving

themselves became the maximum interest of all of them—and each could rely fully upon the steadfast adherence to this definition by all of the others." Ibid., 227. Later, Waltz changed his mind: "In an anarchic domain, a state of war exists if all parties lust for power. But so too will a state of war exist if all states seek only to ensure their own safety." Kenneth N. Waltz, "The Origins of War in Neorealist Theory," in Robert I. Rotberg and Theodore K. Rabb, eds., *The Origin and Prevention of Major Wars* (Cambridge: Cambridge University Press, 1989), 44 (emphasis added).

37. Harold Dwight Lasswell, *Politics: Who Gets What, When, How* (New York: P. Smith [1936], 1950). The classic statement on social power remains Harold D. Lasswell and Abraham Kaplan, *Power and Society: A Framework for Political Inquiry* (New Haven: Yale University Press, 1950).

38. Samuel P. Huntington, "Why International Primacy Matters," *International Security* 17(4) (Spring 1993): 68–69.

39. Spykman, *America's Strategy in World Politics*, 12.

40. See Jervis, "The Future of World Politics: 39–73; Goldgeier and McFaul, "Core and Periphery," 467–91; Stephen Van Evera, "Primed For Peace: Europe After the Cold War," *International Security* 15(3) (Winter 1990–91): 7–57; John Mueller, *Retreat From Doomsday: The Obsolescence of Major War* (New York: Basic Books, 1989); James Lee Ray, "The Abolition of Slavery and the End of International War," *International Organization* 43(3) (Summer 1989): 405–39; George Modelski, "Is World Politics Evolutionary Learning?" *International Organization* 44(1) (Winter 1990): 1–24; Francis Fukuyama, "The End of History?" *The National Interest* (16) (Summer 1989): 3–18; John Lewis Gaddis, "International Relations Theory and the End of the Cold War," *International Security* 17(3) (Winter 1992–93): 5–58.

41. Layne, "The Unipolar Illusion;" Charles Krauthammer, "The Unipolar Moment," *Foreign Affairs: American and the World* 70(1) (1990–91): 23–33; Kenneth Waltz, "America as a Model for the World? A Foreign Policy Perspective," *PS: Political Science and Politics* 24(4) (December 1991): 699; Kenneth N. Waltz, "The Emerging Structure of International Politics," *International Security* 18(2) (Fall 1993): 44–79. Layne predicts that unipolarity "will give way to multipolarity between 2000–2010" (p. 7). Krauthammer makes a similar prediction: "No doubt, multipolarity will come in time. In perhaps another generation or so there will be great powers coequal with the United States, and the world will, in structure, resemble the pre-World War I era" (pp. 23–24). Waltz sees an "emerging world . . . of four or five great powers," including the U.S., Germany, Japan, China, and Russia. Waltz, "The Emerging Structure," 70. Mearsheimer employs the same "balancing logic" in his discussion of the geopolitical future of post-Cold War Europe. See John Mearsheimer, "Back to the Future: Instability in Europe After the Cold War," *International Security* 15(1) (Summer 1990): 5–56.

42. Mearsheimer, "Back to the Future"; Kenneth N. Waltz, *The Spread of Nuclear Weapons: More May Be Better*, Adelphi Paper No. 171 (London: International Institute for Strategic Studies, 1981); Waltz, "Nuclear Myths and Political Realities," *American Political Science Review* 81(3) (September 1991): 731–46.

43. Stephen D. Krasner, "Power, Polarity, and the Challenge of Disintegration," in Helga Haftendorn and Christian Tuschhoff, eds., *America and Europe in an Era of Change* (Boulder, CO: Westview Press, 1993), 22; also see Robert O. Keohane, "The Diplomacy of Structural Change: Multilateral Institutions and State Strategies," in ibid., 43–59.

44. Krasner, "Power, Polarity," 22.

45. Thus, many foreign policy experts currently advocate "less is more" grand strategies for the U.S. in the post-Cold War period. See Eugene Gholz, Daryl G. Press, and Harvey M. Sapolsky, "Come Home, America: The Strategy of Restraint in the Face of Temptation," *International Security* 21(4) (Spring 1997): 5–48; Christopher Layne, "Less is More: Minimal Realism in East Asia," *The National Interest* (43) (Spring 1996): 64–77; Eric A. Nordlinger, *Isolationism Reconfigured* (Princeton: Princeton University Press, 1995); and Barry R. Posen and Andrew L. Ross, "Competing Visions for U.S. Grand Strategy," *International Security* 21(3) (Winter 1996–97): 9–16.

46. Samuel P. Huntington, "America's Changing Strategic Interests," *Survival* 33(1) (January–February 1991): 6. For a related view of current power structures see Richard K. Betts, "Wealth, Power, and Instability: East Asia and the United States after the Cold War," *International Security* 18(3) (Winter 1993–94): 41–43. Josef Joffe, "Bismarck or Britain? Toward and American Grand Strategy after Bipolarity," *International Security* 19(4) (Spring 1995): 101.

47. Joseph L. Nogee, "Polarity: An Ambiguous Concept," *Orbis* 18(4) (Winter 1975): 1193–1224. at p. 1197. Much of the following discussion is drawn from this essay.

48. For studies employing GNP as the sole measure of power, see Bruce M. Russett, *Trends in World Politics* (New York: Macmillan, 1965), 2–4; and A. F. K. Organski and Jacek Kugler, *The War Ledger* (Chicago: The University of Chicago Press, 1980), 30–38.

49. See Jeffrey E. Garten, *A Cold Peace: America, Japan, Germany, and the Struggle for Supremacy* (New York: Times Books–Random House, 1992), 183; Lester Thurow, *Head To Head: The Coming Economic Battle Among Japan, Europe, and America* (New York: William Morrow, 1992); Jacques Attali, *Lignes d'Horizon* (Paris: Fayarde, 1990).

50. President Clinton, "Address to students and faculty at Waseda University, Tokyo, Japan," July 7, 1993," U.S. Department of State Dispatch 4 (28) (July 12, 1993), 486.

51. Quoted in Chalmers Johnson and E. B. Keehn, "The Pentagon's Ossified Strategy," *Foreign Affairs* 74(4) ((July–August 1995), 106. Similarly, Matsataka Ko-

saka, a leading Japanese foreign affairs expert, opines: "Japan [under current conditions] can neither identify itself with Europe and the United States nor live in peace in Asia." Quoted in ibid., 108.

52. Attali, *Lignes d'Horizon.* Attali's work is discussed in Joseph S. Nye, Jr., "Patrons and Clients: New Roles in the Post-Cold War Order," in Haftendorn and Tuschhoff, *America and Europe in an Era of Change,* 98.

53. Mearsheimer, "Back To the Future," p. 7, fn. 5.

54. Richard N. Rosecrance, *Action and Reaction in World Politics* (Boston: Little, Brown, 1963), 79–101, 169–215.

55. Fukuyama, "The End of History?"

56. Kishore Mahbubani, "The West and the Rest," *The National Interest* no. 28 (Summer 1992): 3–13. Also see Matthew Connelly and Paul Kennedy, "Must It Be The Rest Against The West?" *The Atlantic Monthly* (December 1994): 61–84; Kishore Mahbubani, "The Dangers of Decadence: What the Rest Can Teach the West," *Foreign Affairs* 72(4) (September–October 1993): 10–14. For a contradictory view, see Owen Harries, "The Collapse of 'The West'," *Foreign Affairs* 72(4) (September–October 1993): 41–53.

57. Huntington, "The Clash of Civilizations?" Huntington, too, sees a West-against-the Rest conflict, particularly between the U.S. and Confucian-Islamic states.

58. The Correlates of War Project at the University of Michigan employs this type of measurement. See also William B. Moul, "Measuring the 'Balance of Power': A Look at Some of the Numbers," *Review of International Studies* 15 (April 1989): 101–21; Jacek Kugler and Marina Arbetman, "Choosing Among Measures of Power: A Review of the Empirical Record," in Richard J. Stoll and Michael D. Ward, eds., *Power in World Politics* (Boulder, CO: Lynne Rienner, 1989), 75; and Ray S. Cline, *World Power Trends and U.S. Foreign Policy for the 1980s* (Boulder, CO: Westview Press, 1980).

59. Johnston, "Realisms and Chinese Security Policy," p. 40.

60. William C. Wohlforth, "Realism and the End of the Cold War," *International Security* 19(3) (Winter 1994–95): 91–129. For a less sanguine interpretation of future Soviet intentions, see Rajan Menon, "In the Shadow of the Bear: Security in Post-Soviet Central Asia," *International Security* 20(1) (Summer 1995): 149–81.

61. Jervis, "The Future of World Politics."

62. Mearsheimer, "Back to the Future;" Aaron L. Friedberg, "Ripe For Rivalry: Prospects for Peace in a Multipolar Asia," *International Security* 18(3) (Winter 1993–94): 5–33; Betts, "Wealth, Power, and Instability."

63. Friedberg, "Ripe For Rivalry," 6.

64. Arthur Schlesinger, Jr., "Back to the Womb? Isolationism's Renewed Threat," *Foreign Affairs* 74(4) (July–August 1995): 2–8.

65. Joffe, "Bismarck" or "Britain." For the U.S. as an offshore balancer, see Chris-

topher Layne, "Realism Redux: Strategic Independence in a Multipolar World," *SAIS Review* 9(2) (Summer-Fall 1989) pp. 19–44; Layne, "The Unipolar Illusion," pp. 47–51.

66. See Morton A. Kaplan, *Systems and Process in International Politics* (New York: Wiley, 1957), 17, 40–41, 48–40.

67. Terry L. Deibel, "Strategies Before Containment: Patterns for the Future," in Sean M. Lynn-Jones and Steven E. Miller, eds., *America's Strategy in a Changing World* (Cambridge: MIT Press, 1992), 39.

68. Robert W. Tucker, *The Inequality of Nations* (New York: Basic Books, 1977), 3.

69. Raymond Aron, *Progress and Disillusion: The Dialectics of Modern Society* (New York: Praeger, 1968), 160.

70. David Strang, "Anomaly and Commonplace in European Political Expansion: Realist and Institutional Accounts," *International Organization* 45(2) (Spring 1991): 143–62. Also see Alexander Wendt and Daniel Friedheim, "Hierarchy Under Anarchy: Informal Empire and the East German State," *International Organization* 49(4) (Autumn 1995): 689–721; Ian Clark, *The Hierarchy States* (Cambridge: Cambridge University Press, 1989).

71. Morgenthau dealt with this issue in terms of power. See Morgenthau, *Politics Among Nations*: 174–83. I am grateful to Richard Herrmann for pointing this out.

72. Evan Luard, *Types of International Society* (New York: The Free Press, 1976), 207. This section on stratification draws heavily from ch. 9 of Luard's book.

73. R. G. Hawtrey, *Economic Aspects of Sovereignty* (London: Longmans, Green, 1952), 65; Robert G. Gilpin, *War and Change in World Politics* (Cambridge: Cambridge University Press, 1981), 31.

74. Inevitably, however, the system falls into disequilibrium as changes in the actual distribution of capabilities, driven by the law of uneven growth, are not reflected by the hierarchy of prestige, upon which rests the international superstructure of economic, social, territorial, and political relationships. This built-in conflict between prestige and power, which has always been decided by hegemonic war, drives international change. Gilpin, *War and Change*, chap. 5.

75. Richard Louis Walker, *The Multi-State System of Ancient China* (Hamden, CT: The Shoestring Press, 1953), 26–27. For the importance of prestige to the Ch'un-ch'iu states, see ibid., 47–48.

76. John Huxtable Elliott, *Europe Divided, 1559–1598* (New York: Harper, 1968): 108–9.

77. "However great its prosperity and strength, a nation could not be respected if it represented heresy, schism, and the forces of darkness." Luard, *Types of International Society*, 215.

78. Ibid., 92, 215

79. Ibid., 216.
80. Richard B. Elrod, "The Concert of Europe: A Fresh Look at an International System," *World Politics* 28(2) (January 1976), 164.
81. Ibid., 167.
82. Ibid.
83. G. N. Sanderson, "The European Partition of Africa: Coincidence or Conjuncture?" *The Journal of Imperial and Commonwealth History* 3(1) (October 1974): 9.
84. Luard, *Types of International Society*, 220.
85. See, for example, John M. Stopford, Susan Strange, and John S. Henley, *Rival States, Rival Firms: Competition For World Market Shares* (Cambridge: Cambridge University Press, 1991); and Jeffrey A. Hart, *Rival Capitalists: International Competitiveness In the United States, Japan, and Western Europe* (Ithaca: Cornell University Press, 1992).
86. For a discussion, see Jeffrey E. Garten, "Is America Abandoning Multilateral Trade?" *Foreign Affairs* 74(6) (November–December 1995): 50–62.
87. See, for example, Peter Schweizer, "The Growth of Economic Espionage," *Foreign Affairs* 75(1) (January–February 1996): 9–15.
88. Hans W. Maull, "Germany and Japan: The New Civilian Powers," *Foreign Affairs* 69(5) (Winter 1990–91): 91–106.
89. Quoted in Gunther Hellmann, "Goodbye Bismarck? The Foreign Policy of Contemporary Germany," *Mershon International Studies Review* (forthcoming, April 1996).
90. Hans-Dietrich Genscher, *Erinnerungen* (Berlin: Siedler Verlag, 1995), 1016. Also quoted in Hellmann, "Goodbye Bismarck?" p. ?
91. David Marsh, *Germany and Europe: The Crisis of Unity* (London: Mandarin, 1995), 167.
92. Waltz, *Theory of International Politics*: 118–27.
93. Hirsch, *Social Limits to Growth*, 27.
94. Gilpin, *War and Change*, 200–201.
95. Thomas F. Homer-Dixon, Jeffrey H Boutwell, and George W. Rathjens, "Environmental Scarcity and Violent Conflict," *Scientific American* 268(2) (February 1993): 45. For a stinging critique, see Marc A. Levy, "Is the Environment a National Security Issue?" *International Security* 20(2) (Fall 1995): 35–62.
96. Hirsch, *Social Limits to Growth*, 20.
97. Shubik, "Games of Status," 117.
98. Mishan, *What Political Economy Is All About*, 149.
99. Francesco Crispi and Marchese di Rudini as quoted in William L. Langer, *The Diplomacy of Imperialism, 1890–1902* (New York: Alfred A. Knopf, 1965): 272, 281.
100. Friedberg, "Ripe For Rivalry," 27.

101. David Kinsella, "The Globalization of Arms Production and the Changing Third World Security Context," paper presented at the annual meeting of the International Studies Association, Chicago, February 21–25, 1995, p. 5. The phrase, symbolic throw weight, appears in Mark C. Suchman and Dana P. Eyre, "Military Procurement as Rational Myth: Notes on the Social Construction of Weapons Proliferation," *Sociological Forum* 7 (1992): 137–61 at p. 154.

102. Quoted in Eli Heckscher, *Mercantilism, Vol. 2, Mercantilism as a System of Power*, translated by Mendel Shapiro (London: George Allen & Unwin, 1935), 22. For mercantilism and state power, also see William Cunningham, *The Growth of English Industry and Commerce During the Early and Middle Ages*, 2 Vols. (Cambridge: Cambridge University Press, 1890, 1892). For the classic critique, see Jacob Viner, "Power Versus Plenty as Objectives of Foreign Policy in the Seventeeth and Eighteenth Centuries," *World Politics* 1(1) (January 1948): 1–29.

103. Heckscher, *Mercantilism* 2: 21, 24.

104. Findings of 1985 CBS–New York Times poll, as reported in David B. Yoffie, "Protecting World Markets," in Thomas K. McCraw, ed., *America Versus Japan* (Boston: Harvard Business School Press, 1986), 61.

105. Michael Mastanduno, "Do Relative Gains Matter? Americas Response to the Japanese Industrial Policy," *International Security* 16(1) (Summer 1991): 73–74.

106. Quoted in Heckscher, *Mercantilism* 2: 23.

107. Michael J. Boskin, "Macroeconomics, Technology, and Economic Growth: An Introduction to Some Important Issues," in Ralph Landau and Nathan Rosenberg, eds., *The Positive Sum Strategy: Harnessing Technology for Economic Growth* (Washington, D.C., National Academy Press, 1986), 35.

108. Ibid., 35–36.

109. Grieco, "Understanding the Problem of International Cooperation," 303.

110. I am grateful to the anonymous reviewer for pointing this out.

111. Josef Joffe, "How America Does It," *Foreign Affairs* 76(5) (September–October 1997): 24.

112. Donald L. Horowitz, *Ethnic Groups in Conflict* (Berkeley: University of California Press, 1985): 196–97.

113. Waltz, "Conflict in World Politics," p. 464.

114. Milton J. Esman, *Ethnic Politics* (Ithaca: Cornell University Press, 1994), 236. For relative deprivation theory and ethnic conflict, also see Ted Robert Gurr, *Why Men Rebel* (Princeton: Princeton University Press, 1970), and idem, *Minorities at Risk: A Global View of Ethnopolitical Conflicts* (Washington, D.C., U.S. Institute of Peace Press, 1993).

115. See Robert H. Bates, "Ethnic Competition and Modernization in Contemporary Africa," *Comparative Political Studies* 6 (January 1974): 462–64; Paul R.

Brass, "Ethnicity and Nationality Formation," *Ethnicity* 3 (September 1976): 225–41.

116. Robert Melson and Howard Wolpe, "Modernization and the Politics of Communalism: A Theoretical Perspective," *American Political Science Review* 64(4) (December 1970): 1114.

117. Consistent with this argument, Samuel Huntington observes: "The external expansion of the UK and France, Germany and Japan, the Soviet Union and the United States coincided with phases of intense industrialization and economic development." Huntington, "America's Changing Strategic Interests," 12.

118. Nazli Choucri and Robert C. North, *Nations In Conflict: National Growth and International Violence* (San Francisco: W. H. Freeman, 1975). Also see Nazli Choucri, Robert C. North, and Susumu Yamakage, *The Challenge of Japan Before WWII and After: A Study of National Growth and Expansion* (London: Routledge, 1992).

119. Choucri and North, *Nations In Conflict*, 28.

120. The relationship between status inconsistency and international, as opposed to ethnic, conflict has yet to be established. See Thomas J. Volgy and Stacy Mayhall, "Status Inconsistency and International War: Exploring the Effects of Systemic Change," *International Studies Quarterly* 39(1) (March 1995): 67–84.

121. Jack A. Goldstone, "An Analytic Framework," in Jack A. Goldstone, Ted Robert Gurr, and Farrokh Moshiri, eds., *Revolutions of the Late Twentieth Century* (Boulder, CO: Westview Press, 1991), 39.

122. Gilpin, *War and Change*, p. 48.

123. Lucian W. Pye, "China's Quest for Respect," *New York Times* (February 19, 1996), A11.

124. Arnold Wolfers, "The Actors in International Politics," in Wolfers, *Discord and Collaboration: Essays on International Politics* (Baltimore: The Johns Hopkins University Press, 1962): 14–15.

125. E. J. Mishan, *Growth: The Price We Pay* (London: Staples Press, 1969), 100.

126. Ibid., 101.

127. For the connection between political realism and mercantilism–economic nationalism, see Robert Gilpin, *The Political Economy of International Relations* (Princeton: Princeton University Press, 1987), esp. chap. 2; and more recently Gregory P. Nowell, *Mercantile States and the World Oil Cartel, 1900–1939* (Ithaca: Cornell University Press, 1994): 23–25.

128. See Robert Jervis, "Cooperation Under the Security Dilemma, *World Politics* 30(2) (January 1978): 167–214; Charles l. Glaser, "Realists as Optimists: Cooperation as Self-Help," *International Security* 19(3) (Winter 1994–95): 50–90; Thomas J. Christensen and Jack Snyder,"Chain Gangs and Passed Bucks: Predicting Alliance Patterns in Multipolarity," *International Organization* 44(1)

(Spring 1990): 137–68; Ted Hopf, "Polarity, the Offense-Defense Balance and War," *American Political Science Review* 85(2) (June 1991): 475–94; Glenn H. Snyder, "The Security Dilemma in Alliance Politics," *World Politics* 36(4) (July 1984): 461–95; Stephen Van Evera, "The Cult of the Offensive and the Origins of the First World War," *International Security* 9(1) (Summer 1984): 58–107.

129. See Peter Liberman, "The Spoils of Conquest," *International Security* 18(2) (Fall 1993): 125–53; Choucri and North, *Nations In Conflict*; Manus I. Midlarsky, *The Onset of World War* (Boston: Unwin Hyman, 1988); Spykman, *America's Strategy in World Politics*; Sir Halford J. Mackinder, *Democratic Ideals and Reality: A Study in the Politics of Reconstruction* (New York: Henry Holt, 1919); idem., "The Geographical Pivot of History," *Geographic Journal* 23(4) (April 1904), esp. p. 495.

130. See Ludwig Dehio, *The Precarious Balance: Four Centuries of the European Power Struggle* (New York: Knopf, 1962); Gilpin, *War and Change*; George Modelski, *Long Cycles in World Politics* (Seattle and London: University of Washington Press, 1987); A. F. K. Organski, *World Politics*, 2d ed. (New York: Knopf, 1968); A. F. K. Organski and Jacek Kugler, *The War Ledger* (Chicago: University of Chicago Press, 1980); George Modelski and William R. Thompson, *Seapower in Global Politics, 1494–1993* (Seattle: University of Washington Press, 1988); William R. Thompson, *On Global War: Historical-Structural Approaches to World Politics* (Columbia: University of South Carolina Press, 1988); Thompson, "Dehio, Long Cycles, and the Geohistorical Context of Structural Transition," *World Politics* 45(1) (October 1992): 127–52; Charles F. Doran, *Systems in Crisis: New Imperatives of High Politics at Century's End* (Cambridge: Cambridge University Press, 1991); Robert Gilpin, *War and Change in World Politics* (Cambridge: Cambridge University Press, 1981); David P. Rapkin, ed., *World Leadership and Hegemony* (Boulder, CO: Lynne Rienner, 1990); Joshua S. Goldstein, *Long Cycles: Prosperity and War in the Modern Age* (New Haven: Yale University Press, 1988); Fareed R. Zakaria, "The Rise of a Great Power: National Strength, State Structure, and American Foreign Policy, 1865–1908" (Ph.D. dissertation, Harvard University, 1993); and Zakaria, "Realism and Domestic Politics: A Review Essay," *International Security* 17 (1) (Summer 1992): 177–98.

131. Quoted in Gerhard Ritter, *Frederick the Great* (Berkeley: University of California Press, 1968), 66.

3 The Political Economy of Realism

Jonathan Kirshner

What is the political economy of realism? Although there are many examples of realist political economy, there is no clear statement of what core tenets these analyses share. This in turn makes it difficult to identify and assess theories derived from a realist tradition and their shared set of expectations regarding the future. I hope to provide such a baseline in this essay. By building upon basic principles of realist thought, I will specify assumptions and deduce a set of propositions common to realist political economy, and then explore the general consequences of those tenets, and derive a set of more specific expectations.[1]

The first section looks at assumptions realism shares with other approaches, particularly in the context of the rise of liberalism in the late eighteenth century. Section 2 then considers what distinguishes realism in the light of that common ground. It identifies two core divergences from liberalism—statism and the salience of security concerns—and derives from these divergences a number of consequences. Section 3 shows how these in turn informed realist analyses of political economy during the Cold War; the final section raises specific realist predictions for the contemporary international political economy. Parts three and four both attempt to evaluate the performance of realist approaches. It will be seen that such an evaluation is difficult for the Cold War era because many of the relevant outcomes during that time were overdetermined. In the current period, however, there will be numerous issue areas where realist analyses yield distinct expectations from other approaches, offering promising tests of theories derived from competing traditions in the years to come.

I. WEALTH AND POWER IN THE POST-LIBERAL SYNTHESIS

In 1776 came the revolution, with the publication of Adam Smith's *The Wealth of Nations*. Book IV provided an overview of the theory and practice of mercantilism, and then proceeded to dismantle it with devastating critiques.[2] But what was overthrown? For the sake of rhetoric and clarity, Smith simplified mercantilist doctrine and overstated the differences between mercantilism and the liberal alternative he was proposing.[3] While this was true for a number of aspects of mercantilist thought, my focus is solely on those aspects of mercantilism and neomercantilism which inform realism.[4]

In fact, there were important continuities between the classical mercantilists and their liberal challengers. This has been widely recognized. Heckscher saw a fundamental continuity between mercantilism and liberalism as reactions against the political economy of medievalism.[5] Most crucially, each school of thought sought to maximize both power and plenty (as evidenced in Smith's famous support for the navigation acts and subsidies to defense-related industries), and each saw a long-run harmony between those goals.[6]

Still, liberalism did bring many fundamental changes. With regard to its implications for realism, the consequences of the rise of liberalism included three basic conclusions: First, that wealth derived from productive capacity, not precious metals. Second, that trade was positive sum, not zero sum. Third, following from the first two, that the balance of trade and treasure was of sharply less consequence than previously believed. Each of these changes represented an important departure from mercantilist thought.[7]

What separates neomercantilists from the classical mercantilists is that the former read and integrated the teachings of Smith and other liberals into their own philosophies. Neomercantilists reconstituted mercantilism in the light of the liberal revolution, but they did so by incorporating, not rejecting, these three themes. Both Alexander Hamilton and Friedrich List, two of the founding fathers of neomercantilism, accepted much of the teachings of Adam Smith. Hamilton places his arguments in the context of "exceptions" to liberalism.[8] List is, if anything, even more explicit about the extent to which his proposed interventionist measures must be regarded as exceptional. Regarding trade policy, for example, List places limits on the range of goods eligible for protection and the size of any tariff, and emphasizes the temporary measure of the duration of protectionist measures. Despite his sharp critiques of Smith (more about which below), he argues "notwithstanding, we should by no means deny the great merits of Adam Smith."[9]

With the integration of liberal theories of trade, the terms of the debate over this issue shifted to two new issue areas, the *composition* of trade and the *distribution* of the gains (see below). But important areas of agreement also emerged in this era. Most crucially, one can observe a set of shared views regarding economics and power. This is captured in List's statement, *"The power of producing wealth* is therefore infinitely more important than *wealth itself."*[10] Such sentiments are not distinguishable from those of more liberal proponents of free trade, who argue similarly that "National power depends in large measure upon economic productivity" and, "military power depends upon economic strength."[11]

Thus, despite other divergent views, one result of the liberal revolution was the emergence of a synthesis regarding economics and power. As noted above, liberals and mercantilists shared the view that both power and plenty were crucial and complementary aims of state action.[12] Liberals and neomercantilists also share the view that power flows from productive capability and productive capability from economic growth. These are core assumptions upon which realism draws, but they are not uniquely realist positions, and should be considered part of a common foundation shared with liberalism.

> Liberal/Realist Synthesis: Economic growth and capacity are the underlying source of power; economic and political goals are complementary in the long run

This simple statement carries with it a great deal. It broadens considerably the number of elements with which states must be concerned if they hope to survive and prosper in the international system. These include industrial capacity, access to raw materials, and assurance of adequate finance. Additionally, economic growth emerges as an important issue for the sustainability of national security.[13] However, as noted above, these shared views cannot provide the basis for a distinctly realist political economy. Such a conception emerges only when they are combined with assumptions specific to realism.

II. TWO REALIST PROPOSITIONS AND
THEIR CONSEQUENCES

What distinguishes realism from other schools of thought, and particularly from liberalism, are two additional propositions, the first regarding war and the second regarding the state.

Proposition 1: States must anticipate the possibility of war.

This proposition is also quite simply stated, but it is a core tenet associated with realism. It is important to stress that the concern for war (and the significance of statism, below) are best conceptualized as dimensions. Realists need not see a constant "state of war," nor do liberals consider war impossible. Both recognize an international system defined by anarchy in which war is a possible mechanism of resolving disputes and advancing state goals. What distinguishes realists is that they can be placed on that end of a continuum which stresses the likelihood of war, threats of war, and the need for states to shape their policies in the light of this consideration. For E. H. Carr, for example, "Potential war . . . [is] a dominant factor in international politics."[14]

Concern for war was an important aspect of mercantilism,[15] and the view that war was a salient feature of the international system, and was likely to remain so, is one element that was retained in the neomercantilist reconstitution.[16] This is particularly clear in the writings of List, who emphasized the significance of assumptions regarding war in analyses of political economy. "Adam Smith's Doctrine," List argued, "presupposes the existence of a state of perpetual peace and of universal union." But of course, this is not the case. Thus while List recognized the benefits of free trade, he argued that the "influence of war" required states to deviate from some of the policy prescriptions of liberalism.[17]

Proposition 2: The state is a distinct actor with its own interests

The central role of the state is also crucial for realism. As with the significance of war, views regarding statism are not absolute, but are held to varying degrees. Thus, non realists do not deny the existence of an autonomous state, they simply differ as to the extent and consequence of that autonomy. Realists stress the state as a distinct entity from the sum of particular interests; as an entity with the capability and inclination to pursue its own agenda; and as the principal actor in international relations. Once again, this strand of realist thought can be derived from a mercantilist tradition, one that became an even more important element of the neomercantilist reconstruction.

Statism, particularly in evidence with regard to state building—internal unification and external closure—is fundamental for both classical and neo-mercantilists. According to Heckscher, "The state stood at the centre of mercantilist endeavours developed historically: the state was both the subject and the object of mercantilist economic policy." In fact, more than half of Heckscher's massive study is devoted to the study of "Mercantilism as a Unifying System," where, among other things, "The aim was the superiority of the state over all other forces within a country."[18]

The neomercantilist champion of statism and state building is Schmoller.[19] He argued that "What was at stake was the creation of real *political* economies as unified organisms," and that state action was required to bring about "a union for external defense, and for internal justice and administration, for currency and credit, for trade interests and economic life." For Schmoller, mercantilism "in its innermost kernel is nothing but state making."[20] While not all would share this view, the central role of the state, from the perspective of both international and domestic politics, remains a major theme in realist thought.[21]

Four consequences of the realist propositions

From these three foundations—the synthesis on economics and power, and the two realist assumptions regarding the salience of war and the centrality of the state—it is possible to derive a number of interrelated and complementary consequences which form the basic structure of realist political economy. These consequences are not falsifiable predictions, but rough realist generalizations regarding the behavior of states and the nature of international relations.[22]

Consequence 1: The State will intervene when the interests of domestic actors diverge from its own.

From the realist view that the state is a distinct actor with its own interests comes the issue of the extent to which these overlap with the sum of the particular interests of actors within the state. Liberals are more likely to see harmony between the interests of the state and the sum of particular interests.

There is, of course, variation within the liberal camp on this issue, with some arguing that the existence of externalities creates divergences between private and societal levels of optimal production of various goods, which can be corrected by government intervention. Others see almost no scope for such action.[23]

Realists, on the other hand, anticipate that divergences of interest will often arise and that the state will intervene when necessary to defend its interests. These divergences can come from a number of sources, given an autonomous state, but are most likely to arise in regard to issues related to security. This is because in a world where war is possible, states are likely to be very sensitive to national security issues, while, due to a collective action dynamic, individual actors within society are likely to be suboptimally concerned with the common defense. Thus, while power and plenty are complementary in the long run, the state will often be willing to sacrifice short- and medium-term economic gains when tradeoffs present themselves.[24]

This is yet another tradition that survived the transition from classical mercantilism to neomercantilism. Mun was able to distinguish between the interests of the commonwealth, the merchant, and the King, noting for example that there will be patterns of trade by which "the Commonwealth may be enriched . . . when the merchant in his particular shall have no occasion to rejoyce." Similarly, in other conditions the merchant may prosper, "when nevertheless the commonwealth shall decline and grow poor." Other mercantilists held similar views on the potential incompatibility of public and private interests.[25]

List similarly argued that "the interest of individuals and the interest of the commerce of a whole nation are widely different things." Again, this is particularly likely to be the case when the state, due to its greater sensitivity to security concerns or its tendency to have a longer time horizon than individuals, is more willing to accept short-term economic sacrifices in order to reap greater long run rewards. "The nation," List argued, "must renounce present advantages with a view to securing future ones."[26] This contrasts with a liberal perspective, from which List's statism leads "almost insensibly to the concept of the state as an end in itself and the major end of policy, rather than as an instrument for the promotion of individual welfare."[27]

Statism, especially with regard to the divergence of individual and national interests, is also often manifested in the state's search for autonomy. States aim to establish and preserve their independence from three encroachments: those of particular domestic interests, other states, and economic forces.

Given the possibility of war, states will strive for national self-sufficiency, in order to assure the ability to produce the means to fight, as well as to reduce vulnerabilities that would result from the disruption of peacetime patterns of international economic flows. This is an important reason why realists tend to be skeptical of arguments touting the benefits of interdependence. For realists, states are more likely to chafe from the frictions that interdependence will present, rather than being soothed by its multilayered embrace.[28] States may also seek to retain a reservoir of resources, or "war chest." Of course, these actions will direct economic activity along suboptimal paths. Thus complete autarky will rarely be sought—the state will balance its desire for autonomy with its goal of long-run economic growth.[29]

That states will seek to insulate themselves from vulnerability to other states and international economic forces can be traced to Aristotle, and is a mainstay of realist thought.[30] This suggests a reciprocal dynamic: market forces will naturally expand in new directions, which will call forth efforts by states to shape and restrain those flows.[31] Krasner has argued that these concerns can be seen most clearly in small, weak states, who feel the brunt of such vulnerabilities most acutely.[32] However, this concern is plainly visible in even the largest of states, such as the United States at the present time or Great Britain a century ago, at which time dissenters from British liberalism called attention to England's dependence on foreign trade and the dangerous extent to which much of its economic livelihood required the maintenance of peace. They supported state action to reduce these vulnerabilities.[33]

Consequence 2: International political concerns will shape the pattern of economic relations

Another important, related consequence of statism in the context of concerns about war is that states will attempt to shape the pattern of international economic flows to serve their security interests. For realists, politics and the threat of war are crucial determinants of the patterns of economic activity, although these forces are often veiled as behavior becomes routinized.[34] Again, in a broad sense, this view is universally held. One recent study documents how the mere existence of the political border between Canada and the United States, nations with extraordinarily few legal barriers to trade, dramatically skews the pattern of economic activity. This serves as a reminder that the very existence of distinct nations is inefficient from an economic perspective, and can be considered "a standing violation of free trade."[35]

Realists, however, stress the ubiquity of power concerns and the weight of their consequences. Given the possibility of war, for example, states cannot simply allow the market to dictate that they specialize in a production portfolio which does not provide for the domestic manufacture of goods vital for the provision of national defense.[36] When states are faced with threats to their survival, "the subtleties of comparative advantage become a foolish irrelevance."[37]

These concerns function not simply through the overt policies designed to shape the direction of trade, but find expression through and are mediated by more structural factors, such as the balance of power and ideology. As Schmoller argued:

> Does it not sound to us today like the irony of fate, that the same England, which in 1750–1800 reached the summit of its commercial supremacy by means of tariffs and naval wars, frequently with extraordinary violence, and always with the most tenacious selfishness, that that England at the very same time announced to the world the doctrine that only the egoism of the individual is justified, and never that of states and nations; the doctrine which dreamt of a stateless competition of all the individuals of every land, and of the harmony of the economic interests of all nations?[38]

This view was shared by British neomercantilists at the turn of the twentieth century, who argued that free trade policies, which had once served the national interest, were no longer appropriate. Free trade, they argued, was the optimal policy for Britain when it had an economic lead over other states. But mercantilist strategies had been crucial in establishing that lead. Free trade subsequently allowed a relatively advanced England to "crush rival industries in every part of the world, by supplying the markets with goods produced on the better and cheaper methods which were only practiced in England." Neither doctrine was universally appropriate, contrary to the liberal view. Thus, a shift to neomercantilist strategies in Britain was necessary, "to ward off the dangers which threaten her very existence."[39]

Political concerns can shape economic relations in a number of ways. One of the most distinctive aspects of the realist vision of states' search for security is the willingness of states to make economic sacrifices in order to achieve political gains. In this respect realism diverges from liberalism, which tends to emphasize economic ends. It distinguishes realism much more dramatically from other schools of thought, such as neo-Marxism, which holds the opposite view. From the radical perspective, power is used to hold in place a system of international capitalism that enforces economic exploitation: the use of power to accumulate wealth.

As noted above, the realist view reverses this relationship. This process was first described by Hirschman. In his book *National Power and the Structure of Foreign Trade*[40] Hirschman focused on German interwar trading relations. He demonstrated how Germany cultivated a series of asymmetric trading relationships with the small states of southeastern Europe as part of its pre-World War II grand strategy to secure needed raw materials and increase German leverage there. Although inefficient from an economic perspective, redirecting trade to contiguous regions enhanced Germany's autonomy. Focusing on small states increased Germany's political leverage there by making exit more costly for others. This asymmetry, plus the relatively sweet deals Germany offered, exerted, as Hirschman noted, "a powerful influence in favor of a 'friendly' attitude towards the state to the imports of which they owe their interests."[41]

Realists argue these are pervasive characteristics of the international economy: economic relations purposefully shaped along political lines, and the expenditure of wealth in attempts to purchase political influence. These elements have been used by a variety of scholars to explain the pattern of international financial arrangements, commercial policy, monetary relations, and of course, aid, the direct transfer of resources to gain influence.[42]

Consequence 3: International economic cooperation will be difficult to establish and maintain

The difficulty of international economic cooperation, with regard both to reaching agreements and to maintaining them, is another consequence of the propositions of realism. With economic growth underlying long-run military capability, and given concerns for the possibility of war, states will find it difficult to cooperate. Even with the recognition that mutual gains exist, states must still be concerned with the distribution of those gains, lest potential adversaries become relatively more powerful.[43]

Helmut Schmidt stated the realist position quite clearly when he observed, "David Ricardo would certainly not like this state of the world economy." Despite the existence of gains from trade, "What we are witnessing today in the field of international economic relations . . . . is a struggle for the distribution and use of the national product, a struggle for the world product."[44]

Once again, an important contribution in this regard stems from the neomercantilist reformation, after the liberal revolution, of the mercantilist concern for interstate rivalry. Neomercantilists such as Hamilton and List did not deny the gains from trade, but rather raised the question of dynamic comparative advantage: whether specialization imposed by international market forces would put a nation on a trajectory of relatively low growth.[45] If, at the same time, temporary protection or other measures, which, when removed, would allow for specialization in more attractive products, then free trade would not be the optimal policy in the short run. The gains from trade are not denied—rather, this is a classic case of the state imposing short-term costs on society for greater benefits in the long run. Thus the mercantilist concern for the balance of trade is rehabilitated with the neomercantilist concern for the *composition* of trade. This is also one way in which realists can be distinguished from crude protectionists, who tend to stress the overall balance.

Hamilton argued that "the United States cannot exchange with Europe on equal terms." Industry left to itself, will not "naturally find its way to the most useful and profitable employment," because of the "difficulties incident" in initiating enterprise in the context of "superiority antecedently enjoyed by nations."[46] Worse, states may attempt to manipulate their commercial and domestic economic policies in order to shape the trajectory of comparative advantage. These "bounties, premiums and aids" Hamilton declared to be the "greatest obstacle of all." State intervention to manipulate comparative advantage has been a perennial concern of realists, and forms the basis of contemporary arguments for strategic trade and industrial policy.[47]

Even in the absence of concerns for dynamic comparative advantage, realists would still expect cooperation to founder over the distribution of gains in a static setting. Gilpin argues that "the distinction between absolute and relative gains" is "a fundamental difference in emphasis" which distinguishes realism. While this issue has attracted a great deal of attention recently, it too can be traced to the origins of the approach. Writing in German in 1684, P. W. von Hörnigk stated that the wealth and might of a nation depends "principally on whether its neighbors possess more or less of it. For power and riches have become a *relative* matter." A decade earlier, the English mercantilist Coke wrote "if our treasure were more than our Neighboring nations, I did not care whether we had one-fifth part of the treasure we now have."[48]

In contemporary international relations theory, this issue has received a disproportionate share of attention. While the concern for the distribution of mutual gains (the "relative gains" issue) is significant for realist political economy, what ultimately distinguishes realism is not the pursuit of relative gains, but the *motives* behind that pursuit: the existence of anarchy and the concern for security, as I shall discuss below. Actors in the absence of anarchy routinely seek relative, not just absolute gains in their interactions. Thus while realists offer a fundamental motivational difference for state behavior, the behavior itself (pursuit of relative gains) is not incompatible with other approaches to political economy.[49]

While realists expect cooperation to be difficult, there are at the same time exceptions to this rule—exceptions that can also be derived from first principles.[50] As discussed above, states attempting to enhance their influence with other states may make overly generous concessions. This is a reversal of the concern for relative gains, which expands the core of mutually acceptable bargains, and this may be an important feature of asymmetric economic relations. Additionally, structure can also at times mitigate the barriers to cooperation. In a bipolar setting with the expectation of stable military alliances, states' concerns for the consequences of relative gains can be muted with regard to economic relations with allies.[51] Finally, cooperation can often be sustained because present security concerns cause states to discount narrow economic interests.[52]

Consequence 4: Economic change will tend to be associated with political conflict.

Combining the synthesis on economic growth and underlying power with the proposition that states must anticipate the possibility of war leads to some unpleasant realist arithmetic.

Economic change will affect the underlying balance of power. For some states, this will increase perceptions of vulnerability.[53] This can be anticipated even without relying on a realist perspective, since growing states will appear more threatening even if they do not have offensive intentions. For example, consider a state whose economy grows at seven percent per year for ten years. In the tenth year, the absolute level of its annual military spending will be twice what it once was, even if military spending was held constant as a percentage of gross national product. Clearly such conditions are ripe for generating spiral-type conflicts.[54] But realists will expect this problem to be particularly acute, since it is compounded by the fact that the ambitions of growing states may indeed increase. Thus, while all growing states will tend to appear more threatening, some will actually be more threatening, and it may be quite difficult to distinguish one from another. In a world where concerns for war are important, economic change is likely to be a catalyst for political conflict.[55]

This has been stressed by a number of realist scholars, who have emphasized the importance of equilibrium in the international system.[56] According to these approaches, in equilibrium, states are satisfied with or unable to alter the status quo, with the result that given the distribution of power, no state sees benefits from challenging the prevailing order. Economic change, however, will affect states differentially, creating divergences between power and privilege. Thus there is a natural tendency for the system as a whole to drift away from equilibrium over time. It is therefore likely that revisionist states will rise to challenge the status quo, and this challenge is often resolved by war.[57]

III. THE POLITICAL ECONOMY OF REALISM AND THE COLD WAR

How well do realist expectations regarding political economy conform to the pattern of activity observed during the Cold War? Unfortunately, there is no easy answer to this question. As will be seen below, they explain some things quite well, but are less successful at other times. This ambiguity is compounded by a number of significant problems, not the least of which are the dangers inherent in post-hoc analysis, particularly with regard to establishing the criteria for evaluation. Additionally, at times when realist expectations are fulfilled, the outcomes are not clearly distinguishable from the expectations of competing theories. Finally, the Cold War, as a bipolar struggle between market and nonmarket economies, led to analytical specializations within the discipline of international relations that skewed realist analysis. This diverted, with prominent exceptions, much of the attention of realism from international political economy.[58] Still, with these caveats, an evaluation of Cold War realist political economy is possible.

Realism is especially successful in arguing that political concerns will shape the pattern of international economic activity. The rich and expanding economic relations between the U.S. and its allies contrast markedly with the controls placed on trade with the communist bloc.[59] The U.S., from its position of dominance within the Western bloc, actively supported a liberal international order. This conforms with a number of realist expectations.

The U.S. used its wealth to shape preferences and to support political allies against its principal adversary. It championed openness, which was to its advantage as the technological leader and also served to undermine the imperial preference systems which discriminated against American products. It provided the lion's share of the start up costs for new international institutions, and those institutions were in turn shaped by America's vision and served U.S. interests.[60] While much of this is also compatible with other perspectives,[61] there are prominent examples where this is not the case. Important economic flows, such as petrodollar recycling, were shaped by political measures that resulted in patterns clearly at odds with liberal expectations.[62] Additionally, countless other economic relationships—including preferential trading agreements, currency areas, flows of finance and investment, and, of course, aid and economic sanctions—can only be understood as outcomes of international political concerns.[63]

Realist expectations perform quite poorly, on the other hand, regarding the desire of states for autonomy. There have certainly been prominent Cold War examples of statism, most obviously in the case of the Soviet Union. Also, Japan is often portrayed as a strong state mediating and shaping economic forces, particularly with regard to its concerns for economic and national security.[64] Even the U.S. has been accused of seeking "to combine the benefits of liberal internationalism and mercantilist advantage." And the American abandonment of the Bretton-Woods exchange rate system was clearly a reassertion of domestic autonomy from international economic forces.[65] But these episodes have taken place, especially since 1973, in the context of an expanding international economy which has been relentlessly encroaching on state autonomy. This has been manifested in increasingly complex intra-industry and intra-firm trade, larger investment flows, and especially the expansion of financial markets. This latter issue is of particular interest since states engaged in purposeful deregulation of national buffers such as capital controls, and this has led to reduced macroeconomic policy autonomy.[66]

It may be argued that international market forces can at times be used by states to advance policy and enhance their authority vis-à-vis domestic actors. This is certainly true in some cases.[67] However, while this explains the strategic and selective use of such forces by states, it cannot account for the type of wholesale abdication of autonomy that many states have allowed to pass. Additionally, retrospective analyses are likely to overcount the number of "strategic" measures adopted by states, since almost any behavior could be so characterized post-hoc.[68] Still, the "irony of state strength" argument does serve notice that the evaluation of state capacity is more subtle than a simple "states verses markets" conception would suggest.

Finally, with regard to state intervention to preserve autonomy, it should be noted that one clearly stated realist proposition in this regard has been falsified. As discussed above, it was argued that small, weak states would be especially willing to make economic sacrifices to enhance their autonomy. But in the past decade, third world states have generally embraced rather than resisted the international economy.[69]

With regard to realist predictions about the difficulty of international cooperation, it is especially hard to draw any conclusions. There was a great deal of economic cooperation among the advanced industrial powers during the Cold War, which would seem at a glance to cut against the grain of realist expectations. But every element that realists anticipate would mitigate these difficulties, and promote cooperation, was in place. There was stable bipolarity, asymmetry within the alliance, and a clear security threat, three features argued to enhance cooperation and reduce concern for the distribution of gains.

Indeed, American policy behavior, especially in the early Cold War, both promoted the relative gains of others and was fully consistent with realism. Cooperation in the Western alliance was encouraged not only because of the absence of negative security externalities, but also the presence of positive ones: the U.S. wanted its allies to get stronger so that they might better balance against a common threat.[70] This also raises a more general theoretical point: that concerns for relative gains within a bilateral relationship can be muted by the relative gains such a relationship affords vis-à-vis third parties.[71]

Further, it is not clear that evidence of conflicts over relative gains would resolve this issue.[72] For just as realists can explain instances where the concern for relative gains was absent, liberals can explain many fights over relative gains. Liberals would not deny the possibility of conflicts about the distribution of relative gains; these take place in many instances between friendly partners in the absence of threats of force, readily seen, for example, in most transactions between actors within a domestic economy. As discussed above realist analysis in this regard is distinguished principally by its analysis of *underlying motives*, and not necessarily by its expectations regarding state behavior. Realist motives raise the stakes, and supply an additional source of friction. Actors are not concerned simply with others reneging on promises, a sense of distributive justice, or the need to establish a tough reputation for future negotiations, but rather, as Grieco argues, "states in anarchy must fear that others may seek to destroy or enslave them."[73] Thus what distinguishes realists' expectations in practice are not conflicts over relative gains, but *sharper* conflicts over relative gains; with partners walking away from *a significant number* of deals with mutual gains left on the table. For both liberals and realists, then, the "core" of agreements is smaller than the set of mutually beneficial deals. The realist subset is simply smaller still. Distinguishing between these subsets in practice is extremely difficult, to the point that it raises serious questions regarding the tractability of such endeavors. It is not clear that a definitive answer to these questions will ever emerge from retrospective analyses of the Cold War era.

Finally, with respect to the relationship between economic change and political conflict during the Cold War, it is again difficult to reach clear conclusions. The relative decline of the U.S. economy among the advanced industrial states would lead realists to expect a reduction in cooperation. This has certainly been the case with regard to international monetary relations, but less so with regard to other issue areas, such as trade.

International monetary and macroeconomic policies have been punctuated by American unilateralism and characterized by discord, most clearly visible in 1971 with the closing of the gold window by President Nixon, who "spoke exclusively the language of national power and national advantage."[74] The dearth of global monetary cooperation was again prominent in the early 1980s, with the dramatic appreciation of the U.S. dollar, and an administration in Washington that was hostile to the concept of macroeconomic policy coordination. However, this was less the exception than the rule: with a few exceptions, such as the depreciation of the dollar from 1985–1987, international macroeconomic cooperation has been elusive in the past quarter century.[75]

On the other hand, in some areas cooperation has been sustained to a much greater extent than would have been predicted given global economic change. There is clearly greater friction in the U.S.-Japan relationship, and new protectionist pressures have emerged in the international economy.[76] But would realists in 1987, for example, have expected the successful completion of the Uruguay round? Another important Cold War economic change, the oil shocks of the 1970s (especially the initial quadrupling of the world price of oil), worked its way through the international economy more smoothly than might have been expected; the West took no action to seize oil fields.[77] Some conflicts have emerged, and others may yet still emerge, from the economic decline and collapse of the Soviet Union, but that Russia did not go down swinging is a fundamental challenge to realist analysis. Perhaps the most dramatic change in the international economy has been the rise of the Asian economies, and especially China. This has not yet led to political conflict, but here clearly there may be shoes yet to drop.

In summary, while much Cold War history is consistent with realist expectations, there are some "misses" as well. More confounding, there are the problems of distinguishing realist expectations from those of competing approaches and establishing adequate criteria for evaluation in a post-hoc analysis.

IV. REALISM AND THE POST-COLD WAR INTERNATIONAL POLITICAL ECONOMY

One positive aspect of the post Cold War era is that many of the problems associated with evaluating realist theories during the Cold War no longer exist. Obviously, predictions can now be made in advance and the criteria for evaluation established. Further, both bipolarity and international communism, which previously tended to complicate these analyses, have disappeared. Realist predictions can now be less ambiguous and more clearly distinguishable from those of other perspectives. In fact, the coming years are likely to offer excellent laboratories to compare competing theories. This final section presents a number of predictions and evaluates some of the preliminary evidence—of course, the future will speak for itself.

Five Realist Predictions[78]

1. China will become increasingly involved in international conflict

With its dramatic economic growth and large absolute size, China is for realism a prime candidate for conflict and war. Writing in 1988, Kahler argued that international stability was likely to persist "until the elite of another ascendant power (China?) discovers the means to reinforce its military ambitions with economic success."[79] The prospects for conflict in this region have been stressed by other scholars as well.[80] A peaceful China is virtually incompatible with a number of realist theories. At the same time, the liberal perspective would expect contemporary economic change to reduce China's aggressiveness, as economic growth and international trade decentralizes power within China and creates vested interests in continued peace. Growing interdependence will also expand bargaining opportunities and reduce the likelihood that disputes which do arise will spill over into war. Thus China's international behavior in the coming years will offer a distinct test of realist predictions.[81]

Caution must be taken, however, in establishing the criteria of evaluation in this case. China has appeared increasingly aggressive toward Taiwan, for example, but it would be a mistake to draw general conclusions from China's behavior over this peculiar issue area. On the other hand, the threshold can be set too high: China may become increasingly assertive and force prone even in the absence of a great-power war. The initial evidence does suggest that China is increasing its military capability to enhance its international status, and that its buildup is neither motivated by defensive concerns nor in response to an increasingly threatening international security environment.[82] It remains to be seen how these changes affect international politics in the region.

2. States will reassert control over international economic flows

Another clear contrast between liberal and realist expectations has to do with the growth of the international economy. As mentioned above, that expanding economy has made dramatic encroachments on sovereignty in the past quarter century, in trade, investment, and particularly finance.[83] A liberal perspective would be to expect that these changes are irreversible, or at least highly likely to continue. Realists, however, must expect states to find these challenges to autonomy intolerable, or at least highly objectionable, and anticipate that states will attempt to constrain these forces. It is not sufficient for realists to note, however accurately, that there have been periods of history where the international economy imposed even greater constraints on states.[84] Especially given the threats these trends pose to crucial state concerns such as defense autonomy[85] and control over macroeconomic policy, the absence of clear efforts by states to reassert control over many of these flows will challenge fundamental realist conceptions.[86]

There is still no evidence that states, individually or collectively, are attempting to reassert greater control over international market forces. Hints can be seen in the reemergence of a protectionist-isolationist wing in the Republican party of the United States, which dominated the party in the first half of this century. But at this stage these groups and their potential allies on the political left represent a disarticulated politics of dissent that has not influenced policy. More sober proposals designed to provide greater policy autonomy by modulating the balance of power between state and market, such as through small taxes on international financial transactions, have to this point attracted little attention and even less enthusiasm.[87]

3. Multilateral economic cooperation among the advanced industrial states will decline

Many of the changes associated with the end of the Cold War, including the recession of a common military threat and increased economic symmetry among Europe, North America, and Japan, will reduce realist expectations of cooperation.[88] As discussed above, realists consider cooperation inherently difficult under most circumstances, but there can be mitigating factors that allow for increased opportunities: shared security concerns, stable bipolar alliances, and asymmetry. With these factors all receding,[89] states will be even more concerned with relative gains, and less willing to maintain agreements in hard times.[90] While this essay has stressed the difficulty of distinguishing between contrasting expectations regarding the overall level of cooperation, this problem is somewhat less acute in forward-looking analyses where explicit predictions can be established and tested. Good starting points are offered by trade and monetary relations. From the realist perspective, global trade liberalization should stall, and prospects for reforming the international monetary system should be quite slim.[91]

Of the many possible criteria to evaluate realist expectations regarding multilateral cooperation, three barometers stand out. First, regarding international trade, there is the degree to which the transition from the ratification of the Uruguay accords to their implementation in practice is successful. Second is the level of progress toward multilateral management of international monetary and financial relations, given the obvious demand for cooperation in these areas. Fred Bergsten, for example, argues that the international system "most urgently requires . . . supervision and regulation of capital markets."[92] Third, and providing a bridge to the next prediction, is the extent to which broad multilateral cooperation is displaced by narrower substitutes.

4. The global economy will become increasingly characterized by group discrimination

This relates to the previous two predictions. Despite the search for autonomy, it must be recalled that realists also are sensitive to the importance of economic growth. Engaging the international economy provides expanded opportunities and greater prospects for growth. Thus for realists, states face tradeoffs between complete autarky and unfettered internationalism in the pursuit of their multiple goals. Economic discrimination by like-minded states against outsiders (liberalization within the group, with common external barriers) is the realist predicted compromise of the twenty-first century, combining relative autonomy with international economic opportunity. Given concerns for autonomy, there will be a tendency for such discriminatory groups to be regional. But since some states will count fierce adversaries among their close neighbors (precluding intimate economic relations between them), group discrimination will take on a variety of geographic patterns. With this caveat in mind, it is convenient to label group discrimination "regionalism." According to Gilpin, then, "a mixed system of nationalism, regionalism, and sectoral protectionism is replacing the Bretton Woods system of multilateral liberalization." Because of these pressures, he writes, "loose regional blocs are the likely result."[93]

In many cases, regional economies also re-create the asymmetries that no longer exist in much of the international economy. In the context of asymmetry, realists also see greater prospects for cooperation, for reasons discussed above. Thus realists would expect trade, investment, and other economic flows to grow even faster within discriminatory groups, compared with global growth, than could be explained by economic proximity, or even by differential rates of economic growth.[94] Also compatible with realist expectations would be the rise of formal regional agreements and institutions designed to encourage these trends, and the rise of distinct spheres of monetary dominance.

5. European unification will falter

Although realist theory predicts increased regionalism in the global economy, states' concerns for autonomy place limits on how deep regional economic integration is likely to extend. While realists will expect Europe to remain a region with increasing external discrimination and perhaps even greater internal cooperation, this will not lead to political unification. Once again, the end of the Cold War has changed factors that lead to distinct realist expectations. The decline of the Soviet Union removes much of the realist glue binding Western European states together. Similarly, the unification of Germany will change the ways in which all of the states in the region calculate their interests. The pressures placed on the German economy by unification, for example, contributed to the factors which led to the

EMS crisis of 1992, displaying the increasing tension between narrow and regional interests to which recent trends in Europe have contributed. The question of future monetary cooperation in Europe offers a useful gauge of competing theories.[95] The recent stumble would appear to support realist approaches. If the EMU is put on the back burner indefinitely, this would provide further confirmation of realist expectations. If on the other hand, existing informal cooperation is strengthened and progress toward monetary union resumes, the evidence would point in the opposite direction.[96]

CONCLUSION

For a number of reasons it has been difficult in the past to evaluate the political economy of realism. The tradition of realism has generated a heterogenous collection of theories, and the relationships between them have not always been obvious. The problems inherent in post-hoc evaluation and the existence of overdetermined outcomes have further complicated matters. This essay has argued that realist theories share a set of core assumptions that yield distinct expectations. While this does not result in a unique or uniform realist political economy, it does offer a vision of a coherent constellation of realist theories. With the end of the Cold War and the a priori deduction of specific predictions, the coming years will provide the opportunity to test a number of specific realist theories.

ACKNOWLEDGMENT

I thank the other authors in the volume, and especially Ethan Kapstein and Michael Mastanduno, as well as Rawi Abdelal, Tom Christensen, David Edelstein, Karl Mueller, Alan Rousso, and an anonymous reviewer at Columbia University Press, for comments on earlier drafts of this essay.

NOTES

1. This chapter is not, then, designed to be a review of contemporary realist literature. Its goal is to establish the foundations common to realist approaches to political economy.
2. Adam Smith, *An Inquiry into the Nature and Causes of The Wealth of Nations* (Chicago: University of Chicago Press, 1976 [1776]), esp. 1: 450–73, 496–502, 513–24; 2: 3–10, 103–57.

3. Lars Magnusson, *Mercantilism: The Shaping of an Economic Language* (London: Routledge, 1994), 28; J. B. Condliffe, *The Commerce of Nations* (New York: Norton, 1950), 67. W. A. S Hewins, "The Growth of English Industry and Commerce in Modern Times" *Economic Journal* 2 (December 1892): 699. For Smith's caricature, see *Wealth of Nations*, 1: 450–56.

4. It is important to note that this paper does not equate mercantilism or neo-mercantilism with realism. The meaning of realism in the context of political economy is defined explicitly below. Mercantilism and its variants are of great interest because they represent important economic doctrines often associated with and which have contributed to realist thought. However realists will view liberal economic doctrines, such as free trade, as the optimal strategy for some states in certain settings.

   Thus, this essay will not aim to provide a comprehensive definition of "mercantilism." Mercantilist doctrines are heterogenous and many of its crucial concerns, for example theories regarding the importance of the monetary circulation, are not relevant for the study of realism. On these issues see Lars Magnusson (ed.) *Mercantilist Economics* (Boston: Kluwer Academic Publishers, 1993); A. V. Judges, "The Idea of a Mercantile State," *Transactions of the Royal Historical Society* (fourth series) 21 (1939); Jacob Viner, "English Theories of Foreign Trade Before Adam Smith," in his *Studies in the Theory of International Trade* (New York: Harper, 1937); Eli F. Heckscher, *Mercantilism* (2 vols.) (London: George Allen & Unwin, 1935)

5. Heckscher, *Mercantilism*, see for example 1: 26, 456; 2: 13–14, 271, 285, 316, 328; Schumpeter wrote "We have seen that, as far at least as economic analysis is concerned, there need not have been any spectacular break between 'mercantilists' and 'liberals.' " *History of Economic Analysis* (New York: Oxford University Press, 1954), 376. See also William D. Grampp, "The Liberal Elements in English Mercantilism" *Quarterly Journal of Economics* 66(4) (November 1952): 465–501.

6. Smith, *The Wealth of Nations*, 1: 484–5; 2: 28. The classic statement of the mercantilist conception of harmony between economic and political goals is Jacob Viner, "Power Versus Plenty as Objectives of Statecraft in the Seventeenth and Eighteenth Centuries," *World Politics* 1(1) (October 1948): 1–29. While compelling, this paper dramatically overstates the extent to which Heckscher argued that mercantilists were willing to sacrifice wealth in their pursuit of power. Heckscher was aware of the underlying harmony, and his discussion of power is a small part of a large book. See Heckscher, *Mercantilism* 1: 25–26, 29; also Magnusson, *Mercantilism*, 32, 39, 152.

   Viner's treatment of Heckscher's book is surprising given his earlier statement that "It is a work of the highest quality on both the historical and the theoretical sides, and I am happy to find that where we are dealing with the same topics there is no substantial conflict of interpretation or appraisal." Jacob Viner, "English Theories of Foreign Trade Before Adam Smith," p. 3. However, Viner did critique Heckscher's treatment of power, though more subtly, in an earlier review: see *Economic History Review* 6 (October 1935): 99–101.

7. Late mercantilist James Stewart argued: "foreign trade, well conducted, has the necessary effect of drawing wealth from all other nations." *An Inquiry into the Principles of Political Oeconomy* (Chicago: University of Chicago Press, 1966 [1767]), 283, see also p. 363. On the conception of trade as zero-sum, Heckscher stated: "Scarcely any other element in mercantilist philosophy contributed more to the shaping of economic policy, and even of foreign policy as a whole." *Mercantilism* 2: 24. The balance of trade was of great concern to many prominent mercantilists, including Thomas Mun, *England's Treasure by Forraign Trade* (Oxford: Basil Blackwell, 1949 [1664]), indeed, the subtitle of the book is "Or, the Ballance of our Forraign Trade is the Rule of our Treasure," see also esp. pp. 83–86. Richard Cantillion wrote that "above all . . . care must be always be taken to maintain the balance against the foreigner.," *Essay on the Nature of Trade in General* (New York: Augustus M. Kelley, 1964 [1755]), 243. Famed German mercantilist Johann Joachim Becher wrote "it is always better to sell goods to others than to buy goods from others, for the former brings a certain advantage and the latter inevitable damage" (quoted in Heckscher, *Mercantilism*, 2 p. 116). Heckscher argues that "this attitude became crystallized in a demand for an export surplus, a demand which was expressed in every possible way." On this issue see also Frank Whitson Fetter, "The Term 'Favorable balance of Trade'," *Quarterly Journal of Economics* 49(4) (August 1935): 621–45.

8. Alexander Hamilton, "Report on the Subject of Manufactures" (1791), in Arthur Cole (ed.) *Industrial and Commercial Correspondence of Alexander Hamilton* (Chicago: A. W. Shaw, 1928), 248. The Report was revised four times by Hamilton over the course of one year. All five drafts, with Hamilton's own corrections and editorial commentary, are in Harold C. Street (ed.), *The Papers of Alexander Hamilton* 10 (New York: Columbia University Press, 1966). On similarities between Hamilton and Smith, see Edward G. Bourne, "Alexander Hamilton and Adam Smith" *Quarterly Journal of Economics* 8(3) (April 1894): 329–48. While Smith clearly had a profound influence on Hamilton, the roots of Hamilton's thinking can be traced to an important pamphlet he wrote in 1775, "The Farmer Refuted" (New York: James Rivington, 1775), reprinted in *Papers* 1, esp. pp. 122–55. For more on Hamilton, see Edward Meade Earle, "Adam Smith, Alexander Hamilton, Friedrich List: The Economic Foundations of Military Power, in Peter Paret (ed.), *Makers of Modern Strategy* (Princeton: Princeton University Press, 1986), esp. pp. 230–44; Edward C. Lunt,

"Hamilton as a Political Economist" *Journal of Political Economy* 3(3) (June 1895): 289–310, offers a broader but more critical discussion.

9. Friedrich List, *The National System of Political Economy* (London, Longmans, Green, 1885), 308–314; 351 (quote). *The National System* brought to full flower ideas List had been developing for some time. See his *The Natural System of Political Economy 1837 (translated and edited by W. O. Henderson)* (London: Frank Cass, 1983), and "Outlines of American Political Economy" (Philadelphia: Samuel Parker, 1927), reprinted in Margaret E. Hirst, *Life of Friedrich List and Selections From His Writings* (London: Smith Elder, 1909). For more on List, see W. O. Henderson, *Friedrich List: Economist and Visionary 1789–1846* (London: Frank Cass, 1983), Earle, "Adam Smith, Alexander Hamilton, Friedrich List," esp. pp. 243–58; William Notz, "Frederick List in America" *American Economic Review* 16(1) (March 1926): 249–65.

10. List, *National System*, 133 (emphasis in original).

11. J. B. Condliffe, *The Commerce of Nations* (New York: Norton, 1950), 800.

12. See esp. the four features stressed by Viner regarding the mercantilists, in Viner, "Power versus Plenty," 10.

13. On these issues, see Susan Strange, *States and Markets* (New York: Basil Blackwell, 1988); Robert Gilpin, *The Political Economy of International Relations* (Princeton: Princeton University Press, 1987), esp pp. 328–36; Gilpin, *War and Change in World Politics* (Cambridge: Cambridge University Press, 1981); Paul Kennedy, "The First World War and the International Power System," *International Security* 9(1) (1984): 7–40; Kennedy, *The Rise and Fall of British Naval Mastery* (London: Ashfield Press, 1976); Rasler and Thompson, "Global Wars, Public Debts, and the Long Cycle," *World Politics* (July 1983), 489–516; Hans Morgenthau, *Politics Among Nations* (5th ed., rev) (New York: Knopf, 1978), esp. p. 126; Klaus Knorr, *The Power of Nations* (New York: Basic Books, 1975).

14. E. H. Carr, *The Twenty Years' Crisis, 1919–1939* (2nd edition) (New York: Harper, 1964), 109.

15. One of the motives for a trade surplus emphasized by mercantilists was to provide the means to finance war. See for example Henry William Spiegel, *The Growth of Economic Thought* (3rd edition) (Durham, Duke University Press, 1991), 138; Heckscher, *Mercantilism*, 2: 17.

16. Edmund Silberner, *The Problem of War in Nineteenth Century Economic Thought* (Princeton: Princeton University Press 1946), 284.

17. List, *National System*, 347, 316. These sentiments are stressed throughout the work. On p. 120, for example, List, in reference to Smith, states: "Although here and there he speaks of wars, this occurs only incidentally. The idea of a perpetual state of peace forms the foundation of all his arguments."

18. Heckscher, *Mercantilism*, 1: 21 (first quote) 1: 273 (second quote) 1: 273. The discussion of mercantilism as a unifying system takes up 439 of the book's 779 pages. It should be remembered that this emphasis on statism takes place in the context of transition from medieval political economy, and as such is somewhat less "illiberal" than might be assumed by contemporary readers. Heckscher repeatedly emphasizes how from the perspective of *internal* commerce, the options of individuals increased during this period. See 2 pp. 273–74; 282–83.

19. Gustav Schmoller, *The Mercantile System and Its Historical Significance* (New York: Macmillan, 1897). For more on Schmoller, see Nicholas W. Balabkins, *Not by Theory Alone . . . The Economics of Gustav Schmoller and Its Legacy to America* (Berlin: Duncker and Humbolt 1988); F. W. Taussig, "Schmoller on Protection and Free Trade," *Quarterly Journal of Economics* 19(3) (May 1905): 501–11; Thorsten Veblen, "Gustav Schmoller's Economics" *Quarterly Journal of Economics* 16(1) (November 1901): 69–93.

20. Schmoller, *The Mercantile System*, 49, 50 (emphasis in original).

21. As one realist study concluded, "This investigation has shown that the state has purposes of its own." Stephen Krasner, *Defending the National Interest* (Princeton: Princeton University Press, 1978), 300. See also Henri Hauser, *Germany's Commercial Grip on the World* (London: Eveleigh Nash, 1917), 140–45; Robert Gilpin, *U.S. Power and the Multinational Corporation* (New York: Basic Books, 1975), esp pp. 26–32.

22. The realist *approach* to political economy can be assessed, but it is not falsifiable. Specific theories derived from the realist tradition can be falsified.

    It should also be clear that as with the core propositions discussed above, these consequences are neither absolute nor inviolable. Rather, they are held by realists with relatively great intensity, and stressed as particularly significant in explaining state behavior.

23. This issue of externalities was pioneered by A. C. Pigou, *Economics of Welfare* (London: Macmillan 1920), esp pp. 189–96. Coase has argued that size and scope for Pigovian taxes is much smaller than is usually acknowledged. Ronald Coase, "The Problem of Social Cost," *Journal of Law and Economics* 3 (October 1960). Some liberals are quite extreme in their minimalist view of the state, arguing it need not even have a monopoly over the production of currency. See F. A. Hayek, *Denationalization of Money* (London: Institute of International Affairs, 1976).

24. Thus consequence 1 flows from the combination of propositions 1 and 2. This also illustrates how liberal and realist policy prescriptions can diverge from their common base (the liberal/realist synthesis).

25. Mun, *England's Treasure*, pp. 25, 26. On the divergence of national and particular interests, See also Spiegel, *Growth of Economic Thought*, 116, 147 esp.

on the writings of Josiah Child; and Viner "Power Versus Plenty," p. 19. Francis Brewster argued in *New Essays on Trade* (1702), that trade "will find its own Channels, but it may be the ruin of a nation, if not regulated." (Quoted in Heckscher, *Mercantilism* 2: 317).

26. List, *National System*, 269 (first quote), quoted in Silberner, *Problem of War*, 155 (second quote).

27. Condliffe, *Commerce of Nations*, 278.

28. See Kenneth Waltz, "The Myth of National Interdependence," in Charles Kindleberger (ed.), *The International Corporation* (Cambridge: MIT Press, 1970); also Waltz, *Theory of International Politics* (New York: Random House, 1979), chapter 7; Katherine Barbieri, "Economic Interdependence: A Path to Peace or a Source of Interstate Conflict?" *Journal of Peace Research* 33(1) (February 1996): 29–49; and Norrin Ripsman and Jean-Marc Blanchard, "Commercial Liberalism Under Fire: Evidence From 1914 and 1936" *Security Studies* 6(2) (Winter 1996–97): 4–50.

29. Carr, *Twenty Year's Crisis*, 120–24; Heckscher, *Mercantilism*, 2: 31, 40–41, 96, 131, 209–10; Magnusson, *Mercantilism*, 160; Mun, *England's Treasure*, 66. For a contemporary example of the tradeoffs sometimes faced by states, see Irving Lachow, "The GPS Dilemma: Balancing Military Risks and Economic Benefits," *International Security* 20(1) (Summer 1995): 126–48.

30. Aristotle, *The Politics*, translated and edited by Ernest Barker (London: Oxford University Press, 1958), 293–95.

31. Condliffe, *Commerce of Nations*, 435, 832; Robert Gilpin, "Economic Interdependence and National Security in Historical Perspective," in Klaus Knorr and Frank N. Traeger (eds.), *Economic Issues and National Security* (Lawrence: The Regents Press of Kansas, 1977).

32. Stephen Krasner, *Structural Conflict: The Third World Against Global Liberalism* (Berkeley: University of California Press, 1985); see also Robert W. Tucker, *The Inequality of Nations* (New York: Basic Books, 1977).

33. William Cunningham, *The Rise and Decline of the Free Trade Movement* (London: C.J. Clay and Sons, 1904), argued that there were "serious grounds for dissatisfaction" with free trade, which had "rendered England economically dependent on foreign countries." p. 151; see also p. 141. On the U.S., see for example Theodore H. Moran, *American Economic Policy and National Security* (New York: Council on Foreign Relations, 1993), 41–46.

34. Carr, *Twenty Year's Crisis*, 126.

35. John McCallum, "National Borders Matter: U.S. Canada Regional Trade Barriers," *American Economic Review* 85(3) (June 1995): 615–23; Arthur James Balfour *Economic Notes on Insular Free Trade* (New York: Longmans, Green, 1903). It should be noted that Balfour was using this argument as a rhetorical device to support additional deviations from free trade. The rise of dissenters

such as Balfour and Cunningham at this period in history lends support to the realist view that the appeal of economic doctrines is greatly shaped by states' relative positions.

36. Thus consequence 2 flows from the combination of propositions 1 and 2.

37. D. H. Robertson, "The Future of International Trade," *Economic Journal* 48 (March 1938): 11–12.

38. Schmoller, *The Mercantile System*, 80. A modern, general version of this argument is advanced by Krasner, who argues that states' relative position will determine their individual preferences regarding openness and closure in the international system, and the distribution of power and development between them will determine the ultimate extent of openness. Stephen Krasner, "State Power and the Structure of International Trade," *World Politics* 28(3) (1976) pp. 317–47.

39. Cunningham, *Rise and Decline*, 45 (first quote); Cunningham, *The Growth of English Industry and Commerce in Modern Times* (5th ed.) (Cambridge: Cambridge University Press, 1912) See *Part I: The Mercantile System*, on the role of mercantilism in English development; *Part II: Laissez Faire*, 740, 869 (errors of generalizing benefits of liberalism), 870 (second quote). Cunningham also makes the interesting argument that the revival of protectionism in the 1870s stemmed from the Franco-Prussian war, which ended experiments with liberalism by reminding states of the hazards of the international system. (*Rise and Decline*, 86) For more on Cunningham, see H. S. Foxwell, "Obituary: Archdeacon Cunningham" *The Economic Journal* 29 (September 1919): 382–90. Highly critical of Cunningham's work is Hewins, "The Growth of English Industry." Cunningham's arguments serve as a reminder that realists will support "liberal" doctrines such as free trade when they are perceived to serve the national interest.

40. (Berkeley: University of California Press, 1980 [1945]).

41. Hirschman, 29. See also Allan G. B. Fisher, "The German Trade Drive in South-Eastern Europe," *International Affairs* 18(2) (March 1939): 143–70; Antonín Basch, *The Danube Basin and the German Economic Sphere* (New York: Columbia University Press, 1943), esp. p. 178.

42. Herbert Feis states that "The struggle for power among nations left no economic action free." *Europe the World's Banker 1870–1914* (New Haven: Yale University Press, 1964 [1930]), 192. See also Jacob Viner, "International Finance and Balance of Power Diplomacy, 1880–1914," *Political and Social Science Quarterly* 9(4) (March 1929): 408–451; Condliffe, *Commerce of Nations*, pp. 231–2; Hauser, *Germany's Commercial Grip*, 149–51; Feis, *The Diplomacy of the Dollar*, 1965 [1950]; Emile Moreau, *The Golden Franc: Memoirs of a Governor of the Bank of France* (Boulder: Westview Press, 1991), esp. pp. 430–53; Jonathan Kirshner, *Currency and Coercion: The Political Economy of Interna-*

tional Monetary Power (Princeton: Princeton University Press, 1995); David
Baldwin, "The Power of Positive Sanctions," *World Politics* 24(1) (October
1971); George Liska, *The New Statecraft* (Chicago: University of Chicago Press,
1960).

43. Thus consequence 3 is the result of proposition 1 given the liberal/realist
synthesis.

44. Helmut Schmidt "The Struggle for the World Product" *Foreign Affairs* 52(3)
(April 1974): 442. More generally, Gilpin argues that "in a world of scarcity
the fundamental issue is the distribution of the available economic surplus,"
War and Change, 67; See also John Stopford and Susan Strange with John S.
Henley, *Rival States, Rival Firms* (Cambridge: Cambridge University Press,
1991), 204, 209–11.

45. This has also become an important element of criticism from other perspectives
as well. Joan Robinson, reevaluating Ricardo's own example, argued that "the
imposition of free trade on Portugal killed off a promising textile industry and
left her with a slow-growing export market for wine, while for England, exports
of cotton cloth led to accumulation, mechanization, and the whole spiraling
of the industrial revolution." *Aspects of Development and Underdevelopment*
(Cambridge: Cambridge University Press, 1979), 103.

46. Hamilton, "Report on Manufactures," pp. 265, 266. List argued that "under a
system of perfectly free competition with more advanced manufacturing
nations, a nation which is less advanced than those, although well fitted for
manufacturing, can never attain to a perfectly developed manufacturing power
of its own." *National System*, 316. Yet again, we see that views regarding realism
and its consequences are often a matter of degree. Many liberals, for example,
are sympathetic to the concept of temporary infant industry protection. The
seal of approval was offered by the leading classical economist of the mid-
nineteenth century, John Stuart Mill, who wrote this was the "only case" where
"protecting duties can be defensible." *Principles of Political Economy* (revised
edition) (New York: Colonial Press, 1899) 2: 423.

47. Strategic behavior by both governments and firms is emphasized by Hauser,
Germany's Commercial Grip; Cunningham *Rise and Decline of Free Trade*,
108–9; Balfour, *Insular Free Trade*, 25. For contemporary analysis, see Laura
D'Andrea Tyson, *Who's Bashing Whom? Trade Conflict in High Technology
Industries* (Washington: Institute for International Economics, 1992). Note Tyson's emphasis on the composition of trade, deviations from liberal assumptions
which make comparative advantage particularly malleable, and those industries
where strategic behavior is the most likely to affect the trajectory of market
shares, 3–4, 12, 17, 31. See also Douglas A Irwin, "Mercantilism as Strategic
Trade Policy: The Anglo-Dutch Rivalry for the East India Trade" *Journal of
Political Economy* 99(6) (December 1991): 1296–1314; Robert Z. Lawrence

and Charles L. Schultz (eds.), *An American Trade Strategy: Options for the 1990s* (Washington: Brookings, 1990); Paul Krugman (ed.) *Strategic Trade Policy and the New International Economics* (Cambridge: MIT Press, 1986); Gene Grossman (ed.) *Imperfect Competition and International Trade* (Cambridge: MIT Press 1992).

48. Gilpin, *U.S. Power*, 33. Von Hörnigk and Coke are quoted in Heckscher, *Mercantilism*, 2: 22; see also pp. 24, 26, 239. Bacon wrote that princes must remain vigilant "that none of their neighbors do ever grow so (by increase of territory, by embracing of trade, by approaches, or the like), as they become more able to annoy them, than they were." *The Essays or Counsels, Civil and Moral* (New York: Peter Pauper, n.d.), 77. For the modern statement, see Joseph Grieco, "Anarchy and the Limits of Cooperation" *International Organization* 42(3) (Summer 1988): 485–507.

49. On the absolute/relative gains debate, see for example Robert Powell, "Anarchy in International Relations Theory: The Neorealist-Neoliberal Debate," *International Organization* 48(2) (Spring 1994): 313–44; Powell, "Absolute and Relative Gains in International Relations Theory," *American Political Science Review* 85(4) (December 1991): 1303–20; Duncan Snidal, "Relative Gains and the Pattern of International Cooperation," *American Political Science Review* 85(3) (September 1991): 701–26; Robert Keohane, "Institutional Theory and the Realist Challenge After the Cold War," in David Baldwin (ed.) *Neorealism and Neoliberalism: The Contemporary Debate* (New York: Columbia University Press, 1993) and Joseph Grieco, "Understanding the Problem of International Cooperation: The limits of Neoliberal Institutionalism and the Future of Realist Theory," also in Baldwin, *Neorealism and Neoliberalism*. For an example of how difficult it is to distinguish these behaviors in practice, see Peter Liberman, "Trading With the Enemy: Security and Relative Economic Gains," *International Security* 21(1) (Summer 1996): 147–75.

50. Similarly, just as there will be times when realists can anticipate and explain cooperation, there will be conditions under which liberal theorists would predict discord.

51. Joanne Gowa, "Bipolarity, Multipolarity, and Free Trade," *American Political Science Review*, 83(4) (Dec. 1989): 1245–1256.

52. One such example is a realist interpretation of the Tripartite Monetary Agreement of 1936. The rise of the fascist threat reduced the salience of economic disputes among Britain, France, and the U.S. Additionally, the agreement was sustained in the face of gross violations for fear that its termination might strain Western relations in general and signal such discord to others. See Jonathan Kirshner, "Cooperation and Consequence: The Politics of International Monetary Relations," *Journal of European Economic History*, forthcoming.

53. The prized realist pedigree on this issue originates in Thucydides: "What made

war inevitable was the growth of Athenian power and fear which this caused in Sparta." *The Peloponnesian War* (New York: Penguin, 1954), 49. Donald Kagan states that this argument "appears to be right in every particular," *The Outbreak of the Peloponnesian War* (Ithaca: Cornell University Press, 1969), 77.

54. As noted, a sensitivity to the spiral model and the security dilemma are in no way special to realists. See Robert Jervis, "Cooperation Under the Security Dilemma," *World Politics* 30(2) (January 1978): 167–214; Jervis, *Perception and Misperception in International Politics* (Princeton: Princeton University Press, 1976), esp. ch. 3. Once again, the usual caveat on these issues as dimensions hold. The realist emphasis on concerns for war coupled with these problems lead realists to place a much greater stress on their importance and a much greater expectation of conflict. Of course, this does not mean that economic change must lead to war.

55. Thus consequence 3 is the result of proposition 1 given the liberal/realist synthesis.

56. This consequence, then, relates to the realist analysis of *dynamic* economic phenomena: changes in relative growth rates. This is distinct from the analysis of *static* economic phenomena, such as the level of interdependence between states. See the discussion of consequence 1 above and also note 28.

57. Robert Gilpin, *War and Change*; George Liska *International Equilibrium* (Cambridge: Harvard University Press, 1957), also idem, "Continuity and Change in International Systems" *World Politics* 16(1) (October 1963); A. F. K. Organski, *World Politics* (2nd edition) (New York: Knopf, 1968), esp. pp. 364–67; A. F. K. Organski and Jack Kugler, *The War Ledger* (Chicago: University of Chicago Press, 1980); Charles F. Doran, "War and Power Dynamics: Economic Underpinnings," *International Studies Quarterly*, 27(4) (December 1983): 419–40; Paul Kennedy, *The Rise of the Anglo-German Antagonism* (London: Ashfield Press, 1980), esp pp. 291–360.

58. During the Cold War, liberals were overrepresented in the subfield of international political economy, following Robert Keohane, who wrote, "it is justifiable to focus principally on the political economy of the advanced industrialized countries without continually taking into account the politics of international security." *After Hegemony* (Princeton: Princeton University Press, 1984) p. 137. Realists tended to migrate toward security questions, which, during the special conditions of Cold War, often appeared to be detached from political economy. As Kenneth Waltz wrote, "Never in modern history have great powers been so sharply set off from lesser states and so little involved in each other's economic and social affairs." *Theory of International Politics*, 151–52. On the likely erosion of this division, see Jonathan Kirshner, "Political Economy in Security Studies After the Cold War," *Review of International Political Economy* 5(1) (Spring 1998): 64–91.

59. See, for example, Gunnar Adler-Karlson, *Western Economic Warfare 1947–67* (Stockholm: Almqvist & Wiksell, 1968); Michael Mastanduno, *Economic Containment: CoCom and the Politics of East-West Trade* (Ithaca: Cornell University Press, 1992); Bruce Jentleson, *Pipeline Politics: The Complex Political Economy of East-West Energy Trade* (Ithaca: Cornell University Press, 1986).

60. On these issues, see Richard N. Gardner, *Sterling-Dollar Diplomacy in Current Perspective* (New York: Columbia University Press, 1980).

61. John Ikenberry, for example, argues that Gardner and other scholars place too much emphasis on the differences between the U.S. and British conceptions of the postwar order. By ignoring the shared "technical and normative views," and "remarkable discretion" of the architects of that order, realist analyses tend to overstate the significance of the fact that the final plan was much closer to the American proposal than the British. "A World Restored: Expert Consensus and the Anglo-American Postwar Settlement" *International Organization* 46(1) (Winter 1992): 297.

62. David Spiro, *Recycling Power: Petrodollar Politics and the De-Legitimation of American Hegemony* (Ithaca: Cornell University Press, forthcoming).

63. See for example Richard Cooper, "Trade Policy as Foreign Policy" in Robert M. Stern (ed.) *U.S. Policies in a Changing World Economy* (Cambridge: MIT Press, 1987), and his earlier "Trade Policy Is Foreign Policy" *Foreign Policy* 9 (Winter 1972–73): 18–36.

64. Richard Samuels, *Rich Nation, Strong Army: National Security and the Technological Transformation of Japan* (Ithaca, Cornell University Press, 1994).

65. David P. Calleo, *The Imperious Economy* (Cambridge: Harvard University Press, 1982), 123. On the primacy of domestic politics and U.S. unilateralism, see Joanne Gowa, *Closing the Gold Window: Domestic Politics and the End of Bretton Woods* (Ithaca: Cornell University Press, 1983), also John S. Odell, *U.S. International Monetary Policy* (Princeton: Princeton University Press, 1982).

66. Eric Helleiner, *States and the Reemergence of Global Finance: From Bretton Woods to the 1990s* (Ithaca: Cornell University Press, 1994).

67. See G. John Ikenberry, *Reasons of State: Oil Politics and the Capacities of American Government* (Ithaca: Cornell University Press, 1988), as well as his "The Irony of State Strength: Comparative Responses to the Oil Shocks in the 1970s" *International Organization* 40(1) (Winter 1986): 105–37; also Michael Loriaux, *France After Hegemony: International Change and Financial Reform* (Ithaca: Cornell University Press, 1991).

68. Compare, for example, Francesco Giavazzi and Marco Pagano, "The Advantage of Tying One's Hands: EMS Discipline and Central Bank Credibility," *European Economic Review* 32 (June 1988): 1055–1082, and Gian Maria Milesi-Ferretti, "The Disadvantage of Tying Their Hands: On the Political Econ-

omy of Policy Commitments" *The Economic Journal* 105 (November 1995): 1381–1402.

69. Krasner, *Structural Conflict*, esp. chap. 10. Many realists expect small weak states to bandwagon with potentially threatening states, since this strategy might have a better chance at preserving their autonomy than inadequate balancing. Bandwagoning with international market forces, on the other hand, would not preserve autonomy. Krasner predicted, logically, that such states would attempt to insulate themselves from such forces. Steven David, "Explaining Third World Alignment" *World Politics* 43(2) (January 1991): 233–56, also stresses the internal weakness of third world states as a crucial explanatory variable.

70. U.S. behavior was also consistent with a Hirschmanesque interpretation: the use of its economic power to gain influence, shape interests, and support its vision of the postwar international order.

71. I would like to acknowledge Tom Christensen, who has repeatedly emphasized these points with me in conversation. For a related discussion of U.S. early cold war strategy, see his *Useful Adversaries: Grand Strategy, Domestic Mobilization, and Sino-American Conflict, 1947–58* (Princeton: Princeton University Press, 1996).

Somewhat counterintuitively, one could even make the argument that this U.S. behavior in the early Cold War was *more* consistent with realism than with other perspectives, which cannot account for the cultivation of relative gains *for others.*

72. For investigations into this question, see Michael Mastanduno, "Do Relative Gains Matter?" *International Security* 16(1) (Summer 1991): 73–113; Joseph Grieco, *Cooperation Among Nations: Europe, America, and Non-Tariff Barriers to Trade* (Ithaca: Cornell University Press, 1990).

73. Grieco, *Cooperation Among Nations*, 217.

74. Harold James, *International Monetary Cooperation Since Bretton Woods* (Oxford University Press and the International Monetary Fund, 1996), 209.

75. Martin Feldstein, the first chairman of Reagan's council of economic advisers, provides a representative view: "The United States should now explicitly but amicably abandon the policy of international coordination of macroeconomic policy." "Thinking about International Economic Cooperation" *Journal of Economic Perspectives* 2(2) (Spring 1988): 12. On U.S unilateralism, and subsequent events, see Yoichi Funabashi, *Managing the Dollar: From the Plaza to the Louvre* (Washington D.C.: Institute for International Economics, 1988) esp. pp. 65–70; also I. M. Destler and C. Randall Henning, *Dollar Politics: Exchange Rate Policymaking in the United States* (Washington D.C.: Institute for International Economics, 1988) esp. pp. 17–25. See also Jeffrey A. Frankel, "Exchange Rate Policy," in Martin Feldstein (ed.) *American Economic Policy*

in the 1980s (Chicago: University of Chicago Press, 1994). On widespread dissatisfaction with the global monetary system, Peter Kenen, "Summing Up and Looking Ahead," in Kenen (ed.) *Managing the World Economy: Fifty Years After Bretton Woods* (Washington D.C.: Institute for International Economics, 1994), 400.

76. See for example Robert E. Baldwin, "The New Protectionism: A Response to Shifts in National Economic Power," in his *Trade Policy in a Changing World Economy* (Chicago: University of Chicago Press, 1988), and Susan Strange "The Management of Surplus Capacity: Or How Does Theory Stand Up to Protectionism 1970s Style?" *International Organization* 33(3) (Summer 1979).

77. Western states did use force to prevent middle eastern oil from falling into unfriendly hands in the Gulf War.

78. The following are predictions of theories derived from a realist tradition. It should be clear that this tradition can accommodate a heterogenous collection of theories, which may differ in their emphases and in the range of their expectations.

79. Miles Kahler, "External Ambition and Economic Performance," *World Politics* 40(4) (July 1988): 451.

80. Denny Roy, "Hegemon on the Horizon? China's Threat to East Asian Security," *International Security* 19(1) (1994): 149–68; Aaron Friedberg, "Ripe for Rivalry: Prospects for Peace in a Multipolar Asia," *International Security* 18(3) (Winter 1993/4): 5–33.

81. Liberal views on economic relations reducing political conflict can be traced at least as far back as the Manchester School. Richard Cobden advanced these arguments in a speech in Manchester, January 27, 1848. See his *Speeches on Questions of Public Policy* (New York: Klaus Reprint Co., 1970), 233–41. For the modern reconstruction of these views in the form of "complex interdependence" theory, see Robert Keohane and Joseph Nye, *Power and Interdependence* (Boston: Little Brown, 1977).

82. See Alastair Iain Johnston, "Realism(s) and Chinese Security Policy in the Post-Cold War Period," this volume.

83. Helleiner, *States and the Reemergence of Global Finance*; J. Goodman and L. Pauly, "The Obsolescence of Capital Controls? Economic Management in an Age of Global Markets," *World Politics* 46(1) (October 1993): 50–82; Andrew D. Cosh, Alan Hughes, and Ajit Singh, "Openness, Financial Innovation, Changing Patters of Ownership, and the Structure of Financial Markets," in Tariq Banuri and Juliet B. Schor (eds.) *Financial Openness and National Autonomy: Opportunities and Constraints* (Oxford: Clarendon Press, 1992); Raymond Vernon, *Sovereignty at Bay* (New York: Basic Books, 1971); P. Cohey and J. Aronson, "A New Trade Order" *Foreign Affairs* 72(1) (Supplement 1992–

93); Ethan Kapstein, *Governing the Global Economy: International Finance and the State* (Cambridge: Harvard University Press, 1994).

84. See for example, Robert Zevin, "Are World Financial Markets More Open? If So, Why and With What Effects," in Banuri and Schor *Financial Openness and National Autonomy*.

85. On this issue see Ethan Kapstein, "Losing Control: National Security and the Global Economy," *The National Interest* 18 (Winter 1989/90): 85–90; Theodore H. Moran, "The Globalization of America's Defense Industries: Managing the Threat of Foreign Dependence," *International Security* 15(1) (Summer 1990): 57–99.

86. For a discussion of the possible sources and consequences of changing state capacity in the post-Cold War era, see Michael C. Desch, "War and Strong States, Peace and Weak States?" *International Organization* 50(2) (Spring 1996).

87. See for example Barry Eichengreen, James Tobin, and Charles Wyplosz, "Two Cases for Sand in the Wheels of International Finance," *The Economic Journal* 105 (January 1995): 162–72.

88. See for example, John Mearsheimer, "Back to the Future: Instability in Europe After the Cold War" *International Security* 15(1) (Summer 1990): 5–56. On the exceptional stability of the cold war era in general, see John Lewis Gaddis, "The Long Peace: Elements of Peace and Stability in the Postwar International System" *International Security* 10(4) (Spring 1986): 99–142.

89. Some common threats, Cold War alliances, and asymmetries still exist. But threats are decreasingly salient and common, and relevant asymmetries decreasingly pronounced.

90. Note that this discussion relates to *multilateral* cooperation. Realists' mitigating factors may resurface in various bilateral relationships. For example, if China does become increasingly aggressive and threatening, most realists would expect bilateral cooperation between the U.S. and Japan (say) over trade issues, to increase. At the same time, efforts at global trade liberalization could still stall.

91. Liberals need not be so pessimistic, drawing on a tradition that emphasizes both the mutual gains from cooperation and the pacifying consequences of economic interaction. As Hume wrote in 1752, "I shall therefore venture to acknowledge that not only as a man but as a British subject I pray for the flourishing commerce of Germany, Spain, Italy, and even France itself." David Hume, "Of the Jealously of Trade," in his *Essays: Moral, Political and Literary* (London: Oxford University Press 1963 [1742]).

92. Bergsten, "Managing the World Economy of the Future," in Kenen (ed.) *Managing the World Economy*, 360. Regarding international monetary relations, Bergsten argues "The system clearly needs reform. Substantial misalignments

occur with distressing frequency and persist for prolonged periods, often with severe costs for national economies and open trade" (p. 351). On the distinction between reaching and implementing the Uruguay accords, see for example John H. Jackson, "Managing the Trading System: The World Trade Organization and the Post-Uruguay Round Gatt Agenda," also in Kenen (ed.), esp. p. 138.

93. Robert Gilpin *The Political Economy of International Economic Relations*, 395 (first quote), 397 (second quote).

94. Measuring regionalization with a sensitivity to these natural economics can be difficult, but is certainly possible. Also of interest is evaluating whether regional agreements supplement global liberalization or are diverting trade and providing common external protection. On these issues, see Jeffrey Frankel, Ernesto Stein, and Shang-jin Wei, "Continental Trading Blocs: Are They Natural, or Super Natural," *Journal of Development Economics* 47(1) (June 1995): 61–95; and Edward E. Leamer, "American Regionalism and Global Free Trade" *National Bureau of Economic Research Working Paper No. 4753* (May 1994).

95. On this issue, see Joseph M. Grieco, "The Maastricht Treaty, Economic and Monetary Union and the Neo-Realist Research Programme," *Review of International Studies* 21(1) (January 1995): 21–40; also Wayne Sandholtz, "Choosing Union: Monetary Politics and Maastricht," *International Organization* 47(1) (Winter 1993), esp. p. 37.

96. On informal monetary cooperation in Europe, see Rawi Abdelal, "The Politics of Monetary Leadership and Followership: The European Monetary System Since the Currency Crisis of 1992," *Policy Studies*, forthcoming.

4 Realism, Structural Liberalism, and the Western Order

Daniel Deudney and G. John Ikenberry

The end of the Cold War and efforts to explain it have triggered new debates about international relations theory. Equally important, however, is how this epochal development raises new questions about the impact of forty years of East-West rivalry on relations among the great powers of the West. Will the end of the Cold War lead to the decline of cohesive and cooperative relations among Western liberal democracies? Will major Western political institutions, such as NATO and the U.S.-Japanese alliance, decay and fragment? Will "semisovereign" Germany and Japan revert to traditional great power status? Will the United States return to its traditional less engaged and isolationist posture? Our answers depend on the source of Western order: was the Cold War the primary source of Western solidarity or does the West have a distinctive and robust political order that predated and paralleled the Cold War?

Realism advances the most clearly defined—but pessimistic—answers to these questions. Neorealist theory offers two powerful explanations for cooperation within the West: balance of power and hegemony. Neorealist balance-of-power theory depicts Western cooperation and institutions as the result of balancing to counter the Soviet threat.[1] The specter of Soviet military and political expansion provided the incentive for Western countries to ally and cooperate. With the end of that Soviet threat, neorealist balance-of-power theory expects the West, and particularly security organizations such as NATO, to weaken and eventually return to a pattern of strategic rivalry.[2]

A second realist theory holds that American hegemony created and maintained order in the West.[3] The preponderance of American power allowed the United States to offer incentives, both positive and negative, to other Western democracies to form and maintain political institutions. Although the end of the Cold War does not itself signal the waning of American hegemony, many realist theorists argue that America's relative power position has been slowly and inexorably eroding for several decades.[4] So long as Cold War bipolarity produced incentives for Western cooperation, the consequences of the decline of American hegemony were not fully felt. But with the end of the Cold War, those consequences—institutional decay and conflict in the West—will finally manifest themselves. The basic thrust of these realist theories is that relations among the Western states will return to the patterns of the 1930s and early 1940s, in which the problems of anarchy dominated: economic rivalry, security dilemmas, arms races, hypernationalism, balancing alliances, and ultimately the threat of war.

But these realist theories overlook important parts of the story. In the wake of World War II, the United States and its liberal democratic allies created a political, economic, and strategic order that was explicitly conceived as a solution to the problems that led to world war.[5] Importantly, this order predated the onset of the Cold War and was developed and institutionalized at least semi-independently of it. Major features of this order cannot be explained by hegemonic and balance-of-power theories—the Western order contains too many consensual and reciprocal relations for such explanations. Nor can the degree of Western institutionalization, its multilateral pattern, and the stable "semisovereignty" of Germany and Japan be explained by balancing and American hegemony. The timing of this order's creation and many of its salient features provide a puzzle that can be accounted for only by looking beyond realist theories.

Of course, many liberal theories have attempted to understand and explain the distinctive features of the Western political order. But they too fall short in important ways. Theories of the democratic peace, pluralistic security communities, complex interdependence, and the trading state attempt to capture distinctive features of liberal, capitalist, and democratic modern societies and their relations.[6] Their overall picture of the West's future after the Cold War is much more optimistic than that of realism. While offering important insights into the Western order, these liberal theories are incomplete and miss several of its most important aspects. They do not give sufficient prominence to or attempt to explain the prevalence of co-binding security practices over traditional balancing, the distinctive system-structural features of the West, the peculiarly penetrated and reciprocal nature of American hegemony, the role of capitalism in overcoming the problem of relative gains, and the distinctive civic political identity that pervades these societies.

This chapter aims to develop a theory of "structural liberalism" that more adequately captures the unique features of this Western order and builds on the strengths but goes beyond the weaknesses of current realist and liberal theories. Structural liberalism seeks to capture the major components of the Western political order and their interrelationships.

In assessing the claims of structural liberalism, it is important for us to note that conflict within the Western system is not itself contrary to the propositions of structural liberalism. Likewise, the existence of conflict within the West does not in itself validate realist arguments. In holding up "harmony" as the standard of the success of liberal practices, many realists have set a standard that is not only impossible to meet but also deeply misleading concerning the character of liberal political systems.[7] Liberal political systems exhibit endemic conflict, but such conflict is bound and channeled without calling into question the liberal consensus and liberal institutions. In liberal systems, the diversity of actors and interests ensures a continuous, often heated, political struggle with real winners and losers. Indeed, conflict is evidence of the health and vitality of liberal political orders so long as it remains contained and falls short of the use of violence or highly asymmetrical coercion.

The argument unfolds in six sections, each focused on a component of the Western order. The first section examines the security practice of co-binding as a liberal solution to the problem of anarchy. The second explores the penetrated character of American hegemony, the role of transnational relations in American hegemony, and its reciprocal rather than coercive character. The third section analyzes the role of the semisovereign and partial great powers of Japan and Germany as structural features of the Western political order. The fourth section examines structural openness, the political foundations of economic openness, and its solutions to relative gains problems. The fifth section focuses on the distinctive Western civic identity and community and its role in underpinning the liberal institutions in the West. We conclude by summarizing the differing predictions of realism and structural liberalism after the Cold War.

SECURITY CO-BINDING

Neorealism provides a very strong argument relating system structure to unit-level practices. The core of neorealist theory is that states in an anarchical system will pursue a strategy of balancing. Anarchy means that there is no central government that the units can rely on for security; and in such a situation, states seeking security will balance against other states that they perceive to be threats to their security. Balancing has both an internal and external dimension. Internally, it takes the form of the domestic mobilization of power resources (via armament and the generation of state capacity). Externally, balancing typically results in ad hoc, counter-hegemonic alliances in which states join together with other states that fear for their security from threatening or powerful states.[8] Moreover, successful balancing, by undercutting the concentration of power at the system level, tends to reinforce and reproduce anarchy; in effect, balancing and anarchy are co-generative. Likewise, balancing in anarchy tends to strengthen the capacity of the state in its relation with society. That in turn makes the creation of system-wide governance more difficult. This balancing pattern in anarchy has characterized the Western state system both in its early-modern, Europe-centered phase as well as in the global system that has emerged in late-modern times. Because of this long pattern and deep logic, realists expect balancing to be pervasive in international politics wherever anarchy exists.

This realist view overlooks a distinctive practice that liberal states have pioneered and that has given the West a structure unlike anarchy. Neorealists fail to recognize that liberal states practice co-binding—that is, they attempt to tie one another down by locking each other into institutions that are mutually constraining.[9] Binding constraint can be either asymmetrical or symmetrical. Asymmetrical binding is characteristic of hegemony or empire, but liberal states practice a more mutual and reciprocal co-binding that overcomes the effects of anarchy without producing hierarchy. Co-binding does not ignore the problems and dynamics of anarchy, but aims to overcome them. By establishing institutions of mutual constraint, co-binding reduces the risks and uncertainties associated with anarchy. It ties potential threatening states into predictable and restrained patterns of behavior, and it makes balancing unnecessary.

Co-binding practices are particularly suited to liberal states. When it is successful, co-binding reduces the necessity for units to have strong and autonomous state apparatuses. Moreover, the internal structures of democratic and liberal states more readily lend themselves to the establishment of institutions that constrain state autonomy. Just as anarchy gives rise to balancing in traditional great power politics, a community of liberal states gives rise to and is reinforced by co-binding. This co-binding practice, although overlooked by neorealist theory, has a robust logic that liberal states in the West have exhibited.

Co-binding is an important feature of the Western liberal order. While balancing and hegemony played a role in the formation of these Western institutions, co-binding practices were significantly and independently motivated by an attempt to overcome anarchy and its consequences among the Western states. After World War I, the United States sought through the League of Nations to establish a system of co-binding restraints among Western states. It was not fully attempted in practice, however, and to the extent it was, it failed for a variety of reasons.[10] After World War II, the United States and liberal states in Europe sought again to bind themselves through NATO. Although realists dismiss failed efforts at binding as idealistic, and successful post-World War II institutions as the result of balancing, these institutions were mainly created by Europeans and Americans eager to avoid the patterns that had led to the two world wars.

The most important co-binding institution in the West, of course, is NATO. Although the Soviet threat provided much of the political impetus to form NATO, the alliance always had in the minds of its most active advocates the additional purpose of constraining the Western European states vis-à-vis each other and tying the United States into Europe.[11] Indeed, NATO was as much a solution for the "German problem" as it was a counter to the Soviet Union. As the first NATO Secretary General, Lord Ismay, famously put it, the purpose of NATO was to keep the "Russians out, the Germans down, and the Americans in." These aims were all interrelated: to counterbalance the Soviet Union it was necessary to mobilize German power in a way that the other European states did not find threatening and to tie the United States into a firm commitment on the continent.

The NATO alliance went beyond the traditional realist conception of an ad hoc defense alliance. It created an elaborate organization, drew states into joint force planning and international military command structures, and established a complex transgovernmental political process for making political and military decisions.[12] The co-binding character of this alliance is manifested in the remarkable effort its member states made to give their commitment a semipermanent status—to lock themselves in so that it is difficult to exit.

The desire to overcome the dynamics of anarchy also gave rise to an agenda for economic co-binding, particularly in Europe. The European union movement explicitly attempted to achieve economic interdependence between Germany and her neighbors in order to make strategic military competition much more costly and difficult. The first fruit of this program, the European Coal and Steel Community, effectively pooled these heavy industries that had been essential for war making. In its administration of the Marshall Plan, the United States sought to encourage the creation of joint economic organizations in order to foster economic interdependencies that crossed over the traditional lines of hostilities between European states.[13] The United States also supported the creation of political institutions of European union, thereby foreclosing a return to the syndromes of anarchy.[14] American supporters of European reconstruction as well as European advocates of the European community explicitly strove to develop institutions to make Western Europe look more like the United States than like traditional Westphalian states in anarchy.

Faced with this argument, realists might point to significant conflicts between the United States and its allies, such as the 1956 Suez crisis, the Vietnam war, the 1982–83 Euromissiles controversy, and the 1982–83 gas pipeline crisis. But most of these conflicts had their roots not in conflicts internal to the West, but rather in the larger Cold War competition, thus pointing out that bipolarity was as much a source of conflict in the West as it was a source of cohesion. The underlying cause of these conflicts was the fundamental discrepancy between the American perception of the requirements for a global strategy of containment, and the more narrow, regional perspective of the Europeans. Moreover, these conflicts were often resolved in ways that resulted in closer ties, thus both revealing and reinforcing the robustness of Western relations and linkages. The end of the Cold War has reduced this systematic irritant in Western relations.

In sum, security co-binding among Western liberal states has produced a political order that successfully mitigated anarchy within the West in ways that neorealist theory fails to appreciate. Although these institutions created by co-binding practices significantly altered the anarchical relations within the Atlantic world, they fell far short of creating a hierarchy. Because Waltzian neorealism conceives of order as either hierarchical or anarchical, it lacks the ability to grasp institutions between hierarchy and anarchy that constitute the structure of the liberal order.

PENETRATED HEGEMONY

The second major realist explanation for the Western political order is American hegemony. Hegemony theorists, tracing their roots from Thucydides through E. H. Carr, claim that order arises from concentrations of power and that, when concentrated power is absent, disorder marks politics, both domestic and international. In international systems, concentrations of power produce hegemony, which is conceived as a system organized around asymmetrical power relations.[15] Hegemonic theorists argue that Western order is the product of American preponderance, which was at its zenith in the immediate post-World War II years when the major security and economic rules and institutions were established. In this image of the West, order is maintained because the United States has had the capacity and will to compel and others to establish and maintain rules and to provide inducements and rewards to its client states in Europe and East Asia.[16]

Both balance-of-power and hegemonic theories are conventionally viewed as versions of neorealism, but their relationship is much more problematic. In fact, these two versions of neorealist theory have quite contradictory images of order in world politics — one emphasizing that order comes from concentrations of power and the other that such concentrations produce resisting measures. Thus, balance-of-power theory poses a fundamental question to hegemonic theory: why do subordinate powers within a hegemonic system not balance against the hegemon?[17] To answer this question, one must look at the ways in which stable hegemonic orders depart from the simple image provided by hegemonic theory.

The American-centered Western order exhibits far more reciprocity and legitimacy than an order based on superordinate and subordinate relations would expect. American hegemony has had a distinctively liberal cast — one more consensual, cooperative, and integrative than coercive. The distinctive features of this American-centered political system — particularly its transparency, the diffusion of power into many hands, and the multiple points of access to policymaking — have enabled Western European and Japanese allies to participate in the formation of policies for the overall Western system.[18] As a result, American hegemony has been marked by a high degree of legitimacy, without major challenges or efforts to balance against American leadership. In large measure, this system is an "empire by invitation," in which the secondary states have sought American leadership rather than resisted it.[19]

To understand this system, and explain why it deviates from the realist hegemonic model, we must incorporate two factors neglected by realists: the structure of the American state and the prevalence of transnational relations. A distinctive feature of the American state is its decentralized structure, which provides numerous points of access to competing groups — both domestic and foreign. When a hegemonic state is liberal, the subordinate actors in the system have a variety of channels and mechanisms for registering their interests with the hegemon. Transnational relations are the means by which subordinate actors in the system represent their interests to the hegemonic power and the vehicle through which consensus between the hegemon and lesser powers is achieved. This system provides subordinate states with transparency, access, representation, and communication and consensus-building mechanisms. It supplies the means for secondary states to significantly express their concerns and satisfy their interests. Taken together, liberal state openness and transnational relations create an ongoing political process within the hegemonic system without which the system would either be undermined by balancing or the need to be coercive.

The key point is that the open domestic structure of the United States is not simply an anomalous or solely domestic phenomenon, but is integral to the operation of the Western system. The openness and extensive decentralization of the American liberal state provides subordinate powers with routine access to the decisionmaking processes of the hegemonic state relevant to their concerns. And, because the decisionmaking process of the American liberal state is so transparent, secondary powers are not subject to surprises.[20] The fundamental character of the American liberal state is that it is elaborately articulated and accessible to groups and forces emerging from civil societies.[21] The size, diversity, and federal character of the American political system also offers many points of influence and access. The American polity has many of the features associated with international politics—such as decentralization and multiple power centers—and is therefore particularly well prepared to incorporate pressures and influences from liberal societies outside itself.[22] In a large and pluralistic polity, such as the United States, it is relatively easy for foreign actors to represent their interests in forms that more resemble domestic politics than traditional diplomacy.[23]

Transnational relations are a second integral component of the liberal hegemonic system, whose role and significance have not been grasped by either realist or liberal theorists. Realists view transnational relations as derivative of hegemonic power and thus of secondary importance. Hegemony provides a framework within which such interactions can flourish, and realists explain the growth of transnational relations in the post-World War II era as a consequence of American hegemony.[24] Conversely, liberal theorists, who pay a great deal of attention to transnational relations, see them as the beginnings of a system that is expected to eventually displace the state and locate political power in nonstate entities such as multinational corporations, international organizations, and networks of transnational and transgovernmental experts.[25]

Far from being ancillary or derivative, transnational relations are a vital component of the system's operation.[26] Because of the receptiveness of the liberal state and the existence of transnational relations, subordinate states achieve effective representation. Furthermore, transnational connections between the actors in a hegemonic system constitute a complex communication system that is continuously shaping preferences and thus moderating the divergence of interests among actors. Transnational networks also serve to forge a consensus and lobby policymakers throughout the system. In hegemonic systems infused with transnational relations, the legitimacy of the asymmetrical relationships is enhanced. Such processes endow the relations with a degree of acceptability in the eyes of subordinate powers. This in turn reduces the tendency for subordinate powers to resist and, correspondingly, diminishes the need for the hegemon to exercise coercion.[27] Such legitimacy endows hegemonic systems with a greater degree of stability and resilience than what the realist hegemonic model expects. Because of the accessible state structure and transnational state processes, the arrows of influence are not in one direction—from the center to the periphery—as in the hegemonic model, but rather run in both directions, producing a fundamentally reciprocal political order.

In Atlantic relations, the United States and West European states have been tightly linked by transnational forces and influences. The elaborate consultative arrangements in NATO provide venues and forums for European concerns to be registered in the American public policy process.[28] An extensive network of public and private Western institutions exists. Official venues include the G-7 process, the OECD, intergovernmental consultative networks, and the NATO Council. Quasi-official institutions include the Atlantic Council, Council on Foreign Relations, the Atlantic Assembly, the International Institute for Strategic Studies, the Transatlantic Policy Network, and the Trilateral Commission. Extensive social, cultural, and economic networks also span the Atlantic, including business roundtables, parliamentary exchanges, networks of journalists, and common media sources. Taken together, these constitute a dense system of routinized channels for consultation, exchanges of views, dispute resolution, and consensus building. These links ensure that the Atlantic relationship will be consensual more than coercive.

The relationship between the United States and Japan is less extensively institutionalized; however, it also exhibits similar features.[29] Japanese corporate representatives have significant access to the Washington policymaking process and have been able to influence American decisionmaking in areas that affect Japanese interests, particularly in trade policy.[30] This Japanese access has not been reciprocated, but such asymmetry helps compensate for the subordinate role of Japan as an ally. From the Japanese perspective, access to and influence over the Washington process helps Japan cope with the enormous power the United States has over Japan, thus adding legitimacy and stability to the relationship. Viewed from the perspective of the American state, Japanese access is a weakness; viewed from the perspective of the American system, it is a strength.

Faced with this argument, realists might object that America's relations with Europe and Japan still contain significant elements of coercion and conflict, and that the American political system is not fully transparent but is capable of generating shocks and surprises. First, the strongest case of American hegemonic coercion is toward France, which has routinely complained about and actively sought to resist American leadership. France, however, is the most statist and thus its domestic structures are least suitable for participation in the system.[31] But, more generally, "coercion" is endemic to the exercise of power and the processes of politics, and the Western system is not characterized by its absence but by its moderation and reciprocity. Indeed, an American nationalist could object that the Western system coerces the United States into significant commitments and constraints, which is something that fundamentally reflects the European desire to permanently involve the United States in Europe and combat American isolationism.

Second, the American political process is not completely transparent, and it is capable of actions—such as the Nixon shock of 1971, the neutron bomb reversal of 1979, the extension of pipeline sanctions in 1984—that the other actors find surprising and undesirable. But most shocks have related to the prosecution of the Cold War, further demonstrating its potential to produce conflicts in the West, and American actions have hinged upon the concentration of authority in the presidency, which is in significant measure a Cold War artifact. The most salient case of economic surprise within the West was the closing of the gold window; this marked a movement of the system away from American dominance to a more reciprocal system. Overall, coercion has been moderate and surprises infrequent, given the extensiveness and intensity of Western political relations.

In sum, transnational relations are not ancillary or oppositional to the operation of the American hegemonic system as most realists and liberals argue, but are rather integral to its structure and help account for its stability and durability. Transnational relations provide subordinate actors in the system with channels through which their interests can be expressed to the hegemon. Were such relations less robust, the hegemonic system would invite balancing and be more coercive and less legitimate. Realist hegemonic theory has failed to appreciate the significance of transnational relations in the operation of state hegemonic systems and thus furnishes an incomplete picture of the Western system.

Semisovereignty and Partial Great Powers

A third major structural feature of the Western liberal order distinguishing it from the realist image of states in anarchy is the status of Germany and Japan as semisovereign and partial great powers. The "peace constitutions" of Germany and Japan, which in both cases were initially imposed by the United States and the Western allies after World War II, have, contrary to realist expectations, come to be embraced by the German and Japanese publics as acceptable and even desirable features of their political systems. The structure of these states is highly eccentric for realist models, but these are integral and not incidental features of the Western political order.

Realist theories assume that the nature of the units making up the international system are sovereign and, to the extent that they have sufficient capacity, they are great powers. Sovereignty, as understood by realists, is Westphalian sovereignty, which means that states are accorded a set of rights and assume a set of responsibilities, the most important of which is the mutual recognition of each other's autonomy and juridical equality.[32] Moreover, Westphalian sovereignty is understood by realists to be one of the primary means by which the system of anarchical states is institutionalized, thus reinforcing the primacy of the state and the absence of hierarchy characteristic of anarchy, and providing a degree of regularity to anarchy.[33] Central to realist theory is also the concept of the "great power," the exclusive set of states that have sufficient capacity not only to secure themselves but also to exercise influence over surrounding smaller states and to affect the entire system. Integral to this realist notion of the great power is that such states possess a full range of instruments of statecraft, especially a robust military establishment for making good their claims to great power status and influencing the system.[34] Together, Westphalian sovereignty and the great power are enduring features of the realist vision of anarchical society.

Two major states in the Western system, Germany and Japan, do not follow the expected realist pattern, but are semisovereign and partial great powers. It is widely noted that since World War II, Germany and Japan have been "semisovereign" states.[35] Such a label, while partly misleading, is nevertheless essential in capturing their distinctive and eccentric character and roles. As the reconstruction after 1945 progressed, Germany and Japan both sought to be accorded the full panoply of rights and responsibilities of a Westphalian sovereign, and the United States and other Western states were forthcoming with this recognition as part of their reconstruction and reintegration into the international system. However, it is still appropriate to characterize these states as fundamentally semisovereign because in return for sovereign recognition they accepted a role in international relations that was self-constrained in major ways. They were able to gain juridical sovereignty only because they were willing to eschew the full range of great power roles and activities.

At the heart of this odd configuration of juridical sovereignty and effective semisovereignty have been two levels of structure: strong self-imposed constitutional constraints and the integration of Germany and Japan in wider political, security, and economic institutions. German and Japanese domestic political structures that were created during occupation and reconstruction featured parliamentary democracy, federalism, and an independent judiciary—and thus they were much more similar to the liberal American state than the traditional and closed autocratic state.[36] These domestic structures facilitate binding linkages, transnational interaction, and political integration. These structures of constraint and the practice of semisovereignty were anchored in a strong domestic consensus that traditional autocracy and imperialism had catastrophic consequences, which were to be avoided at all costs.[37]

The most important way in which Germany and Japan are eccentric states in the realist model is that they are not playing the traditional role of great powers. Their partial great power status is defined by the discrepancy between their power potential and power mobilization and between the breadth of foreign policy interests and the underdevelopment of their policy instruments. As a product of the American and Western occupations of Germany and Japan, both countries created "peace constitutions" that wrote into their basic law a foreign policy orientation radically at variance with the requirements of great power status and activities. Most important was that their constitutions committed these states to purely defensive military orientations. A powerful expression of this self-restraint is that both Germany and Japan have voluntarily foregone the acquisition of nuclear weapons—the military instrument that more than any other has defined great powers during the last half century. In the postwar period, the international strategic environment has not allowed them to retreat into isolation or maintain neutrality. But their defensive military postures have not been autonomous; instead, they have been elaborately and extensively integrated into multilateral arrangements. In addition to explicitly eschewing great power postures, German and Japanese constitutions contain a strong mandate for an activist foreign policy directed at maintaining international peace and building international institutions.

Although both Germany and Japan are semisovereign and partial great powers, there are important differences between them. Their regional contexts have imposed very different constraints and opportunities.[38] Germany, sharing long-contested land borders with many countries, has pursued its unique postwar role by integrating itself militarily and economically with its neighbors. In contrast, insular Japan was alone in the Far East as a postwar liberal power and therefore its strategic co-binding with the rest of the system has been through the bilateral U.S.-Japanese alliance. Furthermore, the Western reconstruction of Germany along liberal lines was much more intensive, while the early demands of the Cold War led the United States to reconfigure Japan less comprehensively. Partially as a result, domestic political structures in Germany became more liberal and decentralized than in Japan, where strong state capacity remained, particularly in the economic domain. Overall, German integration into the Western political order is much more complete, both in multilateral economic and security systems. One expression of this difference is that German rearmament has been more extensive than Japanese because Germany is more thoroughly bound into the Western order.

The existence of Germany and Japan as semisovereign and partial great powers constitutes a fundamental anomaly for realist theory. The features of these states are not, however, incidental but are integral to the Western political order. The widely held neorealist expectation that Germany and Japan will revert back to great power status poses a test for these competing theories: if this pattern eccentric to realism persists, will the explanatory utility of realism have been compromised? Conversely, should Germany and

Japan return to the normal realist pattern, the Western political order is not likely to endure—and, if it does, the concept of structural liberalism will be called into question.

Structural Economic Openness

A major feature of the Western order is the prevalence of capitalist economies and international institutions dedicated to economic openness. Neorealist theories offer two powerful explanations for the Western liberal economic order, one stressing American hegemony and the other Western alliance within bipolarity. Liberals also claim many explanations, including the rise of "embedded liberalism" among the advanced industrial nations. While providing important insights, these theories are insufficient and miss two crucial dimensions of the political structure and practice of the liberal economic order. First, advanced capitalism creates such high prospects for absolute gains that states attempt to mitigate anarchy between themselves to avoid the need to pursue relative gains. Second, liberal states have pursued economic openness for political ends, specifically by using free trade as an instrument to alter and maintain the motivations and characteristics of other states to make them more politically and strategically congenial.

One powerful realist explanation for the prevalence of open economies in the Western order is hegemonic stability theory.[39] These realists argue that open international orders are created by and must be sustained by the concentration of power in the hands of one state. Hegemonic powers produce and support openness by establishing and enforcing rules, supplying exchange currency, absorbing exports, and wielding incentives and inducements to encourage other states to remain open. Hegemonic stability theorists argue that economic openness in the nineteenth century was made possible by British hegemony and that when British power waned in the first decades of the twentieth century, the open trading system broke down. Likewise, after World War II, the United States, then at the peak of its relative power, provided the leadership to establish Western liberal economic institutions, thereby catalyzing another era of economic openness and high growth.[40] Hegemonic stability theorists maintain that the relative economic decline of the United States has the potential to undermine the openness and stability of this order. Because of bipolarity and American leadership in the Cold War, the effects of American relative decline have not been fully registered, but after the Cold War the expectation is that the system will decay.

Another realist position is that free trade has resulted from bipolarity and the Western strategic alliance.[41] In this view, allied states are less concerned with relative gains considerations than unallied states. Because states are allied, they are at least partially removed from anarchical relations and thus are not as sensitive to relative shifts in economic advance that might result from free trade. Similarly, realist theorists argue that states that are members of a military alliance see relative gains by their allies as adding to the overall strength of the alliance, and therefore they are willing to participate in an open system with their allies. With the decline of bipolarity and the diminished importance of strategic alliances after the Cold War, the expectation of these realist theories is that the free trade order will come under increasing stress.

Liberals also advance powerful arguments about the sources of the Western system of open economies. Of particular note is the proposition that liberal states in the twentieth century have committed themselves to ambitious goals of social welfare and economic stability, which in turn requires them to pursue foreign economic policies that maintain a congenial international environment for realizing these goals.[42] This notion of "embedded liberalism" situates the motivation for open economic policies in the domestic structures of advanced industrial societies, which have changed from laissez-faire to welfare states. As long as Western welfare states retain their commitment to full employment and social welfare, the theory expects that they will remain committed to liberal foreign economic policies regardless of changes in the strategic environment.[43]

These realist and liberal views make important insights, but they neglect two important sources of Western economic openness. Neorealists rightly point out that in an anarchical system, states must be more concerned with relative than absolute gains, and therefore are willing to forego the absolute gains that often derive from economic exchange out of fear that their relative position will suffer.[44] The relative and absolute gains argument is typically seen as an important reason why states will not accept economic openness. In reality, however, it suggests a powerful explanation for why states will take steps to mitigate anarchy. In a world of advanced industrial capitalist states, the absolute gains to be derived from economic openness are so substantial that states have the strong incentive to abridge anarchy so that they do not have to be preoccupied with relative gains considerations at the expense of absolute gains. The assumption of the neorealist argument is that the only alternative to anarchy is hierarchy, but, in fact, liberal states have developed co-binding institutions and practices that make it possible to moderate anarchy without producing hierarchy. The extensive institutions, both strategic and economic, that liberal states have built can be explained as the mechanisms by which they have sought to avoid the need to abandon absolute gains out of the need to pursue relative gains. The Western system of co-binding is highly developed across security, political, and economic realms, and it provides states with confidence that changes in their relative position do not translate into security threats.

Another feature of advanced industrial capitalist society with significant implications for the politics of relative and absolute gains is the uncertainty about how relative gains will be distributed, the high probability that their distribution will fluctuate fairly rapidly, and the many sectors of modern societies that make it likely that patterns of gains and losses will be variegated. Modern industrial economies are characterized by great complexity. This means that states attempting to calculate the relative gains consequences of any particular policy face a high degree of uncertainty about its effects. In highly dynamic markets with large numbers of sophisticated, fast-moving and autonomous corporate actors, it is very difficult to anticipate the consequences of policies and thus the relative distribution of gains and losses. Moreover, the rate of change in advanced industrial capitalism is so great that the distribution of relative gains and losses is likely to fluctuate between countries fairly rapidly. Thus, even if one country can foresee that it will be a loser in a particular period, it can assume that it will experience a different outcome in successive iterations.[45] Finally, modern industrial capitalist societies contain many different sectors and the different sectors in one country may be simultaneously declining and rising as a result of international openness, making it difficult for states to calculate their aggregate relative gains and losses. The multifaceted character of these societies helps ensure that the pattern of relative gains and losses will be highly variegated, thus rendering it unlikely that any one state will be a loser or winner across the board.[46]

A second motivation that Western states have in establishing and maintaining an open economic order is political. The expansion of capitalism that free trade stimulates has the effect of altering the goals and character of other states in the international order in a liberal and democratic direction, thus producing a more strategically and politically hospitable system. Free trade is thus a political instrument for the spread and strengthening of liberal democracy as well as for the security consequences that follow. The collapse of the world economy in the Great Depression and the ensuing political turmoil was a major cause of the retreat of democracy and liberalism in the 1930s, the rise of fascist and imperialist states, the emergence of rival blocs, and ultimately the outbreak of World War II. In reaction to these events, the principal architects of the post-World War II liberal order viewed economic openness as a strategy to avoid regional blocs, trade wars, illiberal regimes, and ruinous imperial rivalry.[47] They understood that a world populated by liberal states would be much more compatible with American interests and the survival of democracy and capitalism in the United States, and they saw economic openness and institutions to spread and stabilize capitalism as powerful instruments for achieving these strategic ends.[48] Thus, contrary to the realist proposition that free trade is the product of political and security structures, the institutions of economic openness are in part the cause of those structures. This proposition suggests that the Western liberal economic order is not fundamentally dependent on bipolarity and American hege- mony, but instead has a powerful independent origin unlikely to be affected by the end of the Cold War.

Realist claims that the Western economic order derives from hegemony and alliance overlooks crucial features of the Western system. The theory of structural liberalism argues that there is a political logic and structure that emerges more directly from capitalism. The character of capitalism provides states with powerful incentives to create structures that replace or mitigate anarchy so as to sidestep relative gains concerns and the impediments they pose to the realization of high absolute gains. Likewise, the dynamic and complex character of modern capitalism frustrates calculations of relative gains and thus the formulation of policies that might seek to advance it. Finally, open economies are themselves the product of a liberal political strategy that seeks to reinforce and spread liberal political structures and their security benefits. In short, the political economy of capitalism and the struc- tural features of the Western political order are much more integrally related than realists suggest, and the viability of this order is likely to be much less dependent on the end of the Cold War and the decline of American hege- mony than they lead us to believe.

CIVIC IDENTITY

The fifth dimension of the Western political order is a common civic identity. The common elements of Western identity take two interrelated and reinforcing forms. The first is the parallel emergence of domestic identities centered around liberalism, democracy, and capitalism—which is now dominant in all Western countries. The second is the emergence of a common Western political identity, which is less hegemonic and tends to be concentrated in elites rather than in the more general public. Together, they have significantly displaced more virulent and xenophobic forms of national identity, producing forms of identity quite at odds with realist expectations. Although difficult to quantify, what Montesquieu called "spirit" is an essential component of any political order. The West's "spirit"—common norms, public mores, and political identities—gives this political order cohesiveness and solidarity. Throughout the Western world, there is an overwhelming consensus in favor of political democracy, market economics, ethnic toleration, and personal freedom. The political spectrum in the West looks increasingly like the narrow "liberal" one that Louis Hartz once identified as distinctively American.[49] Compared to the diversity that characterized Europe as recently as the 1930s, the convergence of political practices and identities within the countries of the West is an important feature whose causes and consequences require explanation.

Realist approaches to international theory largely assume that the separate state units have distinct national identities. Realists emphasize that national identity provides states with legitimacy and serves as a basis for the mobilization of resources against outside threats.[50] For realism, the experience of interstate war serves as an important source of national identity and loyalty because it offers the most potent and emotive symbolism of heroism, battlefield sacrifice, and collective memory of opposition and triumph.[51] Military organizations are one of the most powerful means of socializing individuals into patriotism and veterans organizations constitute a major interest group that reinforces the primacy of the nation-state. For realism, these sociological processes are a crucial link between international anarchy and interstate war and the prevalence of the nation-state as a unit in international system.

No enduring political order can exist without a substantial sense of community and shared identity. Political identity and community and political structure are mutually dependent. Structures that work and endure do so because they are congruent with identities and forms of community that provide them with legitimacy. Conversely, structures and institutions create and reinforce identities and community through processes of socialization and assimilation. These important sociological dimensions of political orders have been neglected by both neorealist and neoliberal theories, which take the preferences of the actors as given and examine only the interaction between interests and structure. As a result, they miss the identity and community dimensions of political order—both national and liberal civic alternatives.

An essential component of the Western political order is a widespread civic identity distinct from national, ethnic, and religious identities. At the core of civic identity in Western countries is a consensus around a set of norms and principles, especially political democracy, constitutional government, individual rights, private property-based economic systems, and toleration of diversity in non-civic areas of ethnicity and religion. Throughout the West, the dominant form of political identity is based on a set of abstract and juridical rights and responsibilities that coexist with private and semi-public ethnic and religious associations. Just as warring states and nationalism reinforce each other, so do Western civic identity and Western political structures and institutions.

Civic identity within the West is intimately associated with capitalism, along with its business and commodity cultures. As Susan Strange argues, capitalism has generated a distinctive "business civilization."[52] Across the advanced industrial world, capitalism has produced a culture of market rationality that permeates all aspects of life. The intensity and volume of market transactions across the industrial capitalist world provide a strong incentive for individual behaviors and corporate practices to converge. One strong manifestation of this convergence is the widespread use of English as the language of the marketplace. Likewise, the universality of business attire across the industrial capitalist world signifies this common business culture.

Another cultural dimension of the Western order is the commonality of commodities and consumption practices. Throughout the advanced industrial world, mass-produced commodities have spawned a universal vernacular culture that reaches into every aspect of daily existence. The symbolic content of day-to-day life throughout the West is centered not on religious or national iconography, but upon the images of commercial advertising. The ubiquitously displayed scenes of the good life are thoroughly consumerist. The demands of mass marketing and advertising place a premium on reaching the largest number of purchasers, thus contributing to the homogenization of identities and the avoidance of polarizing ethnic or religious or racial traits. Further defining popular culture throughout the West is mass entertainment, particularly television, movies, music, and athletic events. Because of increased incomes and cheap transportation, international tourism has become a mass phenomenon. The cumulative effect of this symbolic and popular culture and interaction is to create similar lifestyles and values throughout the West.[53]

Beyond emergence of very similar identities within Western countries, the widespread circulation of elites and educational exchanges has produced a significant and growing sense of shared identity.[54] The advanced industrial countries contain many transnational networks based on professional and avocational specialization. Enabled by cheap air transportation and telecommunications, scientific, technological, medical, artistic, athletic, and public policy networks draw membership from across the Western world and have frequent conferences and events. Also significant is the great increase in the volume of international education activities, most notably the growing transnational character of the student bodies in elite universities, and particularly professional schools. These developments have produced a business, political, cultural, and technical elite with similar educational backgrounds and extensive networks of personal friendships and contacts.[55] The cumulative weight of these international homogenizing and interacting forces has been to create an increasingly common identity and culture—a powerful sense that "we" constitutes more than the traditional community of the nation-state.

As civic and capitalist identities have strengthened, ethnic and national identity has declined. Although it is still customary to speak of the West as being constituted by nation-states, the political identity of Westerners is no longer exclusively centered on nationalism. The West has evolved a distinctive solution to the problem of nationalism and ethnicity that is vital to its operation and inadequately recognized by realists. The Western synthesis has two related features. First, ethnic and national identity has been muted and diluted to the point where it tends to be semiprivate in character. Although not as homogeneous as anticipated by cosmopolitan philosophers of the Enlightenment, the identities of Westerners are largely secular and modern, thus allowing for many different loyalties and sensibilities—none of which predominates. Second, an ethic of toleration is a strong and essential part of Western political culture. This ethic permits—and even celebrates—a highly pluralist society in which muted differences coexist, intermingle, and cross-fertilize each other. Unlike the chauvinism and parochialism of premodern and non-Western societies, an ethic of toleration, diversity, and indifference infuses the industrial democracies.

Many realists forecast that nationalist and ethnic identity will reassert itself in Western Europe in the wake of the Cold War, fueling conflict and destroying liberal democratic society. The virulence of ethnic conflict in the Balkans and elsewhere in former communist lands has revived the specter of the worst of Europe's past. The increase in anti-immigrant violence in Western Europe, particularly in Germany, demonstrates that the West is not immune to a new epidemic of ethnic violence and national war. The opponents of liberal pluralism are a loud but small minority of the alienated and economically dislocated. Their voices are not, however, a cause for a crisis of self-confidence. The ethos of the West remains overwhelmingly tolerant and receptive to diversity. Indeed, the anti-foreigner violence and ethnic ferment have been most revealing in the magnitude of the condemnation they have evoked. Measured by the standards of the past—even the recent past of the 1930s—these episodes are marginal and highlight the strong majorities committed to a liberal civic order.

Contrary to the dominant neorealist and neoliberal theories, identity and community are important components of political order. Identities are not primordial or immutable. Rather they are the product of social, economic, and political forces operating in specific historical contexts. The Western political order is strengthened by and in turn strengthens the distinctive Western civic identity. The continued viability and expansion of capitalism, made possible by Western multilateral institutions, sustain the business, commodity, and transnational cultures that in turn make it more politically feasible to sustain these institutions. Similarly, the success of security binding practices in preserving peace among Western countries reinforces the identity of the West as a political community by allowing memories of war, traditionally generative of conflicting national identities, to fade into an increasingly remote past. While the Cold War and the construction of the Western identity as the "free world" contributed to Western solidarity and helped marginalize memories of international conflict in the West (just as bipolarity contributed to Western institutional development), the Western civic identity has deeper sources that the end of the Cold War does not affect.

REALISM VERSUS STRUCTURAL LIBERALISM AFTER THE COLD WAR

Realism and structural liberalism have very different understandings of the nature of the Western political system, and therefore produce very different expectations about the trajectory of Western relations after the Cold War. In principle, it should be possible to test their different expectations—

to demonstrate the superiority of one over the other. However, during the Cold War such a clean test was elusive because both theories expected that there would be cohesion in the West, but for very different reasons. After the Cold War, a sharp clash between the theories has come to the fore: realist theories expect the Western system to decay as a result of the end of bipolarity and the continuing decline of American power, while the structural liberal theory expects Western order to persist, since the factors that gave shape to the West remain. Events in the first years after the Cold War provide the beginnings of a clean test of the competing theories—a test that will grow sharper as time passes.

Realist theories generate sharp expectations that Western order will decay with the end of the Cold War, and realist scholars have advanced explicit predictions drawn from these theories; balance-of-power theory expects that with the end of bipolarity and the end of the Soviet threat bases of solidarity will decline and conflicts endemic to anarchy will emerge. Without a unifying threat, balance-of-power theory predicts that strategic rivalry among the Western powers will reemerge, and specifically that the NATO alliance will fall apart and movement toward European union will halt and reverse.[56] Realist theories of hegemony have long expected Western order to crumble in the face of declining American power capabilities relative to its Western allies, and with the end of the Cold War—and the end of the masking influence of bipolarity—this theory expects more rapid decay.[57] A corollary expectation generated by realist balance-of-power theory is that the semisovereignty of Germany and Japan will be abandoned and both countries will acquire the full trappings of great power capabilities and ambitions.[58] In the realm of political economy, a corollary expectation of realist hegemony theory is that the liberal trading order will break down and be replaced by trade wars and competing economic blocs. In particular, the U.S.-Japanese relationship is seen as being ripe for increased conflict; with the end of the Soviet threat and the declining significance of the U.S.-Japanese defense alliance, Japan is seen to be free to intensify its mercantilist economic strategies.[59] Finally, realist theory generates the expectations that with the return of anarchy and great power rivalry, nationalism will take a more prominent place in Western identities at the expense of civic identity.[60] The overall prediction of realism is that the future of the West will be much like the pre-Cold War period, characterized by strategic conflict, economic warfare, alliance rivalry, hypernationalism, and ultimately the risk of war.

Structural liberal theory expects a very different pattern for the Western system. Because the institutions and practices that give the Western system its distinctive character are driven largely by internal logics, structural liberal theory posits that the overall cohesion and strength of these institutions will not wane with the end of the Cold War but stand out more clearly. Western practices of security co-binding emerged as responses to fears of anarchy and its consequences, and because this possibility remains a perennial one, the theory expects that co-binding will continue to be practiced, indeed it may become more salient as the assistance and reinforcement of bipolarity and hegemony decline. Similarly, because American hegemony is penetrated and reciprocal, the structural liberal theory does not expect these institutions to decay with the decline of American hegemony—and, if anything, they are likely to become more reciprocal.

On the question of the semisovereignty of Germany and Japan, the structural liberal theory holds that this status, so anomalous to realism, has strong roots in the domestic political systems of these countries, and it is viewed by these states as a successful technique for dealing with the historically grounded fears of their neighbors. From this it follows that semisovereignty is likely to persist and sustain the support of the German and Japanese publics. In the realm of political economy, structural liberalism holds that openness is the product of the imperatives of capitalism rather than balancing and hegemony, and therefore the theory expects that the system will remain and continue to grow in openness. Finally, the evolution toward more complex and similar civic identities, according to structural liberal theory, derives from capitalism, wealth, and the prevalence of liberal norms. Because of this, the theory expects that the end of the Cold War will not contribute to the resurgence of nationalism but that civic identity will continue to be dominant in the West.

It has been less than a decade since the end of the Cold War, and therefore the unfolding of events during this period can provide only preliminary rather than definitive tests of the clash between these competing theories. However, it is striking that the major trends have so far been quite inconsistent with realist expectations and quite consistent with structural liberalism. From the perspective of the last fifty years, it would be difficult to argue that the scope and intensity of conflict between the Western countries have increased measurably since the Cold War's end. Across the whole range of test issues, the pattern has followed structural liberal expectations. Contrary to the realist expectation, the NATO alliance has not begun to decay; Western leaders have unambiguously reaffirmed its central place. After the Cold War,

NATO's role as the provider of order in Western Europe has become increasingly dominant in its purpose.[61] Indeed, the NATO countries have initiated an ambitious program of expansion. The initial entry of the Visegrad countries (Poland, the Czech Republic, and Hungary) during the summer of 1997 signals that NATO is evolving into a security institution that addresses contemporary European security issues. While some advocate and interpret NATO expansion as an insurance policy against Russian resurgence, NATO has simultaneously brought Russia into the formal structure of the alliance through the creation of a NATO-Russian council, and has sought vigorously to reassure Russia that NATO is not an anti-Russian alliance.[62] Consistent with structural liberal expectations, this expansion is widely seen as a way to extend the co-binding pattern of Western security practices to cope with the void created by the end of the Warsaw Pact rather than a balancing measure.[63] Also consistent with structural liberal expectations, Germany has played a key role on supporting NATO expansion to the east, and authoritative German figures speak of the importance of tying Germany within international institutions as well as mitigating anarchy in Eastern Europe.[64]

Also, contrary to realist expectations, efforts toward greater European unity have not reversed but have continued to show the same pattern of two steps forward and one step backward—the pattern evident over the last half century. Reflective of the European view on the relationship between European union and security is Helmut Kohl's defense of further European integration as being necessary in order to avoid a return to anarchy, rivalry, and extreme nationalism.[65] On the question of hegemony, America's major allies have shown no willingness to balance against the United States, and indeed have evinced continued enthusiasm for American leadership. It is striking that the most pointed European criticism of the United States has not been about coercion or heavy handedness, but rather for their perceptions of American unwillingness to lead.[66]

The stability of German and Japanese semisovereignty, expected by structural liberalism, has also continued. The fact that Germany and Japanese defense spending has fallen more rapidly than American spending is a telling indication that these states are not pursuing great power ambitions and capabilities. As a recent analysis indicates, "Germany, of all the states in Europe, continued to promote its economic and military security almost exclusively through multilateral action. . . . [B]edrock institutional commitments were never called into question, and many reform proposals, notably in connection with the EC, aim to strengthen international institutions at the expense of the national sovereignties of member states, including, of course, Germany itself."[67] While Germany and Japan have been seeking a greater political role in international institutions, most notably the UN Security Council, the United States has supported these efforts.

Similarly, developments in the international political economy are inexplicable to realism, but follow the expectations of structural liberalism. The successful completion of the Uruguay round and the evolution of GATT into the World Trade Organization mark a major widening and deepening of the international free trade regime. The intensive discussions of a Transatlantic Free Trade Area also indicate that the momentum of trade liberalization remains strong. As a result, expectations of the rapid emergence of exclusionary and antagonistic trade blocs have not been fulfilled.[68] On the critical case of U.S.-Japanese trade relations, realist expectations of enhanced conflict have been largely confounded. The United States has continued to insist that Japan open its domestic markets and bring its economic practices in line with Western norms, but Japan has not responded with increased intransigence, as the realists expect, but rather has taken major steps toward openness and deregulation—driven by economic necessity as much as American policy. Despite expectations that the post-Cold War domestic realignment in Japan would lead to a strengthened commitment to mercantilist policies and a weakening of U.S.-Japan security arrangements, the Japanese government has affirmed both a commitment to deregulation and greater openness and the primacy of its security treaty with the United States.

Finally, realist expectations that nationalist sentiment would resurge and eclipse civic identities and liberal democratic norms have not been borne out by recent developments. The speed with which the liberal consensus among Western countries responded to incidents of illiberal prejudice and right-wing nationalist violence suggests that liberal identities and values are robust and politically dominant. While there has been an effort on the part of Europeans to exclude non-Europeans from North Africa or people from the lands of the former Soviet empire, the relentless homogenization of cultural life, professional accreditation, educational systems, and business practices has marched onward.

The pattern of events clearly follows the expectations of the structural liberal theory and has so far offered little support for realist expectations. However, the relatively few years of the post-Cold War period indicate that the jury is still out on the ultimate superiority of these competing theories. To escape the implications of these developments, realists might modify their argument with the claim that there has been an overhang in the institutions of the Cold War that accounts for the absence of balancing conflict and institutional decay. However, since key features of the Western system are actually strengthening rather than simply persisting or decaying with imperceptible slowness, this clearly prompts serious doubts about the validity of realist expectations and the theories that generate them.

Conclusion

A principal implication of this chapter for international relations theory is that realist theories of balance of power, hegemony, sovereignty, and nationalism fail to capture the core dynamics of the Western political order. We have demonstrated that the Western political order has five distinctive and important components that together constitute structural liberalism: security co-binding, penetrated hegemony, semisovereignty and partial great powers, structural openness, and civic identity and community. The overall Western political order is a complex composite in which these elements interact and mutually reinforce each other. The overall pattern of these elements and their interaction constitute the structure of the liberal political order—the whole is greater than the sum of the parts. Any picture of the West that fails to bring in all these components will fail to capture its structural character.

As realists point out, American hegemony and the bipolar balance helped form and give cohesion to this order. But the penetrated character of hegemony makes it unlike the realist formulation in its mutual and reciprocal operation. Likewise, Western co-binding institutions and practices are a distinctive and independent response to the problem of anarchy among Western states and not something derivative of bipolar balancing. Overall, the Western liberal world exhibits patterns of political order that lie between traditional images of domestic and international politics, thus creating an unusual and distinctive subsystem in world politics.

Although there is good reason to believe that the Western order has a very robust character, the fact that neither realism nor liberalism captures it very well is not only revealing of their theoretical limitations but also troubling in its implications for the maintaining of this system. Because of the Cold War, it is understandable that *realpolitik* approaches overshadowed liberal ones in policy discourse and practice as well as in academic international relations theory. The hegemonic status of realism has marginalized and displaced the earlier American approaches to international affairs that were more pragmatic and more liberal. The realist characterization of liberalism as idealist and utopian belies its "realistic" sophistication and the extent to which the postwar order was created as a response to the earlier failures of both Wilsonian internationalism and the extreme realism of the interwar period (and its economic blocs, mercantilism, hypernationalism, and imperialism). With the end of the Cold War, the persistence of realism as a dominant approach to international affairs is consequential because of its limited understanding of the Western political order and its inability to provide policy tools for operating within it. Policy agendas derived from realism could also become self-fulfilling prophecies and gradually undermine the Western order, particularly if those agendas include the conversion of Germany and Japan back into "normal" great powers. With the end of the Cold War, it is necessary to recover the theory and practice of structural liberalism so as to chart policy within the Western order.

Liberal theory has also failed to adequately grasp the Western liberal system. The preoccupation of many liberals with building global institutions with universal scope, such as the United Nations, has ironically diverted their attention from understanding and building the liberal order within the West. Similarly, liberal international relations theory is not well situated to understand the Western order because of its lack of accumulation and sense of itself as a long tradition with significant historical accomplishments. Liberal theory's conceptual focus on process over structure and "micro" over "macro" also contributes to its inappropriate theoretical gauge. Also part of liberalism's limitations are the deference it gives realism on security issues and its related focus on "low politics" rather than "high politics." Liberal theory is very heterogeneous and it does capture various components of the Western political order, such as the democratic peace, but it fails to appreciate the West's distinctive history, architecture, and structure. Given the success of the Western liberal order and its centrality within the larger world system, a liberal international relations theory refocused on structure can lay claim to at least equality with realism.

If structural liberalism does capture the logic of the Western political order, then this suggests that the solidarity, cohesion, and cooperation of these countries will outlast the rise and fall of external threats. At the same time, no political order arises purely spontaneously and no political order endures without practices and programs based on an accurate understanding of its nature. In the post-Cold War era, the absence of bipolarity and the waning of American hegemony does remove forces that have contributed to the Western order. Therefore, to sustain this order, it is worthwhile to think about what might constitute a more self-conscious and robust liberal statecraft. A central task of such a liberal statecraft is the formulation of an agenda of principles and policies that serve to strengthen, deepen, and codify the Western political order.

NOTES

1. See Kenneth Waltz, *Theory of International Politics* (Reading, MA: Addison-Wesley, 1979). For extensions and debates, see Robert O. Keohane, ed., *Neorealism and its Critics* (New York: Columbia University Press, 1986).

2. John J. Mearsheimer, "Back to the Future: Instability of Europe after the Cold War," International Security 15 (Summer 1990): 5–57; Mearsheimer, "Why We Will Soon Miss the Cold War," The Atlantic, 266 (August 1990): 35–50; and Conor Cruise O'Brien, "The Future of the West," The National Interest, 30 (Winter 1992/93): 3–10.

3. See Robert Gilpin, *War and Change in World Politics* (New York: Cambridge University Press, 1981).

4. For contrasting views, see Robert Gilpin, *The Political Economy of International Relations* (Princeton: Princeton University Press, 1987); Paul Kennedy, *The Rise and Fall of the Great Powers* (New York: Random House, 1987); Joseph S. Nye, Jr., *Bound to Lead: The Changing Nature of American Power* (New York: Basic Books, 1990); Henry Nau, *The Myth of America's Decline: Leading the World Economy in the 1990's* (New York: Oxford University Press, 1990); Susan Strange, "The Persistent Myth of Lost Hegemony," *International Organization* 41 (4) (Autumn 1987): 551–74. See also the articles in David P. Rapkin, ed., *World Leadership and Hegemony* (Boulder: Lynne Rienner, 1990).

5. See G. John Ikenberry, "Creating Liberal Order: The Origins and Persistence of the Western Postwar Settlement," unpublished paper, 1995; Ikenberry, "Creating Yesterday's New World Order: Keynesian "New Thinking" and the Anglo-American Postwar Settlement," in Judith Goldstein and Robert O. Keohane, eds., *Ideas and Foreign Policy: Beliefs, Institutions, and Political Change* (Ithaca: Cornell University Press, 1993); and Ikenberry, "Rethinking the Origins of American Hegemony," *Political Science Quarterly* 104 (Fall 1989): 375–400.

6. Michael Doyle, "Kant, Liberal Legacies, and Foreign Affairs," *Philosophy and Public Affairs* 12 (1983): 205–35, 323–53; Karl Deutsch, *Political Community and the North Atlantic Area* (Princeton: Princeton University Press, 1957); Robert O. Keohane and Joseph S. Nye, *Power and Interdependence: World Politics in Transition* 2nd Edition (Glenview, IL: Scott, Foresman, 1989); Richard Ro-

secrance, *The Rise of the Trading State: Commerce and Conquest in the Modern World* (New York: Basic Books, 1986). For a survey of liberal theories, see Mark W. Zacher and Richard A. Mathew, "Liberal International Theory: Common Threads, Divergent Strands," in Charles W. Kegley, Jr., ed., *Controversies in International Relations Theory: Realism and the Neoliberal Challenge* (New York: St. Martin's Press, 1995).

7. See Robert Keohane, *After Hegemony: Cooperation and Discord in the World Political Economy* (Princeton: Princeton University Press, 1984), ch. 1.

8. Waltz, *Theory of International Politics*; and Steve Walt, *The Origins of Alliances* (Ithaca: Cornell University Press, 1987).

9. See Daniel H. Deudney, "The Philadelphian System: Sovereignty, Arms Control, and Balance of Power in the American States-Union, 1787–1861," *International Organization* (Spring 1995); and Deudney, "Binding Sovereigns: Authority, Structure, and Geopolitics in Philadelphian Systems," in Thomas Biersteiker and Cynthia Weber, eds., *State Sovereignty as Social Construct* (New York: Cambridge University Press, 1996).

10. See Thomas J. Knock, *To End All Wars: Woodrow Wilson and the Quest for a New World Order* (New York: Oxford University Press, 1992).

11. Mary Hampton, "NATO at the Creation: U.S. Foreign Policy, West Germany and the Wilsonian Impulse," *Security Studies* 4(3) (Spring 1995): 610–56; Geir Lundstadt, *The American "Empire"* (Oxford: Oxford University Press, 1990); David P. Calleo, *Beyond American Hegemony: The Future of the Western Alliance* (New York: Basic Books, 1988), ch. 1; and Joseph Joffe, "Europe's American Pacifier," *Foreign Policy* No. 54 (Spring 1984): 64–82.

12. John Duffield, *Power Rules: The Evolution of NATO's Conventional Force Posture* (Stanford: Stanford University Press, 1995). Martin H. Folly, "Breaking the Vicious Circle: Britain, the United States, and the Genesis of the North Atlantic Treaty," *Diplomatic History* 12 (1988): 59–77. See also Gunther Hellman and Reinhard Wolf, "Neorealism, Neoliberal Institutionalism, and the Future of NATO," *Security Studies* 3(1)(Autumn 1993): 3–43.

13. Michael Hogan, *The Marshall Plan: America, Britain, and the Reconstruction of Western Europe, 1947- 1952* (New York: Cambridge University Press, 1987).

14. Alberta Sbragia, "Thinking about European Future: The Uses of Comparison," in Sbragia, ed., *Euro-Politics: Institutions and Policymaking in the "New" European Community* (Washington, D.C.: Brookings, 1992).

15. See Gilpin, *War and Change in World Politics*; also Gilpin, *The Political Economy of International Relations*, esp. pp. 72–80.

16. See Stephen D. Krasner, "American Policy and Global Economic Stability," in William P. Avery and David P. Rapkin, eds., *America in a Changing World Political Economy* (New York: Longman, 1982).

17. The neorealist argument that secondary states will balance against American

hegemony is made by Christopher Layne: "Proponents of America's preponderance have missed a fundamental point: other states react to the threat of hegemony, not the hegemon's identity. American leaders may regard the United States as a benevolent hegemon, but others cannot afford to take such a relaxed view." Layne, "The Unipolar Illusion," *International Security* 17(4) (Spring 1993): 35.

18. Interestingly, some realists and others have faulted the United States for lacking a centralized and autonomous capacity to make and implement foreign policy. But we argue that it is precisely the absence of these features that have made possible the reciprocal and consensual exercise of American power—and, hence, the stability of the Western order.

19. Geir Lundstad, "Empire by Invitation? The United States and Western Europe, 1945–1952," in Charles Maier, ed., *The Cold War in Europe: Era of a Divided Continent* (New York: Wiener, 1991): 143–68. See also G. John Ikenberry, "Rethinking the Origins of American Hegemony," *Political Science Quarterly*.

20. The importance of liberal state institutions for the effective functioning of a hegemonic system has been noted by scholars who focus on Japan's potential for hegemonic status. The incomplete nature of Japanese liberalism and the difficulty that transnational forces have in influencing the Japanese policy process suggest that Japanese hegemony would be more resisted and more coercive. See Richard Rosecrance and Jennifer Taw, "Japan and the Theory of Leadership," *World Politics*, 42(2) (January 1990): 184–209.

21. See Gianfranco Poggi, *The Development of the Modern State: A Sociological Introduction* (Stanford: Stanford University Press, 1878), esp. ch. 6, "State and Society Under Liberalism and After," pp. 117–49.

22. These characteristics of the American state have been described by many scholars. Stephen Skowronek, *Building a New American State: The Expansion of National Administrative Capacities, 1877–1920* (New York: Cambridge University Press, 1982); and Samuel Huntington, *American Politics: The Promise of Disharmony* (Cambridge: Harvard University Press, 1981).

23. On the connection between domestic structures and transnational relations, see Thomas Risse-Kappen, ed., *Bringing Transnational Relations Back In: Non-State Actors, Domestic Structures and International Institutions* (New York: Cambridge University Press, 1995).

24. See Samuel P. Huntington, "Transnational Organizations in World Politics," *World Politics* 25 (April 1973); and Robert Gilpin, *U.S. Power and the Multinational Corporation* (New York: Basic Books, 1975).

25. See, for example, Wolfgang Handreider, "Dissolving International Politics: Reflections on the Nation- State," *American Political Science Review* 72(4) (1978): 1276–87; and James Rosenau, "The State in an Era of Cascading Politics: Wavering Concept, Widening Competence, Withering Colossus?" in James

Caparaso, ed., *The Elusive State: International and Comparative Perspectives* (Newbury Park, CA: Sage. 1989): 17–48.

26. For an exception, see Susan Strange, "Toward a Theory of Transnational Empire," in Ernst-Otto Czempiel and James N. Rosenau, eds., *Global Changes and Theoretical Challenges: Approaches to World Politics for the 1990s* (Lexington, MA: Lexington Books, 1989), 161–76.

27. See G. John Ikenberry and Charles Kupchan, "Socialization and Hegemonic Power," *International Organization*, 44(3) (Summer 1990): 283–315.

28. See Thomas Risse-Kappen, *Cooperation Among Democracies: The European Influence on U.S. Foreign Policy* (Princeton: Princeton University Press, 1995).

29. See Peter J. Katzenstein and Yutaka Tsujinaka, " 'Bullying,' 'Buying,' and 'Binding': U.S.-Japanese Transnational Relations and Domestic Structures," in Risse-Kappen, ed., *Bringing Transnational Relations Back In*, 79–111.

30. Pat Choate, *Agents of Influence: How Japan Manipulates America's Political and Economic System* (New York: Simon and Schuster, 1990).

31. Viewed from the perspective of great power politics, France's continued pursuit of "first tier" status is a quaint vestige that is possible precisely because its geographic position always allows it to ride free on the American system. Indeed, the degree to which the United States has tolerated the continued French posturing and irritation is a reflection, not of American coerciveness, but of American noncoerciveness.

32. See Michael Ross Fowler and Julie Marie Bunck, *Law, Power, and the Sovereign State: The Evolution and Application of the Concept of Sovereignty* (University Park, PA: Penn State University Press, 1995).

33. See Hedley Bull, *The Anarchical Society* (New York: Columbia University Press, 1977); Barry Buzan, "From International System to International Society: Structural Realism and Regime Theory meet the English School," *International Organization*, 47(3) (Summer 1993): 327–52.

34. See Leopold von Ranke, "The Great Powers," in Theodore von Laue, ed., *The Writings of Leopold von Ranke* (Princeton: Princeton University Press, 1950); Jack Levy, *War in the Modern Great Power System, 1495–1975* (Lexington: The University Press of Kentucky, 1983); and Martin Wight, *Power Politics*, edited by Hedley Bull and Carsten Holbraad (New York: Holmes and Meier, 1978).

35. See Peter J. Katzenstein, *Policy and Politics in West Germany: The Growth of a Semi-Sovereign State* (Philadelphia: Temple University Press, 1987).

36. On American and Western efforts to liberalize postwar German and Japanese political institutions, see John Montgomery, *Forced to Be Free: The Artificial Revolution in Germany and Japan* (Chicago: University of Chicago Press, 1957); John Herz, ed., *From Dictatorship to Democracy: Coping with the Legacies of Authoritarianism and Totalitarianism* (Westport, CT: Greenwood, 1982); Thomas A. Schwartz, *America's Germany: John J. McCloy and the Fed-*

eral Republic of Germany (Cambridge: Harvard University Press, 1991); Robert E. Ward and Sakamoto Yoshikazu, eds., *Democratizing Japan: The Allied Occupation* (Honolulu: University of Hawaii Press, 1987); and Tony Smith, *America's Mission: The United States and the Worldwide Struggle for Democracy in the Twentieth Century* (Princeton: Princeton University Press, 1994), ch. 6.

37. See Ian Buruma, *The Wages of Guilt: Memories of War in Germany and Japan* (New York: Meridian, 1995).

38. See the chapter by Joseph Grieco, this volume.

39. Robert Gilpin, "The Politics of Transnational Economic Relations," *International Organization* 25 (Summer 1971); Charles P. Kindleberger, *The World in Depression* (Berkeley: University of California Press, 1973); Kindleberger, "Dominance and Leadership in the International Economy: Exploitation, Public Goods, and Free Riders," *International Studies Quarterly* 25 (1981): 242–54; Stephen Krasner, "State Power and the Structure of International Trade," *World Politics* 28 (April 1976): 317–47; and Robert O. Keohane, "The Theory of Hegemonic Stability and Changes in International Economic Regimes, 1967–1977," in Ole R. Holsti, Randolph M. Siverson, and Alexander L. George, eds., *Changes in the International System* (Boulder, CO: Westview Press, 1980).

40. See Gilpin, "Economic Interdependence and National Security in Historical Perspective," in Klaus Knorr and Frank Trager, eds., *Economic Issues and National Security* (Lawrence, KS: Regents Press of Kansas, 1977): 19–66.

41. For variations of this argument, see Joanne Gowa, *Allies, Adversaries, and International Trade* (Princeton: Princeton University Press, 1994); and Edward D. Mansfield, *Power, Trade, and War* (Princeton: Princeton University Press, 1994).

42. See John Gerard Ruggie, "International Regimes, Transactions, and Change: Embedded Liberalism in the Postwar Economic Order," in Stephen D. Krasner, ed., *International Regimes* (Ithaca: Cornell University Press, 1983); and Ruggie, "Embedded Liberalism Revisited: Institutions and Progress in International Economic Relations," in Beverly Crawford and Emmanuel Adler, eds., *Progress in International Relations* (Berkeley: University of California Press, 1991). See also Eric Helleiner, *States and the Reemergence of Global Finance: From Bretton Woods to the 1990s* (Ithaca: Cornell University Press, 1994).

43. Conversely, if states abandon their commitment to the welfare state then this motivation for their support of a liberal economic system would decline. Or structural changes in the international economy might be less congenial to domestic welfare commitments, in which states would also pull back from the pursuit of open foreign economic policies. In either case, the liberal order would become "disembedded" and much less robust. See John Gerard Ruggie, "At Home Abroad, Abroad at Home: International Liberalism and Domestic

Stability in the New World Economy," *Millennium: Journal of International Studies* 24(3) (Winter 1995): 507–526.

44. The most systematic discussion of this logic is Joseph Grieco, "Anarchy and the Limits of Cooperation: A Realist Critique of Neoliberal Institutionalism," *International Organization* 42 (1988): 485–507; and Grieco, *Cooperation Among Nations* (Ithaca: Cornell University Press, 1990). For additional discussion and debate, see David Baldwin, ed., *Neoliberalism and Neorealism* (New York: Columbia University Press, 1994).

45. An example of this phenomenon is the high technology sectors. In the late-1980s, Germany and Japan were leading the United States in many areas, but in more recent years this pattern has been reversed.

46. This is a variation on the argument, made by Snidal, that multiple actors (in this case sectors and firms rather than states) complicate the simple calculation of relative gains and therefore mitigates its influence over policy. See Duncan Snidal, "International Cooperation Among Relative Gain Maximizers," *International Studies Quarterly* 35(4) (December 1991): 387–402. The sector focus also yields mixed results in Michael Mastanduno, "Do Relative Gains Matter? America's Response to Japanese Industrial Policy," *International Security* 16 (Summer 1991): 73–113. See also Jonathan Tucker, "Partners and Rivals: A Model of International Collaboration in Advanced Technology," *International Organization* 45(1) (Winter 1991): 83–120.

47. See Robert Pollard, *Economic Security and the Origins of the Cold War, 1945–1950* (New York: Columbia University Press, 1985).

48. See G. John Ikenberry, "Creating Liberal Order: The Origins and Persistence of the Western Postwar Settlement."

49. Louis Hartz, *The Liberal Tradition in America* (New York: Harcourt, Brace, 1955).

50. See Hans Morgenthau, *Politics Among Nations* (New York: Knopf, 1948).

51. George Mosse, *The Nationalization of the Masses* (Ithaca: Cornell University Press, 199x).

52. See Susan Strange, *States and Markets* (New York: Blackwell, 1988).

53. For an analysis of global cultural formations, see Mike Featherstone, ed., *Global Culture* (Newbury Park: Sage, 1990).

54. This second form of common identity is less extensive and institutionalized than the parallel emergence of domestic liberalism, but it is significant in the cohesion it gives the Western system.

55. The United States is the hub of this increasingly open and circulating system of elites. In discussing the globalization of the world economy and rising American competitiveness within it, one reporter argues: "The increased openness of American society appears to be an advantage as well. U.S. graduate schools continue to attract leading foreign students, and entrepreneurs from around the

globe often consider the U.S. the best place to launch an innovative concern. Foreign-born managers are far more prevalent at U.S. companies now than 20 years ago. The top executives of both Apple Computer Inc. and Compaq Computer Corp. are German nationals. Goodyear's Mr. Gibara—born in Egypt— says, "It's a big strength that we have a cadre of multinational managers. We can better relate to other cultures." G. Pascal Zachary, "Behind Stock's Surge is an Economy in which Big U.S. Firms Thrive," *Wall Street Journal*, November 22, 1995, A7.

56. See John Mearsheimer, "Back to the Future," *International Security*. See also Kenneth Waltz, "The Emerging Structure of International Politics," *International Security* 18 (Fall 1993): 44–79; Samuel P. Huntington, "Why International Primacy Matters," *International Security* 17 (Spring 1993): 68–83; Pierre Hassner, "Europe Beyond Partition and Unity: Disintegration or Reconstruction?" *International Affairs* 66 (July 1990): 461–75; Hugh DeSantis, "The Graying of NATO," *Washington Quarterly* 14 (Autumn 1991): 51–65.

57. Robert Gilpin, "American Policy in the Post-Reagan Era," *Daedelus* (Summer 1987): 33–67. Also, Paul Kennedy, *The Rise and Fall of the Great Powers: Economic Change and Military Conflict from 1500–2000* (New York: Random House, 1987).

58. Christopher Layne, "The Unipolar Illusion," *International Security*. For a review of this argument, see Robert Jervis, "The Future of World Politics: Will It Resemble the Past?" *International Security* 16(3) (Winter 1991/92): 39–73.

59. Chalmers Johnson, "History Restarted: Japanese-American Relations at the End of the Century," in Johnson, *Japan: Who Governs? The Rise of the Developmental State* (New York: Norton, 1995). See also Edward Luttwak, "From Geopolitics to Geo-Economics: Logic of Conflict, Grammar of Commerce," *National Interest* No. 20 (Summer 1990); Edward Olsen, "Target Japan as America's Economic Foe," *Orbis* 36(4) (Fall 1992): 491–504; and Erik R. Peterson, "Looming Collision of Capitalisms," *Washington Quarterly* (Spring 1994): 65–75.

60. See Conor Cruise O'Brien, "The Future of the West," *The National Interest* 30 (Winter 1992/93): 3–10; and Owen Harries, "The Collapse of 'the West,'" *Foreign Affairs* 72(4) (September/October 1993): 41–53.

61. John Duffield, "NATO's Functions After the Cold War," *Political Science Quarterly*, 119(5) (1994–95): 763–787.

62. For an overview of issues surrounding NATO expansion, see: Philip H. Gordon, ed., *NATO's Transformation: The Changing Shape of the Atlantic Alliance* (New York: Rowman & Littlefield, 1997).

63. Strobe Talbott, "Why NATO Should Grow," *The New York Review of Books*, August 10, 1995.

64. Voigt Karsten, a member of Germany's parliament who was involved in shaping

Germany's policy toward NATO expansion has observed: "We wanted to bind Germany into a structure which practically obliges Germany to take the interests of its neighbors into consideration." Jane Perlez, "Blunt Reason for Enlarging NATO: Curbs on Germany," *New York Times*, December 7, 1997.

65. Alan Cowell, "Kohl Casts Europe's Economic Union as War and Peace Issue," *New York Times*, October 17, 1995, A10.

66. In the most pointed remarks, President Chirac of France complained during the summer of 1995 that "the Western alliance had no leader." This helped galvanize the Clinton administration to play a more active role in ending the conflict in the former Yugoslavia

67. Jeffrey J. Anderson and John B. Goodman, "Mars or Minerva? A United Germany in a Post-Cold War Europe," in Robert O. Keohane, Joseph S. Nye, and Stanley Hoffmann, eds., *After the Cold War: International Institutions and State Strategies in Europe, 1989–1991* (Cambridge: Harvard University Press, 1993), 34.

68. See Miles Kahler, "A World of Blocs?" *World Policy Journal*, 1995.

5 Preserving the Unipolar Moment: Realist Theories and U.S. Grand Strategy After the Cold War

Michael Mastanduno

Realism is now both the dominant paradigm in the study of international relations and the most challenged. During the 1970s, critics turned to bureaucratic politics and cognitive process models to question realism's emphasis on the unitary rational state, and to interdependence models to challenge its acceptance of the utility and fungibility of military power.[1] The beginning of the 1990s brought a renewed wave of criticism, as realists were faulted for having failed to predict or anticipate the end of the Cold War and the peaceful transition to a new era.[2] In the immediate aftermath of the Cold War, the dark expectation of some realists of renewed security conflict among major powers has not yet been realized, leading critics to the conclusion that realism's days are numbered and that it is more sensible to place bets on domestic politics, international institutions, or constructivism to explain state behavior in the international arena.[3]

Is that conclusion warranted? This chapter takes seriously the challenge of the critics and assesses whether realism is useful in explaining post-Cold War U.S. foreign policy. The Cold War's passing provides an ideal opportunity to examine the impact of international structural change—a variable of central importance to realism—on state behavior. I focus on the United States because realism's traditional emphasis has been on the great powers, and after the Cold War the United States has been the dominant power in the international system.

It is critical to stress at the outset that there is no single "theory of realism" and that realism *per se* cannot be tested, confirmed, or refuted. Realism is a research program that contains a core set of assumptions from which a variety of theories and explanations can be developed.[4] Progress within the research program requires the elaboration and testing of specific realist theories, not only against nonrealist alternatives but also, in the case of competing realist theories, against each other.[5]

Below I focus on two prominent realist theories that offer competing predictions for U.S. behavior after the Cold War. The first is balance-of-power theory, developed most explicitly by Kenneth Waltz.[6] The second is a modified version of the balance-of-threat theory developed by Stephen Walt.[7] I elaborate the logic of each theory and from each I extrapolate specific sets of predictions for U.S. security policy and for U.S. foreign economic policy.[8] I then test these predictions against the (necessarily preliminary) evidence of the post-Cold War era.[9]

The evidence neither fully supports nor fully contradicts either theory. It does reveal a striking pattern: America's post-Cold War security and economic strategies are each explained effectively, but by different realist theories. Balance-of-threat theory accounts for the dominant tendency in U.S. security policy: an effort to preserve America's position at the top of the international hierarchy by engaging and reassuring other major powers. Balance-of-power theory explains the dominant tendency in U.S. foreign economic policy: an effort to mobilize for national economic competition against other major powers. Since each theory provides a plausible explanation for a central aspect of post-Cold War U.S. foreign policy, it would be imprudent to follow the advice of realism's harshest critics and abandon the core paradigm. Yet, realists are hardly in a position to declare victory and go home. The evidence from this single case suggests a need for the further refinement and testing of competing realist theories and for the testing of the stronger realist theories against nonrealist alternatives.

In substantive terms, the realist framework illuminates two key developments in contemporary U.S. foreign policy. First, contrary to those who see U.S. security policy after the Cold War as incoherent or directionless, I argue that U.S. officials have in fact followed a consistent strategy in pursuit of a clear objective—the preservation of America's preeminent global position.[10] This grand strategy of preserving primacy has spanned the Bush and Clinton administrations, notwithstanding differences in their foreign policy rhetoric. It has decisively shaped U.S. relations with Japan, Germany, Russia, and China. Second, America's foreign economic policy has worked at cross-purposes with America's national security strategy. In relations with other major powers, the United States, in effect, has been trying simultaneously to play "economic hardball" and "security softball." U.S. officials have been forced to manage the resulting contradiction in order to prevent the friction generated by its foreign economic policy from spilling over and frustrating the attainment of its primary national security objective.

The next two sections of this article examine U.S. security strategy after the Cold War. I lay out balance-of-power theory, generate predictions, and assess them in light of the available evidence. I then do the same for balance-of-threat theory. The following two sections take up U.S. economic strategy after the Cold War. I apply each theory in the area of foreign economic policy, generate predictions, and compare the predictions to the available evidence. A final section discusses theoretical and policy implications.

BALANCE-OF-POWER THEORY AND U.S. SECURITY STRATEGY AFTER THE COLD WAR

Waltz's balance-of-power theory remains the most prominent neorealist theory of international relations.[11] From the premises that the international system is anarchic and that states are "like units," Waltz derives the behavioral expectation that balances of power will form and recur. Variations in the distribution of capabilities across states produce different configurations of the balance of power. Multipolar balances are likely to be more war-prone than bipolar balances, and in the latter configuration great powers will rely more on internal than external balancing to assure their survival and protect their interests.

Waltz is careful to emphasize that the purpose of his theory is to explain international outcomes, not the foreign policies of particular states. He claims that "the behavior of states and statesmen is indeterminate."[12] This is not entirely convincing, however, because the international structure provides opportunities and constraints that shape state behavior significantly, even if they do not determine it entirely. In a recent article, Waltz himself argues that "neorealist, or structural, theory leads one to believe that the placement of states in the international system accounts for a good deal of their behavior."[13] He suggests, for example, that the similar structural placement of the United States and Soviet Union in bipolarity should have led to "striking similarities" in their behavior. As evidence, he points to convergence in their armaments policies, military doctrines, and intervention habits.[14] International structural theory, then, should be useful in explaining the foreign policies of particular states.[15]

States respond to the particular features of their international structural environment.[16] The end of the Cold War and the collapse of the Soviet Union as one pole in a bipolar system clearly represent significant changes in the international environment. What expectations follow with regard to the national security strategy of the United States?

Balance-of-Power Logic and Predictions

The first task is to characterize the new structure. This is not straightforward, due to the imprecision of measurement that is characteristic of much of the realist literature on polarity.[17] Waltz complicates the issue by suggesting that after the collapse of the Soviet Union "bipolarity endures, but in an altered state," because "militarily Russia can take care of itself."[18] This is hard to square with the more common assessment of realists, shared explicitly by Waltz, that to be a great power a state needs to excel not in one area but across a range of capability attributes. For Morgenthau, the list includes geography, industrial capacity, military preparedness, and more elusive categories such as national character, morale, and the quality of government.[19] Waltz tells us that great power rank depends on how states score on a combination of attributes—size of population, resource endowment, economic capability, military strength, and political stability and competence—although he does not propose anything to serve as a scorecard.[20]

Even without precise measurement, to focus on a range of power attributes leads to the conclusion that the United States is now in a category by itself. Only the United States currently excels in military power and preparedness, economic and technological capacity, size of population and territory, resource endowment, political stability, and "soft power" attributes such as ideology.[21] All other would-be great powers are limited or lopsided in one critical way or another. Thus many commentators and theorists have concluded that the current structure is unipolar. In an article extending Waltz's theory to the post-Cold War era, Christopher Layne opens with the assertion that "the Soviet Union's collapse transformed the international system from bipolarity to unipolarity."[22]

Balance-of-power theory is very clear about the behavioral implications of unipolarity. States seek to balance power, and thus the preponderance of power in the hands of a single state will stimulate the rise of new great powers, and possibly coalitions of powers, determined to balance the dominant state. Layne writes that "in unipolar systems, states do indeed balance against the hegemon's unchecked power."[23] The question is not *whether* new powers will rise and balance, but when; and to Layne the answer is similarly clear—"fairly quickly." Waltz and Layne both anticipate a rapid transition, and each suggests that unipolarity will be transformed into multipolarity by the first or second decade of the twenty-first century.[24] Since neorealists expect a multipolar world to be more conflictual than a bipolar world, it is not surprising that they tend to be pessimistic regarding the prospects for peace and cooperation among great powers.[25]

The overall logic of this argument directs neorealists to focus attention on the calculations and capabilities of those states most likely to rise up and balance the power of the preponderant state. Waltz concentrates on Japan, which he views as "ready to receive the mantle [of great power status] if only it will reach for it," and on the prospects for Germany, China, the European Union, and Russian revival.[26] Mearsheimer, playing out the implications of balance-of-power logic in the regional context, analyzes the incentives for Germany to acquire nuclear capabilities.[27] Layne looks backward as well as forward in seeking to establish that unipolar systems existed in the past and stimulated the rise of new challengers. Like Waltz, he considers Japan to be America's most likely future geopolitical rival and does not count out the possibility of a future hegemonic war between the two.[28]

But what does a unipolar structure imply for the behavior of the state situated at the top of the international hierarchy? The answer suggested by balance-of-power theory is somewhat ironic. On the one hand, the preponderant state in a unipolar system is in an enviable position. It is significantly unconstrained and enjoys wide discretion in its statecraft. The contrast with a bipolar structure, within which that same state is compelled to react to events and tailor policies according to their impact on the bipolar competition, is striking. Yet on the other hand, the preponderant state is helpless to perpetuate this attractive state of affairs. The mere fact of its preponderant power guarantees the rapid rise of competing powers. In short, we should expect the dominant state to savor the unipolar moment, but recognize that it will not last.

Balance-of-power theory suggests further that efforts to preserve unipolarity are bound to be futile and likely to be counterproductive. Instead, the rational strategy for the dominant state is to accept the inevitability of multipolarity and maneuver to take advantage of it. Layne develops the logic most explicitly, and explains the futility of any U.S. effort to preserve its preponderance: "A policy of attempting to smother Germany's and Japan's great power emergence would be unavailing because structural pressures will impel them to become great powers regardless of what the United States does or does not do."[29] Waltz takes a similar position, reflected in his often-quoted statement that "NATO's days are not numbered, but its years are," because potential great powers such as Germany will not tolerate the constraints of a U.S.-dominated institution.[30] Instead of seeking to preserve its preponderance, Layne argues that it is rational for the United States to adopt a posture of "strategic independence," taking on the role of "offshore balancer."[31] Specifically, the United States should extricate itself from its security commitments and forward deployments in Europe and Northeast Asia. It should depend on the dynamics of global and regional balances, and should commit itself militarily as a "last minute" balancer if and only if the balancing efforts of other states fail to prevent the emergence of a new global hegemon.

To summarize, the logic of balance-of-power theory leads plausibly to three predictions of relevance to U.S. security policy in the post-Cold War era. First, we should see the United States, liberated from the confines of the bipolar structure, behaving as an "unconstrained" great power with considerable discretion in its statecraft. Second, we should find evidence that other major powers are, in Waltz's words, "edging away" from the United States and balancing or preparing to balance against it. Third, we should see evidence that the United States accepts the inevitability of multipolarity, which would lead it rationally to disentangle itself from its Cold War commitments and move toward a posture of strategic independence. The evidence at this stage can only be preliminary, but the general tendencies should be clear.

Balance of Power Evidence

There is support for the first prediction, and the evidence is clearest in U.S. intervention policy. Although balance-of-power theory may not be able to predict where and when the United States will intervene, we should see significant differences in the *pattern* of intervention as the international structure changes from bipolarity to unipolarity. More precisely, in the bipolar structure we actually should be able to find a pattern, because the United States was responding to strong constraints and a consistent set of signals from the international system. There was indeed a pattern: the United States intervened fairly consistently to support anti-Soviet or anti-Communist regimes around the world.[32]

In the unipolar structure the international constraints have been lifted, and, in the absence of clear signals from the international structure, intervention policy should become more haphazard and episodic. The U.S. response to the breakup of Yugoslavia is instructive. If that breakup had occurred during the Cold War, managing the ensuing conflict would have been an immediate and overwhelming priority for U.S. foreign policy. The prestige and resolve of the United States and Soviet Union would have been engaged, and there would have been a strong temptation to line up support for opposing sides and engage in a proxy war. As it was, United States was left with considerably more room to maneuver. As the single dominant power, the United States was free to redefine the problem over a five-year period as one not of vital interest, as one of vital interest, as a European problem, as a humanitarian problem, as a war of aggression and genocide, and as a civil war requiring an honest broker to make peace.

The lack of significant constraint is evident in other ways as well. In the bipolar system U.S. officials worried greatly, some would say obsessively, about the costs to U.S. credibility and prestige of failed or aborted interventions. After the Cold War, U.S. officials seem far less concerned about such less-than-successful interventions. In Somalia, the United States moved quickly from a humanitarian mission to a more ambitious nation-building exercise, but abruptly ended its efforts after taking relatively light casualties in a firefight. In Haiti, a U.S.-led intervention attempt was initially turned back by a rock-throwing mob. Subsequently, the United States engaged its prestige publicly with a clear ultimatum to Haiti's rebellious military, only to scramble at the deadline it set itself for a face-saving compromise with the same rebellious leaders in order to avoid a military encounter.

Commentators have searched in vain for a pattern to U.S. intervention policy since the end of the Cold War. After the Persian Gulf intervention, some anticipated that the United States would take on the role of "global policeman" to enforce order in the international system. But U.S. intervention in Iraq was followed by a clear reluctance to intervene in Bosnia, leaving many to speculate that the presence or absence of oil may have been the determining factor. There was no oil in Somalia, but there was U.S. intervention, clearly driven by humanitarian concerns. Yet similar concerns, even more prominently on display in Rwanda, were met by U.S. resistance to intervention.[33]

There is much less evidence in support of the second and third predictions of balance-of-power theory. Since balance-of-power theorists expect the transition to multipolarity to be rapid, by now we should be observing other major powers edging away from and balancing the United States, and we should see the United States disentangling itself from its Cold War commitments, or at least hedging its bets.

Layne and Waltz each provide suggestive evidence of other powers distancing themselves from the United States. Both cite isolated examples of remarks by public officials and academics in the relevant countries suggesting that unipolarity is not a desirable state of affairs. They also point to the desire of Japan and Germany for seats on the UN Security Council, their initial participation in UN peacekeeping efforts, and the role of Germany in forcing the European Community to recognize Croatia's and Slovenia's break from the former Yugoslavia.[34]

The bulk of the evidence to this point, however, does not support balance-of-power theory and suggests that a stronger case might be made for the opposite of the theory's predictions. Rather than edging away from the United States, much less balancing it, Germany and Japan have been determined to maintain the pattern of engagement that characterized the Cold War. German officials continue to view the persistence of NATO and forward deployment of U.S. forces within NATO as the cornerstone of their national security strategy. Japan's official strategy continues to be oriented around the maintenance and strengthening, for a new era, of the U.S.-Japan security treaty. Neither China nor Russia, despite having some differences with the United States, has sought to organize a balancing coalition against it. Indeed, a main security concern for many countries in Europe and Asia is not how to distance from an all-too-powerful United States, but how to prevent the United States from drifting away.

For its part, the United States has been determined to remain engaged. Rather than prepare for multipolarity by disentangling itself from Cold War commitments, the central thrust of post-Cold War U.S. strategy in Europe, North Asia, and the Middle East has been to reinforce and even deepen those commitments. The United States is seeking to preserve the status quo in security relations with its Cold War allies, and is seeking to engage and integrate its Cold War adversaries, Russia and China, into an order that continues to reflect the design and preserves the dominant position of America.

BALANCE-OF-THREAT THEORY AND U.S. SECURITY STRATEGY AFTER THE COLD WAR

The inability of balance-of-power theory thus far to predict effectively U.S. behavior (or that of other major powers) should not lead to the conclusion that "realism" is a useless framework for analyzing international relations after the Cold War. Other theories from within the realist research program may provide more effective explanations. In this section I elaborate the logic and extrapolate predictions for balance-of-threat theory, and apply those predictions to U.S. security strategy.

Balance-of-Threat Logic and Predictions

Stephen Walt expects balancing behavior to be the general tendency in international relations, but he departs from Waltz and his followers on the motivation underlying balancing behavior. Walt argues that balancing behavior is most usefully understood as a response to *threat*.[35] The extent to which states appear as threatening to others depends on a variety of factors, including, but not limited to, the aggregate power resources of the state. Power and threat overlap, but are not identical.[36] Geographic proximity, offensive capability, and aggressive intentions are also relevant considerations.[37] For Walt, "states that are viewed as aggressive are likely to provoke others to balance against them."[38]

The implications of Walt's revision of balance-of-power theory are significant. In a world in which balancing behavior is the norm *and* balancing is a response to threat, it is often rational for states to pursue policies that signal restraint and reassurance. Walt argues that "foreign and defense policies that minimize the threat one poses to others make the most sense in such a world."[39] Jack Snyder similarly contends that aggression that threatens other great powers diminishes a state's security in a balance-of-power system.[40]

The logic of balance-of-threat theory suggests that whether or not states balance a dominant state will depend at least in part on the foreign policy *behavior* of the dominant state. In the current unipolar context, the rapid rise of new powers to balance the United States is not a foregone conclusion. U.S. behavior can affect the calculations of other major states and may help to convince them that it is unnecessary to engage in balancing behavior.[41] By this logic, a rapid transition from unipolarity to "great power rivalry in a multipolar setting" is not inevitable. Unipolarity will not be preserved forever, but balance-of-threat theory implies that it may be sustainable for a meaningfully longer period than balance-of-power theorists anticipate.[42]

This implication is important because unipolarity is a preferred world for the United States. In a unipolar world, security threats to the United States are minimized and foreign policy autonomy is maximized. According to realist logic, any great power should prefer to be a unipolar power, regardless of whether or not it possesses expansionist ambitions. For the state at the top, unipolarity is preferable to being a great power facing either the concentrated hostility and threat of a bipolar world or the uncertainty and risk of miscalculation inherent in a multipolar one.

If balance-of-threat theory is correct in positing that states weigh intentions, and not just capabilities, in deciding whether to balance, what predictions follow with regard to post-Cold War U.S. foreign policy? The most important prediction one can infer from the theory is that, as an overall security strategy, the United States will attempt to prolong the "unipolar moment." If unipolarity is the preferred world for the United States, and if the rapid collapse of unipolarity is not inevitable because balancing is a response to threat, then we should anticipate that U.S. officials will pursue policies aimed at dissuading other states from rising to great power status and, singly or in combination, balancing against the United States.

It is difficult to pin down the specific policies the United States would pursue in the effort to preserve its preeminent position. It is possible, however, to infer general policy predictions from the logic of the theory. For example, it is reasonable to expect that the dominant state in a unipolar setting will rely on multilateralism in its international undertakings.[43] Multilateral decisionmaking procedures may be less efficient, and powerful states are often tempted to act unilaterally. But multilateral procedures are more reassuring to other states and may help to convince them that their preferences matter, and that they are not simply being coerced or directed to follow the dictates of the dominant state.[44]

We must also infer from balance-of-threat theory a set of predictions regarding how the dominant state will deal with potential challengers. Again, intentions matter. Just as the behavior of potential challengers will be affected by how they view the intentions of the dominant state, so, too, the behavior of the dominant state will be influenced by its understanding of the foreign policy intentions of potential challengers. The distinction made in classical realism between status quo and revisionist states is useful here. Hans Morgenthau contrasts the status quo nation, whose foreign policy is oriented toward not challenging the existing distribution of power at a particular time, with the imperialist nation, whose foreign policy seeks a reversal of existing power relations.[45] Imperialist or revisionist states tend to be unhappy with the rules governing the international system and the distribution of benefits within that system. Many other realists have built upon this distinction, including Jack Snyder in his analysis of empire, Randall Schweller in his explanation for World War II, Robert Gilpin in his account of hegemonic war and change, and William Wohlforth in his explanation for the end of the Cold War.[46]

We can infer that the response of the dominant state will be shaped by whether other states are revisionist or status quo oriented in their foreign policy orientation. Balance-of-threat theory should predict policies of accommodation and reassurance from the dominant state in its dealings with status quo states. The purpose of these policies is to reinforce in status quo states the conviction that they are secure and do not need to expand military capabilities significantly and challenge the existing order. Specifically, we should expect the dominant state to avoid, in its own foreign policy, behavior that would be perceived as threatening by status quo states; to help to deter or deflect other threats to the security of status quo states; and to help to provide "outlets" or opportunities for status quo states to demonstrate power or enhance prestige without challenging the existing order.[47]

In dealings with revisionist states, we should anticipate that the dominant state will adopt policies of containment and confrontation. Revisionist states are committed to upsetting the existing international order, and in that sense threaten the primary foreign policy objective of the dominant state. We should expect from the dominant state an effort to organize diplomatic and military coalitions, and at the extreme military action, against revisionist states[48]

Some potential challengers may be neither status quo nor revisionist. They may be "on the fence," uncertain which way their foreign policy will eventually fall. Balance-of-threat theory leads us to anticipate that the dominant state will approach these challengers with policies of accommodation in the hope of nudging them to support the status quo, rather than with policies of confrontation that would drive them unambiguously into the revisionist camp. We should expect the dominant power to adopt the same set of policies predicted for status quo states, and additionally to take steps to integrate these "undecided" states more fully into the existing order so that, by sharing the benefits of that order, they will have less incentive to destabilize or transform it.

The dominant state in a unipolar structure is in a relatively good position to accept the risks inherent in a foreign policy orientation that errs on the side of reassurance. As the sole dominant power it is best able to afford, at least in the short run, to accommodate a state masking revisionist intentions. What would be a "fatal" mistake for a state facing a challenger of equal or greater power is more likely to be a costly but recoverable mistake for the preponderant power in a unipolar setting.

To summarize, the logic of balance-of-threat theory leads to three predictions for U.S. security policy after the Cold War. First, we should expect, as the centerpiece of U.S. grand strategy, an effort to prolong the unipolar moment. Second, we should anticipate that the United States will adopt policies of reassurance toward status quo states, policies of confrontation toward revisionist states, and policies of engagement or integration toward undecided states. Third, we should see the United States emphasizing multilateral processes in its foreign policy undertakings. Before examining the evidence, it is necessary as a preliminary step to discuss the foreign policy orientations of America's potential challengers.

The Status of Potential Challengers

In the current international system, the United States is in the enviable position of not facing any state, or coalition of states, that combines great power capability with clear intent to destabilize the existing order. Instead, the United States faces two potential great powers whose international situation and foreign policy behavior suggest a preference for the status quo, and two others who sit on the fence, with foreign policy intentions and aspirations more uncertain.

Japan and Germany are part of the victorious coalition that prevailed over the Soviet Union in the just concluded hegemonic struggle. Rather than challenging U.S. hegemony, they are currently status quo powers, content to play a subordinate role within a U.S.-dominated system. The cornerstone of German security policy is the perpetuation of NATO, including the maintenance of U.S. forces in Europe and the U.S. nuclear guarantee. In 1994 German Chancellor Kohl described the U.S. presence as an "irreplaceable basis for keeping Europe on a stable footing," and that sentiment is echoed routinely by high German officials.[49] German participation in the West European Union and the Eurocorps has been based on the presumption that European military forces must be integrated into NATO rather than standing as autonomous units.[50]

Japan continues to reaffirm the centrality of the U.S.-Japan Security Treaty, which obliges the United States to defend Japan, if necessary with nuclear weapons, and which leaves Japan a partial military power. A comprehensive report on Japan's post-Cold War security strategy put forth in late 1994 by the Defense Issues Council, a prominent advisory body to the Prime Minister, called for the two countries to "perfect" their bilateral security relationship, which continued to be "indispensable both for the purpose of making Japan's own safety still more certain and for the purpose of making multilateral security cooperation effective."[51] Although its neighbors have been increasing their military spending, Japan's official long-term planning document, released in 1995, called for a *reduction* in military forces and equipment, strongly suggesting a preference for continued reliance on the United States to address regional security threats.[52]

For both Japan and Germany, continuities in foreign policy strategy after the Cold War outweigh major differences. Each state was a major beneficiary of the previous international order, and Germany also shared significantly in the "spoils" of the Cold War settlement by recovering the former East Germany. Future intentions are uncertain, but in the absence of unforeseen threats to their security, Japan and Germany are more likely to support the existing order than to challenge or undermine it.[53]

Russia's predicament and behavior suggest a different assessment. Since 1993 Russia has pursued a more assertive foreign policy, most evident in its coercive and interventionist behavior in the "near abroad" and in its desire to influence events in territorially proximate regions such as the Balkans and the Persian Gulf. None of this should come as a shock: the decline in Soviet/ Russian prestige and influence was so sharp over such a short period of time that one would expect Russia to seek, in the wake of the collapse, to restore some elements of its former great power status and exercise influence as a regional power. Yet, whether that effort will lead ultimately to a renewed strategy of global revisionism is certainly not a foregone conclusion. Russia does not currently possess an expansionist ideology. It has an ongoing need to attend to pressing economic problems at home, and requires international

assistance in that effort. And, after decades of being perceived as a destabilizing force, Russia's leaders have a desire to be treated and respected as
responsible players in the international system, and to share the benefits,
especially economic, of that system. Although tensions between Russia and
the West have increased since the "honeymoon period" of 1990–91, Russia's
overall approach to the West has remained a cooperative one, and Russia
has shown little inclination to enlist others to balance the preponderant
power of the United States.[54]

China's combination of rapid growth, international ambition, and a history of discontent with what it perceives as humiliation at the hands of great
powers makes it a more likely candidate to launch a global revisionist challenge. China's per capita GDP has almost quadrupled since 1978; it continues to develop and modernize its military capability; and it seems increasingly willing to threaten the use of force to achieve its foreign policy
objectives, particularly with regard to Taiwan and the South China Sea.[55]
China has the potential for a destabilizing combination of capabilities and
intentions. Yet even in this case, a revisionist challenge is not inevitable.
China's power position depends on sustaining rapid economic growth over
many years, which, in turn, depends on the maintenance of political stability. Neither are guaranteed. While China, like Russia, seems determined to
throw its weight regionally, it has also exhibited a desire to be respected as
a responsible great power and to share the benefits of the existing international order. And, although U.S.-Chinese relations have been strained by
the 1989 Tiananmen incident, China's post-Cold War military acquisition
pattern does not reflect a strategy of balancing the United States, it has not
tried to organize an anti-American united front, and its economic dependence on the United States has increased.[56]

Balance-of-Threat Evidence

U.S. security policy since the end of the Cold War has conformed, although not completely, to the predictions of balance-of-threat theory. U.S.
officials have sought to preserve America's dominant position through efforts
to convince the status quo states of Japan and Germany to remain partial
great powers, and to integrate the undecided states of Russia and China into
a U.S.-centered international order.[57] U.S. officials have emphasized multilateral coalitions and decisionmaking processes, particularly in cases of military intervention.

To be sure, neither the Bush nor the Clinton administration has advertised, in foreign policy pronouncements, the goal of preventing other states from challenging the preeminent position of the United States.[58] The grand strategy of preserving unipolarity, however, was laid out clearly in the much-discussed Defense Planning Guidance leaked to the press in 1992.[59] The paper concluded that, following the defeat of the Soviet Union, "our strategy must now refocus on precluding the emergence of any future global competitor." The United States "must establish and protect a new order that holds the promise of convincing potential competitors that they need not aspire to a greater role." It must "retain the pre-eminent responsibility for addressing those wrongs which threaten not only our interests, but those of our allies or friends, or which could seriously unsettle international relations." Although U.S. officials publicly distanced themselves from the Guidance at the time it was leaked, its logic and arguments have in fact shaped U.S. security policy.

For example, U.S. policy has been dedicated to dissuading Japan from becoming a "normal" great power by deflecting threats to Japanese security, providing avenues for Japan to exhibit international responsibility despite lacking great power status, and assuring that U.S. behavior does not exacerbate Japanese insecurity. The bilateral security treaty remains the key to the relationship for the United States. Shortly after the collapse of the Soviet Union, U.S. officials had announced plans for a continual reduction in troop levels in Asia, but in 1994 the Pentagon called for a halt in the process in order to allay anxieties among Japanese and Asian officials that the United States might be contemplating a phased withdrawal. On the contrary, U.S. officials have termed their strategy for Asia "deep engagement." It calls for the maintenance of the forward deployment of U.S. forces and a commitment to a stabilizing regional role over the indefinite future. In the words of Joseph Nye, then Assistant Secretary of Defense, "For the security and prosperity of today to be maintained for the next twenty years, the United States must remain engaged in Asia, committed to peace in the region, and dedicated to strengthening alliances and friendships. That is what we propose to do."[60] The U.S. strategy is designed to convince Japan that America will deter possible threats from Russia or China, and that although Japan should contribute to that effort, there is no need for Japan to replicate the U.S. effort by becoming a full great power. The U.S. presence is intended to reassure Japan's neighbors as well, and to dampen incentives for regional arms races generated by insecurity.

U.S. officials have responded to threats that might, if left unattended, create incentives for Japan to develop independent military capabilities. The

U.S.-led war in Iraq served multiple purposes, one of which was to maintain predictable access to Persian Gulf oil, on which Japan depends far more for its economic prosperity than does the United States. The U.S. effort to thwart North Korea's nuclear ambitions was consistent with U.S. nonproliferation strategy in general, and also with the regional strategy of reassuring Japan and discouraging it from having to acquire nuclear capabilities itself. U.S. officials have also been eager to encourage Japan to take on greater international responsibilities that do not require the full attributes of a great power. They have urged Japan to play a greater role in the management of international economic and environmental problems, and have encouraged Japan to take on international peacekeeping obligations, particularly in southeast Asia but in Africa as well.

"Deep engagement" is similarly an apt characterization of the post-Cold War U.S. security strategy in Europe. During the Cold War, the unstated assumption was that NATO's purpose was threefold: to keep the Americans in, the Russians out, and the Germans down. NATO and the European Community were the critical mechanisms to bind Germany and France together and to anchor Germany in a trans-Atlantic political and security community. Following the Cold War and German unification, the United States has continued to pursue a strategy designed to harness the great power potential of Germany while providing for German security in Europe.[61] For U.S. officials, support for German unification and the preservation of NATO with Germany as a full partner within it went hand-in-hand as crucial elements in the post-Cold War settlement.[62] Rather than "edging away" from NATO and the security obligations it imposes, U.S. officials have made clear their intention to transform the alliance and maintain it indefinitely.

The United States has also continued to support European integration, even as members of the European Union contemplate deeper commitments such as monetary and political union and the coordination of foreign and defense policies. Deeper integration has raised the potential for conflict between NATO and emerging European defense cooperation in the Western European Union and Eurocorps. The United States has been willing to support intra-European defense initiatives as long as they remain subordinated to NATO commitments.[63] U.S. officials engineered an arrangement with their European counterparts in 1994 to assure that the Western European Union would utilize rather than replicate NATO's military structure, and that the Eurocorps would come under NATO command during crisis or wartime.[64]

Balance-of-threat theory would anticipate U.S. intervention in conflicts that threaten regional stability and carry the potential for other major powers to develop and project independent military capabilities. America's reluctant and vacillating policy toward the Bosnian conflict between 1991 and 1994 does not square with this expectation. By 1995, however, U.S. strategy coalesced and U.S. officials placed the cohesiveness of NATO at the top of their Bosnian policy agenda. In a critical National Security Council meeting late in 1994, the Clinton administration decided, in the words of one official, that "NATO is more important than Bosnia," and, in deference to its allies, backed away from its commitment to use air power to protect the safe area of Bihac.[65] Subsequently, in an effort to unite NATO and assure that German and Russian involvement was closely coordinated with the United States, U.S. officials hosted and orchestrated a peace settlement among the warring parties and backed their diplomacy with a commitment of 20,000 ground troops.[66]

Turning to the undecided powers, balance-of-threat theory would predict a U.S. attempt to steer Russian foreign policy away from a possible revisionist challenge and toward support for the status quo. We should expect U.S. efforts to avoid threatening Russian security, to provide opportunities for Russia to recover lost prestige, and to integrate Russia into the existing international order. Indeed, the United States was careful not to provoke or humiliate Russian leaders as the Soviet Union collapsed: recall President Bush's concern that the West not be perceived as dancing triumphantly on the ruins of the Berlin Wall.[67] U.S. officials have also reacted cautiously to Russia's internal security problems and have resisted any temptation to encourage or exploit political instability. They essentially condoned Yeltsin's 1993 assault on the Russian Parliament, and their response to Russian aggression in Chechnya has been critical although restrained. Statements of disapproval have been accompanied by the notable absence of sanctions, despite obvious human rights concerns, and by public acknowledgments that Chechnya is part of the Russian federation.[68]

U.S. officials have also tried to bolster Russia's prestige through initiatives intended to highlight Russia's stature as an international actor. Invitations to Russian leaders to attend G-7 summits are one example, and the decision to grant Russia status as the "co-chair" of the U.S.-led Madrid peace conference on the Middle East is another. The Clinton administration worked out a delicate compromise to allow Russian forces to participate in the Bosnian peacekeeping effort under U.S. command when it became evident that Russia desired participation but was unwilling to do so under NATO command.[69] The United States also undertook a major diplomatic effort to ensure Russia's role as a "founding member" and major partner in the construction of a new export control regime, the successor to CoCom, designed to stem the flow of technology and weapons to dangerous states in the developing world. In the interest of furthering Russian economic reform, U.S. officials have facilitated Russia's access to the resources of the International Monetary Fund, to the point of raising questions as to whether Russia has been treated more generously than other recipients.[70] And they have sought to deepen cooperation with Russia in a revitalized United Nations and in the ongoing nuclear and conventional arms control processes.

One apparent anomaly for balance-of-threat theory is the U.S. commitment to NATO expansion. Russian leaders view NATO expansion as a political affront and a threat to Russian security. In the absence of an imminent threat from Russia, balance-of-threat theory would predict that the United States would resist rather than promote the expansion of NATO to Russia's doorstep.[71] Nevertheless, U.S. officials have encouraged NATO expansion and called for extending full membership to an initial group of East European countries in 1999.

The rationale for NATO expansion is multifaceted and complex, and on reflection the initiative is not wholly inconsistent with the U.S. grand strategy of preserving preponderance. NATO expansion extends and institutionalizes the U.S. presence in the historically turbulent zone of instability between Russia and Germany. Rather than as the harbinger of a new containment strategy, it is a hedge not only against future Russian expansion, but also against an independent German *Ostpolitik* and possible German-Russian conflict.[72] The U.S. desire to stabilize Eastern Europe yet not offend Russia has forced U.S. officials into a delicate balancing act. They have stressed publicly that Russia does not hold a veto over NATO expansion, but have clearly been influenced by Russia's concerns. U.S. officials have sought to make NATO "Russia-friendly" through Russian participation in the Partnership for Peace, and they have searched with Russian leaders for a formula that would make NATO expansion politically acceptable to Russia.[73]

For China, as for Russia, balance-of-threat theory would predict a U.S. policy that stressed engagement and integration rather than containment. The overall U.S. approach to China is consistent with this prediction. Assistant Defense Secretary Nye argued in 1995 that "it is wrong to portray China as an enemy. Nor is there reason to believe China must be an enemy in the future. . . . A containment strategy would be difficult to reverse.

Enmity would become a self-fulfilling prophecy."[74] The Clinton adminstration has termed its alternative strategy "comprehensive engagement," and its primary objective, as Kenneth Lieberthal has noted, is to facilitate China's integration into the existing international order on the condition that China accept the rules of that order and not seek to undermine it.[75] In short, the strategy seeks what to many seems improbable: to turn China into a status quo power.

A key element of the U.S. approach is closer defense and security cooperation with China. U.S. officials helped to convince China to join the nuclear nonproliferation regime and have engaged Chinese leaders in high-level dialogues on regional security and defense conversion. In the interest of a broader cooperative relationship, the Clinton administration in May 1994 backed away from the priority it had granted to human rights concerns in China policy and explicitly severed the connection between human rights and the granting of Most-Favored-Nation (MFN) status for China.

Although U.S. officials believe that Chinese "misbehavior" continues to strain the bilateral relationship, their response has been muted. Early in 1996, the Clinton administration determined that Chinese sales of nuclear technology to Iran and Pakistan violated nonproliferation rules, but worked to soften the sanctions it was required by law to impose on China.[76] In March 1996, as China threatened military action against Taiwan, the adminstration responded with "strategic ambiguity"—a display of naval force it hoped would be sufficient to deter China and reassure others in the region without provoking a confrontation with China. In a strong signal of the administration's preference for business as usual, National Security Adviser Anthony Lake stated publicly in the midst of the crisis that the administration planned to renew MFN status for China, even though the State Department's annual human rights report was strongly critical of China.[77]

This review of U.S. relations with potential challengers suggests that balance-of-threat theory provides a strong explanation for U.S. security policy after the Cold War, and one that is more persuasive than that offered by balance-of-power theory. Balance-of-threat theory also anticipates the emphasis in U.S. security policy on multilateral decisionmaking procedures. To be sure, "multilateralism," and especially the United Nations, became targets of opprobrium in the U.S. Congress and in American public opinion after the aborted intervention in Somalia. Nevertheless, as the Persian Gulf and Bosnian crises illustrate, the preferred strategy of the U.S. executive after the Cold War has been to rely on the UN Security Council to authorize the use of force or strong diplomatic initiatives, and then to proceed with U.S.-orchestrated military or diplomatic coalitions.[78] Multilateral decision-making processes help the United States to exercise its dominant power with legitimacy. They are key instruments of statecraft—indeed, of *realpolitik*—for a dominant state that is seeking, in a unipolar setting, to convince other states to cooperate with it rather than to balance against it.

BALANCE-OF-POWER THEORY AND U.S. ECONOMIC STRATEGY AFTER THE COLD WAR

All realists assume that economic relations are a function of and subordinate to political relations; that the state is a distinct actor with its own goals; and that states, in their economic relationships, must remain sensitive to the possibility of military conflict.[79] Both balance-of-power and balance-of-threat theory build on these assumptions, but, as with security strategy, each generates different predictions for U.S. economic strategy after the Cold War. Balance-of-power theory predicts that the primary focus of U.S. foreign economic policy will be to improve America's relative position in economic competition with other major powers. Balance-of-threat theory predicts that the United States will use its economic relationships and power as instruments of statecraft to reinforce its security strategy toward other major powers. In *security* strategy, post-Cold War U.S. behavior has been more consistent with the predictions of balance-of-threat theory. In *economic* strategy, however, U.S. behavior has been more consistent with the predictions of balance-of-power theory.

Balance-of-Power Logic and Predictions

Realists emphasize that international economic interactions among states are inherently competitive, most importantly because of the close connection between economic and military power. Throughout history, the military capabilities of a state have depended on the size and level of development of its economy; great economic powers have become great military powers. If economic power is the basis for military strength, then states that are competitive in the military arena will naturally compete, with a sensitivity to relative position, in the economic arena.

In the contemporary era, however, the connection between economic and military capability is not as tight. Nuclear weapons make it possible to develop formidable military power without having great economic capability.[80] Furthermore, in a nuclear era the prospects for hegemonic war among great powers may be remote, which further diminishes the strategic importance of relative economic position.[81] Do these considerations, for balance-of-power theorists, imply that international economic competition no longer matters?

The answer is clearly no. Waltz, for example, argues that "economic competition is often as keen as military competition, and since nuclear weapons limit the use of force among great powers at the strategic level, we may expect economic and technological competition among them to become more intense."[82] Balance-of-power theorists point to four reasons.[83] First, the prospects for war among major powers may be remote, but they never disappear completely. Today's benign security environment is tomorrow's threatening one, and today's stalemate in military technology is tomorrow's unforeseen breakthrough in military technology. Economic growth rates and technological advantages cumulate, so that small gaps in the present may become large gaps in the future. Second, even in the absence of threats to military security, states worry about foreign policy autonomy. Increases in relative economic capability increase foreign policy autonomy, because economic resources can be used to influence other states and to minimize vulnerability to the influence attempts of others.[84] Third, states compete to enhance national economic welfare. Prosperity, like security, can be shared, and the pursuit of it is not necessarily a zero-sum game. When scarcities exist, however, international economic relations necessarily become more competitive, and states may struggle over access to capital, natural resources, markets, jobs, or advanced technologies. Finally, success in economic competition brings to a state intangible but potentially important benefits in international status and prestige. Governments, like individuals, are probably more concerned with relative rankings than they are inclined to admit. Not every state is obsessed with being "number one," but most states are likely to derive some benefit from a higher ranking in economic competition (or in education, or sports) relative to states they consider to be their peers.[85]

For balance-of-power theory, international economic relations remain an integral part of the ongoing struggle for power and influence among nation-states. But to infer specific predictions for a state's foreign economic policy requires us to recognize again that states respond to the opportunities and constraints of the international structural environment they face. Foreign economic policy depends on the position of the state in the international economic structure[86] and the international security structure.[87]

During the Cold War, U.S. foreign economic policy responded to the incentives of both structures. The emergence of the United States as the dominant economic power led U.S. officials to abandon their traditional policies of economic nationalism in favor of a commitment to construct and maintain a liberal international economy. Bipolarity reinforced this approach in America's economic relations with its principal allies in Western Europe and East Asia. In the interest of strengthening the coalition balancing the Soviet Union, the U.S. officials even permitted their allies to maintain trade (and in the case of Japan, investment) policies that discriminated against the United States.[88]

What should balance-of-power theory predict for U.S. foreign economic policy in the post-Cold War era? The key point is that the U.S. position in both the international economic and security structures has changed. The bipolar structure has given way to unipolarity and the U.S. position in the international economic structure has been in *relative* decline. The United States remains very powerful in absolute terms, but its economic position relative to Japan, Germany, and the European Union is less advantageous now than it was during the 1945–70 period.

We can infer from the combination of unipolarity and declining hegemony that the United States will become more sensitive to relative position in economic competition with other major powers. The Cold War situation was anomalous in two ways. First, when the United States was far ahead, it could afford not to worry too much about how to play—and how others were playing—the game of international economic competition. As others catch up, however, the United States should become more concerned with defending and advancing its relative economic position. Second, the need to meet the Soviet threat prompted the United States to subordinate its relative position in international economic competition to the greater good of fostering the overall economic strength of the Western coalition. In the absence of the Soviet threat, the United States should be less inclined to emphasize overall coalition strength and more inclined to treat other major powers as economic, and potentially geopolitical, competitors.

The logic of balance-of-power theory suggests that in the new structural environment, the position of the United States in international economic competition should become a central foreign policy priority. Specifically, we can infer three types of response. First, we should anticipate an effort by

U.S. officials to cut down the economic costs of foreign policy commitments. At a minimum, expect burden-sharing to become a priority in foreign policy commitments; at a maximum, expect the United States to alter and diminish the commitments themselves.[89] Second, we should expect the United States to become more like other advanced industrial states in terms of assistance to national firms in international competition, with increased emphasis on export promotion policies, industrial policies, and government-industry collaboration. Third, we should expect U.S. officials to try to reverse or at least adjust the "generous" foreign economic policies characteristic of hegemony and bipolarity. They should be less tolerant of asymmetrical trade, technology, and exchange rate policies that gave advantages to principal economic competitors. And, we should expect their commitment to the multilateral free trade system, which was a critical element in the U.S. Cold War strategy, to diminish.

Balance-of-Power Evidence

There is sufficient evidence to support each of these predictions as well as the more general expectation of balance-of-power theorists that changes in the international economic and security structures will prompt the United States to become more sensitive to relative position in economic competition with other major powers.

First, burden sharing—the effort to convince other states to pick up a greater share of the costs of U.S. foreign policy commitments—has become increasingly prominent in U.S. statecraft since the end of the Cold War. U.S. officials have pushed Japan to pay all the yen-based costs and roughly 70 percent of the total costs of maintaining U.S. forces in Japan.[90] During the Gulf War, the Bush administration extracted contributions from other coalition members with a zeal and effectiveness that led some observers to calculate that America made a net profit on the intervention, and others to characterize U.S. forces as mercenaries.[91] The 1994 deal on nonproliferation struck between the United States and North Korea obliges Japan and South Korea to accept a significant part of the cost of providing alternative energy sources to North Korea. U.S. officials have made clear that they expect the members of the European Union to bear the burden of Bosnian reconstruction.[92] No post-Cold War "Marshall Plan" was devised for Russia and Eastern Europe: burden-sharing disputes characterized the Western aid effort for Russia, and for the most part the United States deferred the economic initiative on Eastern Europe to Germany and its European partners.

Second, U.S. officials have taken a series of aggressive steps to assist U.S. firms in international competition. The Clinton administration has elevated export promotion to the very top of the U.S. foreign policy agenda, including the routine use of diplomatic leverage at the highest levels to create opportunities for U.S. firms.[93] The Commerce Department has emulated the Pentagon in dedicating a "war room" to track international competition for major export contracts around the world.[94] A high priority has been placed upon improving America's position in competition for emerging markets across the developing world, and in 1994 President Clinton himself was instrumental in helping U.S. aircraft suppliers outbid their European rivals for a $6 billion order from Saudi Arabia. U.S. officials have made the relaxation of national security export controls—which traditionally disadvantaged U.S. firms more than those in other industrial states—a high priority, especially in areas of U.S. competitive advantage such as computers and electronics. Commercial motivations have also led the Clinton team to weaken restraints on conventional arms sales.

Compared to the governments of other advanced industrial states, the U.S. government still lags in its enthusiasm for civilian industrial policies. Yet an evolution over time is apparent. "Atari Democrats" pushed the idea during the early 1980s without political success. By the late 1980s it became legitimate in the U.S. policy context to promote industrial policy, as long as the primary purpose was defense applications. The Reagan and Bush administrations devoted resources to SEMATECH and encouraged the Defense Advanced Research Projects Agency (DARPA) to fund defense-related civilian technologies such as flat computer-display panels and high-definition television.[95] By the middle of the 1990s, executive officials embraced explicitly the idea of industrial policy directly for commercial applications. DARPA's name dropped "Defense" to become ARPA, and the Clinton administration launched a series of initiatives involving government-business partnerships in industry and advanced technology.[96] The president's often-quoted depiction of economic relations among the United States and other advanced industrial nations as analogous to "big corporations competing in the global marketplace" captures the sentiment underlying these and similar initiatives.

Third, accelerating a pattern that began during the 1970s and 1980s, U.S. officials have become far less tolerant of trade, technology, and exchange rate asymmetries that lend advantage to its primary competitors. Aggressive demands for market access have become the centerpiece of U.S. trade strategy.[97] Struggles with the European Union over aircraft subsidies, broadcasting quotas, and agricultural restrictions reflect this priority, and the concern drove former U.S. Commerce Secretary Robert Mosbacher to demand a "seat at the table" for the United States in order to influence the design of the single European market. Japan, to this point America's most intense industrial and technological competitor, has been an even more prominent target. In trade disputes over satellites, supercomputers, and semiconductors, U.S. officials have sought to disrupt Japan's home market "sanctuary" by countering Japanese infant industry protection and collusive arrangements among Japanese firms and between Japanese government and industry. U.S. behavior in the highly public automotive sector dispute in 1995 was driven in part by similar concerns, as U.S. officials sought to break open the long-term supplier and distributor relationships that shut U.S. firms out of the Japanese market.

U.S. officials have resorted increasingly to the use of exchange rates as a trade weapon in competition with Japan. Since the Plaza Accord of 1985, and in a reversal of the Cold War pattern, the United States has forced Japan to accept a dollar-yen exchange rate that enhances the attractiveness of U.S. exports to Japan and discourages Japanese sales to the United States. The FSX fighter dispute demonstrated dramatically that U.S. officials are no longer willing to encourage, as they did during the Cold War, the transfer to Japan of sensitive U.S. technologies that have commercial significance. The United States wants to stem the flow of critical commercial technologies to Japan and to encourage the "flowback" of Japanese technologies to the United States.[98]

The United States has also begun to counter and emulate the industrial espionage practices that have long been an element of its competitors' national economic strategies.[99] Early in 1995 the French government asked the CIA station chief and his assistants to leave the country in light of accusations that the CIA had been recruiting French officials with responsibilities for GATT negotiations and telecommunications policy. U.S. officials criticized the very public French response as unprecedented in relations among allies but did not deny the allegations.[100] Subsequently, a similar diplomatic controversy broke out with Japan over suspicions that CIA officials had eavesdropped on Japanese officials in an effort to gain advantage for the United States during the auto negotiations. Japan, too, was indignant and demanded explanations. For Japan and France to protest too vigorously is somewhat ironic, but does reflect their discomfort with the idea that the United States might reorient some of its formidable intelligence assets from military collaboration to international economic competition.

Finally, there have been changes in the nature of the U.S. commitment to multilateral free trade. To be sure, U.S. officials continue to support the multilateral system. The successful completion of the Uruguay Round and the replacement of the GATT with the more ambitious World Trade Organization (WTO) were high priorities for both the Bush and Clinton administrations. Nevertheless, the strength and durability of America's commitment to the multilateral system have been questioned by America's trading partners, and with good reason. The Bush administration was willing to risk the collapse of the Uruguay Round at its 1990 deadline, and pinned the blame on its European competitors for refusing to accede to U.S. demands for radical liberalization in the agricultural sector. An uneasy compromise was reached and the round was finally completed in 1993. Subsequently, the United States dealt serious blows to the nascent WTO by refusing to meet deadlines set under the Uruguay Round for new agreements to liberalize trade in telecommunications, financial services, and maritime transport because the proposed accords did not provide sufficient advantages to U.S. firms in overseas markets. U.S. Trade Representative Charlene Barshefsky defended this stand in 1996 by arguing that "with the cold war over, trade agreements must stand or fall on their merits. They no longer have a security component. If we do not get reciprocity, we will not get freer trade."[101]

America's multilateral commitment has also coexisted uneasily since the mid-1980s with the clear determination of U.S. officials to rely on "aggressive unilateralism" in trade policy, even while U.S. tactics have been widely perceived abroad as damaging to the credibility of America's diplomacy and the multilateral system.[102] Aggressive unilateralism exploits the advantages of U.S. economic power and produces quicker results than the more consensual multilateral process. U.S. officials have also devoted considerable diplomatic effort to regional liberalization efforts such as the expansion of NAFTA, while at the same time questioning the need for another comprehensive round of multilateral trade negotiations.[103]

BALANCE-OF-THREAT THEORY AND U.S. ECONOMIC STRATEGY AFTER THE COLD WAR

Earlier I inferred, from the logic of balance-of-threat theory, the prediction that U.S. security strategy after the Cold War would center on the effort to preserve primacy through policies of reassurance and engagement. To develop predictions for U.S. economic strategy requires a bolder extrapolation, because thus far balance-of-threat advocates have devoted relatively little systematic attention to international economic relationships.[104]

Balance-of-Threat Logic and Predictions

Balance-of-power theorists expect intensified economic competition after the Cold War to be a logical counterpart to the renewal of security rivalry among great powers in a multipolar setting. From the perspective of balance-of-threat theory, however, neither the rapid transition to multipolarity nor security conflict among rival great powers is inevitable, because states respond not only to capabilities but also to perceptions of threat and foreign policy intention. Balance-of-threat realists foresee the potential for great power cooperation; they worry that preparation for great power rivalry and possible war might lead to a self-fulfilling prophecy according to the logic of the security dilemma.[105]

Two implications follow for international economic relations. First, if great power rivalry can be held in abeyance and the prospects for war are remote, states can afford to be less concerned about relative gains and relative position in international economic competition. There are other reasons for states to be concerned about relative position, but for balance-of-threat theorists these are less pressing than the likelihood of war.[106] Second, attempts to pursue relative economic advantage might actually prove to be counterproductive, because states respond to perceptions of threat. The pursuit of relative advantage might appear provocative or threatening to other states, triggering the spiral of political tension and rivalry that balance-of-threat theorists hope states will avoid.

We can infer from this logic the general prediction that states will tailor their foreign economic policies to complement and reinforce their national security strategies. Realists generally believe that economic relations are subordinate to political relations; if balance-of-threat theory is correct, we should anticipate that states will use economic relationships as instruments to serve broader political goals.[107] We should expect a state that pursues political confrontation in relations with a revisionist state also to pursue economic confrontation. Since the intentions of a revisionist state are already presumed to be hostile, the purpose of economic confrontation would be to isolate the revisionist state and weaken its capabilities. We should expect a state that pursues a political strategy of reassurance in relations with status quo or undecided states to reinforce that strategy by relying on cooperative economic policies. Economic cooperation might increase the capabilities of an undecided state, but might also shape its foreign policy intentions in a manner desired by the initiating state.[108]

These guidelines suggest the following predictions for U.S. economic strategy after the Cold War. In relations with the status quo states of Japan and the European Union, we should expect the strategy of security reassurance to be reinforced by economic engagement. We should see U.S. officials seeking to minimize bilateral conflicts and to emphasize cooperative initiatives such as the launching of free trade agreements. In relations with Russia and China, states with uncertain foreign policy intentions, we should expect the U.S. political strategy of integration to be complemented by economic strategies of integration and cooperation, as part of the broader effort to steer these states to support the U.S.-centered status quo. For revisionist states, such as Iran and Iraq, we should expect economic containment to reinforce political containment.

Balance-of-Threat Evidence

To what extent have U.S. officials used economic statecraft to reinforce and promote their preferred post-Cold War security strategy? Although the evidence is mixed, the emphasis is clear. U.S. economic strategy thus far has reflected, consistent with balance-of-power theory, a greater concern for the pursuit of relative economic advantage than for using economic relations to support the preferred national security strategies of reassuring and engaging potential challengers.

The tension between security and economic strategy is strongest in U.S. relations with Japan. As Japanese officials sometimes comment, dealing with the United States in economics and in security is like dealing with two different countries. The relationship among U.S. and Japanese security officials has been characterized by a sense of shared objectives, while relations on the economic side have been marked by mistrust and frustration. Disputes have been virtually continuous for a decade: the Toshiba and semiconductor disputes in 1987; the FSX, Super 301, and SII disputes in 1989–90; the Persian Gulf dispute in 1991; President Bush's ill-fated auto sales trip in 1992; conflict over semiconductors again in 1992–93; the collapse of the Framework talks in 1994; and the automotive and economic spying disputes in 1995.[109] Attempts to resolve these disputes call to mind the U.S.-Soviet arms control experience during the Cold War in the sense that each

side approaches the other with suspicion and resentment, and fears its partner will exploit the smallest loopholes or ambiguities as an excuse to renege
on commitments. Instead of the deescalation of economic tensions that
would complement the security strategy of reassurance, U.S. officials have
applied almost relentless economic pressure on Japan.

U.S. economic strategy toward China and the U.S.-China economic relationship have begun to resemble the Japan situation. Concern over China's
mounting trade surplus and frustration over obstacles to market access have
led to political acrimony and threats of economic sanctions and trade wars.
U.S. trade officials speak openly of China as the "next Japan." They view
China as adopting Japan's adversarial economic practices as part of its development strategy, and they are determined not to make the "same mistake"
of subordinating economic interests to security concerns. Then-U.S. Trade
Representative Mickey Kantor expressed the view explicitly in 1995 that the
United States must practice economic confrontation against China earlier
and more aggressively than it did against Japan. He and other trade officials
convinced the White House in early 1996, over the objections of the State
Department, that the United States should continue to confront China over
its intellectual property practices even though confrontation might jeopardize the ability of U.S. officials to moderate China's behavior in its conflict
with Taiwan.[110]

U.S. economic relations with members of the European Union also have
been more a source of tension than of reassurance, with sustained disputes
over agriculture, broadcasting, aircraft, telecommunications, government
procurement and other issues played out bilaterally and multilaterally. Even
U.S. pressure on Japan has tended to have negative repercussions, as European officials have objected that Japanese accommodation to U.S. market
access demands will only force European firms to bear the adjustment costs.
By the mid-1990s these festering economic conflicts, compounded by America's apparent turn away from Europe in favor of Latin America and Asia,
led to concerns on both sides of the transatlantic relationship regarding its
long-term stability. In May 1995 the United States responded, as balance-of-
threat theory would predict, with economic statecraft, in the form of a proposal for a transatlantic free trade agreement. In proposing the agreement,
U.S. officials cautioned that in the absence of "new economic architecture"
across the Atlantic, "natural economic juices may force us much further
apart than anyone conceives of right now."[111] As of the beginning of 1996,
however, plans for a "trans-Atlantic NAFTA" were downgraded to a

more modest dialogue on non-tariff barriers, as both U.S. and EU officials conceded that they were not quite prepared for the arduous negotiations that would be required to launch a free trade agreement.[112]

U.S. economic strategy toward Russia has come closest to meeting the predictions of balance-of-threat theory. As part of the larger effort to encourage Russia to sustain political and economic reforms and a pro-Western foreign policy, U.S. officials have facilitated Russia's dealings with the IMF and the Group of Seven, and have provided funds and technical support to assist Russia in dismantling nuclear weapons and in making the transition to a market economy.[113] The fact that Russia is not a serious economic competitor (or, like China, an emerging competitor) has made it easier for U.S. officials to avoid the kinds of economic conflicts that have characterized U.S. relations with other major powers. Yet, even in this case, U.S. economic statecraft offers only a partial complement to the political engagement strategy. U.S. officials have not offered Russia anything resembling the preferential trade arrangements provided to Western Europe and Japan in their postwar recovery phases, and the U.S. aid program for Russia has caused considerable resentment, with Russian officials complaining that the effort is being driven by U.S. export interests and that the main beneficiaries have not been Russians but American corporations and consulting firms.[114]

CONCLUSION: REALISM AND THE FUTURE OF U.S. GRAND STRATEGY

Realists might be tempted to conclude from this analysis that "realism explains everything," while critics might counter that, by generating contradictory expectations, realism actually explains nothing. Both comments miss the point. Realism *per se* is not an explanation, but a research program from which particular realist explanations can be derived and tested. I assessed two realist theories in this chapter, and the evidence neither fully supports nor fully refutes either one. However, each theory does provide strong insight into a central aspect of post-Cold War U.S. foreign policy and, taken together, they point to an important tension within overall American strategy.

As both realist theories would predict, U.S. strategy has been responsive to the constraints and opportunities of the international structure and to America's position within it. Bipolarity concentrated Washington's attention on the Soviet challenge and drove economic and security strategy in complementary directions. Unipolarity imposes less of a constraint and affords the United States more room to maneuver. After the Cold War, U.S. security and economic strategy have diverged. Security strategy has been more consistent with the predictions of balance-of-threat theory, while economic strategy has followed more closely the expectations of balance-of-power theory.

Further refinement and testing of each theory is needed. Balance-of-power theory confronts a central puzzle in international relations after the Cold War—the absence of balancing at the core of the international system. Unipolarity may indeed prove to be a transition, but for balance-of-power theory the longer unipolarity persists, the more imperative it will become to reconsider the logic of balancing behavior and to reassess the historical evidence that presumably supports the theory.[115] Balance-of-threat theory can explain the persistence of unipolarity, but to do so it must focus on both on the distribution of capabilities and, at the unit level, on foreign policy intentions and behavior. Further advances in balance-of-threat theory require sustained attention to the conceptual and empirical challenges of studying images, intentions, and perceptions of threat in relations among states.[116]

For American officials, the appeal of the security strategy predicted by balance-of-threat theory is not surprising. The temptation to prolong the unipolar moment and the luxuries it affords is a powerful one. That temptation is reinforced by the typical American belief that U.S. power does not threaten anyone, and that the U.S.-led international order provides sufficient benefits so that it is unnecessary for other states to seek to undermine it. The appeal of preserving primacy is also reinforced by inertia—it is easier for American officials to maintain and adjust the practices and institutions of a U.S.-centered international system than to shift to the uncertainty of "strategic independence" in preparation for a multipolar world.

If balance-of-threat theory is correct, then the duration of the unipolar moment will depend not only on the relative distribution of capabilities but also on the effectiveness of U.S. diplomacy. Through policies of engagement and reassurance, U.S. officials can dissuade or at least delay other states from challenging U.S. hegemony and balancing against the United States. The effectiveness of engagement and reassurance, however, will depend on the ability of American officials to meet the following three challenges.

First, Washington must continue to manage the tension between its international economic and security strategies so that economic conflicts do not erode security relationships and eventually trigger a balancing response.[117] Thus far, U.S. officials have tried to square the conflicting demands of their two strategies by resorting to economic brinksmanship, especially in relations with Japan. Their tactic is to extract economic benefits by threatening sanctions, only to search for face-saving compromises under the pressure of deadlines to avoid actually having to initiate or escalate trade wars. Brinksmanship can be effective but it is also risky, especially with trading partners who can muster the resolve to resist.[118]

The next several years should bring a respite in economic tensions with Japan, because U.S. competitiveness has recovered strongly since the late 1980s and at the same time the economic threat from Japan has waned.[119] If China does come to replace Japan as America's principal economic competitor, however, management of the conflicting strategies of economic hardball and security softball will become all the more delicate. More so than Japan has been, China is likely to resist U.S. pressure as a matter of national pride. And, from the perspective of U.S. grand strategy, the security stakes are higher because China is an undecided state rather than a long-standing ally that supports the status quo.

Second, American officials must maintain support at home for the preferred policies of engagement and reassurance. This will not be easy because, as Robert Tucker recently observed, the "great issue" of contemporary U.S. foreign policy is "the contradiction between the persisting desire to remain the premier global power and an ever deepening aversion to bear[ing] the costs of this position."[120] The U.S public indeed has displayed an increasing reluctance to bear the costs of a global engagement strategy, especially when it involves the need to risk American lives in faraway places for the purpose not of meeting an identifiable threat but of maintaining "stability." But that risk is difficult to avoid, because the pursuit of primacy induces the United States to be the stabilizer of last resort in regional crises. In a two-week period early in 1996, U.S. officials found themselves managing the insertion of 20,000 U.S. troops in Bosnia, prepositioning equipment for a possible renewed Iraqi attack against Kuwait, mediating a crisis on the brink of war between Greece and Turkey, and responding to China's military intimidation of Taiwan.[121]

U.S. officials have responded to the domestic constraint by emphasizing "pragmatism" in military interventions—the attempt to avoid excessive commitments, minimize casualties, and emphasize "exit strategies" even at the risk of leaving unfinished business. But the current intervention in Bosnia can still turn sour and future interventions are inevitable if the United States continues to pursue the engagement and reassurance of other major powers. It is hard to imagine that the domestically-acceptable Persian Gulf formula—

clear threat, low casualties, quick settlement, ample external support and financing—can be replicated across a series of regional crises.

Third, U.S. officials must manage what might be called the arrogance of power. The dominant state in any international order faces strong temptations to go it alone, to dictate rather than to consult, to preach its virtues, and to impose its values. In the case of the United States, these temptations are compounded by a democratic political tradition that tends to imbue foreign policy with the values of society and to assure that moral considerations are never far from the surface in discussions of foreign policy.

The United States does succumb to the arrogance of power, as demonstrated by recent conflicts with China over human rights and with America's closest trading partners over the unilateral extension of U.S. sanctions to foreign firms doing business in Cuba, Iran, and Libya.[122] The risks to U.S. grand strategy should be evident. Efforts to impose values or to preach to other states create resentment and over time can prompt the balancing behavior U.S. officials hope to forestall. It is ironic that in a unipolar setting the dominant state, less constrained by other great powers, must constrain itself.

No realist can sensibly expect the current international system to remain in place indefinitely. Eventually, power will check power. But whether or not the transition to a new international order will be prolonged will depend, at least in part, on the skill and resourcefulness of U.S. foreign policy officials. Balance-of-threat theory reminds us to appreciate the classical realist insight that statecraft matters.

ACKNOWLEDGMENT

This chapter appeared under the same title in *International Security* 21 (4) (Spring 1997): 49–88. It is reprinted with permission. For comments and suggestions, I am grateful to Robert Art, Mlada Bukovansky, Dan Deudney, John Ikenberry, Iain Johnston, Ethan Kapstein, Jon Kirshner, Michael Loriaux, Sean Lynn-Jones, and Randy Schweller.

NOTES

1. Graham Allison, *Essence of Decision* (Boston: Little, Brown, 1971); and Robert O. Keohane and Joseph S. Nye, Jr., *Transnational Relations and World Politics* (Cambridge: Harvard University Press, 1972).

2. Charles W. Kegley, Jr., "The Neoidealist Moment in International Studies? Realist Myths and the New International Realities," *International Studies Quarterly* 37 (2) (June 1993): 131–146; and Richard Ned Lebow and Thomas Risse-Kappen, eds., *International Relations Theory and the End of the Cold War* (New York: Columbia University Press, 1995).

3. Prominent realists have responded by pointing out the conceptual and empirical flaws in competing theoretical frameworks. See John Mearsheimer, "The False Promise of International Institutions," *International Security* 19 (3) (Winter 1994–95): 5–49; and Joseph M. Grieco, "Anarchy and the Limits of Cooperation: A Realist Critique of the Newest Liberal Institutionalism," *International Organization* 42 (3) (Summer 1988): 485–507. The "paradigm war" between realists and their critics has been played out in David Baldwin, ed., *Neorealism and Neoliberalism: The Contemporary Debate* (New York: Columbia University Press, 1993); Charles W. Kegley, Jr., ed., *Controversies in International Relations Theory: Realism and the Neoliberal Challenge* (New York: St. Martin's, 1995); and Robert O. Keohane, ed., *Neorealism and its Critics* (New York: Columbia University Press, 1986).

4. The assumptions of the realist research program are that 1) states, or more broadly, territorially organized groups, are the central actors on the world stage; 2) state behavior can be explained rationally; 3) states seek power and calculate their interests in terms of power and the international situation they face; and 4) anarchy is the defining characteristic of the international system, which implies that states ultimately must rely on themselves in an inherently competitive environment. For discussion see Robert O. Keohane, "Theory of World Politics: Structural Realism and Beyond," in Keohane, ed., *Neorealism and Its Critics*: 158–203; Patrick James, "Neorealism as a Research Enterprise: Toward Elaborated Structural Realism," *International Political Science Review* 14 (2) (1993): 123–148; Mearsheimer, "The False Promise of International Institutions," 10–11; and Steven Forde, "International Realism and the Science of Politics: Thucydides, Machiavelli, and Neorealism," *International Studies Quarterly* 39 (2) (June 1995): 141–160. Forde points out (pp. 143–45) that classical realists such as Thucydides and Machiavelli, who ground their arguments in human nature as well as in international structure, might not embrace all of the above assumptions as fully as would contemporary structural realists.

5. Daniel Deudney follows this logic in a recent analysis on U.S. nuclear proliferation policy, arguing that realism is not one theory but a "family of related and competing theories." See Deudney, "Dividing Realism: Structural Realism versus Security Materialism on Nuclear Security and Proliferation," *Security Studies* 2 (3/4) (Spring/Summer 1993): 7–36, quote at p. 8. A recent attempt to test "realism" as opposed to particular realist theories found, not surprisingly, that the "scientific study of realism is difficult because it is often not specific

enough to be falsifiable." See Frank W. Wayman and Paul F. Diehl, eds., *Reconstructing Realpolitik* (Ann Arbor: University of Michigan Press, 1994), 26.

6. Kenneth N. Waltz, *Theory of International Politics* (Reading, MA: Addison-Wesley, 1979). Important applications and extensions include Waltz, "The Emerging Structure of International Politics," *International Security* 18 (2) (Fall 1993): 45–73; Christopher Layne, "The Unipolar Illusion: Why New Great Powers Will Rise," *International Security* 17 (4) (Spring 1993): 5–51; and John Mearsheimer, "Back to the Future: Instability in Europe After the Cold War," *International Security* 15 (1) (Summer 1990): 5–56.

7. Stephen M. Walt, *The Origins of Alliances* (Ithaca: Cornell University Press, 1987). In extending Walt's theory I draw on the classical realist distinction between status quo and revisionist states. See, for example, Hans J. Morgenthau, *Politics Among Nations: The Struggle for Power and Peace*, 5th ed. (New York: Knopf, 1978), chapters 4 and 5.

8. Extrapolation is necessary because balance-of-power and balance-of-threat theory were developed to explain systemic outcomes. Instead, I use them to infer predictions and explanations for the foreign policy of a particular state. And, both theories are usually applied to national security issues. I extend their logic and apply them to U.S. foreign economic policy as well as to U.S. national security policy.

9. Obviously, there are plausible nonrealist explanations of post-Cold War U.S. foreign policy. In this article I confine myself to developing and testing competing realist explanations.

10. In a recent article, Barry Posen and Andrew Ross lay out five possible grand strategies for the United States after the Cold War: neoisolationism, selective engagement, collective security, containment, and primacy. I argue that the United States has in fact chosen to pursue primacy. See Posen and Ross, "Competing Grand Strategies," in Robert J. Lieber, ed., *Eagle Adrift: American Foreign Policy at the End of the Century* (New York: Longman, 1997), 100–134.

11. Waltz, *Theory of International Politics*.

12. Ibid., 68.

13. Waltz, "The Emerging Structure of International Politics," 45.

14. Ibid., 46–49.

15. It is also worth noting that the systemic outcomes of primary interest to structural realists are themselves the results of the foreign policy choices of states, especially the most powerful ones. "Free trade" as a systemic outcome does not occur if the powerful states in the system choose protectionism. "Balancing" does not occur if the major states choose not to balance. For an argument that Waltz's balance-of-power theory should be considered a theory of foreign policy, see Colin Elman, "Neorealist Theories of Foreign Policy: Meaning, Objections, and Implications," paper presented at the annual meeting of the International Studies Association, February 1995.

16. An explicit effort to use international structure to explain foreign economic policy is David A. Lake, *Power, Protection, and Free Trade* (Ithaca: Cornell University Press, 1987). For an argument that international structure decisively shaped the military policies of Latin American states, see Joao Resende-Santos, "Anarchy and the Emulation of Military Systems: Military Organization and Technology in South America, 1870–1930," *Security Studies* 5 (3) (Spring 1995): 190–247.

17. See Richard Ned Lebow, "The Long Peace, the End of the Cold War, and the Failure of Realism," in Lebow and Risse-Kappen, eds., *International Relations Theory and the End of the Cold War*, 26–33.

18. Waltz, "The Emerging Structure of International Politics," 52.

19. Morgenthau, *Politics Among Nations*, chapter 9.

20. Waltz, "The Emerging Structure of International Politics," 50. Earlier, Waltz noted that power is "difficult to measure and compare." Waltz, *Theory of International Politics*, 131.

21. See Joseph Nye, *Bound to Lead: The Changing Nature of American Power* (New York: Basic Books, 1992).

22. Layne, "The Unipolar Illusion," 5. See also Nye, *Bound to Lead*, and Charles Krauthammer, "The Unipolar Moment," *Foreign Affairs* 70 (1) (1990/1991).

23. Layne, "The Unipolar Illusion," 13.

24. Waltz, "The Emerging Structure of International Politics," 50, and Layne, "The Unipolar Illusion," 7.

25. See Mearsheimer, "Back to the Future." Layne argues that "neorealist theory leads one to the expectation that the world beyond unipolarity will be one of great power rivalry in a multipolar setting." Layne, "The Unipolar Illusion," 40. Waltz does argue, however, that nuclear deterrence reduces the probability of war, even in multipolar settings.

26. Waltz, "Emerging Structure of International Politics." This phrase is quoted at p. 55.

27. Mearsheimer, "Back to the Future," 173–76, 190.

28. Layne, "The Unipolar Illusion, 49, 51. In more recent work, Layne concentrates on the hegemonic challenge from China. See Christopher Layne and Bradley Thayer, "The Revolution in Military Affairs and the Future of Stability in Asia," paper presented at the annual meeting of the American Political Science Association, August 1996.

29. Layne, "The Unipolar Illusion," 46–47.

30. Waltz, "The Emerging Structure of International Politics," 76.

31. Wayne, "The Unipolar Illusion," 45–51.

32. See Stephen D. Krasner, *Defending the National Interest* (Princeton: Princeton University Press, 1978).

33. See Alain Destexhe, "The Third Genocide," *Foreign Policy* (97) (Winter 1994–95): 3–17.

34. Waltz, "The Emerging Structure of International Politics," 61–65, and Layne, "The Unipolar Illusion," 35–39.

35. Stephen M. Walt, *The Origins of Alliances*, 21.

36. Layne disagrees, and seeks to disarm Walt's argument and its implications by asserting that "in unipolar systems there is no clearcut distinction between balance of threat and balance of power . . . in a unipolar world, others must worry about the hegemon's capabilities, not its intentions." Layne, "Unipolar Illusion," 13.

37. The fact that Walt includes intentions as one aspect of threat moves balance-of-threat theory away from the purely systemic level. Balance-of-power theory is purely systemic; balance-of-threat theory includes both systemic factors and the kind of unit-level variables that were present in classical realism.

38. Walt, *The Origins of Alliances*, 25.

39. Ibid., 27.

40. Snyder, *Myths of Empire*, 6–9.

41. Waltz concedes something to this argument by suggesting that the "forebearance of the strong [might] reduce the worries of the weak and permit them to relax." Waltz, "The Changing Structure of International Politics," 79. Robert Gilpin reminds us that "an international system is stable if no state believes it is profitable to attempt to change the system." Robert Gilpin, *War and Change in World Politics* (Cambridge: Cambridge University Press, 1981), 50.

42. For a policy argument that implicitly accepts this logic, see Josef Joffe, "Bismarck or Britain? Toward an American Grand Strategy After Bipolarity," *International Security* 19 (4) (Spring 1995): 94–117.

43. This is counterintuitive in that realists generally play down the significance of international institutions. See, for example, Mearsheimer, "The False Promise of International Institutions." Balance-of-threat theory may lend some insight into why dominant states rely on international institutions even though, as Mearsheimer argues, such institutions do not seem to matter in determining war and peace outcomes.

44. David Fromkin wrote recently that "a recurring theme of international politics throughout 6000 years of recorded history is that when a country becomes far more powerful than its neighbors, its greatness is resented and its neighbors band together against it. We ought to anticipate that reaction by acting whenever possible through multilateral groupings, especially the United Nations, because this assures almost every country a sense of participation in making decisions." Fromkin, "We Can Go It Alone. We Shouldn't," *New York Times*, September 29, 1995, p. A31.

45. Morgenthau, *Politics Among Nations*, 42–51.

46. Snyder, *Myths of Empire*; Randall L. Schweller, "Tripolarity and the Second World War," *International Studies Quarterly* 37 (1) (March 1993): 73–104; Robert Gilpin, *War and Change in World Politics*; and William C. Wohlforth,

"Realism and the End of the Cold War," *International Security* 19 (3) (Winter 1994–95): 91–129.

47. Joffe frames a similar set in the form of policy prescriptions for the United States after the Cold War. See Joffe, "Bismarck or Britain?," 117.

48. As a practical matter, it is critical for state officials to detect a potential challenger's intentions effectively and respond appropriately to them. This classic problem of the security dilemma is a difficult one, given uncertainty and the potential for deception. Morgenthau considered it the "fundamental question" of statecraft, and suggested that the answer determines the "fate of nations." Morgenthau, *Politics Among Nations*, 67–68.

49. Kohl is quoted in W. R. Smyser, "Germany's New Vision," *Foreign Policy* (97) (Winter 1994–95): 154. Defense Minister Volker Ruhe, in a 1995 assessment of German security policy, asserted that "without America, stability has never been, and will never be available." Quoted in Rafael Estrella, "Structure and Functions: European Security and Defense Identity (ESDI) and Combined Joint Task Forces (CJTF)," Draft General Report, North Atlantic Assembly, May 1995, para. 44.

50. See Robert J. Art, "Why Western Europe Needs the United States and NATO," *Political Science Quarterly* 111 (1) (Spring 1996): 1–39.

51. Defense Issues Council, *Recommendations for Japan's Security and Defense Capability*, August 12, 1994, reprinted in *FBIS* (East Asia), Oct. 28, 1994, 1–18, quote at p. 6.

52. See Eric Heginbotham and Richard J. Samuels, "Mercantile Realism and Japanese Foreign Policy," in this volume.

53. On Japan, see Peter Katzenstein and Nobuo Okawara, "Japan's National Security: Structures, Norms, and Policies," and Thomas Berger, "From Sword to Chrysanthemum: Japan's Culture of Anti-Militarism," in *International Security* 17 (4) (Spring 1993): 84–150. On Germany, see Timothy Garten Ash, "Germany's Choice," *Foreign Affairs* 73 (4) (July/August 1994): 65–81, and Smyser, "Germany's New Vision."

54. See S. Neil MacFarlane, "Realism and Russian Strategy After the Collapse of the USSR," in this volume. He argues Russia's cooperation with the West actually has been strongest in the area of security policy.

55. Kenneth Lieberthal, "A New China Strategy," *Foreign Affairs* 74 (6) (Nov./Dec. 1995): 35–49.

56. Iain Johnston, "Realism and Chinese Security Policy in the Post-Cold War Period," in this volume.

57. As balance-of-threat theory would expect, U.S. officials have responded to regional powers that have revisionist agendas with confrontation rather than engagement. The war against Iraq, the Clinton administration's subsequent "dual containment" strategy toward Iran and Iraq, and the administration's determination to gain collective support for a confrontational approach toward "rogue"

or "backlash" states demonstrate this point. See Anthony Lake, "Confronting Backlash States," *Foreign Affairs* 73 (2) (March/April 1994): 45–55.

58. The public rhetoric of the Clinton administration has emphasized the need to shift from containment to "enlargement," a somewhat vague doctrine focusing on the strengthening and promotion of democracy, human rights, and free markets worldwide. See *A National Security Strategy of Engagement and Enlargement* (Washington, D.C.: The White House, 1995). After aborted interventions in Somalia and Haiti in 1993, the administration became more pragmatic in practice even though its public statements continued to stress idealist goals. For a critique of Clinton's early foreign policy initiatives, see Michael Mandelbaum, "Foreign Policy as Social Work," *Foreign Affairs* 75 (1) (January/February 1996): 16–32.

59. "Excerpts from Pentagon's Plan: Prevent the Re-emergence of a New Rival," *New York Times*, March 8, 1992, p. A14. For discussion, see Robert Jervis, "International Primacy: Is the Game Worth the Candle?," *International Security* 17 (4) (Spring 1993): 53–54, 64; Benjamin Schwarz, "Why America Thinks It Has to Run the World," *Atlantic Monthly* 277 (12) (June 1996): 92–102; and Posen and Ross, "Competing Grand Strategies," 120–121.

60. Joseph S. Nye, Jr., "The Case for Deep Engagement," *Foreign Affairs* 74 (4) (July/August 1995): 102.

61. Michael Mandelbaum, for example, argues that NATO is still needed "to reassure Germany that it need not arm itself more heavily to remain secure, something that would make Germany's neighbors feel less secure." Mandelbaum, "Preserving the New Peace," *Foreign Affairs* 74 (3) (May/June 1995): 13.

62. See Philip Zelikow and Condoleezza Rice, *Germany United and Europe Transformed* (Cambridge: Harvard University Press, 1995), and Art, "Why Western Europe Needs the United States and NATO."

63. As then-Assistant Secretary of State Richard Holbrooke argued, "It would be self-defeating for the WEU to create military structures to duplicate the successful European integration already achieved in NATO. . . . a stronger European pillar of the alliance can be an important contribution to European stability and trans-atlantic burden sharing, *provided it does not dilute* NATO." Holbrooke, "America, A European Power," *Foreign Affairs* 74 (2) (March/April 1995): 47, emphasis added.

64. Art, "Why Western Europe Needs the United States and NATO."

65. This quote is from Michael Kelly, "Surrender and Blame," *New Yorker*, Dec. 19, 1994, p. 51. See also Ruth Marcus and John Harris, "Behind U.S. Policy Shift on Bosnia: Strains in NATO," *Washington Post*, Dec. 5, 1994, p. A26.

66. See Roger Cohen, "Why the Yanks are Going. Yet Again," *New York Times*, Nov. 26, 1995, sec. 4, p. 1. Reflecting on the administration's Bosnia policy, Assistant Secretary Holbrooke conceded that "It took some time to realize that

we are still part of the balance of power in Europe. We are needed now to bring stability to the vast land mass from the eastern German border to the western Russian border."

67. Zelikow and Rice, *Germany United and Europe Transformed*, p. 105.

68. Holbrooke states that "the Chechnya conflict, terrible though it is, has not changed the nature of U.S. interests." See "America, A European Power," p. 49. Secretary of State Warren Christopher, seemingly struggling to find something positive to say, wrote in 1995 that public debate in Russia over Chechnya and independent media coverage were "reflections of Russia's emerging democracy and civil society." See Warren Christopher, "America's Leadership, America's Opportunity," *Foreign Policy* (98) (Spring 1995): 11.

69. Craig Whitney, "Russia Agrees to Put Troops Under U.S., Not NATO," *New York Times*, Nov. 9, 1995, p. A14.

70. See Richard Stevenson, "Did Yeltsin Get a Sweetheart Deal on I.M.F. Loans?," *New York Times*, March 11, 1996, p. A11. During 1996 IMF negotiations with Russia over a $9 billion loan, President Clinton stated publicly that he wanted the deal to go through. IMF officials denied any U.S. influence or that Russia's treatment or conditions were any less stringent than was the usual practice.

71. Michael Mandelbaum accepts this logic in arguing that Russia is "not destined" to disturb the balance of power in Europe and that NATO expansion is "at best premature, at worst counterproductive." See Mandelbaum, "Preserving the New Peace," 9–12.

72. Barry Posen and Andrew Ross reach a similar conclusion. They argue NATO expansion is being driven less by the need to respond to an imminent Russian threat, and more to "preserve and widen [U.S.] involvement in European affairs," and "to forestall even a hint of an independent German foreign policy in the east." NATO expansion is essentially "the adaptation of a politically familiar vehicle to the task of preserving U.S. primacy." Posen and Ross, "Competing U.S. Grand Strategies," 117.

73. See Andrei Kortunov, "NATO Enlargement and Russia: In Search of an Adequate Response," in David G. Haglund, ed., *Will NATO Go East? The Debate Over Enlarging the Atlantic Alliance* (Kingston, Ontario: Queens University Centre for International Relations, 1996), 69–92; "The Bear Tamer's Next Problem," *The Economist*, February 3, 1996, pp. 19–20; and Jim Mann, "Yeltsin NATO Plan Attracts Interest from Clinton Aides, Central Europe," *Los Angeles Times*, April 22, 1996, p. A10.

74. Nye, "The Case for Deep Engagement," 94.

75. Lieberthal, "A New China Strategy," 43. Warren Christopher writes that it is up to China to decide whether it will be a destabilizing force, but that "American engagement can help encourage it to enjoy the benefits—and accept the obligations—that come with membership in international institutions and ad-

herence to international norms." Christopher, "America's Leadership, America's Opportunity," 12.

76. See Steven Erlanger, "U.S. Set to Impose Limited Trade Sanctions on China," *New York Times*, February 21, 1996, p. A9.

77. Robert S. Greenberger, "U.S. Sends Naval Force Closer to Taiwan," *Wall Street Journal*, March 11, 1996, p. A10.

78. See Bruce W. Jentleson, "Who, Why, What, and How: Debates Over Post-Cold War Military Intervention," in Lieber, *Eagle Adrift*, 61–65.

79. See Robert Gilpin, *The Political Economy of International Relations* (Princeton: Princeton University Press, 1987), and Jonathan Kirshner, "The Political Economy of Realism," in Kapstein and Mastanduno, *Realism and International Relations After the Cold War*.

80. The point is made strongly in Waltz, "The Emerging Structure of International Politics."

81. See Gilpin, *War and Change in World Politics*, 213–219.

82. Waltz, "The Emerging Structure of International Politics," 59.

83. See ibid., and also Layne, "The Unipolar Illusion," 42–45; Samuel P. Huntington, "Why International Primacy Matters," *International Security* 17 (4) (Spring 1993): 68–83; Mearsheimer, "The False Promise of International Institutions," 20–21; and Joseph Grieco, *Cooperation Among Nations* (Ithaca: Cornell University Press, 1990).

84. See David Baldwin, *Economic Statecraft* (Princeton: Princeton University Press, 1985).

85. See Jonathan Mercer, "Anarchy and Identity," *International Organization* 49 (2) (Spring 1995): 229–252.

86. According to hegemonic stability theory, large, relatively productive states prefer openness and seek to organize a liberal world economy, while less efficient states, absent intervention by the hegemonic state, prefer protection or to "free ride" on the open markets of others. As the hegemonic state declines, so does its commitment to the liberal world economy. See Lake, *Power, Protection, and Free Trade*, and Stephen Krasner, "American Policy and Global Economic Stability," in William P. Avery and David P. Rapkin, eds., *America in a Changing World Political Economy* (New York: Longman, 1982), 29–48.

87. Joanne Gowa argues that trade among allies, especially in bipolar systems, will be greater than trade between allies and adversaries. Gowa, "Bipolarity, Multipolarity, and Free Trade," *American Political Science Review* 79 (4) (December 1989): 1245–1266, and *Allies, Adversaries, and International Trade* (Princeton: Princeton University Press, 1994).

88. Robert Gilpin, *U.S. Power and the Multinational Corporation* (New York: Basic Books, 1975), 99–112. Bipolarity also shaped the U.S. approach to its primary adversaries, as economic relations with the Soviet Union, Eastern Europe, and China were carefully restricted so as to avoid contributing to those states' mili-

tary capabilities. See Michael Mastanduno, *Economic Containment: CoCom and the Politics of East-West Trade* (Ithaca: Cornell University Press, 1992).

89. Robert Gilpin derives this policy implication from his declining hegemony argument. See Gilpin, *War and Change in World Politics*, 232–234.

90. Nye, "The Case for Deep Engagement," 98.

91. U.S. Congress, House, Committee on Ways and Means, *Foreign Contributions to the Costs of the Gulf War*, hearings, 102nd Congress, 1st session, July 31, 1995.

92. Christopher Wren, "The G.I.s Don't Carry a Marshall Plan," *New York Times*, Dec. 17, 1995, 14.

93. John Stremlau, "Clinton's Dollar Diplomacy," *Foreign Policy* (97) (Winter 1994–95): 18–35.

94. "Ron Brown, Salesman," *The Economist*, Feb. 25, 1995, 32.

95. "Uncle Sam's Helping Hand," *The Economist*, April 2, 1994, 77–79.

96. Edmund Andrews, "Washington Growing as a Financial Angel to Industry," *New York Times*, May 1, 1994, sec. F, p. 3.

97. See Laura D'Andrea Tyson, *Who's Bashing Whom? Trade Conflict in High Technology Industries* (Washington: Institute for International Economics, 1992); and Jagdish Bhagwati and Hugh Patrick, eds., *Aggressive Unilateralism: America's 301 Trade Policy and the World Trading System* (Ann Arbor: University of Michigan Press, 1990).

98. Michael Mastanduno, "Do Relative Gains Matter? America's Response to Japanese Industrial Policy," *International Security* 16 (1) (Summer 1991): 73–113.

99. See Peter Schweizer, "The Growth of Economic Espionage," *Foreign Affairs* 75 (1) (January/February 1996): 9–15.

100. Thomas Kamm and Robert Greenberger, "France, in Apparent Espionage Spat, Asks Five Americans to Leave Country," *Wall Street Journal*, Feb. 25, 1995, p. A10.

101. See Paul Lewis, "Is the U.S. Souring on Free Trade?," *New York Times*, June 25, 1996, p. D1; and Paul Lewis, "U.S. Rejects Accord to Free Trade in Financial Services," *New York Times*, June 30, 1995, p. D1. In financial services, U.S. officials announced they would grant access to foreign firms selectively, depending on the extent of reciprocal access provided to U.S. firms abroad. The European Union and Japan went forward with the agreement absent the participation of the multilateral system's traditional champion.

102. See Bhagwati and Patrick, *Aggressive Unilateralism*.

103. In the words of Deputy U.S. Trade Representative Jeffrey Lang, "I'm not sure the WTO needs glamorous, big negotiating rounds; we should aim for steady, small steps every year." See Lewis, "Is the U.S. Souring on Free Trade?"

104. An important exception is Jervis, "International Primacy: Is the Game Worth the Candle?"

105. Ibid., 56–57, and Stephen Van Evera, "Primed for Peace: Europe After the

Cold War," in Sean M. Lynn-Jones and Steven E. Miller, eds., *The Cold War and After: Prospects for Peace* (Cambridge: MIT Press, 1993), 193–243. Van Evera writes (p. 218): "If all states accept the status quo and none wish to change it, wars are far fewer. Indeed, if no aggressor state is on the scene, war can only occur by accident or misunderstanding."

106. Jervis, "International Primacy: Is the Game Worth the Candle?," 67–68.

107. As Robert Gilpin points out, "in all historical epochs, realist thinkers have focused on the economic dimensions of statecraft." Gilpin, "Richness of the Tradition of Political Realism," 308. A prominent contribution in this tradition is Albert Hirschman's classic, *National Power and the Structure of Foreign Trade*, rev. ed. (Berkeley: University of California Press, 1980).

108. For a discussion of the use of economic statecraft to shape a target state's capabilities and intentions, see Mastanduno, *Economic Containment*, ch. 2.

109. For background and discussion, see Tyson, *Who's Bashing Whom*; C. Fred Bergsten and Marcus Noland, *Reconcilable Differences? United States-Japan Economic Conflict* (Washington, D.C.: Institute for International Economics, 1993; and Benjamin J. Cohen, "Return to Normalcy? Global Economic Policy at the End of the Century," in Lieber, ed., *Eagle Adrift*, 79–86.

110. David Sanger, "In a Trade Pact with China, the Ghost of Japan," *New York Times*, February 27, 1995, p. D1, and David Sanger and Steven Erlanger, "U.S. Warns China over Violations of Trade Accord," *New York Times*, February 4, 1996, p. A1.

111. Steven Greenhouse, "U.S. to Seek Stronger Trade and Political Ties with Europe," *New York Times*, May 29, 1995, p. A3.

112. Nathaniel Nash, "Showing Europe That U.S. Still Cares," *New York Times*, Dec. 3, 1995, 20.

113. According to one estimate, the United States provided roughly $9 billion in assistance to the former Soviet region between 1990 and 1994. See Charles Weiss, Jr., "The Marshall Plan: Lessons for U.S. Assistance to Central and Eastern Europe and the Former Soviet Union," Occasional Paper (Washington, D.C.: The Atlantic Council, December 1995), 23.

114. See Charles Flickner, "The Russian Aid Mess," *The National Interest* (38) (Winter 1994–95): 13–18, and David Kramer, "Russian Aid (II)," *The National Interest* (39) (Spring 1995): 78–81.

115. A recent, critical examination is Paul Schroeder, "Historical Reality vs. Neo-realist Theory," *International Security* 19 (1) (Summer 1994): 108–148.

116. An important recent contribution is Richard K. Herrmann and Michael P. Fisherkeller, "Beyond the Enemy Image and Spiral Model: Cognitive-Strategic Research After the Cold War," *International Organization* 49 (3) (Summer 1995): 415–450.

117. A forceful argument on the need to bring current U.S. foreign economic policy

in line with foreign and security policy is Henry R. Nau, *Trade and Security: U.S. Policies at Cross-Purposes* (Washington, D.C.: AEI Press, 1995). Nau argues (pp. 1–2) that "Trade policy has been increasingly isolated from other U.S. foreign policy interests in a single-minded pursuit to capture exports and high-wage jobs for the American economy." Economic nationalists argue the opposite: U.S. economic interests are being compromised in the interest of maintaining a questionable security strategy, and security strategy should line up behind the more aggressive international economic strategy even if that means disengaging the United States militarily from Asia. See Chalmers Johnson and E.B. Keehn, "The Pentagon's Ossified Strategy," *Foreign Affairs* 74 (4) (July/August 1995): 104–105.

118. A recent task force report on U.S.-Japan relations prepared for the U.S. government by the National Research Council addressed this problem, and warned that "it is unrealistic to believe that a firewall can be maintained long-term to protect one aspect of the relationship from significant erosion of goodwill in others." The task force recommended a comprehensive dialogue between the two governments to integrate the economic and security aspects of their relationship. See National Research Council, Report of the Defense Task Force, *Maximizing U.S. Interests in Science and Technology Relations with Japan* (Washington, D.C.: National Academy Press, 1995), 81.

119. See Cohen, "Return to Normalcy?," 73–99.

120. Robert W. Tucker, "The Future of a Contradiction," *The National Interest* (43) (Spring 1996): 20.

121. As Posen and Ross note, "Primacy is notoriously open-ended." Posen and Ross, "Competing Grand Strategies," 124.

122. Brian Coleman, "U.S. Envoy to EU Aims to Defuse Anger Over Sanctions on Business with Cuba," *Wall Street Journal*, October 18, 1996, p. A13A.

6 Mercantile Realism and Japanese Foreign Policy

Eric Heginbotham and Richard J. Samuels

Scholars of international relations have largely overlooked Japan in their surveys of great power politics, while students of Japan frequently focus on a single policy-area or on Japan's bilateral relations with specific states and have generally failed to test Japan's larger strategic calculus against international relations theory.[1] Those who have examined Japanese grand strategy typically adopt a structural realist model, under which states are motivated primarily by the fundamental imperative of military security and frequently subordinate other goals to that end. Some scholars, observing divergence from behavior predicted by this theory, have concluded that Japan's foreign policy is nonrealist or otherwise exceptional.[2] In this article, we examine Japan's postwar foreign policy both against structural realism and against what we call mercantile realism, which recognizes technoeconomic security interests—including, but not limited to, those associated with military security—as central considerations of state policy. We conclude that although Japan clearly does not ignore military security, its foreign policy is organized around the goal of advancing its technoeconomic position. Moreover, when tradeoffs must be made between military and technoeconomic security values, the latter frequently take precedent. These findings have implications for the U.S.-Japan relationship, for the broader prospects for peace and prosperity in the coming decades, and for how we reconstruct an international relations theory that explains the behavior of as many of the major powers in the system as possible. Ultimately, we believe that the economic and military security imperatives of state behavior should be reintegrated in a more comprehensive realist theory that captures the complexity of how various economic and military interests are balanced in the short- and long-term to maintain or advance the position of the state in the international system.

In the next section we test Japanese foreign policy against predictions consistent with structural realism and find that it poses a number of problems for this theory. First, structural realists frequently suggest that in cases where economic and military interests cannot be pursued simultaneously, the threat of war will lead each state to subordinate its economic interests to the dictates of maximizing military security. Yet, despite the dramatic growth of defense budgets across East Asia, Japan has adopted a long-term defense plan that will *reduce* the size of its military force. Second, structural realism posits that concerns over relative gains and dependence on goods vital to national defense will convince most leaders to limit the scope of their state's economic engagement with those states deemed to represent the most imminent military threats. Yet, while China is Japan's most important potential military challenger, Japan has shown limited sensitivity toward the distribution of relative economic gains from its trade with China. In fact, Japan has become China's largest trading partner and serves as that country's largest supplier of bilateral and multilateral aid. Ironically, Japan has been far more sensitive to relative gains from trade and investment in its dealings with the United States and the states of Western Europe, its major Group of Seven partners.

Rejecting structural realism as an adequate explanation for Japanese behavior, however, is not to reject all realist-inspired explanations. In the third section of the paper we examine the argument made by Samuel P. Huntington that "for decades Japan has acted in a way totally consistent with the 'realist' theory of international relations, which holds that international politics is basically anarchic and that to ensure their security states act to maximize their power. Realist theorists have focused overwhelmingly on military power. Japan has accepted all the assumptions of realism but applied them purely in the economic realm."[3] We first establish key predictions for a mercantile realist theory of state behavior and test those against observed Japanese foreign policy. We find that not only is Japan's economic and foreign economic policy consistent with the theory, but also that policy in a much broader array of areas—including military and diplomatic—supports Japan's technoeconomic security agenda.

The final section of this paper seeks to explain the origins of Japanese strategic preferences: to show how they are manifest in Japanese institutions and to assess the likelihood of change. We argue that elements of Japanese grand strategy today are consistent with its nineteenth-century strategy, when Japanese survival depended on the rapid acquisition of foreign technology and the modernization of its industrial base. But whereas Japan once pursued policies designed to strengthen its economic base for the purposes of enhancing its military power, today the very concepts of security and power frequently are defined in technological, industrial, and economic terms. Japan's defeat in World War II discredited military measures as a means of enhancing national security, and the hobbling of the state's military bureaucracy has ensured that Japan's powerful economic state organs and their industrial allies have immense influence over the terms by which Japan's security interests are articulated. Japan's prewar economic planning agencies, once in the service of a militarized state, have in effect been liberated both from the burden of war planning and from the constraints of military supervision. The U.S. alliance has provided time for both the new strategic thinking and the domestic structures in which they are embedded to take root. Mercantile realism has persisted beyond the end of the Cold War and the gradual emergence of more challenging strategic realities, and it is likely to be an enduring feature of a wealthy Japan's foreign policy well into the next century.

STRUCTURAL REALISM AND JAPANESE FOREIGN POLICY

Structural realism makes the following set of assumptions: states are the key actors in international relations; they interact in an anarchic environment devoid of rules and enforcers; and, as a consequence of anarchy, much of their behavior is shaped by the possibility of war and the necessity of preparing to deter or defeat military challengers. The threat of war leads each state to maintain its own defense capabilities and to form loose alliances whenever possible with states that share common defense interests. Although structural realists disagree about the foreign policy propositions that derive from the theory, the following are broadly accepted:

1. *States tend to balance against military threats, not bandwagon with them.* Kenneth Waltz writes that "secondary states, if they are free to choose, flock to the weaker side; for it is the stronger side that threatens them."[4] Stephen Walt proposes an important modification, suggesting that "states balance against threats rather than against power alone. Although the distribution of power is an extremely important factor, the level of threat is also

affected by geographic proximity, offensive capabilities, and perceived intentions."[5]

2. *States prefer to maintain independent military capabilities.* Although states will form loose military alliances in order to balance against primary threats, they will guard themselves against the possible defection of allies by maintaining a full array of military forces and will resist the specialization of their military forces in the interests of greater alliance rationality.

3. *Powerful states are more prone to follow predictions 1 and 2 than are weak states.* Both Waltz's and Walt's propositions about state behavior pertain primarily to great powers. Walt observes that "in general, the weaker the state, the more likely it is to bandwagon rather than balance. This situation occurs because weak states add little to the strength of a defensive coalition but incur the wrath of the more threatening states nonetheless."[6]

Contemporary realists have been largely silent on economic issues and on how economic and military security concerns relate to one another. The following propositions capture the most salient observations that have been made on the subject.

4. *States will be highly sensitive to the relative economic gains of other states they consider military threats.* Realists agree that less trade will occur than is rational from a classical economic standpoint.[7] Given that trade may benefit one partner relatively more than the other and that trade involves the specialization of labor between states, states will restrict trade in order to avoid shifts in the balance of power or dependence on trade partners for goods that may be critical in the event of war. The trade-inhibiting effects of differential benefits from trade will be muted within alliances and between partners that are not potential military competitors.[8]

5. *The greater the perceived military threat to a state, the more that state will pay in order to maintain its alliance relationships.* How the costs of a military alliance will be divided among component members will be affected by the relative military dependence of the states involved.[9] When a state faces both a high degree of military threat and the possibility of defection by allies, it will pay relatively more to entangle its partner(s) and reduce the likelihood of abandonment.

Testing Structural Realism against Japan's Cold War Foreign Policy

The crushing defeat Japan suffered in 1945 knocked it cleanly out of the great power ranks. Japan's economy and military power were destroyed, its territory was occupied, and it had little choice but to ally with the United States. That alliance was, however, fully compatible with Prime Minister Yoshida Shigeru's goal to rebuild the Japanese economy behind the protective shield of American military power. Within the alliance Japan did not maintain a fully capable or autonomous military force and did relatively little to contribute militarily to the West's effort to balance Soviet power. But those limitations on Japan's military forces were also consistent with Yoshida's strategy of avoiding any commitment that might slow economic reconstruction. When John Foster Dulles, then chief negotiator of the 1951–52 peace and security treaties, pressed Japan to expand its National Security Force from 110,000 to 350,000 troops, Yoshida refused, fearing that if Japan's forces were larger than absolutely necessary to defend Japan, the United States would ask it to send forces to Korea.[10] In 1952, when the Ministry of International Trade and Industry (MITI) and business leaders pressed Yoshida to rearm and use the arms industry as the locomotive for postwar reconstruction, he declined, siding instead with the Ministry of Finance and the banks' preference for nurturing the commercial economy.[11]

As an American ally, Japan enjoyed access to U.S. markets for industrial products technology, and investment. Japan's Foreign Investment Law of 1950 and other controls, however, effectively excluded U.S. products and capital from the Japanese market. As Japan began to relax legal restrictions in order to join the General Agreement on Tariffs and Trade (GATT) in the 1950s and the Organization of Economic Cooperation and Development (OECD) in the 1960s, its leaders erected a broad array of new nontariff barriers designed to limit foreign investment and imports.[12] Japan also benefited from U.S. influence in Europe, notably pressure forcing the British and the French to accept Japanese entry into the new GATT organization. Japan sacrificed relatively little, and may in fact have gained much, from alliance efforts to contain the Soviet Union during the Cold War. While it was certainly not a completely "free ride," it *was* a cheap and profitable one for Japan.

Neither Japan's economic policy nor its military policy during the Cold War was clearly at odds with the predictions of structural realism outlined above. Japan did join an alliance that worked to balance against the Soviet Union, which it regarded as its primary military threat [proposition 1]. Although Japan failed to maintain a well-rounded and independent defense force and did not expend significant resources to maintain its alliance connections, this too is not necessarily inconsistent with structural realism. Relatively weak powers, like Japan throughout the 1950s and 1960s, are not predicted to balance as actively as more powerful states [proposition 3]. Moreover, the willingness of states to assume the economic leadership of an alliance will, according to structural realism, depend on the relative degree of threat faced by the alliance partners and on the relative size of their economies [proposition 5]. The United States felt that it was engaged in a life or death struggle with the Soviet Union and that U.S. allies on the periphery of the Eurasian land mass were particularly important, since their defection might tip the global balance in favor of the Soviet Union. Given this intense military competition and the vast relative size of the U.S. economy during the 1950s and 1960s, it was unlikely that the United States would object too strenuously to limited cheap riding by allies.

The importance that U.S. policymakers attached to Japan as a military ally is borne out by the 1952 comments of a government official who wrote that "The most highly industrialized country in the Far East must remain outside the Soviet orbit if there is to be a free Asia, and to this end U.S. policy should be directed by whatsoever means are necessary, military or economic, to assist in the establishment of political tranquillity and economic betterment in all of free Asia . . . and until it is clear that Japan can stand firmly on its own feet, the United States must of necessity lend support, even to the extent of providing an unrestricted market for such Japanese goods as American consumers find attractive."[13]

The strength of the U.S. commitment was not lost on Japanese officials who frequently played the alliance card to secure economic concessions. In 1966, for example, Japanese officials warned that continued U.S. pressure over Texas Instruments' attempts to enter Japan could slow the more general process of capital liberalization and harm the overall U.S.-Japan relationship. An editorial in Japan's leading business daily suggested that "American failure to 'understand' Japanese treatment of Texas Instruments and similar foreign direct investment cases might endanger Japan's support for U.S. security policies."[14]

Although Japan's behavior during the Cold War was not necessarily at odds with the predictions of structural realism, it hardly provides decisive validation of the theory. Structural realism claims only to explain the behavior of large states with any degree of reliability. The idea that weak states will be *less* inclined to balance against threats by forming alliances and generating additional military resources serves more as a caveat to the general theory than as a primary prediction. Few structural realists would suggest that a state that refuses to mobilize more than a tiny fraction of its gross national product or available manpower for defense or one that structures its armed forces to provide minimal rear-area services to those of an ally (rather than autonomous, well-rounded national defense capabilities) provides compelling evidence buttressing structural realism.[15]

Perhaps more to the point, it would be difficult to describe Japan in the latter decades of the Cold War as without options in the great power game. By the 1970s Japan's economy had surpassed the Soviet Union's. By the end of the Cold War it was larger in proportion to the U.S. economy than the combined economies of Japan and Germany had been in 1939. While its military capabilities were tiny compared with those of the Soviets' at the end of the Cold War, Japan's military weakness was a result of state policy, not resource limitations. Japan had become very rich, and could easily have become very strong as well. Yet despite the rise of Japan's industrial and financial power and despite its capability to turn itself into a military great power, Japanese foreign policy changed relatively little during the 1970s and 1980s.

Structural realists propose that powerful states are more inclined than weaker ones to balance against threats and maintain independent military capabilities, but they sometimes leave undefined how "powerful states" should be defined. We would suggest that if the term is used to refer to states with strong military capabilities, then there is a sort of circular logic to the theory: powerful military states will prefer to maintain independent military capabilities. If structural realism is to have predictive value, its propositions should address the behavior of states with the existing capability to generate powerful military forces, as well as those that have already done so. Viewed in this light, Japan's behavior at the end of the Cold War begins to diverge from that predicted by structural realism. In 1970, the quintessential realist Herman Kahn suggested that if Japanese economic growth continued the "Japanese will almost inevitably feel that Japan has the right and duty to achieve full superpower status and that this means possessing a substantial nuclear establishment."[16] But Japan did not become a nuclear power and did not aspire to superpower status, at least in the traditional sense of the term. If structural realism did not capture fully Japan's Cold War dynamics, what of its utility *after* the Cold War?

Testing Structural Realism against Japan's post-Cold War Foreign Policy

Structural realist theory predicts a dilemma for post-Cold War Japan. The United States has lost much of its strategic and economic motivation for maintaining its global alliance system. With the collapse of the Soviet Union and the implosion of the Russian economy, U.S. GNP is now 15 times greater than Russia's. Moreover, a new barrier of affiliated states unfriendly to Russian expansion now exists between Russia and Western Europe. Despite China's economic growth, the U.S. economy also is 11 times larger than its economy.[17] Neither China nor Russia could mount a credible direct military threat to the United States in the next ten or fifteen years. Nor could either conquer the Eurasian landmass. Even after reducing defense spending to just over 4 percent of GNP, the U.S. military budget remains more than five times larger than any other single state, and greater than the next ten largest military budgets combined. At the same time, the U.S. share of the world economy declined from around 40 percent in 1950 to around 25 percent by the mid-1990s. Hence the United States is relatively less able to reap the rewards of the free trade system that its military alliance system facilitates.

Given reduced military threats and the relative slippage of American economic strength over time, some U.S. foreign policy elites became more inclined to reexamine the logic, structure, and costs of U.S. alliance commitments.[18] Militarily, the United States undertook to evaluate systematically the need for and costs of maintaining forward deployed U.S. forces on a continuous basis.[19] Economically, the first Clinton Administration took an aggressive approach to promoting U.S. exports, and showed less willingness to tolerate discriminatory trade practices by its allies.[20] In its dealings with Japan, the administration used the threat of economic sanctions to leverage trade concessions; it openly manipulated exchange rates to apply pressure directly on Japanese export-oriented firms; and, until they backed off in 1996, U.S. officials hinted that the security relationship could depend on Japanese willingness to bargain in good faith on the economic front.[21]

Since that time, the regional situation confronting Japan in East Asia has if anything become more uncertain. First, the situation on the Korean peninsula remains unstable. North Korean missiles are now within range of Japan, and there is fear that those missiles could soon carry nuclear warheads. Moreover, although the presence of 50,000 U.S. troops in South Korea is reassuring to Japan, these troops may not remain in place after unification. South Korean military technological and military strength and a history of uneasy Korean-Japanese relations may make a unified Korean peninsula even more a threat to Japan than North Korea is currently.

Despite the passage of time since the Japanese occupation of Korea, anti-

Japanese sentiments in South Korea have not diminished. To the contrary, a 1995 survey of Korean attitudes shows that a record 69 percent of Koreans responded that they "hate" Japan, while only 6 percent responded that they "like" Japan.[22] In this general atmosphere of distrust, defense officials in Japan and South Korea peer across the Tsushima Straits warily. The South Korean navy has grown faster than any other in the region in the last ten years, and much of the rhetoric justifying this growth suggests that the Japanese navy is the competitor.[23] Unresolved territorial disputes also continue to affect the relationship. Japan's extension of 200-mile fishing and mining rights gave increased prominence to the demarcation of islands and waterways. In February 1996 South Korea conducted naval and air exercises around the island of Tokdo (known as Takeshima in Japan) in order to counter Japanese claims to the island.[24] Given these problems, it should not be surprising that some Japanese military analysts view South Korea as a threat and its rapprochement with China as laden with political and even military significance.[25]

Nor has the threat from Russia receded as far from the Pacific as it has from Europe. Russia no longer physically borders Western Europe; however, its borders remain unchanged in the Far East. Because of a lack of resources and maintenance problems, Russia's Far Eastern fleet is largely restricted to port. But it still represents a potentially powerful force in the region and occasionally makes its presence felt. More important, if the Russian economy recovers, the entire fleet, as well as the Far Eastern air force, could be brought up to operational readiness. This has historical precedence, as Japanese strategists are well aware.[26] Given the political uncertainties in Moscow, and the persistent possibility that nationalists could someday gain control of the government, Russia too represents a potential military threat to Japan.

While the latent threats from the volatile Korean peninsula and the Russian Far East are considerable, the growth of China's power looms as Japan's greatest strategic problem. China's military forces are less capable than those the Soviet Union maintained during the Cold War. But China, unlike the Soviet Union, sits between Japan and Southeast Asia, Japan's most important sources of raw materials and one of its most important markets for finished products. In addition, Chinese capabilities are growing. Chinese official defense budgets have grown by 60 percent in real terms since 1989. While this represents a figure that is only half that of Chinese GNP growth, the Chinese National Defense Law, adopted in March 1997 stipulates that henceforth growth in the national economy should be fully reflected in the military budget.

As important as the rise of Chinese power is the question of how China will behave in coming years. Efforts by the Chinese leadership to solidify its domestic position through the use of nationalist symbols and propaganda include the depiction of Japan, with U.S. backing, as a power bent on regional hegemony.[27] Such rhetoric provided the backdrop against which China's long dormant territorial dispute with Japan over the Senkaku/Diaoyu islands was aggravated in the summer of 1996.[28] Moreover, the influence of the military appears to have grown in the last several years. In 1995 conservatives in the military succeeded in pushing Jiang Zemin and other national leaders toward a more confrontational stance on Taiwan independence, culminating in China's launch of missiles across the Taiwan strait in March 1996. With the death of Deng Xiaoping, the influence of the military has further increased: there is greater military representation in the Communist Party Central Committee, and the new National Defense Law requires that educational and media institutions should heighten their efforts at "national defense education."[29]

Japan has two options consistent with structural realism for dealing with its current security challenges. First, it could develop the conventional (and perhaps nuclear) forces necessary to balance against regional threats independent of U.S. assistance, and it could secure military allies among the minor and midsized powers of the region, particularly in Southeast Asia. Alternatively, Japan could work aggressively to offset the natural decline in U.S. alliance motivation by redefining the alliance so that Japan can shoulder a greater portion of military responsibilities within the existing framework; or Japan could be more conciliatory on trade and investment disputes, which, with the end of the Cold War, may assume ever greater importance for U.S. policymakers. Regardless of which strategy it pursues, we should expect Japan to exhibit great sensitivity to the distribution of gains through its trade with China.

The record to date indicates that: (1) although Japan has taken some measures to redeploy its forces into defense positions opposite China, it has not taken measures necessary to balance against China independent of U.S. assistance; (2) despite heightened rhetoric and media attention to the alliance after the 1995 incident in which three U.S. servicemen were convicted of raping an Okinawan schoolgirl, Japan has taken only limited measures to minimize the possibility of U.S. defection; and (3) Japan has shown little sensitivity to the problem of relative gains from trade between itself and China. We examine each point in turn.

Redeployment

To be sure, Japan's military forces are being shifted southward, and in some ways remodeled, to counter Chinese power.[30] Demonstrations of Japanese concern have included the dispatch of Maritime Self-Defense Forces vessels to the disputed Senkaku/Diaoyu islands, the use of Maritime Safety Agency vessels to apprehend "pirates," and political appeals for China to justify its military buildup and make its activities more transparent.[31] Japanese P-3C antisubmarine aircraft have been shifted from northern bases in Hokkaido and Aomori southward to Okinawa. Mobility will be enhanced with the addition of an amphibious assault ship which will be twice the size of any Japanese naval vessel built since World War II that, after minor modifications to the deck, will be able to accommodate Harrier fighter aircraft.[32] Other important additions to Japanese military forces include four Aegis guided-missiles cruisers and four AWACS (airborne warning and control systems) aircraft. Japanese military and diplomatic officials have also initiated or intensified dialogue with virtually all the states of East Asia.[33] In addition, Japan's first postwar military intelligence agency, *Joho Honbu*, was established in late 1995. Much of this activity appears to be designed to help Japan better observe and counter whatever military moves China might mount against Japanese islands ringing the East China Sea.

These measures, however, are limited in scope; and it would be difficult to say that they signal a concerted shift of resources into military assets that could be used independently to balance against China's regional objectives. Although some new capabilities have been added, the new National Defense Program Outline (NDPO), Japan's official long-term military planning document adopted in 1996, calls for the reduction of unit formations in all three services. Almost across the board, personnel and equipment numbers will decline. For example, under the new plan, the number of ground-force tanks will be reduced by 25 percent, the number of maritime-force major surface combatants will decline by 17 percent, and the combined total number of combat aircraft in the maritime and air forces will decline by 14 percent.[34] The government announced in mid-1997 that the defense budget will not be exempt from its program of fiscal austerity. Japan Defense Agency (JDA) officials have been assured that procurement will decline even faster than the NDPO requires.[35]

Reductions in the size of Japan's force structure stand in stark contrast to developments in other parts of the region where regional force structures, particularly naval and air forces, have grown rapidly over the last decade. For example, while the number of major surface combatants in the Japanese Maritime Self-Defenses shrank between 1984 and 1993, the number of major surface combatants in the navies of other Northeast Asian states grew by 64 percent and those of East Asia as a whole (minus Japan) grew by 35 percent.[36]

Given that U.S. security guarantees are currently in force, and that even without U.S. forces the Japanese military would enjoy significant advantages in defensive combat against all potential regional aggressors, Japan's refusal to shift proportionally more resources into the defense sector will not leave the home islands vulnerable to invasion in the near future. Nevertheless, continued limitation on the size of Japan's military force suggests that Japan is not preparing to balance against Chinese military power comprehensively. The lack of significant power-projection capabilities will leave Japan unable to defend her interests in areas distant from the home islands, and will make it difficult for Japan to secure firm allies or create an alliance system in Southeast Asia should strategic circumstances make such a development desirable.

Japanese policymakers are not simply taking the "go slow" approach to the expansion of Japan's force structure. Limitations on the Japanese force structure have been codified in long-term planning documents. The first NDPO was adopted in 1976, and its provisions were faithfully followed for twenty years. It will be difficult to modify the 1996 NDPO quickly, even if strategic circumstances should change. Similarly, although Japan has the technical capability to produce nuclear weapons on fairly short notice (and some analysts have consequently echoed Herman Kahn's 1970 prediction that Japan would go nuclear), Japanese planners are not preparing the population for the introduction of nuclear weapons.[37]

Redefining the Alliance

Although there is little evidence that Japanese planners are thinking seriously about a defense strategy independent of U.S. forces, Japan is doing little substantively, either as a military or economic partner, to make the alliance more appealing to its American ally. During the 1995 crisis over North Korean nuclear program, U.S. defense officials approached their Japanese counterparts about military cooperation in the event of war on the

Korean peninsula. The Japanese side refused to commit to the dispatch of minesweepers and other specialized assets in that eventuality.[38] After the Okinawa rape incident revealed the fragility of Japanese public support for the continued U.S. presence there, Japanese and U.S. officials hustled to reaffirm the alliance. A pair of highly visible rhetorical flourishes of solidarity—the April 1996 Clinton-Hashimoto Joint Declaration and the September 1997 Defense Guidelines—were designed to inject new meaning and confidence to the alliance in a changed security environment. Alliance managers made four claims: (1) the alliance was updated; (2) Japan's defense perimeter was enlarged; (3) the alliance is more reciprocal and balanced; and (4) mutual trust was enhanced.[39] Yet, immediately after the summit, Prime Minister Hashimoto backed away from President Clinton's use of the term "Asia-Pacific" to describe the common defense perimeter. Within months, senior Japanese Foreign Ministry officials sought to reassure Chinese diplomats at a vice-ministerial meeting that "the April 1996 Japan-U.S. joint declaration on security cooperation is not aimed at expanding the sphere of activity or application based on the security treaty."[40] A year later, as new defense guidelines were debated, the Japanese leadership openly split on whether a crisis in Taiwan was included in the geographic expression "area surrounding Japan." In the event, Japan refused to stipulate the contingencies under which it would provide rear area support for U.S. forces or even the geographic scope of the "area surrounding Japan."[41] In short, although there has been much talk about enhanced roles and missions—and Japanese rear area support for U.S. military in particular—the two sides have not articulated clearly what the alliance stands *for*, nor who it is designed to protect *against*.

The United States and Japan have made even less progress on the greatest single irritant in the bilateral relationship, namely, asymmetries in trade and investment. When President Clinton sought numerical targets on Japanese imports, Japanese leaders (especially Prime Minister Hashimoto who was then MITI minister) were hailed as heroes "who could say 'no' " to the powerful Americans. U.S.-Japanese bilateral imbalances in trade and investment persist despite decades of often acrimonious trade talks. Promises of a Japanese "big bang" market liberalization in 2001 are met with widespread skepticism.[42] Despite U.S. officials' proclamations that the alliance depends on Japanese cooperation on trade, despite open moves by U.S. firms to "pass Japan" and move operations elsewhere in the region due to commercial difficulties they encounter in Japan, and despite an ambiguous U.S. China policy, all of which ought to raise the specter of abandonment in Japanese eyes, Japan's economic behavior has not appreciably changed.[43]

Relative Gains

From the perspective of structural realism perhaps the greatest anomaly has been Japan's failure to exhibit a sensitivity to the relative distribution of gains that have accrued to China from its economic relations with Japan and other states. Although Japan has repositioned its military forces nearer China, and although it has made modest efforts to redefine its alliance with the United States, Japan has done little to stifle China's economic growth. To the contrary, Japan has competed vigorously for a major investment presence in China. The Japanese used their influence in the Asian Development Bank and elsewhere to argue for the early lifting of the sanctions imposed on China after the suppression of the Tiananmen demonstrators in 1989, and Japanese business leaders visited China within months to reaffirm the commercial relationship. In fact, Prime Minister Hashimoto reminded his audience at a speech in Tokyo, just before his September 1997 visit to Beijing, that he was the first G-7 finance minister to visit China after Tiananmen.[44] In the late 1990s Japan is China's largest trading partner, and China is Japan's second largest trading partner after the United States. More Japanese official development assistance goes to China than to any other country. As a partial consequence of Japanese and other investments, the Chinese economy has grown at a double-digit pace for more than a decade.

In 1991 Prime Minister Kaifu Toshiki announced that Japan's aid decisions would thenceforth be tied to the recipient state's military and political behavior. However, despite concerns about Chinese nuclear testing, its conventional arms buildup, its military actions in the South China Sea, and its lack of military transparency, the Japanese government announced in December 1994 that annual aid for the three-year period after 1996 would be increased by more than 40 percent.[45] In September 1997 Prime Minister Hashimoto promised Beijing an additional $2 billion concessionary loan package, the largest ever extended. But, of even greater significance, was the report that same month that Japan had broken ranks with (and undercut) the United States and the European Union on the terms for Chinese membership in the World Trade Organization.[46]

Japan is not pursuing these China policies behind a comprehensive U.S. shield. U.S. policy toward China is indeterminate at best. On the one hand, U.S. diplomatic recognition of Vietnam, the visit of Taiwanese leader Lee

Teng-hui, and U.S. military support for Taiwan are all perceived in Beijing as measures designed to contain the growth of Chinese power. On the other hand, the Clinton administration's policy of "engaging" China may clear the way for the United States to reestablish the military-to-military ties and defense industrial cooperation that existed during the Cold War. The United States has not established a clear deterrent posture in the South China Sea area.[47] The ambiguity of U.S. policy, particularly the lack of any comprehensive U.S. promise to protect Japanese interests outside of the areas surrounding Japan, makes the Japanese decision not to pursue a relative gains strategy against the Chinese difficult to reconcile with the core propositions of structural realism.

Japan's economic and foreign aid policies toward China are even more puzzling when considered in the context of its economic policies toward the United States and Western Europe. Whereas Japan is eagerly courting China as an economic partner, its economic relations with other advanced industrial states continue to be difficult. Japan has protected itself against significant import penetration by the other G-7 states by effectively limiting the ability of multinationals to gain control of Japanese companies. Despite the lifting of many formal restrictions on foreign ownership during the 1970s, less than 0.1 percent of all investments in Japan from 1982 to 1992 originated from foreign sources.[48] This is less than one-tenth the level of Germany, the G-7 country with the next lowest ranking.

Japan's reticence to integrate its economy reciprocally with those of Western Europe and the United States, while continuing to deepen its economic relations with China, is perplexing from a structural realist perspective because there seems to be little correlation between the willingness of Japan to engage these states economically and the degree of military threat they pose. Even if one were to make the extreme argument that Japan might view the United States as a potential military threat, it would be extraordinarily difficult to make such a case for the states of Western Europe. None is as populous or as wealthy as Japan; none has a defense budget as large as Japan's; each is so distant from Japan that the projection of force across the gap would be extraordinarily difficult; and finally, none has any territorial or other major unresolved political disputes with Japan, and all are fellow democracies. Structural realists are surely correct that military security concerns sometimes act to inhibit trade and investment flows. At least in the case of Japan's economic relations, however, other considerations would seem to be more important in determining the nature of trade with specific partners.

Japanese foreign policy after the Cold War provides ample evidence that the possibility of war and conquest is not the central concern of Japanese policymakers. Despite great new uncertainties in its relations with both China and the United States, Japan has shown great reluctance to create more independent, robust, or well-rounded military forces. Moreover, it has shown greater concern over Japan's relative economic position vis-à-vis the United States and Western Europe than it has over the rapid expansion of the Chinese economy.

This observation that Japanese behavior does not seem consistent with the predictions of structural realism is not ours alone. Other American defense officials and academics, recognizing this, conclude that Japan has no serious security strategy, or that it is an "economic giant and political pigmy."[49] However, while we find structural realism inadequate as a guide to Japanese international behavior, we would not rush to conclude that Japan is in any way bereft of (or that its norms preclude) strategic thought. Rather, we would first entertain the possibility that Japanese strategy is consistent with the sort of technoeconomic logic referred to by Huntington (and quoted in the introduction to this article). In the following section, we first consider the principles and predictions that would be associated with such a theory and then examine whether Japanese foreign policy is consistent with those predictions.

MERCANTILE REALISM

The idea that technology and national wealth should be given prominence in providing security is hardly unique to the contemporary era. Its disparate antecedents include the nineteenth-century neomercantilist propositions of Alexander Hamilton and Frederick List and the mid-twentieth-century insights of Joseph Schumpeter, E. H. Carr, and Eli Hecksher. We learn from Hamilton and List that states must nurture their manufacturing capacity to remain strong; from Hecksher and Carr that states can use economic power to unify and dominate the system within their sphere; and from Schumpeter that innovation is the most dynamic source of structural change and power in capitalist economies.

Although traditional mercantilists and classical realists have been concerned largely with the connection between national wealth and national military power, we note that policies designed to enhance the technological and economic fortunes of states may be pursued to increase a state's political leverage and independence even in the absence of military-security considerations. In developing predictions consistent with a mercantile version of realist theory, we have entertained the notion that broad segments of the elite in some states might embrace three ideas: (1) the possibility that the efficacy of appeals to arms has, for a variety of reasons, declined dramatically during the course of the twentieth century;[50] (2) the idea that national economic power can be used to constrain the sovereignty or independence of states;[51] and (3) the notion that national economic power can be enhanced through industrial and trade policies designed to create comparative advantage in critical high-tech sectors.[52]

This effort should be seen in a larger context. In its classical formulation, realism was a comprehensive theory of state behavior. Only during the Cold War did it became closely associated with the more narrow logic of military competition. We agree with Randall Schweller that the breadth and full texture of international economic competition has been lost in the structural realists' quest for parsimony. According to Schweller, " . . . scholars and practitioners have been getting off the realist train at various stops over the past decade or so. . . At its core, classical realism is a theory of the state and international competition. It is not, primarily, a theory about how states acquire security or about strictly defense issues. Indeed, the best treatments of realism's intellectual roots are not found in the security side . . . but rather in its more overlooked economic philosophy of mercantilism."[53]

Despite differences in goals, structural and mercantile realism share several common elements. Each is "realist" because each posits states as the most important actors in world politics; each assumes that state behavior is determined by rational national leaders who seek to maximize state power; and each suggests a competition among states for relative power and security. Despite sharing core elements, mercantile and structural realism produce divergent predictions under many global and regional political conditions. These differences involve more than differential rates of military investment or trade policies. They comprise a broad range of preferences, including the question of how elites define threats and select allies, as well as how they conduct themselves with states they find threatening and those they find nonthreatening.

Here we outline several propositions associated with mercantile realism, paying special attention to areas where predictions differ from those of structural realism: (1) security threats are economic as well as military; (2) powerful technoeconomic states will balance against other technoeconomic states; (3) when tradeoffs must be made, technoeconomic interests may be pursued at the expense of political-military interests; and (4) the nationality of firms matters as much or more than the location of production.

Economic Security Threats

Under structural realism, the primary threat to state security is from direct attack. The equivalent of military conquest in mercantile realism is deindustrialization or dependency. States that intervene in their national economies to nurture domestic producers are acting to protect domestic markets from the economic equivalent of direct attack; we would thus expect states to justify these interventions as matters of national security that will therefore entail the sorts of national mobilization and sacrifice associated with military mobilization elsewhere. It follows that the elite cadres of economic bureaucrats in such states should enjoy the same training and status as military officers in the states better described under structural realism. Such states should be particularly sensitive to technological dependency. Given that technological capabilities are essential for prosperity in industrial economies, timely access to technology is a matter of national security. The dangers of excessive dependence are measured as more than "vulnerability" to access denied; there are the opportunity costs of foregone chances to learn and to innovate. Mercantile realists will also worry about exploitation by technological leaders who would use their market power to "tie" (influence purchases), to "rent-seek" (raise prices), to extort by allocating or denying supplies for strategic reasons, and to be predatory by driving another nation's producers from the market entirely.[54] Mercantile realists refer to the consequence of such dependency—the reduction of national firms to assemblers, handlers, and retailers unable to reap the full profits of manufacturing and innovation—as "hollowing" and make it a central focus of strategy.

Economic Balancing Behavior

States may balance both economically and politically against rival industrial powers even when those nations pose little military threat; conversely, close economic and political relations may be pursued with states possessing complementary economies, even when such behavior entails some degree of future military risk. States may adopt a wide array of measures, including strengthening ties with economically less-threatening partners, in order to mitigate this danger. As in structural realism, balancing behavior is most likely to characterize the behavior of major industrial states. Technologically weak states may have little choice but to integrate their economies (bandwagon) with the dominant partner. The economic bloc that would ensue is the mercantile realist analogue to the military alliance in structural realism. Under mercantile realism, states will also balance against others based upon judgment of their strength, position, and behavior, but these judgments will conform to a technoeconomic logic:

Strength

Strength in the mercantile world is not always determined by size, population, or military capability, but also by wealth and technology. While these have hardly been unrelated historically, they are not always covariant and should be distinguished analytically.[55] Mercantile realists will balance against wealthy states that are endowed with technology-intensive industries.

Position

Position in the mercantile world is defined by its industrial structure rather than by its physical geography. States that compete in the same sectors will tend to view one another as threatening, and mercantile realists will minimize intra-industry trade. While military strength is rapidly attenuated across space, technological power, and the ability to profit from it, are not. Hence, in the context of global markets, states far away may pose as big a threat as those that share common borders.

Behavior

States will balance against others that behave as economic predators. Moreover, because the behavior of other states may be misinterpreted under mercantile realism just as it is in the world of structural realism, we can imagine the problem of technoeconomic "security dilemmas" in which defensive efforts made by one state (e.g., to protect infant industries) may be viewed by trading partners as aggressive actions to which they respond with tariffs and other sanctions.

Economic-Military Tradeoffs

Nations may be forced to choose between maximizing technoeconomic values or political-military values. Structural realists argue that when forced to make this choice, states will seek to achieve political-military goals first. Military security is like oxygen, they assert. It is taken for granted until there is too little of it, at which point, states will do anything to get more.[56] Mercantile realists respond that economic security is just as important, adding that once economic security is gone, it is difficult to recover. A state with a powerful technological and industrial base is capable of transforming itself from a military pygmy into a military giant within a short span of time, whereas states with large militaries that allow their industrial and technological base to wither find themselves in a more difficult predicament.[57] They may thus be unable to protect themselves from either economic coercion *or* military threats.

Nationality of Firms

Even in a global economy, mercantile realists assume that firms have (and will retain) a national center of gravity. States therefore seek not only to nurture firms within their borders but also to support national firms abroad. These firms are more comfortable trading with co-nationals sited abroad than they are with foreign-owned entities at home. It follows that outward foreign direct investment can be used to entangle allies and to create dependence that serves national ends, while inward direct investment can be carefully monitored and circumscribed to prevent the same result. Mercantile realists have no difficulty identifying "who is us?" After all, as Laura D'Andrea Tyson put it, mercantile realists know very well that "they are not us."[58] Under structural realism, the physical location of production may be more important, because production assets may be nationalized in the event of war.

Testing Mercantile Realism Against Japanese Foreign Policy

Given that strong military states are also often wealthy states with advanced technology, the predictions of structural realism and mercantile realism frequently are congruent. This, however, is not always the case. Japanese foreign policy is an important case in point. Here we evaluate postwar Japanese foreign policy against each of our propositions in turn.

Economic Security Threats

Japan persistently has acted as if its greatest vulnerabilities have been economic and technological. Foreign penetration of Japanese markets, particularly in manufactured goods, has been perceived as a threat, whether that penetration was by the firms of a military competitor or ally. For example, in 1982 at the height of the Cold War, Wakasugi Kazuo, the director-general of the Trade Policy Bureau of MITI, warned publicly that unless the United States and Europe relaxed their trade and market-opening pressures, Japan might be forced to join the communist bloc.[59]

When economic threats are perceived, Japan's leaders have been willing to sacrifice military values for technoeconomic ones. For example, in the late 1980s, the U.S. Department of Defense (DoD) began a program to improve efficiency in weapons acquisition. The DoD, working with some of its major prime contractors, developed software for an electronic materiel database: the computer aided acquisition and logistical support system (CALS). CALS is designed to shorten development time and reduce inventory, thereby increasing efficiency; contractors including Boeing and General Motors began adapting this integrated product management system for commercial use. According to Japanese press reports: "Japanese companies are afraid that CALS . . . will become the international standard . . . and if Japanese products do not meet the standard they will be kept out of the world market. It could also lead to the disintegration of the Japanese traditional *keiretsu* business practices and to worldwide restructuring since cost/performance could be the driving force for the use of CALS."[60]

The threat that Japanese firms will be excluded from the marketplace, and that traditional supplier relationships will be disrupted by low cost and direct procurement (something *desirable* in the United States) led MITI to budget $17 million in 1997 to develop both a domestic CALS and an international one that excludes U.S. and European firms. The industrial threat posed by the possible imposition of a U.S. procurement standard clearly was given greater weight than considerations of cost in military procurement or than the interests of the U.S.-Japan military alliance. MITI has invited China, Indonesia, Malaysia, and the Philippines to participate in the development of pilot CALS systems in the areas of automobile, electronics, and textile manufacturing. MITI says that it will invite the United States to participate "in the future."[61]

Japan's leaders perceive a range of foreign threats—not the least of which are threats to the sustenance of long-term manufacturing capabilities—including market shifts and technological revolutions. As a result they vigilantly monitor the economy to mitigate the worst effects of each. They also fear "excessive competition"—the fratricidal competition among domestic firms that results in bankruptcies and unemployment. In the Japanese view, the social dislocations of "excessive competition" are as great or greater than the economic costs of excessive concentration in the neoclassical model. Thus firms and sectors are nurtured, and the resulting dense local, regional, national, political, and industrial networks do not facilitate the "cut and run" strategies typical in the United States. Rather, Japanese firms share market pain, and grow together during economic upturns.

The threat of deindustrialization—popularly referred to as "hollowing" in Japan—has never been far from public concern and strategic attention. Perhaps as a consequence, a stronger yen in the first half of the 1990s drew much less investment away from Japan than Western analysts expected. Small and medium-sized manufacturing employment actually rose by 8 percent between 1990 and 1992, stayed flat through 1993–94, and fell just 2 percent from late 1994 to 1995.[62] Thus, Japanese manufacturers added jobs after the bubble burst, despite the high yen, which encouraged even faster investment overseas. That the United States (despite its cheap dollar) lost 12 percent of its manufacturing base during this same period suggests that Japanese strategists place a different value on manufacturing and are willing to pay a higher cost to maintain it.

Finally, there is the issue of technology transfer to Japan's trading partners. Whereas structural realism might predict that states will use technology transfer to strengthen an alliance against military competition, mercantile realism makes no such prediction. During the Cold War it was in the perceived security interest of the United States to encourage U.S. firms to sell technology to Japan (or at least not to intervene when the Japanese demanded such transfers as the cost of gaining access to the Japanese market). The United States provided technology to support its allies. By contrast, in the Japanese case, technology may be traded and transferred within firms, but it is rarely sold at arm's length to unrelated firms. As mercantile realism would predict, there are very few countries with which Japan enjoys a technology trade surplus. Further, those that *do* have a technology trade surplus with Japan are also those—such as China, Thailand, Indonesia, and the United Kingdom—where Japanese investment accounts for a large portion of domestic manufacturing investment. In Japanese practice, technology, like trade, follows investment, and technology is a strategic asset, not a commodity.[63]

Economic Balancing Behavior

During the Cold War Japan seldom had to choose between advancing its political-military or technoeconomic interests. The Soviet Union represented a military security threat to Japan; it did not represent an economic threat, nor did it represent an economic opportunity. For its part, the United States was willing to provide both economic public goods in the form of open markets and military public goods in the form of an extended nuclear deterrent and forward-deployed ground, sea, and air forces. Japan could bandwagon with the United States politically and balance against it economically; thus the general outline of Japan's alliance patterns during the Cold War—that is, a security policy built on an alliance with the United States combined with a protectionist economic policy—is consistent with both conventional and mercantile realism.

In the post-Cold War period, Japanese leaders face difficult choices about how to reconcile technoeconomic with military-political security interests. Intermittent, but intense, U.S. pressure for market access has provoked a heated debate in Japan between those who would suggest an Asia-first strategy and those who would seek to maintain the American alliance. To date, the alliance supporters have prevailed. Yet many Japanese bureaucrats, politicians, and business leaders have openly advocated turning away from the U.S. alliance and toward Asia.[64]

From a mercantile realist standpoint, Japan has significant incentives to pursue an Asia-first strategy. Many Asian economies are highly complementary to Japan's; and Japan enjoys tremendous leverage in its dealing with those states by using its size and technological position to play them off against one another. Japan has not only established wholly owned subsidiaries throughout the region, but it has also replicated entire supplier-producer networks in Asia.[65] The results have been impressive. In 1996 Japan had an $18 billion surplus with members of the Association of Southeast Asian nations (ASEAN) and a $23 billion surplus with Taiwan and the Republic of Korea alone.[66] Japan runs trade surpluses with virtually all its trade partners—rich and poor, agricultural and industrial, those with budget surpluses and those with deficits. These results belie the argument that Japanese trade balances are merely the consequence of low savings and investment abroad.

Economic-Military Tradeoffs

Many of Japan's decisions in the military realm have been driven as much by economic considerations as by strictly military calculations. In 1968 and 1970 Prime Minister Sato Eisaku commissioned studies on Japanese nuclear options. The second of these reports concluded that "the days are gone when the possession of nuclear weapons is a prerequisite for superpower status." The studies were undertaken to provide the intellectual justification for Japan's ratification of the nuclear Non-Proliferation Treaty (NPT). It was hoped that ratification of the NPT would provide both economic and political benefits useful for a Japanese government bent on maintaining high growth. One participant reported that "there was a pressing need to secure nuclear energy for economic growth by joining the treaty. It was therefore urgent that we arm ourselves with a rationale against acquiring nuclear weapons."[67]

The debate over the role of Japan's conventional forces and on whether or not Japan should become a "normal" nation is colored by economic considerations and the exigencies of economic diplomacy. Even those, such as politician Ozawa Ichiro, who use the term "normal" to mean a greater Japanese political and military role in the world, would limit Japanese involvement in operations overseas to U.N.-sponsored and directed missions.[68] Although Japan displays great concern for autonomy in economic affairs, works diligently to acquire and indigenize foreign technology, and resists the foreign ownership of production in Japan, it also displays a far greater willingness than many other states to place its forces under international command. Unlike most "normal" nations, the rationale for the use of military force by a "normal" Japan would be the assumption of greater international burdens. Use of force would not be undertaken in the pursuit of national interests as structural realists would define them. Rather, the use of force would be the burden that Japan would assume in order to maintain its image as a member in good standing of the world community. It is that image, not the use of force per se, that serves Japan's national interests by reinforcing other states' inclinations to continue supporting the free-trade system that makes Japan's prosperity possible.[69]

Whereas the United States is willing to overpay for defense goods to guarantee the autonomy and health of its defense industry, Japan is frequently willing to pay higher factor costs to maintain industrial autonomy. Examples are easy to find. Although Japanese reports in 1995 indicated that acceding to U.S. demands for increased auto parts imports would have enabled Japanese makers to cut costs on those parts by 20 to 30 percent, a rapid shift in supplier relations was judged detrimental to Japan's interests since it might jeopardize Japanese production, employment, and the *keiretsu* system of industrial relations.[70] Japan has shown less sensitivity to the problem of relative gains vis-à-vis one of its greatest potential military competitors than structural realism might predict, while displaying greater sensitivity in its economic relations with the United States and Europe. From the beginning of the U.S. occupation in 1945 until today, Japanese strategists have been more willing to accept U.S. military on their soil than they have U.S. bankers or manufacturers.

Nationality of Firms

As noted earlier, structural realists have made few detailed predictions about national economic priorities, such as whether the ownership of firms or the location of those firms is more important. Although it is therefore difficult to test predictions of structural and mercantile realism with equal certitude, the evidence does suggest three conclusions. First, the logic described by mercantile realism on the question of national ownership does seem to be at work in the Japanese case. Second, Japanese leaders take the question so seriously that they are willing to risk undermining important political-military relationships in the pursuit of Japanese interests in this area. Third, the United States does not pay the same premium for national ownership. Japanese elites are certain that nations and national ownership count, even in a "global economy." The Japanese know exactly "who is us," and prefer to trade with (and transfer technology among) co-nationals.

The 1995 auto parts trade dispute between the United States and Japan illustrates these points clearly. U.S. pressure on Japan to purchase higher volumes of U.S. manufactured automobile parts in 1995 went beyond routine demand-making and threatened to lead to a fuller trade war. The Clinton administration set a deadline by which 100 percent tariffs would be applied to imported Japanese luxury automobiles unless there were "measurable" changes in Japanese procurement of U.S. auto parts. The Japanese reacted vigorously and refused to bow to U.S. pressure. Hashimoto Ryutaro, then Minister of MITI, said "no" to the United States and was hailed as a hero. Ultimately, an agreement was reached that Japan would increase imports of auto parts manufactured by Japanese firms in the United States. The Clinton administration was satisfied that jobs would stay at home, while Japanese firms were pleased to achieve significant cost reductions and retain control and profits. Japan's ability to say "no" to the United States on the ownership of firms and technology and the willingness of the United States to take "no" for an answer are attributable to the difference between the dominant U.S. view that firms do not have a nationality and the prevailing Japanese view that Japanese firms are Japanese wherever they are located.

An even clearer illustration of the emphasis that Japanese leaders place on national ownership and control can be seen in the approach to competitive foreign pressure euphemistically called "development importing" (*kaihatsu yunyu*). Using this approach, when aluminum smelting proved hopelessly uneconomical in the early 1980s, Japanese firms were guided by the government toward collective investment in Brazilian and Indonesian smelters to avoid dependence on foreign ingot.[71] Following the same logic, the liberalization of beef and citrus a decade later was accompanied by the acquisition of cattle ranches and groves abroad.

CONCLUSION

Japanese policymakers and academics commonly argue that economic power is now more salient than military power. The former head of the Mitsubishi Research Institute summarized this position when he wrote that "although national supremacy was once a product of military power, it is now decided primarily by economic power. Economic power is, for its part, decided primarily by the ability to generate technology."[72] Ishihara Shintaro, the conservative politician, and Morita Akio, the former chairman of Sony, called attention to this view when they wrote that production of the microchips used in sophisticated weapons systems abroad gives Japan leverage over even the world's strongest states.[73] Economic power is, in this view, not simply the basis on which military power rests but can be used to safeguard or constrain national sovereignty.

Despite Japan's capability to generate substantial military power, there is no broad-based call for Japan to convert its economic strength into military power and assume regional, much less global, leadership. Rather, many Japanese intellectuals have proposed Japan pursue a division of labor in international society. Noting that that by the end of the Tokugawa era Japan belonged to the merchants and the samurai (warriors) had been reduced to poverty, Amaya Naohiro, the late MITI official, argued that "for a merchant to prosper in samurai society, it is necessary to have superb information-gathering ability, planning ability, intuition, diplomatic skill, and at times the ability to be a sycophant."[74]

Japanese strategists have noted that Japan's history parallels the experience of Renaissance European trading states. Gotoda Masaharu, an LDP (Liberal Democratic Party) politician, argues that "while Mediterranean states such as Genoa, Naples, and Pisa fell one after another, Venetian prosperity continued, giving it a thousand year reign. What enabled Venetian prosperity alone to continue? First, Venice coolly faced the reality that there was no alternative path to making a living by selling their produce overseas. Accordingly, it pursued a wise foreign policy and made no missteps in its foreign policy choices. Secondly, its political and administrative apparatus remained in firm control, internal opposition was overcome, and a comparatively stable social order was maintained domestically."[75] Viewed from this perspective, Japanese efforts to exclude foreign firms from penetrating domestic markets and their willingness to pay a premium for high employment are more understandable. Japanese mercantile realism includes both measures designed to strengthen the technological, industrial, and financial underpinnings of power and measures designed to insulate Japanese society from forces that might ultimately jeopardize the state's ability to pursue a mercantile policy in the long run.

During the 1980s, books and articles held up Japan as the outstanding example of the country whose behavior undermined neoclassical economic theory. Here we suggest that Japan is also a difficult case for orthodox theories of security. Some aspects of Japan's foreign policy are difficult to reconcile with realist theory, when the primary motivation of state behavior is said to be military threat. Of course, structural realists do not claim that all states follow the behavioral imperatives of their theory; rather, they claim that any state which does not will pay a penalty. Japan may ultimately pay a high penalty for its apparent adherence to a different causal model of what makes states succeed or fail. Then again, by following a different, equally rational strategy, it may avoid these costs and emerge stronger and safer than before. Mercantile realism seems to have served Japan well during the period we studied. At a minimum, any comprehensive realist theory should include the logic of technoeconomic competition if it seeks to include Japan in the states the behavior of which it claims to explain.

Some analysts, pointing to the fact that the United States has guaranteed Japanese security, will argue that Japanese behavior is consistent with the precepts of structural realism and that Japan's behavior will change if the U.S. alliance is weakened. While we cannot rule out such a possibility (and while we readily acknowledge that U.S. hegemony abetted the consolidation of the system we describe), we would urge circumspection both toward Japanese foreign policy and structural realism itself based upon our analysis. By now Japan has long had the world's second largest economy—an economy greater in proportion to the world's largest economy than either the Soviet

Union's at the height of the Cold War or Imperial Japan's and Nazi Germany's combined on the eve of World War II. Yet Japan, with all of the makings of a traditional great power, continues to rely on another great power for its military security. While this so-called "free-riding" may be realist—and we argue that it is in fact very consistent with mercantile realism—it is difficult to reconcile with the self-reliant and militarily focused world of great-power competition found under structural realism. A Japan operating under a structural realist model would long ago have begun lobbying to "pop the U.S. cork" from its bottle; it should have been "overproducing" military security since the 1970s.[76] Japan's foreign policy instead consistently reflects a more complex calculus, under which the maximization of military security frequently is subordinated in the pursuit of technoeconomic security interests. Military security is not ignored, but neither is it the predominant focus of a grand strategy designed to enhance comprehensive state power in the long run.

ACKNOWLEDGMENT

The authors gratefully acknowledge the thoughtful critiques of earlier drafts of this essay by Robert Art, Joseph Grieco, Chalmers Johnson, Iain Johnston, Chikako Kawakatsu Ueki, Michael Mastanduno, Randall Schweller, Christopher Twomey, and Stephen Van Evera. This was originally prepared for the Olin Institute conference on "Realism and International Relations After the Cold War," Cambridge, Massachusetts, December 1995.

NOTES

1. See, for example, the essays in two recent compendia on Japanese foreign policy: Gerald Curtis, ed., *Japan's Foreign Policy After the Cold War* (New York: M. E. Sharpe, 1993) and Yoichi Funabashi, ed., *Japan's International Agenda* (New York: New York University Press, 1994). Exceptions are Takashi Inoguchi, *Japan's International Relations* (London,: Pinter, 1994); Chalmers Johnson, "The State and Japanese Grand Strategy," in Richard Rosecrance and Arthur Stein, *The Domestic Bases of Grand Strategy* (Ithaca, N.Y.: Cornell University Press, 1993) and Mike M. Mochizuki, "American and Japanese Strategic Debates: The Need for a new Synthesis," in M. Mochizuki, ed., *Toward a true Alliance: Restructuring U.S.-Japan Security Relations* (Washington, D.C.: Brookings Institution Press, 1997), ch. 2.

2. Peter Katzenstein, *Cultural Norms and National Security: Police and Military in Postwar Japan* (Ithaca, N.Y.: Cornell University Press, 1996) and Peter Katzenstein and Nobuo Okawara, *Japan's National Security: Structures, Norms and Policy Responses in a Changing World* (Ithaca, N.Y.: Cornell University Press, 1993).

3. Samuel Huntington, "Why International Primacy Matters," *International Security* 17 (4) (Spring 1993): 311.

4. Kenneth N. Waltz, *Theory of International Relations* (New York: Random House, 1979), 126.

5. Stephen Walt, *The Origins of Alliances* (Ithaca, N.Y.: Cornell University Press, 1987), 5.

6. Waltz, *Theory*, 134 and Walt, *Origins*, 29.

7. This rationale can be found in Waltz, *Theory*, 104–7. For realist critiques of institutionalism which make similar points, see Joseph Grieco, "Anarchy and the Limits of Cooperation: A Realistic Critique of the Newest Liberal Institutionalism," *International Organization* 42 (Summer 1988): 497–500 and John Mearsheimer, "The False Promise of International Institutions," *International Security* 19 (Winter 1994/95): 21.

8. Joanne Gowa, *Allies, Adversaries, and International Trade* (Princeton: Princeton University Press, 1994), 53 proposes that "free trade is more likely within than across alliances." See also Grieco, "Anarchy and the Limits of Cooperation," p. 501 and Arthur Stein, "The Hegemon's Dilemma: Great Britain, the United States, and the International Economic Order," *International Organization* 38 (Spring 1984): 364–67.

9. See Glenn Snyder, "The Security Dilemma in Alliance Politics," *World Politics* 36 (July 1994): 471–72.

10. John Dower, *Empire and Aftermath: Yoshida Shigeru and the Japanese Experience, 1878–1954* (Cambridge: Harvard University Press, 1979), 388–89.

11. Richard Samuels, *"Rich Nation, Strong Army": National Security and the Technological Transformation of Japan* (Ithaca, N.Y.: Cornell University Press, 1994), ch. 3.

12. Edward J. Lincoln, *Japan's Unequal Trade* (Washington, D.C.: Brookings Instititution, 1990), 15 provides a full analytical summary of Japanese nontariff barriers. For a discussion of measures to discourage foreign investment, see Mark Mason, *American Multinationals and Japan* (Cambridge, MA: Council on East Asian Studies, Harvard University, 1992).

13. Jerome Cohen, *Economic Problems of a Free Japan* (Princeton: Princeton University Center for International Studies, 1952), 89.

14. Mason, *American Multinationals*, 183.

15. Since 1976, the Japanese defense budget has remained essentially fixed as a percentage of GNP (around 1 percent by Japanese accounting practices or 1.5 percent by NATO accounting standards).

16. Herman Kahn, *The Emerging Japanese Superstate: Challenge and Response* (Englewood Cliffs, N.J.: Prentice-Hall, 1970), 165.

17. GNP figures are from the World Bank, *World Development Report* (1994), 166–67.

18. See, for example, Eric A. Nordlinger, *Isolationism Reconfigured: American Foreign Policy for a New Century* (Princeton: Princeton University Press, 1995) and Eugene Gholz, Daryl G. Press, and Harvey M. Sapolsky, "Come Home America: The Strategy of Restraint in the Face of Temptation," *International Security* 21 (4) (Spring 1997): 5–48.

19. The United States reduced the number of forward-deployed military personnel in Western Europe, where the threat has receded most dramatically, from over 300,000 in 1989 to approximately 100,000 in 1997. U.S. forces have been withdrawn entirely from the Philippines, where the United States had been asked to pay a larger sum for basing rights.

20. On the increased assertiveness of U.S. economic policy, see Michael Mastanduno, "Preserving the Unipolar Moment: Realist Theories and U.S. Grand Strategy after the Cold War," *International Security* 21 (4) (Spring 1997): 49–88.

21. Department of Defense Office of International Security Affairs, *United States Security Strategy for the East-Asia Pacific Region*, February 1995.

22. *Asahi Shimbun*, July 29, 1995, 1. A survey done in seven major East Asian cities showed that while a majority of the people interviewed in Southeast Asia (Bangkok, Manila, Singapore, and Jakarta) responded that "Japan had become a country which could be trusted," those in Seoul, Beijing, and Shanghai responded that it had not. *Asahi Shimbun*, August 13, 1995. These feelings help explain why a novel by a little-known author about a Korean nuclear attack on Japan sold two million copies in its first ten months in 1993 and why the popularity of President Kim Yong-Sam rose in 1994 after he ordered the destruction of the National Museum in Seoul, a structure originally built to house Japanese occupation authorities. See Katsuhiko Kuroda, "'Nichi-Kan Kakusenso Shosetsu' no Kiken" ("The Danger of a 'Japan-South Korean Nuclear War Novel'"), *Bungeishinju*, June 1994.

23. The official South Korean Defense White Paper listed Japan as a potential military threat in 1992. Under U.S. pressure, explicit references were subsequently deleted.

24. *New York Times*, February 15, 1996, 5.

25. See, for example, Shinju Butei, "Kan-Chu Kokko Juritu to Nichi-Kan Kankei" ("Korean-Chinese Normalization and Japanese-Korean Relations"), *Bôei Kenkyû* (5) (1992).

26. According to *Foreign Media Note*, August 12, 1993, a military analyst, Goro Saito, pointed out in *Gunji Kenkyu*, May 1993 that Moscow had recovered from the chaos of the Russian Revolution to field formidable Soviet forces in

Siberia and the Maritime Province and argued that Japanese need "to learn from history the risk of Japan's northern threat recovering." p. 2.

27. For Chinese propaganda towards Japan, see *Asahi Shimbun*, September 14, 1995. On the larger effort to inspire nationalism, see *Far Eastern Economic Review*, November 9, 1995, 21–26.

28. Following harsh rhetoric from China on the issue, the central government ultimately apparently became alarmed at independent calls by student organizations for even tougher measures. The police were called upon to prevent further independent student agitation, and the government softened its own rhetoric.

29. See *Jiefangjunbao*, March 19, 1997, for full text of National Defense Law and *Asahi Shimbun*, September 19, 1997 for data on Central Committee representation. The official Chinese military budget passed in March 1997 called for a 15 percent increase in defense spending—about the same rate as national economic growth.

30. *Asahi Shimbun*, May 14, 1994, 13. Michael Green and Benjamin L. Self, "Japan's Changing China Policy," *Survival* (Summer 1996).

31. See for example, Shigeo Hiramatsu, "China's Naval Advance: Objective and Capabilities," *Japan Review of International Affairs* (8) (Spring 1994); *Beijing Review*, November 5–11, 1995; and "Murayama to Raise Spratlys Issue with Li Peng," *FBIS*, March 9, 1995, 4.

32. The Maritime Self-Defense Force announced its intention to procure "Harrier-2 plus" fighters in April 1995. See the report in *Tokyo Shimbun*, April 28, 1995 in *FBIS-EAS-95-083*, May 1, 1995.

33. In Southeast Asia, there has been active cooperation with regional states. For example, Japan coordinates its efforts toward Burma and Indochina with Thailand, where strong political and military ties have been reinforced by high levels of foreign aid, exchange programs for military officers, and constant high level contact between diplomats. See, *Asahi Shimbun*, *March 13, 1995*. See also *Japan Digest*, March 20, 1995.

34. "Shinboei Keikaku Taiko" ("The New National Defense Program Outline"), *Asahi Shimbun*, November 29, 1995.

35. JDA procurement officer interview, September 18, 1997, Tokyo. The rise of the yen and the growth of the Japanese economy has resulted over the decades in the steady rise of Japanese defense spending in constant dollar terms. By FY 1996 the Japanese defense budget reached almost $60 billion, easily the second largest defense budget in the world. Yet given the continued unwillingness of the Japanese to increase the share of GNP devoted to defense and the high price of domestically produced defense goods, even that amount is insufficient to produce a force with substantial power projection capabilities.

36. IISS, Military Balance 1993–94, Map insert titled "Asia: the Rise of Defense

Capability, 1984–1993. "Primary surface combatants" refers to combatant naval ships over 1,000 tons."

37. For realist predictions of the nuclearization of Japan, see Christopher Layne, "The Unipolar Illusion," *International Security* 17 (Spring 1993) and Waltz, *Theory*, 1993. As noted earlier, Kahn, *The Emerging Japanese Superstate*, 1970, is of particular interest in this regard. On Japan's technical capabilities and the concerns that Japan's plutonium-based energy program has engendered, see Eugene Skolnikoff, T. Suzuki and K. Oye, *International Responses to Japanese Plutonium Programs* (Cambridge, MA: Center for International Studies, Massachusetts Institute of Technology, 1995).

38. *Asahi Shimbun*, November 26, 1995, 1.

39. Patrick Cronin," The US-Japan Alliance Redefined,"*Strategic Forum*, (75) (May 1996).

40. Yoshitaka Sasaki, "New Order in the Asia-Pacific Region and Japan's Non-Military Role," unpublished paper presented to the Abe Fellows Symposium, December 19, 1996, p. 10.

41. See the Office of the Secretary of Defense (Public Affairs), *Joint Statement of the U.S.-Japan Security Consultative Committee on the Completion of the Review of the Guidelines for U.S.-Japan Defense Cooperation* , No. 507–97, September 23, 1997. Kajiyama Seiroku, Japan's Chief Cabinet Secretary, resigned soon after being scolded by LDP Secretary General Kata Koichi for asserting that Taiwan was "naturally included" within this area. See *Asahi Shimbun*, September 3, 1997.

42. Some refer to the "Big Bang" as a "Big Whimper." *The Daily Yomiuri*, February 3, 1997, 6.

43. A 1995 DOD East Asian strategy statement (the so-called "Nye Report") warns that "if public support for the relationship is to be maintained over the long term, progress must continue to be made by both sides in addressing fundamental economic issues." Department of Defense Office of International Security Affairs, *United States Security Strategy for the East-Asia Pacific Region*, February 1995, 10. In a 1995 column, Thomas Friedman argued that "We are being played for fools. Japan will only change when we use the full strategic and economic weight of the U.S. to make it clear to Tokyo that a failure to open all its markets, with concrete results, will lead to a crisis in the U.S.-Japan strategic relationship—not just economic ones—and to specific retaliation against Japanese exports." *New York Times*, March 26, 1995, 15.

44. Prime Minister Ryutaro Hashimoto, "Seeking a New Foreign Policy Toward China," Speech to the Yomiuri International Economic Society, August 28, 1997.

45. Peter Evans, "Japan and the United States Diverge on Assistance to China," *Japan Economic Institute Report* No. 19A (May 19, 1995). Japan protested Chi-

nese nuclear testing in May 1995, and suspended grant aid for the coming year. However, given that grant aid represents only one quarter of all Japanese ODA to China, given the limited nature of reductions in that aid, and given that Japan maintained its far more significant ($6 billion) yen loan package, it is clear that the use of ODA for leverage on military issues, is a secondary consideration at most. See *Sankei Shimbun*, May 24, 1995.

46. A *Financial Times*, September 16, 1997 story as reported in the *Japan Digest*, September 22, 1997.

47. For example, although the U.S. has a defensive alliance with the Philippines, it declared that that treaty commits the U.S. only to the defense of the main islands, not to the defense of the Spratlys. That clarification came in the weeks following the Chinese seizure of a reef in that island group long claimed by the Philippines. Nor were U.S. military assets mobilized to combat piracy by Chinese vessels, many with military markings, against selective targets (including Japanese ships) in the South and east China Sea areas during the early and mid-1990s.

48. Keidanren, "Tokushu: Sangyo no Kudoka ni Oeru" ("Special Issue: Responses to Industrial Hollowing"), *Gekkan Keidanren*, March 1995, 21. See Lincoln, *Japan's Unequal Trade*, 1990. See also Henri-Claude De Bettignies, "Japan and E.C. '92," in Craig C. Garby and Mary Brown Bullock, *Japan: A New Kind of Superpower?* (Washington, D.C.: Woodrow Wilson Center Press, 1994), 81, who suggests that "if one word can characterize the European-Japanese economic relationship, it is probably imbalance. Whether one looks at trade, investment, or people, the key feature remains disequilibrium, increasing over the years."

49. Michael Blaker, "Evaluating Japan's Diplomatic Performance," in Gerald Curtis, ed., *Japan's Foreign Policy* (New York, M. E. Sharpe, 1993), 3, argues that Japanese policymakers simply "cope" with crises and have "no calculated strategy." See also Charles Krauthammer, "The Unipolar Moment," *Foreign Affairs* 70 (1) (1990/91): 24.

50. A broad range of realists and nonrealists alike have made these arguments. For essays on both sides of the issue, see Sean Lynn-Jones and Steven E. Miller, *The Cold War and After: Prospects for Peace* (Cambridge: MIT Press, 1994).

51. David Baldwin, *Economic Statecraft* (Princeton: Princeton University Press, 1985); Stephen Krasner, *Defending the National Interest: Raw materials Investment and U.S. Foreign Policy* (Princeton: Princeton University Press, 1978); The classical analysis is Albert O. Hirschman, *National Power and the Structure of Foreign Trade* (Berkeley: University of California Press, 1945 [1980]); For a test of Hirschman's "asymmetric trade dependence" hypothesis in the contemporary Asian context, see Davis B. Bobrow, Steve Chan, and Simon Reich,

"Trade, Power, and APEC: Hirschman Revisited," forthcoming in *International Interactions*.

52. Paul Krugman, ed., *Strategic Trade Policy and the New International Economics* (Cambridge: MIT Press, 1990).

53. Randall Schweller, "Realism and the Present Great Power System: Growth and Positional Conflict Over Scarce Resources," paper prepared for the Olin Institute conference on "Realism and International Relations After the Cold War," Cambridge, Massachusetts, December 1995, 46.

54. This analysis is from George Gilboy, "Technology Dependence and Manufacturing Mastery," unpublished paper, Massachusetts Institute of Technology, Department of Political Science, Cambridge, 1995. See also Theodore Moran, *American Economic Policy and National Security* (New York: Council on Foreign Relations Press, 1993).

55. Russia in the nineteenth century was a first-rate military power, yet its industrial and technological base was second-rate. Spain in the sixteenth century, or China today, may also be regarded as strong military states without comparable economic or technological strength. Contemporary states such as Switzerland and Singapore stand out as examples of states with limited military capabilities but strong technological and financial ones.

56. See Joseph S. Nye, Jr., "The Case for Deep Engagement," *Foreign Affairs* 74 (4) (July/August 1995) for the use of this metaphor.

57. The best example of an economic superpower transforming itself rapidly into a military great power is the United States, which had been spending only 1.5 percent of its GNP on defense in the two decades before World War II. In 1939 the U.S. produced only a quarter as many military aircraft as Germany. Yet, by 1941 it was producing well over twice as many military aircraft as Germany. [See Paul Kennedy, *The Rise and Fall of the Great Powers* (New York: Random House, 1987), 324, 332, 354.] The reverse example is sixteenth-century Spain. Not only did Spain's relentless wars weaken its financial position, but mercantile policies specifically designed to amass gold reserves for military operations rather than to promote manufactures also enervated Spanish industry. Ultimately, Spain lost its edge over England and even the United Provinces in both military technology and in the relative ability to finance military operations.

58. The debate over "Who is Us?" was initiated by Robert Reich, "Who is Us?," *Harvard Business Review* (January/February 1990). See also Laura D'Andrea Tyson, "They Are Not Us: Why American Ownership Still Matters," *The American Prospect*, No. 4 (Winter 1991).

59. Chalmers Johnson, "La Serenissima of the East," *Asian and African Studies* 18 (1) (March 1984): 59.

60. *Foreign Media Note*, August 23, 1995, 1. This English-language compendium

cites reports in *Nikkan Kôgyô Shimbun*, July 25, June 5, and May 29, 1995; *Nikkei Sangyô Shimbun* July 13, July 31, 1995; *Nikkei Mechanical* May 1, 1995; *Nihon Keizai Shimbun*, July 28, 1995.

61. Ibid., 2.

62. Sofuchô Tôkeikyoku, ed., *Rodoryoku Chosa Nenpo (Annual Report on the Labor Force Survey)* (Tokyo: Sofuchô Tokeikyoku, 1994), Table 6. On responses to hollowing, see Keidanren, *Gekkan Keidanren*, 1995; see also National Institute for Research Advancement (NIRA), "Sangyo no Kudoka to Chiiki Keizai" ("Industrial Hollowing and Regional Economics"), *Seisaku Kenkyo* 8 (2) (February 1995).

63. For more on differences between the U.S. and Japanese strategic treatment of technology, see U.S. Congressional Office of Technology Assessment (1994). For comprehensive data on Japanese technology trade see Kagaku Gijutsu Chô and Kagaku Gijutsu Seisaku Kenjyûjo, ed., *"Nihon no Gijutsu Yushutsu no Jittai: Nihon no Gijutsu, Shinhon to tomo ni Ajia E" (The Actual Condition of Japanese Technology Technology trade: Japanese Technology and Capital Together toward Asia),* (Tokyo, 1997).

64. See Michael Green and Richard J. Samuels, "Recalculating Autonomy: Japan's Choices in the New World Order," *NBR Analysis* 5 (4) (December 1994) for how these choices are framed by politicians and bureaucrats. See also Kazuo Ogura, "Ajia no Fukken no Tamemi" (In the Interest of Asia's Revival), *Chuo Koron*, July 1993 and Shigeki Tejima, "Sekkyoku shisei ni tenjita Nihon no kaigai toshi" ("Japanese Overseas Investment Turns Active"), *Shukan Toyo Keizai*, 1994.

65. Michael Borrus, "Left for Dead: Asian Production Networks and the Revival of U.S. Electronics," MITJP Working Paper No. 96–24 (Cambridge: MIT-Japan Program, 1996). John Ravenhill, "Japanese and U.S. Subsidiaries in East Asia: Host Economy Effects," MITJP Working Paper No. 96–07 (Cambridge: MIT-Japan Program, 1996).

66. China is nearly alone among Japan's trading partners to enjoy a bilateral trade surplus ($19 billion in 1996). Trade data are from the Japanese Ministry of Finance web page: http://www.mof.go.jp/trade-at/199638c.htm.

67. *Asahi Shimbun*, November 13, 1994.

68. Ichiro Ozawa, *Blueprint For A New Japan* (Tokyo: Kodansha, 1994).

69. This argument is made explicitly by Ozawa, ibid.

70. *FBIS*, June 6, 1995, 1–2.

71. Richard Samuels, "The Industrial Destructuring of the Japanese Aluminum Industry," *Pacific Affairs* 56 (3) (Fall 1993): 495–509. See Mark Tilton, "Informal Market Governance in Japan's Basic Materials Industries," *International Organization* 48 (4) (Autumn 1994) for more on upstream integration overseas by Japanese firms.

72. Noboru Makino, "Kokka no Haken wa Gijutsuryoku de Kimaru" ("National Supremacy is Decided by Technological Strength"), *Chuo Koron* (July 1990), 111.

73. Shintaro Ishihara and Morita Akio, *"No" to Ieru Ajia (The Asia That Can Say "No")* (Tokyo: Kappa Hard, 1989), 14.

74. Cited in Kenneth Pyle, *The Japanese Question: Power and Purpose in a New Era* (Washington, D.C.: The AEI Press, 1992), 38.

75. Masahara Gotoda, *Seiji To Wa Nanika? (What is Politics?)* (Tokyo: Kodansha, 1988), 97. Johnson, "La Serenissima of the East," 1984, also offers a compelling comparison between Japan and Venice.

76. The "cork in the bottle" metaphor is from General Henry Stackpole, former commandant of U.S. Marines in Japan. *Washington Post*, March 27, 1990.

7 Realism and Russian Strategy after the Collapse of the USSR

Neil MacFarlane

From 1993 to 1996, Russia's relations with the West gradually deteriorated while Russia reasserted itself at the expense of the other newly independent states on the territory of the former Soviet Union. Some have explained this in terms of the increasing influence of realism in Russian foreign policy after a short honeymoon of liberal institutionalism.[1] Others have contested this interpretation. For example, Robert Legvold has taken exception to what he perceived to be the deterministic quality of realist argumentation and its excessive focus on systemic variables. Policy consistent with the dictates of realism, in his view, was not systemically determined, but was largely a product of domestic politics and the choices of the Russian leadership; national leaderships could choose either "Waltzian" or "Wilsonian" definitions of self-interest, since "self-interest is a highly subjective matter and honest people can disagree over the best way to achieve it":

> The extent to which realist theory attempts to turn it into an objective matter by basing self-interest on the struggle for power also offers no way out . . . There is, in short, nothing about the essence of international politics or the imperatives created by states that says, at this juncture, facing the problems that it does, Russia should better pursue a Monroe Doctrine in the near abroad and a *droit de régard* [sic] in Central Europe than seek international regimes and multilateral machinery protecting its interests in these areas.[2]

Legvold's objection is interesting and challenging. To what extent was and is evolving Russian foreign policy consistent with the deductive propositions and predictive dimension of international realism? To what extent does it depart from these aspects of realist theory? And how does one explain both the congruence of theory and practice and the departures of the one from the other?

Closer analysis of the problem reveals other puzzles. First, given the frequent assumption in realist theory that the state is a rational unitary actor, how does one account for realist outcomes in Russian behavior where the state is hardly unitary or monolithic, where there is a wide diversity of opinion on the meaning of "the national interest,"[3] and where the state's control over Russian persons and organizations active internationally is often notional?

Second, Russian foreign policy is played out in at least two more or less distinct arenas: the other former Soviet republics, and the broader international system. The regional and global agendas of Russian policymakers operating on a realist calculus of international relations may diverge. The pursuit of a realist regional agenda might conflict with that of a broader realist agenda toward international actors outside the former Soviet Union. How, then, would one account from a realist perspective for the choices of policymakers?

In this chapter, I begin with a summary of basic propositions of realism concerning the behavior of states in the international system, and how, in deductive terms, these propositions generate hypotheses regarding Russian behavior. I follow this with a discussion of the evolution of Russian foreign policy in the post-Soviet era. I do not deal in detail with Soviet foreign policy during the Cold War. Although the exploration of continuity and change between the Cold War and post-Cold War eras might be useful in assessing the significance of systemic and structural influences on Russian foreign policy, space is limited, and contemporary Russia is a product in large part of the radical discontinuity constituted by the end of the Cold War.

I argue that the distribution of power at the regional level has favoured a strategy of assertion and consolidation by Russia in the "near abroad." At the broader systemic level, the rapid decay of Russia's position in international relations leaves it with two options: balancing and bandwagoning. The balancing option has proven difficult to exercise in the current international system. Consequently, realist theory would suggest a continuation of the retreat from the confrontational rhetoric and policy of the Cold War and of the more accommodative behavior characteristic of the Gorbachev era. This is also favored by Russia's dependence on the other great powers for material assistance and the maintenance of status. This does not imply simple surrender to the desires of the West in general and the United States in particular. But one would expect that—to the degree that there is a correlation between the deterioration in state power and the pursuit of cooperative behavior—as Russia's power declined, the cooperative content of its approach to the West would grow.

The two strategic agendas are in tension with each other. Russian behavior follows the predictive propositions of realism *within* the former Soviet region. It is not entirely consistent with predictions derived from Russia's changing position in the global balance. While Russia's economy continues to contract and its military power continues to atrophy, it has abandoned the liberal internationalist focus of its foreign policy and is behaving in an increasingly confrontational manner. In particular, it has been unwilling to curb its regional ambitions in order to stabilize its relations with the United States and NATO,[4] while farther abroad, its attitude on arms transfers to powers hostile to the West, on the conflict in the former Yugoslavia, and on NATO expansion, among other issues, suggests that the limits on its willingness to cooperate are narrowing. Russia is in fact willing to challenge the West on such issues, even if this risks substantial complication in its relationship with Western states.

This apparent departure from the theory may reflect significant second image influences. However, it also reflects the fact that Russia retains substantial resources of power in international relations that are often missed at first glance. Notably, Russia's weakness is itself a source of strength in the relationship with other great powers in the system. Recognition of these sources of power helps resolve the apparent tension between global and regional agendas and goes some distance toward explaining the apparent departure of Russia from the agenda dictated by its deteriorating position in the post-Cold War distribution of power.

THE THEORETICAL FRAMEWORK

The question addressed in this chapter is whether realism can account for Russian behavior in international relations better than alternative theoretical perspectives, such as, at the systemic level, neoliberal institutionalism, or, at the unit level, those focusing on domestic politics and political culture.

The basic propositions of realism are highly contested, and the theoretical framework itself admits of considerable pluralism. Many realists would so characterize themselves without accepting the structural revisions of a Kenneth Waltz. For "classical" realists, the essence of international relations lies in the egoistic pursuit of national interest in an essentially anarchic environment, rather than in the determining influence of structure on the choices of states. It allows an important place for judgment and for motivation in the explanation of outcomes.[5] To take a second example, some would argue that state-centricity is essential to the theory. Others would argue that it is an "analytical convenience." As one author put it with reference to older exemplars of realism: "State-centrism is a superfluous principle in classical realism: the predominance of power and self-interest in international affairs abides, with all its consequences, whether states are the sole actors in that realm or not."[6]

The same author rightly notes that for "classical" realists, the assumption of rationality is not necessary, and much of the realist literature gives space in explanation to such variables as motivation and judgment, and, for that matter, to speculation regarding human nature, as is evident in the work of Hans Morgenthau and Reinhold Niebuhr.[7]

Despite the considerable pluralism in realist perspectives, most would accept the following propositions as basic to the realist perspective on international relations. First, the primary actor in international relations is the state. The state is capable of unitary and rational action. It operates in a systemic framework characterized by anarchy; that is, states are autonomous actors in a system without a supreme authority above them. Resources in this system are finite and scarce. The scarcity of resources in the system dictates competition for control over them. The absence of an authority above states means that they must rely on their own devices to assure their security. As Paul Kennedy put it in a discussion of the meaning of grand strategy:

> The history, geography, and culture of each country on our planet are unique . . . but there are some unifying elements, deriving from our common humanity. One of them is the demand placed on all the polities of this world, whether ancient empires or modern democracies, to devise ways of enabling them to survive and flourish in an anarchic and often threatening international order that oscillates between peace and war, and is always changing.[8]

This in turn accounts for the fact that, in the realist tradition, international politics is essentially about power and the competition for it. Some have argued that national interest itself can be boiled down to the pursuit of power.[9] Given that power is a relational concept, states are sensitive to relative gains in the distribution of power.[10] This poses considerable constraints on their capacity to cooperate, since the gains from cooperation are not necessarily distributed equally among cooperating states. The significance of relative gains and, consequently, the constraints on cooperation are likely to be particularly strong in the realm of military affairs (as opposed to, say, trade). Charles Lipson pointed out in this context that regimes are much rarer in security than in economic affairs, because the "immediately and potentially grave losses to a player who attempts to cooperate without reciprocation," and the "risks associated with inadequate monitoring of others' decisions and actions" were much higher in the former than in the latter realm. He noted that in this context the incentive to defect is higher, concluding that "it is this special peril of defection, not the persistence of anarchy as such, that makes security preparation such a constant concern."[11]

Given that, according to the theory, states are inherently self-interested competitive entities, and given the intimate connection between wealth and power, sensitivity to relative gains is evident in the economic realm as well. Consequently, and *ceteris paribus*, prospects for cooperation are limited here as well. Moreover, economic instruments can and will be used by states in the competition for power when military means are, for whatever reason, deemed inappropriate. Strategy, the effort to relate means to ends, includes both military and economic dimensions.[12]

In addition, most states pursue both welfare and power. Assuming that the two objectives are distinct yet simultaneously pursued, the basic realist point is that the principal objective of states is to maximize their own utility and, equally important, prevent relative decline in their own utility relative to that of other states. That is, the utility functions of states are not independent, but interrelated.

Given the uneven distribution of capabilities in the system and the uneven development of states, few states have the capacity to assure their survival on their own. As Steven van Evera and Stephen Walt have argued, in seeking cooperative solutions to their security dilemma, states do have a choice. They can bandwagon with, or balance against, potential threats in their environment. Most realists would agree that states balance against, rather than bandwagon with, threats, because this choice carries a higher probability of maintaining autonomy.[13] This presumes, however, the existence of similarly interested states with whom one can balance. Moreover, it is generally accepted that weak states (i.e., "states with illegitimate leaders, weak governmental institutions, and/or little ability to mobilize economic resources") are likely to bandwagon, because, in part, of the severity of domestic threats to them.[14]

There is a further, dynamic aspect to realism, concerning not so much the position at any given time of a state in the system, but trends over time in the distribution of power and their effects on state strategy. Rising powers attempt to appropriate resources at the expense of other states. Declining powers attempt to save what they can through preventive war, retrenchment, or appeasement.[15] One might expect this strand of the discussion to have particular relevance to Russia, given the dramatic change in its position in the global balance of power. Since 1991, its position has been one of weakness and the trend has been one of decline.

It is also worth noting that much of the structural realist literature focuses not so much on the details of a single state's approach to international relations—as I do in this chapter—as on the patterned quality of international relations in general. Waltz, among others, has stressed that his is not a theory of foreign policy; its focus is on the structure of the international system. He would, I suspect, be among the first to admit that there is a substantial range of choice for states in the international system. Classical realism is more congenial to this project, as it leaves substantial room for the characteristics of specific states and the motivations and judgments of their leaders.

My own perspective on realism is minimalist and nondeterminist. It is realist in the belief that states in general act in a self-interested fashion to further their own ends (survival, welfare) in an anarchic system. They seek to retain or expand their power and control over resources. They are sensitive to their relative position in the system and to trends affecting that position. Beyond these basic propositions, other motivations may intrude into the calculus of decision. How leaders relate means to these ends is a matter of judgment. Both dimensions leave considerable space for domestic political influences and leadership characteristics to affect the choices and behavior of states. Systemic characteristics and environmental factors constrain choice and predispose states to certain kinds of patterned behavior, but they do not determine anything.

One potential problem with this analysis and with realism in general is that of nonfalsifiability. Self-interested behavior of almost any type (viz. balancing, bandwagoning, confrontation, and appeasement) may be rendered consistent with the theory. Indeed, the simultaneous pursuit of all of these alternatives in different contexts and on different issues may be explained in realist terms. One is left wondering what the theory could not explain. I address this problem in greater detail later in this chapter, and suggest a number of actual or potential policies that could falsify the realist perspective.

THE APPLICATION OF REALIST THEORY TO RUSSIAN FOREIGN POLICY

What does this discussion of international realism imply for Russia? It emerged from the Cold War as a weak state internally. Its position in the balance of power had deteriorated rapidly and substantially. Russia's military position and alliance structure in Europe had largely collapsed while that of its principal post-World War II adversary remained largely intact. The collapse of the USSR deprived Russia of control over its immediate periphery. The discrediting of Marxism-Leninism had stripped the Soviet state of its ideological basis, requiring the definition of an alternative form of legitimation. The economy was in free fall, with a 39 percent decline in GDP from 1990–93, and a further 16 percent decline in the first quarter of 1994.[16] Signs of growth returned only in 1996–97, and these were stalled further by the consequences of instability in emerging markets in the last months of 1997 and through 1998.

Russia and the Newly Independent States

On the other hand, power is relative and relational, and the situation of Russia's newly independent neighbors, with the possible exception of the Baltic republics, was even worse. (See Tables 7.1 and 7.2.)

It should be acknowledged that, in many instances, these data are approximations. However, the point of the table is to give a picture of the relative power and power potential of the former Soviet states. There is no reason to believe that the lack of precision in data acquisition biases the results sufficiently to draw into question the accuracy of the basic picture.

The first aspect to note in this table is the sheer difference in size, and therefore, potential power, between Russia and the rest. The second is that, although the decline in GNP and the rate of inflation in the Russian economy have been notable, they are hardly the most impressive in the bunch. One need only compare Russian inflation with that of Ukraine, the second most powerful state in the region, to grasp this point.

In assessing the relative economic power of the Russian Federation in the former Soviet space, however, one should look beyond the gross indicators of economic weight and performance to examine the nature of dependencies among the constituent republics of the USSR at the time of dissolution. The spatial structure of production and exchange in the USSR greatly favored the Russian Federation. Infrastructure was routed from the republics to the center with the result that very few links to the outside world not controlled by Russia existed, with the exception of the western republics. The other republics, moreover, were (and in a number of instances still are) heavily trade dependent on the Russian republic. There is no question that Russian was sensitive to disruption of trade with the other republics. However, the impact of disruption or diversion for Russia and its neighbors was

TABLE 7.1 Macroeconomic Indicators for the former Soviet Republics (1993)

Country	Population (1989) (millions)	GNP 1993 ($billions)	GNP Chg (1990–93)	% Chg in Consumer Prices (1991–93)	Debt 1994 ($billions)
Russia	148.92	1,160	−35	804	85
Ukraine	51.85	54.2	−34.6	1,535	1.6
Kazakhstan	17.407	18.2	−31.3	907	2
Belarus	10.491	16	−25.7	846	1.3
Uzbekistan	22.318	14	−11.8	528	?
Turkmenistan	3.987	3.8	−16.2	513	?
Tajikistan	5.897	2.5	−50.2	862	?
Kyrgyzstan	4.684	2.9	−34.4	751	?
Georgia	5.682	2.3	−66.2	3,664	.09
Armenia	3.421	1.9	−56.7	630	.011
Azerbaijan	7.462	4.4	−44.3	486	.082
Moldova	4.472	4.1	−36.7	779	.2
Estonia	1.623	1.7	−36.7	445	.1
Latvia	2.622	1.6	−49.6	394	.1
Lithuania	3.833	2.9	−54.5	552	.1

Sources: IISS, The Military Balance, 1994–5 (London: Brassey's, 1994), General Accounting Office, Former Soviet Union: Creditworthiness of Successor States and U.S. Export Guarantees GAO/GGD-95-60 (Washington, DC, 1995), pp. 84, 89.

asymmetric. The other republics were in most cases more susceptible to the vulnerabilities of asymmetric interdependence, in large part as a result of the focused nature of their markets and the high degree of specialization in production.

Similar comments can be made about the balance of military power in the region. Russia possesses a massive military advantage over its neighbors. Although the state of repair of much of the equipment in the Russian Federation is subject to question, the readiness of many of its units dubious, and (to judge from Chechnya) their combat effectiveness less than ideal, the same is true of the militaries of the other former Soviet republics. They

TABLE 7.2 The Military balance in the Former Soviet Union

Country	Military Personnel	Tanks	Combat air	Helicopters	Artillery
Russia	1,520,000	19,000	2,150	2,851	20,650
Ukraine	542,000	4,775	846	204	3,685
Kazakhstan	40,000	624	133	44	1,850
Belarus	98,400	2,348	349	40	1,579
Uzbekistan	25,000	179	126	43	325
Turkmenistan[a]	11,000	530	171	20	345
Tajikistan[b]	2–3,000	?	?	13	?
Kyrgyzstan	7,000	204	0	65	3,685
Georgia[c]	?	48	2	1	60
Armenia	60,000	128	6	7	225
Azerbaijan	86,700	325	46	18	343
Moldova	11,850	0	27	8	61
Estonia	3,500	0	0	1	0
Latvia	6,950	0	0	5	45
Lithuania	8,900	0	0	3	0

[a] Turkmenistan's armed forces are under formal joint (Russian-Turkmen) control.

[b] Tajikistan has not yet formally constituted its armed forces.

[c] Georgia's armed forces are in a process of reconstitution after their rout in the 1992–3 campaign in Abkhazia. Enumeration has also been difficult as a result of the presence of large numbers of paramilitary formations occasionally cooperating with the army. The largest of these, Mkhedrioni, is currently being suppressed and disarmed by the Georgian government.

Source: IISS, The Military Balance, 1995–96 (London: Oxford University Press, 1995).

suffer the additional problem that many of their officers were (and are) of
Russian extraction. The demise of the USSR left substantial (though decreasing) numbers of Russian troops on the soil of the other republics. Leaving aside the jointly controlled forces in Turkmenistan, more than 90,000
personnel in Russian-controlled military units are in the other former Soviet
republics (mainly in Ukraine, Armenia, Georgia, Moldova, and Tajikistan).[17]
Azerbaijan is the only former Soviet republic outside the Baltics that is free
of Russian military forces.[18] For the most part, these units are far more formidable than the armies of their host countries. All of this leaves aside the
question of nuclear weapons. By 1997, Russia was the only remaining nuclear power in the regional system.

Arguably, Russia possessed certain sociopolitical advantages as well. In
contrast to many of the other former Soviet republics, Russia did not have
a significant problem with compactly settled ethnic minorities, with the
exception of the Northern Caucasian jurisdictions. While much was made
of the possibility that Russia might go the way of the former Soviet Union,
dissolving into ethnically based subordinate jurisdictions, such an expectation ignores certain aspects of the ethno-demography of the Federation.
There are eleven autonomous republics within the Russian Federation in
which Russians are *not* a majority of the population. With the exception of
those in the Northern Caucasus, they are surrounded by areas in which
Russians are a majority. Together these autonomous jurisdictions constitute
approximately 13.9 million people, or 9 percent of the total population of
147.3 million at the time of the 1989. The same census reported that some
83 percent of the total population of the Russian Federation were ethnic
Russians.

Although the war in Chechnya demonstrated that, in this particular region of the Russian Federation, intercommunal violence could cause substantial pain, the potential for effective challenge to the territorial integrity
of the Russian state on the part of minorities is very limited.[19] The contrast
with Georgia, for example, or, for that matter, Ukraine, is striking. As we
will see, the ethnic diversity of the populations of many of Russia's former
Soviet neighbors creates vulnerabilities that are comparatively easy to exploit.
One element of that diversity, in fact, presents particularly attractive opportunities for the Russian Federation. The russophone diaspora of some 25
million people distributed throughout the former Soviet Union, although
in some respects a liability, represents a significant potential resource in
Russia's policy toward its neighbors.[20]

If one accepts Gilpin's proposition that a state will expand at the expense of other members of the system until the perceived costs of such expansion equal the perceived benefits, then Russia would be likely to expand its influence at the expense of its neighbors in the region.[21] The distribution of power in the region favors a revisionist strategy on the part of Russia. Sensitivity to the possibility of relative gains by powers external to the post-Soviet space that might take advantage of the region's confusion to establish themselves would strengthen this conclusion.[22] Finally, as Russian analysts themselves have argued, the reestablishment of a position of leadership in the former Soviet region may be a prerequisite for reestablishment of the global stature of Russia.[23]

Such a strategy would seem particularly attractive since the weaker neighbors of Russia were perceived to be generating negative externalities for Russia in the form of migration that the Russian Federation lacked the resources to absorb, economic dislocation as a result of the rupture of links of interdependence, and potential spillover of local conflict outside the Federation into border regions of Russia. In addition, Russia faced serious problems resulting from the absence of established and policed borders with its neighbors. Control of narcotics and arms trafficking, for example, required effective border interdiction. There were no effective borders within the territory of the former Soviet Union between Russia and the other republics. Such facilities existed on the former Soviet borders that fell for the most part under the jurisdiction of other former Soviet republics.

To summarize, realist theory would suggest, all other things being equal, that the distribution of power weighted toward the Russian Federation and the negative consequences of lack of control over its neighbors would favor a policy of assertion of Russian power at the expense of the Federation's neighbors. Russia would attempt to use political, military, and economic instruments to control the other former Soviet republics.

RUSSIA AND THE REST

Within the global arena the Russian position was far more problematic. During the Cold War, Russia had been the core of a multinational state and associated alliance system that formed one of the two poles of the international system. The USSR was generally recognized in military terms as at least the equal, if not the superior, of the United States. Although the economic performance of the Soviet Union and its allies left much to be desired, particularly as the dilemmas of transition from extensive to intensive economic growth in centrally planned systems began to take their toll, the USSR nonetheless was the center of one of two competing economic systems in the global economy.

This position began to erode considerably in the late 1980s. Owing to internal crisis and a reconceptualization of its place in the international system, the USSR implemented a substantial retrenchment from its alliance commitments in Eastern Europe and its farther flung commitments in the Third World. The position collapsed in 1991 with the implosion of the Soviet state. In the meantime, after a recession at the beginning of the 1990s, the Western economies recovered and continued healthy growth into the 1990s. The combination of shrinkage in Russia and stasis and then expansion in the West rapidly widened the economic gap between the two. Russia is now substantially dependent on Western financial resources to stabilize its budget, and resuscitate its economic base.

The withdrawal from forward bases in the former German Democratic Republic, the former Czechoslovakia, Poland, and Hungary fundamentally altered the place of Russia in the European conventional military balance. The collapse of the Warsaw Pact deprived the USSR of its principal allies. The scrambling of former Warsaw Pact states—and, for that matter, many of the non-Russian former Soviet republics—for inclusion in Western po-litical (the Council of Europe), economic (the EU), and military (NATO) multilateral structures posed the prospect of a substantial expansion of the sphere of influence of the Western alliance at the expense of Russia. The Russian fleet was in port, its blue water capability rusting away, while the army lacked the funds properly to house and feed, let alone train, its units. The incapacity of the Russian state to sustain levels of military expenditure has had a profound impact on the readiness of Russian nuclear and conven-tional forces. The consequences of the fiscal crisis in the Russian defense sector are evident in the poor performance of land forces in Chechnya.

In short, there has been a profound global erosion in the Russia's position. Realist theory suggests that a state in such circumstances, and concerned about its deteriorating position, would seek to balance against the United States and its Western allies.

The problem was that the external balancing option was weak. The power-political advantages—from the Russian perspective—of balancing through alliance with lesser powers such as Iraq, Iran, North Korea, and/or Cuba were (and are) hard to fathom. The logical candidate is China, which is emerging as a key economic and military actor in the Pacific Rim and which has problems of its own with the West. There are other more specific reasons why Russia might seek substantial improvement in its relations with China. Notably, Russia has a long frontier with China that it cannot afford to defend. China provides a substantial market both for Siberian natural resources and Russian armaments. China is also a source for light manufactured goods and agricultural products for the Russian Far East, allowing the latter to compensate for supply problems along the west-east axis of the Russian transportation system. Finally, both Russia and China share an interest in the stability of the new Central Asian states, since both are vulnerable to the spillover of ethnically and religiously based disorder there.[24] Moreover, as the events of 1996–97 in Xinjiang suggest, China is facing a destabilizing demonstration effect of independence in Central Asia. Arguably, all these factors favor rapprochement between the two states.

However, although China's relations with the West are strained on an array of issues from human rights through China's military buildup to its trading practises, the creation of an alternative pole in the system—based on an alliance between Russia and China—would require a level of tension in China's relations with its Western and Asian economic partners that is difficult to conceive, given the priorities of China's leadership in current circumstances. China requires orderly economic and stable politico-military relations with Western states to continue its surge of growth.

Moreover, for Russia, China is as much a threat as it is an answer to the country's security problems. The demographic and economic weight of China is exercising an increasing economic pull on the eastern regions of the Russian Federation. The regions bordering China are underpopulated and their population continues to shrink as a result of emigration. There is considerable illegal Chinese immigration into the Russian Far East.[25] The difference between Russian and Chinese rates of economic growth suggests that Russia will be left ever farther behind in the economic balance between the two states. Russia and China have a long history of conflict over these areas and of cultural animosity. This gives the Chinese reason for concern over the possibilities of a nationalist turn in Russian politics and of Russian recovery to a point where Russia might once again seek to assert itself in the Far Eastern region. For all these reasons, there are, in the abstract, significant limits on the attractiveness for each side of reliance on the other. The predictive dimension of realism in this context would suggest a limited rapprochement that falls short of a full balancing strategy.

The limitations on balancing options, coupled with the decline in Russia's position in the distribution of power and Russia's dependence on West-

ern assistance and economic involvement, suggested a strategy of appeasement and cooperation. In this sense, the predominance of the liberal
internationalist perspectives of "new thinking" in the early period after the
demise of the USSR, and the close and cooperative ties with the United
States and the other Western states during this period are consistent with the
predictive dimension of realism.

Such a strategy was also suggested if one accepts modification of the
balancing-bandwagoning dichotomy to include domestic as well as external
threats. Close relations with the Western community would arguably
strengthen the Russian leadership in the face of its internal opposition. Moreover, the "promise of rewards"—the capacity to reallocate resources away
from defense expenditure and reform the domestic economy without needing to preoccupy oneself with imminent or potential strategic threats from
the main historical adversary, as well as flows of Western assistance—recommended bandwagoning for profit.[26]

It is worth stressing that this accommodation would, in theory, include
Japan—one of the principal potential sources of capital and expertise for
Russian recovery and a logical market for Russian raw material exports.
There are fewer potential longer term threats emanating from Japan than
from China. Indeed, one could argue that the development of stronger re-
lations with Japan would serve as a means of balancing potential threats from
China in the Russian Far East.

The overall problem for a realist explanation is that, at first glance, the
two vectors of Russia's expected strategy contradict one another. A strategy
of assertion and suppression in the former Soviet Union is likely to create
tensions in relations with the West, since Western states have assumed commitments to the sovereignty of the other former Soviet republics, and since
any successful reconsolidation of the former Soviet space might be perceived
by Western states to be threatening, particularly as Western strategic and
economic interests in the newly independent states gradually expand, as they
are doing in the Caspian Basin. This in turn would make Western states
more likely to balance against rather than cooperate with Russia.[27]

RUSSIAN CONCEPTUALIZATION OF FOREIGN POLICY AND INTERNATIONAL RELATIONS

The maturation of Russian foreign policymaking from 1991–96 produced several more or less authoritative statements of Russian strategy in the
"near abroad."[28] I focus on six—the Foreign Policy Concept of the Russian

Federation,[29] the descriptions of Russian military doctrine,[30] the "Russian National Security Concept for 1994,"[31] Andranik Migranyan's analysis of Russian interest in the "near abroad," from January 1994,[32] Boris Yeltsin's Decree of September 1995 on Russian relations with CIS states,[33] and the theses of the Council on Foreign and Defense Policy of May 1996.[34] As a group, they are indicative of a wider evolution in the views of policy analysts and the attentive public.[35]

Several themes run through these documents. First is the focus on state interest as the basic underpinning of national strategy. As the Russian National Security Concept for 1994 put it: "The main threat is the weakening of power and statehood, " in the context of a "fundamental change in Russia's position in the world community and in its mutual relations with foreign states."[36] This is frequently coupled with a critique of previous "liberal" or "utopian" policy for insufficient attention to matters of Russian interest.

With regard to the newly independent states, which are identified as the first priority of Russian foreign policy, most of these documents stress that Russia is surrounded by a region of weak states that are in many instances incapable of controlling negative spillovers into Russia itself. The major failure of early Russian foreign policy was its inattentiveness to the centrality of policy vis-à-vis the near abroad.[37] Citing Russian military doctrine, one of the basic dangers to the Russian Federation is "existing and potential local wars and armed conflicts, particularly in the vicinity of Russian borders."[38] Moreover, powers external to the former USSR may take advantage of Russian inattentiveness or weakness to establish strategic positions at Russia's expense.[39]

This problem was judged to be particularly serious along the southern periphery of the former Soviet Union. Turkey pursued an ambitious strategy of deepening its relations with the turkic states of the former Soviet Union, as well as with Georgia, in 1992–96. This extended in a less dramatic way to the establishment of ties with North Caucasian Muslim peoples such as the Chechens. Much of the Russian strategy in the Caucasus discussed below may be explained at least partially in terms of an effort to contain this initiative.[40] More recently, the United States has come to be seen as a regional threat, seeking to acquire control over the region's important natural resources. Also frequently encountered is insistence on the need to control the borders of the former Soviet Union in order to limit cross-border contraband in weapons and drugs, and the spread of ideologies (e.g., Islamic fundamentalism) that are perceived to be antithetical to the interests of the

Russian Federation.[41] This identification of Russian strategic preoccupations in the near abroad reveals a strong sensitivity to issues of interest, power, competition, and relative gain. It predisposes Russian policymakers toward actions to control this space and limit involvement of other powers. Together, these factors favor a Russian interest in cooperation among former Soviet states, but, even in declaratory doctrine, this is not to be cooperation among equals on the basis of mutually recognized common interests, but instead on Russian leadership and the others' acquiescence.[42] Their discussion of institutional manifestations of Russian control is reminiscent of Gilpin's discussion of hegemonic cooperation.

With regard to the West, the early embrace of interdependence and cooperation in security and economic relations was well expressed recently by Sergei Rogov, the director of the USA-Canada Institute, who points out that the Russian leadership felt that:

> to provide favorable conditions for reform at home, Russia had to adopt a foreign policy which would reject Bolshevism's ideological dogmas, not only doing away with the legacy of the confrontation of the Cold War era, but also joining the "civilized world," that is, the Western community, at an early date. Accordingly Russia was prepared to accept US leadership without qualification.[43]

This has been replaced by a deep disillusionment with the fruits of this attempt at cooperation,[44] a growing suspicion of Western intentions regarding Russia perhaps best typified in the commentary on NATO expansion, and a reemphasis on the primacy of specific Russian interests distinct from those of Western states.[45] The latter often translates—at least at the declaratory level—into advocacy of the balancing strategy inherent in Eurasianism.[46] The earlier comprehensive quality of cooperation with the West has been replaced by a far more differentiated and less ambitious agenda of cooperation based not so much on universal liberal values as on convenience and interest. There are areas in which the benefits of cooperation exceed the cost, and where cooperation is therefore desirable. There are those in which cost exceeds benefit, and where, consequently, cooperation does not make sense. This strongly resembles the classical realist approach to cooperation, whereby states cooperate to the extent that, and as long as, it suits them. When it doesn't, they don't, with institutions and norms having little autonomous impact on their behavior.

This equivocal and self-interested approach to the issue of cooperation is also evident in economic policy. Russia remained strongly interested in broadening and deepening economic ties to the West. This was cast, however, not so much in the rhetoric of globalism as in terms of Russian national interest. As the Foreign Policy Concept put it in 1993,

> Without economic rebirth, Russia cannot become a full-fledged member of the club of great powers at the end of the 20th and beginning of the 21st centuries, and, consequently, it will be more difficult to defend its own interests and the interests of Russians in the international arena.

Disillusionment with the fruits of the relationship with the West has been accompanied by increasing interest in alternative relationships. In 1993, Yeltsin himself, in comments during his first trip as president of an independent country to China, stressed that Russia's foreign policy could not be oriented in an exclusively Western direction, but had to face both east and west. Similar comments were made during the president's visit to India. The "Foreign Policy Concept" criticized the Soviet era's production of policies that tended to isolate the USSR from its Asia-Pacific neighbors, and stressed the possibilities for more cooperative relationships there as a means of "ensuring Russia's independent role in the polycentric system of regional international relations." It went on to call for a deepening relationship with China. Significantly, however, it warned against any steps that might reproduce a re-creation of Cold War confrontation in the region between a Sino-Soviet bloc and the United States.[47] It is also noteworthy that, in the section of this document on the Asia-Pacific dimension of Russian foreign policy, the discussion of relations with China was preceded by that concerning Russo-American relations in the region.

Discussion of balancing alternatives revived in the face of NATO's expansion project and also the turn in Russian domestic politics evident in the elections of December 1995. Defense Minister Pavel Grachev, for example, asserted in November 1995 that any expansion of NATO would produce a Russian search for allies, not only in the CIS, but also in "the Middle East and Far East."[48] Both India and China have been mentioned in this regard. Boris Yeltsin responded to the 1997 decision to invite three Central European states to join NATO by noting that Russia would engage China more deeply in response to enlargement.

Russian Strategy in the Former Soviet Union

The principal focus in this discussion of Russian behavior is on the newly independent states of the former Soviet Union, since this is, by Russian admission, the first priority of their foreign and security policy. In examining Russian strategy in the newly independent states, I focus on three components: Russian national security policy vis-à-vis the other newly independent states; Russian foreign economic policy in the region; and Russian policy toward regional cooperation. The first displayed an increasingly clear propensity to use force or the threat of force to expand Russian influence over the other former Soviet republics until the war in Chechnya. The second suggested a consistent pattern of manipulating the dependencies of the other former Soviet states to obtain compliance with Russian economic and politico-security interests. The third indicated an increasingly clear Russian effort to structure regional cooperation in such a way as to establish Russian leadership and control over regional organizations. All three directions are consistent with the predictive component of realism outlined previously.

Decisionmakers responded to the interests and concerns outlined in the previous section in a patterned way in national security policy. One element was the use of force, officially or unofficially, to interfere in the affairs of other republics in order to enhance Russian influence and/or prevent gains on the part of potential state and non-state adversaries. The best example was Tajikistan, where the Russian Army intervened in force to sustain an unrepresentative ex-communist regime in the face of attacks on it by a democratic and Islamic opposition. The intervention occurred in response to a request from Islam Karimov, the President of Uzbekistan, and other Central Asian leaders who had even more to fear from instability in Tajikistan than Russia did.[49] In justifying the intervention, Yeltsin stressed that, given the lack of established border control within the former Soviet space, the border of Tajikistan with Afghanistan was the border of Russia. The result has been the establishment of significant Russian force along the Central Asian perimeter of the former Soviet Union. This intervention was accompanied by substantial Russian pressure on the Central Asian states to deepen cooperation (under Russian control) in the area of border control.

The Transcaucasus provided other examples.[50] Here, elements of the Russian military assiduously manipulated the civil conflicts in the region (notably the Nagorno-Karabakh conflict between Azerbaijan and Armenia and the conflicts between Ossets and Abkhaz on the one hand and Georgians on the other in the Republic of Georgia) in order to return the governments of the region to a position of subservience. In the case of Georgia, Russian forces stationed in Abkhazia assisted the secessionist movement up to the point that the Georgians were driven from the region. At this stage, Georgia abandoned its previous unwillingness to join the Commonwealth of Independent States (CIS), signed a number of economic agreements binding the republic to Russia, and ultimately accepted a military cooperation agreement that provided, among other things, for a twenty-five year Russian lease on three military bases within its borders.[51] Armenia has signed a similar agreement concerning the status of Russian forces and followed that up in 1997 with a bilateral treaty that amounted to an alliance. Azerbaijan is the only country in the Transcaucasian region with no Russian forces within its borders, but it has been under significant Russian pressure to allow a return of the Russian military, coordination of air defense systems, and joint border control.[52] Many have interpreted Russian support of the Armenian side in the Nagorno-Karabakh dispute as a means of bringing Azerbaijan to heel.

A third example might be the Russian manipulation of the Crimea dispute to elicit Ukrainian concessions on the Black Sea Fleet question and compliance with Ukrainian commitments to denuclearization, as well as a more compliant general direction in Ukrainian foreign policy. Here the pluralistic quality of the Russian foreign policy formulation process has worked to Russian advantage. Although the government itself studiously avoided any demonstration of commitment to Russian secessionist forces in the Crimean parliament, the State Duma repeatedly expressed support for the transfer of Crimea to Russian sovereignty and supported the Crimean government against Kyiv, underlining the possibility of change in official policy.[53] The success of Russian pressure is evident in Ukraine's formal accession to the Nonproliferation Treaty (NPT) in October 1994, and the general improvement in Russian-Ukrainian relations subsequent to the election of Leonid Kuchma as president, typified by the initialing of a treaty of friendship and cooperation in February 1995 and the conclusion of a bilateral treaty in 1997. The Russian Federation's failure to interfere with the Ukrainian Government's suppression, in early 1995, of the Crimean constitution and presidency reflected not only Russia's preoccupation with the analogous case of Chechnya, but also recognition that the Russians had essentially obtained what they wanted.

The mention of Azerbaijan and Ukraine brings me to the second dimension of the discussion—the use of economic instruments to pursue strategic objectives. In the case of Ukraine, the central question was that of energy debt. In 1995, Russia was providing more than two-thirds of Ukraine's oil and 60 percent of its natural gas (the balance coming from Turkmenistan via pipelines transiting Russian territory). The critical issue from the Ukrainian perspective was Russian willingness to tolerate the accumulation of debt through the unpaid export of natural gas supplies without which the Ukrainian economy would grind to a halt. The incapacity of Ukraine to pay precluded the search for alternative sources of supply to this energy-poor economy and created a deep and asymmetrical dependence on Russia. The results were exacerbated by Russia's (and other CIS suppliers') move to world price levels for energy. Energy dependence, coupled with the termination of official transfers from Russia to Ukraine, caused Ukraine in 1993 to have an annual trade deficit with the other CIS states of some $2.5 billion dollars, owing Russia more than $1 billion for energy imports, and being in substantial arrears with Turkmenistan as well. By 1995, according to some reports, the Ukrainian energy debt to Russia had risen to $4.3 billion.[54] Energy debt was used as a lever in negotiations regarding the disposition of the Black Sea Fleet. It was intended, for example, that a substantial portion of the Ukrainian share be sold back to Russia in return for diminution of debt. Ukraine is hardly alone in this respect.[55] Between 1992 and 1994, it was estimated that these factors had resulted in a cumulative debt of the non-Russian former Soviet republics to Russia of $15 billion, or about 15 percent of their cumulative 1994 GDP.[56]

More concretely, Russia has on occasion demonstrated its willingness to use its control over energy transport infrastructure to coerce its neighbors into compliance with Russian foreign policy objectives. A concrete example is the experience of Kazakhstan. The Kazakhstani authorities concluded an agreement with Chevron in 1993 for a $20 billion U.S. investment in the development of the Tengiz oil field. Initially, the oil was to be exported to Western markets along existing and improved Russian pipeline routes terminating at Novorossiisk on the Black Sea.

It transpired, however, that Russian authorities were unhappy with their exclusion from the Tengiz development and their share of other Kazak energy development projects. They sought to take advantage of their monopoly position in the pipeline sector to extort rents at the expense of both the Kazaks and their foreign partners.[57] They also exploited the vulnerabilities that resulted from the hub and spokes pattern of energy transport in the region to coerce the Kazaks into compliance by interrupting the flow of oil to the energy complex in Southeastern Kazakhstan in 1994.[58] From a geopolitical perspective, this had the effect of limiting the extent to which Western firms might replace Russia in the critical energy sector of Central Asia, and making the point to the Kazaks that, if they wanted to get back on their feet, it would be with Russian help. Chevron responded to its unforeseen transport costs by putting its Tengiz development on hold, reducing its level of planned investment and ultimately splitting its equity stake with Mobil in order to spread future risk and inviting the Russian corporation LUKOil to take a stake as well. Russian behavior in this instance suggests a desire to extract a substantial share of the profits of development of critical natural resources in the other former Soviet republics, and to control the access of these states to the international marketplace.

A similar conclusion can be drawn about Russian behavior regarding energy production and development in the Transcaucasus. Azerbaijan negotiated for several years with a consortium led by British Petroleum to develop offshore reserves. The Azerbaijanis attempted to mollify Russia by granting LUKOil 10 percent of Azerbaijan's 30 percent stake in the project. In September 1994, negotiations came to fruition in a $7 billion deal for offshore development. At this stage, the Russian Foreign Ministry weighed in, rejecting the deal on the basis that ownership of offshore resources in the Caspian was unresolved since the Caspian Sea, as a lake (*sic*), was not covered by international laws concerning offshore resource zones. The Foreign Ministry took the view that LUKOil participation in the project might imply Russian recognition of Azerbaijan's authority over the a section of the Caspian shelf. This resulted in substantial delay of the project in question; this, in turn, interfered with economic recovery and political stabilization in Azerbaijan.

This story also has a pipeline dimension. The preferences of the majority of consortium partners were for transport in the short term via Georgia to Supsa and the Black Sea, and in the longer term via Armenia and Eastern Turkey to terminals on the Mediterranean. This option had the advantage from the point of view of Azerbaijan and Georgia of reducing dependence on Russia, as well as (in the Georgian instance) providing a much-needed infusion of hard currency to assist in economic recovery. Russia vociferously resisted this variant, insisting that Azerbaijani oil be exported via Russia to Novorossiisk. Turkey attempted to shortcircuit this option by enacting (in July 1994) more stringent restrictions on tanker traffic through the Bosporus and Dardanelles. Russia has responded with a proposal to ship the oil by tanker to Burgas (Bulgaria), where it would be offloaded into a new pipeline that would terminate in Alexandropoulis, Greece (a prospect no doubt difficult for the Turks to swallow). The fact that the Russian section of pipeline transits Chechnya no doubt goes some considerable distance toward explaining the Russian operation to suppress the Dudaev regime in Chechnya.

In the autumn of 1995, the development consortium selected the Georgian option. The Georgians and Azerbaijanis, along with their international partners, attempted to reassure Russia by agreeing that existing volumes of oil exported from Azerbaijan would continue to use Russian pipelines and that the new pipeline would carry only "new" oil. In other words, the project implied no loss for Russia in absolute terms. Nonetheless, the decision reportedly resulted in a flying visit to Baku by two Russian deputy foreign ministers who read Geidar Aliev the riot act. The result was a reversal and acceptance of the Russian option.[59] Ultimately a compromise was achieved whereby Azerbaijan's oil would travel on both routes once they were rehabilitated. The first of Azerbaijan's new oil began to flow in the autumn of 1997 via Novorossiisk. The Georgian pipeline was scheduled to come on line in late 1998. The "relative gains" dimension of Russian behavior on this issue should be obvious.

Both the economic and military discussions have international institutional components as well. The Russian government has manipulated the collective security and peacekeeping agreements of the Commonwealth of Independent States in such a way as to provide an institutional *imprimatur* for unilateral intervention in pursuit of its own foreign and defense policy objectives. The peacekeeping force in Tajikistan, for example, operates under a CIS mandate renewed at regular intervals, but is heavily dominated by Russian forces who report to the Ministry of Defense in Moscow. The CIS peacekeeping force in Georgia was installed only after Georgia had capitulated to Russia on the question of membership in the CIS. It is composed exclusively of Russian troops and also reports to Moscow. In short, Russia has dominated the military and security dimensions of multilateral cooperation in pursuit of its own strategic objectives. Where the organization has not been useful in this regard, Russia has bypassed it in concluding asymmetrical bilateral agreements, such as those concerning status of forces in Armenia, Georgia, and Armenia and military cooperation in Turkmenistan and Kazakhstan.

Similar patterns are evident in multilateral economic cooperation. The paradigm case is the (ultimately failed) ruble zone project of 1992–93. Here Russia offered cooperation in the supply of liquidity to other former Soviet states in return for the deposit of these states' hard currency reserves in the Russian State Bank in Moscow and effective Russian control over monetary policy.

More recently, Russia has been seeking closer multilateral cooperation on matters of border control and air defense with the peripheral states of the former Soviet Union,[60] as well as in the area of trade. Yeltsin's September 1995 decree on Russian policy toward the other newly independent states makes clear that such efforts—and indeed foreign, security, and trade policy issues in general—should occur under Russian leadership.[61] In short, in all three dimensions of Russian policy in the former Soviet Union, both documentary evidence and the empirical record are consistent with the predictive dimension of realist theory.

By way of conclusion, it is worth noting that Russia's capacity to pursue a hegemonic agenda in the former Soviet region has depended importantly on at least one permissive condition—the unavailability of serious balancing options for the other newly independent states. This condition may be weakening as the United States and the EU states gradually increase their political and economic involvement in the CIS states, and notably in Ukraine, the Transcaucasus, and Central Asia. This may reduce the vulnerability of these states to Russian politico-military and economic pressure. However, this does not alter the basic conclusion thus far regarding the utility of the realist logic in accounting for Russian behavior toward its neighbors.

RUSSIAN STRATEGY TOWARD THE REST

Matters are not as simple in Russia's relations with the West. On the one hand, ample evidence exists of durability in the most fundamental aspects of the Gorbachevian project of cooperation with the West on security issues. In fact, the Russian-American arms control arrangement suggests the opposite of Lipson's point cited above. The most developed aspects of Russian cooperation with the West lie in the realm of security, even though this is the area in which, theoretically, sensitivity to relative gains should be most intense. This is the one area in which Russia might be said to be embedded in the core of international relations and in which "strategic partnership" with the United States exists.

Implementation of the INF Treaty moved forward more or less smoothly. Russia is generally complying with the provisions of the two major arms control agreements at the strategic level—START I and II—despite the failure to ratify the latter. Russia actively cooperated with the United States in facilitating Ukrainian compliance with the Lisbon Protocol on the application of the non-proliferation regime in the former Soviet Union.[62]

With one critical reservation (to be discussed), Russia complied with the provisions of the CFE Agreement. It implemented the troop withdrawal provisions of the two plus four agreement on German unification. It completed the withdrawal of its forces from the former Warsaw Pact states. The Russian government on the whole cooperated for much of the period with Western agendas in the UN Security Council, such as the maintenance of sanctions on Libya and on Iraq, despite fairly substantial costs to Russia. It did not allow its reservations regarding Western policy toward Serbia and Bosnia-Herzegovina to prevent the West from escalating its involvement in that war. In instances where Russian preferences in the former Soviet region ran directly counter to Western preferences, and where these preferences are made unambiguously clear (viz., the question of Russian troop presence in the Baltic Republics), it abided by them. This behavior is consistent with the deductive propositions based on change in the distribution of power outlined in Section III.

However, there are elements of tension in these smoothly operating areas of Russian-Western relations. There were disagreements on the pace of reduction in strategic ballistic missile arsenals and on ballistic missile defense, and Russia ignored forcefully expressed Western opposition to sales of missile technology to India and of conventional arms.[63] Moreover, Russia intensively sought revision of flank limits in the CFE Treaty, particularly as these concerned Russian deployments on the southern flank. Russia unilaterally violated these limits during its action in Chechnya. Moreover, the Russian government, or elements thereof, courted significant problems in the relationship with the United States through the proposed transfer of nuclear technology and (reportedly) ballistic missile expertise to Iran in the face of sustained and vociferous American disapproval.

In the former Yugoslavia, when push came to shove, Russia did not interfere with UN-sanctioned escalation in Bosnia in 1995, the Croat offensive in Krajina, and the subcontracting of military functions to NATO in the

context of UN efforts to secure a cessation of hostilities.[64] However, it resisted, and on occasion acted unilaterally to prevent, specific acts of force
against the Bosnian Serbs, as it did in February 1994 in its redeployment of
peacekeepers from Croatia to areas around Sarajevo when the Bosnian Serbs
were under threat of air attack. Moreover, the United States and its European
allies—in escalating the use of force in the area—have had to rely on broad
interpretations of early UNSC resolutions on the conflict, since it is improbable that Russia would have supported new broader mandates. In the
context of impending settlement of the conflict, Russia continued to oppose
NATO command of the peacekeeping venture likely to follow signature of
a peace accord in Bosnia. Once the IFOR plan came into effect, they refused
to accept the subordination of Russian forces in Bosnia-Herzegovina to the
NATO command structure. Finally, Russian policy in the former Soviet
region has more than occasionally acted as an irritant in relations with Western powers ostensibly committed to the autonomy of the non-Russian former
Soviet republics and attracted by the economic opportunities they present.

The deepest disagreement between Russia and the West concerned the
role of NATO in Europe in general and NATO expansion in particular.
Russian commentary on NATO has suggested that they view the organiza-
tion as an artifact of the Cold War, and as an inappropriate basis for strengthening European security. They regarded NATO expansion into the former
Warsaw Pact zone as a hostile act deleterious to the national security of the
Russian Federation. This sentiment spanned the political spectrum.[65] As
former U.S. Defense Secretary William Perry put it, Russian reaction to
NATO expansion "ranges from being unhappy to being very unhappy . . .
This is not just one or two officials expressing a view, this is a very widely
and very deeply held view in Russia."[66] In practice, they substantially delayed
their adherence to the Partnership for Peace, and then—when the expansion
project was approved in Brussels in December 1994—walked away from
formally signing the partnership agreement they had negotiated. This was
followed by Yeltsin's warning of a descent into "Cold Peace" at the Budapest
OSCE meetings.

Although this lies in the realm of speculation, one cannot resist the conclusion that these obstreperous Russian positions on matters outside their
immediate region are linked to their objectives within that region. Yeltsin's
warning at the Budapest Summit was followed closely by the military action
against Chechnya.

Of course, his remarks may simply have reflected his rage at NATO's decision to proceed with expansion. Alternatively, they may have been the result of a judgment that to proceed in relations with the West as if nothing had happened would have courted domestic political disaster. However, this hard line in Budapest also served a strategic purpose. The fanning of a sense of crisis in Russia's relations with the West served as an instrument of dissuasion in anticipation of a highly negative Western response to impending events in Chechnya. Yeltsin was reminding his Western counterparts that a radical deterioration in relations with Russia could cause them significant problems.

There is evidence of more concrete strategic tradeoffs in Russian-Western relations. It appears, for example, that in 1994 the Russian Federation granted its approval in the Security Council for the American-led intervention in Haiti in return for Security Council endorsement of the Russian peacekeeping role in Georgia.[67] Elsewhere in 1994, Russia granted its cooperation in the creation of the heavy weapons exclusion zone around Sarajevo in return for the creation of the five-power "Contact Group" that ended Russian exclusion from the diplomatic process in the former Yugoslavia and restored it to status as a major player in the Balkan diplomatic process. In 1995, the escalation of NATO bombing of Serb positions coincided with NATO acceptance in principle of a revision in CFE flank limits that essentially gave the Russians what they wanted in the south.

This suggests that the issues were linked. Russia held back on the Bosnian question in return for Western concessions on a CIS issue. In this respect, there are grounds to doubt the view of those who argue that events in Bosnia-Herzegovina in July and August 1995 indicate a deepening marginalization and powerlessness of Russia.[68] Instead, Russia was trading off concessions on less important issues for flexibility on more important ones.

Likewise, as NATO moved toward a decision on enlargement, pressure increased for formal adoption of revisions to CFE flank limits. As the revised flank limits came into effect quite closely with the May 1997 enlargement decision, this too may have contained elements of a quid pro quo.[69] In the same vein, although acknowledging that there was little they could do to forestall the process, Russian diplomats extracted what they could,[70] including a charter in which NATO stated that it had no intention of deploying nuclear weapons or substantial new forces on the territory of new member states, accepted the establishment of a Russia-NATO Permanent Joint Council, and accepted in principle the necessity of a substantial CFE adaptation to take NATO enlargement into account.[71]

In short, the picture one gets in the politico-military realm is somewhat different from that forecast by realist theory. For reasons noted previously, from the perspective of structural analysis, the weakness of Russia, the continuation of its decline in 1992–97, and the failure of balancing options to emerge should produce a deepening of cooperative behavior on the part of Russia. However, since 1991 Russia has moved away from a position of more or less complete acquiescence to Western preferences and has become increasingly assertive in defending its own interests and status in the relationship with the West, even when these considerations impede cooperation and risk alienating their Western partners. It appeared to be using its leverage across a broad range of issues to secure Western concessions, particularly on CIS issues. This reflects the principal focus on power and interest characteristic of realist theory, but departs from the predicted behavior of weak powers with few balancing options. Moreover, it also suggests a capacity to extract concessions that is difficult to explain in terms of the distribution of capabilities prevailing at the time.

Turning to economic strategy with respect to the West, a realist analysis would suggest that Russia would seek to manipulate the levers of economic policy to manage Russia's opening to the international economy in such a way as to maximize Russian relative gain. In trade, this meant a reorientation in activity toward hard currency exchange with partners outside the CIS. This has occurred. Vladimir Popov reported in 1994 that trade with the near abroad diminished by a factor of two between 1992 and 1994, while Russian exports and imports shifted dramatically to the far abroad. This reorientation was particularly evident in the energy sector, where the ratio of exports to the near versus the far abroad was approximately 2.5 to 1 in 1991, and 1 to 3 in 1994.[72] The same redirection was evident in the dramatic growth of Russian export of nonferrous metals during this period. The export of aluminum to foreign markets, for example, grew by a factor of three between 1991 and 1993. Although the substantial involvement in natural resources trade of private actors often acting outside the Russian regulatory framework creates problems in speaking of a Russian strategy in trade, the evolving pattern appears to be one of emphasizing natural resource export as a basis for financing Russian recovery.[73]

This was accompanied by an increasing effort to control expansion of imports through duties, excise taxes, and value added taxes on imports.[74] More recently, the Russian government has implemented further duties to protect key sectors. In short, the strategy in trade appears to be one of maximizing relative gain through expansion of export and control of import activity.

The final area in the economic sphere is that of arms transfers. After a radical decline in arms exports from their 1980s levels, the Russian government has quite deliberately reorganized the sector to facilitate export to hard currency markets. Its export policies show little attentiveness to issues of regional stability and also, as is evident in transfers to Iran and China, little regard for Western preferences. The point is, apparently, revenue maximization.[75]

Although Russia is constrained in its capacity systematically to pursue economic strategies that maximize Russian relative gain at the expense of its Western economic partners by, most notably, its need for access to Western markets, Western technologies in key sectors, and IMF support of currency stabilization, the self-interested thrust of the policy is clear. This is consistent with realist analysis as it relates to behavior of states in the international economy.

Realist analysis also performs reasonably well in accounting for Russia's relations with China. Those relations display a limited balancing quality. Russia has moved actively since 1991 to resolve issues that have caused tension. The best example is that of border demarcation. This has involved Russian cession of territory to China in several instances, despite considerable domestic opposition. Russia resumed military sales to China in 1991, and by 1995 was selling submarines, late-generation tanks, and Su-27 aircraft along with the technology to produce them. In 1997, the disillusionment of both states with NATO enlargement was evident in the April summit between Yeltsin and Jiang Zemin, in which the two rejected the idea of "unipolar" domination and reemphasized their strategic partnership.

On the other hand, although political relations are better than they have been in decades, there is no substantial evidence of efforts to institutionalize such cooperation through alliance building, or of practical cooperation in wider international relations. Both, moreover, are combining their more cooperative policies with efforts to balance against one another as insurance. This is evident, for example, in the Russian cultivation of South Korea and China's vigorous effort to develop relations with the non-Russian CIS republics.[76]

However, Japan is the logical balancer for Russia with respect to China. There was no real progress in the development of relations with Japan, despite the obvious geopolitical and economic advantages. The key issue remained the Kurile Islands and particularly those that Japan referred to as its Northern Territories. Russia continued to refuse to abandon these islands, while the significance of their return in Japanese domestic politics was such that little progress in bilateral relations was possible so long as the issue remained unresolved. It is possible—though not very credible—to account in realist terms for Russia's reluctance to make the necessary concessions to move the relationship forward. The islands do have some strategic value in retaining the Sea of Okhotsk as a secure bastion for the submarines of Russia's Pacific Fleet. Moreover, concession on territorial issues may encourage further demands from other states.

The latter argument, however, lacks credibility since Russia is already making territorial concessions with China. The former seems stretched, given the diminishing strategic significance of nuclear weapons in Russian national security doctrine and the obvious costs to Russia associated with lack of progress in its relations with Japan. By contrast, unit level explanations focusing on the symbolic significance of the islands in domestic political discourse and the potential domestic costs of giving them away are more compelling. Realist theory does not help much here.

To sum up, the record of realist theory in explaining Russia's relations with major actors outside the former Soviet Union is mixed. It helps little with regard to Japan, but performs better concerning China and Russian foreign economic strategy in general. Perhaps the most significant problem is that the level of Russian cooperation with the West is lower than one would expect from a deductive analysis of the implications of change in the distribution of power for Russian policy. Notably, Russia's positions on NATO enlargement, the wars in the former Yugoslavia, and, arguably, on trade and investment are less accommodating than predicted.

WEAKNESS AS STRENGTH

Following Waltz's schema, if a theory produces hypotheses that do not pass observational tests, then one can reject the theory or refine its assumptions, definitions, and/or hypotheses.[77] One promising possibility here is a revisitation of the characterization of power relations. Arguably, the problem is that the discussion of Russia's place in the global distribution of power was excessively simplistic. In the first place, it was insufficiently differentiated, and paid inadequate attention to several areas where Russian power

remains considerable. Moreover, it paid insufficient attention to the relational aspect of power, and more specifically to Western vulnerabilities in
the relationship with Russia.

In this context, and contrary to the frequently encountered image of a
Russia prostrate in the face of American unipolarity and the discipline of
the international market, Russia possesses significant assets in its struggle for
survival and autonomy of decision. First, the Russian nuclear deterrent remains intact. How one assesses this factor depends strongly on assumptions
concerning the significance of nuclear weapons in contemporary world politics, and particularly their relationship to state power and the distribution of
power among states. The significance attributed to nuclear weapons in the
balance of power has both diminished and altered in substance. In the Russian case, the deterrent role of these weapons has lessened considerably. The
Russian deterrent appears to have developed an "existential" quality, di-
vorced from immediate threat assessment, strategy, or force restructuring.
Nonetheless, the presence of substantial numbers of strategic nuclear weapons and the infrastructure to maintain them in Russia retains considerable
significance in its strategy toward the West. Their presence lies at the core
of Russian leverage over the West, and they are, consequently, a key remaining element of Russia's national power, although not in a traditional
sense.

It is the Western—and particularly the American—concern to ensure the
integrity of the Russian nuclear force, and to prevent diversion of nuclear
materials, delivery capabilities, and the human capital of the former Soviet
nuclear weapons industry to potential proliferators that gives Russia substantial leverage in its dealings with the West.[78] So does the American desire to
ensure continuing Russian cooperation in the implementation of START I
and II and the Conventional Forces in Europe Treaty. These factors are
practically the sole basis for retention of Russian status as a great power in
the international system as a whole. Russian defection from these agreements
would have serious implications for the development of American defense
policy. This is not merely a matter of Russian state policy. To the extent that
a collapse of law and order in Russia may jeopardize the security of weapons
and nuclear stocks, there is a Western interest in sustaining the Russian state.

The Western and American interest in preventing Russian defection from
these arms control agreements—coupled with the existence within the domestic political arena of groups that consider these agreements a betrayal of

the Russian national interest—creates a potential for blackmail by Russian policymakers. *Après moi, le déluge* is a powerful means of turning weakness into strength.

In the economic realm, the matter of Russian debt is also illustrative. Russia inherited 61.3 percent of the estimated $67 billion external debt of the Soviet Union. By the end of 1993, Russian debt amounted to some $87 billion, having increased $9 billion in 1993 alone.[79] The external debt of the Russian Federation continued to grow through the middle of the decade as Russian enterprises became active on international bond markets. While these debts are indicative of Russian dependence on external financial support, they also suggest a strong and growing Western interest in preventing Russian default on its obligations, an interest evident in the repeated deferrals of debt service and extension of new credit characteristic of 1992–95, and the widespread concern expressed over instability in Russian markets in late 1997.

The gradual entry of Russia into global commodity markets created additional vulnerabilities for Western producers. This was clear in the devastating impact that uncontrolled (and often illegal) exports of Russian raw materials, notably metals, had on prices in already weak international commodities markets in 1992–93.[80] Although the general recovery of the international economy in the mid-1990s vitiated this effect, it remained the case that the potential disruption of international markets associated with Russian entry gave Western states a substantial incentive to cooperate with Russia, a factor evident in the prolonged negotiations on quotas for Russian aluminum production in 1993–94.

Russia also enjoys a number of political/institutional assets. The most notable is permanent membership of the United Nations, which gives Russia leverage over Western efforts to develop multilateral responses to specific problems, such as Bosnia-Herzegovina or Iraq. The value of this asset was evident in late 1997 during the crisis over Iraqi expulsion of UN inspectors, when Russia joined France and China in a successful effort to forestall US-led, UN-mandated military action against Iraq, and then mediated a compromise permitting the return of the inspectors. The latter suggests a further asset that may in future have considerable utility. As a result of historical relations and current activities, Russia may be useful as an *interlocuteur valable* in relations with a number of states that the United States has considerable difficulty in dealing with, not least Iraq and Iran.

Finally, Western states were (to a degree) vulnerable, or perceived themselves as vulnerable, to the social consequences of instability in the former
Soviet Union and contiguous zones of Europe. The internationalization of
criminal activity originating in the former Soviet Union is a case in point.
Most generally, many Western policymakers and analysts take the view
that including Russia in the framework of post-Cold War Europe is preferable to leaving Russia outside the status quo. Russia remains that country in
Europe with the largest population, the largest military establishment, and
the largest resource base for future economic development. A German analyst, reflecting a degree of amnesia, put it this way in December, 1995:
"The basic problem of European security remains what it has been since
the Napoleonic Wars. Russia is too big for Europe."[81] Recent economic data
suggest that the bottom may have been reached in Russia's economic decline
and that its economy is rebounding.[82] Western states face a future in which
Russia will resume its central place in the balance of power in Europe. The
question for them is whether—when it does—Russia will be integrated into
the structure of the system or it will be left on the fringes with an incentive
to challenge the post-Cold War settlement.[83]

In all these respects, Russia retains considerable assets in its relations with
the dominant coalition of powers in the international system. Realist theory
would suggest an opportunistic effort to take advantage of Western vulnerabilities to maintain maximal access to Western assistance and markets and
to limit so far as possible Western efforts to reap the strategic benefits of
victory in the Cold War (viz. NATO enlargement). Closer to home, it would
predict Russian efforts to take advantage of these vulnerabilities to restrain
Western challenges in the newly independent states and to limit efforts to
influence sovereign choices in domestic policy.

In concrete terms, while the record shows that the leverage produced by
perceived weakness is insufficient for extracting the desired level of Western
assistance in economic recovery, it did enhance Russia's autonomy of decision in the former Soviet Union. The best example was the lack of substantial Western response to the reassertion of Russian military power and
political control in the CIS in 1993–96. The smaller states of the region
found themselves without meaningful international defense against Russian
manipulation of military and economic power. Western concern about the
weakness of the current government of Russia also impeded the operation-
alization of NATO expansion and elicited a level of accommodation to Rus-

sian concerns on former Yugoslav issues and on NATO enlargement that would have been unlikely otherwise. In this sense, weakness itself is a source of power.

CONCLUSION

As already noted, the possibility that realism explains not merely the co-operative phase in 1992 of Russian relations with the West, but also the turn to a more self-interested, assertive, and occasionally confrontational strategy and limited balancing in later years raises the obvious question of whether there is anything that realism could not explain—or to put it another way, whether realism as applied to Russian foreign policy is nonfalsifiable.

There are, however, possible developments in Russian policy that would strain the explanatory capacities of the realist tradition. Most notably, Russia has a clear and unambiguous interest, given the current and prospective distribution of power in the international system, in pursuing and strengthening the network of arms control arrangements that constrain the United States, since it would lose any unrestrained arms competition. An abandonment of the START process could not be explained in terms of the realist calculus. That such a development is possible, as a result of trends in current Russian domestic politics, suggests that there are limits on the utility of realism in this instance and that realism in this version can be disconfirmed. Moreover, as we already noted, there are important areas of Russia's foreign relations that cannot simply be explained in terms of international realism, particularly the development of the relationship with Japan.

Nonetheless, the above analysis suggests that realism has considerable utility in understanding the general lines of Russian strategy in international affairs. This is particularly true when the focus is on the fundamentals of international realism, which stress that states operate in an anarchical environment, that state policy is rooted in self-interest, and that it is sensitive to the distribution of power in the international system and to relative change in that distribution.

To return to the point raised by Robert Legvold, it is true and obvious that leaders have choices when they formulate foreign policy. And it is equally true that Russian leaders could have chosen to sustain their liberal internationalist perspectives and policies of the early years. Realism does not maintain that states must follow the "dictates" of the international distribution of power. It does, however, suggest that the systemic environment predisposes the choices of leaders and the behavior of states in certain directions and discourages others. In the Russian case, the liberal institutionalist option was disadvantaged in at least two respects. The Western states, although professing their friendship for Russia and their appreciation of the positive impact that change in the USSR had on their own interests and position in world affairs, were reluctant to weave Russia into the web of institutional linkages (NATO, the OECD, the G7, the European Union, etc.) that together arguably formed a regime stabilizing expectations and facilitating cooperation in the West. The proposed inclusion of a number of Central European states in NATO and the rejection of Russian calls for a strengthening of pan-European structures of cooperative security intensified Russian perception of exclusion. Since the Russians were left outside these structures by the choice of Western powers, it is not obvious that Russia could choose the liberal institutionalist alternative in the conjuncture of the early and mid-1990s. It apparently was not there.

With regard to the near abroad, there was no web of regimes similar to that affecting international politics in Western Europe. Few states of the region (including Russia), moreover, were stable internally. Since a degree of internal predictability is a necessary prerequisite for stable partnership in foreign relations, it is not clear that the liberal institutionalist choice was present in the near abroad either. To put it another way, there was an institutional deficit in the former Soviet Union. Moreover, given the legacy of Russia's relations with the other states of the former Soviet Union, a Russian effort to construct consensual regimes in the area would be problematic at best. Consequently, and to return to Legvold's terms, there was something about "the essence of international politics or the imperatives created by states that says, at this juncture, facing the problems that it does, Russia should better pursue a Monroe Doctrine in the 'near abroad' and a *droit de regard* in Central Europe than seek international regimes and multilateral machinery protecting its interests in these areas."[84]

This leaves open the question of how these systemic factors impinged on the policy process. Although there is no space here to go into detail, they were clearly mediated by the domestic political process.[85] At first glance, the post-1993 degree of consensus among relevant political circles on the realist agenda suggests that domestic politics is not the principal locus of explanation. On the other hand, issues such as the fate of the diaspora, local conflicts in the former Soviet republics, the treatment of the Serbs by the West, the various forms of partnership with NATO, and the structure of Russia's economic relations with the West were (and are) all hotly debated in Russian political circles. One might, in fact, interpret the gradual conversion of the "westernizers" dominating the foreign policy bureaucracy to a russo-centric agenda in the face of substantial pressure from their parliamentary and other critics as evidence that their concern to sustain their domestic position determined the change in their foreign policy perspectives. Had they not embraced the cause of the diaspora and the Serbs, and had they not waffled on Partnership for Peace and resisted NATO expansion, they would have been even more vulnerable to criticisms for abandoning Russia's national interest and status as a great power.[86]

However, this is not a full explanation. The question remains as to why such issues were salient in domestic politics. If it is true that their salience reflected popular and elite insecurities about instability in the near abroad and its implications for Russia, as well as resentment of loss of status in the international system and unequal treatment by the Western powers, then one might be led to the Gourevitch argument[87] that, far from domestic politics determining unit level behavior in the system, systemic trends strongly affect domestic political processes relating to foreign policy within the units. The truth in the Russian case presumably lies somewhere in between, with foreign policy being the result of interconnected processes operating at both systemic and unit levels. The only claim being made here is that systemic factors clearly favored certain policy outcomes consistent with the predictive apparatus of realism outlined above, and that the record shows a reasonably close relationship between empirical outcomes and predictions. This suggests that, in this case anyway, the theoretical apparatus of realism has substantial power as an instrument for explaining and predicting Russian international behavior.

By way of conclusion, we should note that this is an "easy" case. Russia exists at the center of a group of weak states in an underinstitutionalized and especially anarchic periphery of the international system. Its connections to the established network of institutions and norms of European "international society" are fragile, and the military/political stresses that the regional subsystem place on Russia's changing state apparatus are strong.[88] The implications are clear. The relevance of realism to Russian strategy is case-specific in at least two senses. First, it reflects the particular circumstances of Russia at this point in its history, rather than some immutable logic of international politics, or, for that matter, the "Russian soul." And, second, conclusions drawn from this case are not obviously generalizable, particularly with reference to states at the "core" of the international political system.

ACKNOWLEDGMENT

The author is grateful to colleagues at Dalhousie University and Dartmouth College for their critical reactions to the analysis. The comments of an anonymous reviewer for Columbia University Press were very useful in finalizing the analysis.

NOTES

1. S. Neil MacFarlane, "Russian Conceptions of Europe," *Post-Soviet Affairs* 10 (3) (July–September 1994): 234–69.
2. Robert Legvold, "A Comment on Adomeit and MacFarlane," *Post-Soviet Affairs* 10 (3) (July–September 1994): 272–73.
3. As one analyst of Russian foreign policy put it: "Moscow continues to lack a comprehensive blueprint of its national interests. All too often, the notion of national interests appears to have become a fig leaf behind which various economic or political groupings—from Russian arms merchants to oil or atomic energy interests to ultranationalist parliamentary groupings—advance their own agendas." Stephen Foye, "A Hardened Stance on Foreign Policy," *Transition* 1 (9): 40.
4. As discussed below, the Baltic Republics are a qualified exception to this generalization. Russian forces, under American and other Western pressure, have more or less completely withdrawn from their territory. This reflects the fact that European and American interest in Baltic sovereignty has been greater than that vis-à-vis the other former Soviet republics.
5. Or, as one author put it, "classical realism clearly offers more scope for voluntarism than does structural realism." David Haglund, "Must NATO Fail? Theories, Myths, and Policy Dilemmas," *International Journal* 50 (Autumn 1995): 665.
6. Steven Forde, "International Realism and the Science of Politics," *International Studies Quarterly* 39 (2) (June 1995): 144.
7. For Morgenthau's situating of realist theory in considerations of human nature, see Hans Morgenthau, *Politics among Nations*, 5th Edition (New York: Knopf, 1978), 3.
8. Paul Kennedy, ed, *Grand Strategies in War and Peace* (New Haven: Yale University Press, 1991), 6.
9. See Morgenthau, *Politics among Nations*, 5.
10. On this point, see Joseph Grieco, "Anarchy and the Limits of Cooperation," in David Baldwin, ed., *Neorealism and Neoliberalism* (New York: Columbia University Press, 1993), 127: "Thus realists find that the major goal of states in any relationship is not to attain the highest possible individual gain or payoff. Instead, the fundamental goal of states in any relationship is to prevent others

from achieving advances in their relative capabilities." For the record, power is defined in this paper as the capacity of one actor to make another do what the latter would not otherwise choose.

11. Charles Lipson, "International Cooperation in Economic and Security Affairs," in Baldwin, ed, *Neorealism and Neoliberalism* (New York: Columbia University Press, 1993): 71–72.

12. On the relationship between economics and security and the need to integrate the study of security into a broader analysis of "statecraft," see, inter alia, David Baldwin, "Security Studies and the End of the Cold War," *World Politics* 48 (1) (October 1995): 117–41.

13. See Stephen Walt, *The Origins of Alliances* (Ithaca, NY: Cornell University Press, 1987). For a summary of some of the criticisms of Walt's argument, see Randall L. Schweller, "Bandwagoning for Profit," *International Security* 19 (1) (Summer 1994): 72–107. It might be objected that the balancing/bandwagoning dichotomy does not apply in Russia's relations with the Western community, since the latter is not a threat. However, it is clear that important elements of the Russian foreign policy elite do perceive Western political, cultural, and economic penetration, as well as the persistence of NATO, to be threatening to both security and values.

14. See Schweller, "Bandwagoning for Profit," p. 78, on this point.

15. On these points, see Robert Gilpin, *War and Change in World Politics* (Cambridge: Cambridge University Press, 1981), passim.

16. Vladimir Popov, et al., *The Russian Economy: Survey of 1994 and Forecasts for 1995* (Middlebury, VT: Geonomics, 1995), 9, 16. The authors note that by 1994, Russian GDP was approximately one half the level of 1989 (p. 8).

17. IISS, *The Military Balance, 1995–96* (London: Oxford University Press, 1995), 119. This figure includes ground forces, naval forces (primarily the base at Sevastopol), and border forces.

18. However, Russian technicians continue to man the air defense radar at Kabala.

19. Moreover, although the Russian military operation in Chechnya has demonstrated considerable ineptitude, the Russian willingness and capacity to reduce to rubble those who defy them serves as a reasonably effective deterrent to emulation of the Chechen challenge by other disaffected minorities.

20. For a useful profile of Russian minorities in the other former Soviet republics, see "The New Russian Minorities: A Statistical Overview," *Post-Soviet Geography* 34 (1) (1993): 1–27.

21. See Gilpin, *War and Change in World Politics*, 10.

22. On this point, see Sovet po Vneshnei I Oboronnoi Politike, "Vozroditsya li Soyuz?," *Nezavisimaya Gazeta* (May 23, 1996).

23. R Ovinnikov, "SNG ne obuza dlya Moskvy," *Nezavisimaya Gazeta* (April 16, 1994).

24. On this point, see Peter Rutland and Ustina Markus, "Russia as a Pacific Power," *Transition* (August 1995).

25. On this point, see Ol'ga Zakharova, etal., "Nelegal'naya immigratsia v prigran-ychnykh raionakh Dal'nego Vostoka," *Mirovaya Ekonomika i Mezhdunarodnye Otnoshenia* (1994) (12): 11–21.

26. The term is from Schweller, "Bandwagoning for Profit."

27. For an example, see Zbigniew Brzezinski, "The Premature Partnership," *Foreign Affairs* 78 (2) (April/May 1994): 67–82.

28. I take as authoritative official statements of foreign policy, national security, and military doctrine. The analyses of individuals, such as Andranik Migranyan and Sergei Karaganov, both close foreign policy advisers to the president at various times, also plausibly reflect official thinking on these subjects.

29. MID, "Kontseptsia Vneshney Politiki Rossiiskoi Federatsii, 25 yanvarya 1993g," *Document (1)615/IS*. For a complete translation, see *Foreign Broadcast Information Service-USR* (Central Eurasia), 93–037 (March 25, 1993), 1–20.

30. See the description of "The Basic Provisions of the Military Doctrine of the Russian Federation" adopted by the Russian Federation Security Council in October 1993, in *Rossiiskie Vesti* (November 18, 1993), 1–2. See also Igor Tishin, "National Interests and Geopolitics: A Primer on the "Basic Provisions of the Military Doctrine of the Russian Federation," *European Security* 4 (1) (Spring 1995): 107–31.

31. 35 RAU Corporation, "Russian National Security Concept for 1994," Obozre-vatel', special supplement, December 14, 1993

32. Andranik Migranyan, "Rossia i Blizhnee Zarubezh'e," *Nezavisimaya Gazeta* (January 12, 1994), 1, 4.

33. "Ukaz Prezidenta Rossiiskoi Federatsii ob Utverzhdenii Strategicheskogo Kursa Rossiiskoi Federatsii c Gosudarstvami-uchastnikami Sodruzhestva Nezavisi-mykh Gosudarstv" 9 (40) (September 14, 1995): 1–8.

34. *Nezavisimaya Gazeta* (May 23, 1996). A full English translation (by John Hen-riksen of the Center for Science and International Affairs at Harvard University) is posted on the World Wide Web at http://www/columbia.edu/sec/dlc/ciao/wps/cfd01.

35. On this point, see MacFarlane, "Russian Conceptions of Europe," pp. 250–54.

36. "National Security Concept," pp. 2–3.

37. Migranyan, "Rossia i Blizhnee Zarubezh'e," p. 4.

38. "Basic Provisions of Military Doctrine," p. 2. See also "Kontseptsia Vneshnei Politiki," 1. For a specific comment on this subject with regard to conflict in the Republic of Georgia, see *Rossiiskaya Gazeta* (August 31, 1993), 7.

39. On this point, see "Basic Provisions of Military Doctrine," p. 3.

40. Lowell Bezanis, "On New Footing with Turkey?," *Transition* 1 (10) (June 23, 1995), 41.

41. Kontseptsia Vneshnei Politiki," p. 4. Or as Presidential adviser Migranyan put it: "This leads to the conclusion that the entire geopolitical space of the former Soviet Union is the sphere of vital interests of the Russian Federation. So there would be no doubt on the question of what was meant by vital interest, I was led to the parallel with the 'Monroe Doctrine.'" Migranyan, "Rossia i Blizhnee Zarubezh'e," p. 4. See also "Theses of the Council on Foreign and Defense Policy."

42. As Yeltsin's recent decree on relations with CIS states put it: "[Among] the basic tasks of Russian policy towards the states of the CIS is the strengthening of Russia as a leading force in the formation of a new system of interstate political and economic relations on the territory of the post-Soviet space" "Ukaz Prezidenta," p. 1. The document goes on to advocate the creation of a customs union and payments union, and the development of common foreign and defense policies. In a rather revealing passage of this document, Yeltsin noted that, although participation in this process of integration was "voluntary," the attitude of other CIS members to the integrative approach he was putting forward "will be an important factor defining the scale of economic, political, and military support from the Russian side" (p. 2).

43. Sergei Rogov, "Russia and the United States: A Partnership or Another Disengagement," *International Affairs* (Moscow) 7 (1995): 3.

44. Migranyan, "Rossia i Blizhnee Zarubezh'e," p. 4; Andrei Kozyrev, "The Lagging Partnership," *Foreign Affairs* (May–June 1994): 59–70.

45. Ibid., 61–62.

46. On this point, see David Kerr, "The New Eurasianism: The Rise of Geopolitics in Russia's Foreign Policy," *Europe-Asia Studies* 47 (6) (1995), 977–88.

47. See "Kontseptsia Vneshnei Politiki," p. 13.

48. *Krasnaya Zvezda* (November 1, 1995), p 3.

49. This is an interesting example of the propensity for smaller states to trade away autonomy in return for the public good of stability, underlining the partly voluntary quality of regional hegemony. Karimov and his colleagues clearly viewed Russia as a threat to their freedom of action, but saw the instability typified by the Tajik conflict as the greater threat. They were, consequently, willing to support an expanded Russian military role in the region.

50. For a more extended discussion of the nature of Russian strategy in the Transcaucasus, see S. Neil MacFarlane, "The Structure of Instability in the Caucasus," *Internationale Politik und Gesellschaft* (October 1995).

51. The military cooperation agreement remains unratified by the Georgian Parliament. The Georgian and Armenian cases are part of a broader pattern of Russian pressure on the governments of the other former Soviet republics to formalize Russian base rights See, for example, Dan Ionescu, "Russia's Long Arm and the Dniester Impasse," *Transition* 1 (19) (20 October, 1995): 14.

52. On this point, see Elizabeth Fuller, "The 'Near Abroad': Influence and Oil in Russian Diplomacy," *Transition* 1 (6) (April 28, 1995): 34.
53. For a useful analysis of the Crimean question in Russian-Ukrainian relations, see Ustina Markus, "Shoring up Russian Relations," *Transition* 1 (6) (April 28, 1995): 57.
54. Ibid., 58.
55. In September 1993, Russia and Ukraine had agreed that Ukraine would sell its share of the fleet to Russia to redeem energy debt. In April 1994, Yeltsin and Ukrainian President Leonid Kravchuk confirmed this approach, proposing that Ukraine would sell part of its half of the fleet to Russia. In June, 1995, Yeltsin and Kravchuk's successor, Leonid Kuchma, signed the Sochi Agreement, according to which the fleet would be divided in half and that Ukraine would sell 60% back to Russia. For a useful discussion of the evolution of these discussions, see Ustina Markus, "Black Sea Fleet Dispute Apparently Over," *Transition* 1 (13) (June 1995). The issues of basing, and how precisely to divide the fleet were finally resolved in 1997. Russia and Ukraine signed an agreement involving Russian leasing of two bays at Sevastopol and a month later transferred thirty-five submarines and other vessels to Ukraine, with more to follow. IISS, *The Military Balance, 1997/1998* (Oxford: Oxford University Press for the IISS, 1997), 102.
56. GAO, *Former Soviet Union: Creditworthiness of Successor States*, 108.
57. The only available exit route for Kazakhstan's oil from the Tengiz field is via existing pipelines, at least 640 kilometers of which pass through the Russian Federation. Chevron made its initial investment decision based on assurances from the Russians that this capacity would be available for its oil. Russia, however, has failed to honor its commitments. The Caspian Sea Pipeline Consortium—which controls the relevant pipeline, and in which Russia is a key player—has presented terms that in Chevron's judgment make proceeding with the Tengiz project unprofitable. See Anne Reifenberg, "Dream Clashes with Pipeline Politics," *Wall Street Journal*, as reprinted in *The Globe and Mail* (October 30, 1995), p.B24.
58. The oil and gas fields of western Kazakhstan are connected to the Western Siberian industrial complex in the Russian Federation. Eastern and southern Kazakstan is supplied with fuel by pipeline from the oil producing centers of the Ob River Basin. There is no pipeline connection between the oil producing and oil-consuming regions of Kazakstan. On this point, and its link to Russian pressure for a share in the development of the Karachaganak gas field, see *Central Asia Monitor* 4 (1994): 9.
59. Interviews with Georgian diplomatic personnel (Charlottesville, October 1995).
60. In November 1995, CIS Defense Ministers concluded an agreement on joint air defense, whereby Russia will finance the upgrading of jointly managed air

defense systems in Georgia, Kyrgyzstan, Tajikistan, Armenia, Kazakhstan, and Uzbekistan. Moldova, Azerbaijan, Turkmenistan, and Ukraine refused to participate in the joint system. Scott Parrish, "Russia Contemplates the Risks of Expansion," *Transition* 1 (23) (December 15, 1995): 12.

61. Yeltsin, "The Strategic Course of Russia," 1.

62. Although one would hardly argue that they were jeopardizing their interests in so doing, since full implementation of the protocol would leave Russia as the only nuclear power in the former Soviet Union and would deny nuclear capability to the largest potentially hostile state in the region—Ukraine.

63. On this point, see Sumner Benson, "Can the United States and Russia Reshape the International Strategic Environment?," *Comparative Strategy* 14 (1995): 241–48.

64. In the context of the levels of analysis debate, and in particular the debate over the weighing of domestic versus systemic determinants of foreign policy, it is noteworthy that in its late stages, Russian acquiescence in NATO escalation proceeded in the face of substantial parliamentary disillusionment. Following the July 1995 NATO air strikes against Serbia, the Duma passed a resolution calling for Russian withdrawal from sanctions against Serbia by a vote of 246–0, and passed a resolution condemning the air strikes by a margin of 277–1. See Scott Parrish, "Twisting in the Wind: Russia and the Yugoslav Conflict," *Transition* 1 (20) (1995): 29.

65. As one observer put it in December 1995, "Not a single political figure approves of the idea, and the leaders of every major Russian political party, from Yegor Gaidar to Vladimir Zhirinovsky, have openly opposed any enlargement of the alliance." Parrish, "Russia Contemplates the Risks of Expansion," p. 11.

66. Cited in James Hoagland, "Advice for Avoiding Bad Trouble in U.S.-Russian Relations," IHT (10/1/97): 8.

67. This has been confirmed by interview with diplomats involved in these deliberations.

68. For example, Parrish, "Twisting in the Wind . . .", passim.

69. It is noteworthy that newly independent states such as Georgia and Azerbaijan, who balked at ratification of the flank revisions, came under heavy American pressure to sign on.

70. One prominent Russian analyst referred to this as a process of damage control. See Sergei Oznobishchev, "Cooperation between Russia and NATO: Doubts and Prospects," *Prism* 10 (2): 1.

71. For the text, see gopher://cc1.kuleuven.ac.be:/71/00/lsvarch/NATODATA/LOG9705.E.6044.

72. Vladimir Popov, *Ekonomicheskie Reformy v Rossii: Tri Godya Spustya* (Moscow: Rossiiskii Nauchnyi Fond, December 1994), 46–47.

73. Popov refers in this context to the export of raw materials as the "locomotive" of Russian recovery, ibid., 52.

74. In 1993, for example, the government imposed a 20% VAT on almost all imported goods, as well as 15–20% customs duties; see Victor Kurierov, "External Economic Relations," in *Geonomics, The Russian Economy: Survey of 1993 and Forecasts for 1994* (Middlebury, VT: Geonomics, 1994), 72.

75. For a useful summary of these developments, see "Russia's Defence Industry: Firing Back," *The Economist* (December 2, 1995), 72–73.

76. See Ustina Markus, "To Counterbalance Russian Power, China Leans toward Ukraine," *Transition* (September 22, 1995), 34–36.

77. Waltz, *Theory of International Politics*, 13.

78. It may also translate into significant economic advantage. In 1992, the United States agreed to pay Russia more than $10 billion for 500 metric tons of weapons grade uranium from dismantled Soviet weapons. Andreas Heinrich and Heiko Pleines, "Russia's 'Nuclear Flea Market' Tempts Smugglers," *Transition* (November 17, 1995), 11.

79. World Bank and Planecon data, as cited in GAO, *Former Soviet Union*, 59, 65, 76.

80. On this point, see David Haglund and S Neil MacFarlane, *Change in the Former Soviet Union and Its Implications for the Canadian Minerals Sector.* (Kingston, ON: Centre for Resource Studies, 1994).

81. Conversation with author, Herstmonceux Castle, United Kingdom, December 8, 1995.

82. Data from 1994 suggest dramatic improvement in the Russian inflation rate, a stabilization in the ruble/dollar exchange rate, a slowing in the rate of GNP reduction, increases in real disposable income and retail sales, an increases in export revenues See Popov (1995), et al., passim. This continued into 1995, despite the temptations of reflating the economy in advance of the parliamentary elections of December 1995. Inflation continued to drop in 1996 and 1997 while some evidence emerged of expansion in output in key sectors of the Russian economy, leading some to conclude that Russian growth rates had once again become positive.

83. For an interesting examination of this point, see John Erickson, "The Russians Are Coming—But Not Just Yet," *Queen's Quarterly* 102 (2) (Summer 1995): 297–312.

84. Legvold, "Comment on Adomeit and MacFarlane," pp. 272–73.

85. For a discussion of domestic politics and Russian foreign policy formulation, see MacFarlane, "Russian Conceptions of Europe," pp. 262–265.

86. Ironically, this may also have been the result of democratization itself. Matthew Evangelista has argued that one of the factors assisting in the radical redefinition

of foreign policy perspectives during the Gorbachev era was the nature of authoritarian political structure. This made it possible for a small group of experts to lobby for substantial change without equivalent input from parties negatively affected by the change and who might have effectively opposed it if they had had similar access. See Matthew Evangelista, "The Paradox of State Strength: Transnational Relations, Domestic Structures, and Security Policy in Russia and the Soviet Union," *International Organization* 49 (1) (Winter 1995): 1–38. From the perspective of this essay, the implication is that the more pluralistic the process becomes, the more difficult it is for a political leadership to ignore the perspectives of interest groups (e.g. the military) or opinion clusters (e.g. the nationalists) whose preferences were ignored in the flirtation with liberal internationalism.

87. Peter Gourevitch, "The Second Image Reversed: The International Sources of Domestic Politics," *International Organization* 32 (2) (Autumn 1978): 881–912.

88. This point recalls the analysis of the differences in the international relations between "core" and "periphery" in James Goldgeier and Michael McFaul, "A Tale of Two Worlds: Core and Periphery in the Post-Cold War Era," *International Organization* 64 (2) (Spring 1992): 467–91. See also Barry Buzan's conception of international society in terms of "concentric circles" of commitment to norms and institutions. Barry Buzan, "From International System to International Society: Structural Realism and Regime Theory Meet the English School," *International Organization* 47 (3) (Summer 1993): 349.

8 Realism(s) and Chinese Security Policy in the Post-Cold War Period

Alastair Iain Johnston

      Why try once again to test realist theory, this time on the behavior of states in the post-Cold War period, when it has, apparently, been so bad at prediction and explanation in the past?[1] One justification is that even if realist hypotheses do not do particularly well in explaining a range of cases, there is still some portion of these where these hypotheses do work. China would seem to be a good candidate. A a number of observers of Chinese foreign policy have remarked on the realpolitik nature of Chinese behavior,[2] but there is still some controversy over how realpolitik, and over the roots of this realpolitik. Adding or subtracting the China case from the number of cases that realists can claim to explain well is important for advancing IR theory's understanding of major-power behavior, which heretofore has rested largely on the European or American cases. Indeed, the question of Chinese balancing during the post-Cold War period ought to be as "most likely" a case for realism as any. With a rapid and massive shift in polarity after the collapse of the USSR, realism should be optimistic about confirming predictions about balancing from a major state with no prior alliance ties to the U.S. and a skeptical approach to international institutions such as China.

Some realists might object to this single-country empirical focus. Those who purport to rest their explanations entirely on system structure would argue this is an unfair test of their theory. They argue that their models work *as if* unit-level characteristics and variables are essentially irrelevant. They go on to suggest that even if these unit-level characteristics are different and have some effect on the behavior of particular states, in the aggregate these deviations cancel each other out. But when looking at specific cases, the structuralists would argue, one should expect some role for unit-level characteristics, since one is not looking at an aggregation of actors. So, they would conclude, don't be surprised if their predictions don't work on individual states such as China.

One could counter, however, that China is a major power, and it is major powers that should be more acutely sensitive to structural constraints (since they, not small states, are likely to be the target of rising hegemons). Thus major powers are more likely to such reflect the modal characteristics of the aggregation of the actors. This ought to make them amenable to tests of realist theory.[3] I will take up the question of whether structural realism embodies expectations about the foreign policy behavior of individual states in a moment. But the point here is that while *one* single-country test of realist propositions is not sufficient to confirm or undermine realist claims, realists ought to be concerned about the cumulative implications of *many* single-country major-power tests. If the number of major-power cases in which behavior uniformly deviates from the direction expected by realism grows too large it is doubtful that realists' claims about systemic outcomes will be right.

One of the problems with testing realist theory, of course, is deciding what it is. We often find ourselves bracketing or qualifying realism with adjectives such as "standard," "mainstream," "old fashioned," "baseline," "traditional," as though it were obvious what was meant by these descriptors. More often, it seems, these adjectives are used to avoid acknowledging the problem of realism's indeterminateness, particularly at the actor level, and to infuse materialist realist theory with far more coherence than really exists. As Wayman and Diehl argue, realism is not so much a theory as it is a "cluster of models, assumptions, hunches, hypotheses, and parameter estimates held together by their common focus on concepts including and related to national material capabilities, power, perceived power, major-power status, revisionist and status quo powers, coalition formation via the balance of power, resolve and commitment."[4]

Instead of trying to distill an intersubjectively acceptable version of realist theory, I will test four versions of realism. Three of these would be considered the predominant strains of contemporary realism and are readily identified with prominent scholars who claim to be working in the realist tradition.

Two versions of realism fall within the neorealist camp—that is, they derive their predictions from system-level variables: balance of power realism, identified with Waltz; and power maximization realism as exemplified by Mearsheimer. The other two versions fall outside of neorealism because they rely heavily on the explanatory role of nonsystemic variables: balance-of-threat realism, as explained by Walt; and what could be called identity realism, which draws on work in social-psychology and constructivist IR theory that suggests an ideational basis for realpolitik behavior.

The structure of the essay is essentially a simple interrupted time-series design, where the X treatment is "the end of the cold war" as defined by a change in the value of the key independent variable for each theory. One then observes trends in the dependent variable before and after the X treatment to see if there is a significant variation that is consistent with the expectations of the theory.[5] To telegraph my argument, I find that Waltz's balance of power and Walt's balance-of-threat theories are not useful explanations of Chinese security behavior. Chinese security policy is not reacting to the end of the Cold War in ways these theories predict. Power maximization realism provides a relatively accurate *description* of Chinese security behavior. But it gets the explanation wrong, or at least it is incomplete. China's power maximizing behavior in the post-Cold war period is not rooted in insecurity generated by structural changes in the international system. The drive to increase relative capabilities predates the shift of global military capabilities toward the U.S. direction. Moreover, although this drive persists under near-unipolarity it is not because the Chinese believe this structural condition is especially dangerous for China at the moment—indeed Chinese assessments describe the post-Cold War period as the most benign period in Chinese strategic security since at least 1949.

I argue here that identity realism provides a more nuanced understanding of the origins, timing, and content of Chinese security policy spanning the Cold War-Post Cold War transition. It does so by helping us understand two critical features of Chinese foreign policy in this transition: The first is why Chinese leaders believe that this relatively peaceful era provides a window of opportunity to increase relative capabilities relatively rapidly so as to enhance China's international status, rather than security. The second is why Chinese leaders believe that the primary dangers in their environment come from threats to the achievement of higher status emanating from challenges to the cohesiveness of internal order. One consequence is that the Chinese leadership has tried to intensify popular identification with the regime and the nation-state, with the result that we have seen a somewhat starker "oth-ering" of the external environment and a consequent hardening of realpolitik discourse and behavior.

REALISMS AND THEIR PREDICTIONS

Balance of Power Realism

Waltz's balance of power realism makes a simple prediction about a major power's behavior: it ought to balance against whichever state appears to be trying to establish a dominant or hegemonic position in the system. If ever one ought to see such balancing, it ought to be when there is such a dramatic change in the systemic distribution of power that it leaves another power in a commanding position. The end of the Cold War—essentially the disap-pearance of one of the poles in a bipolar system—was precisely such a mo-ment of dramatic redistribution.[6]

Thus, if the end of the Cold War constitutes a change in an independent variable of some type, for balance of power theory it must signify a change in polarity if it is to have any observable implications for variation in the foreign policies of major powers. This raises the question of how to deter-mine whether there has been a change in polarity. Waltz notes simply that power is "difficult to measure and compare": How it is measured and dis-tributed are "empirical" questions and "common sense can answer" them.[7]

One place to start is simply to use relative shares of world military expen-ditures as a measure of power.[8] The key question, obviously, is what partic-ular distribution of this measure would constitute different types of polarity? Neorealists provide no insights. For simplicity's sake I use Modelski's com-monly used categories: a state that possesses 50 percent or more of system-wide military expenditures is the unipole; two states that, combined, possess 50 percent or more of system capabilities, with each having 25 percent or more, are the two bipoles; and any other distribution is multipolar.[9]

The question for balance of power theory, then, is: with the collapse of the Soviet Union did the distribution of system capabilities change enough to constitute a change in polarity? Depending on the source for military expenditures (ME) one uses, one arrives at somewhat different estimates. According to Arms Control and Disarmament Agency (ACDA) data in 1987 the U.S. and Russian shares of world expenditure were about the same at around 30 percent. This distribution met Modelski's definition of bipolarity.

By 1993 the U.S. share increased somewhat to 34 percent of world military expenditures, but the Russian share dropped dramatically from about a third to less than a sixth (see figure 8.1). These shares do not meet Modelski's criteria for unipolarity, but neither does this fit his definition of multipolarity: Rather, this distribution slips between the definitional cracks because the U.S. has such a commanding lead in military capabilities over the next contender (Russia). According to IISS military expenditure figures, however, in 1992 the ME shares stood at 43.5%, 7.1% and 4.0% for the U.S., Russia and China respectively.[10] This distribution doesn't quite fit Modelski's categorization of unipolarity either, since the U.S. has less than 50 percent and three or more states have more than 5 percent each, but neither is it multipolarity, given the clear lopsidedness. The U.S. would need only a few percentage points more for the system to be unipolar. Thompson recognizes this and calls this kind of distribution asymmetrical multipolarity or *near unipolarity* .[11] Regardless of which data set one uses, however, both show a very clear redistribution of capabilities beginning in 1991 with the collapse of the USSR. In military power terms, the U.S. is the dominant actor.[12] It is obvious that this differs from the distribution of power for most of the Cold War. Thus it is plausible to assume for the purposes of testing balance of

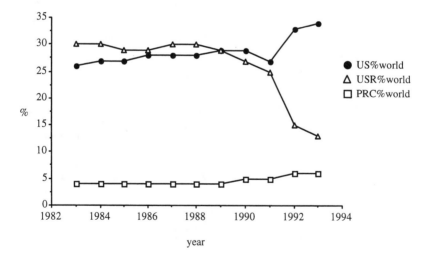

FIGURE 8.1 U.S., Russian and Chinese shares of world military expenditure

Source: ACDA 1995 World Military Expenditures.

power theory that the end of the Cold War (set at 1991), constituted a shift in polarity from a bipolar to a near-unipolar or highly asymmetrical multi-polar system, where the U.S. is the one candidate hegemon.

Balance of power theory therefore makes the following general prediction. **H.A:** In order to maximize security in an anarchical competitive environment where the use of force is the *ultima ratio* of state behavior, states balance against a rising state (or coalition of states) that is, or threaten(s) to emerge as, the dominant actor(s) in the system. China, therefore, ought to be bal-ancing against the United States. More specifically: **H.A1:** We should expect that military expenditures and trends in acquisition and doctrine reflect the particular needs of militarily balancing against the candidate hegemon. This first hypothesis predicts that China ought to be increasing its military ex-penditures and adjusting its force posture to deal with the United States as the emergent post-Cold War hegemon. As figure 8.2 suggests, however, if China is balancing internally against the United States its military spending, adjusted for inflation, does not reveal much single-minded effort to concen-trate resources on military capabilities after 1991. Or at least the statistics are inconsistent. The Pentagon's *East Asia Strategy Report* of February 1995 pro-vides one of the more alarmist estimates of real growth in Chinese military expenditures (ME)—40 percent from 1989 through 1994, or about 8 percent per year.[13] The United States General Accounting Office, however, estimates only a 6.4% real growth between 1987 and 1993.[14] ACDA figures for constant ME also suggest relatively slow but steady growth after 1989.

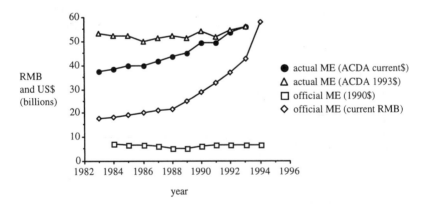

FIGURE 8.2 Chinese military expenditures 1981–1994

Sources: SIPRI

Military expenditures as a percentage of GDP and central government expenditures also do not indicate a "storming" approach to military power. That is, the economy is apparently not becoming increasingly militarized to deal with the large structural shift in power after 1991. Whether counting nominal or real military expenditures, these percentages have dropped over the 1980s and 1990s, showing no obvious reaction to the emergence of the United States as the dominant hegemon or as the one remaining superpower (see figure 8.3).

Of course, one could argue that since the dominant hegemon's own military expenditures have declined in real terms in the 1990s, the net relative change is quite significant. In the post Cold War period the United States share of world military expenditures increased, but the ratio of its spending to China's decreased from about 6.6: 1 in 1988 to 5.3:1 in 1993 (using ACDA figures). The ratio of the Soviet/Russian spending to China's dropped from 7.2:1 in 1988 to about 2:1 in 1993 (see figure 8.4). Thus China narrowed the power gap with both states in the post Cold War period. Still, this change is not so much a function of deliberate Chinese balancing against the U.S. as it is the unpredicted collapse of a major military spender, the Soviet Union.

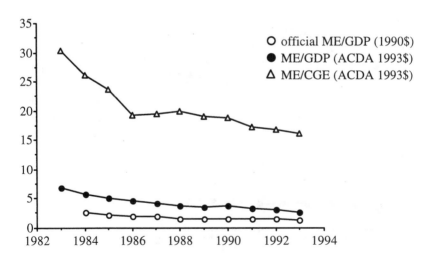

FIGURE 8.3 Chinese military expenditures as a percentage of GDP and Central Government Expenditures

Source: SIPRI

Internal balancing is not limited to overall increases in military expenditures. A balancing state could also be expected to develop operational capabilities designed to deal with potential military threats from the system hegemon. Chinese military acquisition patterns after the collapse of the USSR do not indicate a particularly alarmed balancing directed at the United States Rather the PLA is modernizing to deal with a range of contingencies from border conflicts with India, to naval conflicts over the South China Sea, to operations against Taiwan. There is some discussion in military writings on modern high-tech war to suggest that the U.S., among other high-tech militaries, is the standard that China should aim for.[15] But these trends in doctrinal thinking were rooted in the "strategic decision" of 1985 to shift China's force posture away from dealing with a Soviet blitzkrieg and toward the management of local, limited high-tech wars. This shift was reinforced with more vigor after the U.S. Gulf War, but its origins are in the mid-1980s, not the post-Cold War redistribution of power. This shift in doctrine has been reflected in the creation of rapid reaction forces (numbering variously between 200,000–500,000 or about 10–25 percent of the PLA).[16] However, these, again, are multidirectional, multipurpose forces, and training is not preoccupied with a single superpower enemy the way Chinese

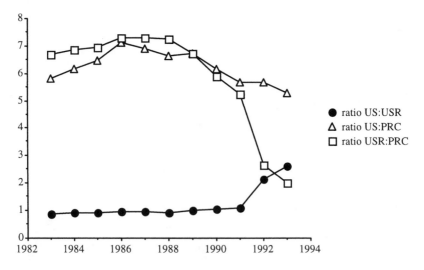

FIGURE 8.4 Military Expenditure Ratios

Source: ACDA

military force posture, doctrine, and training were focused on the USSR in the 1970s and 1980s.[17]

As for quantitative indicators of military capabilities, there has in fact been a decline in the size of the PLA, from about 3 million in 1985 to about 2.5 million in 1990. These numbers held steady through 1995. This reflects a decline in the ground forces as the PLA slowly shifts from anti-Soviet missions to rapid reaction to local wars along its borders. Acquisitions and deployment of major weapons systems also show no particularly rapid pattern of arming after 1991 (see figure 8.5), and in qualitative terms most of the weapons modernization going on still leaves the PLA a generation or two behind Western militaries. PLA acquisition specialists admit that Chinese weapons are "now roughly 15–20 years behind those of advanced nations."[18]

Military exercises and combined arms exercises at the group army level have picked up in frequency after the collapse of the USSR, but U.S. army analysts do not detect any specific enemy or contingency in mind in these exercises. Rather, the focus is on rapid reaction to potential local wars along China's periphery, and on an overall effort to increase the operational flexibility of a very backward force.[19] Some smaller unit exercises have been directed at a potential conflict with Taiwan.[20]

Naval modernization has been only indirectly aimed at U.S. power in the Pacific. Rather, the predominant driver appears to be to secure control over

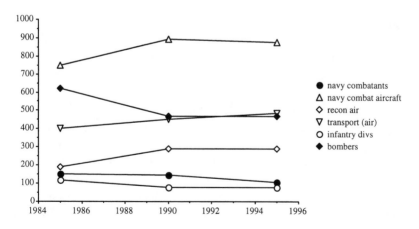

FIGURE 8.5 Weapon Deployment Trends

Source: IISS, *Military Balance* 1985, 1990, 1995

resources in territorial waters claimed by China in the East and South China Seas. A secondary goal is to be able to control SLOCs that are used by the United States and Japan. Consonant with these goals, naval doctrine has shifted from the coastal defense of the mainland to active defense of maritime economic, resource, and strategic interests. This means developing an operational capability that should extend to the interdiction of enemy SLOCs and attacks on enemy bases within the first island chain around China (running roughly from Kamchatka Peninsula to east coast of Japan, east coast of Philippines and east of Indonesian archipelago), and to the protection of Chinese long-distance SLOCs.[21] This is reflected in the somewhat more concentrated effort in the 1990s to build a blue-water surface navy. Naval acquisition is focusing on missile frigates, submarines, supply ships, V/STOL-capable aircraft carriers (there are apparently plans for between three and five of these), a fleet air arm, marine and rapid-deployment force, plus C3I, expanded berth, and operational command systems that are more mobile.[22] Naval exercises and operations have extended progressively farther away from coastal waters beginning in 1980. In the words of one participant in a 1988 conference on military futures held at the PLA Air Force Command College in Beijing, in the next century China should try to exercise effective control over its territorial waters, recover occupied islands, and "move towards international waters, the core being to seek the rights we deserve in international waters."[23] But these goals, and the initiation of this kind of thinking, predate the emergence of the United States as the lone superpower.[24]

As for nuclear modernization there are internal discussions among strategists about whether China needs to develop a limited warfighting capability to deter conventional war, nuclear war, and intrawar escalation in future high-tech local wars.[25] Possibly to this end, China is developing more accurate, mobile land-based ICBMs, and a second generation of SLBM. Obviously, the United States is a potential adversary in this conceptualization — along with Russia and a future nuclearized Japan. But the interest in limited nuclear war capabilities developed in the mid to late 1980s, prior to the collapse of the USSR; thus it cannot be attributed to the emergence of the United States as the dominant power in the system. While it takes time for new systems to come on line, thus far, according to the Natural Resources Defense Council, the numerical size of the Strategic Missile Forces has not increased much after the fall of the USSR.[26] Again, this may change if China's acquisition is guided by limited warfighting thinking (the relationship between those who think about doctrine and those who make R&D

and acquisition decision is unknown), and if the United States proceeds with development of THAAD ballistic missile defense systems. But the primary impetus in nuclear modernization has not been the redistribution of power after 1991.

H.A2: A second hypothesis generated by structural balancing theory is that states will also balance against the existing or emerging hegemon(s) by joining, or constructing, loose security alliances aimed at containing the hegemon. At the same time the state should try to loosen or undermine any alliance structures that buttress the hegemon's power. At a minimum the state should be signaling to other potential adversaries of the hegemon an interest in loose coordination of policies on the basis of the realist principle that an enemy of my enemy is my friend. This hypothesis suggests that Chinese diplomacy after the Cold War ought to be driven by a search for allies and partners with whom to coordinate in balancing against the United States

A simple question to ask first is whether China is, in fact, acting less cooperatively toward the United States after the end of the Cold War. This would be a reflection of China's identification of the United States as the emerging hegemon, and the calculus that, at the very least, China should not be accommodating such a power. A quick and dirty look at quantitative events data suggest that, indeed, China's behavior toward the United States in the last few years has been obviously less cooperative than in much of the 1980s.[27] There is a moderate negative correlation between Chinese military expenditures in constant dollars and the intensity ($r = -26$) and proportion ($r = -.22$) of cooperative actions directed toward the United States from 1984 to 1994.[28] Certainly this is consistent with the analysis of outside observers that Sino-U.S. relations in the 1990s have been troubled, to say the least, by disputes over trade, proliferation, human rights, and the Taiwan question. One does not see now the degree of strategic coordination that existed between the two countries during the 1980s, for instance.

However, as the percentage of cooperative and conflictual actions indicate (figure 8.6), the precipitous drop in overall cooperative behavior occurred in 1989, prior to the collapse of the USSR. This shift was triggered primarily by the June 4 crisis and the effect this had in souring both U.S. and Chinese perceptions of the intentions of the other in a range of other issues.

Even if the initial trigger of this decline in Chinese cooperative signaling were the legacy of June 4, perhaps the emergence of the United States as the dominant state in the system in 1991 perpetuated or injected new life into China's calculus? If so, one expectation might be that China should try, at a minimum, to improve relations with potential adversaries of the United States, and, at a maximum, to coordinate policies with them. The principle ought to be a soundly realpolitik one—the enemy of my enemy is my friend. The quantitative events data suggests a fair degree of ambiguity on this score.[29] The KEDS/PANDA data show a reduction in the ratio of conflictual to cooperative actions in relations with Iran after 1991. The pattern is similar for reported Chinese actions toward Iraq. The data set shows no change in the pattern in relations with Cuba—the small N of Chinese actions all being coded cooperative.

Another expectation from balancing theory is that China ought to be trying to consolidate relations with existing allies and strategic partners, particularly those whose relations with the United States have declined. The exemplar, of course, is Pakistan. The N is too small to say much with confidence (the addition of only a couple of recorded actions could change the cooperative:conflictual proportions quickly), but the PANDA data suggest that China's signaling has been somewhat more conflictual after 1991. Relations with Pakistan remain close as the Chinese continue to believe that

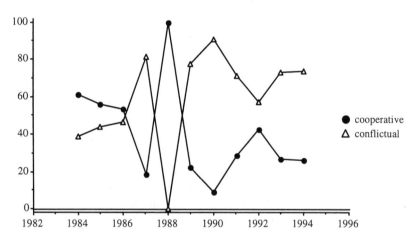

FIGURE 8.6 PRC actions directed at the United States: percentage cooperative and conflictual

Source: KEDS/PANDA (counting only WEIS scores over |1|, so as to reduce error from coding ambiguous actions)

arming Pakistan will help divert Indian military resources away from China, but in the November 1997 Sino-U.S. agreement to implement the 1985 nuclear cooperation agreement China essentially pledged to stop all assistance to Pakistan's nuclear weapons program. As for PRC signaling toward its one formal ally, and sworn adversary of the United States, North Korea, the ratio of conflictual to cooperative actions did not change over the 1991 divide. Arguably, these data have not captured a deterioration in Beijing-Pyongyang relations as China has used behind-the-scenes pressure to convince the North Korean regime to adopt an economic reform program and to rejoin the NPT, pressure for which the U.S. government has openly thanked the PRC. Indeed, while China still has a military alliance with North Korea, Beijing has signaled that it does not consider this to be a particularly hard and fast commitment.[30]

Anecdotal evidence is consistent with this mixed picture. There was some speculation in the early 1990s about an evolving Iran-PRC axis, though the cooperation on nuclear power development, arms sales, and trade, began well before 1991. The Chinese motivation is not only to have at least some voice and presence in another region (as major powers must, in Beijing's view), but also to ensure positive relations with a major energy supplier, and to maintain good relations with a radical Islamic state in order to understand better the more sensitive political-strategic issue of Islamic fundamentalism on and within Chinese borders. However, there is little evidence of a foreign policy axis emerging. Indeed, in order to preserve relatively constructive relations with the United States, in November 1997 China provided a written, private guarantee to the United States that it would avoid any new nuclear technology cooperation with Iran and would phase out existing commitments.

According to Waltz's balancing theory, we might also expect China to be trying to undermine American relationships with other major players in the system, including American allies. However, most Chinese analysts and officials continue to indicate privately a preference for a continuing U.S. security relationship with Japan so as to restrain Japanese military power, at least for the time being.[31] As for South Korea, China has moved quickly to consolidate friendly political and economic relations with Seoul — with formal normalization in 1992 — even though the ROK is a formal American military ally. As yet there is no evidence that China is trying to undermine this alliance, despite perfunctory calls for a reduction in U.S. military forces in the peninsula.

Sino-Russian relations have improved since 1991, despite Chinese invective directed at Yeltsin in for undermining socialism in the Soviet Union. The two countries have negotiated settlements for most of the disputed border areas, and in 1996 they concluded, along with three central Asian republics, an unprecedented multilateral CBM treaty placing limits on peacetime military operations along their border. China has also made a couple of high profile purchases of weapons systems—SU27s have been delivered, as well as some transport aircraft and four batteries of SA-10 SAMs; and there are persistent reports of Russian weapons specialists working in Chinese military industries. However, none of this signals anti-American security coordination. Indeed, some Chinese elites are worried about Russian-American military collusion against China. The 1995 Clinton-Yelstin communique pledging joint development of TMD systems raised concerns in Beijing. Moreover, there are serious perceptual problems in the Sino-Russian relationship, not the least of which are Russian fears that China is deliberately flooding Siberia with workers and businesspeople. Russian Minister of Defense Grachev has termed this a "peaceful invasion." Chinese exports to Russia as a percentage of Chinese exports to the United States stood at about 6 percent in 1994–95. Chinese trade with Russia accounted for about 2 percent of China's total trade, as compared with 15 percent for trade with the United States

In general, there is little evidence of the kind of security coordination with American adversaries directed at the United States in the 1990s that China developed with the United States and its allies against the Soviet Union in the 1970s and 1980s. At that time U.S.-PRC security cooperation involved, among other shared interests, highly sensitive exchanges of intelligence,[32] arms sales, the coordination of assistance to the Afghanistan resistance and the Nicaraguan contras, and American incorporation of Chinese concerns into U.S.-Soviet arms control agreements (such as the INF Treaty). China is not trying to manufacture an anti-American united front, nor is it obviously trying to undermine American security commitments to other states.

Finally, if China were balancing against the United States due to a post-1991 structural shift in power one might also expect China to try to reduce its economic dependence on the United States As Gowa argues, trade can create security externalities.[33] If a state perceives that the relative gains of economic interaction may be used to develop the military power of potential adversaries, then it has an incentive to reduce its trade with these adversaries

and to diversify its economic linkages with more strategically reliable partners.[34] Although China has carried a trade surplus with the United States
for a few years, and thus, materially, the relative security externalities are in
China's favor, Chinese leaders tend to discount these kinds of externalities
and focus on how China's dependence has made it more vulnerable to
threats to cut off or limit trade. Indeed, they have even called for reducing
China's trade dependence on the United States This has not happened,
however. China's dependence has increased over time. In the mid 1980s
about 10 percent of China's trade was with the United States By 1993 the
figure stood at about 14 percent, and for the year from August 1994 through
August 1995, the figure is 15 percent.[35] Exports to the United States as a
share of all of China's exports jumped even more dramatically after 1991
(See figure 8.7). Chinese military expenditures are positively correlated with
the percent of China's total trade that is with the United States (r = .67).
In other words, if China is balancing against the United States, it is not
trying very hard to reduce the negative security externalities of trade with its
adversary.

   H.A3: A final hypothesis is that a state's policy processes should reflect
the specific balancing calculus embodied in H.A1–2.[36] That is, if, as balance
of power theory suggests, realpolitik actors are those who choose to balance,

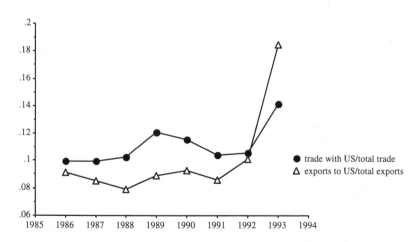

FIGURE 8.7 China's trade dependence on the United States ($billions)

Source: *Almanac of China's Foreign Economic Relations and Trade*, 1988–1995.

then we should expect to find with some high probability that the decision-making discourse reflects a realpolitik worldview, and specifically, that these decisionmakers view the rising hegemon as the target of their balancing choices. Thus one hypothesis would be that with the emergence of hegemon, the discourse ought at least to stress the need to balance against, rather than accommodate, the hegemon.

Much of the more authoritative Chinese discourse on the nature of the international system accepts that the system is, or close to, unipolar, though this conclusion is not a consensus position. It emerged as the predominant line only after the Soviet coup (which suggests that treating 1991 as the end of the Cold War has some face validity). This unipolar assessment was signaled by a lead article in *World Economics and Politics*, the authoritative internal circulation journal of the Institute of World Economics and Politics, written by He Fang, a senior foreign policy specialist in the State Council's Center for International Studies. He argued that "it must be acknowledged that the U.S. really does possess all-round superiority in political, economic and military affairs, and in science and technology."[37] The official line acknowledges, in a roundabout way, the unipolar characteristics of the system by arguing that the system is in a transitionary stage to multipolarity from unipolarity.[38]

However, the policy conclusions that He Fang and others have drawn from this transitional unipolarity are that China should accommodate the United States on certain issues, or at least try to avoid preventing any dramatic downturn in relations. As researchers from the China Institute of Contemporary International Relations—the rough equivalent to the analytic side of the CIA—implied in an article in *World Economics and Politics* in 1993, because of China's economic ties, its technological and developmental goals, and its relatively weak "comprehensive national strength" (*zong he guoli*) balancing against the United States could be very costly.[39] Glaser reported that by the end of 1992 the dominant position was that China could not counterbalance U.S. power but should try to improve relations with it. Economic reform, market access, and technology transfers all dictated accommodation, not competitive balancing.[40] In a fascinating study of about 130 Chinese foreign policy, business and academic elites in 1991–1992, Wang Jianwei even found substantial support for, or at least understanding of, the United States as a world leader, despite China's being subject to considerable bullying from the United States. Surprisingly, almost 40 percent of the respondents expressed varying degrees of "appreciation of or support for American leadership in world affairs" because the system needed a leader and the United States was less overbearing and dangerous than other contenders.[41] Even after Taiwan President's Lee Teng-hui's visit to the United States in June 1995 pushed Sino-U.S. relations to a new low, the Chinese leadership has apparently been keen on avoiding any irreparable damage to the relationship. Thus, contrary to Layne's expectations that eligible great powers should be striving to help create a multipolar system,[42] China may be vaguely hoping for the emergence of one; but it is not expending much economic or political capital to hasten its arrival or to weaken American hegemony.

Power Maximization Realism

This realism is most clearly identified with John Mearsheimer, with certain elements shared by Morgenthau. Essentially the argument is that states seek to maximize relative power or capabilities. While Morgenthau's starting point was greed in human nature, Mearsheimer derives his offensive realist propositions from the characteristics of structure. For Mearsheimer, states want to maximize relative power because the uncertainty and fear generated by anarchy puts a premium on being prepared for attack from other actors in the system.[43] Since the probability of such an attack is a function of whether the defender can credibly deter or eliminate threats, this probability decreases as the defender's relative capabilities improve. States therefore seek to maximize their instruments of control over other states. There is no *a priori* logical barrier in this realism to states preferring pre-emption, or at the very minimum superior capabilities if possible. "Since the desire to attain a maximum of power is universal, all nations must always be afraid that their own miscalculations and the power increases of other nations might add up to an inferiority for themselves which they must at all costs avoid."[44]

This suggests that for power maximization realism, states must always be essentially dissatisfied with relative position, even if all they seek is to maximize security. They want to maximize relative capabilities since this is what makes them most secure in anarchy. This is where power maximizers have a beef with defensive positionalists. The latter argue that states seek mainly to preserve their relative position rather than to improve it.[45] But to power maximizers this axiom does not really warn against trying to improve one's own relative capabilities. By increasing one's own relative share of capabilities, by definition one prevents any increase in the relative capabilities of the other, and more effectively so. Given the fear generated by uncertainty under anarchy, it makes little sense only to try to freeze the status quo in relative capabilities; one can never be sure the other side will be content with the status quo. This means that, *ceteris paribus*, states will prefer to maximize offensive, power projection capabilities.

What, then, is the critical structural independent variable for power maximization realism? One could argue that, in principle, there should be no obvious variation in the interest in improving improve relative capabilities.[46] That is, it should be a constant feature of state policy. But the ability to realize this interest is affected by at least two exogenous material constraints: the drain on resources that this single-minded pursuit to improve relative capabilities brings; and the probability that these efforts might compel a counter-coalition to form. We should expect to see the pace of power maximization to pick up as these costs decline, which will happen when other states are unable or unwilling to race or coalesce.[47] The state will then exploit this opportunity to rapidly increase relative capabilities. Thus one should expect that in periods where other states are reducing their military capabilities, the state should increase its efforts to improve its own. Alternatively, a change in the systemic power distribution toward unipolarity might provoke power maximizing behavior. Even though the costs of this behavior may be quite high (given a state is "racing" with a unipole), the costs of not balancing against the unipolar are potentially very high as well.[48]

Power maximization realism would therefore make the following general prediction: **H.B.** States act primarily to increase their relative military power. More specifically: **H.B1**: a state will increase its military spending and step up the development of power projection capabilities when the opportunity to improve relative capabilities is low cost (e.g., when others are standing still or reducing their relative capabilities). Power maximization realism arguably allows for enough intentionality in the behavior of units such that they will calculate strategically to exploit opportunities for improving relative capabilities. Gilpin, for one, argues that differential rates of growth in power have a dynamic effect on state behavior by altering the "cost of changing the international system, and therefore the incentives to changing the international system."[49] Did, then, the end of the Cold War constitute a change in this cost for China, and if so a change in which direction?

Arguably, the collapse of the Soviet Union reduced this cost to China quite dramatically. For one thing it reduced the Russian ability to race the Chinese and to preserve existing ratios in capabilities. Indirectly, as well, the

Russian ability to maintain existing capabilities ratios was constrained by a series of bilateral arms control agreements with the United States in the late 1980s (e.g., INF, START). For another it marked the end of a period of relatively sizable increases in U.S. military spending, and it saw the retrenchment of the military industrial complex as U.S. political leaders searched for a peace dividend.

Finally, the collapse of the USSR constituted the end of bipolarity. While the United States at present constitutes the predominant military power, according to Layne other players ought to be working especially hard to prevent the consolidation of U.S. hegemony. Thus with end of the Russian and American competition, and with the limited success in U.S. Congressional efforts to consolidate U.S. hegemony by increasing military expenditures in an era of low threats, the Chinese have both a window of opportunity and an extra incentive to increase their share of world capabilities in a relatively short period. Both factors are products of changes in global distributions of power after 1991.

Hypothesis **H.B1** therefore suggests that the recent upturn in Chinese military expenditures ought to be due primarily to the reduced costs of "racing" with Russia and the United States. Moreover, internal maximization strategies are more realistic now, given the payoffs from economic growth in the 1980s. The same data used to test **H.A1** applies here. If the post-1991 period presents a window of opportunity to shift substantially more resources in the military's direction, the ME/GDP and ME/CGE data suggest this is not being exploited with much fervor. Additionally, this increase in ME began prior to the collapse of the USSR—that is, prior to the opening of this window. The pace of these improvements has generally not picked up much with the collapse of the Soviet Union, as the figures on military procurement indicate. In those areas where acquisition has increased since 1991, it is not clear these will be sustained. For instance, one quick fix to close the relative capabilities gap would be to rely on arms imports. According to SIPRI, however (using a composite measure of cost, lethality, and technical sophistication), there was a sharp jump in the arms imports index in 1992, accounted for primarily by China's acquisition of SU-27s and SAMs, but the figures for 1993 and 1994 were much lower, suggesting this may have been a one-time jump.

In short, as I noted in the discussion of **H.A1**, the motivation for the slow but steady modernization of Chinese military capabilities—particularly its power projection forces—is more consistent with the desire to improve relative power than it is with the goal of balancing the system hegemon. But the pace of military modernization seems slower than power maximization might expect.

H.B2: unilateral efforts to improve relative capabilities will be supplemented by efforts to build a coalition to help the state's relative capabilities improve (e.g., by providing technology, military assistance, or support for cooperative arrangements that constrain the relative power of others). It will, however, be sensitive to the costs this coordination carries for the autonomy of the state. These coalitions will be loose, with low levels of mutual coordination.

The evidence for this hypothesis is essentially similar to that for **H.A2**. China is not obviously trying to construct an anti-American united front; it has improved relations with American allies in East Asia, and it would, for the most part, prefer to maintain stable political, military and economic relations with the United States One might be able to argue from a power maximization position that China ought to be trying to maintain relatively good relations with the United States so as not to provoke a militarized response that increases the cost to China of arming, or that shuts the Chinese off from to the economic and technological benefits of the U.S. market. But power maximization theory suggests states will guard their autonomy carefully, and thus might be reluctant to become to closely entwined economically with a potential adversary.

H.B3: There should be evidence in the policy process that is consistent with general calculus embodied in **H.B1–2**. Decisionmakers therefore ought to see or portray the international system as anarchical, in which unitary actors pursuing the maximization of power are locked into competitive relationships that lead most often to conflict. Decisionmakers also ought to be arguing that in such a world it is best to maximize relative capabilities.

Arguably many Chinese officials and analysts do indeed accept that the nature of world politics is essentially zero-sum and that competition is the primary feature of the system. As one recent article in the authoritative internal circulation journal, *World Economics and Politics*, put it, systemic anarchy renders all interdependence asymmetric, and asymmetric relationships are essentially ones involving zero-sum power political struggles. As long as gains are asymmetric, the basis for conflict exists. Interdependence can accentuate interstate conflict by trampling on the sovereignty of nation-states, by preventing them from controlling their economic, military and political resources, and by providing opportunities for states to interfere in the internal affairs of others. The basic characteristic of the international system, therefore, is that states pursue short-term benefits by adopting policies harmful to others.[50]

It is interesting to note that in Chinese-language analyses, particularly after the collapse of the USSR, one rarely sees the term "new world order" (*shijie xin zhixu*) to describe the Chinese leaders' normative vision of world politics (see figure 8.8).[51] Rather the preferred term is "new international order" (*guoji xin zhixu*). The former connotes a system in which a hegemon is the primary impetus behind this order.[52] Moreover, a new *world* order connotes a system of interstate norms which undermines state sovereignty, ostensibly in the search for cooperative solutions to global problems. In a new *international* order, however, the sovereign state remains the unit of analysis, and the primary objective of this order is to preserve the sovereignty and independence of states.[53]

This does not mean that the system is imminently dangerous, only that states should be prepared for potential threats. Indeed, some analysts explicitly identify the relatively benign security environment of the 1990s as precisely the one in which China can make strides in narrowing the military gap with other major powers without having to divert resources away from economic development. As weapons experts in the military wrote, "The rela-

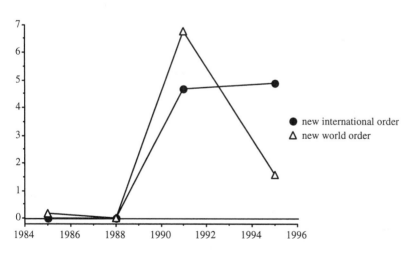

FIGURE 8.8 Average frequency of terms per article in *Shijie jingji yu zhengzhi*, 1985–1995.

tively peaceful international climate and our friendly relations with our neighbors are providing fine external conditions for PLA weapons development."[54] As an internal circulation 1993 book for military cadres stressed in reference to the navy,

> At present our navy faces a tremendous opportunity for development that is has not had before: the international environment is moving toward detente, the national economy is in the midst of rapid development, the reform and opening policy has become a state policy, the people's "ocean consciousness" is in the process of strengthening, the Central Military Commission has given a great deal of attention to the development and construction of the navy, and the development and expansion of the navy has received the understanding and support of knowledgeable people in all spheres of life.[55]

On balance, Chinese behavior appears to be more consistent with power maximization realism than with balance-of-power realism. In particular, China's goal in its security policy is more consistent with the desire to maximize relative capabilities as insurance in a potentially dangerous world than it is with the intention to balance against a rising hegemon.

I am leery, however, of jumping to the conclusion that power maximization realism has been confirmed. The main problem has to do with the motivation behind Chinese power maximizing behavior. In this version of realism the driving force behind state behavior is ultimately fear of insecurity in an anarchical environment. Long-term interests and goals are exogenous (security in an anarchical world) while shorter term goals and interests (the means to these long-term goals) are endogenous, shaped by particular power distributions and the opportunities these present for power maximizing behavior. The problem is that in the Chinese case a critical driver of its long-term goals is not security *per se* but status. Indeed, elements of Chinese realpolitik are sometimes put almost as a conscious choice. Writing in 1988, one analyst at a military conference on East Asian strategy noted, "In the early 21st century we must utilize the Soviet-U.S. detente, and the advantageous opportunities presented by their partial retreat from the Asia-Pacific region, to speed up the development of our diplomacy, throw off the limitations of ideology, adopt flexible diplomacy and gradually expand our country's influence, increase our status and effectiveness in the Asia-Pacific region."[56]

The status arguments behind power maximization are explicit and implicit in internal discussions about why China needs nuclear weapons, why
it needs aircraft carriers, and why it needs to control the South China Sea.
In each of these cases a powerful argument is that these are signs that China
has "stood up" in world affairs. Indeed, Chinese foreign policy discourse
since 1949 has been replete with status-related language,[57] and foreign policy
behavior since 1949 has been aimed, in part, at protecting "national self-
respect" (*minzu zizun*), at enhancing China's "international position" (*guoji
diwei*).[58] The most visceral, hence deeply ingrained, emotional reaction to
Western criticism of China's record on human rights or its foreign policy
behavior, is usually a heartfelt recitation of the 100 years of humiliation that
China suffered at the hands of Western imperialism, including the loss of
territory through "unequal treaties." Thus when Chinese leaders and analysts
talk about the post Cold War period being the most advantageous for China
since 1949 (*zui you li de guoji huanjing*) this is not simply a reference to
the relatively low level of security threats, but also to China's influence in
international institutions and in world economics and politics in general.[59]
    This drive for status is not directly structurally determined. It may be a
product of structure at time t, but its persistence at time t + 1 is independent
of structural conditions (e.g., China's drive for major-power status has been
a persistent policy goal of leaders inherited from the legacy of weakness in
the face of imperialism in the nineteenth century). It is this historically
generated, ideationally propelled and politically institutionalized interpretation of China's place in international politics that explains the persistence
of power maximization behavior, independent of a structurally determined
drive for security. The disconnect between structural threat and/or structural
opportunity to increase relative capabilities is illustrated by Deng's remark
in 1984 that if China could quadruple its national wealth by the end of the
century, it could devote more resources to military capabilities.[60] A major
policy study commissioned by the State Council in 1984, called "China
2000," was explicit that in the 1990s more resources would be devoted to
the PLA and to hinterland development.[61] It is hard to say to what degree
the study is still guiding the state's development strategy. But the point of
both examples is that regardless of broad structural transformations in the
international system, Chinese leaders have taken it for granted that China
needs to increase its military power in the not-too-distant future.[62]
    Some Chinese strategists now also speak of the need for "survival space"
(*sheng cun kongjian*) and for strategic frontiers that extend horizontally into

the Indian Ocean, the South China Sea, the East China Sea, and vertically into space. But they have spoken of these "soft frontiers" at least since 1987, and not specifically in reaction either to U.S. hegemony or post-Cold War opportunities to increase relative capabilities for security reasons.[63] Advocates of naval modernization and the development of the "near ocean defense strategy" (*jin hai fangyu zhanlue*) speak not only of protecting shipping lanes, fishing grounds, and SLOCs, but also of increasing China's "national awesomeness" (*guo wei*) and expanding its "political influence" (*zhengzhi yingxiang*).[64] As some proponents of naval modernization have put it: "If we are to be a world great power, we must not merely cast our eyes at the continental land, but must also look toward the oceans, and we must have a strong "ocean consciousness" [*haiyang guan*]. If we don't have a strong and powerful ocean force, it is very difficult to enter the ranks of the world's powerful states."[65]

Status is not unrelated to security, of course. Status buys deference to one's interests; it buys access to states and international institutions. But as Schweller points out, there are states that have revisionist tendencies not because the present structures make them insecure, but because the present structures do not allow them to appropriate other goods (e.g., status and deference).[66] In China's case, there is a fair degree of evidence that, at the moment, it is not security maximizer, but a "prestige maximizer."[67]

How serious the damage, then, to power maximization theory if it gets the motivation for China's power maximizing behavior wrong? I think it is quite serious since it means that the theory gets a basic prediction, **H.B1**, wrong: immediate security fears are not the the obvious driving force behind China's military policies in the 1990s, and the opportunities to improve relative capabilities with the collapse of the USSR emerged *after* China began to increase its military expenditures and power projection forces.

Balance-of-Threat Realism

Balance-of-threat theory, as developed by Walt, predicts that states will balance against the primary threat as defined by aggregate power, geographic proximity, offensive power, and aggressive intentions (a component of which is ideology that may affect perceptions of enemy intentions). The primary threat may or may not be the dominant power in the system.

The theory is fairly indeterminate, however. For one thing, as Walt acknowledges, it does not provide any *a priori* aggregate weighting system for the four key variables. Each variable could lead to predictions about behavior that contradicted the other.[68] This raises problems of falsifiability. For another, virtually any perception of threat drives the model, and the threat need not be to strategic/territorial interests, as is the focus of traditional realism. Threat can mean threat to the domestic politics and the internal legitimacy of a regime.[69] Again this introduces a great deal of indeterminacy into the theory, since if one finds balancing behavior in the absence of a military threat to the territorial integrity or strategic interests of a state, one can always claim that the threat is in fact to the internal legitimacy of the state, an altogether more subjective, flexible, hence manipulable definition of threat. To make the theory testable, then, I think it has to define threat in more "traditional" realist terms—as a military threat to the territorial integrity or military security of the state. Threats to the legitimacy of the regime may be derivative of strategic threats, but they should not be included in an amorphous independent variable.

Finally, Walt's theory is not clear about what happens when when one threat ends or declines. Is it necessarily succeeded by another? Do states require or expect that one threat will be followed by another? Balance-of-power theory suggests there is a constant shifting of the target of balancing: once one hegemon is balanced against, then the system balances against the initial balancing state or coalition.[70] But Walt is unclear about this. If threats are constructed—that is if we assume, as I think Walt has to, that the crucial variable is threat *perception*—which interprets the meaning of military power, geographic proximity, and offensive doctrines—then the replacement of an old threat by a new one is not automatic. So once the threat disappears, balancing behavior should cease.[71]

H.C: The general prediction is that states balance against the primary threat. Thus with the collapse or end of that threat (in the absence of the appearance of another) we should see the end of balancing behavior until another threat emerges.

This first step in testing this this general hypothesis, and its derivatives, is to show that variation in Chinese internal and external balancing behavior is consistent with variation in *perceptions* of the primary threat (either the disappearance of the old threat and/or the appearance of a new one). There is little doubt that the collapse of the USSR signaled the end of a long-standing military threat to China, and the major impetus behind China's force posture and alliance behavior from the late 1960s through the late 1980s. The question is whether Beijing sees newer and imminent threats at present or over the horizon. The evidence on this is ambiguous. Perhaps indicative of this, a major PLA conference consisting of a wide range of strategic and operational analysis institutions held in late 1993 to determine precisely this question came to a range of estimates. According to Hong Kong reports of the conference, about 60 percent of the attendees believed primary threat in the next century will be Japan, 40 percent believed it would be the United States, while 10 percent thought it would be a resurgent Russia.[72]

Nonmilitary analysts seem divided as well. During the sharp downturn in relations in mid 1995, some analysts apparently concluded that U.S. policy was determined to keep China divided and weakened, to prevent it from challenging U.S. hegemony.[73] Others have observed, however, that American foreign policymakers are not engaged in a monolithic conspiracy to contain, divide, and weaken China, but are themselves being buffeted about by conflicting domestic interests, the division of powers, and other peculiar features of U.S. policy process.[74] While some hardline analysts believe that the United States is trying to encircle China—*vide* U.S. efforts to control political and economic reform in Russian, U.S.-Vietnamese normalization, American promotion of multilateral security institutions in East Asia, improved U.S.-Indian relations, the promotion of Taiwanese efforts to increase their international status[75]—even they are willing to concede that this strategy is largely political and economic in nature: "If one looks at it from a purely military security angle, [the United States] does not constitute a realistic threat."[76] The general assessment that China operates in the most benign strategic environment since 1949 still stands.

If the perceived threat is not clear, or as Chinese leaders proclaim, relatively low, then according to balance-of-threat theory we should not expect to see much internal or external balancing. On this score the evidence suggests this version of realism does not do a particularly good explanatory job.

H.C1: As the threat declines or disappears a state will slow down, stop, or reverse the rate of growth in its military expenditures and in its development of any power projection capabilities that could be used against the former threat.[77] Arguably this hypothesis is disconfirmed by the continued, if moderate, real growth in Chinese military expenditures and military power projection capabilities in the 1990s. Of course, these power resources are not necessarily directed at Russia, but they could well be. They could be used against Russian capabilities in East Asia, Central Asia, or against Russia itself. More generally, however, military modernization is directed at multiple possible contingencies, one of which is considered imminent (anti-Taiwan operations).

H.C2: As the threat declines or disappears, a state will withdraw from, or cease seeking alliances that aggregate capabilities, and will draw down efforts to break apart existing or real coalitions that favor the former threat. Consistent with this proposition, given the collapse of the Soviet threat, China is no longer trying to build a united front directed at Russia, as it did in the 1970s and 1980s. Given that there is no consensus yet as to the degree to which the United States constitutes a clear strategic security threat, we should also not expect to see alliance building against it. And indeed, as I noted, despite problems in the Sino-U.S. relationship the Chinese are still interested in developing closer military ties with the United States, in part to acquire technology, training, information about command and control and operations through these exchanges.

The problem for the theory is that it is not clear that the end of the Cold War *per se* had much to do with this diffusion of potential targets of Chinese military power. On the one hand, though Soviet threat was, in the Chinese view, declining somewhat over the 1980s, this was debated inside China well into the Gorbachev period. His reforms were viewed as an effort to restore Russia's ability to vie for hegemony and China was still a potential target. In this sense, the collapse of USSR in 1991 could be viewed as the critical change in the independent variable. Indeed, sometimes the Chinese discourse will speak of the end of the Cold War and the breakup of the Soviet Union in the same breath. On the other hand, Sino-Soviet relations were "normalized" in 1989. The Soviets unilaterally met China's conditions for normalization, and in doing so reduced the operational military threat against China (e.g., by withdrawing forces from Mongolia). U.S.-Soviet arms control, particularly the INF agreement, also improved China's security. All of these changes preceded 1991. So, as the theory predicts, the decline in the threat has led to a decline in external balancing efforts and a diffusion of internal balancing efforts. But it is not clear that the decline of this threat and the end of the Cold War are the same thing.

H.C3: As the threat declines or disappears, so does the assessment of threat in policy process. Since this theory relies heavily on subjective judgments about threat (given the potential role of ideology in defining threat), it is even more important for its validity that ideas and discursive practices are consistent with behavior. Indeed, in this theory these practices are at times causal, not ephiphenomal.

There is no doubt that Chinese threat assessments are consistent with an end to the Soviet threat. Chinese commentary on its relatively friendly external environment is not just public posturing: internal circulation papers written by top analysts in the intelligence and foreign policy communities generally endorse this assessment as well.[78] The problem for the theory is that if Chinese leaders were balancing against threats, the discourse would be inconsistent with the behavior outline in **H.C1**. That is, even though China's threat environment is relatively benign, its internal balancing behavior in particular is inconsistent with the behavior the theory predicts given this change in environment. If the behavior were consistent with the discourse, one might expect to see Chinese leaders arguing in favor of slowing down the military modernization program, now that threats have declined.

Identity Realism

This form of realism has heretofore been unexplicated in any detail, but it flows from work in social constructivism and social psychology on group identity formation and intergroup conflict. Much of this disparate literature essentially holds that the creation of in-group identities leads directly to the devaluation of out-groups. This in turn leads to competitive interpretations of the relationship with the out-group. The creation of and intensification of group identities, then, positively correlates with the degree of competitiveness with the out-group.[79] Thus the initial motivation for self-help behavior is not the survival of the group (state) but its creation.

The literature is murky about the reasons for this out-group devaluation, however. Some explanations rest on individual material interest.[80] But Kinder and Sears's work on racial prejudice shows that the devaluation of the out-group is not obviously interest-driven among most members of the group. Put another way, the in-group does not resent or distrust the out-group because of some tangible threat to in-group's interests (as neorealism/realism would posit, whether because the out-group is a predator or is structurally compelled to compete). Rather it is socialized and learned—whether or not a tangible threat exists—and is reinforced by pressures to conform. In symbolic racism the cognitive structure of this devaluation is based on dramatically differentiating the values of in-group and those of out-group: the other is seen as morally unalike (e.g., blacks are lazy, criminal, don't work hard, are unpatriotic etc, among other stereotypes).[81] The cognitive structure of nationalism and nation-state identity is probably akin to symbolic racism in its normative condemnation of the other. That is, identity creation must be based on stereotypes of self and other, not just on evidentiary-based arguments about conflicting material interests. The persistence of the former in the absence of the latter suggests identity construction is not epiphenomenal to the state's need to mobilize resources in a given competitive anarchy (just as the persistence of symbolic racism even when no concrete interests are threatened by blacks suggests that racial conflict is a constructed, not an economic, fact). Rather the causal arrows run the other way: identity construction, and its intensity, determine anarchy and how much fear and competition results. Applied to international relations, then, the literature would suggest that changing intensities of in-group identity affect the degree of outwardly directed realpolitik behavior, regardless of changes in structural environment.[82] Moreover, variation in in-group intensity will explain variation in the targets of this realpolitik. That is, weak or porous in-group identification provides greater cognitive space for identifying, at least in part, with other groups. To the extent that identity expands to these groups, they no longer serve as logical targets of realpolitik behavior.[83]

In sum, if there is an increase in the intensity of identity—or efforts to intensify identification—we should expect to see more competitive behavior directed at the out-group. As the boundaries of the in-group expand or contract we should expect a change in the degree of competitive behavior directed at the those actors comprising the old in-groups and out-groups at time t.

What might an identity explanation of realpolitik consider to be the critical independent variable explaining this initial variation in intensity of identity? Unfortunately there is no clear guidance from either the social psychology literature or constructivist work in IR theory. One obvious possibility that flows from the symbolic basis of identity is as follows: a threat to the legitimacy of the in-group's composition, or to forms of legitimate organization, or to its cohesion and its values, rather than specifically to the material interests of the group, leads to efforts to shore up in-group identity. Thus threats to the in-group will vary depending on self-evaluations of the content of the primary valuations of the group. Put another way, identities have two elements: The first is the group specific values associated with the self-perceived role of the group—the content of identity. The second is the cross-group tendency to devalue out-groups. The specific content of the identity will tell the group what it ought to value, and thus how to define what and who threatens its integrity. The second element tells the group how it ought to react to these threats, namely in a realpolitik fashion. Thus competitive strategies will be adopted toward threats that are determined by the specific content or legitimacy of the (predominant) identity. The content of in-group identity is not given by position in the international system, as essentially structural realism would argue: indeed, empirically this content varies far too much across states similarly and differently positioned for it to be determined by material structures. Democratic identities shared by members of a European security community are provided neither by anarchy nor by different distributions of power under anarchy.

This does not mean that identity realism ignores material, structural variables. Identity realism acknowledges that structural variables—namely changes in relative capabilities—are important steps in predicting state behavior. But these are important because the realpolitik ideology that is a creation of in-group formation interprets changes in relative capabilities in particular ways. Identity creation makes a group sensitive to relative capabilities only to the extent that, given the prior content of the group's identity, the group believes it is in a competitive relationship with an out-group. But the logic of the argument suggests that this sensitivity varies as intensity and scope of identity varies. So changes in relative capabilities matter between in-group and out-group, but they matter more as in-group intensity increases and the out-group is more starkly devalued. Conversely they matter less the less intense the in-group identity, and by definition, the less starkly the other is devalued, even though the groups exist, technically, in anarchical relations. They matter not at all between groups that believe they are part of a larger in-group.

This addresses a problem that other realisms have had difficulty with— an inability to account for variations in the intensity of realpolitik behavior and variation in the responses of different groups to similar changes in relative capabilities. Some realists have tried to account for the variation in competitiveness by invoking offense-defense balances and their effect on the intensity of the security dilemma.[84] That is, the competitiveness of groups increases when offense dominates and the security dilemma is especially acute. This has nothing to do with in-group identity intensities—these are epiphenomenal—but with offensive-defense balances. But this still begs the question why one state would necessarily interpret another state's offensive advantage as threatening if, say, the states are in a friendly relationship.

If self-help is a product of group identity creation, then it is in the interests

of the group to preserve the high evaluation of the in-group and the devaluation of the out-group. Institutions are thus necessary to uphold, socialize,
and transmit identity, and by doing so they perpetuate realpolitik interpretations of the out-group across time. It is in the group's interest to do this,
in part to prevent free riding. One would therefore expect to see the institutionalization of self-help axioms accompanied by norms that delegitimate
the out-group and that punish those whose identities are loose enough to
allow defection from the group.[85] Hence the language used to intensify in-
group identities, in effect, compels marginals, or those on the fringe of the
group, to declare themselves for or against the group. The threat implicit in
this language is that those who do not, or those who try to straddle identities
are threats to the integrity of the group, and thus are beyond the moral pale,
no different than the out-group. This stark othering deters members of the
group who might defect.[86]

Thus realpolitik becomes an institutionalized ideology stressing the
"linked fate" of the in-group,[87] the dangers of the disorder in the environment
beyond the group, and the dangers presented by marginal members.[88] As
Hobbes argued, domestic cohesion around the state-as-in-group—the Levi-
athan—requires this ideology.[89] The group therefore needs to provide arguments about the competitiveness of the environment in order to reinforce
in-group identification. This is what realpolitik as ideology does. Arguments
about the inherently competitive and dangerous external world might be
supplied, for example, through official interpretations of the group's history,
the accepted language of strategic debate, or policy process structures that
marginalize certain voices and interests.[90] Together, realpolitik ideologies
and their institutions are designed to prevent groups from perceiving security
dilemmas as the basis of insecurity. The logic of in-group creation compels
a group to emphasize that insecurity comes from the predisposition of out-
groups to threaten it. Thus from an identity realist perspective, the institutional struts of realpolitik should also be essential focii of research.

To summarize, identity realism would make the following general predictions: **H.D**: the greater the intensity of in-group identity, the greater the
devaluation of the out-group, the more competitive the policies directed at
the out-group. The root cause of this increasing intensity of identification is
a challenge to the legitimacy of the content of a group's identity. So, in the
Chinese case there are three issues. First, to what extent has there been an
increase in the intensity of in-group identification and a concomitant increase in the devaluation of out-groups? Second, to what extent is this

change, if there has been one, a function of the end of the Cold War? Third, to what extent has this change correlated with any change in the competitiveness or coerciveness of Chinese realpolitik behavior? I will address this last question when I come to the specific hypotheses **H.D1–3**.

As to the first issue, I have no good indicator for intensity of identity. I am not alone on this score. Until very recently, the literature on identity is remarkably free of any effort to think about indicators of the scope and intensity of in-group identification. Some of the literature that measures patriotism and nationalism has used, in combination with other survey tools, 5-point Likert scales. One might also use Osgood semantic differential procedures, or a "meta-contrast" ratio.[91] But these are applied to surveys, not to the content analysis of historical documents. When one has to rely on content analysis, applying these methods is difficult—one has to rely on groups of well-trained coders to judge where the author of an article or document might place her/himself on a scale with no reference to the ideas of the author other than what exists in the article.[92]

In lieu of rigorous measures of the intensity and exclusiveness of in-group identity, I rely for the moment on a mix of anecdotal indicators: the degree to which nationalist symbols have replaced Marxist-Leninist ones in the public and decisionmaking discourse on China and its role in international relations; the degree to which discourses about China's relationship to the outside stresses the former's uniqueness and differentness;[93] and the language used to describe marginal or fringe actors (e.g., the discourse used to describe those whose identities are suspect, or potentially more diffuse: the more the group is interested in excluding fringe actors, or deterring their defection from the group, the shriller the discourse used to describe them).

The common, and probably accurate, observation from China specialists is that with the collapse of Marxist-Leninist ideology as a force for social cohesion and political legitimacy, the regime has turned with more urgency to a victimization discourse,[94] and to a new amalgam of appeals to an ancient, glorious Confucian past,[95] barely disguised racialist discourses on the greatness of the Chinese people,[96] "Asian" ways toward human rights and political and economic development,[97] and characterizations of conflict in the international system as residing increasingly in differences in culture and social structure, among other stark appeals to Chinese identity.

Much of this discourse has been embodied in the ubiquitous adjectival phrase "Chinese characteristics" (*zhongguo tese*) used to modify a dizzying array of activities: China is building socialism "with Chinese characteristics";

artists and musicians are urged to produce cultural products with "Chinese characteristics"; academics are tasked with developing social science theories "with Chinese characteristics."There is, to be sure, a great deal of perfunctoriness in all of this, but it reflects a broader interest the regime has in wrapping valued behavior in allegedly unique cultural characteristics, and implicitly devaluing alternatives by labeling these foreign, different, and alien. I have not done any rigorous frequency count of the term, but my sense is that it became a shriller, more ubiquitous and more reactionary concept after June 1989.

The regime has also implicitly attacked those with marginal identities or who might try to hold multiple identities by once again delegitimatizing "cosmopolitanism." The critique of cosmopolitanism (*shijie zhuyi*) picked up after June 1989, in part because the regime believed that some democracy activists saw themselves as part of a broader global historical ideological trend. Some scholars who worked on issues relating to cultural convergence (*wenhua qutong*) through internationalization of national economies had to drop their research focii. In some internal circulation materials the "open consciousness" (*kaifang yishi*) prior to June 4 was blamed for the proliferation of such unpatriotic concepts as "citizen of the world" (*shijie gongmin*), "global village consciousness" (*diqiu cun yishi*), "convergence theory" (*qutong lun*), as well as "foreign worshiping" behavior and the negation of the cultural legacies of the Chinese ethno-nation.[98] The regime also critiqued the concept of the "new world order," in part because the core unit of analysis in the term is the globe rather than the nation-state. In sum, there is important evidence that the regime has attempted, at least, to intensify identification with the Chinese state using symbolic cues with deep resonance in the socialization of the Chinese people.

It is clear the regime has thought fairly carefully about the politically instrumental purpose of these nationalist discourses. In what may have been the summary of an explicit research project on the uses of direct nationalism, an analyst with the State Council Information Office—the office charged with controlling information into and out of China—wrote in 1995 that nationalism could have a number of functions. Among the positive ones were unification of a people and nation, and preservation of the nation-state in the face of external aggression.[99]

The second question is when did this process begin? This has a bearing on the third question, namely, whether there is a correlation between this discourse and China's security policy. One thing is fairly clear: the efforts to increase the intensity of identification with the Chinese state—while never absent in post 1949 history, of course—picked up before the collapse of the Soviet Union but after June 4, 1989. This should not be surprising. The protests against the regime and the aftermath of the crackdown in June 1989 constituted an unprecedented crisis in the regime's legitimacy. The initial discourse was especially shrill in its accusations of foreign efforts to overthrow socialism in China through "peaceful evolution."

In essence, June 4 provided information to the regime that "revealed" not only that the outsiders were trying to undermine the integrity of the in-group, but also that they held much different approaches to the inviolability of internal affairs. In other words, June 4 provided information to Chinese leaders that suggested more work needed to be done to intensify in-group identification (so as to maintain the legitimacy of the in-group political status quo) and also suggested that differences with the out-group were larger, more pressing, and involved higher and more competitive stakes than they had previously acknowledged.

The talk about peaceful evolution has been toned down in volume since 1991, but it is clear that the regime does not believe the crisis in internal legitimacy has passed. The crisis has been accentuated or at least perpetuated, in Chinese eyes, by American pressure on China on human rights, U.S. support for the internationalization of Taiwan's foreign policy, and the condescending way that the United States has described China as a violator of international norms of behavior in a range of issues. The crisis of legitimacy has been accentuated as well by a deep concern about other processes of identity creation or consolidation within China, namely in Tibet, among Muslims in Xinjiang, and among island-born Taiwanese (hence the seriousness with which the Chinese leadership takes the crisis with the United States over Taiwan's status).[100]

The end of the Cold War, in a sense, only indirectly explains this process of fostering more exclusive in-group identification. Chinese leaders argued that, as China's strategic value to the United States has declined with the collapse of the USSR, the U.S. use of human rights to threaten China's political stability reveals the true essence of U.S. hegemonism and power politics, thus accentuating the differences between the two social systems. The primary charge leveled at the United States has been that it wants to "divide and westernize" (fenhua xihua) China, and to prevent it from gaining its rightful status as a great power. The U.S. threat is not aimed directly at China's territorial integrity or military security, but rather at the vision of

China as a sovereign, independent, great power, both economically and militarily. The end of the Cold War, then, did not make this in-group–out-group differentiation inevitable. Rather it reinforced information about in-group–out-group differences that were made especially apparent with the events of June 4.

To reiterate, this intensified identity discourse is primarily a function of a regime of shaky legitimacy trying hard to convince its people that only the Communist Party can lead China to its place of greatness in the face of external adversaries. This discourse has, as I noted, sharpened after June 4, with the decline of even relatively benign interdependence themes of the 1980s.[101] The discourse is not a product of the end of the Cold War, and the emergence of the United States as the lone superpower. It is therefore not an epiphenomenon of structurally induced balancing behavior. The discourse may be an ephiphenomon of the leadership's quest for legitimacy, but it would not cue the desired identification in the population if there were not fertile ideational ground for such symbols.

Thus identity issues have had two effects: the crisis of legitimacy has compelled greater efforts to foster identification with the Chinese state as led by the CCP, and the symbolic content of the identity discourse is determined by a historically rooted identity as a victimized great power. Indeed, some political insiders in China have explicitly recognized the importance of cultivating nationalist sentiments and an "enemy psychology" (*diqing xinli*) to gird the population for competition with the United States and to prevent internal disorder along the lines of June 1989. The language should stress that the U.S. intention is to exterminate China (*mie wang zhongguo*), as stark a zero-sum image as one can imagine.[102] The net hypothesized effect of the interplay of these two components of identity should be a more intense, or harder, realpolitik behavior toward out-groups, regardless of changes in material structures.

How well, then, does identity realism do in explaining change in Chinese security policy? At a very general level, of course, one could argue that it does a very good job establishing the necessary conditions for the realpolitik core of Chinese behavior. Like any most other states, *ceteris paribus*, the creation of Chinese state identity entails devaluing external actors and portraying the external environment as conflictual. This process creates relationships under anarchy and interprets them as conflictual: hence an overarching preference for realpolitik behavior. This preference ought to persist regardless of changes in material structures. The rhythm of realpolitik behavior, in other words, ought to be out of sync with changes in material power, but in tune with changes in the intensity of identification as required by the internal cohesiveness of the group. As for more specific predictions about security policy, one can deduce the following:

H.D1: *Ceteris paribus* the greater the intensity of in-group identity, the greater the devaluation of the out-group, and thus the greater the increase in military expenditures and arming directed at the out-group. Most importantly, for our purposes, the intensification of the identity discourse correlates temporally with the push to increase real military expenditures and improve military operational capabilities in the late 1980s. Moreover, the primary driver of this modernization program—achieving the status of a great power—is consistent with the content of Chinese identity as reflected in the preeminence of realpolitik ideology and institutions. Contrast this with the other realisms that predict security not status will be the primary goal, and that a change in military expenditures and acquisitions should be a function of the change in power distributions at end of the Cold War in 1991.

H.D2: the greater the intensity of in-group identity, the greater the devaluation of the out-group, the greater the effort to seek alliances that constrain or balance against the out-group. These alliances may be tighter than one might expect if there is a greater probability that allies will be identified as members of the in-group. If there is no such identification, then loose, temporary security coordination will be preferred. Therefore, China ought to support relatively tight alliances with states that are perceived to share similar in-group values. Otherwise it should prefer loose alliances against the devalued out-group. In many respects the post-June 1989 discourse on identity has stressed China's uniqueness and its determination to preserve the sovereignty and autonomy of the state. Thus it has not sought or joined tight security coalitions aimed at devalued out-groups like the United States But neither has it sought or joined loose coalitions aimed at containing U.S. power. This is a problem for the argument if indeed the starkness of in-group–out-group differences has been accentuated.

China's global human rights diplomacy is more consistent with the argument, however. Part of the discourse on human rights has stressed the common approaches to the relationship between the individual and the state shared by such Asian states as Singapore and Malaysia. As the theory would expect, this common discourse has been reflected in Chinese efforts to construct a coalition of states opposed to Western pressure on human rights, particularly human rights defined in terms of individual political and civil liberties.

H.D3: the greater the intensity of in-group identity, the greater the devaluation of the out-group, the starker and more denigrating the images the policy discourse will present of the out-group, the more the in-group will use these images to mobilize in-group identities. Discourse about strategic threats will follow *from* discourses about threats to the valuational integrity of the in-group (e.g., strategic competition will flow from perceived valuational competition, not the other way around).

As a first crack at measuring an increasing sensitivity to the independence and autonomy of the Chinese state (which, for most realists, ought not to vary), a randomly sampled set of articles from an internally circulated, authoritative journal on international relations, *World Economics and Politics*, was content analyzed. These were coded for the frequency of specific terms that reflected judgments about the conflictual nature of the international environment and about degree of congruence between "national interests" and the interests of other actors.[103] Specifically, each article was coded for the frequency of concepts that tapped into two different poles of thinking about the international system and China's relationship to it—a hard realpolitik pole in which the system is highly conflictual, and in which independence, sovereignty, and national interest are of primary importance, and an interdependence pole where cooperation, the predominance of global interests, and international institutions characterized the system. My assumption is that the more frequent the concepts that cluster around the former pole, the more likely that Chinese analysts stress China's identity as an independent, autonomous actor with fewer common interests or values shared with other states. The more frequent the concepts that cluster around the latter pole, the more likely that Chinese analysts accept more porous identity boundaries with outside actors, and acknowledge some common interests and values.

This is, to be sure, a very rough indicator. Nonetheless, one does see a jump in the references that describe the international system as conflictual and that stress national interests and the Chinese version of a new international order (which is based on the enhancement of the independence and sovereignty of states) after 1988 but before 1991. As figure 8.9 shows, after 1988, not after 1991, the cumulative frequency of conflictual images takes off on a trajectory at a rate that exceeds the cumulative frequency of cooperative references. This is what one should expect if the legitimacy crisis of 1989 were driving the efforts to intensify in-group identity and realpolitik ideology.

CONCLUSION

Given the messiness of the realist theories I have tested here, I feel somewhat less concerned about the messiness of my conclusions. One thing is clear: the first three realisms do not come through with flying colors, even though I tried to create ideal test conditions for each of them. Balance-of-power realism is problematic for a number of reasons. First, the intensification of China's military modernization efforts has preceded, rather than followed from, a substantial structural shift in power in favor of the United States Second, China is not determinedly internally or externally balancing against the United States, despite this structural shift. Third, despite the emergence of the United States as the predominant military power in the system, China is becoming more, not less, dependent on trade with the it. Finally, despite this shift, and despite the recognition in the security policy discourse that the present system is highly asymmetrical, if not unipolar, Chinese decisionmakers have not determined that the United States is China's primary military adversary or the primary target of its balancing behavior. They continue to argue that from China's perspective the post-Cold War period is highly competitive but for the moment relatively benign strategically.

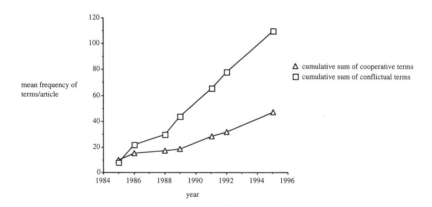

FIGURE 8.9 Content analysis of *Shijie jingji yu zhengzhi*

At first glance, power maximization realism does a better job accounting for much of Chinese security policy. Chinese military modernization has proceeded as the costs of trying to maximize relative capabilities have declined with the collapse of the USSR. The Chinese policy discourse is also consistent with power maximization's assumptions about the competitive nature of the environment and the need to exploit opportunities to increase relative power. The difficulty with the theory, however, is that, again, much of this behavior precedes the collapse of the USSR and the reduction in costs of power maximizing. Moreover, it is not clear that the motivation behind power maximization is security as much as it is status—a driver that is much harder to attribute to systemic anarchy and changing power distributions, as Schweller has noted. The fact that both balance-of-power and power-maximization versions of structural realism get what should be an easy, "most likely" case wrong is, or ought to be, profoundly troubling for those who believe that anarchy and polarity are critical variables in explaining the security policies of major powers. In other words, their disconfirmation in this particular case ought to be weighted quite heavily for defenders and critics of structural realism alike. If not in this case, then when *does* balancing occur for material structural reasons?[104]

Balance-of-threat realism is not a particularly good explanation of Chinese security policy either. In general, China's military expenditures and modernization of operational capabilities are on a gradual upward trajectory even though the primary security threat has essentially disappeared. China is not balancing against any identifiable military threat at the present, and decisionmakers and strategists are divided about which state may constitute the next security challenge. Although the United States presents the most foreign policy headaches for the regime, even hardline analysts do not believe the United States presents an imminent military threat. Indeed, for the most part Chinese decisionmakers consider the post-Cold War security environment to be, on balance, the least threatening since the founding of the People's Republic.

As for identity realism, the discussion here is a first cut at exploring a constructivist perspective on realpolitik behavior. To be sure, this version of realism has been the most difficult to operationalize, and hence to test convincingly. Two things can be said for it, however. First, the *timing* of China's discourse about international relations and its role in the system is consistent with the acute accentuation of the regime's legitimacy crisis in 1989. Identity realism would expect under this condition that the regime try to foster greater in-group identification with the Chinese state and CCP leadership. Second, the *content* of this discourse is also consistent with identity realism's expectations. In order to intensify in-group identification the regime ought to stress the uniqueness of the in-group, the potential dangers of the external environment, and the valuational differences between in-group and out-group. Hence, the intensification of nationalist symbols, the invocation of traditional cultural values, the relative increase in conflictual images of international relations, the denunciation of Western interference in the internal affairs of sovereign states and the illegitimacy of U.S. "hegemonistic" foreign policy, among other manifestations. This discourse, by definition, is a realpolitik one, and the timing and content of behavior ought to be a consistent with it.

The difficulty for the identity argument, however, is that this intensification of realpolitik discourse and behavior is relatively minor in comparison with the long-time realpolitik nature of Chinese foreign policy. There are deeper roots to Chinese realpolitik than the effort to intensify in-group identities after 1989. As I have argued elsewhere,[105] and as ought to be clear by the failure of the Chinese to respond in the 1990s in ways predicted by the two structural realisms, it is not at all obvious that structural anarchy explains these deeper realpolitik impulses. Much more work needs to be done on the interplay between deeply historical identity creation and state responses to the contemporary identity crises that they face.

Unit-level constructivists might argue that there are unit-level ideational structures or identities that can produce realpolitik behavior through specific interpretations of the intentions of out-groups, and these are sustained through the production of histories and symbols institutionalized in education systems and decisionmaking processes that stressed hostility, rivalry, threat, and competition. I would argue that this production is inherent in in-group identity construction, and should lead constructivists to a somewhat more pessimistic view of the persistence of realpolitik behavior. Systemic constructivists would have to argue that there are global ideational structures—interpretations of actors and their intentions—that are competitive, self-regarding ones but that are produced and reproduced independent of material structures. This may be part of the Chinese story if one were to argue that the Chinese have consciously adopted an idea of major-power behavior that was normatively acceptable and descriptively standard earlier in this century, and have perpetuated this model even as other major powers have moved on to definitions of major-powerhood based on soft power attributes. In what one might call a normative product cycle, Chinese leaders have inherited "sunset" concepts of sovereignty, independence, autonomy, and security because these appeared to have worked well in producing national power and status for major powers in the past.

In either case, a constructivist focus on social interaction—namely in-group identity construction—can provide important insights into the nature of realpolitik behavior, not just into the "deviant" cases on which constructivism heretofore has concentrated. I do not think the China case has necessarily resolved the debate between ideational and material explanations of realpolitik behavior. But I hope it starts one.

ACKNOWLEDGMENTS

I would like to thank the following people for their input and feedback on this project: Tom Christensen, Dale Copeland, Jeff Frieden, Ethan Kapstein, Peter Katzenstein, Mike Mastanduno, Jack Snyder and the members of the project on realism in the post-Cold War period.

NOTES

1. Vasquez found that most of what he classified as realist hypothesis that have been tested in the quantitative literature have accounted for little of the variance in dependent variables of interest. See John A. Vasquez *The Power of Power Politics: A Critique* (New Brunswick: Rutgers University Press, 1993) and his "Realism as a Degenerative Paradigm" *American Political Science Review* (December 1997). See also Frank Wayman and Paul Diehl, eds., *Reconstructing Realpolitik* (Ann Arbor: University of Michigan Press 1994) for a series of quantitative tests of realist propositions that also find that the "theory" lacks predictive and explanatory power. In his qualitative analysis of alliance behavior in modern European history, Schroeder argues that structural realist predictions do not work particularly well in accounting for the wide number of reasons for states joining or leaving alliances. Paul Schroeder, "Historical Reality vs Neo-realist Theory" *International Security* 19 (1) (Summer 1994): 108–48.

2. Andrew Nathan and Robert S. Ross, *The Great Wall and the Empty Fortress: China's Search For Security* (New York: Norton, 1997); Samuel S. Kim *China In and Out of the Changing World Order* (Princeton: Princeton University World Order Studies Program Occasional Paper No. 21, 1991); Peter Van Ness *Revolution and Chinese Foreign Policy: China's Support for Wars of National Liberation* (Berkeley: University of California Press, 1971); Gerald Segal *De-*

fending China (New York: Oxford University Press, 1995); Thomas J. Christensen, "Chinese Realpolitik" *Foreign Affairs* 75 (5) (September/October 1996): 37–53.

3. As Elman points out, Waltz seems to be of two minds on whether great powers are more or less likely to behave consistently with the dictates of the theory. See Colin Elman "Neorealist Theories of Foreign Policy: Meaning, Objections and Implications" (Paper Presented to ISA Annual Meeting, Chicago, February 1995), 27–28; and Kenneth Waltz, *Theory of International Politics* (Reading MA: Addison Wesley, 1979), 198–99, 194, 195).

4. Wayman and Diehl, *Reconstructing*, 26; see also Brian M. Pollins, "Cannons and Capital: The Use of Coercive Diplomacy by Major Powers in the Twentieth Century" in ibid., p. 41.

5. There are a number of caveats, however. First, given that the Cold War has only recently ended the number of post-test observations is quite small. So if the observations suggest the X treatment has had little or no effect on the dependent variable, it may be simply that there has not been sufficient time for an effect to show up. Second, there is the problem of identifying in which class of independent variables the "end of the Cold War" belongs. The different theories might treat the "end of the Cold War" as a change in different variables. Balance of power might view it as a change in polarity; power maximization theory as change in the opportunity to maximize capabilities; and balance of threat as a change in threat. So the fairest thing to do is to interpret the end of the Cold War as a change in that independent variable on which each theory focuses. Finally there is the potentially arbitrary nature of the dependent variable. In this chapter I focus on the dependent variables of interest to realism: military expenditures and capabilities, and alliance behavior. If the theories don't do well under these ideal conditions, then there is little reason to believe they'd do better in explaining change in other kinds of dependent variables (e.g., behavior in economic affairs, environment diplomacy, and international institutions).

6. One often hears the claim that Waltz's balancing theory is a theory of systemic outcomes and not a theory of foreign policy of individual states. Thus it is pointless to test it to explain the behavior of any one particular actor. [e.g., William Wolforth, "Realism and the End of the Cold War" *International Security* 19 (3) (Winter 1994/5): 101; Christopher Layne, "The Unipolar Illusion: Why New Great Powers Will Rise" *International Security* 17 (4) (Spring 1993): 9]. This argument is not convincing. In a number of places Waltz implies that his theory leads to certain probabilistic expectations that states are likely to act to prevent other states or coalitions from dominating the system. I have difficulty seeing why this is not a prediction about how individual states will behave. Systemic balances are the consequences of the behavior of the units, but the

behavior of the units that produced this outcome is a particular type of behavior, namely balancing behavior. It is hard to see how a balancing outcome is produced if most of the major actors in the system were to refuse to balance. Indeed, the theory cannot ignore intentionality, for as Waltz himself notes, in, say, a bipolar system secondary states "if they are free to *choose*, flock to the weaker side" (emphasis added) (Waltz, *Theory* p. 127). They choose to do so because they are realpolitik actors who calculate that to preserve and strengthen themselves they should act in ways that prevent other states from dominating the system (ibid., 117). See also Waltz's most recent prediction about Chinese balancing against the United States in Kenneth Waltz, "Reply" *American Political Science Review* 91 (4) (December 1997): 916. For a sophisticated argument that Waltzian neorealism is indeed a theory of foreign policy see Elman, "Neorealist Theories," especially pp. 31–32.

7. Waltz, *Theory*, 131.
8. This is not so arbitrary a decision as it sounds. Sullivan has found that the correlation coefficients among different indices, including COW's six power indicators, Ray Cline's formula for national strength, Clifford German's complex measure of national power, and GNP, are quite high, sufficient to make these indices interchangeable for most uses. Interestingly, he finds a strong correlation between subjective perceptions of national power rankings among states and their actual rankings using GNP and military expenditure indices. This suggests that power indicators based on military expenditures or GNP considered *alone*, are probably sufficient as a first crack at measuring relative power and its distribution. See Michael P. Sullivan *Power in Contemporary International Politics* (Columbia: South Carolina University Press, 1990), 110–17.
9. George Modelski, *World Power Concentrations: Typology, Data, Explanatory Framework* (Princeton: Princeton University Press 1974). Modelski's categories are somewhat arbitrary but they makes intuitive sense, and they correlate with the U.S. and Soviet capabilities shared during the Cold War, a period most people accept was a bipolar one.
10. This calculation uses an unofficial revision of the IISS figures for China's official budget. As a rough rule of thumb the official budget may undercount by a factor of three.
11. William Thompson, *On Global War* (Columbia: South Carolina University Press, 1988), 209–10, emphasis added.
12. Layne's subjective judgment is that the United States constitutes the unipole. See Layne, "Unipolar Illusion."
13. DOD (Department of Defense) (1995) *East Asia Strategy Report* (Washington: USGPO, February).
14. GAO (General Accounting Office) (1995), "National Security: Impact of

China's Military Modernization in the Pacific Region" (Report to Congressional Committees, GAO/NSIAD-95–84, June), 3.

15. Guan Jixian, *Gao jishu jubu zhanzheng zhanyi* (Campaigns in high tech limited wars), (Beijing: National Defense University Press, 1993).

16. Dennis Blasko, et al, "Training Tomorrow's PLA—A Mixed Bag of Tricks" (unpublished paper, Hong Kong, October 19, 1995). p. 19.

17. Shambaugh reports, however, that since at least 1991, the PLA has conducted war games at the Academy of Military Sciences where the the United States has been tagged as the simulated enemy. See David Shambaugh, "The Insecurity of Security: The PLA's Evolving Doctrine and Threat Perceptions Towards the Year 2000" *Journal of Northeast Asian Studies.* 13 (1) (Spring 1994): 3–25.

18. Ma Fajing and Dan Yuntian, "Discussion of PLA Weapons Development Problems," *Xiandai bingqi* (Modern ordnance) No. 6 (June 1993) JPRS-CAR-93–075 (October 12, 1993), 35. See also Ken Allen, et al. (1995) *China's Air Force Enters the Next Century* (Santa Monica: The RAND Corporation).

19. Blasko, "Training," p. 22.

20. Chongpin Lin "Beijing and Taipei: Dialectics in Post Tiananmen Interactions" *China Quarterly* no. 136 (December 1993): 770–804; Chongpin Lin, "The Power Projection Forces of the Peoples Liberation Army" (Paper presented to American Enterprise Institute 6th Annual PLA Conference, Coolfont, West Virginia, June 1995).

21. Liao Wen-chung, "China's Blue Waters Strategy in the 21st Century: From the First Islands Chain to the Second Islands Chain" (Taipei, Chinese Council of Advanced Policy Studies, Occasional Paper, September, 1995). See also John Garver, "China's Push Through the South China Sea: The Interaction of Bureaucratic and National Interests" *The China Quarterly* No. 132 (December 1992), 999–1028.

22. Liao, "China's Blue Waters."

23. Shen Zhiyan, "21 shiji chu Sulian zai Ya-Tai diqu de junshi zhanlue dongxiang." [Trends in Soviet military strategy in the Asia-Pacific region in the early 21st century] *Ya-Tai de xuanwo* [The Asia-Pacific Vortex] (Beijing, Academy of Military Sciences Press, 1989), 43, and Hua Zhongting and Tang Cheng, "Huan he, jing zheng, wu bei" [Detente, conflict, military preparations] in ibid, 12–24.

24. See, for instance, the discussion of off-shore, blue-water naval operations in an internal study materials published at the National Defense University in December 1987, in Liao, "China's Blue Waters," appendix 4. What the document calls "near ocean defense strategy" includes operations to defend the South China Sea, reunify Taiwan with the mainland, protect scientific activities,

ocean shipping, fishing industry, etc.—a list that goes well beyond traditional coastal defense strategy.

25. Alastair Iain Johnston, "China's New 'Old Thinking': The Concept of Limited Deterrence" *International Security* 20 (3) (Winter 1995/6): 5–43.

26. Robert S. Norris and Andrew S. Burrows and Richard W. Fieldhouse, *British, French and Chinese Nuclear Weapons* (Boulder, CO: Westview Press 1994) p. 359.

27. I used the Kansas Events Data System/Protocol for the Assessment of Nonviolent Direct Action (KEDS/PANDA) data base. These events are machine-coded reports from Reuters wire service. I culled only official government statements, actions directed at government actors/targets from 1984–1995. This reduced the N substantially from 11759 to 1410 over 10 years, with all states as targets. So this final list does not reflect the totality of interactions by all actors across the two states, but does capture, hopefully, the trends in cooperative and conflictual signaling from China. For a discussion of the caveats in using KEDS/PANDA, see Doug Bond and Joe Bond, "Protocol for the Assessment of Nonviolent Direct Action (PANDA) Codebook for the P24 Data Set" (Unpublished paper, Program on Nonviolent Sanctions and Cultural Survival, Harvard University, May 1995). On average the computer miscodes about 25% of the observations. I discovered this in the small N country cases as I read through the headlines and compared these with the coding. I excluded these observations in the small N data sets, but not on the China-U.S. set. Here I assumed that given the N (360) cooperative events coded as conflictual and conflictual events coded cooperative will cancel each other out. Weighted WEIS scores as developed by Goldstein are supplied as well. See Joshua S. Goldstein, "A Conflict-Cooperation Scale for WEIS Events Data" *Journal of Conflict Resolution* 36 (2) (June 1992): 369–85.

28. Intensity refers to the mean yearly WEIS scores for Chinese actions directed at the United States As ME moves up, the scores drop, meaning the actions are coded less cooperative. The proportion refers to the percentage of all actions that are cooperative, according to weighted WEIS scales. As ME increases, the proportion of cooperative actions decreases. I used ACDA figures in 1993 dollars. If one uses official ME the correlation coefficients increase to r = -.53 and r = -.42 respectively.

29. I don't provide mean WEIS scores for these countries because the N of observations is too small. The means could change dramatically with the inclusion of a few additional events in the following country cases. Instead I coded all the headlines as cooperative or conflictual by reading them, and by looking at the KEDS/PANDA event category (categories above number 372 are essentially conflictual). Admittedly this misses the more fine-tuned information available

using weighted WEIS scores, but as I noted, aggregate scores are potentially too volatile with small numbers of observations.

30. *Korea Times*, November 16, 1995 as reported in North East Asia Peace and Security Network Daily Report, November 16, 1995.

31. See Bonnie Glaser, "The Chinese Security Perspective on Soviet/Russian-Japanese Relations" in T. Haregawa et al eds., *Russia and Japan* (Berkeley: University of California Press, 1993), 223; Banning Garrett and Bonnie Glaser, "Multilateral Security in the Asia-Pacific Region and its Impact on Chinese Interests: Views from Beijing" *Contemporary Southeast Asia* 16 (1) (June 1994): 22–23; Christensen, "Chinese Realpolitik." This does not mean that the Chinese support any and all forms of U.S.-Japanese security cooperation. The possibility of TMD deployments in Japan are viewed with alarm, for instance. American support for a more militarized Japan, in the context of Sino-U.S. conflict, is also viewed with concern. But this is an argument for preserving relatively good relations with the United States, not competitively balancing against it.

32. Indeed, there is no public evidence that the joint listening posts set up in Xinjiang province in the early 1980s have been closed down, even though Sino-U.S. relations have entered unstable times of late.

33. Joanne Gowa, *Allies, Adversaries and International Trade* (Princeton: Princeton University Press, 1994).

34. Edward D. Mansfield and Rachel Bronson, "Alliances, Preferential Trading Arrangements, and International Trade" (Paper presented to Olin Institute National Security Seminar, Harvard University, November 1995), 2–3.

35. *China Monthly Statistics* No. 9 (1995): 35–39. Chinese statistics on bilateral trade do not count exports reprocessed and exports from Hong Kong. U.S. data do include these exports, thus U.S. figures for China's market dependence are even higher—roughly double that of the Chinese figures.

36. Waltz argues that a theory should not necessarily fall if its assumptions are empirically wrong or inaccurate (*Theory*, 8, 119). Consistent with the spirit of his positivism, however, if the theory stands we should be able to generate additional empirical predictions that are consistent with the theory. Even if the policy discourse is an ephiphenomenal artifact of the processes that the theory suggests are at work, it ought to be an important *indirect indicator* of balancing behavior. That is, it ought to be rare to find a deep discourse that does not stress balancing when a state is indeed balancing. Nonstructuralists would argue, of course, that the discourse reflects an intentionality that has a causal effect on state behavior and, in turn, on systemic outcomes. Either way, I would argue, H.A3 is an important hypothesis to test.

37. He Fang,"Shijie geju yu guoji xingshi" [Global system and the international

situation] *Shi jie jingji yu zhengzhi* [World economics and politics] No. 11
(1991). As Ross has convincingly shown, this article signaled not only the "hegemony" of the unipolarity argument, but also a period of Chinese concessions
to the United States on MTCR, trade reform, and prison labor. This is not
entirely consistent with balancing against the dominant player in the international system. Robert S. Ross, "Two Level Games and Sino-U.S. Bargaining"
(Unpublished paper, Harvard University, 1995).

38. Du Gong, ed., *Zhuanhuan zhong de shijie geju* [The world structure in tran-
    sition] (Beijing: World Affairs Press 1992), 6–7.
39. Yan Xuetong et al., "Dangqian wo guo waijiao mianlin de tiaozhan he renwu"
    [The challenges and tasks that our country's foreign policy currently faces] *Shi
    jie jingji yu zhengzhi* [World economics and politics] No. 24 [1993]).
40. Glaser, "Chinese Security Perspective," 225–26. My impression from discus-
    sions with specialists in Beijing in the spring of 1996 is that there is still con-
    siderable debate in the Chinese leadership circles on the nature of American
    hegemony.
41. Wang Jianwei, *United States-China Mutual Images in the Post-Tiananmen Era:
    A Regression or Sophistication?* (Ann Arbor: University of Michigan, Political
    Science Department, PhD diss. 1994), 268–69. Wang's intensive interviews
    with 127 members of Chinese foreign policy elite and foreign policy analysts,
    businessmen, and scholars from June 1991 to March 1992, before and after the
    collapse of the USSR, revealed a general agreement that the United States was
    among other descriptors, "all-out champion, first class military power, the sole
    superpower, number one in the world" (p. 263 note 14). Conservatives, of
    course, do see unipolarity as potentially threatening to China's economic, po-
    litical interests and internal cohesion. See Wang Chiming's concern that the
    United States is moving to encircle China strategically in Asia, as exemplified
    by the U.S. interest in multilateral security institutions in East Asia that might
    "lasso" (*tao zhu*) China. Wang Chiming, "Shixi wo guo zhoubian huanjing
    zhong de 'Meiguo yinsu' " [Preliminary analysis of the 'American factor' in the
    environment around our country's periphery] *Shi jie jingji yu zhengzhi* [World
    economics and politics] No.1 (1994): 56–61. As of late 1997—there was still
    some debate in the leadership whether, even though the United States is the
    only superpower, it is on the decline (and therefore should be challenged) or
    is increasingly dominant (and therefore should be accommodated on some
    issues). The difficulty of accommodation on most of the major irritants in the
    relationship is due to domestic political constraints—the relatively weaker post-
    Deng leadership—not a consensus view that U.S. power is on the decline.
42. Layne, "Unipolar Illusion," p. 3, fn.1; p. 9.
43. John Mearsheimer, "Back to the Future: Instability in Europe After the Cold

War" *International Security* 15 (1) (Summer 1990): 12; John Mearsheimer, "The False Promise of International Institutions" *International Security* 19 (3) (Winter 1994/5): 11–12.

44. Morgenthau, cited in Bruce Bueno de Mesquita and David Lalman "Power Relationships, Democratic Constraints, and War" in Wayman and Diehl, *Reconstructing* p. 170.

45. Joseph Grieco, "Anarchy and the Limits of Cooperation: A Realist Critique of the Newest Liberal Institutionalism" *International Organization* 42 (3) (Summer 1988): 499.

46. The problem for power maximizing realism arises, as Glaser's work implies, when defense has a decisive and long-term advantage over offense. If defense dominates to this extent, then no amount of effort to improve relative capabilities will lead to an offensive advantage. Moreover, if defense dominates, a power maximizing state ought still to feel secure enough that it need not drive for offensive advantage. Thus under conditions of nuclear deterrence, assured second strike deterrence, even power maximizing states should ease up in their effort to achieve decisive advantage. See Charles Glaser, "Realists as Optimists: Cooperation as Self-Help" *International Security* 19 (3) (Winter 1994/5): 50–90. If a state continues to maximize relative power even when defense dominates, this suggests there is some other, nonstructural basis for its dissatisfaction. We then need to term to the unit-level sources of dissatisfaction, as Schweller suggests we do.

47. It is not clear how power maximization realism would explain why these states would be unwilling, short of their collapse, if they too are power maximizers without making ad hoc assumptions about the characteristics of the units.

48. Layne, "Unipolar Illusion".

49. Robert Gilpin, *War and Change in World Politics* (Cambridge: Cambridge University Press, 1991), 94–5.

50. Zhao Huaipu and Lu Yang, "Quanli zhengzhi yu xianghu yicun" [Power politics and interdependence] in *Shijie jingji yu zhengzhi*, [World economics and politics] No.7 (1993): 36–41. See also He Xin's description of the international economic system as one populated by developed country "wolves" and developing state "sheep" whereby policies that are advantageous for the former are not similarly advantageous for the latter. Evidently there are few opportunities for joint gains. See He Xin, "Wang Zhen tongzhi tanhua jiyao" [Record of key points in conversation with Comrade Wang Zhen" (1991.4.17) in He Xin (1993) *He Xin Zhengzhi Jingji Lunwen Ji—Nei bu yanjiu baogao* [Collected political and economic writings of He Xin—internal circulation research reports] (Harbin, Heilongjiang Education Press 1993) p. 325. See also the discussion of the zero-sum nature of competition for ocean resources,Yang Zhiqun, "Officer's Forum—Brown Water, Blue Water—Thoughts on Naval

Theory" *Jianchuan Zhishi* [Naval and Merchant Ships] (February 1994) JPRS-CAR-94-031 (May 13, 1994): 34.

51. This figure shows the average frequency of the terms "new world order" and "new international order" used in a randomly sampled selection of articles from *World Economics and Politics*. The drop in the former after 1991 is due to a conscious decision to critique the term after its prominence in the global discourse on international relations after the Gulf War. See below for a discussion of the coding procedures.

52. For a similar reason, China's leaders do not like the term "new thinking" (*xin siwei*), as it is too closely identified with Gorbachev's destruction of communist rule in the Soviet Union.

53. Li Shisheng, "Guanyu guoji xin zhixu ji ge wenti de tan tao." [Discussion of several questions relating to the new international order] *Shijie jingji yu zhengzhi*. [World Economics and politics] No. 10. (1992): 43–44.

54. Ma and Dan, "Discussion of PLA" p. 34; see also Wang Pufeng et al, eds., *Xiandai guofang lun* [On modern national defense] (Chongqing: Chongqing Publishing House, 1993), 67.

55. Zhang Zhaozhong and Guo Xiangxing, *Xiandai haijun qishi lu* [A record of the inspiring modernization of the navy] (Beijing: People's Liberation Army Press, 1993), 26–27.

56. Shen, "21 shiji chu" p. 43.

57. Mao noted in 1958 that if China didn't have nuclear weapons, it would "count for nothing" (*bu suan shu*). Huang Cisheng and Wang Lincong, "Shilun Mao Zedong de he zhanlue sixiang" [Preliminary discussion of Mao Zedong's thinking on nuclear strategy] in *Quan jun Mao Zedong junshi sixiang xueshu taolun wen jing xuan* [Selected essays from the all-Army academic meeting on Mao Zedong's military thought] (Beijing: Academy of Military Sciences Press, 1992), 602. See also his comments just before the Great Leap Forward and the second Quemoy-Matzu crisis in 1958 that China had to increase industrial production and military power so that John Foster Dulles would sit up and take notice of China's stature. See Thomas J. Christensen, *Useful Adversaries* (Princeton: Princeton University Press, 1996).

58. Gu Yan, "Duli zizhu shi Mao Zedong waijiao sixiang de linghun" [Independence and self-reliance is the spirit of Mao Zedong's foreign policy thought] *Shijie jingji yu zhengzhi*. [World Economics and politics] (1994): 32. Position in this context is hierarchical, implying rank and status. *Minzu* is a hard-to-translate term that in its usage in the 1980s and 1990s blurs the division among nation, ethnicity, and race.

59. For a definition of this benign environment purely in security terms see Yan, "Dangqian" p. 22. For a definition that implies improvements in China's status see Gu, "Duli Zizhu."

60. Cited in Wan Ming, "Yuan Diplomacy: China's Economic Statecraft since 1978" (Unpublished paper, Center for International Affairs, May 1994), 31 fn. 90.

61. Carol Hamrin, *China and the Challenge of the Future: Changing Politics Patterns* (Boulder: Westview Press, 1990) p. 124.

62. The argument here agrees substantially with Samuel Kim's speculation that China's military buildup has less to do with balancing against threats or hegemons and more to do with prestige and status. See his "China in the World in Theory and Practice." in Samuel S. Kim ed., *China and the World* (Boulder, CO: Westview Press 1994), 13–14.

63. These arguments were first made most forcefully in an article in *Jiefangjun Bao* (Liberation Army Daily) in 1987. The purpose of the development of "three dimensional" military capabilities was to "protect China's legitimate rights and interests"—no mention of security threats here. See Xu Guangyu "Pursuit of Equitable Three Dimensional Strategic Boundaries" *Jiefangjun Bao* (April 3, 1987) in JPRS-CAR-88–016 (March 29, 1988): 38. The status issue was also prominent in Lt. Cmdr. Yang Zhiqun's praise of blue-water navies. "When a country has the humiliation of being chased out of an ocean, today when it has an extremely great oceanic interest, its navy will patrol the blue water." His meaning—China's navy needs to restore control over those blue water areas that rightfully belong to China. See Yang, "Officer's Forum," 34.

64. See "Curriculum Research Materials: General summary of discussions on building the strategic theory of the airforce and navy" (National Defense University, December 12, 1987) in Liao, "China's Blue Waters," 18.

65. Zhang and Guo, *Xiandai haijun* p. 27.

66. Randall Schweller, "Bandwagoning for Profit: Bringing the Revisionist State Back In" *International Security* 19 (1) (Summer 1994): 72–107; and Schweller "Neorealism's Status-Quo Bias: What Security Dilemma?" *Security Studies* 5 (3) (Spring 1996): 225–58.

67. The term was suggested by Tom Christensen, personal correspondence, May 1996.

68. Stephen Walt,*The Origins of Alliances* (Ithaca: Cornell University Press 1987), 26. For instance, the theory would predict that, given a geographically proximate state with overwhelming military power and an offensive doctrine, Canada ought to be balancing against the United States On the other hand, Walt's theory could also argue that this absence of balancing is not an anomoly because perceptions of intent suggest Canada need not worry. In this case the threat perception variable would clearly overwhelm the effects of the other three variables in Walt's theory. In particular, this case would seem to be an instance of ideological solidarity (illustrated by the fact that the end of the Soviet threat

has not led Canada to worry more about an American threat). Ideological solidarity, in this case, is a function of shared political and cultural traits, in other
words shared democratic identities.

69. See Walt's description of Nasser's fears about the U.S. threat, in ibid., p. 69.

70. Though if this is so, then it suggests that the balancing coalition at time t is
violating one of neorealism's assumptions that states will not act to increase
relative capabilities to the point where others form counterbalancing coalitions
and thus threaten its security at time t + 1. If this axiom did hold for the
balancer at time t, then it should have held as well for the state that sought
hegemony at time t - 1. If it had held, then it should have been prudent enough
not to seek hegemony at t - 1, and therefore it should not have provoked balancing at time t, which, in turn should not have provoked counterbalancing at
t + 1. As Schweller (and Wendt) points out, the process of balancing and
counterbalancing requires the presence of a predator state that seeks power
regardless of the cost to security. See Schweller, "Bandwagoning"; Schweller,
"Neorealism's Status Quo Bias"; and Alexander Wendt, "Anarchy is What States
Make of It: The Social Construction of Power Politics" *International Organization* 46. (1992): 391–425; Alexander Wendt, "Collective Identity Formation
and the International State" *American Political Science Review* 88 (2) (June
1994): 384–96.

71. This assumes states are not power maximizers and do not take advantage of
opportunities to maximize relative capabilities once they are secure. Walt is not
all that explicit about whether states are "defensive positionalist" or power maximizers, though he appears to lean toward the former. See Walt, *Origins*, p. 9,
where he notes that states balance when their security position is threatened.

72. Zong Lanhai, "Zhong gong yiding guoji tou hao diren" [The Chinese com-
munists determine their main international adversary] *Cheng Ming* No.195
(January 1994): 16–18.

73. Wang Jianwei, "Coping with China as a Rising Power (New York: Council on
Foreign Relations, Asian Project Working Paper, July 1995), 7; Wang Jisi, "U.S.
Policy Toward Taiwan and Sino-U.S. Relations" *Wen Wei Po* (Hong Kong)
(August 19, 1995) in FBIS-CHI-95–177 (September 13, 1995): 6–7; Wu Peng,
" 'Zhongguo weixie' lun pouxi" [An analysis of the "China threat" theory] *Shijie
jingji yu zhengzhi* (World economics and politics) No. 10 (1993): 3.

74. Song Baoxian, "A Great Debate on U.S. Policy Toward China" *Wen Wei Po*
(Hong Kong) (August 19, 1995) in FBIS-CHI-95–177 (September 13, 1995):
7–8; Kuan Wen-liang, "Pro-Taiwan U.S. Congressmen Abandon Elections
One After Another—On Absence of Anti-China Foundation in U.S. Society"
Wen Wei Po (Hong Kong) (September 9) in FBIS-CHI-95–181 (September
19, 1995): 15–17; Yuan Ming and Fan Shiming, " 'Leng zhan' hou Meiguo

dui Zhongguo (an quan) xingxiang de renshi" [China's security role in post-Cold War American security perceptions] *Meiguo yanjiu* [American Studies] 9 (4) (Winter 1995): 7–29.

75. Wang, "Shixi wo guo," 56–57.

76. Ibid., p. 60.

77. This is potentially a dodgy prediction. It is not clear in realist theories whether the relationship between threat and military expenditures ought to be linear or stepwise. On the one hand, one could argue that, given the role of uncertainty in producing self-help behavior, a decline in threat (measured objectively) should not produce a monotonic decline in balancing behavior. Rather the absence or virtual absence of threat may be necessary for a reduction in expenditures to begin. Measured subjectively, of course, a decline in threat is a decline in uncertainty about likelihood of attack, and thus should be linearly related to a decline in expenditure.

78. Yan, "Dangqian," 22; Wang, "Shixi wo guo," 56.

79. Marc Ross, *The Culture of Conflict: Interpretations and Interests in Comparative Perspective* (New Haven: Yale University Press 1993; Jonathan Mercer, "Anarchy and Identity." *International Organization* 49 (2) (Spring 1995): 229–52; Daniel Druckman, "Nationalism, Patriotism, and Group Loyalty: A Social Psychological Perspective," *Mershon International Studies Review* 38 (Supplement 1) (1994); Eugene Burnstein et al "How the Mind Preserves the Image of the Enemy: The Mnemonics of Soviet-American Relations" in William Zimmerman and Harold Jacobson eds., *Behavior, Culture and Conflict in World Politics* (Ann Arbor, University of Michigan Press, 1993); Chester A. Insko et al., "Individual-Group Discontinuity as a Function of Fear and Greed" *Journal of Personality and Social Psychology* 58 (1) (1990): 68–79.

80. It sometimes pays individually to call oneself a member of a group. But the attractiveness of group identification is not entirely self-interestedly material, nor are the sanctions against violating group identity entirely material. Experimental research has found that perception of shared identity leads to an "empathetic altruism" where the interests of others in the group are taken to be one's own interests. (See John C. Turner, *Rediscovering the Social Group: A Self-Categorization Theory* (London and New York: Basil Blackwell, 1987), p. 65. And the source of shared identity is not necessarily interpersonal interest or interdependence, but perceived interpersonal similarity according to some socialized criteria of prototypicality. Nor are the symbolic cues that trigger identity-enforcing or -dissolving behavior uniformly material ones. Beyond this, however, there are a number of hypothesis about out-group devaluation. One possibility is that in-group identity creation by definition requires a devalued out-group, so as to reveal exactly why the in-group ought to exist. This opens the door to attribution effects and justifications for violence. Another possibility

is that political entrepreneurs have an interest in accentuating in-group–out-group differences so as to consolidate their leadership. Still another hypothesis is that individuals have a psychological need to enhance their self-worth and status by belonging to a valued group. Finally, the devaluation of the out-group may increase the efficiency of the in-group in the production of benefits through coordination.

81. Donald R. Kinder and David O. Sears, "Prejudice and Politics: Symbolic Racism versus Racial Threats to the Good Life" *Journal of Personality and Social Psychology* 40 (3) (1981): 414–31. The mere anticipation of interacting with an out-group can lead to more competitive interpretations of the out-group's likely behavior, even though the structural conditions of interaction with this group are not yet clear. See Willem Doise, *Groups and Individuals* (Cambridge: Cambridge University Press, 1978), 118.

82. An identity theory of realpolitik is important for at least three reasons. First, since the findings on the relationship between group formation and in-group–out-group competition in the experimental social psychology and cultural anthropology literature are so robust, it makes sense to see if these have implications for interstate relationships. Second, an identity theory of realpolitik introduces a third overarching category of realism by placing the origins of self-help behavior in the characteristics of group formation and membership, placing the theory between neorealism's focus on the the the causal attributes of system structure and classical realism's stress on human nature. Finally, an identity realism is one potential route for a constructivist contribution to explaining realpolitik. If constructivists are to challenge materialist realism they will have to explain both the so-called deviant cases and the allegedly nondeviant ones.

83. This leads to two conclusions. First, as the intensity of identity varies so must the degree to which the other is devalued, alienized and thus feared. This means uncertainty varies. If uncertainty varies while technical anarchy persists, then the causal connection between structural anarchy and uncertainty/fear is severed. Thus the scope and intensity of identity of the in-group can expand or contract while anarchy remains constant. Second, it is possible for a decentralized community identity to form without the complete subsumption of all actors into a bigger group. This means that, technically, anarchy can exist among independent actors who share a group identity. Thus Western European states can operate under conditions of anarchy, while sharing identities as members of a democratic European community. These shared identities lead to the interpretation of changing relative power capabilities in ways that structural realism would be unable to predict. Again this suggests that anarchy and self-help behavior are causally disconnected. It is precisely because the boundaries of identity communities can move, that it becomes possible to create larger or smaller pockets of low-competition relationships. This means, in principle, that

if in-group identity were global then no intergroup relationship would be affected by anarchy.

84. Glaser, "Realists as Optimists."

85. Russell Hardin, *One For All: The Logic of Group Conflict* (Princeton: Princeton University Press, 1995), 74–75.

86. This raises the possibility that identity discourses are used instrumentally by political leaders to buttress their political power, and thus ought properly to be seen as elements in strategic "diversionary" behavior by elites. There is no doubt this is often the case. But leaders can chose only those discourses that find resonance among relevant constituencies, that is, in groups where these are deeply internalized. Race baiting may be used instrumentally by Republicans in elections, but as Kinder and Sears indicate, this works only among whites who have internalized "symbolic racist" values. Race baiting is also likely to be used by those who, ironically, devalue the importance of racism as a central feature of American society. Thus the decision to chose a particular political instrumentality is constrained both by the values of the political entrepreneur and by the values of the target population. Instrumentality does not, therefore, reduce the causal importance of identity.

87. Ross, *The Culture of Conflict*, 176.

88. This tendency of groups to institutionalize a realpolitik world view is reinforced by the cost of acquiring and processing information that suggests the world is not so competitive. Since information is costly, the most authoritative sources will be from within the group. People are much more easily convinced by arguments coming from those within the in-group, since there is a prior expectation that one is more likely to agree with their views (Turner, *Rediscovering*, 100, 154). This creates a vicious circle of interpretation of new data that reinforces realpolitik beliefs. Put in Bayesian updating terms, prior beliefs about the realpolitik nature of the environment are reinforced by the a realpolitik likelihood function. Thus new data—new events whose probability of occurring might suggest that a less competitive state of the world exists—is interpreted as confirming rather than challenging priors. Posterior beliefs do not change. Identity realism would argue that this realpolitik likelihood function is a product of group identity formation, not structural anarchy. On Bayesian updating and the parallels between rational choicers' concept of the likelihood function and constructivists' concept of ideology see Robert H. Bates and Barry R. Weingast, "A New Comparative Politics: Integrating Rational Choice and Interpretivist Perspectives" (Cambridge: Center for International Affairs, Working Paper No. 95–3, April 1995): 35–36.

89. See David Campbell,*Writing Security: United States Foreign Policy and the Politics of Identity* (Minneapolis: University of Minnesota Press, 1992), 61–68. On the role of images of external danger and disorder as mechanisms of con-

trol—specifically the delegitimization of non-realpolitik views of strategy in policy discourses—see also Robin Luckham, "Armament Culture," *Alternatives* 10 (1) (1984), and Bradley S. Klein, "Hegemony and Strategic Culture: American Power Projection and Alliance Defence Politics," *Review of International Studies* 14 (1988). On the relationship between identity creation, control, and disorder see Harrison White, *Identity and Control: A Structural Theory of Social Action* (Princeton: Princeton University Press, 1992).

90. One indicator, then, of the intensity of in-group identification would be the discourse used to describe marginals—the more intensive in-group identity is the less acceptable multiple identities are in the discourse.

91. Osgood semantic differentiation asks a respondent to place her/himself along a seven-point scale between two binary opposite terms used to describe potential attitudes toward a particular item. A meta-contrast ratio refers to the "ratio of the average difference perceived between in-group and out-group members over the average difference perceived between in-group members." The smaller the denominator (e.g. the more closely in-group values converge), and the larger the numerator (e.g. the more divergences between group values) the greater the ratio, or the higher the measure of intensity of identification. See Margaret Wetherall, "Social Identity and Group Polarization" in Turner, *Rediscovering*, 155.

92. Glenn Chafetz has tried to measure the degree of identification between groups, essentially a measure of affect, by coding public statements about other states on a nine-point positive-negative scale. See Glenn Chafetz, "An Empirical Analysis of International Identity Change" (Paper presented to American Political Science Association Annual Meeting, Washington, D.C., August 28–31, 1997). It is not clear, however, that this measure captures deeply internalized, "taken-for-granted" assessments of other actors, or whether it simply measures the current state of amity-enmity in an interstate relationshup.

93. Social psychological work on group identity and intergroup conflict has shown that the preemptive devaluation of out-groups protects the sense of uniqueness of the in-group. Thus the intensity of group discourses that stress its uniqueness would also seem to be a logical indicator of in-group solidarity and out-group devaluation.

94. This works because of the intense socialization in particular interpretations of modern history. As one example, the first of a recently produced two-volume set on modern Chinese history written for Chinese youth is entitled, *National Shame*. It lists more than eighty instances of shame and insult to China, almost all of which were perpetrated by foreigners or Chinese working on behalf of foreign interests (the companion volume is entitled, *National Prowess*). See Che Jixin, ed., *Guochi* [National shame] (Jinan: Shandong Friendship Publishing House, 1992). The victimization has resonance even among Western-

educated intellectuals. See for example, Wang, *United States-China*, p. 267. The regime also expertly exploited the U.S. Congressional opposition to China's bid for the 2000 Olympics—the United States denied China a "chance" to show off its national spirit and energy—resulting in a surge of anti-americanism even among intellectual critics of the regime. See Jeremy Barme,"To Screw Foreigners is Patriotic: China's Avante-Garde Nationalists" *The China Journal* No.34 (July 1995): 214, and Wang, "Coping with China," 8.

95. See, for instance, the paean to traditional Chinese Confucian cultural values in a lengthy article on political education in the military written by Minister of Defense Chi Haotian. See "Build An Ideological Great Wall to Resist Corruption and Prevent Degeneration" *Renmin Ribao* (People's Daily) (August 10, 1995) in FBIS-CHI-95-188 (September 28, 1995): 30–31. See also a recent book on China's traditional ethics issued by the State Education Commission, Luo Guojie, ed., *Zhongguo chuantong daode* [China's traditional morality] (Beijing, People's University Press, 1995).

96. The racialist elements of the Chinese nationalist discourse is an extremely sensitive and difficult-to-handle issue, but too important to ignore. There is ambiguity as to which Chinese China's leaders refer to when invoking nationalism—ethnic Chinese, citizens of the PRC? Who is it that must "stand up" and take their place in the sun? Conservative nationalists have referred to the threat from "white culture." They will condemn those who are perceived to damage the national interest, like dissidents, as race traitors (*han jian*) (see for instance He Xin, "Weilai Zhong Mei guanxi" [Sino-U.S. relations in the future] (September 7, 1992) in He, *He Xin zhengzhi jingji*, 125). Conservative nationalists will distinguish between conflict based on socialist-capitalist ideology and issues like human rights on the one hand, and clashes of national interest on the other. However, the boundaries between racial-national interest and state interest are blurred. He Xin has characterized the conflict with the United States—namely American efforts to "peacefully evolve China"—as a conflict of "national-ethnic interests" (*minzu li yi*], not ideology (nor state interests— *guojia li yi*). See ibid., and He Xin, "Guanyu 'zuo' ji yishi xingtai gaige wenti de sikao" [Thoughts on the problem of the 'left' and ideological reform] (July 2, 1992) in ibid., p. 136. While He Xin is personally not so influential as he was in the late 1980s and early 1990s—he was close to Premier Li Peng for a time—his views are probably fairly representative of conservative nationalist voices in Beijing. On the racialism in modern Chinese nationalism see Frank Dikotter, *The Discourse of Race in Modern China*. (Stanford: Stanford University Press, 1992).

97. Andrew Nathan, "Human Rights in Chinese Foreign Policy" *The China Quar-*

terly No. 139 (September 1994): 622–43; Chen Jie, "Human Rights: ASEAN's New Importance to China." *Pacific Review.* 6 (3) (1993).

98. Wei Cizhu, "Zou chu aiguozhuyi jiaoyu 'wuqu' de duice silu" [Countermeasures for the road out of "error zones" in patriotic education], *Neibu wengao* [Internal manuscripts] No. 21 (1990): 8–9). See also Chen Xiushan, "Qutong lun pingxi" [A critique of convergence theory], *Neibu wengao* [Internal Manuscripts] No. 19 (1989): 5–8.

99. Hua Qing, "Jiekai minzuzhuyi shenmi de mianmao" [Open up the mysterious face of nationalism] *Shijie jingji yu zhangzhi* [World economics and politics] No. 7 (1995): 69–71). The more negatively described ones included the manufacturing of national hatreds and irrational ethno-national passions. There were implicitly distinguished from more progressive uses, as in the Chinese case.

100. On increase in the autonomous construction of ethnic identities inside China, the self-outing of people who previously saw themselves as Han Chinese, see Dru Gladney, "China's Ethnic Awakening" *Asia Pacific Issues* (East West Center) No. 18 (January 1995); Yitzhak Shichor, "Separatism: Sino-Muslim Conflict in Xinjiang," *Pacifica Review* 6 (2) (1994): 71–82. For a high-level expression of the dangers of Muslim separatism, fueled by Islamic revival worldwide, see the remarks by then-Vice President Wang Zhen in He Xin, "Wang Zhen tongzhi tanhua jiyao" [Record of key points in conversation with Comrade Wang Zhen" (April 17, 1991) in He, *He Xin zhengzhi jingji.*

101. Arguably one found in the mid 1980s, when the military challenge to China (from the USSR and Vietnam) was greater than the 1990s, and when China's integration into economic institutions was lower, the discourse was less shrilly realpolitik. Contrast, for instance, Zhao Ziyang's discussion of foreign policy in his report to the 13th Party Congress in 1987 with Jiang Zemin's report at the 14th Party Congress of 1992. Zhao stressed disarmament and development themes, while Jiang's was replete with references to preserving state sovereignty and independence. One was also more likely to find somewhat more sympathetic discussions of multilateral security institutions (e.g. summits, CBMs, crisis management centers, etc.) in the mid 1980s than one finds now. See for instance, Yu Shaoqiu, "Xi fang guoji chongtu yu weiji de kongzhi lilun pingshu" [Critique of Western theories on international conflict and the control of crises] in *Shijie jingji yu zhengzhi.* [World economics and politics] No. 7 (1986). Three of the realisms tested here would have a difficult time explaining the shift in discourse over the 1980s and 1990s. Identity realism's prediction that in the face of a severe legitimacy crisis the state will make greater efforts to intensify in-group identities is consistent with this shift in discourse.

102. He, "Weilai Zhong Mei," 126; He Xin, "Qianfu weiji yu qianjing yuce—dangqian Zhongguo nei wai xingshi de yanjiu baogao." [Hidden crisis and pro-

spective predictions—research report on the current internal and external situation] (September 25, 1989) in He, *He Xin Zhengzhi jingji*. Note this is similar to the rhetorical strategy of invoking Croatian fascism among Serbs: even though the probability of extermination is low, it is greater than zero, given modern history in China. Thus the effects of American strategy would be disastrous for China. This expected utility, manufactured through the invocation of historically rooted symbols, then rallies support for regime. Bates and Weingast, "A New Comparative Politics."

103. Although this has been the official journal of Institute of World Economics and Politics at the Chinese Academy of Social Sciences, in practice it has been a forum for policy-relevant scholarship on IR topics from specialists from a wide range of institutes including the military, the Foreign Ministry, and the intelligence community. Thus, it has some degree of face validity as a source of authoritative thinking about IR and China's role in the world. The procedures were kept simple. Ten articles were randomly selected from each of seven years spanning the 1989 and 1991 divides. All references to the eleven terms, including pronouns, were counted for each article (N = 1772). The number of references to each term in each article was then averaged, giving a yearly mean. The chart represents the cumulative sum of these yearly means. The terms were clustered into roughly opposing cooperative and conflictual concept categories. The cooperative terms were: cooperation (*hezuo*), interdependence (*xianghu yicun/yilai*); international interest (*guoji liyi*), new world order (*shijie xin zhixu*); and international organizations (*guji zuzhi*]. The terms signifying conflict were: power politics/hegemonism (*qiangquan zhengzhi/baquanzhuyi*); conflict/contradictions (*douzheng, maodun*); sovereignty (*zhuquan*); independence (*duli*); national interest (*guojialiyi*); and new international order (*guojixinzhixu*). I thank Robert Ross for lending me his copies of the journal, and Fu Jun and Qiu Dong for doing the coding work. We were, unfortunately, unable to find complete runs for 1987, 1990, 1993 and 1994.

104. In preciously few instances if one accepts in combination the very different work of Vasquez, Schweller, and Schroeder.

105. Alastair Iain Johnston, "Cultural Realism and Strategy in Maoist China" in Peter Katzenstein ed., *The Culture of National Security: Norms and Identity in World Politics* (New York: Columbia University Press, 1996).

9   Realism and Regionalism: American Power and German and Japanese Institutional Strategies During and After the Cold War

Joseph M. Grieco

It was suggested in the early 1990s that the end of the Cold War and the loss of a common Soviet challenge to the advanced industrial democracies might split the world political economy into three main competing blocs centered around Germany in Europe, the United States in the Americas, and Japan in East Asia.[1] Since 1990 countries in many parts of the world have sought to construct or strengthen regional economic institutions.[2] In Western Europe these efforts have led to robust (albeit sometimes tumultuous) regional economic institutionalization, and in the Americas there has been significant initial movement toward institutionalization of regional economic diplomacy.[3] However, institutionalization of economic relations has failed to take hold in East Asia.[4] The only active arrangement in the region at present—the Association of South East Asian Nations (ASEAN)—has few accomplishments to its credit.[5] Most interesting from the viewpoint of the present discussion is that proposals to form an economic arrangement restricted to East Asian countries—the East Asian Economic Group (EAEG), and, later, the East Asian Economic Caucus (EAEC)— have failed so far to garner support or operational significance. At present, the only serious regional diplomatic effort aimed at economic liberalization—the Asia-Pacific Economic Cooperation forum (APEC)—is designed explicitly *not* to be a wholly East Asian regional entity and instead to be trans-Pacific in its membership and goals.[6]

The variance one observes in regional economic institutionalization in

Western Europe and East Asia is due in substantial measure to the marked differences in the policy preferences and strategies of the most powerful states in the two areas, Germany and Japan. In brief, Germany has sought very clearly to define its national interests and strategies in terms of formal European institutions. In contrast, Japan has not had such an institutionalist orientation regarding its neighbors. Japan has made no significant effort to help establish a uniquely East Asian economic arrangement, and indeed, as is described below, it rejected invitations in the early 1990s by countries in the region to undertake such a leadership role. Instead, it accepted what has become an essentially American-inspired program through APEC for trans-regional as opposed to intraregional economic diplomacy.

This chapter addresses two main questions. First, why, in the face of an apparently similar stimulus—the end of the Cold War—have Germany and Japan responded so differently on the issue of regional economic institutions? Second, can modern realist theory help us understand the differences observed in German and Japanese preferences for regional economic institutions? To pursue these questions, the next section provides a description of Germany and Japan's recent policy preferences regarding regional economic arrangements. This is followed by a section in which the differences observed in German and Japanese preferences for such arrangements are shown to constitute an empirical puzzle for students of international politics if these differences are examined in light of liberal institutionalist ideas about the functional bases of international collaboration or from the viewpoint of important realist propositions about hegemonic leadership.

The third main section then puts forward a realist-inspired analysis that seeks to help account for the strong German bias in favor of regional institutions and the equally pronounced Japanese aversion for such arrangements to date. The main thesis presented in the section is that a part of the explanation for the difference in German and Japanese interest in regionalism centers around the current level and role of American power in the two regions. A second line of analysis is that differences in geostrategic circumstances at the outset of the Cold War in West Europe and East Asia, combined with differences in American grand strategy in the two regions, set the countries in the two areas on different trajectories regarding their interest in regionalism and amenability to institutionalized economic cooperation, trajectories that are still in evidence today despite the end of the Cold War. The final section analyzes the implications of this case study of realist theory and American policy.

German and Japanese Preferences for Regional Economic Institutionalization

For almost half a century, the Federal Republic of Germany has worked resolutely to define and pursue its national economic interests in terms of European institutions. Ever since it became a sovereign state in 1949, the Federal Republic has worked closely with its neighbors—in particular, France—to construct the region's main economic arrangements: the European Coal and Steel Community in 1951, the European Economic Community in 1957, and the European Communities in 1967.[7]

Germany has also played a key role—again, with France and, to some degree, Great Britain—in more recent European Community efforts to develop important new programs for trade (the Single Market Program in 1985), and internal Community decisionmaking (the Single European Act of 1987).[8] In addition, Germany has been vital in EC (now European Union, or EU) efforts to construct special arrangements aimed at enhanced institutionalized European monetary cooperation: the "snake in the tunnel" in 1971, the European Monetary System in 1979, and, with the Maastricht Treaty of 1992, a posited trajectory for full Economic and Monetary Union perhaps by the turn of the century.[9] Germany has also taken on a leading role in EU negotiations to expand trade with the former Soviet satellite countries, and eventually to expand the European Union to include such countries as Hungary, Poland, and the Czech Republic.[10]

In contrast, Japan has been indifferent and even hostile to proposals for regional economic institutionalization in East Asia. Japan has made no significant effort to help establish an East Asian institutionalized arrangement aimed at regional economic liberalization and integration. Indeed, the diplomacy during 1990 and 1991 surrounding the ill-fated East Asian Economic Group suggests that Japan has made a clear-cut choice against regional institutionalization, at least for the present.

In December 1990, in the wake of the failure of the GATT countries to bring the Uruguay Round to completion on schedule, and in the face of new efforts at European Community integration and the ongoing talks surrounding the North American Free Trade Agreement, Malaysia's Prime Minister, Mahathir Mohamad, suggested that the East Asian countries should establish their own East Asian Economic Group (EAEG).[11] The group, as envisioned by the Malaysian government, would be composed of the six member countries of ASEAN—Brunei, Indonesia, Malaysia, the Philippines, Singapore, and Thailand—plus China, Japan, South Korea, Taiwan, Hong Kong, Vietnam, Cambodia, and Laos, *but not* Australia, New Zealand, or the United States.[12] Mahathir's Foreign Minister, Rafidah Aziz, suggested in March 1991 that such an arrangement could serve as a pressure group for East Asia in the Uruguay Round in a manner similar to that being pursued by the Cairns Group of agricultural producers. However, she also left open the possibility that such a group might evolve into an East Asian common market at some future point.[13] Thus, Malaysia's foreign policy leaders appear to have thought of EAEG as being at the minimum a Uruguay Round lobbying group, and at the maximum a nucleus for a potential fullblown formal trade bloc in East Asia, one that would exclude a number of Pacific Rim countries, most notably the United States.

Malaysia's EAEG proposal appears never to have had a good chance for success. Singapore was the only country in the region to offer even qualified official support for the proposal.[14] In contrast, in early January 1991, Indonesia's Foreign Minister and Trade Minister both expressed doubts about the idea of a regional arrangement, and indicated that it required fuller consultations among the ASEAN partners.[15]

Moreover, the key country in the EAEG would have been Japan, and that country was markedly disinclined to pursue such a proposal. In late April 1991, Japan's Prime Minister, Toshiki Kaifu, indicated that his government would react to the proposal only after Malaysia had worked with its ASEAN partners to develop a more complete view on what EAEG would entail.[16] However, Kaifu was more clearly and categorically hostile to the proposal a month later: he was quoted as saying that, "At a time when we are trying to build a free trade system, we shouldn't create problems and misunderstandings with the aimless establishment of lots of small groups." He was reported further to acknowledge that he had taken a "cool and impassive approach" toward the proposal, but that "I am thinking from a global perspective, one that will benefit Asia."[17]

In early October 1991 Mahathir acknowledged that he did not have support even within ASEAN for an EAEG. He then tried to solicit support for a more modest and less formal arrangement, an East Asian Economic Caucus (EAEC), which in response to an Indonesian proposal the ASEAN countries agreed in July 1993 would operate solely within the framework of APEC.[18] However, Japan was unattracted even to this approach to East Asian regional economic institutionalization. In November 1991, Koichi Kata, the Chief Cabinet Secretary, made it clear that Japan would not participate even in an informal East Asian caucus given that the latter would exclude the United States.[19] Malaysia did attain modest ASEAN support for an EAEC.[20] However, by July 1993 Japan and South Korea made it clear that they would not join the Caucus.[21] During the spring of 1995 Mahathir continued to press for an EAEC, but specified that Australia and New Zealand would not be included because they were not "Asian countries."[22] This appears to have given Japan an opportunity to put even more distance between itself and the EAEC proposal: the Japanese government indicated during the summer of 1995 that it would support establishment of the EAEC only if all other APEC countries endorsed such an effort, which was unlikely in light of strong U.S. objections to the EAEC concept (discussed below), *and* only if the proposed Caucus included Australia and New Zealand.[23]

Prime Minister Mahathir has sometimes suggested that EAEC could go forward without Japan.[24] However, it is clear that few countries in the region are or will become interested in an EAEC that does not include Japan. For example, when the Japanese government announced in April 1995 that it would not attend an ASEAN-proposed meeting on the EAEC proposal, the prospective host, Thailand, canceled the meeting.[25] Given Japan's strong and now sustained opposition to the EAEC, the organization's future can only be considered highly bleak.

JAPANESE AND GERMAN PREFERENCES FOR REGIONALISM AS A PUZZLE FOR INTERNATIONAL THEORY

In light of the country's decisive role in the failed diplomacy surrounding East Asian economic institutionalization during the 1990s, we need to ask in the first place whether it is surprising that Japan elected not to pursue institutionalization as would have been entailed by the EAEG and EAEC proposals, especially in light of Germany's strong support for regionalism in Western Europe. Indeed, one might suggest that Japan has been disinclined to pursue formal regional institutionalization because it does not need it to enjoy the benefits of close regional economic integration. Why, then, should it be expected that Japan would incur the inevitable costs associated with institutionalization?

Three points can be made in response to this question. First, there are grounds to suggest that Japan did in fact seriously consider both the EAEG and the EAEC institutional options. Over the years there have been reports that senior Japanese officials in the Ministry of Foreign Affairs, the Ministry of Finance, and the Ministry of International Trade and Industry (MITI) were sympathetic to the EAEG and, later, the EAEC proposals.[26] Regarding the latter, for example, Japanese Foreign Minister Yohei Kono attended an ASEAN-sponsored informal planning session regarding EAEC hosted by Thailand in July 1994.[27] Finance Minister Masayoshi Takemura was quoted in early 1995 as saying that the Japanese people were becoming sympathetic to the idea of holding talks "amongst East Asians."[28] And Toshiki Kaifu, president of the New Frontier Party, indicated in early 1995 that Japan should keep open its option to participate in EAEC.[29] It should also be noted that there has been a broader debate in the Japanese bureaucracy in recent years on whether Japan should develop a stronger Asian orientation in its foreign policy, and at least some of these "Asia-first" advocates viewed the EAEC proposal with interest.[30] Finally, there were arguments within the Japanese business community—specifically, among officials connected with the Keidanren, Japan's main business organization—in favor of the EAEC concept.[31]

Second, and as highlighted in the next section, two different U.S. administrations worked hard to bring about the failure of the EAEG and the EAEC. At the core of this effort was the application of significant pressure on Japan to ensure that it would reject both proposed arrangements. Given these sustained, high-level U.S. efforts directed at a number of East Asian countries and especially Japan, it might be inferred that the proposals had some regional credibility, including possible Japanese interest in them. Thus, while there were clearly problems with Malaysia's proposals for EAEG and EAEC, including insufficient consultation on Malaysia's part with Japan and even its ASEAN partners, the proposals elicited interest in some Japanese policy circles, and it was sufficiently serious that it drew increasingly harsh criticisms from the United States (and, it should be noted, Australia).

Third, from the viewpoint of existing systemic international theory, it might have been expected that Japan would be interested by the early 1990s in the construction of a formal East Asian economic arrangement. From the viewpoint of arguments within the liberal institutionalist tradition, for example, the Japanese government might have been expected to react to changes that occurred during the past decade in Japan's trade patterns by developing a significant interest in the formation of such an arrangement. Drawing on that tradition's functionalist logic, a country should become motivated to establish a formal regional trading regime if and as its trade is becoming more regionally concentrated: as such a country becomes more dependent on its regional partners for trade, it should experience a greater functional need for and interest in attaining the certainty and stability of access to those partners that might result from formal arrangements.[32]

To obtain a sense of whether Japan could have been expected to develop a functional interest in East Asian regional institutionalization, Figure 9.1 presents data on changes from the 1970s through the early 1990s in the percentage of Japan's overall exports going to the countries (except Vietnam, Cambodia, and Laos) that would have composed the EAEG/EAEC. For purposes of comparison, the figure also presents data on Germany's regional concentration of exports in connection with its EC fellow-members and the United States' regional export concentration in regard to its NAFTA partners.

The figure indicates that for many years Germany has had a much higher percentage of its exports going to its EC partners (now expanded from 12 to 15) than Japan has had in regard to its potential EAEG/EAEC partners in East Asia. This certainly helps account for Germany's stronger preference for European regionalism compared to Japan's lower preference for Asian institutionalization. However, at least two features about the data in Figure 9.1 suggest that Japan ought to have developed a stronger preference for a regional arrangement in recent years. First, Japan's export dependence on East Asia, while not approaching that of Germany's in respect to Western Europe, has been growing quite significantly: the recipients of roughly one-fourth of Japan's total exports during the 1970s and the bulk of the 1980s, Japan's proposed EAEG/EAEC partners became the recipients of roughly one-third of Japan's total exports during the late 1980s and early 1990s. Second, while the regional export concentration levels of both Japan and the United States have grown in the past decade—that is, both have begun to look somewhat more like Germany in Western Europe—Japan's regional export dependence actually has exceeded that of the United States in recent years (an average of about 34% for Japan between 1990 and 1994 compared to 29% for the United States during the same period). In light of the way in which the United States responded to growing regional trade dependence, its development of NAFTA, it is surprising that Japan reacted so differently, essentially rejecting regional institutionalization, in the face of a similar stimulus, an acceleration of Japanese trade dependence on its own region.

Just as functional institutionalism has difficulties in accounting for the

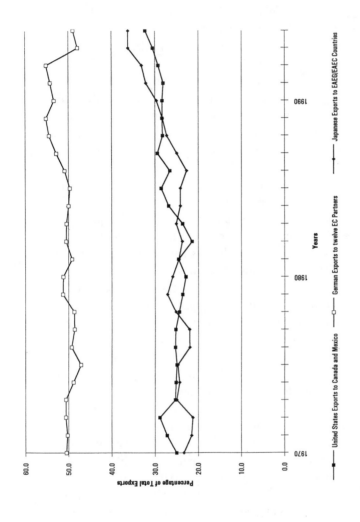

FIGURE 9.1 Percentage of Total Exports of Germany, Japan, and the United States to Regional Partners, 1970–1994

Sources: International Monetary Fund, *Direction of Trade Statistics Yearbook* (Washington, various years); and Republic of China, *Taiwan Statistical Data Book* (Taipei, various years).

divergence between Germany and Japan with regard to their preference for regional economic institutions, so too realist theory has difficulties in explaining that divergence. From a realist viewpoint it might have been expected that, in light of the end of the Cold War, the erosion of bipolarity, and the possible reduction in American attention to East Asia, Japan would turn to regional institutionalization as a form of insurance that its close ties with its East Asian neighbors would continue in a stable, predictable context. Yet, the end of the Cold War and bipolarity have not caused Japan or, for that matter, Germany, to shift their preferences regarding regionalism.[33] Japan was highly disinclined to pursue regionalist policies during the Cold War, and this has not changed since 1989. The Federal Republic was highly regionalist in its foreign economic policy during the Cold War, and it has stayed on (and indeed reinforced its commitment to) that course since reunification with the eastern zone. Hence, in the face of a momentous change at the international level—the end of the great Soviet-American struggle that had defined the basic structure of the international system for half a century—we see little significant change in the behavior of two very powerful secondary countries toward their neighbors in regard to regional institutions. This continuity in Japanese and German policies concerning regional institutionalization in the face of international structural change raises questions about whether it has been the polarity of the international system that has been driving the behavior of these two key states in an important policy domain.

Moreover, it might have been expected that as Japan became more hegemonic in East Asia it would have the capacity and, more importantly, would develop the desire to provide the leadership necessary to construct regional arrangements for the area. This line of analysis—that a regional hegemon is at least a necessary condition for regional economic institutionalization— would appear to be confirmed in the case of regional cooperation in North America, where the United States in 1990 accounted for more than 80 percent of that area's economic activity. However, while Germany was the site for about one-fourth of Western Europe's gross domestic product in 1990, Japan at that time was the origin of almost three-quarters of the economic activity of the countries that would have constituted the EAEG/ EAEC.[34] Hence, while Japan enjoys a much more pronounced overall hegemonic position in East Asia than Germany does in Western Europe, and approaches the United States' overall hegemonic position in North America, Japan has not presented evidence that it is as willing as either Germany or the United States to exercise leadership in regional economic institutions in the post-Cold War era.

REALIST THEORY AND GERMAN AND JAPANESE PREFERENCES FOR REGIONALISM: THE IMPACT OF AMERICAN POWER AND STRATEGY

The discussion above suggests that, from the viewpoint of both functional institutionalism and realism, it is puzzling that Japan continues to have a weak preference for regional institutions, and especially while Germany continues to have a strong preference for such institutions. The discussion below suggests that the resolution of this puzzle may be found in the character and level of American power and strategy during the Cold War and since its conclusion.

To develop this argument, it may be helpful to begin with Japan and its refusal to support the EAEG and EAEC proposals. Japan's disinclination to pursue either approach was due to many factors, including domestic institutional characteristics that make foreign policy innovation by that country quite difficult.[35] But one that was clearly of major importance to Japan was the strong opposition expressed by the United States to both options, and particularly to the prospect of Japan's becoming a part of either proposed arrangement. The United States began to voice its opposition to Malaysia's EAEG proposal early in 1991.[36] Vice President Dan Quayle, in an address in May, said that the United States would "not welcome" an arrangement from which it was excluded.[37] In addition, in early November a letter from Secretary of State James Baker was submitted to the Japanese government and other prospective EAEG members specifically requesting that they not support the proposal.[38]

This opposition continued with the change in U.S. administrations, and in regard to Malaysia's fallback proposal for a Caucus rather than a more ambitious Group. For example, after being provided details in May 1994 on the Malaysian proposal for an EAEC, including the idea that the Caucus would operate within but not be responsible to APEC, the Clinton Administration formally presented its view to Japan and Thailand, then ASEAN chair, that the arrangement should not be pursued by the East Asian countries.[39] Assistant Secretary of State Winston Lord explained in July that the proposal had "seemed to [be] a more ambitious concept than we had been led to believe," and "we don't want to see anything develop that would have a dividing line down the Pacific."[40] Similarly negative statements about the EAEC were made by senior administration officials in September 1995, with Joseph Nye, Assistant Secretary of Defense, suggesting (and perhaps issuing as a warning) the view that he believed that East Asian countries had rejected the EAEC because they recognized that, had they moved down a path leading to exclusion of the United States, "we would probably withdraw our security presence."[41]

There is good evidence that at least a part of Japan's reticence to pursue either the EAEG or the EAEC option was in fact related to U.S. opposition to both ideas. For example, in explaining Japan's opposition to the EAEC proposal in November 1991, Chief Cabinet Secretary Kato specifically cited the United States' important economic and security role in the region.[42] Similarly, according to the *Nikkei Weekly*, while Japanese officials had revisited the idea of supporting the EAEC proposal in the first half of 1994, they decided that "at a time when close cooperation with Washington is vital in dealing with North Korea, diplomatic wisdom dictates Japan should not do anything that could unsettle its relations with the U.S." The report also quotes Foreign Minister Yohei Kono as emphasizing in a recent meeting with his Malaysian counterpart the view that, "If EAEC is embarked on without the support of the U.S. and other nations, its value will be halved."[43] Japan's decision not to attend the April 1995 proposed ASEAN-sponsored meeting in Thailand was apparently heavily based on a desire not to alienate the United States.[44] Finally, in explaining why Japan continued to avoid the EAEC option, in July 1995 the spokesperson for Japan's Foreign Minister noted in a press conference that, "As you know the United States is still very much opposed to the idea of the EAEC . . . [and] some other countries are opposed to the EAEC as well."[45]

The United States pressured Japan to reject both the EAEG and the EAEC proposals, and Japan rejected those proposals at least in part so as not to provoke the United States. American policy preferences thus help to account for Japan's disinclination to pursue a wholly East Asian economic grouping in the early 1990s. But to say that the United States opposed Japanese support for East Asian economic institutionalization and that this helps account for the low preference on Japan's part to pursue such an option raises another question: what about Germany and the EC/EU? Why, in light of the United States' vigorous efforts to press Japan to reject the EAEG and the EAEC, do we not see similar efforts by the United States to seek to influence Germany to forestall the further development of the Community? There are at least three reasons why American policy toward Germany and the EC has differed from that toward Japan and East Asian economic institutionalization. First, while the United States believes that the EC has had a basically positive impact on U.S. trade interests, there is great concern that an East Asian trade would have a manifestly negative effect on U.S. commercial interests in that region, especially if it were centered around Japan. The United States has on occasion raised concerns about European institutionalized integration. For example, it has repeatedly voiced complaints about the Community's Common Agricultural Policy, it has insisted on its GATT rights and requested compensation when the EC expanded to include such countries as Spain and Portugal, and it has expressed concerns about such recent EC policy initiatives as the Broadcasting Directive.[46] However, the United States has viewed the EC/EU as, on balance, a trade-creating arrangement, and it certainly recognizes that Germany has been a leading force for economic openness within the Community.

In contrast, U.S. officials in the early 1990s specifically voiced their concern that an EAEG would promote closure of Asian markets to the United States, and would do so precisely because it would be decisively driven by Japan. As one news report indicated in October 1991, "Despite claims to the contrary, U.S. officials say, Mahathir's proposed East Asian Economic Group (EAEG) could—in a worst-case scenario—develop into a protectionist bloc prone to shedding traditional values of open markets," and it went on to specify that, "The obvious tendency would be to emulate the Japanese model of development through industrial policy, managed trade and mercantilism, a model that draws vociferous complaints of unfairness from the West." Indeed, it was because the United States wanted to counter this prospect of a closed East Asian arrangement that it pressed for the development of Australia's APEC proposal; for example, an American official was quoted in the October 1991 news report as saying about APEC as an alternative to EAEG that, "Our goal is to get all these countries into the camp of open markets rather than see them take the Japanese approach of more managed trade."[47]

A second argument draws more explicitly on realist-oriented work by Albert Hirschman and Kenneth Waltz on the political effects of asymmetric economic interdependence. A basic insight resulting from their respective analyses is that if one partner in an interstate economic relationship would sustain fewer losses than the other partner were the relationship terminated, then, other things being equal, the former would enjoy greater influence in the relationship.[48] This insight can allow us to assess various bilateral relationships in terms of differentials in potential influence; in particular, it suggests that even if the United States wanted to pressure both Germany and Japan to slow or reverse economic institutionalization in their respective regions, America's capacity to so influence Germany would be substantially less than it would be in regard to Japan.

There are, for example, sharp differences that exist between Japan and Germany in terms of their respective stakes in the American export market. This can be observed in Figure 9.2, which provides data on the percentage of total exports from Japan and Germany going to the United States from 1970 to 1994. The figure shows that Japan has needed the United States export market much more than has been true of Germany. For example, while during the early 1990s about 7 percent of Germany's total exports went to the United States, about 29 percent of Japan's went to that market. Hence, even if the United States wanted both Japan and Germany to forgo regional economic institutionalization in the trade issue-area, it is in a much more powerful position to press this interest in regard to the former than to the latter.

A similarly higher level of Japanese export dependence on the United States compared to Germany can be observed in Figure 9.3, which presents data on exports from each country to the United States as a percentage of their respective gross domestic products from the 1970s to the early 1990s. Again, Japan has experienced a higher level of dependence on the United States for its overall economic growth and well-being than has Germany. For example, while approximately 2.6% of Japan's national annual economic activity during the early 1990s was composed of exports to the United States, about 1.5% of Germany's GDP during this period took the form of exports to the U.S. market.

In addition, Figure 9.4 provides evidence that, as a basis for importing goods and services from the rest of the world, Japan has needed its bilateral trading relationship with the United States much more than Germany has relied on its American ties. The figure presents data on the percentage of imports by Japan and Germany from countries other than the United States that are covered by Japanese and German net exports to (that is, their respective trade surpluses with) the United States. The figure indicates that almost one-fourth of Japanese imports from countries other than the United States between 1990 and 1993 was paid for by that country's net exports to

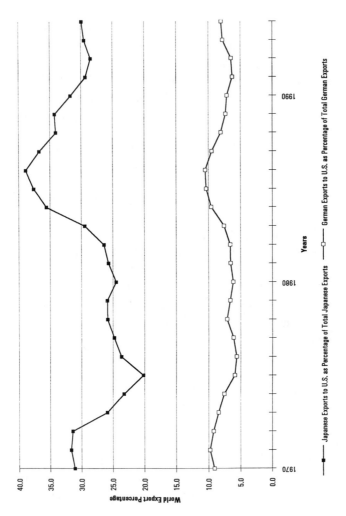

FIGURE 9.2 Percentage of Total Exports of Germany and Japan to the U.S., 1970–1994

Sources: International Monetary Fund, *Direction of Trade Statistics Yearbook* (Washington, various years).

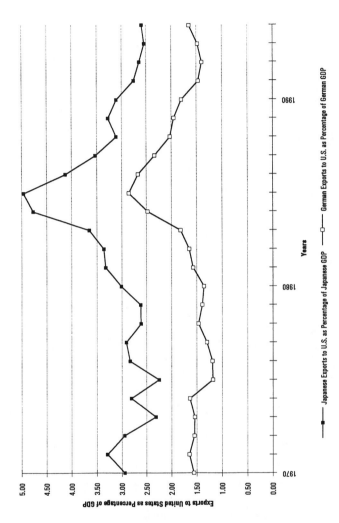

FIGURE 9.3 Japanese and German Exports to United States as a Percentage of their Gross Domestic Product, 1970–1994

Sources: International Monetary Fund, *Direction of Trade Statistics Yearbook* (Washington, various years); and Organization for Economic Co-Operation and Development, *National Accounts*; *Main Aggregates*, Vol. 1 (Paris, various years).

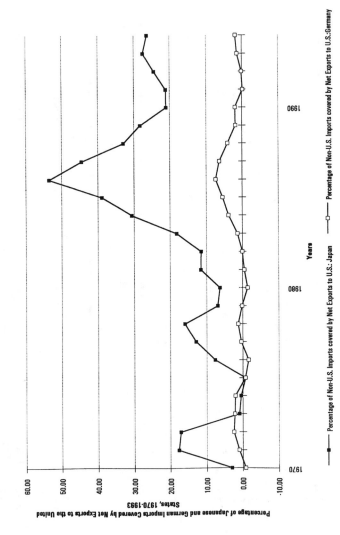

FIGURE 9.4 Japanese and German Non-U.S. Imports Covered by Net Exports to the United States, 1970–1994

Sources. See Figure 3.

the United States; the comparable figure for Germany during those years was substantially less than 1 percent.

These data suggest that Japan is markedly more dependent on the United States export market than is Germany. This acute Japanese trade dependence would certainly help account for Japan's reluctance to be supportive of EAEG and EAEC if this entailed a confrontation with the United States. Of course, that this was true in the case of EAEG and EAEC does not mean that Japan is helpless in all its political-economic dealings with America. Indeed, in other issue-areas, such as high technology and especially finance, U.S.-Japanese relationships are more symmetrical, with each having strong interests in maintaining favorable ties with the other, and it is likely that the United States may be reluctant to press its position in some trade issues (like automobiles) because of its interests in those other nontrade issue-areas. However, Japan does not appear to have found the EAEG and EAEC proposals to be so important or promising to use any leverage arising from the symmetrical vulnerability in those nontrade issue-areas as a way of parrying U.S. pressures against EAEG and EAEC.

Another key factor contributing to asymmetrical interests between Japan and the United States on the one hand and Germany and the United States on the other concerns the respective security situations of the two regional powers in the wake of the Cold War. Since the late-1980s, Japan has faced a wider and more serious array of security challenges than Germany, and for that reason Japan may be more interested in maintaining good relations with its U.S. ally *as a security question* than is true of Germany. Germany's security position has improved dramatically since 1989: its main threat since 1945, the Soviet Union, no longer exists; the main military alliance that had been directed at the Federal Republic, the Warsaw Treaty Organization, also no longer exists; Russia at present is not simply interested in good relations with Germany, it positively needs German economic assistance; even if Russia were to turn authoritarian at home and adventurist abroad, it would do so with highly diminished military capabilities; and a number of independent states now lie between Russia and Germany, greatly increasing the difficulties that Russia would have in exercising a military threat. For these reasons Germany is interested today in U.S. security ties not so much as a counter to real, immediate threats but as insurance against theoretical, distant contingencies.

Japan's situation is quite different. There is, in the first place, the immediate danger that North Korea might now have, or will soon possess, a capability to threaten Japan with nuclear weapons. In addition, and perhaps more ominously in the near future, China is a rapidly growing economic force in East Asia, and there are disturbing signs that it wants to revise the political and perhaps even the territorial order of the region.[49] Thus, Germany remains interested in a solid security relationship with the United States as a matter of prudence; for Japan the military alliance with the United States is a matter of necessity.

This discussion of asymmetries in Japanese and German interests in the good will of the United States may help account for Japan's acute responsiveness to American objections to a uniquely East Asian economic arrangement. But there is one final set of factors that must be highlighted as we try to understand why the United States came to view regionalism in Western Europe and East Asia so differently, and why institutionalization has varied so markedly in the two parts of the world: the differences in the geostrategic circumstances of the Cold War in East Asia and Western Europe, the way in which these geostrategic differences caused the United States to develop very different political-military strategies for the two regions, and the direct and profound impact that these differences in U.S. strategies had on the trajectory of intraregional relations in the two areas.[50]

As John Ikenberry emphasizes in an important essay, the United States sought at the conclusion of World War II to help construct a genuinely multilateral ("one-world") economic order based on the Bretton Woods negotiations on monetary matters and the talks on the ill-fated International Trade Organization. As World War II ended and competition between the United States and the Soviet Union intensified, however, the United States was compelled to turn from its original plans for a multilateral global order to a European "third force" option. That is, the United States abandoned full world multilateralism and sought instead to promote the development of a Western Europe that was both strong and autonomous *and* linked closely to America through joint economic and security institutions. The United States would continue to work with Western Europe through the Bretton Woods agreement and the fallback to the ITO, the General Agreement on Tariffs and Trade, or GATT. But these efforts would be supplemented by specifically Euro-American projects. The early military-institutional manifestations of this new strategy were the Truman Doctrine of 1947 and the North Atlantic Treaty of 1949; its first economic elements were the Marshall Plan of 1948 and, as its main European operating entity, the Organization for European Economic Cooperation (OEEC), established in

1948, as well as the European Payments Union (EPU), founded in 1950.[51]

In pursuing this "third force" option, the fundamental political-military problem for the United States *and* its Western European allies from the late 1940s (and indeed throughout the Cold War) was crystal clear. First, the Soviets enjoyed massive conventional military superiority. Second, there was no way the United States could commit sufficient ground troops to offset that superiority. Third, while nuclear weapons *might* ensure deterrence, this became less credible as the Soviets developed a more deadly nuclear arsenal. Fourth, if there were to be a realistic chance that the West could employ conventional military forces to defeat and thus to deter a Soviet conventional military attack, the prospects for such a Western strategy would be greatly augmented if the Soviet thrust could be stopped at the West's geographic and political front line—West Germany. Finally, there was one and only one Western European state with sufficient manpower and potential military-industrial capability to contribute decisively to Western conventional power, and the motive to turn that potential capability into actual power—the Federal Republic of Germany.[52]

This last fact created profound misgivings in Germany's World War II victims, and especially in France. The solution to which the Western Europeans turned, and for which the United States gave strong and vitally important support, was to allow Germany to rebuild its economy, and later its armed forces, within the framework of regional economic and security institutions.[53] In this way, Germany's neighbors believed, German power would be shared with and managed by its Western European partners, and those partners would be able to cooperate with but not be dominated by that key country.[54] The institutions for this strategy in the economic domain were of course the European Coal and Steel Community and, later, the European Economic Community and the European Communities; in the security domain they were the North Atlantic Treaty Organization (after the proposal for a European Defense Community was defeated by the French parliament in 1954) and, to a lesser degree, the Western European Union.[55]

The West German government was highly attracted to this approach for several reasons. First, European integration allowed Germany to undertake reindustrialization. Second, it created a context within which Germany reattained sovereignty and a larger voice in European affairs. Third, the reemergence of Germany within the framework of European institutions permitted and fostered the relegitimization of the German state both within Germany and within the European and world system.[56]

Hence, from the beginning of the Cold War, to have any real chance of pursuing their fundamental goal of preventing the domination of Western Europe by the Soviet Union, the Western European countries and the United States needed an industrialized, militarily potent West Germany. To have German economic and military power available to the Western alliance without also permitting German hegemony in Europe, its neighbors pursued and the United States promoted the creation and development of NATO and what has become the European Union. It is of course an open question as to whether Germany's neighbors have succeeded in limiting German power through institutions; Germany's near-total domination of recent EU diplomacy regarding Europe's path to EMU suggests that this strategy has serious limitations.[57] But the Western Europeans remain committed to this strategy and the Americans continue to embrace the goal of European economic integration and institutionalization.

For Germany, European integration has yielded tremendous economic benefits. It has, as noted above, also permitted German reentry into European and world affairs. Finally, the diplomacy of the European Community and now the Union makes it clear that no important European initiative can move forward without German support, and none can survive German opposition. The case of EMU shows in fact that Germany now dominates— in a tactful, diplomatic, but unambiguous way—the key characteristics of important European institutional initiatives. The Community at first gave the Germans a way by which they could again be a part of civilized Europe; now it provides them with a vehicle for exercising great and growing power discreetly and without arousing substantial resistance or even very much resentment.

As the Cold War commenced in East Asia in the late 1940s, the United States shifted its attention in Japan from democratization and decartelization to economic recovery.[58] As a part of that "new course" strategy, the United States sought to encourage the reestablishment of trade between Japan and its East and Southeast Asian neighbors (with the notable exception of China) without necessarily creating formal regional institutions to accomplish that goal.[59] Later, and as the Cold War intensified in that part of the world, the United States came to favor the establishment of regional economic institutions that would involve Japan. For example, Burton Kaufman reports that as a part of a containment strategy in Asia in the wake of the Korean War and the French defeat in Indochina, President Eisenhower and Secretary of State John Foster Dulles expressed in late 1954 the view that Japan was the key U.S. ally in the region and that it was essential to support it by fostering closer economic ties between that country and those in Southeast Asia. Further, Kaufman reports that in October 1954 U.S. foreign aid chief Harold Stassen proposed to Asian countries participating in the Colombo Plan that they band together to establish an organization similar to the OEEC in Europe, and the Eisenhower administration sought from 1954 through 1956 to obtain approximately $200 million from Congress to be distributed through such an Asian regional aid arrangement.[60]

However, even before Congress declined to provide these resources, thirteen Asian countries met in May 1955 in Simla, India, to discuss how that proposed U.S. aid could be employed, and they formally rejected the idea that they should form a regional organization to dispense the resources. They suggested instead that the monies be provided directly to the participating Asian recipients.[61] The problem, Kaufman reports, was Japan: "With memories of World War II fresh in their minds, the countries of the region were reluctant to establish commercial relations with their former captors," and, in addition, "they feared that their own interests would be dwarfed by an economically resurgent Japan supported by the United States."[62]

Given that the United States was pursuing a controversial embargo of most trade with Japan's traditional critical commercial partner, China, and that most of the countries in the region were averse to reestablishing economic ties with Japan, the United States supported Japan through direct assistance and military procurement and through sponsorship of that country's application to join the GATT. Japan became a member of the GATT in 1955, but almost half of its new partners immediately invoked the safeguard provisions of the agreement and severely limited Japanese access to their markets.[63] American support for Japan then turned to the more complete opening by the United States of its market to Japanese goods, as well as the continuation of massive U.S. military orders that had begun with the outbreak of the Korean war in June 1950.[64] Thus, while the United States sought to promote Asian regionalism in the early to mid-1950s, Japan's potential partners rejected this option. They, as Germany's partners in Western Europe, were extremely fearful and suspicious of Japan. But unlike Germany's European partners, they could not overcome that fear and suspicion and undertake the construction of institutionalized regional economic ties with their former oppressor.

This difference in outcomes was surely due in part to the fact that Germany was not so far ahead of its European partners economically as Japan was in comparison to its Asian neighbors. But, in addition, in the early-to-mid 1950s such countries as South Korea and the Philippines did not need direct Japanese military support, and the United States also did not believe it needed Japan to help support these countries.[65] As noted above, the geographic circumstances and military situation in Western Europe—Germany as a front-line state in the West's stand against the USSR, and the need perceived by Germany's neighbors for that country's industrial and military capabilities in order to make that stand—served in part to catalyze an interest on the part of those neighbors in constructing European institutions as a way of managing the reconstitution of German power. In contrast, the geographic and political-military conditions that obtained in East Asia at the outset of the Cold War made Japan a less important potential partner for the United States and for the noncommunist countries in the region.[66] As an island-nation, Japan itself was less vulnerable to direct conventional military threats from the Soviet Union than was West Germany. Moreover, resolution of Japanese security concerns (for example, internal subversion) would not directly affect the capacity of other noncommunist countries in the region to defend themselves.[67] In addition, for these countries, American hegemonic air and naval and nuclear power was seemingly sufficient to maintain their security. There was, by consequence, little interest on the part of these countries in security ties with Japan.[68] Finally, while the United States saw German conventional military re-entry into the European power equation as vital to its defense strategy for the continent, the United States was able to devise for Japan an important role in America's Asian strategy—most importantly, permitting the establishment of huge American air and naval bases on Japanese soil on the basis of the U.S.-Japanese Security Treaty of 1952—without needing that country to take on more affirmative roles or, relatedly, to be a part of formal security arrangements with its Asian neighbors.[69]

Thus, while constraints on American power led the United States in the first half of the 1950s to promote regional institutionalization in Western Europe as a way of incorporating German power into Western defenses, American military and economic hegemony in East Asia in the mid-1950s made such institutionalization of Japanese power unnecessary in its part of the world.[70] The United States appeared in those first years of the Cold War to be able to extend effective security guarantees to Asian countries without Japan's direct assistance, and American security guarantees to both Japan and its neighbors made it less necessary for Japan and those neighbors to reconcile and develop more advanced modes of formal cooperation among themselves. When Malaysia urged its East Asian neighbors to begin to think about Japanese-led regional institutionalization in the early 1990s, those countries had no track record of active collaboration with that country, and because Japan and its neighbors had had no material need to effect reconciliation with one another, the former still evoked hostility and suspicion in the latter. At the same time, while the United States was not so hegemonic economically that it could tolerate what it thought might become an exclusivist economic bloc, it was still important enough to those Asian countries, including the core potential regional partner, Japan, to terminate or at least delay the establishment of an arrangement.

IMPLICATIONS FOR REALIST THEORY AND AMERICAN POLICY

Modern realist international theory has placed a great deal of emphasis on the polarity of the international system as a master-cause of differences in state behavior. By consequence, the end of the Soviet-American Cold War during 1989 and 1990, and the end thereby of bipolarity (and if that did not end bipolarity, then surely the collapse of the USSR in 1991 did) should have had profound consequences not just for the United States and Russia, but also for such important second-tier powers as Germany and Japan.[71] It might have been expected that the profound changes at the international structural level would prompt changes in the preferences of these important second-tier countries regarding regional institutionalization. Yet, as suggested above, one observes not change but continuity: Germany was interested in economic institutions before 1989–91, and has remained so after those watershed years; Japan was disinclined to support formal regional arrangements before the great transition, and has remained uninterested in such arrangements. Thus, something besides polarity and polarity shifts must be influencing German and Japanese preferences for regional institutions.

The analysis of this chapter suggests that, whatever might be the actual efficacy of polarity arguments in modern realist theory, those arguments ought to be supplemented by other realist propositions, at least in regard to the question of regionalism. There are at least two such arguments that are not grounded in realism's focus on how particular distributions of power in the international system affect state preferences and behavior, but are related to realism's core ideas that in the context of interstate anarchy, differences in state power and differences in political-military circumstances sharply delimit the preferences and actions of states both in the military field and in the international political economy.

First, and with respect to the sources of state power in the anarchical international environment, earlier realist arguments about the impact of asymmetries in interdependence on national influence ought to be given renewed attention in contemporary realist theory. The discussion in this chapter suggests that it is precisely such asymmetries in the trade field that have made Japan vulnerable to American pressures regarding East Asian economic institutionalization. Second, this discussion underlines the core realist view that political-military conditions and circumstances decisively affect the range of economic relationships that states may pursue and attain. In the present case, the intersection of the Cold War in Europe and NATO's need for a German military contribution to manage that conflict helped to bring about the initiation and flourishing of West European institutionalized cooperation in the economic realm; in contrast, the onset of the Cold War in Asia and the United States' capacity to carry out that struggle on its own probably doomed institutionalized economic cooperation among countries in that part of the world.

Finally, this discussion highlights the point, which is not necessarily based on realist ideas, that differences in political-military strategies in one period may have lasting, path-determining consequences on later opportunities for institutional development among countries that otherwise share common interests. That is, even if the United States were not actively to oppose the formation of an East Asian arrangement at present, it is quite likely that the manner in which regional relationships evolved during the Cold War has left the East Asian countries ill positioned to build such a bloc. For example, one main consequence of the combination of Cold War conflicts and American bilateralist economic and security ties with key countries in East Asia is that the area is now characterized by a remarkably low level of institutionalization either among governments or among private actors.[72] This characteristic of the region in turn reduces the opportunities for the "nesting" of new arrangements in more established frameworks, and the possibilities for the development of the habits of trust and cooperation — that is, international "social capital" — needed to pursue such arrangements.[73]

Regarding policy implications, the diplomacy surrounding the EAEG and the EAEC makes it clear that the United States is adamantly opposed to an exclusively East Asian economic arrangement, and that it still retains the capacity to derail efforts aimed at the formation of any such arrangement. Yet, it is possible that if the EU or NAFTA (or an expanded agreement covering the bulk of the Americas) were to turn seriously inward, or, even more ominously, if the United States were to press Japan too vigorously on bilateral trade matters, then as a defensive measure Japan might turn seriously to institutionalized regionalism in East Asia. Hence, we are brought back to the point that Japan's preferences for regionalism in East Asia are now and will continue to be driven by perceptions of America's policy toward Asia. If the United States were to persuade itself that multilateralism through the new World Trade Organization (WTO) is ineffective, or that strong forms of regionalism might spur progress in multilateralism, then the resulting U.S. tilt away from the WTO might well prompt Japan to undertake the formation of a closed bloc in East Asia.[74] If this were to occur, the consequences would be highly damaging to the world trading system: the EU would in all likelihood accentuate its more closed as opposed to its more liberal characteristics, and the United States in turn might respond to developments in both areas with even stronger regional projects of its own and more strident unilateralism around the world.

Thus, the United States must be especially careful in exercising its continuing great power in world economic matters. If there is a risk that regionalism might evolve in the years ahead in ways harmful to the multilateral trade order, the magnitude of that risk is probably being determined not by dynamics in East Asia or even in Western Europe, but by choices made by the United States. The United States today and for the foreseeable future is the only country that can sustain or seriously threaten the world economic order; its decisions will determine to a disproportionate degree whether the international economy will become more or less open in the years to come.

ACKNOWLEDGMENT

I thank Peter Feaver for suggesting that I seek to connect current trends in regionalism to U.S. political-military decisions during the early years of the Cold War. I also thank Ajin Choi and Imke Risopp-Nickelson for their excellent research assistance, and Eric Heginbotham, Ole Holsti, Ethan Kapstein, Kozo Kato, G. John Ikenberry, Michael Mastanduno, David Priess, Randall Schweller, Scott Cooper, and Beth Simmons for their helpful comments on an earlier draft of the paper. I thank the Josiah Charles Trent Foundation and the Duke University Arts and Sciences Research Council for their generous financial support for this project.

NOTES

1. See Lester Thurow, *Head to Head: The Coming Battle Among Japan, Europe, and America* (New York: Morrow, 1992), 11–25, 65.
2. Citing data from the World Trade Organization (WTO), the *Economist* reported in 1995 that of the total of 109 regional trade arrangements notified to the GATT/WTO between 1948 and 1994, approximately one-third were established between 1990 and 1994: see "The Right Direction?," *Economist*, September 16, 1995: 23–24. For helpful analyses of trends in economic regionalism as of the early 1990s, see Jeffrey J. Schott, "Trading Blocs and the World Trading System," *The World Economy* 14 (March 1991): 1–18; Robert C. Hine, "Regionalism and the Integration of the World Economy," *Journal of Common Market Studies* 30 (June 1992): 115–122; International Monetary Fund, "Regional Trading Arrangements," annex to *World Economic Outlook* (Washington, May 1993), 106–115; Vinod K. Aggarwal, "Comparing Regional Cooperation Efforts in the Asia-Pacific and North America," in Andrew Mack and John Ravenhill, eds., *Pacific Cooperation: Building Economic and Security Regimes in the Asia-Pacific Region* (Boulder, CO: Westview Press, 1995), 40–65; and Stephan Haggard, *Developing Nations and the Politics of Global Integration* (Washington: Brookings Institution, 1995).
3. These efforts are described in John Whalley, "CUSTA and NAFTA: Can WHFTA Be Far Behind?," *Journal of Common Market Studies* 30 (June 1992): 125–41; Luigi Manzetti, "Economic Integration in the Southern Cone," *North-South Focus* (North-South Center, University of Miami, December 1992); Bill Hinchberger, "Mercosur on the March," *Institutional Investor* 27 (March 1993): 107–12; Sebastian Edwards, "Latin American Economic Integration: A New Perspective on an Old Dream," *World Economy* 16 (May 1993): 317–38; Gary Clyde Hufbauer and Jeffrey J. Schott, with Diana Clark, *Western Hemisphere Economic Integration* (Washington: Institute for International Economics, 1994), especially pp. 97–129; and Felix Pena, "New Approaches to Economic Integration in the Southern Cone," *The Washington Quarterly* 18 (3) (Summer 1995): 113–22.
4. For additional arguments highlighting the limitations on what Miles Kahler calls "hard" regionalism through formal institutions in Asia (and the Americas), see Kahler, "A World of Blocs: Facts and Factoids," *World Policy Journal* 12 (Spring 1995): 19–27, and especially p. 24; Robert A. Manning and Paula Stern, "The Myth of the Pacific Community," *Foreign Affairs* 73 (November/

December 1994): 79–93; and Peter J. Katzenstein, "Regionalism in Comparative Perspective," *Cooperation and Conflict* 31 (June 1996): 123–59. Jeffrey Schott foresaw at the beginning of the 1990s that prospects for East Asian hard regionalism were unfavorable: see Schott, "Trade Blocs and the World Trade System," pp. 14–15. Even Lester Thurow expressed doubts about a Japan-based economic block in the Pacific Rim: see *Head to Head*: 250–51.

5. For this view see, for example, Rolf J. Langhammer, "ASEAN Economic Cooperation: A Stock-Taking," *ASEAN Economic Bulletin* 8 (November 1991): 147; Ippei Yamazawa, "On Pacific Economic Integration," *Economic Journal* 102 (November 1992): 1525; and Bilson Kurus, "Agreeing to Disagree: The Political Reality of Asean Economic Cooperation," *Asian Affairs* 20 (Spring 1993): 28–41. In February 1992 the ASEAN countries agreed to cut trade barriers through an ASEAN Free Trade Area (AFTA), but they have encountered serious implementation problems: see Michale Vatikiotis, "Market or Mirage," *Far Eastern Economic Review* (April 15, 1993): 48–50; "Malaysia: List Threatens AFTA," *Business Times* (Malaysia), Nexis, April 29, 1995; and "ASEAN Differences Over Tariff Cuts For Raw Farm Products May Drag On," *BNA International Trade Daily*, Nexis, May 5, 1995.

6. For a useful analysis of APEC's goals and strategies, see Gary Hufbauer and Jeffrey J. Schott, "Toward Free Trade and Investment in the Asia-Pacific," *The Washington Quarterly* 18 (Summer 1995): 37–45. On the diplomacy surrounding the establishment of APEC, see Andrew Elek, "The Challenge of Asian-Pacific Economic Cooperation," *The Pacific Review* 4 (4) (1991), especially pp. 324–26.

7. For overviews of the diplomacy surrounding the construction of European regional institutions, see F. Roy Willis, *France, Germany, and the New Europe, 1945–1967* (Stanford: Stanford University Press, 1968); John Gillingham, *Coal, Steel, and the Rebirth of Europe, 1945–1955: The Germans and the French From Ruhr Conflict to European Community* (Cambridge: Cambridge University Press, 1991); and Derek W. Urwin, *The Community of Europe: A History of European Integration Since 1945* (London and New York: Longman, 1991). It should be noted that the Federal Republic of Germany, established in 1949, was not part of the negotiations leading in April 1948 to the establishment of the first key post-World War II Western European economic organization, the Organization for European Economic Cooperation (OEEC), which coordinated efforts by Western European countries to make use of reconstruction aid provided by the United States under the auspices of the Marshall Plan.

8. See Andrew Moravcsik, "Negotiating the Single European Act: National Interests and Conventional Statecraft in the European Community," *International Organization* 45 (Winter 1991): 19–56; David R. Cameron, "The 1992 Initiative: Causes and Consequences," in Alberta M. Sbragia, ed., *Euro-Politics: In-*

stitutions and Policymaking in the "New" European Community (Washington: Brookings Institution, 1992), 23–74; and Geoffrey Garrett, "International Cooperation and Institutional Choice: The European Community's Internal Market," *International Organization* 46 (Spring 1992): 533–60.

9. On the overall development of European monetary cooperation see Loukas Tsoukalis, *The Politics and Economics of European Monetary Integration* (London: Allen & Unwin, 1977); Peter Ludlow, *The Making of the European Monetary System* (London: Butterworth, 1982); Jonathan Story, "The Launching of the EMS: An Analysis of Change in Foreign Economic Policy," *Political Studies* 36 (1988): 397–412; and especially Horst Ungerer, *A Concise History of European Monetary Integration: From EPU to EMU* (Westport, CT: Greenwood, 1997). On the negotiations surrounding the Maastricht Treaty and EMU, see, in addition to Ungerer, Wayne Sandholtz, "Choosing Union: Monetary Politics and Maastricht," *International Organization* 47 (Winter 1993); and Joseph M. Grieco, "State Interests and Institutional Rule Trajectories: A Neorealist Interpretation of the Maastricht Treaty and European Economic and Monetary Union," *Security Studies* 5 (Spring 1996): 176–222.

10. See George Kolankiewicz, "Consensus and Competition in the Eastern Enlargement of the EU," *International Affairs* 70 (July 1994): 488–90; Lily Gardner Feldman, "Germany and the EC: Realism and Responsibility," *Annals of the American Academy of Political and Social Science* 531 (January 1994): 40–41; and especially Michael Mihalka, "The Bumpy Road to Western Europe," *Transition: Issues and Developments in the Former Soviet Union and East-Central and Southeastern Europe* 1 (January 30, 1995): 72–78.

11. For a helpful analysis of the background to Malaysia's EAEG proposal, see Linda Low, "The East Asian Economic Grouping," *The Pacific Review* 4 (1991): 375–82.

12. This list was reported in UPI, "Malaysia Pushes for New Trade Bloc," *UPI International*, Nexis, February 1, 1991.

13. "Japan Seen as Leader of New Group, Trade Official Says," *Kyodo News Service*, Nexis, April 1, 1991.

14. "Singapore Supports Formation of Asian Economic Group," *Kyodo News Service*, Nexis, January 13, 1991; "Singapore Urges Japan to Join EAEA [sic]," *Jiji Press Ticker Service*, Nexis, August 15, 1991; also Haggard, *Developing Nations and Global Integration*, 68.

15. "Indonesia Wants to Study East Asian Trading Bloc Plan," *Reuters: Reuters Library Report*, Nexis, January 8, 1991. One problem regarding Mahathir's proposal was that he had failed to consult with Indonesia or other ASEAN partners prior to presenting the EAEG idea at an official dinner in China. On Indonesia's resentment about this, see "Mahathir Hints East Asia Economic Group Lacks Consensus," *Kyodo News Service: Japanese Economic Newswire*, Lexis,

October 7, 1991; and Bilson Kurus, "The ASEAN Triad: National Interest, Consensus-Seeking, and Economic Cooperation," *Contemporary Southeast Asia* 16 (March 1995), especially pp. 409–410.

16. Lai Kwok Kin, "Kaifu Sidesteps Controversial Asian Economic Group," *Reuters Money Report*, Nexis, April 28, 1991.

17. "Tokyo Cold Shoulders East Asian Economic Group," *Agence France Presse*, Nexis, May 21, 1991; and Charles P. Wallace, "Southeast Asia Warms to Trade-Bloc Plan," *Los Angeles Times*, Nexis, June 1, 1991, which also includes part of the Kaifu statement quoted in the text.

18. "Mahathir Hints East Asia Economic Group Lacks Consensus," *Kyodo News Service: Japan Economic Newswire* Nexis, October 7, 1991; Lai Kwok Kin, "Asia to Speak Out on Trade Through New Caucus," *Reuters*, Nexis, October 9, 1991; and Moon Ihlwan, "Indonesia Seeks to Refine Regional Forum Plan," *Reuters: Reuter Library Report*, Nexis, January 27, 1992.

19. "Japan Links EAEC and Regional Security," *Kyodo News Service: Japan Economic Newswire*, Nexis, November 12, 1991.

20. Bill Tarrant, "Malaysia, Indonesia to Promote East Asian Trade Group," *Reuters: Reuter Library Report*, Nexis, July 17, 1993.

21. Lai Kwok Kin, "Mahathir Asks Japan to Back East Asian Caucus," *Reuter Asia-Pacific Business Report*, Nexis, January 14, 1993; "Miyazawa Urges Support U.S.-Backed APEC, Rejecting Malaysian Call for Asia Bloc," *International Trade Reporter*, Nexis, January 27, 1993; and Moon Ihlwan, "U.S., Japan, S. Korea Still Wary of Asia Caucus," *Reuters: Reuter Library Report*, Nexis, July 27, 1993.

22. See "Australia, New Zealand Denied EAEC Membership, Mahathir Says," *BNA International Trade Daily*, Nexis, May 30, 1995.

23. K. T. Arasu, "Japan All But Rules Out Joining EAEC," *Reuter European Business Report*, Nexis, July 31, 1995; and "Malaysia Disappointed with Japan's Stance on EAEC," *Kyodo News Service: Japan Economic Newswire*, Nexis, August 3, 1995.

24. See, for example, "Mahathir Says Japan Not Needed to Start Asia Group," *Reuters World Service*, Nexis, October 25, 1994.

25. See "Japan Tentatively Decides to Skip Meeting for East Asian Economic Group," *BNA International Trade Daily*, Nexis, April 12, 1995; and Nusara Thaitawat, "Thailand: ASEAN Postpones Informal EAEC Meet," *Bangkok Post*, in *Reuter Textline*, Nexis, April 13, 1995.

26. See Karl Schoenberger, "Asia Seeks Leading Role in Pacific's Destiny," *Los Angeles Times*, Nexis, October 21, 1991; Satoshi Isaka, "Tokyo Mulls Participation in East Asian Economic Caucus," *Nikkei Weekly*, Nexis, January 10, 1994. It should be noted that China also offered some support for East Asian regional institutionalization: see "China Supports East Asian Trade Group,"

Agence France Presse, Nexis, June 14, 1993, in which a Chinese Foreign Ministry spokesman said after a meeting between Prime Minister Mahathir and Premier Li Peng that the latter "in the most explicit terms expressed his support for that proposal advanced by Malaysia." Also see Ho Kay Tat, "China Will Back EAEC Even If Japan Opts Out," *Business Times*, Nexis, November 12, 1994.

27. See "Japan to Attend Informal 'EAEC Luncheon' in Bangkok," *Agence France Presse*, Nexis, July 22, 1994; and Siti Rahil, "Japan Joins 'EAEC Luncheon' but not EAEC," *Kyodo News Service: Japan Economic Newswire*, Nexis, August 1, 1994.

28. See "Japan Warming Up to EAEC, Says Takemura," *Agence France Presse*, Nexis, January 13, 1995.

29. "Kaifu Favors Japan Joining EAEC," *Daily Yomiuri*, Nexis, February 2, 1995.

30. On the general debate about Asia vs. America in Japan's foreign policy, see Eugene Brown, "The Debate Over Japan's Strategic Future," *Asian Survey* 33 (June 1993): 543–59. The interest in the EAEC proposal by the Japanese foreign policy officials who are Asia-oriented is reported by Eric E. Heginbotham and Richard J. Samuels, "Mercantile Realism and Japanese Foreign Policy During and After the Cold War," in this volume.

31. See "Japanese Business Group Considers Urging Government to Join EAEC," *Agence France Presse*, Nexis, December 7, 1994; "In Japan, A Swing Toward Fellow Asians and Away from the West," *International Herald Tribune*, Nexis, December 12, 1994; Nobuyuki Oishi, "Keidanren Officials Step Behind EAEC," *Nikkei Weekly*, Nexis, December 19, 1994.

32. This line of analysis is derived from functionalist international theory, which suggests that governments are most likely to accept the need for and costs of establishing institutions if, and as, the latter meet specific needs arising from some form of functionally-specific international interaction involving mutual interests. For the early functionalist argument about institutions, see David Mitrany, *A Working Peace System: An Argument for the Functional Development of International Organization*, rev. ed. (London: Oxford University Press for the Royal Institute of International Affairs, 1944). This functional logic was applied to the question of formal regional institutionalism in Western Europe in the 1950s and 1960s by such scholars as Ernst Haas and Philippe Schmitter, and in the 1980s its was applied to broader, multilateral regimes by such scholars as Robert Keohane. See Ernst B. Haas, *The Uniting of Europe: Political, Social, and Economic Forces, 1950–1957* (Stanford: Stanford University Press, 1958); Haas, "Technology, Pluralism, and the New Europe," in Joseph S. Nye, Jr., ed., *International Regionalism* (Boston: Little, Brown, 1968), 149–76; and Philippe Schmitter, "Three Neo-Functional Hypotheses," *International Organization* 23 (Winter 1969): 161–67. On regime theory see Robert O. Keohane,

After Hegemony: Cooperation and Discord in the World Political Economy (Princeton: Princeton University Press, 1984).

33. The discussion in this volume by Heginbotham and Samuels, "Mercantile Realism and Japanese Foreign Policy," also places emphasis on continuity as opposed to change in Japanese foreign policy since the end of the Cold War.

34. I present this argument more fully in "Systemic Sources of Variation in Regional Institutionalization in Western Europe, East Asia, and the Americas," in Edward Mansfield and Helen Milner, eds., *The Political Economy of Regionalism* (New York: Columbia University Press, 1997), 164–87. In that essay I also suggest that in terms of trade dependence, Germany does not occupy a very different position in Western Europe (18.3% of EU exports go to that country) than does Japan in relationship to the countries that would have formed the EAEG/EAEC (Japan receives 14.6% of their exports).

35. On this general point see Peter J. Katzenstein and Nobuo Okawara, "Japan's National Security: Structures, Norms, and Policies," *International Security* 17 (Spring 1993): 84–118; and Peter Preston, "Domestic Inhibitions to a Leadership Role for Japan in Pacific Asia," *Contemporary Southeast Asia* 6 (March 1995): 355–74.

36. See "Malaysia Pushes for New Trade Bloc," *United Press International*, Nexis, February 5, 1991; "U.S. Reaction to Proposal for East Asian Economic Group," *Central News Agency*, Nexis, March 15, 1991.

37. Charles P. Wallace, "Regional Economics: Southeast Asia Warms to Trade-Bloc Plan," *Los Angeles Times*, Nexis, June 1, 1991.

38. "Japan Asked Not to Back Mahathir's Scheme," *Jiji Press Ticker Service*, Nexis, November 5, 1991. The United States did not mince words about its expectation that the EAEG should not be pursued: at an APEC meeting in Seoul in November, Secretary Baker is reported to have said to Korean Foreign Minister Lee Sang Ock that "Malaysia didn't spill blood for this country—but we did." See Don Oberdorfer, "U.S. Lobbies Against Malaysian Trade Plan," *Washington Post*, Nexis, November 14, 1991.

39. Siti Rahil, "U.S. Tells Japan it Opposes EAEC," *Kyodo News Service: Japanese Economic Newswire*, Nexis, June 15, 1994.

40. "Proposal on Asian Trade Bloc Called Surprisingly Detailed," *BNA International Trade Daily*, Nexis, July 21, 1994.

41. Anthony Rowley, "US Warns Against Its Exclusion from Proposed EAEC," *Business Times*, Nexis, September 5, 1995; also see comments by Jeffrey Garten, Undersecretary of Commerce, reported in *Agence France Presse*, Nexis, September 22, 1995.

42. "Japan Links EAEC and Regional Security."

43. Satoshi Isaka, "Japan Under Pressure to Take Sides on Trade Caucus," *Nikkei Weekly*, Lexis, July 25, 1994.

44. See "Japan Tentatively Decides to Skip Meeting for East Asian Economic Grouping."

45. K. T. Arasu, "Japan All but Rules Out Joining EAEC."

46. See Tim Josling, "Agricultural Trade Issues in Transatlantic Trade Relations," *World Economy* 16 (September 1993): 553–74; Youri Devuyst, "GATT Customs Union Provisions and the Uruguay Round: The European Community Experience," *Journal of World Trade* 26 (February 1992), especially pp. 25–26; and Jon Filipek, "Culture Quotas: The Trade Controversy Over the European Community's Broadcasting Directive," *Stanford Journal of International Law* (Spring 1992): 323–70.

47. All quotations in this paragraph are reported in Schoenberger, "Asia Seeks Leading Role in Pacific's Destiny."

48. Albert O. Hirschman, *National Power and the Structure of Foreign Trade* (Berkeley: University of California Press, 1969), 13–40; Kenneth N. Waltz, "The Myth of National Interdependence," in Charles P. Kindleberger, ed., *The International Corporation: A Symposium* (Cambridge: MIT Press, 1969), 205–23; and Waltz, *Theory of International Politics* (Reading: Addison-Wesley, 1979), 152–60.

49. On the potential danger of a Chinese threat to East Asian security and stability, see Aaron L. Friedberg, "Ripe for Rivalry: Prospects for Peace in a Multipolar Asia," *International Security* 18 (Winter 1993/94): 5–33; Richard K. Betts, "Wealth, Power, and Instability: East Asia and the United States After the Cold War," *International Security* 18 (Winter 1993/94): 34–77; Dennis Roy, "Hegemon on the Horizon? China's Threat to East Asian Security," *International Security* 19 (Summer 1994): 149–68; Gerald Segal, "East Asia and the "Constrainment" of China," *International Security* 20 (Spring 1996): 107–35; David Shambaugh, "Containment or Engagement of China? Calculating Beijing's Responses," *International Security* 21 (Fall 1996): 180–209; and Allen Whiting, "Asean Eyes China: the Security Dimension," *Asian Survey* 37 (April 1997): 299–322.

50. On the manner in which U.S. national security interests and constraints at the outset of the Cold War fundamentally shaped U.S. preferences and policies as it constructed the post-World War II international economic order, see Robert Gilpin, *U.S. Power and the Multinational Corporation: The Political Economy of Foreign Direct Investment* (New York: Basic, 1975). For an important recent investigation of the ways in which alliance relations of states drive their commercial integration, see Joanne Gowa, *Allies, Adversaries, and International Trade* (Princeton: Princeton University Press, 1994).

51. G. John Ikenberry, "Rethinking the Origins of American Hegemony," *Political Science Quarterly* 104 (1989): 375–400.

52. On the centrality of West German conventional forces to NATO strategy—a

point that was seen even as the German army was just being reconstituted in the early 1950s—see Wolfram F. Hanrieder, *Germany, America, Europe: Forty Years of German Foreign Policy* (New Haven: Yale University Press, 1989), 40–42.

53. For an overview of U.S. internal documents highlighting the support of the United States for European cooperation as a way of both strengthening Europe and dealing with German power, see Geoffrey Warner, "Eisenhower, Dulles, and the Unity of Western Europe, 1955–1957," *International Affairs* 69 (April 1993): 319–29. For interesting recent analyses of this point that are closely based on primary sources, see Klaus Schwabe, "The United States and European Integration, 1947–1957," and Gustav Schmidt, " 'Tying' (West) Germany into the West—But to What? NATO? WEU? The European Community?," both in Clemens Wurm, *Western Europe and Germany: The Beginnings of European Integration, 1945–1960* (Oxford and Washington: Berg Publishers, 1995), 115–35 and 137–74.

54. In this regard it should be stressed that the idea that institutionalization served as a postwar strategy by which France and other European countries sought to limit and channel German power was articulated in early postwar realist thinking about European economic cooperation, that is, in Hans Morgenthau's discussion of the European Coal and Steel Community in the second edition of his *Politics Among Nations: The Struggle for Power and Peace* (New York: Knopf, 1958), 497–98, and his discussion of the European Communities in the third (1966) edition, pp. 531–34.

55. For historical analyses of early postwar European economic cooperation in which the problem of managing German power is a focus of attention, see Michael Hogan, *The Marshall Plan: America, Britain, and the Reconstruction of Western Europe, 1947–1952* (Cambridge: Cambridge University Press, 1987), especially p. 64; and Gillingham, *The Rebirth of Europe*, 174, 364–66. On Western European efforts—themselves prompted by significant U.S. pressure to bring about German rearmament—to build a uniquely European defense entity between 1950 and 1954 that would include but constrain Germany, the failure of that effort, and the subsequent admission of Germany into NATO at the end of 1954, see Willis, *France, Germany, and the New Europe*, 130–197.

56. The recognition by West Germany's Chancellor Konrad Adenauer that Germany's partners needed that country's conventional capabilities, and wanted them incorporated and constrained through institutions, *and that this approach afforded the new West German state important political and diplomatic opportunities in European affairs*, is discussed in Hanrieder, *Germany, America, Europe*, 9, 38–39. Similarly, Adenauer recognized that European economic institutions presented important opportunities for Germany to reintegrate itself in European diplomacy; see Hanrieder pp. 233–34, 246–48.

57. See, for example, Lionel Barber, "Bonn Sets Agenda for Monetary Union," *Financial Times* (October 2, 1995): 2.

58. For an interesting comparison of Germany and Japan in the early Cold War, see James R. Kurth, "The Pacific Basin Versus the Atlantic Alliance: Two Paradigms of International Relations," *The Annals of the American Academy of Political and Social Science* 505 (September 1989), especially p. 36.

59. See William S. Borden, *The Pacific Alliance: United States Foreign Economic Policy and Japanese Trade Recovery, 1947–1955* (Madison: University of Wisconsin Press, 1984), 109–42.

60. Burton I. Kaufman, "Eisenhower's Foreign Economic Policy with Respect to East Asia," in Warren I. Cohen and Akira Iriye, eds., *The Great Powers in East Asia 1953–1960* (New York: Columbia University Press, 1990), 106–7.

61. Ibid., 115.

62. Ibid.

63. On the importance assigned in 1955 by the Eisenhower Administration to obtaining Japan's acceptance by a reluctant GATT membership, see Borden, *Pacific Alliance*, 179–80.

64. On the vital role of U.S. military orders in Japan's economic recovery between 1950 and 1952, see Richard J. Samuels, *"Rich Nation, Strong Army": National Security and the Technological Transformation of Japan* (Ithaca: Cornell University Press, 1994), especially pp. 133–43; Borden, *Pacific Alliance*, 143–49; Kaufman, "Eisenhower's Foreign Economic Policy," pp. 116–17; and Richard B. Finn, *Winners in Peace: MacArthur, Yoshida, and Postwar Japan* (Berkeley: University of California Press, 1992), 267–79.

65. For a useful discussion of Japan's role in the Cold War, see Barry Buzan, "Japan's Defense Problematique," *The Pacific Review* 8 (1) (1995), especially pp. 29–31. Finn points out that the outbreak of the Korean War did lead to a decision by General MacArthur, as supreme commander of the allied powers in Japan, to bring about a limited rearmament of Japan; however, these forces had no power-projection capability; see Finn, *Winners in Peace*, 263–66.

66. On the impact that differences in geography made on the military problems facing the United States in Western Europe and Asia with the onset of the Cold War, see Betts, "Wealth, Power, and Instability," p. 45, at which he argues that "The conventional Soviet military threat was more manageable in Asia than it was in Europe."

67. On the impact of geography on Japan's strategic interests in world politics after the Pacific War, see Buzan, "Japan's Defense Problematique," especially pp. 25–26.

68. On this point see Donald Crone, "Does Hegemony Matter? The Reorganization of the Pacific Political Economy," *World Politics* 45 (July 1993): 507.

69. For a helpful discussion of the negotiation of the U.S.-Japan security treaty, as

well as Japan's peace treaty with the United States and other allied powers, see Finn, *Winners in Peace*, 270–312.

70. For this argument in regard to Asia see Crone, "Does Hegemony Matter?," pp. 501–25.

71. For powerful arguments along these lines, see John J. Mearsheimer, "Back to the Future: Instability in Europe After the Cold War," in Sean Lynn-Jones and Steven E. Miller, eds., *The Cold War and After: Prospects for Peace*, expanded edition (Cambridge: MIT Press, 1994), 141–92; and Kenneth N. Waltz, "The Emerging Structure of International Politics," *International Security* 18 (Fall 1993): 44–79.

72. As Barry Buzan and Gerald Segal suggest, "Perhaps the most alarming aspect of East Asian security is the virtual absence of effective multilateralism," and they go on to observe that, "What is distinctive about Asia is its combination of several industrialised societies with a regional international society so impoverished in its development that it compares poorly with even Africa and the Middle East." See Barry Buzan and Gerald Segal, "Rethinking East Asian Security," *Survival* 36 (Summer 1994): 15.

73. On the concept of nesting, see Vinod Aggarwal, *Liberal Protection: The International Politics of Organized Textile Trade* (Berkeley: University of California Press, 1985). Aggarwal uses his nesting logic to reach the conclusion that APEC has been an extremely weak regime: see "Comparing Regional Cooperation Efforts in the Asia-Pacific and North America," in Andrew Mack and John Ravenhill, eds., *Pacific Cooperation: Building Economic and Security Regimes in the Asia-Pacific Region* (Boulder, CO: Westview Press, 1995), especially p. 51. In this I am drawing upon the insights of Miles Kahler, who, basing his analysis on Robert Putnam's work on social capital, makes the important point that the Pacific region as a whole is characterized by a low level of interstate social capital: see Kahler, "Institution Building in the Pacific," in Mack and Ravenhill, eds., *Pacific Cooperation*, 29–30; and Putnam, with Robert Leonardi and Raffaella Y. Nanetti, *Making Democracy Work: Civic Traditions in Modern Italy* (Princeton: Princeton University Press, 1993).

74. On the possibility that the United States could overemphasize regionalism see Jagdish Bhagwati, "Regionalism Versus Multilateralism," *The World Economy* 15(5) (September 1992), especially pp. 540–42.

10 Realism and Reconciliation: France, Germany, and the European Union

Michael Loriaux

The governments of Western Europe have engaged in the most ambitious experiment in progressive international political reform in history. That experiment would seem to fly in the face of realist theory, which invites us to conceptualize nation-states as self-interested actors pursuing self-help policies within an anarchical system, in which politics is conditioned by the competition for power. But many facets of the history of European integration do in fact conform to realist expectations. Before World War II, international politics in Western Europe was power politics. The disruptive effects of power competition were contained only by hegemonic intervention by the United States. Today, some cooperative ventures, particularly in monetary relations, are conditioned by European efforts to cushion their economies against the destabilizing effects of U.S. self-help policies designed to alter the terms of the postwar hegemonic arrangement.

But there remains an aspect of European integration that realism cannot explain: the robustness of Franco-German reconciliation and cooperation in promoting integration following reunification. According to realist theory, we should expect Germany to act more hegemonically in Europe. We would expect France and Great Britain to balance German power. But Germany resists the hegemonic temptation, France's relationship with Germany remains close, and France's relationship with Great Britain remains more distant. But there is a way to reconceptualize realism so that it does allow for this peculiarity, which I discuss in the conclusion.

I have adopted a different method of inquiry from that of most of the other chapters. Trained as a historian, I tend to resist the idea that history can be treated as a warehouse of data with which to test social science theories. The textual evidence underdetermines theoretical statements, particularly in modern times, for which the sheer volume of documentation is overwhelming. Moreover, historical texts are prone to divergent interpretations. The historian makes sense of the mass of evidence by weaving narratives around it, the narrative being a more supple and adaptable mental construct than nomological theory. But narratives, even though they adhere more closely to the evidence, are nevertheless subject to the same objections as nomological explanations: they are also underdetermined by the evidence, and the evidence is still susceptible to a variety of interpretations. Modern historians have become more aware of this fact, and as a result have become more willing to recognize that narratives, which provide guidance through the bewildering maze of historical evidence, appeal more or less intentionally to some normative or ideological principle or preference for guidance. History, in this conceptualization, becomes a site of debate among scholars of different normative sensibilities. That debate is refereed—but not always decided—by the archives.[1]

My approach to the theme of this book is informed by this observation. I seek to assess the extent to which realism, conceived as a normative sensibility, warranted (at least hypothetically) by some more or less rational understanding of how "the world works," can credibly guide the historiography of the European Union. Or, turning the proposition around, I seek to assess the extent to which the history of the European Union can serve as a warrant for being a realist.

U.S. Hegemony and the Origins of the European Union

Realism helps us understand European integration because it informs two concepts, hegemony and what I call "geopolitical internationalism," that illuminate many aspects of European and U.S.-European relations.

Power competition in Western Europe traditionally centered on control of the Rhineland, the industrial core of continental Western Europe since the end of the nineteenth century. The Rhine itself is one of the principal inland waterways of the world, linking Rotterdam, the world's busiest seaport, with the industrial hinterland of the Ruhr, the upper Rhine, the Main, the

Saar, and the Neckar. Continental Europe's industrial heartland reaches out from Rotterdam and Antwerp to southern England, the oil fields of the North Sea, and the rest of the world. In the south, through deeply cut Alpine passes, the Rhineland economy tugs at Milan, Turin, Genoa, and Italy's industrialized north. At the Rhineland's hub, Western Europe's coal and steel core extends from Lorraine to the Ruhr. The steel industry has declined, but the industrial supremacy of the Rhineland has not. From Basel to Rotterdam, from Lille to Frankfurt and Stuttgart, the geographical basin of the Rhine remains the industrial, commercial, and financial heart of the Western European economy today.

Geopolitically, the Rhineland, whose economic preeminence was already visible in late Antiquity, was among the last regions of Western Europe to be integrated into the emerging nation-state system. The Treaty of Vienna (1818) was the principal instrument of that integration. It consolidated France's claim to Lorraine and Alsace, recognized England as the guarantor of the sovereignty and integrity of the Netherlands and Belgium (following independence) as buffer states, and installed Prussia on the banks of the middle Rhine. But the Vienna settlement antedated the industrial era and the rise of the Rhineland as an industrial powerhouse. Prussia developed the Rhineland's economic potential and aggressively harnessed the region's industries to its military machine. By the end of the nineteenth century the German Reich, unified under Prussian leadership, was the premier industrial power of Europe.

The defeat of Germany in 1919 and again in 1945 created the opportunity to renegotiate the partition of the Rhineland. The dominance of Rhenish industry was such that all great powers of the West had a stake in the settlement. The French had wanted to keep the Rhineland away from the Prussians, the British then wanted to keep it away from the French, and now the Americans wanted to keep it away from the Russians. This competition for control of the Rhineland generated a discernible parallelism in the diplomatic histories of the two postwar periods. The first phase of those histories was dominated by French efforts to detach the Rhineland from Germany and make it a sovereign state, subject to French influence. British and American resistance caused that plan to collapse. Subsequently, the French adopted a strategy that one might call "geopolitical cartelism." They sought to create, in collaboration with the Germans and without the Americans, some more or less exclusivist and mercantilist arrangement with Germany such that their claims on the industrial wealth of the Rhineland would be given some satisfaction, and German sovereignty over the Ruhr constrained. Those efforts were little more than embryonic in 1923. Representatives of the French steel industry met with their German counterparts, with the authorization of the French Foreign Ministry, to explore solutions to the reparations problem that might prove beneficial to both parties. They agreed on a plan that involved the transfer of a number of mines to French ownership, a long-term contract guaranteeing the delivery of German coke to French mills, and a second long-term contract whereby German mills would agree to buy a part of the semi-finished goods produced by French industry. English and American opposition put an end to these efforts.

But after World War II, the United States supported French efforts to enter into this kind of mercantilistic relationship with Germany. The United States wanted to reunify the three western zones of occupied Germany to implement its strategy of containment of the Soviet Union. The French resisted. Neither concessions nor Marshall aid swayed them. No compromise was in sight as late as March 1949 when European foreign ministers prepared to meet in Washington to lay the groundwork for the North Atlantic Treaty Organization (NATO). In this context, Secretary of State Dean Acheson appealed to French Foreign Minister Robert Schuman: "I believe that our policy in Germany, and the development of a German Government which can take its place in Western Europe, depends on the assumption by your country of leadership in Europe on these problems."[2]

The French seized that offer, and achieved what has since been recognized as the single most decisive step in the creation of the European Union. They proposed the establishment of a European Coal and Steel Community that placed the entire French and German outputs of coal and steel under a single European High Authority, and created a common, cartelized market for coal and steel products. The French accepted West German reunification in exchange for secure access to the resources of the Ruhr, multilateral control over the allocation of the industrial wealth of Europe's steel-producing core, and secure European markets for French steel-producing firms. The success of the Monnet Plan of Economic Reconstruction and Modernization was predicated on this diplomatic success.

In the beginning, European integration was hegemonically mediated. Working under hegemonic constraint-cum-sponsorship, France pursued its strategy of geopolitical cartelism in a way that is perfectly compatible with realist expectations. Germany responded by deploying a more inclusive policy of "geopolitical internationalism," which is no less compatible with realist expectations. The Germans showed generally strong support for multilateralism, but only because those arrangements provided the most expeditious way to regain equality of status with the victorious powers and curry Western support for territorial reunification. France, however, continued to work to institutionalize its cartel relationship with Germany and to construct a viable European rival to the Atlantic alliance, because this was the most expeditious way to maximize control over the way Germany used its resources. In pursuit of that strategy, de Gaulle, who returned to power in 1958, gave strong support to West German claims on East Germany, and, in the first years of his presidency, adopted a decidedly anti-Soviet foreign policy. De Gaulle and German Chancellor Konrad Adenauer signed the Franco-German Treaty of Reconciliation in January 1963, just as de Gaulle vetoed Great Britain's entry into the Common Market and rejected American proposals to participate in the Multilateral Nuclear Force. But de Gaulle's ambitions collapsed at the point of success. The German Bundestag refused to abandon the strategy of geopolitical internationalism in favor of this cartel relationship with France. It voted unanimously to append a preamble to the treaty that emphasized the importance of "entente between the free peoples—with a particularly close cooperation between Europe and the United States," and added a pointed reference to Great Britain's exclusion from the Common Market.[3] Adenauer retired soon thereafter and the government of Germany passed to the more liberal and pro-American Ludwig Erhard.

France's strategy of geopolitical cartelism ultimately failed. France reacted to this failure by adopting a unilateralist, even exploitative orientation in foreign policy. Through brinkmanship in the Common Market, de Gaulle forced passage of the Common Agricultural Policy (which essentially required Germany to subsidize French agriculture), and the formal recognition of the "unit-veto" in Common Market affairs. During this same period, France withdrew its forces from the integrated NATO command structure and adopted a more sympathetic policy toward the Soviet Union.

DIPLOMATIC FAILURE AND FRENCH INTERNATIONALISM

After having failed to draw Germany into a tightly construed cartel relationship, French policy eventually turned decisively cooperative and more inclusively internationalist, both in the 1920s and the 1970s. In both cases, the turnabout in policy had the same cause: diplomatic failure compounded by financial weakness. In 1923, the occupation of the Ruhr by the French provoked British and American opposition. The House of Morgan and the governor of the Bank of England made it clear to the French that they "could not advance sizable loans to Germany [needed for reparations payments] unless unilateral sanctions were banned."[4] The French, financially strapped and in the grip of currency crisis, began to withdraw from the Ruhr in 1925. In the interwar period, as in the post-World War II period, U.S. involvement in European politics generated new international institutions. The Bank for International Settlements (BIS), established as executor of the Young Plan in 1929, is the dean of contemporary international organizations, and is set symbolically in Basel on the banks of the Rhine, where it materializes the link between the competition for control of the Rhineland and the development of institutions of economic cooperation in Europe.

The French welcomed involvement by American financiers, given the free fall of the franc on currency markets and the budget deficits that the occupation of the Ruhr had spawned. The Germans, meanwhile, persisted in their strategy of geopolitical internationalism. They had been seeking to enlist American involvement since 1921. In 1924, the *Auswärtiges Amt* expressed the hope that "the United States could somehow be persuaded to invest large sums of idle and unproductive money in German industry. Not only would Germany's capitalistic system benefit, but its economic recovery and the revision of the Versailles treaty would almost certainly be accelerated."[5]

Having relinquished all unilateral or cartelistic claims on the Rhineland, the French now invested in efforts to internationalize it, that is, to contribute to the success of multilateral agreements and institutions that placed constraints on Germany's sovereign power to exploit the wealth of the Ruhr. In other words, the French themselves embraced geopolitical internationalism. But whereas the Germans adopted geopolitical internationalism in order to gain equality of status with the other great powers, the French adopted it in order to institutionalize and confirm international constraints on German sovereignty. The French now looked to the League of Nations and the United States to secure respect of those articles of the Treaty of Versailles that regulated German activity in military matters, and secured the partial transfer of German wealth to the allies through reparations. In 1925, France agreed to admit Germany to the League; in 1927, France and the United States acted together to win adherents to the Kellogg-Briand pact, one of the foremost expressions of the liberal reformism of the period, and when Ger-

many and Austria entered into a trade alliance, the French suggested that
the plan be extended to all European countries.[6]

In similar fashion, French diplomacy turned more aggressively supportive
of integrationist institutions after 1969. Pompidou, who succeeded de Gaulle
as president of France, could not sustain the unilateralist thrust of Gaullist
policy. Hostility toward Germany left France isolated in Europe. The French
responded, as in 1924, by embracing and even championing the cause of
internationalism. Pompidou approved Great Britain's entry into the Common Market. He supported the project for Economic and Monetary Union
as a means to back France out of the diplomatic cul-de-sac in which de
Gaulle had left it.

It is true that the monetary crisis of 1969–1973 delayed implementation
of the plan as a bitter feud erupted between France and Germany regarding
Europe's response to the pending breakdown of the Bretton Woods system
of fixed exchange rates. But the French altered the general orientation of
their monetary policy in 1974 under the leadership of the new president,
Valéry Giscard-d'Estaing, and adopted a strong franc policy (for reasons analyzed in greater detail below). France and Germany resolved their monetary
differences, solidified their relationship, and assumed joint leadership within
the European Community. France and Germany led the campaign to create
the European Monetary System in 1978, to admit Greece to the European
Union in 1981 and Spain and Portugal in 1986, to abolish custom controls
at the frontier (the Schengen agreements of 1985 signed with Benelux and
Spain), to revise the Treaty of Rome and promulgate the Single European
Act in 1986, to establish a plan for Economic and Monetary Union in 1989,
to endorse the principle of political union in 1990, to create the Eurocorps
in 1991, to reform the Common Agricultural Policy in 1992, and to admit
Austria, Finland, Sweden, and Norway in 1994.[7]

CHANGE IN THE HEGEMONIC ORDER AND EUROPEAN
ECONOMIC COOPERATION

France and Germany adopted strategies of geopolitical internationalism
in response to pressures and incentives created by American actions. But, as
the preceding litany of achievements makes plain, French and German internationalism endures, even though the hegemonic order that spawned it
is being gradually dismantled. Enduring Franco-German internationalism
and leadership in Europe now constitute, at least in part, a response to

American efforts to "alter the terms" of its hegemonic relationship with its allies, efforts informed by American perceptions of decline relative to the rising economies of Europe and especially East Asia.

Monetary integration provides an illustration. The post-World War II hegemonic order was composed of institutions and arrangements that gave states the means to manage and direct capital in a way that preserved political stability within the framework of an open international economic order and export-led growth.[8] States were empowered to direct capital to accomplish political tasks: neutralize political opposition through subsidies and clientelism, nurture the development of an indigenous industrial and financial elite, and develop a strong industrial base that facilitated participation in an open trade order and contributed to the military strength of the alliance.

France and Germany took advantage of these hegemonic arrangements in different ways. France entered into a thirty-year partnership with inflation. Although inflation did not always manifest itself in consumer price increases, money supply growth was always rapid, even in times of apparent price stability, as, for example, during the post-Korean War recession. Price inflation at other times was held in check by administrative controls. Despite periods of price stability, rapid growth in the monetary base, due to credit expansion, generated endemic inflationary pressures in France that dominated economic policymaking for much of the post-World War II period. To contain and channel those pressures to productive use, successive governments patched together a complex system linking banks to public finance agencies to semi-public lenders to post office checking accounts, all attached to and directed by the Treasury, "the sanctuary inside the temple of the Ministry of Finance, the economic apex."[9] Through this system, the French irrigated the economy with inflationary money in a more or less controlled fashion. Elsewhere, I describe the development of an "overdraft economy" in which economic activity, rather than being regulated and directed by market forces, was driven by the growing dependence of industry on credit accounts managed by lending institutions under direct or indirect state control. The state was typically reluctant to impose rigorous standards, fearing the economic and political repercussions of doing so. The overdraft economy thus became a source of "soft constraints," as described by Janos Kornai in his study of the former socialist regimes of Eastern Europe.[10]

The institutional constraints of the overdraft economy generally succeeded in containing inflationary pressures. But the dikes gave way on more than one occasion. When the French overdraft economy spun out of control, as it did in 1948, 1954, 1957, 1969, 1975, and 1981, the only tool the French could wield effectively was that of external adjustment—devaluation of the franc (or, as in 1954, manipulation of trade restrictions in a way that mimicked the effect of a devaluation). In other words, France's overdraft economy was viable because the international monetary order, structured by a hegemonic United States, made it possible for France to achieve adjustment with the help of (and at the expense of) the international community.

Germany responded differently to the opportunities created by the hegemonic order in international monetary relations. In Germany, economic growth was accorded the highest priority as the means to solve a number of difficult political issues.[11] But Germany's international situation all but ruled out French-style interventionism, while institutional decentralization under the federal constitution—itself the legacy of occupation—complicated state intervention even in the form of Keynesian demand management.[12] The government therefore spurred growth by promoting exports, and promoted exports by pegging the Deutschmark to an external parity that was undervalued relative to the dollar.[13] The strategy would never have worked had not Bretton Woods conferred on central banks a monopoly on operations on the currency market. Absent that monopoly, the Deutschmark would have been bid up by traders long before 1971.[14]

But in the mid-1960s, the United States began to neglect and finally abandon its hegemonic commitments in monetary relations. It started to indulge in inflationary policy itself under the dual pressure of war in Vietnam and domestic social unrest. American policy aggravated inflationary pressures and monetary instability world-wide. American policy had begun to turn predatory.[15] The United States could indulge in inflation, yet ignore the potential trade and monetary effects of inflation, at least for a time, because the American currency was the principal medium of international trade. Germany reacted to imported inflationary pressures by imposing a rigorous stabilization plan in 1966. As the international monetary system grew more unstable, America's allies called for the devaluation of the dollar. Unwilling to revalue the Soviet Union's gold stock by devaluing the dollar, and increasingly intolerant of the asymmetric trade and monetary arrangements that characterized the hegemonic order, the United States refused to devalue and insisted that other countries revalue. As the crisis worsened, Germany suspended the mark's fixed parity in May 1971, letting it float upwards as the market dictated. But the French refused that course. They were vehemently critical of American policy. Having devalued in August

1969, they naturally rejected revaluation in 1971. They tried to forge a common European front against American demands that currencies be revised upward, but met with opposition from the Germans, who had coopted floating rates into their war on inflation.[16]

The final collapse of the fixed rate system in 1973, however, altered French monetary interests, and initiated a complete turnabout in policy. Floating rates gave rise to the threat of destabilizing spirals of inflation and currency depreciation, notably in the trade-dependent economies of Western Europe.[17] Floating rates, despite the predictions of economic theory, made the defense of the currency more necessary than before. France opted for a hard currency in 1974, but the overdraft economy's soft constraints on firms rendered ineffective the anti-inflationary policy needed to support a strong currency. Toothless when implemented with sensitivity to the fragile financial position of French firms, it was devastating when given more bite. Without hegemonic validation, the French overdraft economy was not viable. Persistant currency weakness ended in the near-collapse of the French overdraft economy in the early 1980s. The government, under Socialist direction, effected a dramatic policy U-turn and implemented a series of deep liberalizing reforms designed to give the French economy the means to deploy a strong currency policy.

Monetary cooperation with Germany became essential both to France's efforts to stabilize the franc and to reform the structures of its political economy. Those efforts help explain France's current interest in the single currency. Although a system of fixed exchange rates among European currencies would go far toward addressing the problems that floating rates create for open economies, the system would still leave France paying a "risk premium" levied on domestic interest rates for past sins. The single currency would equalize interest rates across member countries (though not across all individual borrowers) and render national economies invulnerable against speculative movements into the mark (which would cease to exist).[18] Inversely, countries that are not in the midst of reforming the structures and mores of their political economy—notably Great Britain—tend not to share France's concerns, and thus attach importance to the defense of monetary sovereignty.

German interest in monetary integration fluctuates. The French approached the Germans as early as 1974 with a plan to reform the European currency float in a way that facilitated participation by weak-currency countries. The Germans rebuffed the French proposal, complaining that it asked them in effect to absorb French inflation. That complaint has informed Germany's attitude toward monetary integration on many occasions. Their attitude alters, however, when a drop in the dollar sends speculative money into the mark, bidding it up to values that threaten export markets. At such times, Germany shows greater interest in European monetary integration. It is in such circumstances that Germany agreed with France in 1978 to create the European Monetary System (which bore a close resemblance to the French plan of 1974). But at the time of this writing, the dollar is high, and the Germans are displaying muted approval of the single currency.

Turning from monetary integration to commercial and financial deregulation, we find in other cooperative actions similar efforts to shelter national economies against the stress generated by the dismantling of the hegemonic order. Following the New Economic Policy (NEP) of Richard Nixon and the attendant scuttling of Bretton Woods, the second major shock that the United States unleashed on the world economy was "Reaganomics." Like the NEP, Reaganomics was a reaction to the perception that America was declining as a hegemonic power. It was designed to reanimate the American economy through supply side economics and fiscal stimulus, while generating the funds needed to upgrade the U.S. military, particularly the navy, by stimulating economic growth. But because taxes were cut at a time when the Federal Reserve Board was clamping down on inflation, Reaganomics created a sizable budget deficit that "the Fed" refused to monetize. International capital was siphoned into American Treasury bills by high interest rates. Investors bid the dollar up to record levels as they exchanged foreign currencies to buy U.S. bonds. Europeans responded by deregulating their capital markets in order to compete more effectively for capital's favors. The London Stock Exchange submitted to the "Big Bang" of liberalizing reform, while France, under a Socialist government, introduced the last word in capitalism: a financial futures market on the Chicago model.[19]

Deregulation, which occurred on a global scale, endowed capital with a measure of "structural power" that it had lacked during the half century that it was constrained by the rules of the hegemonic order. In this new financial environment, Europeans had to devise ways to make European firms more competitive. Because of financial globalization, a firm's survival depends more and more on the size of its capital base and its ability to realize economies of scale and invest in research and development. Larger firms require larger markets, and the path to larger markets in Europe passes through EU trade liberalization and deregulation.[20] The single European act, along with other measures, launched the Europeans on the Herculean task of revising and harmonizing their national regulatory codes regarding production and trade.

CHANGE IN THE HEGEMONIC ORDER AND EUROPEAN MILITARY COOPERATION

Geopolitical internationalism and the gradual dismantling of the post-World War II hegemonic order also help explain European security initiatives. In the early 1960s, French geopolitical cartelism informed efforts to improve France's security relationship with Germany, just as it informed France's interest in building the Common Market. That effort culminated in the Franco-German pledge to develop a "common conception" of defense, inscribed in the Treaty of 1963. But the Bundestag's adjunction of the pro-Anglo-Saxon preamble led to a period of French unilateralism in security affairs, as in economic affairs, that lasted from about 1965 to about 1975. During that period, France withdrew from NATO's integrated command structure and organized its national defense around its nuclear *force de frappe*, one element of which was the deployment of tactical missiles whose range, at 80 miles, presupposed the existence of targets in Germany. De Gaulle also worked to position France as a mediator between East and West, and thus provide Germany with a supplementary demonstration of just how indispensable France was to the achievement of German security interests.

But American and German rapprochement with East bloc countries in the late 1960s and early 1970s caused that strategy to collapse. The French had alienated their allies, but now lost, too, the hope of being the principal mediator between East and West. France faced possible isolation. In security as in economic relations, France abandoned unilateralism and embraced the strategy of geopolitical internationalism.

The missile crises of the late 1970s and early 1980s and suspicions of German "Finlandization" reinforced French fears of isolation by raising the specter of German unilateralism. The Pax Americana had been predicated on German diplomatic and military semi-sovereignty, which the Germans accepted in return for America's and NATO's commitment to their security and eventual reunification. The bargain had flaws, since NATO's policy of graduated response, designed to make nuclear deterrence credible, seemed to designate the German homeland as the future battleground in a nuclear war between the super-powers. The installation of new weapons technologies in the late 1970s and early 1980s revived fears and dissatisfaction with the terms of that bargain. Official reluctance and popular opposition to the new weapons raised fears in France that Germany might denounce the bargain and reclaim full diplomatic and military sovereignty. France responded by showing solicitude for Germany's security concerns, moving toward a more forward defense posture that included Germany in its defense perimeter, and deemphasizing deterrence. Fear of German unilateralism prompted Mitterrand to speak in defense of the installation of Pershing missiles before the German Bundestag in 1982. French efforts were rewarded by an agreement to regularize meetings between the French and German ministries of defense. In 1987, Germany proposed the formation of a mixed Franco-German military brigade. In the beginning, the brigade only symbolized Franco-German cooperation, but by 1992, under the impetus of Franco-German efforts to forge political union, it turned into a division of 35,000 troops, in which other EU countries were invited to participate.[21]

The collapse of the Cold War's bipolar international structure forced the wholesale reexamination of the national defense requirements and regional security arrangements that constituted the hegemonic order in security affairs. The disintegration of the Soviet Union rendered all but useless the mass conscript armies and armaments that were designed to resist a large scale Warsaw Pact invasion. Both France and Germany substantially cut military expenditures and decreased the size of their militaries. France, at this writing, has embarked on a radical reconfiguration of its military forces and the defense industries that support them. President Jacques Chirac argued that France should have the capacity to mobilize and rapidly project abroad a force of about 50,000–60,000 troops. He complained that France could now project a force of only about 10,000 troops effectively, far fewer than Great Britain. In both the Gulf War and Yugoslavia, the French found it difficult to maneuver effectively and independently. The British, who moved to a professional army many years ago, were much better able to acquit themselves of the tasks required in these two operations. Chirac has advocated reforms that will reduce the size of the armed forces from 500,000 to 350,000 by 2002.[22] He has scuttled mass conscription altogether, and experts in his entourage claim that the long-term goal is an army of 130,000 troops. Similarly, the French have begun to restructure their arms industry. The powerful military aviation firm Dassault has been forced to merge with Aérospatiale. Other restructurings are being examined in order to preserve

France's once flourishing arms industry, which has suffered from its inability to adapt quickly to the lessons of the Gulf War.[23]

The German Bundestag has also been debating the future of its conscript army. Germany committed 4.9 percent of gross domestic product to defense in 1963. That figure remained near 4 percent throughout the 1970s and 1980s, but has now sunk to 2 percent. The size of the German army has fallen precipitously from 500,000 at the time of the fall of the Berlin Wall to 340,000 at this writing, which is 30,000 fewer than the number allowed by the "2 + 4" agreements on reunification. Following the move to a professional army in the United States, Canada, Great Britain, and the Benelux countries in the 1970s, Germany debated a similar move. But Germany's front-line position in the Cold War argued against such a move. Today, the advocates of an all-volunteer army foresee a force of 250,000 or even as few as 200,000 troops. Critics of the idea maintain that Germany's key geopolitical position between the "stable" democracies of Western Europe and the "unstable" democracies of Eastern Europe still requires a mass "republican" military based on conscription.[24] But German youths themselves are unsympathetic to conscription—fully one-third of German conscripts declare themselves conscientious objectors and opt for civilian service.[25]

The Soviet collapse has also forced Germany and its allies to reexamine the issue of multilateral security arrangements. Germany's support for internationalist institutions in the past was motivated in no small part by the desire to win international support for territorial reunification and readmission to the community of great powers. But Germany remains internationalist, even though it has achieved the goals that internationalism was designed to achieve. Its enduring internationalism derives in part from its continued dependence on the United States, the principal military power of the Atlantic Alliance, for the resolution of new challenges arising from the collapse of the Soviet empire. But it is not certain that military dependence will continue to breed an attitude of diplomatic deference. Because geography exposes Germany to the repercussions of political instability in Eastern Europe, Germany has supported Eastern European demands to join NATO (and the EU). Inversely, and for the same reason, Germany is more sensitive than the United States to the risk of alienating Russia. U.S.-Russian discord, fomented by a measure of American arrogance, conflictual interests in the exploitation of energy resources in the former Soviet republics, and the threat of Islamic fundamentalism along Russia's southern flank, has tempted Germany to assume greater independence in foreign policy.[26]

Feeding that temptation is the fact that, whatever Germany's degree of dependence on America's security umbrella, the Cold War security "bargain" with NATO is no longer meaningful in the post-Cold War world. During the Cold War, Germany was not invited to engage in interventions "out of area," that is, beyond the frontiers of the defensive NATO alliance. But since the collapse of the Soviet Union, NATO itself has begun to operate "out of area," thus forcing the Germans to reconceptualize their obligations. The UN-sponsored intervention in Somalia, given its humanitarian nature, had already disoriented those who, on the anti-militarist left, opposed enlarging Germany's military role. Germany provided noncombatant troops to the mission in Somalia, but only after acrimonious debate. The NATO intervention in Yugoslavia was even more difficult for the Germans because they bore some responsibility for the crisis. It took a decision by the German Federal Constitutional Court in July 1994 to determine that the deployment of German troops "out of area" in conjuction with a collective security organization did not violate the federal constitution.[27] Germany sent 14 Tornado jets to support the rapid reaction force of British, French, and Dutch troops in Bosnia, and on September 1, 1995, German warplanes engaged in their first combat mission since World War II. But it is of at least symbolic importance that they did not fire a shot on that mission. In application of the Dayton accords 4,000 German troops joined the 10,000 French troops, 13,000 British troops, and 20,000 American troops in policing the Bosnian peace. Growing responsibilities in international security affairs have begun to translate into greater diplomatic activity and independence.

As Germany has been wrestling with the diplomatic and military ramifications of reunification and the end of the Cold War, France has been trying to tie Germany down institutionally to Europe, even at the expense of its own independence. The Bosnian debacle illustrates this orientation. Germany, for a host of reasons, showed great sympathy with demands for Slovenian and Croatian independence. The French and the Americans were less sympathetic, fearing the destabilizing effects of Yugoslavia's disintegration. The French in particular feared that the multiplication of what Mitterrand referred to as the "tribes" of Eastern Europe would tempt or perhaps even compel Germany to increase its diplomatic and military role in the region, leading to the reconstitution of a "Mitteleuropa" that would reinforce Germany's hegemonic weight in Europe and turn its priorities eastward.[28]

Franco-German differences over Yugoslavia became acrimonious during the summer of 1991. But in the end, Germany, as a matter of principle, placed European solidarity ahead of its desire to recognize Slovenian and Croatian independence, while the French conceded to the negotiated dismantlement of the Yugoslav federation under European Union auspices. The European-sponsored negotiations, presided over by Britain's Lord Carrington, took place as Bosnian Serbs pressed their territorial claims by arms. But the German government, goaded by outrage in German public opinion, showered strong criticism on the Carrington negotiations. When European foreign ministers met to discuss the Maastricht treaty on December 16, 1991, the German delegation compelled the European Union to recognize the two breakaway republics, threatening unilateral recognition if Europe did not act in concert. Although Germany succeeded in forcing through a botched and vague "conditional recognition" of independence by the Europeans, its strongarm tactics made a bad impression and prevented the Europeans from making greater progress on the issue of political union. Germany found itself isolated in Europe as a result of its first autonomous act of diplomacy since World War II. Its isolation was compounded by persistent complaints of German monetary hegemony, provoked by the Bundesbank's refusal to ease upward pressure on interest rates in the wake of reunification.

The Bosnian crisis ended in fiasco. But the fiasco had the effect of strengthening rather than weakening European unity. The embarrassment caused by European disunity in the crisis, and French and European nervousness before the prospect of German unilateralism, rekindled European efforts to strengthen the Union. That integrationist reflex was reinforced by U.S. arrogance. As the German Defense Minister Volker Rühe observed, the French decision in May 1995 to send Rapid Intervention forces to Bosnia to support troops operating under UN command, along with NATO air strikes and the successful Croatian military operation, played an important role in bringing the warring parties to the negotiating table.[29] But the Europeans were practically excluded from the Dayton negotiations. European members of the Contact Group had to remonstrate before being allowed to see and approve documents that were being submitted to the negotiating parties. Their ire was such that they walked out of the press conference that followed the conclusion of the accords.[30] The crisis and the humiliation prompted the creation of a study group to find ways to improve the capacity of the European Union to define and defend a common foreign policy, perhaps by creating a post of "EU Foreign Minister" to coordinate a common security and foreign policy.[31]

But the specter of German unilateralism and hegemony in Europe stirred the French to tighten their relationship with NATO as well. It is no coincidence that three weeks following Germany's first combat mission in Bosnia, NATO aircraft stationed in Germany joined French air units in the first NATO exercise to be staged in France since Paris withdrew from the integrated military command in 1966. France joined action to symbol by declaring in February 1996, that it intended to collaborate more actively with NATO's integrated command structure. In a sparsely attended address to the joint houses of the U.S. Congress, Chirac maintained that the United States' military presence was still essential to the security of Europe. But he called for a reform of NATO that would "enable the European allies to assume fully their responsibilities, with the support of NATO facilities, wherever the United States does not wish to engage its ground forces."[32] Dissensions between France and the United States regarding the devolution of responsibilities, however, has prevented France, as of this writing, from rejoining the integrated command structure.

THE LIMITS OF REALISM: THE SPECIAL FRANCO-GERMAN RELATIONSHIP

Because it informs the concepts of hegemony and Franco-German geopolitical internationalism, realism helps make sense of the history of European integration. It explains the origins of European integration, and it sheds light on initiatives in economics and security that Europeans have deployed in response to the gradual unraveling of the hegemonic order. But realism fails to clarify a key aspect of that history: the enduring strength of the Franco-German relationship. Post-reunification Germany, the most populous country in Europe after Russia (80 million inhabitants to France's 55 million), produces 35 percent of the gross domestic product of the European Union, and is the premier exporting economy in the world, ahead of the United States and Japan (France is fourth). Germany is potentially hegemonic within the European Union. Moreover, it has gained all that it sought to gain from its strategy of geopolitical internationalism. But Germany has so far shown no interest in assuming the mantle of regional hegemon. It continues to value close cooperation with France, even at the expense of what many perceive to be its national interests. For its part, France has never succumbed to the temptation to balance German power in Europe by allying itself more closely with, say, Great Britain.

This does not mean that the French are unconcerned by the prospect of

German hegemony in Europe. Such fears were very apparent in the months preceding German reunification. Moreover, the Bundesbank's unwillingness to take the interests of Germany's neighbors into account as German interest rates climbed in response to budget deficits spawned by reunification contributed significantly to opposition to the Maastricht agreements in France. Pierre Chevènement, a leftist critic of Maastricht, complained that Europe had become a "financial Holy Roman Empire." Germany "with its demographic, industrial, and financial power, 'geocentric' within the continent and primary beneficiary of the enlargement of the European Community," was falling prey to the temptation to use European integration to "extend itself" through the creation of "a second mark," the imposition of free trade, and through the creation of dependent relations with Eastern Europe.[33] But French diplomacy in the 1980s and early 1990s continued to show a distinct preference for good relations with Germany before any other country, including Great Britain. Indeed, Great Britain was the odd-man-out in the European Union. When political and monetary union met with strong opposition from Britain's Conservative government, France worked closely with Germany to isolate Britain in Europe.

It is true that, at times, the French seemed poised to shift their attention to Britain, particularly during the period of reunification, during the Bosnian conflict, and during the international flap over French nuclear testing. In the first case, the collapse of the Soviet empire and the fall of the Berlin Wall on November 9, 1989 inaugurated a period of diplomatic forcing by a Germany that was intent on seizing the opportunity to win recognition of its territorial claims and its equality of status within the community of great powers. Germany abandoned the more cautious internationalism of the previous decade and, while generally not acting without consulting its allies, nevertheless took actions that placed those allies before a *fait accompli*. On November 28, Kohl proposed his ten-point plan for reunification without giving the French advanced notification.[34] The principle of reunification was contested by no one, and was approved by the European Council on December 9. But the timetable was judged precipitous, particularly by France and Great Britain.[35] Both France and Great Britain wanted to submit the issue of reunification to the attention of the Conference on Security and Cooperation in Europe (CSCE).

During the months following the collapse of the Wall, French policy was marked by verbal support for German reunification. That support was qualified only by insistence on the principle of respect for existing frontiers,

particularly the Oder-Neisse. But France also indulged in *realpolitik* ma-
neuvering to slow reunification and gain some control over it.[36] As early as
November 10, Mitterrand announced his intention to visit East Germany
and other Eastern European countries, adding that "reunification was not
the only future modality of relations between the German states, between
the German entities that represent the German people." When Germany
acted without consultation to extend the benefits of the Schengen agreements (on free passage of goods and peoples among France, Germany, and
Benelux) to East Germans, France withdrew from the arrangement temporarily to signify its opposition to the presumption that treaties with West
Germany somehow applied automatically to East Germany.[37]

The British reaction to the prospect of German reunification was, if anything, more skeptical and hesitant than the French one. Mitterrand and
Thatcher met on several occasions in the months following the collapse of
the Wall. At the European Council summit of December 8 and 9, 1989,
Mitterrand and Thatcher held private conversations, during which, according to Thatcher, Mitterrand observed that "at moments of great danger in
the past France had always established special relations with Britain and he
felt that such a time had come again." Thatcher concurred: "If there was
any hope now of stopping or slowing down reunification it would only come
from an Anglo-French initiative."[38] Despite their shared misgivings regarding
German unification, and despite their shared desire to involve the CSCE,
Mitterrand and Thatcher were unable to agree on a common policy. The
stumbling block was the European Union, toward which Mitterrand was
already looking to blunt the impact of German reunification on the balance
of power and influence in Europe. He proposed that the EU proceed with
the implementation of the Single European Act, agree on economic and
monetary union, and draw up a European social charter.

When Mitterrand and Thatcher met again in January, the French were
still complaining bitterly of being consulted by the Germans only after the
fact. But Mitterrand again refused the idea of closer cooperation with
Thatcher to delay reunification. Thatcher writes: "Essentially, he had a
choice between moving ahead faster towards a federal Europe in order to
tie down the German giant or to [defend] French sovereignty and the striking
up of alliances to secure French interests." In Thatcher's mind, "he made
the wrong decision."[39] But Mitterrand was equally critical of Thatcher, who,
he believed, was unrealistic in her opposition to German reunification.
"Only the full participation of Germany in this [European] construction

makes it possible to look with serenity on the inevitable reunification of the two Germanies."[40] Mitterrand's sentiments were shared unambiguously—for reasons we will explore below—by Helmut Kohl: "Germany's house—our common house—can only be constructed under a European roof. This must be the objective of our policy."[41]

Kohl's aggressive stance on German reunification gave his Christian Democratic Union (CDU) victory in the East German elections of March 18, 1990. On the 18th of May, the two CDU governments of West and East Germany signed a treaty of economic, monetary, and social union, a prelude to rapid and complete reunification. On July 16, the United States and the Soviet Union announced their agreement on the modalities of reunification. Mikhail Gorbachev acquiesced in the reunified Germany's membership in NATO in exchange for limits on the size of its army (370,000 troops), its renunciation of nuclear, chemical, and biological weapons, and the payment by Germany of a substantial indemnity. By that time, France and Germany had already settled their differences and turned their energies to the further development of the EU. They had issued a joint communiqué on March 13 stating their intention to work together toward European political union, and confirmed the "fundamental role of the Franco-German relationship in the context of the current evolution in Europe" and the need to intensify contacts at all levels. Franco-German initiatives were again setting the agenda at European Council meetings. On April 18, a joint letter by Mitterrand and Kohl placed the discussion of German reunification, political union, and monetary union by 1993 on the agenda of the Council meeting of April 28. The French also informed the United States of their strong desire that the American military presence in Europe be maintained, and began reexamining their relationship with NATO. The Franco-German summit that preceded that meeting marked the renewal of close bilateral relations, and in May, the French took an unusually active role in the effort to redefine the future role of NATO. The temptation to play the "English card" was a dim memory.

On April 19, 1990, Mitterrand and Kohl called for an intergovernmental conference on political union to examine the adoption of qualified majority rule in ministerial councils and the definition of a common European foreign and security policy. The European Council, composed of EC heads of state, debated the joint proposal ten days later and again in June, and agreed to convene a conference to draw up a plan for political union by the end of 1992. To give impetus to the negotiations, Kohl and Mitterrand penned a joint letter to the European heads of state on December 6, 1990, which laid out in greater detail their common conception of political union. In this letter, they again called for, among other things, the adoption of qualified majority rule in community affairs, and "a veritable common security policy that would lead in the future to a common defense policy."[42] In February 1991, France and Germany proposed again that the Europeans commit themselves to the development of a common defense, and that, in the interim, the Western European Union be considered the military arm of the European Community.[43] Kohl and Mitterrand addressed their colleagues on the topic of common defense again in October, and announced the enlargement of the joint Franco-German military units, which would become the kernel of a future European military corps.

Franco-British relations warmed again in 1995 following the election of the less determinedly Europeanist Jacques Chirac to the French presidency. Relations between the two governments had already been strengthened by close military cooperation in Bosnia, and shared exasperation with German diplomacy in that unstable region. Great Britain's tacit approval of French nuclear tests in the Pacific (despite a general outcry in the Commonwealth countries), combined with Germany's muted disapproval and the European Commission's rather clumsy efforts to exercise its oversight prerogatives (in application of the Euratom Treaty of 1957), was another sign of possible realignment within the EU power structure.[44]

But nothing came of it. At the Franco-German summit of December 7, 1995, Kohl and Chirac reaffirmed their commitment to Maastricht and European Union and, in a pointed reference to Britain, warned that they would not tolerate unilateral vetoes of further integration efforts. At the same summit, they reaffirmed their commitment to qualified majority voting, anathema to de Gaulle, but not to the Gaullist Chirac; they proposed to study voting weighted according to population; and they announced the joint development of a new reconnaissance satellite, to the chagrin of the United States which had been seeking to enter into partnership with Germany in this endeavor.[45] Pierre Séguin, like Chirac, dropped his opposition to Maastricht and called upon like-minded critics to drop their short-sighted opposition to monetary union and to engage in a constructive examination of the ways in which the European Union could formulate a response to the challenge of economic globalization.[46]

Just as France has not sought to balance German power by moving closer to Britain, France has not displayed any particular concern over Germany's rapidly expanding economic power and political and cultural influence in Eastern Europe. In contrast to the interwar period, when French geopolitical internationalism was complemented by the active construction of counter-vailing military alliances with the countries of Eastern Europe, as well as by efforts to forge such alliances with Great Britain and Fascist Italy, French diplomacy in recent years has shown little interest in this endeavor.[47]

REALISM, SKEPTICISM, AND THE NEED FOR NORMS OF PRUDENT CONDUCT

We asked at the outset if realism could inform a narrative reconstruction of postwar European integration. We saw that it succeeds quite well, to the extent that it informs the two conceptual vehicles that help structure that narrative, European geopolitical internationalism and American hegemony. Realism fails, however, when we try to make sense of the survival and re-inforcement of Franco-German mutual preference as the U.S. hegemonic order comes undone, particularly since the end of the Cold War. Realism would lead us to expect greater German self-sufficiency, and greater French energy in developing countervailing alliances. Geopolitical internationalism fails in both cases. Germany no longer has any use for that strategy, and France has shown little if any interest in closer countervailing alliances with Great Britain and other countries, even within the framework of existing international institutions.

The notion of "structural liberalism," developed here by Daniel Deudney and John Ikenberry, might provide an attractive alternative explanation. Although Europeans would bristle at the idea that American hegemony is a "penetrated hegemony," as Deudney and Ikenberry maintain, we nonethe-less have no difficulty recognizing "security binding" in the European alli-ance, the enduring and self-imposed semi-sovereign status of the region's most potentially powerful state, and structural openness. Nor is it inexact to speak of a common civic identity, though that identity is currently contested by an appreciable groundswell of nationalist populism.

But there is no need to abandon realism, since there is a way to amend realism so that it becomes more relevant to an understanding of France's and Germany's enduring special relationship and joint leadership of the European Union.[48] It involves going back to the classical sources of realist thought, beyond even the reconstruction provided here by Randall Schweller, to the recovery of one of the central themes of the classical realist tradition: its skepticism. R. B. J. Walker disputes the claim that there is such a thing as a "realist tradition," calling it a "hyperelastic label" that self-styled realists have applied to a hodgepodge of great thinkers in order to fabricate a tradition that in fact does not exist. Yet in spite of his best efforts to deny the existence of a realist tradition, Walker, in a superb exploration of the philosophical foundations of contemporary international relations thought, appends one and the same epithet—skeptical—to every great thinker that realists include in their tradition. Thus Walker writes of a "Rousseauean skepticism," a Machiavellian challenge to "universalist pretensions," a Weberian acquiescence "in a complex and widespread skepticism about modernity that characterised much socio-political theory and philosophy at the turn of the century." In a more general characterization of realism, Walker writes: "Whether in terms of the Nietzschean challenge to prevailing theories of progress, or of the barbarities of a war to end all wars, the seminal sources of realism in international political theory were acutely aware that the clash between philosophies of history grounded in Enlightenment optimism and their radical rejection constituted the starting point for almost any serious discussion of politics."[49]

What, then, is this skeptical component of realist thought? Realism, Robert Gilpin writes, is basically an attitude of "pessimism regarding moral progress and human possibilities."[50] But that attitude can be justified in a variety of ways. For the structuralist, anarchy impedes moral progress. For the classical realist, the "will to power" makes moral progress unattainable. For Gilpin himself, uneven growth in the international political economy and the subsequent rise to power of revisionist states perpetually sows the seeds of hegemonic war. But of all possible justifications of realist pessimism, perhaps the most unproblematic, though least well understood, is simple doubt or skepticism regarding either the will of humankind to live according to the dictates of reason or, more radically, regarding the capacity of reason itself to identify a "best way" to live or to organize society. One finds skepticism regarding the human will in Augustine, Rousseau, and Reinhold Niebuhr.[51] One finds the more radical skepticism regarding the capacity of reason itself to identify a path toward the good in Thucydides, Machiavelli, Hobbes, and E. H. Carr.[52] This latter expression of skepticism is particularly apposite in these "late modern" times when the ideologies of both Marxism and liberalism have been so forcibly contested.

Realism, however, is not coterminous with skepticism. Realism represents a "conservative reaction" to skepticism, a desire to act to create or impose some sort of political order in defiance of skepticism. It is this conservative reaction to fundamental doubt regarding the human will or reason that produces realism's core features: its statism and its concern with power and the distribution of power. The state provides the arena in which order is imposed, and power is the means with which we impose and defend it.

But that same reaction can produce other conclusions. Hume, not only a skeptic, but one of the early apologists of balance of power politics, claimed that philosophy's incapacity to discover the path to moral perfection forces us to acknowledge the usefulness of the norms and maxims of the "common life."[53] Though our skepticism inclines us to look on such norms and maxims critically, these same norms and maxims contribute effectively to the acquittal of the ordinary tasks of human survival. Inversely, the rejection of those norms on the basis of some religious, philosophical, or ideological "enthusiasm" is frequently a source of disorder and violence. We should use our skepticism to combat such "enthusiasms" and nourish respect for the norms of the common life in order to preserve peace and order. One encounters a similar though philosophically less developed sentiment in Hedley Bull's effort to marry realist prudence with respect for international law.[54]

By exploring the skepticism that lurks at the core of realist thought we gain additional purchase on the phenomenon of Franco-German reconciliation. Why, we asked, do France and Germany remain so committed to their peculiar relationship? It is because the principle of Franco-German reconciliation and mutual preference, the byproduct of the hegemonically brokered multilateral settlement of the long contest for the Rhineland, has in time congealed to become a norm of the "common life," a norm of prudent policy, a demarcation criterion that discriminates between the "normal" and the "abnormal" in foreign policy. It has become a customary commitment that stands between German policy and the ideological enthusiasms that once endowed it with recklessness, that is, the "imperialist" enthusiasm that challenged British supremacy on the seas before World War I and the "nationalist" enthusiasm that engendered such a cavalier attitude toward international law and norms in the 1930s. Simultaneously, that commitment stands between France and the *realpolitiker* instinct to develop balancing alliances to contain reunified Germany's power.[55]

This appeal to the understanding that France and Germany are bound by a special relationship, and the treatment of that understanding as a norm of prudent policy, explains aspects of French and German policy that have eluded our efforts so far. We noted, for example, some ambivalence in German attitudes toward the single currency. How can ambivalence sustain such a radical and ambitious policy goal? Helmut Schmidt, in response to the project's German critics, claimed that "progress toward European integration is not an affair of German idealism, but corresponds to Germany's vital, long-term, strategic interest in peace—if it were to be rejected, then we would face a third anti-German coalition. Compared with this goal of vital importance, technical fault-finding with the currency union and self-righteous criticism of the bureaucracy in Brussels are at best a secondary concern."[56]

As we read this passage, we ask what might cause Schmidt to fear that rejection of monetary union would produce an "anti-German coalition?" He cites no mechanism, and no mechanism that might produce that effect is immediately apparent. In justification of his fears, we find nothing more than the suspicion that any departure from the ideal of European integration will threaten the norm of Franco-German reconciliation and mutual preference, and the conviction that that norm has helped French and German statesmen conduct themselves prudently so as to preserve and consolidate the long peace. Elsewhere Schmidt admonishes his Social Democratic colleagues, as they wrestle with the temptation to capitalize on opposition to the single currency: "look after our friendship with France; it is the most precious good that has come to us in the twentieth century."[57]

The commitment to European Union is an affair of realist prudence born of skepticism. It is an affair of "high politics" that has engaged statesmen in a *fuite en avant* or "forward retreat" into the albeit imperfectly conceptualized path of political and economic integration. Integration is embraced not because it is valued *per se*. It is true that integration promotes some common interests in the realms of money, trade, and security. But integration European-style, as opposed to NAFTA-style, is valued primarily because it provides the vehicle for preserving norms that have proven themselves to be effective touchstones of prudent politics. The Europeans—above all the French and the Germans—embrace integration because they fear that the prudential norms they have developed in the postwar period will become inoperative if the pan-European ideal loses strength.

French and German diplomacy is replete with appeals to the ideals of European unification that contain nothing more substantive than the reaffirmation of this shared attachment to the norm of reconciliation. Germany, following its heavy-handed advocacy of Slovenian and Croatian independence, turned immediately to the task of mending its relations with France by promoting more energetically the idea of political and monetary union, even though political debate in Germany manifested considerable doubt about the benefits of either. France, following its decision to resume nuclear testing, turned immediately to Germany to lay to rest any suspicion that the new French government was revising policy toward Germany or the European Union, even though political debate in France bore the imprint of fears of German hegemony in Europe. The motivation in each case was not merely the fear of isolation. Germany's sympathies with the breakaway republics were widely shared. France's nuclear arrogance was not widely admired, but it was secretly applauded by the British government and tacitly approved by other nuclear powers. As mentioned above, observers predicted a new Franco-British alliance in Europe, and were subsequently surprised when Chirac reaffirmed France's attachment to its special relationship with Germany. The prudent reflex, embodied in the norm of Franco-German preference, prevailed.

Attention to the skepticism inherent in realism leads us to voice doubts—realist doubts—regarding the theory of structural liberalism, which, we conceded above, has *prima facie* explanatory power. My claim that mutual Franco-German preference is valued as a norm of prudent policy raises a central question: do liberal institutions suffice to constrain behavior, or is it not indeed restrained behavior, guided by deference to shared norms of prudential conduct, that assures the durability of the institutions?[58] The realist is the first to remind us how often institutions (and even power structures) have crumbled before the onslaughts of revolutionary or revisionist enthusiasms. The realist as skeptic counsels us to resist those enthusiasms and admonishes the statesman to respect, for reasons of prudence, existing norms and the institutions they legitimate if only because they define what the international community understands to be normal conduct. This kind of prudent adherence to norms of reconciliation and cooperation, and the desire to strengthen those norms through institutional and legal development, informs France's and Germany's ambitious integrationist enterprise today.

NOTES

1. An example is the debate between Bruce Cumings, *The Origins of the Korean War* (Princeton: Princeton University Press, 1981–1990) 2 vols., and John Lewis Gaddis, *The United States and the Origins of the Cold War, 1941–1947*

(New York, Columbia University Press, 1972). If I indulge in this methodological parenthesis, it is because the field of political science is currently undergoing one of its recurrent "totalizing crises," spawned by the conviction that
there is a "best way" to study politics. That conviction is set forth most forcefully
in Gary King, Robert O. Keohane, and Sidney Verba, *Designing Social Inquiry:
Scientific Inference in Qualitative Research* (Princeton: Princeton University
Press, 1994). But the argument is constructed on philosophical sand. It assumes
that nature is of "one kind," accessible to one method of inquiry. See John
Dupré, "Metaphysical Disorder and Scientific Disunity," in Peter Galison and
David J. Stump, eds., *The Disunity of Science: Boundaries, Contexts, and Power*
(Stanford: Stanford University Press, 1996). It also eschews the problem of ref-
erence—see, for example, Barry Stroud, *The Significance of Philosophical Skepticism* (Oxford: Oxford University Press, 1984)—that has so exercised philosophers of science since the publication of Thomas Kuhn, *The Structure of
Scientific Revolutions* (Chicago: University of Chicago Press, 1970) 2nd ed. The
problem of reference can be credibly dealt with by adopting an instrumental
criterion of truth—see Richard Rorty, "Is Natural Science a Natural Kind" in
Ernan McMullin, ed., *Construction and Constraint* (Notre Dame: University
of Notre Dame Press, 1988) and Arthur Fine, "Science Made Up," in Galison
and Stump, eds., *The Disunity of Science*—but nomological political science
does not fare particularly well when measured by this criterion. See Charles
Taylor, "Interpretation and the Sciences of Man" in Taylor, *Philosophy and the
Human Sciences* (Cambridge: Cambridge University Press, 1985). However,
the application of instrumentalism to any method of social science may be
problematic, given normative disagreement over the goals being pursued. See
Mary Hesse, "Theory and Value in the Social Sciences," in Christopher Hook-
way and Philip Pettit, eds., *Action and Interpretation: Studies in the Philosophy
of the Social Sciences* (Cambridge: Cambridge University Press, 1978). In this
view, all social science—not just history—becomes a site of moral debate.

2. Alan Milward, The *Reconstruction of Western Europe* (Berkeley: University of
   California Press, 1984), 392.
3. Alfred Grosser, *Affaires extérieures: la politique de la France, 1944–1989* (Paris:
   Flammarion, 1989), 185.
4. Henry Blumenthal, *Illusion and Reality in Franco-American Diplomacy, 1914–
   1945* (Baton Rouge: Louisiana State University Press, 1986), 135.
5. Blumenthal, *Illusion and Reality*, 130–131. See also p. 119.
6. Blumenthal, *Illusion and Reality*, 140. Blumenthal argues that the French
   sought to halt and diminish Anglo-Saxon penetration in Europe. But such fears
   are meaningful only in the context of French fears of growing German power,
   which, from the French perspective, the Anglo-Saxon powers tolerated and
   abetted. Compare with French attitude toward *Zollverein* in the nineteenth

century: see Raymond Poidevin and Jacques Bariéty, *Les Relations Franco-allemandes, 1815–1975* (Paris: Armand Colin, 1977), 38–43.

7. The chronicle of European integration can be found in Pierre Gerbet, *La Construction de l'Europe* (Paris: Imprimerie Nationale, 1994). Norway did not ratify the treaty.

8. Michael Loriaux, "Capital, the State, and Uneven Growth in the International Political Economy," in Michael Loriaux, Meredith Woo-Cumings, Kent Calder, Sylvia Maxfield, and Sofia Perez, *Capital Ungoverned: Liberalizing Finance in Interventionist States* (Ithaca: Cornell University Press, 1996).

9. John Zysman, *Governments, Markets, and Growth: Financial Systems and the Politics of Industrial Change* (Ithaca: Cornell University Press, 1983), 114.

10. In the terms of my analysis, the overdraft economy generated "moral hazard" in the French political economy. Loriaux, *France after Hegemony: International Change and Financial Reform* (Ithaca: Cornell University Press, 1991) pp. 90–95, 284–88.

11. Klaus H. Hennings, "West Germany," in Andrea Boltho, ed., *The European Economy* (Oxford: Oxford University Press, 1982) p. 479.

12. Such intervention was difficult despite the relatively large size of the public sector. See Sima Liberman, *The Growth of European Mixed Economies: 1945–1970* (New York: Wiley, 1977), ch. 2.

13. Note that the government, not the *Bundesbank*, was accorded the responsibility for determining the exchange rate of the D-mark under fixed rates. The *Bundesbank* was empowered to defend that rate. Hennings, "West Germany," p. 475.

14. Speculators under Bretton Woods technically bought foreign currencies from the central bank, thus challenging the central bank to satisfy demand for foreign currencies at prices that were fixed by international agreement.

15. See Eric Helleiner, *The Reemergence of Global Finance: States and the Globalization of Financial Markets* (Ithaca: Cornell University Press, 1994), 13.

16. See Gerbet, *La construction de l' Europe*, 299–308, 342–50.

17. Loriaux, *France after Hegemony*, 24–31. Currency depreciation (like devaluation) raised the price of imported goods. If the demand for those goods was inelastic, currency depreciation could result in a vicious circle whereby depreciation and inflation fed off each other. Inversely, attacking inflation could cause the currency to appreciate again, negating whatever commercial benefits were being sought in the first place. Overshooting of equilibrium currency values by an inherently nervous currency market ruled out "finessing" this dilemma through "fine tuning."

18. This observation applies as well to other traditionally weak currency countries of the "Club Med," who experience the same need as France to implement a strong currency policy to fight vicious circles of inflation and depreciation.

Antonio Guterres, leader of Portugal's opposition Socialist Party, writes: "Interest rates are the fundamental reason why I am a defender of the single currency. This will be the only way to make sure that we stop paying a risk premium, and to have interest rates equal to other countries, like Germany," *Diario Economico*, August 24, 1995. Capital flight into the single European currency would create pressures to lower interest rates, whereas currently capital flight into the mark creates pressures to raise interest rates in economies that seek to defend a D-mark parity.

19. See Philip G. Cerny, "From Dirigisme to Deregulation? The Case of Financial Markets" (Paper presented at the International Conference on Thirty years of the French Republic, Paris, June 1988). See also Loriaux, "Capital, the State, and Uneven Growth," in Loriaux et al., *Capital Ungoverned.*

20. See Jack Hayward, ed., *Industrial Enterprise and European Integration: From National to International Champions in Western Europe* (New York: Oxford University Press, 1995).

21. Françoise Manfrass-Sirjacques, "La coopération militaire depuis 1963," in Henri Ménudier, ed., *Le Couple Franco-Allemand en Europe* (Asnières: Publications de l' Institut d' Allemand d' Asnières, 1993).

22. Reuters, February 22, 1996. See also Josette Alia, "Chirac et les soldats de l'an 2000," *Le Nouvel Observateur*, Feb. 22–28, 1996.

23. Airy Routier, "Les dessous d' une opération commando," *Le Nouvel Observateur*, Feb. 29–March 6, 1996.

24. See Theo Sommer, "Wehrpflicht oder Berufsheer: Fünf Argumente gegen eine Armee aus lauter Freiwilligen. *Die Zeit*, March 8, 1996.

25. See Werner A. Perger, "Grosser Schritt: Pazifisten, Militärs, und der Minister," in *Die Zeit*, Dec. 22, 1995.

26. See Christian Schmidt-Häuer, "Der Kalte Krieg is noch lange nicht vorbei," *Die Zeit*, March 8, 1996.

27. See Christoph Bertram, "Präzedenzfall?" in *Die Zeit*, December 22, 1995.

28. Hans Stark "La Yougoslavie et les dissonances franco-allemandes," in Henri Ménudier, *Le Couple franco-allemand en Europe* pp. 225–36. See also the provocative essay of James Kurth, "Mitteleuropa and East Asia: The Return of History and the Redefinition of Security," in Meredith Woo-Cumings and Michael Loriaux, *Past as Prelude: History in the Making of a New World Order* (Boulder, CO: Westview, 1993).

29. Interview in *Die Zeit*, December 8, 1995.

30. Henri Guirchoun, "Dayton: Les coulisses de la 'pax americana,' " *Le Nouvel Observateur*, Nov. 30–Dec. 6, 1995.

31. Reuters, Sept. 22, 1995. That idea was not retained at the European summit of 1996.

32. Reuters, February 1, 1996.

33. Pierre Chevènement, "Lettre à un ami allemand, *Le Nouvel Observateur*, May 19–25, 1994.

34. Indeed, it is uncertain how much advance notice Kohl even gave his own foreign minister, Dietrich Genscher.

35. See the commentary on the 1996 conversation between George Bush, François Mitterrand, Mikhail Gorbachev, and Margaret Thatcher, in *Die Zeit*, March 15, 1996.

36. See Kristin Stehouwer, "France and German Unification: The Transition to a New Europe," Ph.D. dissertation, Northwestern University, July, 1997, from which much of the material in these several paragraphs is taken.

37. The legal foundations of Mitterrand's position may have been contestable, since economic exchanges between the two Germanies were already treated as "inter-German" trade by EU law, and thus not subjected to EU tariffs.

38. Margaret Thatcher, *The Downing Street Years* (New York: HarperCollins, 1993), 796.

39. Thatcher, *The Downing Street Years*, 798.

40. Passages quoted are taken from an interview of François Mitterrand by Jean Daniel, published in *Le Nouvel Observateur*, Jan 18–24 1996.

41. In Gerbet, *La Construction de l' Europe*, 450.

42. Quoted in Gerbet, *La Construction de l' Europe*, 453.

43. Following the collapse of the European Defense Community project in 1954, Great Britain proposed that Germany and Italy be admitted to the 1948 Brussels Treaty, a mutual security treaty among France, Great Britain, and the Benelux countries. The enlarged security pact was named the Western European Union. This arrangement reaffirmed Great Britain's commitment to France's security, provided a common framework within which Germany was permitted to rearm, and paved the way for Germany's admission to NATO. The coordination of defense strategy, however, was left entirely to NATO, and the WEO evolved into a rump institution, though a useful one to the extent that it became the vehicle through which Great Britain was associated with the Common Market countries prior to its admission in 1972. See Gerbet, *La Construction de l' Europe*, 154–55, 453–61, 498–501, et passim.

44. See Jürgen Krönig, "Die 'French Connection,' " in *Die Zeit*, Sept. 22, 1995. See ibid. Klaus Peter Schmid, "Mehr Bomben, Weniger Europa," and Theo Sommer, "Chiracs Muster ohne Wert."

45. Peter Norman and David Budhan, "Franco-German Summit Warning on EU Reform," *Financial Times*, December 8, 1995.

46. Reuters, February 15, 1996.

47. See K. S. Karol, "Europe de l'Est: la vague allemande," *Le Nouvel Observateur*, January 25–31, 1996

48. Realists whom I know are content with the orthodox definition. For this reason,

REALISM AND RECONCILIATION

I prefer to designate the perspective I develop here simply as "prudential skepticism." But I would argue that prudential skepticism is a central component of the realist tradition.

49. R. B. J. Walker, *Inside/Outside: International Relations as Political Theory* (Cambridge: Cambridge University Press, 1993). The term "hyperelastic" is found on p. 17. The passages cited are found on pp. 4, 47, 56, 110.

50. Robert Gilpin, *The Political Economy of International Relations* (Princeton: Princeton University Press, 1986), 304.

51. On Augustine, see Michael Loriaux, "The Realists and Saint Augustine: Skepticism, Psychology and Moral Action in International Relations Thought," *International Studies Quarterly* 36 (1992). On Rousseau, see Stanley Hoffmann and D. Fidler, eds. *Rousseau on International Relations* (Oxford: Oxford University Press, 1992), introduction. See also Reinhold Niebuhr, *Human Nature and Destiny* (New York: Scribner, 1942).

52. On Machiavelli, see Walker, *Inside/Outside*, chap. 2. On Hobbes, see Cornelia Navari, "Hobbes and the Hobbesian Tradition in International Thought," *Millennium*, 11 (1982), and Donald W. Hanson, "Hobbes and the Highway to Peace," *International Organization* 38 (1984). On Thucydides, see J. Peter Euben, *The Tragedy of Political Theory: The Road Not Taken* (Princeton: Princeton University Press, 1990), chap. 6, and Sara Monoson and Michael Loriaux, "The Illusion of Power and the Disruption of Moral Norms: Thucydides' Critique of Periclean Policy," *American Political Science Review* 92 (1998). See also E. H. Carr, *The Twenty Year's Crisis, 1919–1939* (New York: Harper and Row, 1964).

53. David Hume, *Enquiries Concerning Human Understanding and Concerning the Principles of Morals*, edited by L. A. Selby-Bigge, revised by P. H. Nidditch (Oxford, Clarendon Press, 1975). See Donald W. Livingston, *Hume's Philosophy of Common Life* (Chicago: University of Chicago Press, 1984) 3rd ed., 28–31.

54. See Hedley Bull, *The Anarchical Society: A Study of Order in World Politics* (New York: Columbia University Press, 1977).

55. In this construction, realism is not incompatible with constructivism.

56. Helmut Schmidt, "Deutsches Störfeuer gegen Europa," *Die Zeit*, Oct. 6, 1995.

57. Helmut Schmidt, in a speech prepared for but not delivered at the Mannheim Congress of the Social Democratic Party. Published in *Die Zeit*, Dec. 1, 1995.

58. This question applies as well to Peter Katzenstein's analysis, "Taming of Power: German Unification, 1989–1990," in Woo-Cumings and Loriaux, eds., *Past as Prelude*.

11 Neorealism, Nuclear Proliferation, and East-Central European Strategies

Mark Kramer

The end of the Cold War and the collapse of the Soviet Union ushered in a new era. The contours of the post-Cold War system have not yet congealed, but enough time has passed to allow for some preliminary judgments about the emerging international order and the effects it has had on state strategies. Although most specialists on international relations have welcomed the recent changes in world politics, a small number have been pessimistic from the outset, warning that the demise of bipolarity would increase the risk of war and spur many more countries to seek nuclear weapons. This pessimistic view, while not confined to any single group of scholars, has been especially pronounced among proponents of structural realism.

As early as 1990, John Mearsheimer warned that the emerging post-Cold War order would be far more dangerous than the old bipolar system. He predicted that the Nuclear Non-Proliferation Treaty (NPT) "will come under increasing stress in the post-Cold War World" because "the international system's new architecture creates powerful incentives to [nuclear] proliferation."[1] In particular, Mearsheimer believed that the buildup of a sizable nuclear force by Ukraine was "inevitable . . . regardless of what other states say and do."[2] Mearsheimer also warned that Germany and, even more, "the minor powers of Eastern Europe would have strong incentives to acquire nuclear weapons" in the post-Cold War era:

Without nuclear weapons, these Eastern European states would be open to nuclear blackmail from the [former] Soviet Union and, if it acquired nuclear weapons, from Germany. No Eastern European state could match the conventional strength of Germany or the [former] Soviet Union, which gives these minor powers a powerful incentive to acquire a nuclear deterrent, even if the major powers had none. [Thus,] a continuation of the current pattern of ownership [of nuclear weapons] without proliferation seems unlikely.[3]

Although Mearsheimer hedged this last prediction by stating that the East European countries might not actually begin building nuclear forces "until the outbreak of crisis," he consistently emphasized that the end of the Cold War was bound to give a strong fillip to nuclear proliferation both in Europe and elsewhere.

Subsequent developments failed to bear out Mearsheimer's expectations. Far from increasing, the number of nuclear weapons states initially decreased by one, when South Africa unilaterally dismantled its small arsenal.[4] That development was offset by the nuclear explosive capability that Pakistan displayed in 1998, but outside South Asia no new nuclear weapons states emerged. The two leading candidates for nuclear rivalry in Latin America — Argentina and Brazil — agreed in 1990–91 to cooperate in disbanding their nuclear weapons programs.[5] In 1994 Ukraine joined Belarus and Kazakhstan in signing the NPT as a non-nuclear weapons state and agreed to transfer to Russia the nuclear missiles and warheads left on Ukrainian territory after the Soviet Union collapsed. More generally, the NPT was extended for an indefinite period in May 1995, something that would have been almost inconceivable if the Cold War had still been under way.[6]

The disjuncture between this empirical evidence and Mearsheimer's predictions raises important questions about the structural realist conception of international politics. In making his predictions, Mearsheimer explicitly adduced structural realist arguments — an approach also adopted by numerous other scholars who argued, on the basis of neorealist premises, that nuclear weapons would spread rapidly in the post-Cold War era.[7] One of the questions to be explored here is whether these arguments were truly consonant with structural realism and, if so, what that would imply. Is there a way of reconciling the theoretical claims with observed trends? What modifications, if any, are needed in the structural realist outlook? Are broader aspects of the paradigm thrown into doubt?

In answering these questions, this essay will proceed in four stages. The first section will consider why a structural realist approach might lead one to expect that nuclear proliferation would increase in the post-Cold War era. The second part will examine the security strategies of four East-Central European states—Poland, the Czech Republic, Hungary, and Ukraine—to explain why all decided not to acquire their own nuclear weapons. The third section will consider how one might square the empirical evidence with hypotheses derived from the structural realist framework. The final section will offer conclusions about the relative merits and shortcomings of structural realism in explaining nuclear proliferation.

The chapter as a whole will seek to account for a system-level result (the lack of nuclear proliferation in Europe in the 1990s) by analyzing unit-level phenomena (the choices made by individual European states). At first glance, this may seem an odd way of evaluating structural realism, which originally was designed to explain systemic results, not foreign policy decisions. Most proponents of neorealism have moved away from (or at least modified) that premise, but a few still insist that the focus must be exclusively on systemic phenomena, which, they claim, can be understood only as the aggregate result of states' actions.[8] In their view, the structures of international politics are analogous to market outcomes in oligopolistic sectors of an economy. Just as theories of oligopolistic competition do not specify what any particular firm will do, so too, the argument goes, a structural analysis of international relations cannot specify what any particular state's foreign policy will be. The validity of this argument, however, is highly problematic. Neorealist theory does in fact make important predictions about state behavior and state goals, both explicitly and implicitly. These predictions, as shown below, yield a number of hypotheses about states' foreign policies, including policies on nuclear weapons. The hypotheses can then be tested against the empirical record (i.e., the record of states' foreign policy decisions) to help determine whether the underlying principles are accurate. An analysis of foreign policy decisions is especially crucial in understanding the systemic result discussed in this chapter—the lack of nuclear proliferation in Europe—which could have been fundamentally altered by the actions of a single state. Only by focusing on unit-level calculations will it be possible to explain why Mearsheimer and others went astray in predicting that nonnuclear states in Europe would seek nuclear weapons.[9]

The four countries selected for scrutiny here were chosen for a number of reasons. All four are former European Communist states (or parts of states) that were left without formal security arrangements after Communism collapsed. In addition, all were mentioned by Mearsheimer as plausible candidates to acquire nuclear weapons in the post-Cold War world, and indeed they all (especially Ukraine) did consider that option before deciding to forgo nuclear arms. All four were temporarily left with Soviet nuclear warheads and delivery vehicles on their soil after 1989. (As discussed below, these were withdrawn in 1990 from Poland, Hungary, and Czechoslovakia, and by 1995 from Ukraine.) Finally, all four were technologically sophisticated enough to build at least a small number of nuclear weapons if they had so chosen, albeit at enormous cost. The question to be explored here is why none of the four proceeded with that option.

It is worth noting that this chapter makes no judgment about the merits (or lack thereof) of the policies of the four East-Central European countries. The question of whether the world will be better or worse off if more states acquire nuclear weapons has been the subject of heated debate in recent years.[10] Discussion of this matter long predates the end of the Cold War—indeed, it began almost as soon as the first bombs were dropped on Hiroshima and Nagasaki—but it has taken on a new edge in a world that is no longer bipolar. This chapter, however, will not seek to determine whether nuclear proliferation in East-Central Europe would be good or bad. Although normative questions about the spread of nuclear weapons are certainly important, there is no way to make any firm judgments without greater empirical evidence. If more states in the region deploy nuclear weapons (as one would expect from the neorealist paradigm), the experiences of these countries over time will provide data that can be used to resolve the normative debate. For now, the more interesting question is why, contrary to some forecasts, nuclear proliferation did not occur in the 1990s.

REALIST PERSPECTIVES ON NUCLEAR PROLIFERATION

The analytical approach known as realism has a long and varied tradition among observers of international politics. Over the past two decades, most of the debate about realism has focused on the "structural" realist (or "neorealist") framework first expounded at length in 1979 by Kenneth Waltz.[11] Waltz's landmark book, *Theory of International Politics*, posits that state strategies are shaped primarily by structural features of the international system. Although Waltz and other structural realists do not deny the importance of unit-level behavior (i.e., domestic politics) in determining a particular state's foreign policy, they argue that the units (i.e., states) are not operating in a vacuum. The choices facing state leaders, according to the neorealist para-

digm, are always sharply constrained by structural factors, notably the anarchic ordering of the international system and the unequal distribution of
capabilities. Waltz acknowledges that under conditions of anarchy, states
"are free to do any fool thing they choose," but he emphasizes that "they are
likely to be rewarded for behavior that is responsive to structural pressures
and punished for behavior that is not."[12] Expectations of these costs and
benefits should in the end, according to Waltz, cause states to heed structural
pressures when deciding "to do some things and to refrain from doing
others."

The neorealist view has come under challenge from numerous quarters.
One such challenge has been posed by the "constructivist" school, which
rejects almost all the premises of neorealism.[13] A more formidable challenge
has come from proponents of "neoliberal institutionalism," who, unlike the
constructivists, share many of the assumptions of neorealism.[14] The major
difference between the neoliberal institutionalists and the neorealists is that
the former believe that norms, international regimes, international organizations, and other institutions can moderate the structural effects of the
international system. Institutionalists see ample grounds for cooperation
among states on important issues, provided that institutions are in place to
dispel or at least mitigate each side's fears that the other side (or sides) will
cheat. These institutions thereby reduce the transaction costs of cooperation
and ensure that the benefits of cooperation greatly exceed the costs. By
contrast, structural realists argue that inducements for cooperation and the
facilitating role of institutions are usually outweighed by the systemic pressures that states encounter. (The main exceptions are when states form an
alliance against a common threat or when a hegemonic state is able to
induce cooperation through both positive and negative means.) Some neorealists do attach importance to international institutions, but most argue
that institutions give little more than a "false promise" of lasting
cooperation.[15]

The contentious debate about Waltz's book should not deflect attention
from the broader realist enterprise, including several recent efforts to modify
and improve on the structural paradigm.[16] Too often, critics of neorealism
have resorted to straw men and caricatures. The aim in this article is quite
different. Because structural realism has been so important and controversial
in the field of international relations, the focus here is primarily on that
brand of realism; but the discussion has been carefully tailored to ensure
that structural realist propositions about nuclear proliferation are set forth

and tested as fairly as possible. This section begins by laying out a structural realist framework for judging nuclear proliferation in the post-Cold War world. It then derives hypotheses from that framework, which can be tested against concrete evidence from East-Central Europe as presented in the following two sections.

Systemic Pressures

Structural realists broadly agree that the international system is anarchic and decentralized. Although diplomacy, international law, and international regimes provide elaborate "rules of the game," no supranational government exists that can, if necessary, impose its will on a recalcitrant unit (or units) within the system to prevent or rectify a breach of the rules. The lack of a superordinate authority contrasts with the makeup of most states, whose governments are responsible for enforcing domestic rules and for helping to resolve conflicts among individuals or groups.[17]

The anarchic structure of the system, according to the neorealist paradigm, ensures that most states at least occasionally will feel threatened by one or more other states. Even if these fears are unwarranted, government leaders must treat the perceived threats seriously. Some structural realists, such as John Mearsheimer and Robert Gilpin, contend that most of the perceived threats are indeed genuine.[18] They argue that states constantly strive to outdo their rivals and to amass power at their rivals' expense. This view, commonly known as "offensive realism" (or "hyperrealism") is not shared by some other neorealist scholars such as Kenneth Waltz and Joseph Grieco.[19] Waltz and Grieco maintain that states are chiefly interested in preserving their current position, rather than in constantly seeking to improve it.[20] This view is usually called "defensive realism." The offensive-defensive split among neorealists has important theoretical implications, but the point to be emphasized here is that all structural realists, even those who subscribe to defensive realism, believe that conditions of anarchy necessarily spawn perceptions of threat.

Neorealists also agree that the prevalence of anarchy ensures that states will never be fully confident about the willingness of outsiders to come to their aid in an emergency. Hence, every state must operate in a self-help manner. Even when a state harbors expansionist or revisionist ambitions, that state (like all other states) will want to ensure its own survival first and foremost. Most neorealists argue that this imperative will induce states to pursue both internal and external "balancing" against existing and potential adversaries.[21] Internal balancing is the effort that a state makes to marshal its own resources (through defense spending, conscription, etc.) to counter perceived threats. Internal balancing minimizes reliance on outsiders and therefore is the preferable route of action, *ceteris paribis*.[22] For some states, however, external balancing—that is, the pursuit of alliances—is a crucial supplement to internal balancing. A relatively small state confronted by a much larger and hostile neighbor will have a particular incentive to seek allies.[23]

Nevertheless, even for small states, external balancing is likely to be viewed as problematic. The neorealist paradigm suggests that allied states will remain suspicious and mistrustful of one another, fearing that today's allies could be tomorrow's enemies. Even when State A is willing to ally itself with State B against State Z, structural realists would expect State A to try to limit its cooperation, for fear that State B's relative gains might one day be turned against State A. State A also will be constantly mindful that in an emergency State B might forsake its alliance obligations or be unable to fulfill them.[24] Hence, most neorealists would expect that State A will be reluctant to depend solely, or even predominantly, on external balancing, especially when it has viable alternatives.

If allied guarantees are viewed as inherently problematic from the neorealist standpoint, nuclear guarantees against a nuclear-armed adversary must be deemed especially problematic because they require the guarantor (State B) to risk nuclear destruction on behalf of another state (State A). Officials in State A will be aware that State B, like other states, places the highest premium on its own survival, and that if war breaks out State B will be loath to commit suicide merely to defend a distant ally. Thus, from the neorealist perspective, nuclear guarantees should have very little credibility with State A and other countries that are under State B's nuclear umbrella. This point was emphasized by Robert Rothstein three decades ago in his discussion of alliances and small powers: "Nuclear guarantees do no more than increase the probability of future support; they do not make that support certain. Under the circumstances, if [State A] feels threatened, and if it has the technical means to do something about it, the guarantee can only have an interim significance until [State A] can build its own nuclear capability."[25] Although neorealists acknowledge that less-than-credible nuclear guarantees may be enough to deter potential aggressors, they argue that those guarantees provide little or no reassurance to State A.[26]

Hypotheses About Post-Cold War Europe

These various systemic constraints should, according to the neorealist paradigm, be even stronger in post-Cold War Europe. One of the central tenets of neorealism is that the distribution of power within the system determines how and when states cooperate on security issues. If that is so, the recent shift from bipolarity to multipolarized unipolarity—and perhaps eventually to full-fledged multipolarity—should further reduce the attractiveness of external balancing (i.e., reliance on allies) and bolster European states' incentives to pursue internal balancing.[27] The reasons for this are threefold:

First, the post-Cold War order in Europe is likely, in the neorealists' view, to be more war-prone (though not necessarily more unstable) than the old bipolar order.[28] This is so for two reasons. First, the demise of bipolarity and the disintegration of several multiethnic states (Yugoslavia, the Soviet Union, Czechoslovakia) have produced a much greater number of potentially conflictual dyads in the region.[29] Second, the end of the bipolar nuclear standoff in Europe may reduce the inhibitions that some European states had during the Cold War about resorting to military force against one another. To the extent that European governments believe these two developments have increased the risk of war, they will be strongly inclined to ensure that their states can be defended against potential enemies.

Second, the end of bipolarity and the dissolution of the Warsaw Pact, according to most neorealists, will cause future alliances in Europe to be more fluid and uncertain, raising doubts about the credibility of new allied guarantees. The threat posed by the Soviet Union provided a crucial rallying point for the North Atlantic Treaty Organization (NATO) and other U.S. alliances. From the neorealist perspective, the disappearance of that threat not only casts doubt on the *raison d'etre* of NATO, but also suggests that future alliances, if formed at all, will be relatively loose and ephemeral. The option of external balancing may therefore be deemed inadequate for European states that face serious military threats.

Third, the sharp cuts in U.S. strategic nuclear forces mandated by the Strategic Arms Reduction Treaties (START), as well as the general contraction of U.S. overseas commitments in the post-Cold War era, may further erode the credibility of U.S. nuclear guarantees. One of the reasons that the U.S. nuclear arsenal was so large during the Cold War was to provide flexibility and a margin of error for extended deterrence.[30] The elimination of thousands of U.S. strategic warheads is bound to have an impact on the perceived viability of extended deterrence. Although the United States has been willing, through its support for the expansion of NATO, to bring additional European states under its nuclear umbrella, the umbrella may well be viewed in the future with ever greater skepticism by those it is designed to protect.[31] That is why many neorealists expect that U.S. allies (or prospective allies) in the post-Cold War world will increasingly want "a hedge against . . . the inevitable risks of abandonment."[32]

In combination, these three factors can be seen, from the neorealist perspective, to create a strong inducement for vulnerable European states to emphasize internal balancing over external balancing. What is less clear is whether internal balancing in itself will be of much use. If a relatively small European state (State A) is confronted by a much stronger and potentially hostile neighbor (State Z), internal balancing may well be ineffective unless State A acquires nuclear weapons. Nuclear weapons, unlike conventional arms, can give State A the capacity to inflict "unacceptable damage" on State Z, partly offsetting the disparity of power between the two sides. State Z will still be much stronger overall than State A, but the A-Z dyad will be far less war-prone if, as Kenneth Waltz has long argued, nuclear weapons enable "the weak to deter the strong."[33] If a particular dyad is highly unequal and the two states in question are antagonistic (or potentially antagonistic), structural realists would expect the smaller state to seek (or at least be very interested in seeking) nuclear weapons.[34]

In any given case, however, several factors might militate against a nuclear option. For example, even if State A faces a clear-cut military threat, it might believe that it has sufficient conventional strength to deter or, if necessary, to overcome that threat. In addition, State A might fear that an attempt to build nuclear arms would provoke alarm among rival states, perhaps causing them to seek nuclear weapons of their own (if they did not already have them) or to take other military steps (including a preemptive attack) that would offset State A's action. This is the nuclear dimension of the more general "security dilemma."[35] Alternatively, State A might forgo nuclear deployments if it has sufficient confidence in allied nuclear guarantees. The credibility of such guarantees, as noted above, has always been problematic, but they may be credible enough to induce State A to eschew the risks and costs of a nuclear program.[36]

Whatever the precise circumstances, neorealists would argue that the paramount factor driving State A's decision about nuclear weapons (assuming that State A has the capacity to produce such weapons) will be the magnitude of the external threats to State A's security and the possibility of coping with those threats either through conventional forces or through alliances. Neorealists do not deny that other factors, such as a desire for prestige, may play some role in decisions about nuclear weapons, but they argue that these considerations are bound to be overshadowed by security concerns. This theme was highlighted by Kenneth Waltz in 1981 when he predicted that "nuclear weapons will spread from one country to another in the future for the same reasons they have spread in the past," above all because of fears of external threats.[37] That point has been reaffirmed in the post-Cold War era by numerous other structural realist scholars.[38]

On that basis, it is possible to formulate three sets of neorealist hypotheses about nuclear proliferation in post-Cold War Europe, taking as given that State A has ample technological prowess:[39]

(H-1) If State A decides to build nuclear weapons, it will do so because of major external threats to its security. (This hypothesis is formulated from the standpoint of defensive realism. An offensive realist might reformulate it as: "If State A decides to build nuclear weapons, it will do so either to counter external threats or to intimidate and dominate rival states.")

(H-2) The main alternatives to a nuclear weapons program for State A, especially the prospect of relying on outside nuclear guarantees against a nuclear-armed adversary, will be much less feasible in the post-Cold War era.

(H-3) If State A refrains from acquiring nuclear weapons, it will do so for one (or more) of six reasons, listed here in descending order of importance:

(a) it does not face any urgent external threats;

(b) it believes it can cope with urgent threats by non-nuclear means;

(c) it has obtained what it believes is a reliable nuclear guarantee from outside powers;

(d) it is concerned that a nuclear weapons program might spur rival states to take countermeasures, including the possibility of a pre-emptive attack;

(e) it is unable or unwilling to commit the economic resources needed to support a viable nuclear weapons program; or

(f) it is concerned about the political and diplomatic costs of a nuclear weapons capability.

This third hypothesis, too, is couched in defensive realist terms. An offensive realist would add a seventh possible reason—"it does not harbor expansionist ambitions"—and place it at the top of the list. From the neo-realist standpoint, only considerations (a) through (e) in (H-3) should have a decisive bearing on State A's policy. Point (f) can do no more than rein-force a decision made on the basis of one or more of the other factors. Point (f) will not be sufficient in itself to determine the outcome. Or at least that is what one would conclude from the structural realist literature. Whether that is in fact the case will be explored in the next two sections.

NUCLEAR WEAPONS AND EAST-CENTRAL EUROPEAN STRATEGIES

This section turns first to the cases of Poland, the Czech Republic, and Hungary, which are similar enough that they can be discussed together. It then shifts to the case of Ukraine, which for a variety of reasons needs to be treated separately. The aim here is not to provide an exhaustive analysis of each state's security strategy. Instead, this section briefly considers the main external threats perceived by the four states, the role of nuclear weapons in dealing with those threats, and the reasons that non-nuclear options were chosen.

Poland, Czech Republic, Hungary

Poland, the Czech Republic (the main successor to Czechoslovakia), and Hungary have pursued broadly similar security strategies since 1989. To be sure, the three states have differed somewhat in their perceptions of threats and the ways of coping with them. For example, Hungary, unlike Poland and the Czech Republic, must be ready for conflicts with Romania, Serbia, and Slovakia. Similarly, Poland was concerned for a while (in late 1989 and the first half of 1990) that a reunified Germany might seek to redraw the border between the two countries.[40] Nevertheless, despite these variations, the three states generally have been concerned about the same major threat (a possible militant resurgence in the former Soviet Union) and have pur-sued roughly the same means of forestalling, or if necessary countering, that threat.

Perceptions of External Threats

The collapse of Communism in East-Central Europe in 1989, the dis-solution of the Warsaw Pact in mid-1991, and the demise of the Soviet Union in December 1991 removed the security framework that had been imposed on East-Central Europe during the Cold War era. As auspicious as all those developments were, officials in the region perceived that their countries had been left in a "security vacuum," a phrase used over and over in the early and mid-1990s to convey a sense of political-military unease and vulnerability. The end of Soviet hegemony in East-Central Europe eliminated the chief source of the region's periodic crises in the postwar era, but other dangers soon emerged. The new East European governments found themselves having to contend with a number of serious threats without the benefit of a security framework to replace the one that had collapsed.

Initially, the most salient of the threats confronting the new governments was continued uncertainty about the political future of the Soviet Union. Even before the reformist trends in Moscow turned sour in late 1990 and early 1991, apprehension about Soviet political developments was readily apparent in all the East-Central European states. Hungarian foreign minister Geza Jeszensky consistently warned in 1990 that events could take a sharp turn for the worse in the Soviet Union, and that any such reversal would have ominous implications for the Warsaw Pact countries:

> Only recently has the Soviet Union become a trustworthy partner in efforts to truly liberate the Hungarian people. . . . But there are different trends in Moscow and they are in conflict with one another. . . . Our major problem is that it is difficult to predict the direction of processes in the Soviet Union.[41]

Polish officials had begun to speak in even gloomier terms by mid-1990 about "the threat of a conservative overthrow" in Moscow, which would cause "the USSR to disintegrate into parts that would not only be riven by *internal* conflicts, but would also be prone to unleash some sort of *external* conflict, if only to provide the population with easy victories and conquests. [We cannot] assume there will automatically be peace [with the Soviet Union] in the future."[42]

The concerns expressed by these East European officials took on a new sense of urgency after the abrupt resignation of Soviet foreign minister Eduard Shevardnadze in December 1990, coupled with his warnings about "reactionary" elements who were pushing the Soviet Union toward a new "dictatorship."[43] This sense of urgency was heightened still further by the violent crackdown in the Baltic republics in January 1991, which prompted all the East European governments to condemn the Soviet Union and to threaten to withdraw immediately from the Warsaw Pact. (The Pact was not due to be formally abolished until July 1991.) A top aide to the Polish president, Lech Walesa, warned at the time that the Polish government could "no longer rule out the possibility that Russian generals are thinking about regaining Eastern Europe."[44] Although most East European officials assumed that the Soviet High Command had grudgingly come to accept the demise of the Warsaw Pact, many were still uneasy about what would happen if the Soviet armed forces acquired a larger political role or, worse yet, launched a coup. Even the then-foreign minister of Poland, Krzysztof Skubiszewski, who had tried to defuse the most extreme speculation about Soviet policy in the region, admitted to a few misgivings about "the Soviet Army's Stalinist desire to win back territory, expand Soviet borders, and regain a military presence" in central Europe.[45]

In addition to concerns about a hardline backlash in Moscow, other important external problems emerged after the collapse of the Warsaw Pact, notably the deepening war in Yugoslavia, the rise of ethnic assertiveness in some parts of Eastern Europe, and the general sense of "not knowing what is going to happen in our part of the world now that the straitjacket of the Soviet Army has been removed."[46] These factors clearly induced all the East-Central European governments to look for new security arrangements. Still, the overriding long-term concern in Warsaw, Prague, and Budapest remained the future of Russia. When the Soviet Union disintegrated at the end of 1991, the urgency of the threat diminished sharply, but the fragility of democratic changes in Russia left many in East-Central Europe apprehensive.

Polish, Czech, and Hungarian concerns about Russia mounted in the first half of the 1990s as a result of the increasingly nationalist tone of Russian political discourse, the confrontation at the Russian parliament building in October 1993, the strong electoral showing of Vladimir Zhirinovsky's quasi-fascist party in December 1993, the resurgence of the Russian Communist Party in 1995–96, and the vehement campaign that Russian leaders waged against East European efforts to join NATO. By early 1994 top Polish officials were warning of a "resurgence of imperialist thinking in Moscow," a concern aggravated by Zhirinovsky's proclaimed goal of retaking eastern Poland.[47] Czech president Vaclav Havel expressed similar concerns about the "chauvinistic, Great Russian, crypto-Communist, and crypto-totalitarian forces" that might someday regain ascendance in Moscow.[48] Although in public all the East-Central European governments continued to affirm that their countries "are not threatened at present," they acknowledged that conditions in Russia "are far from stable" and that "the end of the Cold War has by no means eliminated the possible sources of military danger" in Moscow.[49] Widespread misgivings about Russia were also evident in opinion polls in the three East European states, particularly Poland and the Czech Republic. From 1994 through 1997, more than two-thirds of respondents in Poland said they believed there would be a "renewed imperial threat" from Russia "within the next five to ten years."[50] Surveys in the Czech Republic in 1995 and 1996 showed that roughly three out of every five citizens believed "Russia will present a threat to our country in the future."[51]

Russia's efforts to prevent the East European states from joining NATO evoked particular worries about Moscow's long-term intentions. In early 1995 Havel expressed dismay that Russia was trying to "dictate to other countries which alliances they can belong to."[52] Polish leaders, too, said they were "baffled" by the intensity of the Russian campaign, warning that Moscow was moving back to "the shadow of the Cold War."[53] A highly publicized document released by top-ranking Polish government officials (and former officials) in October 1995 claimed that Russia was trying to "retain a belt of militarily, politically, and economically weak states around it and to increase its presence in these areas over time until its renewed strength will permit outright spheres of influence to be reestablished."[54] The authors of the report left no doubt that if Russia persisted in its "aggressive stance," it would soon pose a "real threat" and plunge Europe into a "cold peace."

Anxiety in Poland, Hungary, and the Czech Republic was further piqued by Russia's growing propensity to rely on overt nuclear threats in its campaign against NATO expansion. These threats were linked with a new military doctrine approved by the Russian government in November 1993, which affirmed that "if an attack is launched against Russia by a country allied with a state that possesses nuclear weapons"—as all the NATO countries obviously are—"Russia retains the right to use nuclear weapons and to deliver a preemptive nuclear strike against the adversary."[55] Shortly after this doctrine was adopted, General Gennadii Dmitriev warned that if the East-Central European countries "are dreaming about entering NATO, they should realize that by doing so, they will immediately be placed on the list of targets for Russian strategic nuclear forces, with all the consequences this entails."[56] Subsequently, Polish commentators expressed concern that Russia was "stationing nuclear missiles in Kaliningrad and targeting them at Warsaw and

Krakow."[57] In the fall of 1995, a senior officer on the Russian General Staff asserted that if the Czech Republic and Poland were admitted into NATO, "the coordinates of targets located on Czech and Polish territory will be entered into the flight plans of Russian long-range nuclear missiles."[58] This threat was echoed in early 1996 by a top official at Russia's Atomic Energy Ministry, Georgii Kaurov, who warned that Russia would be "obliged to neutralize the danger" of NATO expansion by "targeting nuclear weapons at military sites in Eastern Europe."[59]

Ordinarily, these sorts of threats would have been regarded as mere bluster, but the "Zhirinovsky factor" in Russian politics changed the calculus, at least somewhat. On many occasions both before and after the December 1993 elections in Russia, Zhirinovsky was quoted as being eager to use nuclear weapons in pursuit of state interests.[60] Although Zhirinovsky's political fortunes declined sharply after 1994, the reports of his loose talk about nuclear strikes—irrespective of the accuracy of some of those reports—left a distinct residue of unease in East-Central Europe.

This unease necessarily affected Polish, Czech, and Hungarian security strategies. Although the Polish defense minister acknowledged that it was "impossible to ignore the fact that Russia remains a huge country and a nuclear superpower," he and other Polish officials expressed "outrage and condemnation" after the barrage of Russian threats in October 1995, which they characterized as "nuclear blackmail."[61] Hungarian military experts also denounced the Russian statements, noting that "this is the first time in more than 30 years that nuclear weapons are being used not only as a deterrent, but as a threat."[62] The same point was emphasized by Czech officials, who argued that "nuclear threats are inappropriate in the post-Cold War era," and warned that the Czech government would "firmly resist any form of Russian nuclear blackmail."[63]

Quite apart from Russia's nuclear arsenal, the conventional force imbalance in East-Central Europe also posed daunting problems for military planners in East-Central Europe. Under the limits originally set by the Conventional Forces in Europe (CFE) Treaty in November 1990, the combined military strength of the Visegrad states (Poland, Hungary, and Czechoslovakia) was meager compared to the Soviet armed forces. This disparity was mitigated somewhat by the dissolution of the Soviet Union in late 1991 (see table 11.1, p. 406), but even now the Polish, Czech, and Hungarian armies combined are dwarfed by the Russian army. The then-chief of the Polish General Staff, General Tadeusz Wilecki, warned in 1996 that "the huge asymmetry of military power in Central Europe" could leave Poland and other states in the region "vulnerable to a stronger army."[64]

The disproportion in Moscow's favor is even greater than it may seem, because the Russian Army still has tens of thousands of heavy weapons deployed east of the Urals, which are not covered by CFE (see table 11.1, p. 406). Most of those weapons were initially relocated there by the Soviet government in 1990 to ensure that they would be exempt from the treaty's limits.[65] This equipment generally has not been maintained in working order, but much of it could be rendered operational in an emergency, provided that enough lead time was available. If a severe crisis were to erupt in Europe, thousands of weapons could eventually be activated and shifted back to western Russia to augment Russian ground and air forces. The weaponry located east of the Urals thus could vastly magnify the force imbalance in East-Central Europe. Although the process of transporting such large amounts of hardware back to Europe would be very costly and might take as long as several months, the redeployments in 1990 showed that the task is eminently feasible.[66]

Combined with the deep uncertainty about the future of Russian politics, the military equation in East-Central Europe was inevitably a source of unease in the Visegrad countries. Although all the governments in the region publicly averred that "no external danger currently exists," the potential threat from Russia loomed just below the surface.

Nuclear Weapons Policies

Despite concerns about a possible backlash in Moscow, the Czech, Polish, and Hungarian governments all decided not to acquire nuclear weapons as a hedge. Each of the three governments seriously considered the nuclear option for at least a brief while; but the possibility of building nuclear weapons was never openly promoted—and was only rarely mentioned in public—by senior political or military figures. Instead, the main objective for Poland, Hungary, and the former Czechoslovakia after 1989 was to get all Soviet nuclear weapons removed from the region as soon as possible. That endeavor proved eminently successful.

By October 1990, less than a year after Communism collapsed, all Soviet tactical nuclear warheads and delivery vehicles had been pulled out of Hungary and Czechoslovakia. Withdrawals from Poland were completed the following year. By the end of 1990, the Czechoslovak government had reasserted full national control over facilities that had been designated as nuclear warhead dispensing areas (for Czechoslovakia's weapons) under a secret bilateral agreement of February 1986. The Czechoslovak army also reclaimed the three military bases in western and southern Bohemia—Bilina, Bela pod Bezdezem, and Misov—that had been warhead storage sites for the Soviet Union's own nuclear missiles under an agreement dating back to December 1965.[67] Similarly, the Hungarian army regained control of the former Soviet nuclear weapon depots near Dombovar, Baj, and Nagyvazsony in western Hungary.[68] In April 1991 the Polish army reclaimed the former nuclear munitions sites near Sypniewo when Soviet missile units finally pulled out.[69] The dismantling of all these facilities, combined with the withdrawal of Soviet theater nuclear weapons and the disintegration of the Warsaw Pact, made the whole region a de facto nuclear-free zone.

Even before the Soviet withdrawals were completed, the East European governments gave at least some consideration to the possibility of acquiring their own nuclear weapons. The acquisition of a viable nuclear force (as opposed to just one or two explosives) would have been extremely expensive for the three countries even if they had pursued the matter jointly; but it would have been possible. The industrial and technical capacity of the East European states was clearly sufficient to design and build nuclear explosives.[70] All three countries were long-standing members of the elite Nuclear Suppliers' Group, and they had many well-trained nuclear scientists and advanced nuclear power facilities. Czechoslovakia had long provided uranium to the Soviet Union for weapons applications.[71] Moreover, all three countries had substantial numbers of nuclear-capable delivery vehicles, which could have been equipped with nuclear warheads. (Until 1989, in fact, that is precisely what would have happened if a crisis had arisen. Soviet nuclear warheads would have been installed on some of the East European missiles, which then would have been brought under direct Soviet command.[72]). Czechoslovakia, in particular, had secretly obtained forty-eight SS-23 missiles and eight SS-23 launchers from the Soviet Union between 1986 and 1988, apparently because Soviet leaders wanted to circumvent limits imposed by the Intermediate-Range Nuclear Forces (INF) Treaty in December 1987.[73] Although nuclear warheads for the SS-23s had not been provided, the nuclear-capable missiles remained in service in the Czech Republic long after Communist rule ended.

In addition to having the *capacity* to acquire nuclear weapons, the East European countries had considerable *motivation* to do so, not least to deter the former Soviet Union. A U.S. Government survey in late 1991, based in part on reports from intelligence specialists, concluded that the acquisition of nuclear weapons by the East European states was "conceivable," albeit "not very likely at the moment."[74] The report described the circumstances that might prompt Hungary, Poland, or the Czech Republic to seek nuclear arms:

> [I]t is conceivable that the Eastern Europeans could be driven toward the development of nuclear weapons if it appeared that the Soviet Union had irrevocable designs on them, if they gave up all hope that the West was prepared to extend a meaningful security guarantee, and if they feared that war was inevitable. Another theoretically possible set of conditions would involve the acquisition of nuclear weapons by one or more western Soviet republics as part of the breakup of the Union. This might trigger proliferation throughout the region, as one Eastern European state after another concluded that it could not go without nuclear weapons as long as its neighbors possessed them. . . . These states do face some very real threats, whether from the Soviet Union, from their neighbors, or from ethnic turmoil in the region; in extreme circumstances nuclear weapons may look to be attractive as the ultimate credential for independence, as an equalizer for an inferior position in a security relationship (especially with the Soviet Union), and as a cheap means of defense. Those circumstances do not seem to be very likely at the moment, but they cannot be definitively ruled out over the longer term.[75]

This analysis is remarkably similar to what East European officials themselves argued during interviews in the early 1990s. They affirmed that, *in extremis* (i.e., if no alternatives were feasible), their governments would have to "take a serious look at the nuclear option."[76] Polish and Czech concerns about this matter revolved largely around the former Soviet Union, whereas Hungarian concerns were somewhat broader. As early as July 1989, senior Hungarian officials expressed anxiety about Romania's apparent attempt to build nuclear weapons.[77] Although some of the Hungarian claims may have been overstated, recent disclosures have confirmed that Romania had a nuclear weapons project, including plutonium extraction efforts, under way throughout the 1980s.[78] Hungarian leaders may therefore have had some justification for wanting to counter that threat.

In the end, however, all three East European governments decided against the nuclear option. With varying degrees of finality, they gradually announced that they would not seek to develop nuclear weapons of their own to fill the void left by the Soviet withdrawals. The tone was set in late 1990 by the Czechoslovak government's declaration that Czechoslovakia "will not produce any nuclear weapons or other weapons of mass destruction, and will never make the effort to produce them. Nor will it allow the deployment of such weapons on its territory."[79] The Czechoslovak government also indicated that it would cease exports of uranium for military purposes to the Soviet Union.[80] In addition, the Czechoslovak authorities pledged that they would dismantle their SS-23 launchers and missiles, though they later refrained from doing so. In mid-1993 a senior officer on the Czech General Staff, General Jiri Divis, acknowledged that "the SS-23 complexes and missiles are still in service, and we will probably keep them for some time, particularly because it would be expensive to destroy them."[81] He emphasized, however, that the missiles were equipped only with conventional "high-explosive fragmentation warheads," adding that "our retention of the SS-23s does not alter or detract from our basic decision, after a careful review, to forgo the production of nuclear weapons."

Poland and Hungary both followed Czechoslovakia's lead. The Polish government barred the Soviet Union from "transporting nuclear weapons through Polish airspace or by Polish rail or road" either during or after the withdrawal of the Western Group of Soviet Forces from Germany.[82] All Soviet nuclear weapons in Germany had to be removed by sea. The Polish authorities also announced in March 1991 that they would unilaterally eliminate all their nuclear-capable missiles, "retrain the missiles' crews, and provide the crews with new duties."[83] This decision should have affected some 60 Frog-7 and 32 Scud-B launchers and missiles, but the Polish army ended up keeping roughly 40 of the Frog-7s. Senior Polish officials later indicated that they would rely on "self-defense," including nuclear deterrence, as a last resort if no other options proved feasible, but they consistently emphasized their determination to seek more "advantageous" and "credible" alternatives.[84]

The decision on nuclear weapons in Hungary was even firmer and more explicit, despite some initial wavering. In November 1990 the new Hungarian defense minister, Lajos Fur, pledged that Hungary would unilaterally dismantle all its nuclear-capable missiles and launchers, which amounted to some 24 Scud-B missiles, 9 Scud launchers, 107 Frog-7 missiles, and 18 Frog launchers. This action, according to Fur, was intended to "promote European peace and a good relationship with our neighbors" and to "inspire other countries to take similar steps."[85] Subsequently, when the expense of scrapping the weapons became clear, Hungarian military officials said they would try to sell the Scuds and Frogs back to the Soviet Union (or some other country), rather than dismantling them.[86] That shift in approach, however, did not lessen Hungary's commitment to get rid of all its nuclear-capable missiles and launchers. By February 1991, the last Hungarian missile unit had been disbanded; and shortly thereafter, Fur enunciated the "basic principle" that Hungary would "never again permit weapons of mass destruction to be stationed in the country."[87]

Thus, the trend in East-Central Europe after 1990 was decidedly against nuclear deployments. Even when apprehension in the region was piqued by instability in Russia and the growing strength of Russian nationalist forces, the Polish, Czech, and Hungarian governments gave few indications that they would change their minds about acquiring nuclear arms. Only in one respect did the non-nuclear commitment of the three states diminish, albeit it in a way fully compatible with their own non-nuclear status. In their bids to join NATO, the East-Central European governments pledged that they would be willing, if necessary, to have U.S. tactical nuclear weapons stationed on their soil, a practice long followed by some other non-nuclear member-states of NATO such as Germany, Italy, and Belgium. In the latter half of 1995 Polish leaders affirmed that "Poland would have nothing against" U.S. nuclear deployments on Polish territory "if the alliance deems them necessary"; and Czech president Havel declared that it would be "perfectly normal" and "reasonable" if NATO sought to deploy nuclear weapons on Czech soil "when the Czech Republic becomes a member of the alliance."[88] Hungarian officials were far more discreet about the matter, but privately indicated that they, too, would consider permitting appropriate U.S. deployments. Moreover, all three of the East-Central European states flatly rejected a proposal by Ukraine to establish a nuclear-weapon-free zone in central Europe.[89]

These declarations of willingness to accept U.S. nuclear deployments were issued even though NATO had never asked any of the East European governments to make such an offer. An official *Study on NATO Enlargement*, released in September 1995, explicitly indicated that states hoping to join the alliance would *not* be required to host nuclear munitions. Although the study averred that "new members should be eligible to join [NATO's] Nuclear Planning Group and its subordinate bodies and to participate in nuclear consultation during exercises and crisis," it emphasized that "there is *no a priori requirement* for the stationing of nuclear weapons on the territory of new members."[90] This principle was strengthened in February 1997

when the NATO governments formally announced that "the Alliance has
no intention, no plan, and no reason to deploy nuclear weapons on the
territory of new members; nor does it foresee any future need to do so."[91]
That pledge was reaffirmed numerous times in 1997, most notably at the
July summit in Madrid of the NATO heads-of-state.

Even if NATO had declined to rule out the hypothetical deployment of
allied nuclear forces on Polish, Hungarian, and Czech territory, the fundamental decisions by the East-Central European governments to eschew *their
own* nuclear weapons would not have changed. After an initial period of
hesitation (when it was still unclear whether membership in NATO would
be feasible), the Polish, Hungarian, and Czech authorities all determined
that they should forsake any effort to build nuclear arms and instead meet
their security needs through external balancing.

Alternatives to Nuclear Weapons (I): Sub-Regional Balancing

Initially, many officials in East-Central Europe hoped to contend with
future security threats by relying mainly on a pan-European organization
like the Conference on Security and Cooperation in Europe (CSCE, now
OSCE).[92] Those hopes, however, proved illusory, as it became clear that the
use of CSCE for most security functions was impractical. The organization
was too unwieldy in its decisionmaking, and it had no military forces at its
disposal even for very limited missions. The governments in Prague, Warsaw,
and Budapest soon realized that other arrangements would be needed to fill
the "military vacuum" and "deep political void" created by the disintegration
of the Warsaw Pact. As the Polish defense minister put it: "We are not a
superpower; therefore, we must seek allies."[93]

Beginning in 1990, two schemes were proposed for the states of East-
Central Europe to cooperate in balancing against external threats. The first
idea, the so-called Visegrad Triangle (later renamed the Visegrad Group),
did come to fruition, but it never took on the functions or appearance of a
military alliance. The other proposal, for an alliance ranging from the Baltic
to the Danube, never got off the ground. In both cases, the East-Central
European states decided that other considerations (discussed below) were
more important than the prospect of intra-regional balancing.

The Visegrad Group

Polish leaders took the initiative in 1990 in promoting a form of subregional security cooperation with Hungary and the former Czechoslovakia.
Polish officials even spoke hopefully about the possible establishment of an

"organized alliance" over the longer term.[94] In April 1990 the leaders of the three (later four) countries held preliminary discussions at Bratislava, but those discussions were almost entirely symbolic and had no specific agenda. Five months later, the deputy foreign and defense ministers from the three sides met near the Czechoslovak-Polish border, in Zakopane, to consider the idea of a trilateral security framework. That session was followed in November 1990 by a higher-level meeting in Budapest, and by another gathering of the deputy foreign ministers in Prague in late December 1990. A fifth session, involving the foreign ministers of the three countries, took place in Budapest in mid-January 1991; and a climactic sixth meeting, which brought together the presidents and prime ministers of the three states, was held in the Hungarian city of Visegrad the following month.[95] That session marked the true beginning of what came to be known as the "Visegrad Triangle" (and then the "Visegrad Group" after the split of Czechoslovakia).

Shortly before the Visegrad summit, Bulgarian and Romanian officials expressed interest in joining a subregional organization if the other three countries ended up forming one.[96] The Romanian overtures were promptly rebuffed by the Visegrad participants (led by Hungary), but the Bulgarian

TABLE 11.1 Comparisons of Total Force Strength (Autumn 1995)

Country	Tanks	ACVs[a]	Artillery	Aircraft	Helicopters	Troops
Russia[b]						
Total	19,000	34,820	20,650	4,300	2,600	1,520,000
European	6,400	11,480	6,240	3,280	870	998,800
Ukraine	4,080	5,050	3,400	1,090	270	450,000
Czech Rep.	957	1,367	767	215	36	67,000
Hungary	835	1,600	840	170	39	70,000
Poland	1,730	1,590	1,610	412	80	234,000

[a] Armored Combat Vehicles

[b] Total holdings for Russia (in the upper line) include tens of thousands of forces east of the Urals (i.e., in the Asian part of Russia), which are not restricted by the Conventional Forces in Europe Treaty. Many of these Asian-based weapons have not been maintained in working condition. The lower line gives the number of Russian weapons based west of the Urals, which are covered by CFE.

Source: International Institute for Strategic Studies, The Military Balance, 1995–96 (London: IISS/Oxford University Press, October 1995), pp. 75–120.

request encountered a somewhat more favorable response. Even so, Bulgarian leaders were too optimistic in concluding that "the 'troika' will eventually expand and become a 'group of four.' "[97] The Visegrad participants were all well aware that trilateral cooperation on issues such as military strategy, defense planning, and weapons procurement would be difficult enough without bringing in other East European countries whose political stability and economic status were problematic at best.

Indeed, it soon became clear that even with the participation of just Poland, Hungary, and Czechoslovakia, no multilateral security arrangement was going to emerge. Although Hungarian leaders acknowledged the desirability of "some kind of closer [military] cooperation among the three countries when some kind of identity of interests can be shown," they were reluctant to undertake any major commitment, for fear that Poland would try to make the organization into an anti-German coalition.[98] To be sure, both Hungary and Czechoslovakia later displayed some interest in pursuing military cooperation with Poland, including joint air defense efforts and the possibility of a subregional military consultative group.[99] The appeal of such an arrangement increased as the domestic situation in the Soviet Union grew more turbulent. Moreover, the Hungarian and Czechoslovak governments signed a bilateral military treaty in January 1991, and both of them subsequently concluded similar bilateral treaties with Poland.[100] The three states also began joint air defense operations in early 1991 to make up for the integrated air-defense network they had formerly shared with the Soviet Union.[101]

Nevertheless, the Polish government's hopes of taking these arrangements much further by forming a full-fledged security organization went unfulfilled. The bilateral military agreements that the three states signed were limited in scope and contained no provisions for automatic assistance in the event of an attack. Moreover, at no point did either Hungary or Czechoslovakia express interest in merging the treaties into a broad, trilateral military agreement, much less a quadrilateral pact with both Poland and Bulgaria, or a pentagonal arrangement that included Romania as well. On the contrary, Czechoslovak and Hungarian leaders said explicitly at the time that they did not intend to form a "new alliance" or "bloc" at the subregional level.[102] Even Polish officials eventually conceded that it was premature to "conclude a military alliance," though they still hoped to "formulate a common approach to questions of security and regional stability."[103]

A further obstacle to military cooperation among the Visegrad countries came, ironically enough, when the Soviet Union broke apart. This development seemed to eliminate, or at least mitigate, the most exigent threat to the East European states, and hence it removed the main incentive for pursuing joint military efforts in the first place. Most East European officials argued that it made far more sense, in those circumstances, to press for membership in NATO rather than trying to make the Visegrad framework into a quasi-alliance.[104] The efficacy of the Visegrad arrangement was also attenuated by the split of Czechoslovakia. Under the leadership of prime minister Vaclav Klaus, the Czech government initially was much warier of developing close security ties with the other Visegrad countries, for fear of being held back in its drive to obtain membership in the European Community (later renamed the European Union) and NATO. The Czech Republic's shift toward a "go-it-alone" approach between 1992 and 1995 did not obviate the prospects of subregional military cooperation altogether, but it did mean that the Visegrad Group was largely dormant for nearly three years. Not until mid-1996, when the Czech government began consulting with Poland and Hungary to coordinate their efforts to join NATO, did the Visegrad structure revive; and even then its chief function was geared toward NATO, not toward the group itself.[105]

Thus, even though officials in Hungary, Poland, and the Czech Republic were still concerned about the security vacuum in East-Central Europe, they all had concluded by 1994 that the only way to fill that vacuum was through an extension of NATO, not through the creation of a mini-alliance system.[106] This judgment was especially compelling in light of the military forces deployed by the Visegrad states. Even if the four governments had committed themselves wholeheartedly to a separate military alliance, their combined armies would have been unable to handle anything except relatively low-level threats (see table 11.1, above). So long as concerns persisted about the possible emergence of military dangers "to the east," the Visegrad states had an incentive to look to the great powers, both inside and outside Europe, for protection.

"From the Baltic to the Danube"

In February 1993 President Leonid Kravchuk of Ukraine proposed the creation of a formal or semi-formal alliance "from the Baltic to the Danube," comprising the three Baltic states (Latvia, Lithuania, and Estonia), Poland, the Czech Republic, Slovakia, Hungary, Austria, Belarus, and Ukraine. This idea went nowhere.[107] Even in Ukraine itself many experts regarded the proposal to be unwise or infeasible, and all the other states included under the proposal (with the partial exception of Belarus) were distinctly hostile to the idea. In Poland, for example, two senior officials argued that Ukraine merely "wants to carve out a hegemonic role for itself and to be the dominant power in a new military bloc in East-Central Europe. That would just be the Warsaw Pact all over again, with Ukraine in place of the Soviet Union."[108] This sort of response to Kravchuk's proposal, though deliberately overstated, was very much in accord with what neorealists would expect about the importance that states attach to relative gains.[109] Most of the Visegrad and Baltic countries were averse to forming any local alliance with Ukraine—even a potentially beneficial alliance—for fear that Ukraine would thereby gain undue military influence in Eastern Europe and possibly even develop into a subregional hegemon.

Critics of the "Baltic-to-Danube" proposal also maintained that Ukraine was hoping to exploit the other states in a bid to "surround" Russia. Although officials in most of the East-Central European countries were concerned about the possibility of a militant resurgence in Moscow over the longer term, they believed that the thinly disguised anti-Russian orientation of Kravchuk's plan would merely increase the likelihood of a worst-case scenario. In that sense, the Ukrainian proposal fit in well with the kind of external balancing one would expect to find under the structural realist paradigm, whereas the desire of the other Central European states to avoid isolating Russia reflected a sensitivity to the security dilemma (vis-à-vis Russia) as well as concern about the relative gains Ukraine might derive.

Kravchuk's proposal was further undermined by the inception of NATO's Partnership for Peace in January 1994. Because this new entity was depicted as a vehicle for Poland, Hungary, and the Czech Republic (and other former Communist states) to gain eventual membership in the Western alliance, the East European governments were more determined than ever to avoid being entangled in subregional organizations that might impede their admission into NATO. Kravchuk's stillborn proposal remained nominally under consideration during the first few months of 1994, but the idea was not taken up by the new Ukrainian president, Leonid Kuchma, when he assumed office in June 1994. Nor was any further mention made of it later on.

Throughout the region, then, the consensus by the mid-1990s was that intraregional groupings would play little or no role in East-Central European security in the future. The governments in Hungary, Poland, the Czech Republic, and other countries were convinced that the only viable way to fill the security vacuum in East-Central Europe was through an extension of NATO, not through the creation of a mini-alliance system. Only in Ukraine and to some extent Belarus (before the election of Aleksander Lukashenka) was there ever any sentiment for the establishment of local alliances and military groupings directed against Russia, and that sentiment quickly ebbed when other states displayed no interest.

Alternatives to Nuclear Weapons (II): Looking to NATO

Beginning in 1989, and particularly after the Soviet Union's collapse, the East-Central European states looked increasingly to NATO, both implicitly and explicitly, to fill the vacuum left by the demise of the Warsaw Pact. Even before the Polish, Hungarian, and Czechoslovak/Czech governments started openly pursuing full membership in NATO, they set about establishing firm ties with the alliance and with individual member-states. By 1991, exchanges between top Polish, Hungarian, and Czechoslovak military-political officials and their Western counterparts had become so frequent and extensive that they rarely drew more than passing notice any longer.[110]

In March 1991, Vaclav Havel became the first East European head of state to visit NATO's headquarters; and a few weeks later, Lech Walesa became the second. During their visits the two presidents expressed strong interest in forging much closer ties with NATO, including the possibility of formal membership over the longer term if Western countries would agree. Havel emphasized that the alliance "should not be forever closed" to the East European states, and he expressed hope that Czechoslovakia would eventually become a "regular NATO member" even if it "cannot become one at the moment."[111] The same view was expressed by Polish and Hungarian leaders.

Equally noteworthy was the expansion of direct military contacts between the East-Central European countries and the Western alliance. Even before the upheavals of 1989, Hungary tentatively began to establish military-diplomatic exchanges with NATO countries.[112] After 1989, those contacts rapidly multiplied and became much more wide-ranging not only for Hungary but for all the East-Central European states. By the fall of 1991 military-educational exchange programs were fully under way, bringing officers from the former Warsaw Pact countries to military academies in the West, and vice versa.[113] The East-Central European states also assigned permanent military representatives to NATO. Czechoslovak leaders proposed formal cooperation with NATO on anti-aircraft defense and civil defense when the chief of NATO's Military Committee, General Vigleik Eide, visited their country in April 1991.[114] In addition, Czechoslovakia sought close bilateral military relations with some of the smaller NATO members, notably Spain, Belgium, and the Netherlands.

Furthermore, all three of the East-Central European governments began approaching the United States, Germany, Great Britain, and France about the possibility of obtaining weapons and support equipment in the future. By purchasing Western-made arms, they hoped to eliminate or at least reduce their logistical dependence on the former Soviet Union and establish greater commonality with NATO. As early as May 1990 the French government expressed tentative support for French-Polish military coproduction ventures, including joint development, engineering, and manufacturing arrangements, as well as exchanges of technical knowledge. Later that year the French government also indicated its readiness to "set up arms cooperation and sell military technology" to Hungary.[115] Polish and Hungarian officials received nearly as favorable a response when they visited the United States, from which Poland was particularly eager to obtain F-16 fighters.[116] Despite severe constraints imposed by shortages of hard currency and lingering export controls (which were not fully lifted until February 1995), the East-Central European states by early 1991 had made clear their desire to shift away from former Soviet arms manufacturers toward greater ties with the West.

Equally important, the Polish, Czechoslovak, and Hungarian governments sought to establish concrete military cooperation with NATO and to "side with the West" as much as possible on key international issues.[117] During the Persian Gulf war in early 1991, all the East-Central European states contributed military personnel and equipment to the American-led multinational force, in contrast to the Soviet Union, which refrained from taking part at all.[118] Czechoslovak, Hungarian, and Polish units were placed under direct American and British command (except for a few personnel who were primarily under Saudi command), and they served alongside American soldiers. In addition, the East-Central European countries provided use of their airspace and airfields to NATO for military purposes before, during, and after the war. Hungary and Czechoslovakia gave Germany permission to fly combat aircraft over their territory in early 1991, something that would have been inconceivable when the Warsaw Pact still functioned. Both countries also allowed the United States to send many hundreds of military transport and cargo flights through their airspace during the war itself.[119] In addition, Hungary permitted the American planes to land and refuel at Hungarian air bases.

Poland, for its part, offered crucial intelligence support for the war effort.

Because Polish construction and engineering firms had done extensive work in Iraq for many years, Polish officials in 1990 were able to supply detailed information about Iraqi military facilities and precise maps of Baghdad to the United States.[120] Poland also turned over valuable technical data about Iraq's air defense systems, tanks, fighter aircraft, and other weaponry, which had been bought mainly from Warsaw Pact countries. Most dramatically of all, Polish intelligence officials masterminded the escape of six key U.S. intelligence agents who had been inadvertently trapped behind Iraqi lines when the crisis broke. The success of this operation, as a senior Polish diplomat later exclaimed, "proved to the Americans that we [in Poland] are a reliable partner who can carry out sensitive, delicate missions on behalf of the American government."[121]

Following the Soviet Union's collapse, the military links between NATO and the East-Central European states grew exponentially, both in number and in scope. All the Visegrad governments designed their new military doctrines and restructured their armed forces with an eye to facilitating eventual membership in NATO. Political and military cooperation between the alliance and the former Warsaw Pact states greatly increased, as evidenced by the joint operations in regions contiguous with the former Yugoslavia. Beginning in 1992, Hungary allowed NATO AWACS aircraft to use Hungarian airspace and bases while monitoring the conflict, and Hungarian MiG fighters were deployed as escorts for the AWACS to ward off any potential interference by Serbian planes. The Czech, Polish, and Hungarian governments also cooperated with NATO countries in peacekeeping efforts in Croatia, Kurdistan, Liberia, and Bosnia-Herzegovina, not only by contributing troops, but also by permitting the use of air bases, refueling facilities, and supply lines. The declared aim of this cooperation, for all three countries, was to show that "we are determined to join NATO, and nothing can change our minds."[122] The East European states also expressed keen interest in taking part in other peacekeeping missions that NATO might organize in the central Eurasian region.

Furthermore, even before NATO established the Partnership for Peace (PfP) in January 1994, the Visegrad states had been taking a direct part in the alliance's high-level military and political deliberations. In June 1993, Hungary became the first non-NATO country to host the alliance's annual meeting on military security issues and crisis management. Hungary also was the first East European country to set up a bilateral military working group with the United States to deal with all aspects of security issues that might confront NATO. Poland and the Czech Republic quickly followed suit. In addition, the Czechs established secure, high-level communications links with Western countries in mid-1996, using encryption hardware purchased from the Motorola Corporation.[123] The system replaced the top-secret network that once connected all the Warsaw Pact countries.

By the mid-1990s, NATO's military and political ties with Poland, Hungary, and the Czech Republic had become so close that it was almost possible to regard the three states as *de facto* members of the alliance. Although the *de jure* role of the Visegrad countries through 1997 was limited primarily to membership in the North Atlantic Cooperation Council (NACC) and the PfP, the *de facto* role that those countries assumed long before July 1997 (when they received formal invitations to join NATO) was more important than the contributions of at least a few existing members of the alliance.

Even so, the NATO governments initially were reluctant to consider any formal additions to their ranks. Until late 1994, the NATO countries generally tried to discourage the East-Central European states from seeking membership in the alliance. Several factors acccounted for this stance, chief among them concern about Moscow's reaction. The East-Central European states were undeterred by the cool reception they initially encountered and continued to express their interest in joining NATO, but they clearly were uneasy about the West's position. Indeed, the Czech and Polish governments were wary of joining NACC and the PfP, for fear that these organizations were little more than ploys by NATO to avoid offering genuine membership. In the end, all the former Warsaw Pact states did sign up for PfP, but they remained apprehensive about NATO's seeming unwillingness to offer full-fledged membership. As the Russian campaign against NATO enlargement gathered pace, disquiet in East-Central Europe increased. Senior Polish, Hungarian, and Czech officials complained both publicly and privately that NATO was far too deferential to Russia's objections, and at times they even spoke openly about a "betrayal" and a "second Yalta."[124]

At no time, however, did the three East-Central European states fundamentally alter their strategic priorities. Having geared their security strategies overwhelmingly toward the goal of NATO membership, they were determined to do whatever was necessary to achieve it. Although it took longer than expected to attain that goal, their efforts finally paid off.

Ukraine

Ukraine regained its independence in December 1991 after some seventy years under Soviet rule. The new Ukrainian state experienced many severe

internal problems during its first seven years, including a catastrophic economic decline between 1992 and 1997, occasional ethnic unrest in Crimea,
and a growing political divide between the eastern and western portions of
the country.[125] These difficulties inevitably took their toll on Ukrainian security strategy. Although most Ukrainians acknowledged that the gravest
threats to Ukraine's survival as an independent state came from within, officials in Kiev were also constantly mindful of the country's external situation, notably its proximity to Russia. Ukraine is contiguous with seven countries (Moldova, Romania, Hungary, Slovakia, Poland, Belarus, and Russia)
at the crossroads between Europe and Asia, but the long border with Russia
is by far the most important.[126] Ukraine's continued dependence on Russia
for vital energy supplies (which were sold at highly subsidized prices long
after 1991), the extensive trade links between Russia and Ukraine, the presence of some 11.3 million ethnic Russians in Ukraine (out of a total population of 52 million), and the troubled history of Russian-Ukrainian relations
affected all aspects of Ukrainian strategy in the 1990s, including decisions
about nuclear weapons.

Perceptions of External Threats

From the moment the Soviet Union was dissolved, Ukraine's relations
with Russia were marked by periodic tensions and recriminations. Although
most Ukrainian officials did not expect that Russia would try to re-conquer
Ukraine through military force in the near future, they would not exclude
the possibility of a large-scale conflict at some point down the road. Even
in the near term, some Ukrainian officials were worried that a low-level
military clash between the two former Soviet republics—perhaps over territorial issues—could escalate into something much larger than either side
had anticipated. Such a conflict, if it had transpired, would undoubtedly
have worked to Ukraine's disadvantage. The Ukrainian army was one of the
largest in Europe and was relatively well-equipped (primarily because sizable
stocks of front-line weaponry were left on Ukrainian territory after the Soviet
Union collapsed), but it would have been no match for the Russian army.
Ukrainian officials were under no illusions that Ukraine's conventional
forces could have repulsed a full-scale Russian attack.[127] The key problem
for Ukrainian military officials, therefore, was how to make a prospective
attack so costly that Russian leaders would not want to pay the price of
"victory."

Initially, the chief points of contention between Ukraine and Russia were the division of the Black Sea Fleet (which both sides claimed), the status of Crimea (a peninsula in Ukraine inhabited mainly by ethnic Russians), and the deployment of nuclear weapons on Ukrainian territory. Although none of these disputes led to a military conflict, the series of disagreements reinforced Ukrainian leaders' suspicion that the large majority of Russians, whether government officials, military officers, or ordinary citizens, had not yet fully accepted the fact of Ukrainian independence.[128] Ukrainian leaders often expressed concern that ultranationalist and imperial-minded forces in Russia might yet succeed in stirring up public sentiment in favor of an aggressive policy on behalf of the ethnic Russians living in the Crimea, Odessa, and the Donbass region. They feared that Russian hardliners and security force personnel could manipulate domestic politics in Ukraine to provoke civil conflict that would create an opportunity and pretext for Russia to undertake more overt military intervention. Although the rebuff of the hardline revolt in Moscow in October 1993 briefly eased those concerns, the strong electoral showing of Zhirinovsky's ultranationalist forces in December 1993 caused many in Ukraine to fear that hardline elements in Moscow would eventually gain sway.[129]

Apprehension in Kiev remained high in 1994 and 1995, as the tone of Russian politics veered in a more nationalist direction (symbolized by the war in Chechnya) and the Russian Communist party experienced a strong resurgence. Minatory statements by Russian military officers, including a remark about Ukraine's place "on the list of targets for Russian strategic nuclear forces," boosted tensions still further.[130] Nevertheless, Ukrainian relations with Russia began to improve after mid-1994 because of the election of Leonid Kuchma as president. Kuchma had made clear during the electoral campaign that he favored closer ties with Russia. His surprisingly wide victory in July 1994—by a 52 to 45 margin—over the incumbent, Leonid Kravchuk, provided the impetus for a more conciliatory policy toward Russia. This new approach was not so drastic that it led to a full-scale rapprochement between Russia and Ukraine; on the contrary, most Ukrainian leaders remained highly suspicious of Russia's intentions, and bilateral disputes persisted over the Black Sea Fleet and other issues. Even so, the acrimonious and threatening atmosphere of 1992 and 1993 was at least partly alleviated. Ties between the two countries remained uneasy and tense after mid-1994, but the threat of armed conflict receded.

A sign of how much the relationship had improved came in mid-1995 when a vote of independence by the Crimean parliament provoked a crackdown by the Ukrainian government. Had such a step been taken in 1992 or 1993, Russia undoubtedly would have responded very harshly and perhaps made some effort to provide direct aid to the Crimean government; but Kuchma's action provoked barely a murmur of protest from Moscow.[131]

Relations between the two countries continued to improve after 1995, despite periodic glitches and disruption. At a summit in Kiev in late May 1997, Russian Prime Minister Viktor Chernomyrdin and Ukrainian Prime Minister Pavlo Lazarenko signed long-awaited agreements on the leasing of military facilities in Crimea and the division of the Black Sea Fleet. At that same meeting, Kuchma and Russian president Boris Yeltsin signed a historic "treaty on friendship, cooperation, and partnership," which recast the bilateral relationship as a "strategic partnership."[132] The treaty marked the first time that Russia unequivocally affirmed the "territorial integrity" of Ukraine and the "inviolability of [its] existing borders."

Despite this general improvement of relations, most Ukrainian officials still harbored little doubt that the only serious external threat to Ukraine over the long term would come from Russia. Ukraine's military planning and deployments remained geared toward deterrence of a Russian attack.[133] Ukrainian leaders realized that the limited detente between the two countries could easily be reversed, particularly if Communist and ultranationalist forces regained a dominant position in Russia.

At the same time, one key factor—the awareness, on both sides, of how disastrous a conflict would be even if no nuclear weapons were used— helped keep the relationship free of hostilities. Large-scale fighting would almost certainly have disrupted the flow of oil and natural gas through the pipelines extending from Russia to Ukraine and into Central Europe, causing vast economic upheaval throughout Europe. Hostilities between Russia and Ukraine might also have caused an accident at one of the five nuclear power stations in western and southern Ukraine, scattering highly radioactive debris all around the region on a scale far eclipsing even the 1986 Chernobyl disaster.[134] Because the potential consequences of a Russian-Ukrainian military confrontation would have been so inimical and long-lasting, it was hardly surprising that officials in both countries sought to avoid a direct clash.

Nevertheless, Ukrainian leaders were well aware that a militant backlash in Russia could have ominous consequences for their own country. Although they acknowledged that internal problems posed the greatest threat to Ukrainian security in the near term, they would not rule out the prospect of a serious external danger in the future.

Nuclear Weapons Policies

When the Soviet Union split apart in December 1991, Ukraine inherited some 46 SS-24 intercontinental ballistic missiles (ICBMs), 130 SS-19 ICBMs, and 45 Bear-H and Blackjack heavy bombers equipped with roughly 600 nuclear-armed AS-15 air-launched cruise missiles (ALCMs). The Ukrainian government soon asserted "administrative" control over these weapons, and Ukrainian troops were sent to guard the bases. At no time, however, did Ukraine have operational command of any of the nuclear arms. Operational control remained exclusively in Moscow.[135] Moreover, Ukraine itself had relatively few technicians who could provide regular servicing and upkeep for the missile silos. As a result, that task had to be performed mainly by Russian specialists.

In October 1991, two months before the dissolution of the USSR, the Ukrainian parliament adopted a Proclamation for the Non-Nuclear Status of Ukraine, which included a pledge "not to accept, produce, or acquire nuclear arms."[136] Soon thereafter, the new Ukrainian government promised to relinquish the nuclear warheads and delivery vehicles on its territory by the end of 1994 and sign the NPT as a non-nuclear weapons state. These statements and pledges reaffirmed the commitment to non-nuclear status adopted by the Ukrainian parliament in its original declaration of "sovereignty" in July 1990.[137] Before long, however, the Ukrainian government became increasingly hesitant about following through on its commitments. A lively debate emerged in Ukraine, with views divided roughly along three lines.

Some experts and officials argued that Ukraine should not insist on preconditions before relinquishing the nuclear weapons on its soil. They pointed out that the warheads were, and would remain, under Russia's operational control and thus would contribute nothing to Ukrainian security. Indeed, the weapons, in their view, actually *detracted* from Ukraine's security in six key ways: by posing an ecological threat to Ukrainian territory if they were inadequately maintained; by spurring other nuclear powers (notably the United States) to continue targeting the silos in Ukraine; by causing tensions in Ukraine's relations with the United States and other Western countries; by giving Russia a pretext for a hostile relationship with Ukraine;

by forcing Ukraine to renege on its international commitments; and by draining funds and resources that might otherwise be devoted to Ukraine's non-nuclear armed forces.[138] Those who wanted to get rid of the SS-19s, SS-24s, and AS-15s also noted that Ukraine had to rely on Russian technical personnel to service and repair the weapons. This arrangement, they argued, meant that the missiles, far from symbolizing Ukrainian sovereignty and independence, were instead a sign of Ukraine's dependence on Russia. Hence, in their view, the sooner Ukraine got rid of the warheads and missiles, the better.

For a brief while this position guided Ukrainian policy, but it was soon eclipsed by the views of those who favored a conditional relinquishment of the weapons on Ukrainian territory. Although the "conditionalists" were in favor of joining the NPT as a non-nuclear weapons state and transferring the ICBM and ALCM warheads to Russia for dismantling, they insisted that Ukraine, in return, must be given adequate security guarantees and financial compensation. Some of the officials and legislators who subscribed to this position believed that the "security guarantees" could simply be a formal pledge by the permanent members of the United Nations (UN) Security Council, whereas others were determined to obtain much more far-reaching guarantees, including full membership in NATO and a mutual security treaty with the United States.[139]

Views about what would constitute adequate "compensation" also varied widely. Some Ukrainian officials were willing to be reimbursed only for the costs of transferring the warheads and dismantling the missiles (citing figures of as much as $2.5 billion to $3.0 billion), whereas others insisted on additional payment for the fissile material removed from the warheads. Those in Ukraine who were skeptical about this latter demand argued that the United States would be unwilling to pay much for stocks of either plutonium, which would be difficult to adapt for civilian purposes, or highly enriched uranium, which would be expensive to convert into fuel for nuclear power plants when there was already a huge glut of nuclear fuel on the world market. The notion that the weapons must be "worth something" was simply an illusion, in their view.

In addition to those who were willing to give up the ICBMs and ALCMs either conditionally or unconditionally, a relatively small but vocal group of officials, legislators, and specialists in Ukraine, led by a former high-ranking military officer, General Volodymyr Tolubko, were in favor of retaining all the weapons. Initially, when Ukrainian elites and the Ukrainian public were committed to the goal of a non-nuclear Ukraine, the influence of the pro-nuclear activists was negligible. By early 1993, however, sentiment in Ukraine began shifting in a broadly pro-nuclear direction. The dominant reason for this shift was the growing anxiety among experts as well as the public about a potential threat posed by Russia.[140] No doubt, as Peter Lavoy's analysis of "nuclear mythmakers" would suggest, the pro-nuclear lobby in Ukraine tended to exaggerate the urgency of the Russian threat.[141] Still, it is unlikely that their appeals would have made much headway if there had not been mounting unease about Russia within the Ukrainian population as a whole.

Despite the growing influence of the pro-nuclear camp, the condition-alists ended up carrying the day. In January 1994 Ukrainian president Leonid Kravchuk signed an agreement with his U.S. and Russian counterparts that laid the basis for Ukraine to give up its missiles and become a non-nuclear state in return for joint "security guarantees" and financial compensation.[142] This agreement, as well as other issues connected with Ukraine's nuclear status, sparked controversy within the Ukrainian parliament in the leadup to Ukraine's presidential elections in June and July 1994.[143] Following the election of Kuchma, however, the pro-nuclear lobby was put on the defensive. By mid-November 1994, Kuchma persuaded the parliament to approve Ukraine's accession to the NPT as a non-nuclear weapons state and the dismantling of all remaining nuclear missiles on Ukrainian territory. The overwhelming vote in favor of these steps marked the climax of the nuclear debate in Ukraine. In a speech to parliament just before the vote, Kuchma outlined numerous factors that warranted a non-nuclear status for Ukraine, most of which were similar to the points raised by those who had been opposed all along to keeping or building nuclear weapons (see above).[144] In addition, Kuchma was able to stress that Ukraine had been granted its demands for security guarantees and financial compensation, demands that both Russia and the United States initially had opposed.

The Ukrainian parliament's action paved the way for Kuchma's formal ratification of the NPT at a summit in Budapest of the CSCE heads of state in early December 1994.[145] From that point on, Ukraine upheld its initial non-nuclear commitments. By the end of 1995, some 90 percent of the 1,900 strategic nuclear warheads once located in Ukraine had been transferred, well ahead of schedule, to Russia for disassembly. The remaining warheads were shipped to Russia from storage facilities near Pervomaisk in the spring of 1996. In early June 1996 the final batch of nuclear warheads were removed from Ukraine in a ceremony marking the country's non-nuclear status.[146]

Much the same occurred with Ukraine's strategic delivery vehicles. As of November 1995, all 46 of the SS-24 ICBMs and 80 of the 130 SS-19 missiles in Ukraine had been dismantled, and work on the remaining weapons continued at a brisk pace in 1996 and 1997. Under bilateral agreements signed in Sochi in late 1995, Russia agreed to buy 32 of the remaining SS-19s from Ukraine as well as 19 Blackjack bombers, 25 Bear-H bombers, and 300 AS-15 cruise missiles. The two sides also agreed at Sochi that Russia would be given all equipment formerly used for the training and maintenance of tactical nuclear weapons and strategic bombers.[147] The Sochi deals sparked praise and satisfaction in both Moscow and Kiev. Although Russia had always maintained operational control of the nuclear weapons in Ukraine, it was ironic that, in the end, Ukraine's grave economic problems spurred Ukrainian leaders to display "keen interest" in adding (if only marginally) to the nuclear potential of the very country with which Ukraine might someday again be bitterly at odds.

Alternatives to Nuclear Weapons: Potential Alliances

Even before Ukraine formally agreed to relinquish all the nuclear weapons left on its territory, Ukrainian leaders had begun to explore the possibility of external balancing (i.e., the creation of a new alliance or entry into an existing alliance). The situation was complicated somewhat because Ukraine's declaration of sovereignty in July 1990 had indicated that the country would be "permanently neutral" (*postiino neitral'na*) and "would not participate in any military blocs."[148] Ukrainian officials continued to emphasize those objectives after gaining independence in late 1991. The rationale for Ukrainian "neutrality," however, was mainly to eschew any continuation of security ties with Russia, rather than a strict policy of non-alignment per se. This became evident in May 1992 when Russia invited the other members of the Commonwealth of Independent States (the loose coalition of former Soviet republics) to conclude a Treaty on Collective Security, which committed the signatories to provide "all necessary assistance, including military assistance," to any member that came under attack.[149] Several former Soviet republics in Central Asia and the Caucasus agreed to sign the treaty, but Ukrainian officials refused to have anything to do with it and emphasized that Ukraine would not be joining any post-Soviet military alliances or blocs sponsored by Russia. Thus, to the extent that

Ukraine did eventually consider the possibility of creating or joining a military alliance, the goal clearly was to balance against Russia.

One such effort, as mentioned earlier, occurred in 1993 when Ukrainian president Kravchuk broached the possibility of forming a Baltic-to-the-Danube constellation, which would have encompassed Ukraine, the three Baltic states, Poland, Belarus, the Czech Republic, Slovakia, Hungary, Bulgaria, Romania, and Austria.[150] This proposal, first advanced in February 1993 and then elaborated a few months later in a document on "The Strengthening of Regional Stability and Security in Central and Eastern Europe," met with a distinct lack of enthusiasm in the other countries, with the partial exception of Belarus. Czech, Polish, and Hungarian leaders were especially wary of embarking on any arrangement that might impede their entry into NATO and the European Union (EU). They also were uncertain about the future stability of Ukraine. When Polish president Lech Walesa traveled to Kiev in late May 1993, he informed Kravchuk that Poland (and, implicitly, the other East-Central European countries) would not pursue the Ukrainian leader's idea because they wanted to rely on existing "Euroatlantic structures of security."[151] In subsequent months, Kravchuk rarely mentioned the proposal again, and Kuchma abandoned it altogether.

As an alternative to a subregional alliance, Kuchma gradually bolstered Ukraine's ties with NATO. He was cautious in pursuing the matter so that he would avoid antagonizing Russia, but in 1995, 1996, and especially 1997, Ukraine slowly but steadily drew closer to NATO. In February 1994, Ukraine became the first member of the Commonwealth of Independent States (CIS) to join NATO's Partnership for Peace, and signed a full-fledged agreement on partnership the following year. Over the next few years, Ukraine took an active part in many PfP military exercises (including exercises on Ukrainian territory) and countless other PfP activities, in contrast to Russia, which only belatedly and grudgingly joined the PfP and sharply limited its participation.[152] The Ukrainian government also sent a peacekeeping unit to help NATO's efforts in the former Yugoslavia and even permitted the Ukrainian troops to serve under NATO command.

Although Ukraine formally retained its commitment to nonalignment, Ukrainian officials took some important steps to seek greater alignment with the West. The new Ukrainian constitution, adopted in 1996, made no mention of neutrality or nonalignment, and a landmark document on Ukrainian national security, issued in January 1997, explicitly endorsed "integration into international security structures."[153] Increasingly, Ukrainian officials emphasized that they would pursue "cooperation with the CIS" but full-fledged "integration into Europe," including NATO.[154] That approach underlay the accord that Ukraine signed with NATO in July 1997 during the Madrid summit of allied heads-of-state.[155] Although the "NATO-Ukrainian Charter on a Special Partnership" was not a binding agreement and offered Ukraine little that was not already covered by PfP and NACC, it vividly symbolized the growing ties between Kiev and the Western alliance. Ukrainian leaders did their best to allay any concerns Russia might have about Ukraine's closer relationship with NATO (most notably by calling for a nuclear-weapon-free zone in East-Central Europe), but there was little doubt that the trend sparked unease in Moscow, especially when senior Ukrainian officials began intimating that Ukraine might seek outright membership in the alliance in the early twenty-first century. One of the reasons that Russian leaders were so eager to establish a "strategic partnership" with Ukraine in the bilateral agreement they signed in May 1997 was to slow down Ukraine's *rapprochement* with NATO.

In the absence of a militant, hardline backlash in Moscow, Ukrainian leaders were disinclined to seek formal admission into NATO, not only because of the likely repercussions in Russia, but also because of the wrenching internal changes that would have been required in Ukraine itself. Occasional statements by Ukrainian officials about the prospect of eventual membership in the alliance did not necessarily adumbrate a realistic effort to join. Moreover, even if the political situation in Russia had taken a disastrous turn, and even if Ukraine had adopted far-reaching political and economic reforms, it is questionable whether the NATO countries themselves would have been willing to consider granting membership to Ukraine. The closer ties between Ukraine and NATO were important for symbolic reasons, but they did not automatically afford Ukraine any greater protection than it had before.

Alternatives to Nuclear Weapons: Security Guarantees

If a state is unable to become a full-fledged member of an alliance, it might still pursue another form of external balancing, namely, security guarantees. That is precisely what Ukrainian leaders sought when they promised to gain parliamentary approval of their decisions to eliminate the nuclear weapons based on Ukrainian soil and to sign the NPT as a non-nuclear weapons state. In return, Ukraine ultimately received security pledges from the United States, Great Britain, and Russia.[156] Through these pledges, as formally enunciated in the January 1994 trilateral agreement and at the CSCE/OSCE summit in December 1994, the three guarantors offered general assurances of respect for Ukraine's independence and sovereignty, promised to "refrain from the threat or use of force against the territorial integrity or political independence" of Ukraine, promised to assist Ukraine via the UN Security Council "if Ukraine falls victim to aggression or is subject to threats of aggression with nuclear weapons," and reaffirmed the principle in the CSCE Final Act that "changes of borders can be carried out only through peaceful means and by mutual agreement."[157] The guarantors also promised to "refrain from economic coercion" against Ukraine, an assurance that the Ukrainian authorities had avidly sought because of Russia's periodic threats to halt oil and natural gas shipments to Ukraine unless prices were increased to world levels and payment arrears were resolved.

At first glance, these security pledges might seem far-reaching and expansive, but in fact they went no further than the commitments undertaken by the United States, Britain, and the Soviet Union many years earlier in the NPT, the Helsinki Final Act, and the UN Charter. Even the provision about "economic coercion" was merely a word-for-word restatement of a pledge in the Helsinki Final Act. Initially, Ukrainian leaders had demanded much more ambitious military, political, and economic guarantees—even Kuchma had spoken at one point about the need for an explicit U.S. nuclear guarantee—but the commitments they ended up accepting were surprisingly modest. Still, the very fact that Ukraine received guarantees at all (as well as financial compensation) was itself, as Kuchma emphasized to the parliament, a symbolic victory for the "national interests, prestige, and security of the Ukrainian state."[158]

ASSESSMENT AND IMPLICATIONS OF STRATEGIC CHOICES

Structural realism would lead one to believe that one or more of the four states covered in this essay, especially Ukraine, should have sought their own nuclear arsenals. Under anarchy, with states forced to rely primarily on self-help in maintaining their security and ultimately their survival, the nuclear option should be attractive if highly reliable alternatives are not available.[159] In the cases examined here, all four states were potentially threatened by a formidable nuclear and conventional power, Russia, whose future political complexion and foreign policy seemed uncertain at best. Russian military officials explicitly raised the possibility of targeting nuclear weapons against all four of these countries, particularly Ukraine (see above). Until the mid-1990s, Poland, Hungary, and the Czech Republic had no assurance that they would ever become members of NATO. Indeed, for at least a few years, Polish, Czech, and Hungarian leaders feared that their countries would be left permanently outside the alliance. Even when the Visegrad states finally were invited to join NATO—a status that would provide them with U.S. (and British/French) nuclear guarantees—the reliability of those future guarantees was problematic from the neorealist perspective.[160] The security guarantees that the United States extended to Ukraine in January and December 1994 were even less credible, in part because of the reaction that followed. Although the guarantees did not go beyond existing pledges, a few prominent members of the U.S. Congress expressed concern about the nature of U.S. commitments vis-à-vis Ukraine.[161] Reservations also were voiced in Congress during hearings in 1997 and 1998 on the proposed admission of Poland, Hungary, and the Czech Republic into NATO.[162] Because the Ukrainian and Central European governments were well aware that the United States was reluctant to extend full-fledged security guarantees to them, one might have expected them to be doubtful about the "protection" they were being offered. After all, a commitment provided with extreme reluctance would not normally be deemed highly reliable.

Nevertheless, despite these many uncertainties, none of the four states in question pursued a nuclear weapons capability. All four had the physical *capacity* to build nuclear warheads (at enormous expense), and they also had substantial numbers of nuclear-capable delivery vehicles left over from the Communist era. Even so, they chose not to realize their nuclear potential. In Hungary, Poland, and Czechoslovakia, the decision to forgo the production of nuclear weapons stirred very little public controversy. In Ukraine, the debate was more protracted and emotional than expected, but the Ukrainian government and parliament eventually agreed to relinquish the nuclear missiles and warheads on Ukrainian territory and to accept a permanent non-nuclear status under the Non-Proliferation Treaty. Afterward, Ukrainian officials made no effort to build nuclear weapons of their own, despite being confronted by a nuclear-armed Russia.

This outcome runs counter not only to the logic of structural realism, but also to explicit predictions made by Waltz, Mearsheimer, and other neorealist scholars, including those cited above. In 1981 Waltz listed a number of factors that could prompt states to seek nuclear weapons.[163] Most of these were pertinent to Ukraine, Poland, Hungary, and the Czech Republic in the first half of the 1990s: the absence of any allied nuclear guarantees; a desire to deter an enemy possessing a much stronger conventional army; and a desire to deter an enemy at an acceptable cost. Although Waltz proposed these factors while the Cold War was still on, the relevance of them seems, if anything, even greater in the post-Cold War era. Yet none of the factors spurred the East-Central European states to press ahead with a full-fledged nuclear weapons program.

The neorealist paradigm would lead one to expect that if states perceive themselves in a "security vacuum" and are confronted by a much larger, potentially hostile, and seemingly volatile state, they will seek to balance against that state as soon as possible. The reality in East-Central Europe in the early to mid-1990s was far more complex. All four states, including Ukraine, refrained from pursuing the most potent form of *internal* balancing—the acquisition of nuclear weapons. Moreover, except for Ukraine, they were unwilling to engage in external balancing with one another against the most likely threat. The Visegrad Group never took on the functions of a genuine military alliance, despite early hopes to that effect in Poland. Although the Visegrad states agreed in March 1993 to coordinate certain aspects of their national security policies, very little coordination of military affairs actually occurred. The Ukrainian government broached the possibility of a regional alliance "from the Baltic to the Danube" in early 1993, but that proposal was summarily rejected by the other governments involved, and the new leaders in Ukraine soon abandoned the idea themselves.

Explanations of the outcomes in Poland, Hungary, and the Czech Republic do not pose any insurmountable difficulties for the neorealist perspective, but the case of Ukraine does raise important questions. Hence, as before, the two will be considered here separately.

Poland, Hungary, Czech Republic

Rather than pursuing either internal balancing (i.e., the deployment of nuclear weapons) or intraregional external balancing, the Polish, Czech, and Hungarian governments pinned their hopes entirely on the United States and NATO. This approach yielded contradictory results. On the one hand, Poland, Hungary, and the Czech Republic sought to avoid the impression that they (and other former Warsaw Pact states) were "ganging up" against Russia; this was one of the factors that caused them to reject Ukraine's proposal for a "Baltic to the Danube" constellation. On the other hand, the three countries sought security guarantees from, and full membership in, NATO. In effect, they were trying to redefine their subregion to make it come formally under NATO's auspices. (For this reason, the three states repeatedly drew a distinction between "Central Europe" and "Eastern Europe.") Hopes of gaining membership in NATO were more than enough to dispel any notion that the Polish, Czech, and Hungarian governments might have had of seeking nuclear weapons. Even though there was still a risk that events in Russia would take a disastrous turn (a development that might have given sufficient motivation for the East-Central European states to acquire nuclear arms), the prospect of NATO membership was seen as a vastly preferable alternative to internal balancing.

The willingness of the East-Central European states to place such a high premium on NATO, despite the alliance's initial reluctance to take on new commitments, underscores the continued credibility of allied security guarantees, including nuclear guarantees. Indeed, the very reluctance of NATO to accept new members increased the appeal to nonmembers of the prospect of membership in the alliance. Polish, Czech, and Hungarian officials claimed that "if NATO takes its commitments so seriously, those are the kinds of guarantees we want to have."[164] The views of the East-Central European states on this matter make an interesting contrast with the neorealist contention that "the end of bipolarity means that superpower guarantees . . . will be reduced and weakened. . . . The accelerated proliferation of weapons of mass destruction will be an early and noticeable consequence of this change."[165] Far from losing faith in U.S. guarantees, the East-Central European states wanted those guarantees more than ever, and they were willing to forgo other key options.

The deep cuts projected in U.S. strategic nuclear forces under START (see table 11.2, p. 433) were large in percentage terms, but they still left—and will leave—the United States with a vast, highly accurate, and flexible arsenal with which to underwrite its nuclear guarantees for many years to come. Beyond a certain minimum level, the absolute size of U.S. strategic forces mattered far less than the perceived willingness of the United States to uphold its commitments. The link between arms reductions and nuclear proliferation is by no means artificial, but the notion that reductions implemented during the 1990s (and the cuts envisaged for later years) were large enough to undermine extended deterrence is problematic. The chief question in the 1990s was whether foreign governments still believed the United

States would fulfill its treaty guarantees to allies. Developments in East-Central Europe suggested that they did.

The reorientation of the East-Central European states toward NATO also belied oft-heard predictions of NATO's demise. Alliances can have greater staying power than most neorealists anticipated. Although the Warsaw Pact collapsed very quickly, it never was a genuine alliance. A voluntary and cohesive entity like NATO can take on a life of its own. NATO's main original goal—the deterrence of Soviet expansion—was no longer relevant after 1991, but the alliance by then had evolved into a key organ for the "pluralistic security community" of democratic industrialized states.[166] As such, it was able to survive in a strategic environment very different from the one in which it was founded. With the gradual entrenchment of democracy in Poland, Hungary, and the Czech Republic, those countries became informal members of the pluralistic security community. The enlargement of NATO merely formalized that status.

This development sheds intriguing light on one of the main points of contention in neorealist discussions, namely, the proper way to conceive of "balancing" and "bandwagoning." Some neorealist scholars, including Kenneth Waltz, have argued that states tend to balance against the strongest state in the system, forming an overall balance of power.[167] Waltz concedes that certain states may be inclined to bandwagon (i.e., align themselves) with the strongest state, but he believes that this action (which he sees as the opposite of balancing) ultimately will not keep the remaining states from preserving or restoring the system's balance. Other analysts, notably Stephen Walt, have contended that when states decide whether to balance or bandwagon, they focus not on the strongest state in the system, but on the state they perceive as most threatening.[168] Although the most threatening state may also be the strongest, that need not always be the case. Walt's "balance-of-threat" approach thus differs from Waltz's "balance of power," but the two approaches are similar in treating balancing and bandwagoning as opposite behaviors. A third group of neorealist scholars, especially Randall Schweller, have argued that both Waltz and Walt draw too much of a contrast between balancing and bandwagoning.[169] Schweller maintains that aggression, not bandwagoning, is the real opposite of balancing, and that bandwagoning is far more common than either Waltz or Walt suggests.

The integration of Poland, Hungary, and the Czech Republic into the West's pluralistic security community may not conclusively resolve this debate, but three key points are worth highlighting:

First, what occurred with Poland, Hungary, and the Czech Republic was *both* balancing *and* bandwagoning. The three states were seeking to balance against Russia (to gain a hedge against untoward developments rather than against an existing threat), yet they were also bandwagoning with the dominant group of states (i.e., the Western pluralistic security community, of which NATO was the chief organ). This outcome supports Schweller's contention that balancing and bandwagoning should not be seen as inherently opposite activities. Although in some cases states will choose either to balance or to bandwagon, in this case the two forms of behavior went hand in hand.

Second, the determination of the East-Central European states to join NATO highlights the nonmilitary dimension of bandwagoning. Although scholars have differed over what they see as the motivations for bandwagoning—some view it as driven primarily by "defensive" concerns, while others believe it is more often a form of scavenging or predation—they have tended to define it as a purely military activity.[170] However, the bandwagoning of the East-Central European states with NATO was only partly spurred on by military concerns. Equally important was the desire of the East-Central European countries to join the Western community of democratic states. They saw membership in NATO and the European Union as crucial steps toward, and symbols of, that goal. Indeed, throughout the 1990s, East European officials consistently emphasized the nonmilitary benefits of joining NATO. They cited the important role that NATO played in bolstering democratic polities in Spain, Portugal, and Greece after those countries emerged from many years of dictatorship, and they argued that the alliance could serve as an equally effective stabilizer for the democratic changes and sweeping economic reforms underway in their own societies.[171]

Third, the bandwagoning of the East-Central European states with NATO bears out a simple definition of bandwagoning as "joining the stronger coalition," rather than the definition proposed by Walt as "aligning with the source of danger."[172] Poland, Hungary, and the Czech Republic perceived no danger at all from NATO; quite the contrary. Nor were their efforts to join NATO coerced in any way by the alliance. Far from pressuring the East-Central European states to seek membership in the alliance, as Walt's theory would suggest, the NATO governments initially did their best to discourage the former Warsaw Pact countries from applying. Yet even the cool reception that the East-Central European states experienced did little to dampen their eagerness to bandwagon with NATO.[173]

One final point about Polish, Hungarian, and Czech security strategies is worth noting. So great was the desire of the three states to be admitted into NATO that the mere prospect of qualifying for membership constrained their foreign and domestic policies in important ways. As noted earlier, their bids to join NATO caused them to refrain from forming a subregional alliance and to forgo any pursuit of nuclear weapons. The prospect of NATO membership also had a direct impact on the internal complexion of the East-Central European states, all of which knew that they must be genuine democracies and must foster strong civilian control of their militaries if they were to have any chance of getting into the alliance.[174] Those requirements, and others laid out in NATO's September 1995 report, influenced key legislation in all three countries and helped guide the formulation of numerous provisions in Poland's new constitution, adopted in 1997. The constitution placed the Polish army and general staff directly under the command of civilian leaders, thus eliminating earlier ambiguities in Poland's civil-military relations.[175]

The requirement that prospective members of NATO undergo far-reaching internal democratization was viewed by East-Central European leaders themselves as a salutary influence for the whole region. In their view, the alliance's democratizing effect would continue long after, as well as precede, the actual expansion of NATO. In part for this reason, Hungarian officials supported allied membership not only for Hungary, but for Hungary's traditional rival, Romania:

Hungarian-Romanian relations and the question of joining NATO are of fundamental importance from the standpoint of regional security. . . . If a country wants to become a member of NATO, it will have to ensure that all its policies conform with European norms. These European norms do not permit the use of the army to solve internal ethnic problems. That is why Romania's rapprochement with NATO and the European Union must be supported.[176]

The same view was expressed by leaders of the Hungarian community in Romania, who vigorously endorsed "Romania's membership in NATO [because it] would be a guarantee that the army would never be used against the civilian population."[177] They acknowledged that democracy alone would not remove ethnic tensions, but they claimed it would greatly increase the likelihood that all sides would confront their differences peacefully. This outcome, in turn, they argued, would effectively eliminate the risk of an armed conflict between Hungary and Romania and the potential for a spillover. In that sense, the prospect of NATO membership was seen as a powerful force for regional peace and stability.

In other ways as well, the criteria set forth by NATO promoted conciliatory external policies in East-Central Europe, notably by requiring that prospective members not be embroiled in territorial disputes with their neighbors. Hungarian officials realized early on that they had to try to resolve long-standing tensions with Slovakia and Romania, lest these disputes thwart Hungary's chances vis-à-vis NATO. As the Hungarian defense minister noted in late 1994:

We should not only establish cooperation with NATO members and evince our determination to do so, but should also demonstrate this intention in our relations with neighboring countries. For I am convinced that NATO would not admit countries between whom there is a conflict situation or lack of understanding, or between whom the level of military trust is not high enough to permit them to be admitted into a joint military organization.[178]

Hungary's efforts in this regard paid off dramatically in 1996 and 1997. In September 1996, Hungarian leaders signed a momentous treaty with Romania regarding Transylvania and the status of ethnic Hungarians in Romania. The agreement helped bring a swift improvement in the treatment of Romania's Hungarian community.[179] Subsequently, Hungary concluded similar treaties with Slovakia and Ukraine. Although the deteriorating political situation in Slovakia under Vladimir Meciar prevented a full abatement of bilateral tensions, Hungary's efforts to ease frictions with its neighbors won strong approval from NATO.[180] The same was true of Poland's successful bid to sign major bilateral agreements with Lithuania and Ukraine, which forestalled any possible tensions concerning borders or the status of ethnic Polish minorities in those countries. Even the Czech Republic finally proved willing in early 1997 to sign a bilateral declaration with Germany regarding the status of Sudeten Germans, an issue that had divided the two countries for more than fifty years.[181] The document required significant concessions by both sides. Had the prospect of NATO membership not loomed, the Czech government would have had very little incentive to resolve the matter.

The willingness of the Hungarian, Czech, and Polish governments to pursue these crucial domestic and foreign issues in accordance with NATO's norms and expectations—well before they could even be certain of membership in the alliance—was a sign of the far-reaching impact of the alliance on East-Central European state strategies. Developments in Poland, Hungary, and the Czech Republic after 1990 lend considerable weight to the notion that regimes and institutions can have a strong effect on crucial aspects of state behavior.[182] In that sense, it is not surprising that the drive for NATO membership precluded any effort by the East-Central European states to reverse their earlier decisions not to acquire nuclear weapons.

Ukraine

Ukraine's willingness to forgo nuclear weapons casts doubt on some basic tenets of structural realism. To be sure, it might be possible for neorealists to discount Ukraine's decision to give up the ICBMs, ALCMs, and warheads on its soil. After all, the Ukrainian government had no operational command of those weapons, and it would have been dangerous for Ukrainian scientists to try to salvage any of the fissile material from the warheads.

The only people who can safely dismantle nuclear warheads are those who helped design them, and the ex-Soviet design laboratories are all located in Russia.[183] Thus, despite John Mearsheimer's prediction in 1993 that Ukraine's retention of ICBMs and ALCMs was "inevitable," one can make a strong case from a neorealist perspective that giving up the weapons actually made sense.

What is not so easy to explain is Ukraine's decision to sign the NPT as a non-nuclear weapons state. One might be tempted to dismiss this step as purely cosmetic, noting that countries like Iraq and North Korea secretly developed nuclear weapons in recent years despite being signatories of the NPT. In Ukraine's case, however, the decision to sign the NPT was of much greater importance, bringing an end to many months of impassioned debate about how best to ensure the country's security. Top-ranking Ukrainian military officials underscored the adjustments that would be necessary:

We must now consider how to prepare our armed forces to fight a war using only conventional weapons. . . . It is clear that if a state (like Ukraine) forgoes an entire class of arms—nuclear, which can serve as a deterrent—it must develop an alternative of some sort. The alternative must be a type of weapon that would successfully deter an aggressor under the new circumstances. High-precision weaponry can perform that function.[184]

The evidence that Ukraine's accession to the NPT marked a genuine turning point in Ukrainian security strategy creates particular difficulties for the structural realist paradigm. Most neorealists would agree that vulnerable states usually seek to balance, either internally or externally, against powerful enemies. Although some Ukrainian officials might have hoped that high-technology weapons could provide Ukraine with a satisfactory alternative to nuclear arms for the purpose of balancing against Russia, it is far from clear that this is the case. Precision-guided munitions and other sophisticated weapons tend to be very expensive, and Ukraine's defense budget was, and has remained, insufficient to finance a massive procurement program.[185] Even if greater funding had been available, it is highly unlikely that Ukraine could have fielded a conventional army capable of thwarting a full-scale Russian attack. Furthermore, as Mearsheimer noted, even if Ukraine could somehow have acquired an overpowering conventional deterrent, "a nuclear-free Ukraine would still be vulnerable to Russian nuclear blackmail."[186]

Nor did Ukraine have many options for external balancing. Despite the close ties that Ukrainian officials sought with NATO, there was little chance that Ukraine would be formally admitted into the alliance, if only because of the severe complications such a step would have created vis-à-vis Russia. Early on, a few Ukrainian officials expressed interest in joining NATO, but when their overtures met with a lukewarm response, they abandoned the idea and returned to their earlier pledge that Ukraine would remain "non-aligned."[187] This policy of nonalignment did not prevent Ukraine from establishing much closer ties with NATO in the latter half of the 1990s, but the prospect of full-fledged membership for Ukraine still seemed remote. Similarly, Ukraine's hopes of forging an intraregional alliance, as proposed by Kravchuk in early 1993, were dashed, and no other subregional military alliances involving Ukraine seemed practical or efficacious. The security guarantees that Ukraine received in January and December 1994 were a form of external balancing, but, as noted above, those pledges added nothing to existing great-power commitments in the NPT, Helsinki Final Act, and UN Charter. Pro-nuclear officials and opposition members in Ukraine, including Kravchuk, denounced the guarantees as a mere "illusion."[188] Even Kuchma acknowledged that the statements were "above all a political document."[189] Skepticism about the value of such pledges was evident in the West as well. In mid-1993 a neorealist analysis of nuclear proliferation emphasized that states generally "want a hedge against the potential unreliability of alliance guarantees" and that "such worries will likely be even stronger" for a new state such as Ukraine:

> Those who believe that international commitments to Ukrainian security can substitute for [Ukraine's] possession of a nuclear capability must explain why Ukrainians will comfortably conclude that their international patrons would run grave risks, perhaps facing off against the Russians, to ensure Ukrainian interests.[190]

This assessment, made less than a year before the Ukrainian government took its first big step toward renouncing nuclear weapons, is a faithful sum-

TABLE 11.2 Projected Effects of Start I and Start II on U.S. Strategic Forces

	Number at End of Cold War (1990)	Number Under START I	Number Under START II
total strategic warheads/bombs	12,646	8,556	3,500
of which:			
ICBM warheads[a]	2,450	1,400	500
SLBM warheads	5,760	3,456	1,728
on D-5s[b]	768	1,920	960
bomber/ACLSMS	4,436	3,700	1,272
on B-2s[c]	0	320	272

[a] ICBM = Intercontinental Ballistic Missile; SLBM = Submarine-Launched Ballistic Missile; ALCM = Air Launched Cruise Missile

[b] With a range of 12,000 km and a CEP (probable circular error) of only 90 m, the D-5 (Trident II) SLBM is the most accurate strategic missile ever built. Each of the D-5's eight warheads has a yield of 300 to 475 kilotons.

[c] The projected force of 20 B-2 Stealth bombers will be equipped with advanced conventional munitions as well as B-83/B-61 nuclear bombs. The much-upgraded B-52H bombers will carry the rest of the airborne nuclear force, primarily in the form of advanced ALCMs.

Source: U.S. Department of Defense

mary of what most structural realists would have expected at the time.[191] It is not easy, on the basis of neorealist principles, to explain why those expectations went unfulfilled.

Despite the doubts expressed both inside and outside Ukraine, the government in Kiev ultimately was willing to accept a very limited set of commitments rather than the explicit U.S. nuclear guarantees that Kuchma had once declared were necessary. Part of the reason for this change of heart was undoubtedly the economic benefits that Ukraine stood to gain by forswearing nuclear status. Under an agreement with Russia, Ukraine was able to secure stable supplies for its nuclear power reactors (a crucial part of Ukraine's energy sources) as compensation for recycled fissile material.[192] Russia also promised to continue selling vitally needed oil and natural gas to Ukraine. The United States provided Ukraine with hundreds of millions of dollars to dismantle the SS-19s and SS-24s and to transfer the warheads to Russia, and also extended a huge amount of economic and technical assistance to Kiev, which had been held up earlier when the nuclear issue was still unresolved. The European Union contributed additional economic and technical aid.[193] By the mid-1990s, Ukraine was the single largest recipient of Western financial aid in the former Communist world, a status due primarily to Kiev's decision to forswear nuclear weapons. In light of the drastic problems that the Ukrainian economy was suffering, this Western (and Russian) assistance was of no small importance, especially at a time when serious economic reforms were finally being considered (though not ultimately adopted).

Ukraine's decision to renounce nuclear weapons was also strongly affected by questions of international credibility. From 1990 to 1992, the Ukrainian government repeatedly pledged to adopt a non-nuclear status. Later on, amidst growing tensions with Russia and the vigorous lobbying of pro-nuclear groups in Ukraine, Ukrainian leaders came under pressure to renege on their earlier commitments. The implications of such a move, however, would have been so grave that Kravchuk and Kuchma were able to fend off the lobbyists' pressure. Despite growing tensions with Russia, the vast majority of Ukrainian officials did not want their country to be branded a pariah. Even many of the pro-nuclear advocates said that Ukraine should keep its nuclear weapons only on a "temporary basis."[194] Kravchuk never disavowed the earlier non-nuclear pledges, and Kuchma was determined to uphold them in deeds as well as words.

These inhibitions on Ukrainian policy suggested that the non-nuclear norm embodied in the NPT (and in the broader nuclear nonproliferation regime) had taken on a life of its own.[195] The stigma attached in recent years to aspiring nuclear states like Iraq, North Korea, and Iran was indicative of the growing weight of the non-nuclear norm. Had the NPT never existed, it is doubtful that Ukrainian officials would have felt the need to offer a non-nuclear pledge in the first place. It is also doubtful that, in the absence of the NPT and the nonproliferation regime, Ukrainian leaders would have been so loath to renege on their country's non-nuclear promises, or that U.S. pressure on Ukraine could have been applied so effectively. Realists have tended to downplay or even dismiss the role of norms in shaping state behavior, but the importance of the non-nuclear norm in the Ukrainian case indicates that a reassessment is in order. Ukrainian leaders, even those who were wary of adopting a non-nuclear posture, were cognizant of the benefits they could gain by acting in accordance with the norm of nonproliferation.

Despite the concrete economic and political advantages that Ukraine derived from its renunciation of nuclear weapons, the decision still seems difficult to square with the neorealist paradigm. Most neorealists would agree that "insecurity is the driving force behind national security policy, and [that] highly insecure states are the most likely to acquire nuclear weapons."[196] Ukraine seemed to qualify as such a state, yet it chose not to pursue nuclear weapons despite the lack of satisfactory military alternatives. A unit-level explanation of this outcome might cite the shift from Kravchuk to Kuchma, which clearly made an important difference in Ukraine's foreign policy, especially policy toward Russia. That factor alone, however, was hardly sufficient. After all, important steps in the denuclearization of Ukraine had begun under Kravchuk with the relinquishment of all tactical nuclear weapons as of May 1992, an agreement on the transfer of strategic warheads to Russia in 1993, and the trilateral agreement of January 1994.[197]

To a certain extent, the case of Ukraine may simply be an example of "hiding" (to use Paul Schroeder's term), whereby Ukraine "assumed a purely defensive position in the hope that the storm [would] blow over."[198] Prominent neorealists, including Waltz, have argued that "hiding" is an option only for small states, not for a large state like Ukraine. When a large state is confronted by a more powerful rival, the risks of "hiding" are thought to be too great.[199] For Ukraine, however, the alternatives to "hiding" either were infeasible or would have posed serious risks of their own. So long as the political situation in Moscow did not take a disastrous turn, Ukrainian leaders had ample reason to hope that the "storm" would indeed blow over. If the external environment had been far more adverse, Ukrainian officials might well have reconsidered their whole stance on nuclear weapons. Although the transaction costs of a policy reversal would have been huge, Ukraine eventually could have built a nuclear force (at great expense) if circumstances had so warranted. But in the absence of a grave setback in Moscow, Ukrainian leaders viewed non-nuclear "hiding" as the most viable route to pursue while they sought, with only partial success, to build up Ukraine's internal strength and cohesion.

One final point is worth noting about the implications of the Ukrainian case for nuclear proliferation in general. Neorealist analyses have often suggested that the demise of bipolarity would encourage the spread of nuclear weapons, but the experience with Ukraine shows that, in some instances, the end of the Cold War actually facilitated efforts to *prevent* nuclear proliferation. During the Cold War the extent of U.S. and Soviet cooperation to stem the spread of nuclear weapons was inherently limited.[200] The end of the fierce bipolar rivalry permitted much greater cooperation in extending security guarantees and other side-payments to potential proliferators to steer them away from the nuclear option. That is precisely what happened with Ukraine. Efforts of this sort in any part of the world, much less in East-Central Europe, would have been impossible during the Cold War. Admittedly, this example is not enough to invalidate the view that more states will eventually acquire nuclear arms in the post-Cold War world, but it does show that, contrary to many forecasts, the effects of moving away from bipolarity were by no means uniformly conducive to nuclear proliferation.

IMPLICATIONS FOR THE NEOREALIST-NEOLIBERAL DEBATE

Four broad conclusions pertaining to international relations theory can be drawn from this essay.

First, structural realism is no more useful than neoliberal institutionalism in explaining the state strategies of Poland, the Czech Republic, and Hungary. At the very least, structural realist analyses of these states' policies are in need of important qualifications. In particular, many neorealists tended to underestimate the continuing appeal of nuclear guarantees in the post-Cold War era.[201] Despite longstanding doubts about the credibility of extended deterrence, nuclear guarantees remained a highly attractive option in the 1990s, even when other means of balancing were available. The

Czech, Polish, and Hungarian cases also demonstrate that some states will pursue membership in military alliances (i.e., external balancing) for non-military as well as military purposes. For these three states, external balancing was congruent with, and inseparable from, a form of nonpredatory band-wagoning. Until recently, most neorealists had treated balancing and band-wagoning as opposite behaviors, but the findings here suggest that the relationship between the two can be far more complicated.[202]

Second, although the nuclear weapons policies and broader security strategies of Poland, Hungary, and the Czech Republic can be understood for the most part through either a neorealist or a neoliberal institutionalist prism, developments in those three countries in the 1990s clearly buttressed one of the key tenets of the institutionalist literature, namely, that institutions can place sharp constraints on state behavior, both formally and informally. The mere prospect of gaining membership in NATO helped ensure that Poland, the Czech Republic, and Hungary made no effort to build nuclear weapons. In many other ways as well, the prospect of allied membership had a far-reaching impact on these states' external policies and even their internal complexion, as discussed above. The extent of NATO's influence on the East-Central European states—years before they were actually invited to join the alliance—bears out the prediction made by Jack Snyder in early 1990 that Western institutions like NATO and the European Union could have a highly beneficial effect in the former Warsaw Pact countries.[203]

By moderating the East European states' behavior, the prospect of NATO membership largely undercut one of the main phenomena that neorealists expected to see in East-Central Europe: a highly competitive struggle for security. Most proponents of neorealism argue that, in a self-help world, states never regard their own security and well-being to be positively linked with the security and well-being of their rivals.[204] Developments in East-Central Europe in the 1990s raised doubts about that premise. Hungary strongly supported NATO membership for its chief rivals, Romania and Slovakia, in the hope that the alliance's criteria would help solidify democratic changes in Romania and Slovakia, which in turn would eliminate the risk of a future conflict with Hungary. At least implicitly, Hungary's approach was based on the notion that established democracies never (or almost never) go to war with one another.[205] Similarly, Poland championed the interests of two potential rivals, Lithuania and Ukraine, in their bids to be integrated into NATO. Polish leaders consistently stressed that Polish security and well-being could not be assured unless Poland sought to bolster the security and well-being of its neighbors. The Czech Republic initially was less inclined to engage in "other-help" (the alternative to self-help) than Hungary and Poland were, but by 1995–96 the Czech government, too, increasingly emphasized the need for a coordinated approach.[206] To the extent that this shift toward other-help was fostered by NATO either directly or indirectly, it went beyond the far-reaching cooperation that Charles Glaser has shown can result purely from each state's pursuit of self-help.[207]

Third, structural realism is much less useful than neoliberal institutionalism in explaining the case of Ukraine. Ukraine hesitated before agreeing to relinquish the nuclear arms on its territory and before signing the NPT as a non-nuclear weapons state; but by December 1994 it had consented to both steps. Despite the continued possibility of a future confrontation with Russia, the Ukrainian government was willing to forswear the most potent means available of deterring Russian aggression. The only security benefit Ukraine got in return was a rather tenuous set of great-power pledges — pledges that, from the neorealist perspective, should have had little concrete influence on Ukrainian policy. Although it is possible from an institutionalist perspective to explain why a Ukrainian nuclear deterrent proved not to be "inevitable" (to use Mearsheimer's phrase), this explanation is not compatible with the underlying precepts of structural realism.

Fourth, overall, then, neoliberal institutionalism fares better than structural realism in explaining why the East-Central European states refrained from seeking to acquire nuclear weapons in the post-Cold War era. Neoliberal institutionalists give due weight to the norms and institutional constraints that were salient in East-Central Europe in the 1990s. This by no means implies that international institutionalism is always — or even often — of greater explanatory value than neorealism, but at least in this one important case the institutionalist approach is superior.

NOTES

1. John J. Mearsheimer, "The Case for a Ukrainian Nuclear Deterrent," *Foreign Affairs* 72 (3) (Summer 1993): 61.
2. Ibid., 58.
3. John J. Mearsheimer, "Back to the Future: Instability in Europe After the Cold War," *International Security* 15 (1) (Summer 1990): 36.
4. "South Africa Is First to Dismantle All of Its Covert Nuclear Weapons," *The Chicago Tribune*, 20 August 1994, 15. For a useful overview of the South African program and the decision to eliminate it, see David Albright, "South Africa's Secret Nuclear Weapons," *ISIS Report* 1 (4) (May 1994): 1–19.

5. Tom Zamora Collina and Fernando de Souza Barros, "Transplanting Brazil's and Argentina's Success," *ISIS Report*, 2 (2) (February 1995): 1–11. This episode as well as the South African case is also covered in Mitchell Reiss, *Bridled Ambition: Why Countries Constrain Their Nuclear Capabilities* (Washington, D.C.: Wilson Center Press, 1995), 7–43 and 45–87.

6. The indefinite extension of the NPT would have been extremely unlikely had there not been far-reaching reductions underway in the U.S. and ex-Soviet nuclear arsenals. Those reductions were made possible by the end of the Cold War. If the U.S. and former Soviet nuclear forces had still been at the same levels that they were in the mid-1980s and if U.S. and Soviet nuclear test programs had still been active, numerous Third World signatories of the NPT would have used that as a pretext to renounce or at least weaken the treaty.

7. See, for example, Benjamin Frankel, "The Brooding Shadow: Systemic Incentives and Nuclear Weapons Proliferation," *Security Studies* 2 (3/4) (Spring/Summer 1993), 37–78; Kenneth N. Waltz, "The Emerging Structure of International Politics," *International Security* 18 (2) (Fall 1993): 66–67; and Bradley A. Thayer, "The Causes of Nuclear Proliferation and the Utility of the Nuclear Nonproliferation Regime," *Security Studies* 4 (3) (Spring 1995): 463–519.

8. The original formulation was laid out in Kenneth N. Waltz, *Theory of International Politics* (New York: McGraw-Hill, 1979), 110 ff. Waltz has reiterated his view in many subsequent writings, including "Reflections on *Theory of International Politics*: A Response to My Critics," in Robert O. Keohane, ed., *Neorealism and Its Critics* (New York: Columbia University Press, 1986), 322–45, esp. 326–27. For a recent exchange on the question of unit-level versus system-level analysis, see Colin Elman, "Horses for Courses: Why *Not* Neorealist Theories of Foreign Policy?" *Security Studies* 6 (1) (Autumn 1996): 7–51, with a response by Waltz, "International Politics Is Not Foreign Policy," *ibid.*: 54–57, and a rejoinder by Elman, "Cause, Effect, and Consistency: A Response to Kenneth Waltz," *ibid.*: 58–61.

9. This point is reinforced by an intriguing article which shows that a particular unit-level phenomenon (the domestic influence of a nuclear weapons "lobby") has made a critical difference in potential nuclear-weapons states. See Peter R. Lavoy, "Nuclear Myths and the Causes of Nuclear Proliferation," *Security Studies* 2 (3/4) (Spring/Summer 1993): 192–212. Although Lavoy's argument presupposes that state leaders perceive external security threats, the article demonstrates that the magnitude of these threats is often exaggerated by "nuclear mythmakers." According to Lavoy, this unit-level phenomenon (i.e., the exaggerated perceptions) ultimately can drive the whole policy. That notion is of relevance to the cases discussed here, especially Ukraine.

10. See, for example, Scott D. Sagan and Kenneth N. Waltz, *The Spread of Nuclear Weapons: A Debate* (New York: Norton, 1995) and the exchanges it inspired in "The Kenneth Waltz-Scott Sagan Debate—The Spread of Nuclear Weap-

ons: Good or Bad?" *Security Studies* 4 (4) (Summer 1995): 695–810; the exchange between Jordan Seng, "Command and Control Advantages of Minor Nuclear States," and Peter D. Feaver, "Neooptimists and the Enduring Problem of Nuclear Proliferation," with Seng's response, "Optimism in the Balance: A Response to Peter Feaver," all in *Security Studies* 6 (4) (Summer 1997): 48–92, 93–125, and 126–36, respectively; David J. Karl, "Proliferation Pessimism and Emerging Nuclear Powers," *International Security* 21 (3) (Winter 1996/1997): 87–119, and the ensuing exchange involving Karl, Peter D. Feaver, and Scott D. Sagan under the same title in *International Security* 22 (2) (Fall 1997): 185–200; Martin van Creveld, *Nuclear Proliferation and the Future of Conflict* (New York: The Free Press, 1993); Peter D. Feaver, "Command and Control in Emerging Nuclear Nations," *International Security* 17 (3) (Winter 1992/93): 160–87; Peter D. Feaver, "Proliferation Optimism and Theories of Nuclear Operations," *Security Studies* 2 (3/4) (Spring/Summer 1993): 159–91; Benjamin Frankel, ed., *Opaque Nuclear Proliferation: Methodological and Political Implications* (London: Frank Cass, 1991).

11. Waltz, *Theory of International Politics*. The terms "structural realism" and "neorealism" are used here interchangeably. The literature about structural realism, both pro and con, is so vast by now that a thick book would be needed to catalog it all. For recent overviews of, and contributions to, the debate, see Michael E. Brown, Sean M. Lynn-Jones, and Steven E. Miller, eds., *The Perils of Anarchy: Contemporary Realism and International Security* (Cambridge: The MIT Press, 1995); the two-volume collection edited by Benjamin Frankel, *Roots of Realism* and *Realism: Restatements and Renewal* (London: Frank Cass, 1996); Ethan B. Kapstein, "Is Realism Dead? The Domestic Sources of International Politics," *International Organization* 49 (4) (Autumn 1995): 751–74; Charles W. Kegley, Jr., ed., *Controversies in International Relations: Realism and the Neoliberal Challenge* (New York: St. Martin's Press, 1995); David A. Baldwin, ed, *Neorealism and Neoliberalism: The Contemporary Debate* (New York: Columbia University Press, 1993); Barry Buzan, Charles Jones, and Richard Little, *The Logic of Anarchy: From Neorealism to Structural Realism* (New York: Columbia University Press, 1993); the special issue on "Theorien der Internationalen Beziehungen" of *Osterreichische Zeitschrift fur Politikwissenschaft* (Vienna) 22 (2) (1993); Robert Powell, "Anarchy in International Relations Theory: The Neorealist-Neoliberal Debate," *International Organization* 48 (2) (Spring 1994): 313–44; Kenneth N. Waltz, "Realist Thought and Neorealist Theory," *Journal of International Affairs* 44 (1) (Spring/Summer 1990): 21–37; and Robert O. Keohane, ed., *Neorealism and Its Critics* (New York: Columbia University Press, 1986). An article by John A. Vasquez, "The Realist Paradigm and Degenerative versus Progressive Research Programs: An Appraisal of Neotraditional Research on Waltz's Balancing Proposition," *American Political Science*

Review 91 (4) (December 1997): 899–912, provoked spirited responses in the same issue from Kenneth N. Waltz, Thomas J. Christensen and Jack Snyder, Colin Elman and Miriam Fendius Elman, Randall L. Schweller, and Stephen M. Walt. The responses are especially useful in elucidating different neorealist approaches.

12. Kenneth N. Waltz, "Evaluating Theories," *American Political Science Review* 91 (4) (December 1997), 915.

13. For a good sample of this literature, see three articles by Alexander Wendt, "Anarchy Is What States Make of It: The Social Construction of Power Politics," *International Organization* 46 (2) (Spring 1992): 391–425; "Collective Identity Formation and the International State," *American Political Science Review* 88 (2) (June 1994): 384–96; and "The Agent-Structure Problem in International Relations," *International Organization* 41 (3) (Summer 1987): 335–70. See also Richard K. Ashley, "The Geopolitics of Geopolitical Space: Toward a Critical Social Theory of International Politics," *Alternatives* 12 (4) (October 1987): 403–34; John G. Ruggie, "Territoriality and Beyond: Problematizing Modernity in International Relations," *International Organization* 47 (1) (Winter 1993): 139–74; Christian Reus-Smit, "The Constitutional Structure of International Society and the Nature of Fundamental Institutions," *International Organization* 51 (4) (Autumn 1997): 555–89; Robert W. Cox, "Social Forces, States, and World Orders: Beyond International Relations Theory," *Millennium: Journal of International Studies* 10 (2) (Summer 1981): 126–55; Richard K. Ashley, "Untying the Sovereign State: A Double Reading of the Anarchy Problematic," *Millennium: Journal of International Studies* 17 (2) (Summer 1988): 227–62; Richard K. Ashley, "The Poverty of Neorealism," *International Organization* 38 (2) (Spring 1984): 225–86; Cynthia Weber, *Simulating Sovereignty: Intervention, the State, and Symbolic Exchange* (New York: Cambridge University Press, 1995); and selected essays in Peter Katzenstein, *The Culture of National Security: Norms and Identity in World Politics* (New York: Columbia University Press, 1996).

14. For important statements of this view, see the neorealist-versus-neoliberal collections adduced in note 11 *supra*. For additional presentations of the neoliberal institutionalist argument, see Andrew Moravcsik, "A Liberal Theory of International Politics," *International Organization* 51 (4) (Autumn 1997): 513–53; Robert O. Keohane, *International Institutions and State Power* (Boulder, CO: Westview Press, 1989); numerous essays in Robert O. Keohane, Joseph S. Nye, Jr., and Stanley Hoffmann, eds., *After the Cold War: International Institutions and State Strategies in Europe, 1989–1991* (Cambridge: Harvard University Press, 1993); Arthur A. Stein, *Why Nations Cooperate: Circumstance and Choice in International Relations* (Ithaca: Cornell University Press, 1990); Robert O. Keohane, "International Institutions: Two Approaches," *International*

Studies Quarterly 32 (4) (December 1988): 380–94; Lisa L. Martin, *Coercive Cooperation: Explaining Multilateral Economic Sanctions* (Princeton: Princeton University Press, 1992); Robert O. Keohane and Joseph S. Nye, *Power and Interdependence: World Politics in Transition*, 2nd ed. (Boston: Little, Brown, 1989); Kenneth A. Oye, ed., *Cooperation Under Anarchy* (Princeton: Princeton University Press, 1986); Judith Goldstein and Robert O. Keohane, eds., *Ideas and Foreign Policy: Beliefs, Institutions, and Political Change* (Ithaca: Cornell University Press, 1993); and Robert O. Keohane, *After Hegemony: Cooperation and Discord in the World Political Economy* (Princeton: Princeton University Press, 1984). For a critique, see John J. Mearsheimer, "The False Promise of International Institutions," *International Security* 19 (3) (Winter 1994/95): 5–49. See also the responses to Mearsheimer's article (particularly the one by Martin and Keohane) as well as Mearsheimer's rejoinder in the forum "Promises, Promises: Can Institutions Deliver?" *International Security* 20 (1) (Summer 1995): 39–93.

15. Mearsheimer, "The False Promise of International Institutions," 5–49. Among those who highlight the importance of institutions are Stephen D. Krasner, "Global Communications and National Power: Life on the Pareto Frontier," *World Politics* 43 (3) (April 1991): 336–66; Stephen D. Krasner, "Sovereignty: An Institutional Perspective," in James A. Caporaso, ed., *The Elusive State: International and Comparative Perspectives* (Newbury Park: Sage Publications, 1989), 69–96; and Joseph M. Grieco, "State Interests and Institutional Rule Trajectories: A Neorealist Interpretation of the Maastricht Treaty and European Economic and Monetary Union," in Frankel, ed., *Realism: Restatements and Renewal*: 261–306. For a critical view, see Wayne Sandholtz, "Institutions and Collective Action: The New Telecommunications Movement," *World Politics* 45 (2) (January 1993), 45–67.

16. These include recent works by Stephen M. Walt, Joseph M. Grieco, Randall L. Schweller, Michael Mastanduno, Ethan B. Kapstein, Charles L. Glaser, and numerous other scholars cited here.

17. The statement here is deliberately qualified (referring to "most" states rather than all states) to take account of a criticism made of Waltz's theory. The complexion of some states—particularly "failed" states (or "quasi-states") and states undergoing civil wars—is such that they, too, might be described as anarchic. In some Latin American and African countries, in Lebanon, in Cambodia, in Afghanistan, and in some of the former Soviet republics, private groups and even individuals are able to operate in flagrant breach of domestic law with impunity. These types of states, however, are the exception rather than the rule, and their existence does not necessarily undercut the contrast usually drawn between state structures and the structure of the international system. For fur-

ther comments on variance in state structures, see Robert H. Jackson, *Quasi-States: Sovereignty, International Relations, and the Third World* (Cambridge: Cambridge University Press, 1990); I. William Zartman, ed., *Collapsed States* (Boulder, CO: Lynne Rienner, 1995); Joel S. Migdal, *Strong Societies and Weak States* (Princeton: Princeton University Press, 1988); Charles Tilly, *Coercion, Capital, and European States, AD 990–1990* (Oxford: Blackwell, 1990); Gideon Gottlieb, *Nation Against State: A New Approach to Ethnic Conflicts and the Decline of Sovereignty* (New York: Council on Foreign Relations Press, 1993); and John W. Meyer, "The World Polity and the Authority of the Nation-State," in Albert Bergesen, ed., *Studies in the Modern World System* (New York: Academic Press, 1980), 109–37.

18. Mearsheimer, "The False Promise of International Institutions," 5–49; Robert G. Gilpin, *War and Change in World Politics* (New York: Cambridge University Press, 1981); Robert G. Gilpin, "No One Loves a Political Realist," in Frankel, ed., *Realism: Restatements and Renewal*: 3–26; and Eric J. Labs, "Beyond Victory: Offensive Realism and the Expansion of War Aims," *Security Studies* 6 (4) (Summer 1997): 1–49.

19. On the offensive-defensive realist divide, see Fareed Zakaria, "Realism and Domestic Politics: A Review Essay," *International Security* 17 (1) (Summer 1992): 190–96; Randall L. Schweller, "Neorealism's Status-Quo Bias: What Security Dilemma?" in Frankel, ed., *Realism: Restatements and Renewal*: 90–121; Benjamin Frankel, "Restating the Realist Case: An Introduction," ibid., esp. xiv–xviii; Randall L. Schweller and David Priess, "A Tale of Two Realisms: Expanding the Institutions Debate," *Mershon International Studies Review* 41 (1) (April 1997): 1–32; Jack Snyder, *The Myths of Empire: Domestic Politics and International Ambition* (Ithaca: Cornell University Press, 1991), 9–13; and Mearsheimer, "The False Promise of International Institutions," 9–12.

20. Waltz, *Theory of International Politics*: 91–93; and Joseph M. Grieco, "Understanding the Problem of International Cooperation: The Limits of Neoliberal Institutionalism and the Future of Realist Theory," in Baldwin, ed., *Neorealism and Neoliberalism*: 301–38, esp. 303. See also Joseph M. Grieco, *Cooperation Among Nations: Europe, America, and Non-Tariff Barriers to Trade* (Ithaca: Cornell University Press, 1990), 37–40; Charles L. Glaser, "Realists as Optimists: Cooperation as Self-Help," in Frankel, ed., *Realism: Restatements and Renewal*: 122–63; and Stephen M. Walt, *The Origins of Alliances* (Ithaca: Cornell Univeristy Press, 1987).

21. Whether this expectation is well-founded—especially for states that are not faced with important external threats (or potential threats)—is a different matter. Randall Schweller has averred that "in the absence of a reasonable external threat, states need not, and typically do not, engage in balancing." See Randall

L. Schweller, "Bandwagoning for Profit: Bringing the Revisionist State Back In," *International Security* 19 (1) (Summer 1994), 105. Paul Schroeder goes still further in arguing that "in the majority of instances" between 1648 and 1945 balancing "just did not happen. In each major period in these three centuries, most unit actors tried if they possibly could to protect their vital interests in other ways." Balancing, Schroeder adds, was "relatively rare, and often a fallback policy or last resort." See Paul Schroeder, "Historical Reality vs. Neo-Realist Theory," *International Security* 19 (1) (Summer 1994): 116, 118.

22. Waltz, *Theory of International Politics*, 168–70. See also James D. Morrow, "Arms Versus Allies: Trade-Offs in the Search for Security," *International Organization* 47 (2) (Spring 1993): 207–33.

23. On the particular problems facing small states, see Robert L. Rothstein, *Alliances and Small Powers* (New York: Columbia University Press, 1968); Michael Handel, *Weak States in the International System*, 2nd ed. (London: Frank Cass, 1990); Miriam Fendius Elman, "The Foreign Policies of Small States: Challenging Neorealism in Its Own Backyard," *British Journal of Political Science* 29 (2) (April 1995): 101–19; and Annette Baker Fox, "The Small States in the International System, 1919–1969," *International Journal* 24 (4) (Autumn 1969): 751–64.

24. Thomas J. Christensen and Jack Snyder, "Chain Gangs and Passed Bucks: Predicting Alliance Patterns in Multipolarity," *International Organization* 44 (2) (Spring 1990): 137–68.

25. Rothstein, *Alliances and Small Powers*, 316.

26. On what is needed to deter a potential aggressor versus what is needed to reassure State A, see Robert Jervis, *The Meaning of the Nuclear Revolution: Statecraft and the Prospect of Armageddon* (Ithaca: Cornell University Press, 1989), esp. 78–99. For a classic discussion of this nexus, see Michael Howard, "Deterrence and Reassurance," *Foreign Affairs* 61 (2) (Winter 1992/93): 309–324

27. The term "multipolarized unipolarity" is an inversion of the "unipolarized multipolarity" discussed in Barry Buzan, "New Patterns of Global Security in the Twenty-First Century," *International Affairs* 67 (3) (July 1991): 437. The extent of U.S. preeminence in the post-Cold War system warrants the emphasis on a unipolar structure, with some elements of multipolarity now visible. Contrary to the declinist literature of the 1980s, unipolarity has, if anything, increased in the 1990s. Over time, a multipolar system may well emerge, but movement in that direction has been slower than forecast in Christopher Layne, "The Unipolar Illusion: Why New Great Powers Will Rise," *International Security* 17 (2) (Spring 1993): 5–51. For a pointed critique of the historical claims in Layne's article, see Schroeder, "Historical Reality vs. Neo-Realist Theory," 130–48.

28. For many years Kenneth Waltz argued that bipolar systems are inherently more stable than multipolar systems. See, for example, Kenneth N. Waltz, "The Stability of a Bipolar World," *Daedalus* 93 (3) (Summer 1964): 881–909; Waltz, *Theory of International Politics*: 163–76; and Kenneth N. Waltz, "War in Neorealist Theory," in Robert I. Rotberg and Theodore K. Raab, eds., *The Origins and Prevention of Major Wars* (New York: Cambridge University Press, 1989), 44–48. But in 1993 Waltz said that he had been "mistaken" in "conflating peace and stability." He averred that rather than being more stable, bipolar systems are merely less war-prone than multipolar systems. See Kenneth N. Waltz, "The Emerging Structure of International Politics," *International Security* 18 (2) (Fall 1993): 45. Waltz's retraction has gained relatively little attention, however. Almost all recent discussions of multipolarity versus bipolarity have still focused on questions of stability rather than war-proneness.

29. See Mearsheimer, "Back to the Future," 14–15. For analyses that question this view, see Bruce Bueno de Mesquita, "Risk, Power Distributions, and the Likelihood of War," *International Studies Quarterly* 25 (4) (December 1981): 541–68; Charles W. Ostrom, Jr. and John H. Aldrich, "The Relationship Between Size and Stability in the Major Power International System," *American Journal of Political Science* 22 (2) (1978): 743–71; and Frank Wayman, "Bipolarity, Multipolarity, and the Threat of War," in Alan Ned Sabrosky, ed., *Polarity and War* (Boulder, CO: Westview Press, 1985), 115–44.

30. Paul K. Huth, *Extended Deterrence and the Prevention of War* (New Haven: Yale University Press, 1988).

31. Frankel, "The Brooding Shadow," 37–78; Thayer, "The Causes of Nuclear Proliferation and the Utility of the Nuclear Nonproliferation Regime," esp. 503–5; George H. Quester and Victor A. Utgoff, "U.S. Arms Reductions and Nuclear Proliferation: The Counterproductive Possibilities," *The Washington Quarterly* 16 (1) (Winter 1993): 129–40.

32. Avery Goldstein, "Understanding Nuclear Proliferation: Theoretical Explanation and China's National Experience," *Security Studies* 2 (3/4) (Spring/Summer 1993): 215.

33. Kenneth N. Waltz, *The Spread of Nuclear Weapons: More May Be Better*, Adelphi Papers No. 171 (London: International Institute for Strategic Studies, Autumn 1981), esp. 13–19, 26–28.

34. Some neorealists contend that small states are more likely than large states to engage in "hiding" (i.e., remaining on the sidelines in the hope that existing threats will dissipate) rather than balancing. But that was not the case with the three smallest states examined here (Hungary, the Czech Republic, Poland), whereas it may well apply to the largest (Ukraine), as discussed below.

35. Among numerous sources on the security dilemma, see Robert Jervis, "Cooperation Under the Security Dilemma," *World Politics* 30 (2) (January 1978):

167–214; Glenn H. Snyder, "The Security Dilemma in Alliance Politics," *World Politics* 36 (4) (July 1984): 461–95; and Robert Jervis, *Perception and Misperception in International Politics* (Princeton: Princeton University Press, 1976), 58–113. For an illuminating critique of the defensive realist assumptions that underlie these discussions, see Schweller, "Neorealism's Status-Quo Bias," 90–121.

36. For a pessimistic view of this matter, see Frankel, "The Brooding Shadow," 37–78. See also Quester and Utgoff, "U.S. Arms Reductions and Nuclear Proliferation," 129–40.

37. *The Spread of Nuclear Weapons: More May Be Better,* 8. Waltz offers similar arguments in his recently published exchange with Scott Sagan, *The Spread of Nuclear Weapons: A Debate* (cited in footnote 12 *supra*).

38. See, for example, Goldstein, "Understanding Nuclear Proliferation," 213–55; Thayer, "The Causes of Nuclear Proliferation and the Utility of the Nuclear Nonproliferation Regime," 463–519; Avner Cohen and Benjamin Frankel, "Opaque Nuclear Proliferation," *Journal of Strategic Studies* 13 (3) (September 1990): 14–44; and Robert D. Blackwill and Albert Carnesale, eds., *New Nuclear Nations: Consequences for U.S. Policy* (New York: Council on Foreign Relations Press, 1993).

39. This assumption is warranted because all four states covered here could, at very great cost, have built nuclear forces if they had so decided, a point discussed further below.

40. See, for example, "Mazowiecki: Bez dwuznacznosci w sprawie granic," *Gazeta wyborcza* (Warsaw), February 22, 1990, 1; Janusz Reitter, "Po co te wojska," *Gazeta wyborcza* (Warsaw), February 14, 1990, 1; Valerii Masterov, "'Proshchanie slavyanki' k zapadu ot Buga," *Moskovskie novosti* No. 23 (June 10, 1990): 12; Maria Wagrowska, "Bron i polityka," *Rzeczpospolita* (Warsaw), May 9, 1990, 7; and Valentin Volkov, "Pol'sha-Germaniya: Trevogi i nadezhdy," *Literaturnaya gazeta* No. 15 (April 11, 1990): 11.

41. Interview in "Magyarorszag az uj Europaban," *Magyar Nemzet* (Budapest), October 13, 1990, 7.

42. "Zmierzch blokow," *Zolnierz rzeczypospolitej* (Warsaw), September 6, 1990, 3 (emphasis in original).

43. See, for example, Waldemar Gontarski, "Odejscie Eduarda Szewardnadze: Sprzeciw wobec dyktatury," and Jadwiga Butejkis, "Moze za wczesnie spiewac requiem?" both in *Rzeczpospolita* (Warsaw), 21 December 1990, 1, 7. See also the interview with Czechoslovak foreign minister Jiri Dientsbier in "Vstupujeme do dramatickeho obdobi," *Lidove noviny* (Prague), January 4, 1991, 7.

44. Statement by Andrzej Drzycimski, cited in Kazimierz Groblewski, "OKP u prezydenta: Wybory parlamentarne jesienia?" *Rzeczpospolita* (Warsaw), January

18, 1991, 1. On this same point, see "Prezydent Havel nie odwiedzi republik baltyckich," *Slowo powszechne* (Warsaw), January 29, 1991, 2.

45. "Nic o Polsce bez Polski: Rozmowa z ministrem spraw zagranicznych prof. Krzysztofem Skubiszewskim," *Gazeta wyborcza* (Warsaw), January 24, 1991, p. 1.

46. Comments of then-Polish deputy defense minister Janusz Onyszkiewicz, cited in Ruth Graber, "Poland Revises Defense Strategy," *The Christian Science Monitor*, June 26, 1990, 3.

47. "Brak wizji Europy budzi demony: Udzielone w ostatnim tygodniu wywiady prezydenta Lecha Walesy na temat polityki zagranicznej," *Rzeczpospolita* (Warsaw), 8–9 January 1994, 20; "Prezydent i rzad o NATO: Zbyt krotki krok we wlasciwym kierunku," *Rzeczpospolita* (Warsaw), January 11, 1994, 1; and "Bez alternatywy: Kontrowersje wokol amerykanskiej propozycji," *Rzeczpospolita* (Warsaw), January 12, 1994, 23.

48. "Chci Evropu evropskou, Evropu vsech jejich narodu a statu," *Hospodarske noviny* (Prague), December 2, 1994, 1, 23.

49. Interview with Polish defense minister Zbigniew Okonski in "Silna armia — bezpieczne panstwo," *Polska zbrojna* (Warsaw), October 26, 1995, 6; and interview with Colonel Zygmond Temesvari, Hungarian military attache in Moscow, "Sotrudnichestvo — vygodno nashim stranam," *Nezavisimoe voennoe obozrenie* (Moscow) No. 9 (May 16, 1996): 1.

50. Centrum Badania Opinii Spolecznej, "Czy Rosja nam zagraza" (N = 1,117), June 1993, June 1994, December 1994, February 1995, April 1995, July 1995, December 1995, April 1996, July 1996, December 1996, April 1997, and June 1997.

51. "Verejne mineni a hrozba Ruska," *Respekt* (Prague), No. 26 (June 24–30, 1996): 10.

52. Interview in "Gefahr eines neuen Jalta," *Der Spiegel* (Hamburg), No. 7 (February 13, 1995): 136–38.

53. Comments of Witold Waszczykowski, cited in Bernard Osser and Laure Mandeville, "L'Europe centrale inquiete mais resolue: A Varsovie, Prague et Budapest, les atermoiements des Occidentaux, tres a l'ecoute de la Russie, ont cree un malaise," *Le Figaro* (Paris), November 4–5, 1995, 2.

54. The report, "Polska-NATO," was jointly authored by Andrzej Ananicz, Przemyslaw Grudzinski, Andrzej Olechowski, Janusz Onyszkiewicz, Krzysztof Skubiszewski, and Henryk Szlajfer.

55. "Osnovnye polozheniya voennoi doktriny Rossiiskoi Federatsii," *Rossiiskie vesti* (Moscow), November 18, 1993, 2–3. The doctrine was approved by the Russian Security Council on November 2, 1993 and enacted that same day by Directive No. 1883 of President Boris Yeltsin.

56. Cited in Aleksandr Zhilin, "Voennaya politika i voina politikov," *Moskovskie novosti* (Moscow), No. 47, (November 21, 1993): C10.

57. Osser and Mandeville, "L'Europe centrale inquiete mais resolue," 2.

58. Igor' Korotchenko and Mikhail Karpov, "Rossiiskye yadernye rakety budut perenatseleny na Chekhiyu i Pol'shu: Takoe predlozhenie gotovit General'nyi shtab Vooruzhenykh sil RF na sluchai real'nogo rasshireniya NATO na vostok," *Nezavisimaya gazeta* (Moscow), October 7, 1995, 1.

59. "Nevernyi perevod slov," *Nezavisimaya gazeta* (Moscow), February 20, 1996, 1.

60. It is often difficult to pin down some of the more lurid quotations attributed to Zhirinovsky. In some cases his "remarks" may have been embellished before appearing in Russian or Western newspapers. See the careful discussion of this matter in Vladimir Kartsev with Todd Bludeau, *Zhirinovsky!* (New York: Columbia University Press, 1995), 157–65, esp. 160–61. Even so, it is clear that on occasion Zhirinovsky has been willing to speak about the possible use of nuclear weapons. Moreover, the universal *perception* in East-Central Europe is that Zhirinovsky is a potentially reckless and aggressive figure.

61. "Silna armia—bezpieczne panstwo," 6; Andrzej Lomanowski, "Sprawa stacjonowania w Polsce broni atomowej: Moskwa nie krzyczy," *Gazeta Wyborcza* (Warsaw), October 6, 1995, 6; and comments by Eugeniusz Mleczak, representing the Polish defense ministry, as cited in Oskar Filipowicz, "Jadrowy szantaz," *Trybuna Slaska* (Katowice), October 10, 1995, 1–2.

62. Interview with Peter Deak and Laszlo Magyar in "Politika es realitas hatalom," *Nepszava* (Budapest), October 11, 1995, 1, 9.

63. Interview by the author with Jan Kohout, head of security affairs in the Czech foreign ministry, in Prague, December 17, 1995.

64. Interview in "Wojsko ma prawo sie bronic," *Polityka* (Warsaw), September 9, 1996, 3.

65. Army-General V. N. Lobov, "Puti realizatsii kontseptsii dostatochnosti dlya oborony," *Voennaya mysl'* (Moscow), No. 2, February 1991, 16. See also the interview with the military economist V. Litov in "Nasha bezopasnost' i parizhskii dogovor," *Sovetskaya Rossiya* (Moscow), January 9, 1991, 5; the interview with then-Soviet foreign minister Eduard Shevardnadze in "Edouard Chevardnadze: 'Notre probleme, le votre, c'est de reussir la perestroika . . .'," *Le Figaro* (Paris), 22–23 December 1990, esp. 4; the interview with Col.-General Nikolai Chervov, deputy chief of the Soviet General Staff, in "Kam sa podeli tanky?" *Verejnost* (Bratislava), January 8, 1991, 4; Joseph Harahan and John C. Kuhn, III, *On-Site Inspections Under the CFE Treaty: A History of the On-Site Inspection Agency and CFE Treaty Implementation, 1990–1996* (Washington, D.C.: U.S. Department of Defense/On-Site Inspection Agency, 1996), 200–201; and the interview with Army-General Mikhail Moiseev, chief of the Soviet General

Staff, in "Oborona: Korni i krona," *Pravitel'stvennyi vestnik* (Moscow), No. 9, (February 1991: 10–11.

66. The swift redeployment of some 57,000 heavy weapons in 1990 was an extremely impressive logistical feat, but it absorbed so much of the USSR's rolling stock during the harvest season that it was one of the main factors behind the near-breakdown of Soviet food distribution in 1990–91. See "Nasha bezopasnost' i parizhskii dogovor," 5.

67. Jan Brabec, "Jaderne hlavice pod Bezdezem," *Respekt* (Prague), No. 13, 25–31 March 1991, 6; "Tajne smlouvy s otaznikem: Stanovisko Generalni prokuratury," *Lidove noviny* (Prague), June 14, 1991, 2; and "Ustava nebyla porusena: Jaderne zbrane umisteny legalne," *Obcansky denik*, June 14, 1991, 2.

68. "Antall, Nemeth on Presence of Nuclear Weapons," Hungarian News Agency (MTI), April 23, 1991.

69. Maria Wagrowska, "Bron atomowa byla w naszym kraju," *Rzeczpospolita* (Warsaw), April 9, 1991, 1, 7.

70. See, for example, Ian Anthony, "Restructuring the Defence Industry" and "International Dimensions of Industrial Restructuring," in Ian Anthony, ed., *The Future of the Defence Industries in Central and Eastern Europe*, SIPRI Research Report No. 7 (Oxford: Oxford University Press, 1994), 58–90 and 91–106, respectively.

71. Karel Kaplan and Vladimir Pacl, *Tajny prostor Jachymov* (Ceske Budejovice: K Klub/ACTYS, 1993).

72. This was specified in top-secret agreements signed by the Soviet Union and Czechoslovakia on December 15, 1965 ("Dohoda mezi vladou CSSR a vladou SSSR o opatrenich ke zvyseni bojove pohotovosti raketovych vojsk") and February 21, 1986 ("Dohoda mezi vladou CSSR a vladou SSSR o rozmisteni zakladen s jadernymi naboji na uzemi CSSR"). The Soviet Union concluded similar agreements with Poland on February 25, 1967 ("Uklad o przedsiewzieciu majacym na celu podwyzszenie gotowsci bojowej wojska") and Hungary in mid-1965. The same arrangements were in place for East Germany under a series of agreements signed in the early 1960s.

73. "Jak je to s raketami," *Lidova demokracie* (Prague), March 29, 1990, 1; and "Nase armadu v novem duchu," *Lidova demokracie* (Prague), April 12, 1990, 1. The secret transfer of these missiles (and of other SS-23s sent to East Germany and Bulgaria) was discovered fortuitously in March 1990, when West German officials happened to notice the East German SS-23s in a training exercise. See "Kein Geheimnis, um Raketen der NVA: Sprecher des Veteidigungsministeriums," *Neues Deutschland* (East Berlin), 8 March 1990, 3; and Rainer Funke, "Die NVA rustet Raketen ab—wann folgt die Bundeswehr?" *Neues Deutschland* (East Berlin), March 16, 1990, 1. Following the disclosure of the East

German missiles, Czechoslovak and Bulgarian officials acknowledged that their countries, too, had secretly received SS-23s from the Soviet Union at around the time the INF Treaty was signed in December 1987. See also Captain Sergei Sidorov, "Novyi doklad—na zaigrannyi lad," *Krasnaya zvezda* (Moscow), March 20, 1991, 5. On the relationship between the transfers and Soviet compliance with the INF Treaty, see U.S. Government, The White House, Office of the Press Secretary, *Annual Report on Soviet Noncompliance with Arms Control Agreements*, February 15, 1991, esp. 11–13.

74. Jeffrey A. Larsen and Patrick J. Garrity, *The Future of Nuclear Weapons in Europe: Workshop Summary*, Report No. 12 (Los Alamos: Center for National Security Studies/Los Alamos National Laboratory, December 1991), 4.

75. Ibid., 15.

76. Interview with Maciej Kozlowski, department chief in the Polish foreign ministry, in Cambridge, MA, November 30, 1995. Very similar remarks were made in interviews by the author with several dozen high-ranking military and political officials in the three countries, including General Anton Slimak, then-chief of the Czechoslovak General Staff, in Prague, July 3, 1990 (and a follow-up interview with Slimak in Bratislava, July 6, 1993); Ambassador Ivan Busniak, head of European affairs in the Czechoslovak/Czech Foreign Ministry, in Prague, June 27, 1990 and June 24, 1993; General Antal Annus, deputy chief of the Hungarian General Staff, in Budapest, July 8, 1990; Geza Jeszensky, Hungarian foreign minister from 1990 to 1994, in Cambridge, MA, January 30, 1998; Colonel Tibor Koszegvari, director of the Hungarian Defense Ministry's Institute for Strategic and Defense Studies, in Budapest, July 8, 1990, July 7, 1991, and July 4, 1993; Laszlo Szendrei, Hungarian state secretary of defense, in Budapest, July 3, 1993; General Jiri Divis, head of the Foreign Relations Directorate of the Czechoslovak/Czech General Staff, in Prague, July 17, 1991 and June 25, 1993; Tomas Pstross, deputy foreign policy adviser to Czech president Vaclav Havel, in Prague, June 26, 1993; Bronislaw Komorowski, Polish deputy national defense minister, in Warsaw, June 20, 1990; and Janusz Onyszkiewicz, then-Polish deputy national defense minister (later minister), in Warsaw, June 21, 1990.

77. See the interview with then-foreign minister Gyula Horn in *La Repubblica* (Rome), July 16–17, 1989, 15.

78. "Romania Planned Atom Bomb," Rompress (Romanian State News Agency), May 26, 1993, based on a lengthy account in the Bucharest daily *Evenimentul Zilei*. The Romanian nuclear weapons program was centered in the Institute of Nuclear Power Reactors in Pitesti.

79. "Vojenska doktrina Ceske a Slovenske Federativni Republiky," *Report* (Prague), April 11, 1991, 7. For a virtually identical statement earlier on, see "Armadu

jen k obrane: L. Dobrovsky zduvodnil vojenskou doktrinu," *Lidova demokracie* (Prague), November 9, 1990, 7.

80. "Melo to prijit driv," *Lidova demokracie* (Prague), October 23, 1990, 2.

81. Interview by the author, in Prague, June 25, 1993.

82. Dariusz Fedor, "Wielki rodwrot za wielpie piemiadze," *Gazeta wyborcza* (Warsaw), December 12, 1990, 7.

83. Statement by defense minister Piotr Kolodziejczyk, in "Wojsko na mniej tajemnic," *Rzeczpospolita* (Warsaw), April 18, 1991, 2.

84. See, for example, Andrzej Karkoszka, "A View from Poland," in Jeffrey Simon, ed., *NATO Enlargement: Opinions and Options* (Washington, D.C.: National Defense University Press, 1995), 75–85, esp. 78–80. Karkoszka was a top official in the Polish national defense ministry.

85. "Spokesman on Dismantling Missiles, Pact Summit," Budapest Domestic Service, November 16, 1990; "Defense Minister's Announcement on Arms Reduction" and "Spokesman on Foreign Military, Economic Relations," MTI, November 16, 1990; and interview with Colonel Gyorgy Keleti, Hungarian defense ministry press secretary, on Budapest Domestic Service, November 16, 1990. See also the interview with General Gyorgy Szentesi, head of the department for international relations and security policy at the Hungarian defense ministry, in "Negyszemkozt Szentesi Gyorggyei," *Nepszabadsag* (Budapest), November 24, 1990, 1, 4; and "Military Rocket Unit To Be Dismantled," Budapest Domestic Service, December 5, 1990.

86. "USSR To Be Asked To Buy Back Scuds, Frogs," Hungarian News Agency, 4 February 1991.

87. On the elimination of the missile units, see "Independent Missile Unit Disbands 1 Feb," MTI, February 1, 1991, and the interview with Hungarian deputy defense minister Mihaly Boti, Budapest Domestic Service, February 2, 1991. On the pledge by Fur, see "Defense Minister Outlines New Defense Principles," MTI, March 22, 1991.

88. See, for example, Pawel Wronski, "Niebezpieczne deklaracje: Reakcja na 'atomowe' wystapienie Okonskiego," *Gazeta wyborcza* (Warsaw), October 2, 1995, 3; and Jerzy Jachowicz and Pawel Wronski, "Ulubione wojsko prezydenta," *Gazeta wyborcza*. (Warsaw), 10 August 1995, 3. On Havel's statement, see "Pristi rok se bude jednot o vstupu republiky do NATO, tvrdi Havel," *Mlada fronta dnes* (Prague), October 5, 1995, 2

89. "Zayava Prezydenta Ukrainy," *Uryadovyi kur'er* (Kiev), 6 June 1996, 3. See also "Vystup Prezydenta Ukrainy L. Kuchmy u Seimi Respubliky Pol'shcha," *Polityka i chas*, No. 7 (July 1996): 82–85.

90. North Atlantic Treaty Organization, *Study on NATO Enlargement*, Brussels, September 1995, 20 (emphasis added).

91. U.S. Department of State and Department of Defense, *Report to the Congress on the Enlargement of NATO: Rationale, Benefits, Costs, and Implications*, Washington, D.C., February 1997, 13–14.

92. In December 1994 the CSCE was renamed the "Organization for Security and Cooperation in Europe," or OSCE.

93. Interview with then-defense minister Zbigniew Okonski in "Silna armia—bezpieczne panstwo," *Polska Zbrojna* (Warsaw), October 26, 1995, 1, 6.

94. See, for example, the comments of Janusz Onyszkiewicz in Dariusz Fedor, "Nowa armia," *Gazeta wyborcza* (Warsaw), November 16, 1990, 1. See also Miroslaw Cielemecki, "Manewry pod giewontem: Byc moze wojskowym udalo sie to, co do tej pory nie wyszlo politykom," *Przeglad tygodniowy* (Warsaw), No. 40 (October 7, 1990): 6.

95. Kazimierz Woycicki, "Szansa dla Europy Srodkowej: Zblizenie polsko-czechoslowacko-wegierskie," *Zycie Warszawy* (Warsaw), February 16–17, 1991, 1, 4; Jan Kunc, "Tristranny summit ve Visegradu," *Obcansky denik* (Prague), February 15, 1991, 1; "Wojsko—to sprawa nas wszystkich," 1–2; Cielemecki, "Manewry pod giewontem," 6; and Yu. Gatselyuk, "Bez uchastiya SSSR," *Izvestiya* (Moscow), September 21, 1990, 3.

96. See "Prezidentite Zhelyu Zhelev i Vatslav Khavel razgovaryakha v Praga," *Duma* (Sofia), February 5, 1991, 1. See also the interview with Bulgarian foreign minister Viktor Vulkov in "Varshavskiyat dogovor ostana bez mundir i pagoni: Iztochna likvidira blokovata kolektivna sigurnost," *Otechestven vestnik* (Sofia), February 26, 1991, 1.

97. Interview with Bulgarian president Zhelyu Zhelev in "Sudurzhatelno sutrudnichestvo," *Zemedelsko zname* (Sofia), No. 29, April 19, 1991, 1, 4.

98. "Keznyujtas es Kezfogas," *Nepszabadsag* (Budapest), June 24, 1994, 1.

99. Interview with Czechoslovak foreign minister Jiri Dientsbier in "Tato cesta nie je na preteky," *Narodna obroda* (Bratislava), January 23, 1991, 5.

100. On the Czechoslovak-Hungarian military agreement, see "Smlouva mezi armadami: Vojenske vztahy s Madarskem," *Lidove noviny* (Prague), January 22, 1991, 2. See also "Schuzka ministru v Budapesti," *Obcansky denik* (Prague), January 22, 1991, 1, 7; and the interview with Czechoslovak defense minister Lubos Dobrovsky in "Nova vojenska doktrina statu," *Verejnost* (Bratislava), January 29, 1991, 6. On the Polish-Hungarian agreement, see "Minister obrony narodowej zakonczyl oficjalna wizyte na Wegrzech," *Polska zbrojna* (Warsaw), March 21, 1991, 1. On the Polish-Czechoslovak agreement, see "Minister obrony CSRF z rabocza wizyta," *Polska zbrojna* (Warsaw), February 28, 1991, 1–2.

101. Interview with Polish defense minister Piotr Kolodziejczyk in "Wojsko ma mniej tajemnic," 2. On the demise of the Warsaw Pact's Unified Air Defense

System, see Rolf Berger, "The Rise and Fall of the WTO's Unified Air Defence System," *Jane's Intelligence Review* 4 (7) (July 1992): 291–94. Berger was the final commander of the air and air-defense forces of the East German *Nationale Volksarmee*.

102. Interview with Hungarian foreign ministry state secretary Tamas Katona in "Katona Tamas: Csak eg, csak eg," *Nepszava* (Budapest), March 15, 1991, 9.

103. "Warszawa-Praga-Budapeszt: Jestesmy dopiero u progu wspolpracy," *Rzeczpospolita* (Warsaw), April 18, 1991, 7.

104. See, for example, "Rozhovory s NATO," *Pravda* (Bratislava), September 30, 1993, 2.

105. "Zeme se o vstupu do NATO dozvedi koncem roku," *Mlada fronta dnes* (Prague), July 24, 1996, 2.

106. Barbara Sierzula, "Grupa Wyszehradzka nie istnieje," *Rzeczpospolita* (Warsaw), 15–16 January 1994, 23; "Vaclav Havel: Doba velkych spolecnych gest pominula," *Mlada fronta dnes* (Prague), November 3, 1994, 7; "Cesko, Polsko a Mad'arsko jsou na stejne urovni," *Lidove noviny* (Prague), December 2, 1994, 7; "Imrich Andrejcak: Zapadni orientace Slovenska je nezpochybnitelna," *Hospodarske noviny* (Prague), November 20, 1994, 4; and the interview with Hungarian foreign minister Laszlo Kovacs in "Kovacs Laszlo: Amerikanak fontos a NATO-igen," *Magyar Nemzet* (Budapest), December 10, 1994, 7.

107. "Bezpecnostna politika Ukrainy a Stredna Europa," *Medzinarodne otazky* (Bratislava) 2 (3) (1993): 3–17.

108. Interview by the author with Jan Kuriata, Polish deputy national defense minister, and with Colonel Adam Marcinkowski of the Polish General Staff, in Warsaw, July 1, 1993. See also Stephen R. Burant, "International Relations in a Regional Context: Poland and Its Eastern Neighbors—Lithuania, Belarus, Ukraine," *Europe-Asia Studies* 45 (3) (1993): 395–418.

109. For various perspectives on the relative gains problem, see Joseph M. Grieco, "Anarchy and the Limits of Cooperation: A Realist Critique of the Newest Liberal Institutionalism," *International Organization* 42 (3) (Summer 1988): 485–507; Michael Mastanduno, "Do Relative Gains Matter? America's Response to Japanese Industrial Policy," *International Security* 16 (1) (Summer 1991): 73–113; Duncan Snidal, "Relative Gains and the Pattern of International Cooperation," *American Political Science Review* 85 (3) (September 1991): 701–26; Robert Powell, "Absolute and Relative Gains in International Relations Theory," *American Political Science Review* 85 (4) (December 1991): 1303–1320; plus other essays in Baldwin, ed., *Neorealism and Neoliberalism*. See also the lively interchange among Grieco, Powell, and Snidal in "The Relative-Gains Problem for International Cooperation," *American Political Science Review* 87 (3) (September 1993): 729–43.

110. For a more detailed assessment of these activities, see Mark Kramer, "NATO, Russia, and East European Security," in Kate Martin, ed., *Russia: A Return to Imperialism?* (New York: St. Martin's Press, 1995), 105–61.

111. "Nas prezident byl prvni" and "Prijimame podanou ruku: Z projevu prezidenta CSFR Vaclava Havla v bruselskem sidle NATO," both in *Obcansky denik* (Prague), March 22, 1991, 1–2.

112. Zolton D. Barany, "The Western Contacts of the Hungarian Army," RAD Background Report No. 231 (East-West Relations), *Radio Free Europe Research*, December 29, 1989.

113. Interview with Hungarian defense minister Lajos Fur in "Negyszemkozt honvedelmi miniszterrel," *Nepszabadsag* (Budapest), September 10, 1990, 5; interview with Hungarian deputy defense minister Erno Raffay in "Pozegnania," *Przeglad tygodniowy* (Warsaw), No. 42 (October 21, 1990): 8; "Droga ku bezpieczenstwu," *Zolnierz rzeczypospolitej* (Warsaw), September 12, 1990, 3; "Sprzet z ZSRR, wiedza z Ameryki," *Gazeta wyborcza* (Warsaw), April 9, 1991, 2; "Delegacja MON zakonczyla oficjalna wizyte w RFN: Wracamy z precyzyjnym planem dalszego dzialania," *Polska zbrojna* (Warsaw), November 30– December 2, 1990, 1–2; and "Aus der Bundeswehr: Studium," *Wehrtechnik* (Bonn) 23 (1), January 1991, 69.

114. "Hoste z NATO v Brne: Nova bezpecnost," *Lidove noviny* (Prague), April 25, 1991, 2.

115. Interview with General Laszlo Borsits, chief of the Hungarian General Staff, in *Nepszabadsag* (Budapest), December 17, 1990, 1, 5.

116. "Bialo-czerwone F-16—jesz nie teraz" and "Format krotkiej wizyty: Temat na dzis," both in *Polska zbrojna* (Warsaw), December 6, 1990, 2 and 1, respectively.

117. Interview with Hungarian deputy foreign minister Tamas Katona in "NATO es valtozas," *Nepszabadsag* (Budapest), January 10, 1991, 1.

118. Hungary sent a military medical unit of 37 people to Saudi Arabia; Poland contributed two military vessels with a total of 150 people, plus another 150 medical specialists for two military hospitals in Saudi Arabia; and Czechoslovakia sent a regiment of nearly 200 anti-chemical warfare specialists.

119. "Bez munice nad CSFR," *Zemedelske noviny* (Prague), February 14, 1991, 2; and "Popov, Mutafchiev i Danov otgovaryat na deputatski vuprosi," *Duma* (Sofia), February 22, 1991, 1.

120. Witold Beres, *Gliniarz z "Tygodnika": Rozmowy z bylym ministrem spraw wewnetrznych Krzysztofem Kozlowskim* (Warsaw: BGW, 1991), esp. 73–78.

121. Cited in John Pomfret, "Escape from Iraq," *The Washington Post*, January 17, 1995, p. A-27.

122. Cited in Jane Perlez, "Bosnia: Proving Ground for NATO Contenders," *The New York Times*, December 9, 1995, 6. For further background on East Eu-

ropean states' cooperation with NATO countries in recent peacekeeping missions, see Stephane Lefebvre, "Hungarian Participation in IFOR," *Jane's Intelligence Review* 8 (2) (February 1996), 57; A. L. Zaccor, *Polish Peacekeepers and Their Training* (Fort Leavenworth: Foreign Military Studies Office, August 1993); and Jaromir Novotny, "The Czech Republic—an Active Partner with NATO," *NATO Review* 42 (3) (June 1994): 12–15.

123. "Tajne vladni telefonni spojeni povede na zapad: Vlastni zprava," *Pravo* (Prague), June 19, 1996, 1.

124. See, for example, "Rzeczywistosci i sposobnosci Polski," 1–2; and "Stapanie po kruchym lodzie: Sekretarz generalny NATO uda sie do Moskwy," *Rzeczpospolita* (Warsaw), March 11, 1996, 5.

125. On political and economic developments in independent Ukraine, see Taras Kuzio, *Ukraine Under Kuchma: Political Reform, Economic Transformation, and Security Policy* (Basingstoke: Macmillan, 1997); Adrian Karatnycky, "Ukraine at the Crossroads," *Journal of Democracy* 6 (1) (January 1995): 117–30; Peter Hole *et al.*, *Ukraine*, IMF Economic Review Series (Washington, D.C.: International Monetary Fund, November 1995); Gerhard Simon, "Probleme der ukrainischen Staatsbildung," *Aussenpolitik*, No. 1 (1994): 67–78; V. S. Nebozhenko, *Sotsial'na napruzhenist' i konflikty v Ukrainskomu suspil'stvi* (Kiev: Abrys, 1994); Oleksandr Kovalenko, *Ukraina: Sotsial'na sfera u perekhidnyi period* (Kiev: Osnovy, 1994); Chrystyna Lapychak, "Ukraine's Troubled Rebirth," *Current History* 92 (10) (October 1993): 337–41; Alexander Duleba, "Povolebna Ukrajina: Najdiskutovanejsie otazky vnutropolitickeho vyvoja a zahranicna politika," *Medzinarodne otazky* (Bratislava) 3 (4) (1994): 69–80; Ilya Prizel, "Ukraine Between Proto-Democracy and 'Soft' Authoritarianism," in Karen Dawisha and Bruce Parrott, eds., *Democratic Changes and Authoritarian Reactions in Russia, Ukraine, Belarus, and Moldova* (New York: Cambridge University Press, 1995), 330–69; Roman Solchanyk, "The Politics of State-Building: Centre-Periphery Relations in Post-Soviet Ukraine," *Europe-Asia Studies* 46 (1) (January 1994): 47–68; and "A Survey of Ukraine," 18-page supplement to *The Economist*, May 7, 1994.

126. For two brief but very useful assessments of Ukraine's strategic situation, see Sherman W. Garnett, *Keystone in the Arch: Ukraine in the Emerging Security Environment of Central and Eastern Europe* (Washington, D.C.: Carnegie Endowment for International Peace, 1997); and Taras Kuzio, *Ukrainian Security Policy*, Washington Paper No. 167 (Westport, CT: Praeger, 1996). Ukraine had latent disputes with Moldova and Romania over the status of northern Bukovina and southern Odessa oblast, but these differences remained submerged and were greatly overshadowed by the frictions with Russia. Ukraine and Romania signed an agreement in early June 1997 that largely resolved their remaining territorial differences.

127. See, for example, "Vystup Ministra oborony Ukrainy generala armii Ukrainy V. G. Radetskogo," *Narodna armiya* (Kiev), December 6, 1993, 1–2.

128. Nikolai Churilov and Tatyana Koshechkina, "Public Attitudes in Ukraine," and Leonid Kistersky and Serhii Pirozhkov, "Ukraine: Policy Analysis and Options," both in Richard Smoke, ed., *Perceptions of Security: Public Opinion and Expert Assessments in Europe's New Democracies* (Manchester: Manchester University Press, 1996), esp. 192–94 and 216–18, respectively. See also Roman Solchanyk, "Russia, Ukraine, and the Imperial Legacy," *Post-Soviet Affairs* 9 (4) (October–December 1993): 358–62; and Jeremy Lester, "Russian Political Attitudes to Ukrainian Independence," *Journal of Communist Studies and Transition Politics* 10 (3) (June 1994): 193–233.

129. "Perspektyvy Ukrainy pisla vyborov u Rosii," *Holos Ukrainy* (Kiev), December 28, 1993, 2.

130. Comment by General Gennadii Dmitriev, cited in Zhilin, "Voennaya politika i voina politikov," 10.

131. Chrystyna Lapychak, "Crackdown on Crimean Separatism," *Transition* 1 (8) (May 26, 1995): 2–5. Moscow's restraint may have been partly intended to reciprocate for Kuchma's low-key and muted statements about Russia's intervention in Chechnya earlier in the year, but the chief reasons for Russia's discretion were the general improvement in bilateral relations and a recognition in Moscow that the Crimean leader, Yurii Meshkov, had lost almost all of his popularity.

132. "Dogovor o druzhbe, sotrudnichestve i partnerstve mezhdu Rossiiskoi Federatsiei i Ukrainoi," May 31, 1997, in *Diplomaticheskii vestnik* (Moscow), No. 7 (July 1997): 35–41. For the various agreements on Crimea and the Black Sea Fleet signed by Russian prime minister Viktor Chernomyrdin and Ukrainian prime minister Pavlo Lazarenko, see "Rossiya-Ukraina: Dokumenty o rossiisko-ukrainskom sotrudnichestve," *Diplomaticheskii vestnik* (Moscow), No. 8 (August 1997): 29–41.

133. Ustina Markus, "Recent Defense Developments in Ukraine," *RFE/RL Research Report* 3 (4) (January 28, 1994): 26–32. The assessment here is also based on four lengthy interviews by the author with General Konstyantin Morozov, the former Ukrainian defense minister, in Cambridge, MA, May-June 1994.

134. A. Kachinsky, *Kontseptsiya riziku u svitli ekologichnoi bezpeky Ukrainy*, Working Paper No. 14 (Kiev: Ukrainian National Institute for Strategic Studies, November 1993), esp. 21–25.

135. See the comments by Colonel Oleksandr Serdyuk, central administrative head of the Ukrainian Strategic Nuclear Forces, reported in "Yaderni rakety u derzhavnoi strategii Ukrainy," *Narodna armiya* (Kiev), October 31, 1995, 1; and the comments by the Ukrainian presidential adviser and chief weapons scientist, Viktor Baryakhtar, "Problemy likvidatsii yaderno-raketnogo oruzhiya dislotsi-

ruyushchego na territorii Ukrainy," *Vooruzhenie, Politika, Konversiya* (Moscow), No. 2 (November 1994): 48–51. See also Bruce G. Blair, "Russian Control of Nuclear Weapons," in George Quester, ed., *The Nuclear Challenge in Russia and the New States of Eurasia* (Armonk, NY: M. E. Sharpe, 1995), 65–69.

136. "Prohloshennya 'Pro bez"yadernyi status Ukrainy'," *Molod' Ukrainy* (Kiev), October 25, 1991, 1.

137. "Deklaratsiya pro derzhavnyi suverenitet Ukrainy vid 16 lipnya 1990 roku," in *Ukraina na mizhnarodnii areni* (Kiev: Zbirnyk dokumentiv, 1993), 10.

138. See, for example, Serhii Pirozhkov and Volodymyr Selivanov, "Natsionalna bezpeka Ukrainy: Suchasne rozuminnya," *Visnyk Akademii Nauk Ukrainy* (Kiev), No. 3 (September 1992): 11–25.

139. Sergei Zgurets, "Ukraine nuzhna ne yadernaya bulava, nuzhny garantii," *Narodna armiya* (Kiev), December 21, 1993, 3.

140. On the reasons for the shift in Ukrainian opinion, see Franz-Josef Meiers, *Die Denuklearisierung der Ukraine: Wunsch oder Wirklichkeit*, Report No. 5 (Bonn: Forschungsinstitut der Deutschen Gesellschaft fur Auswartige Politik, April 1994), esp. 5–11.

141. On the concept of "nuclear myths," see Lavoy, "Nuclear Myths and the Causes of Nuclear Proliferation," 192–212.

142. For the text, see "Trekhstoronnee zayavlenie prezidentov Rossii, SShA, i Ukrainy," *Diplomaticheskii vestnik* (Moscow), Nos. 3–4 (February 1994): 18–20.

143. See the coverage in *Cherhova sesiya Verkhovnoi rady Ukrainy: Byuleten'* (Kiev), Nos. 13–14 (1994), esp. 124–27.

144. "Vystup Prezidenta Ukrainy Leonida Kuchmy na sessii Verkhovnoi Rady Ukrainy 16 listopada 1994 r.," *Uryadovyi kur'er* (Kiev), November 17, 1994, 1.

145. "Uspikh planovanii i vystrazhdanii," *Holos Ukrainy* (Kiev), December 7, 1994, 1–2.

146. "Vyvoz yadernykh boepripasov s territorii Ukrainy zavershen," *Segodnya* (Moscow), June 4, 1996, 1. Ukraine thus joined Kazakhstan and Belarus, which had relinquished all nuclear warheads on their territory as of mid-1995. The only warheads still outside Russia after mid-1996 were in Belarus, where a few warheads on SS-25 mobile missiles were not transferred to Russia until November 1996.

147. "Vitcyznany rakety emitsnyuyut' rosiis'ku yadernu potuzhnist'," *Holos Ukrainy* (Kiev), November 28, 1995, 1.

148. "Deklaratsiya pro derzhavnyi suverenitet Ukrainy vid 16 lipnya 1990 roku," 10.

149. "Dogovor o kollektivnoi bezopasnosti," *Krasnaya zvezda* (Moscow), May 23, 1992, 1.

150. "Bezpecnostna politika Ukrainy a Stredna Europa," 4–5.

151. Maja Narbutt, "Polska, Ukraina i ta trzecia: Lech Walesa w Kijowie," *Rzeczpos-polita* (Warsaw), May 26, 1993, 1, 23; and Maja Narbutt, "NATO-bis w od-wrocie? Prezydent Walesa nie poparl ukrainskiej inicjatywy utworzenia strefy bezpieczenstwa," *Rzeczpospolita* (Warsaw), May 25, 1993, 1.

152. "Vzaemodiya pid praporom NATO," *Holos Ukrainy* (Kiev), September 4, 1997, 3.

153. "Kontseptsiya natsional'noi bezpeky Ukrainy," *Uryadovyi kur'er* (Kiev), January 6, 1997, 3.

154. Oleksandr Kupchyshyn, "Spivrobitnytstvo—z SND, integratsiya—z evropoyu," *Polityka i chas* (Kiev), No. 7 (July 1996): 13. One of the most explicit statements about Ukraine's desire to be integrated into NATO came during the visit by Foreign Minister Hennadyi Udovenko to NATO headquarters in April 1997; see "Vystup ministra H. Udovenko na zasidanni NATO," *Uryadovyi kur'er*, April 17, 1997, 3.

155. "Khartiya pro osoblyve partnerstvo mizh Ukrainoyu ta Orhanizatsieyu Pivni-chnoatlantychnoho dohovoru," *Holos Ukrainy* (Kiev), July 11, 1997, 1–2.

156. Separately, France and China indicated that they, too, would abide by these commitments, thus giving them the imprimatur of all five permanent members of the UN Security Council.

157. "Trekhstoronnee zayavlenie prezidentov Rossii, SShA, i Ukrainy," 18–19.

158. "Vystup Prezidenta Ukrainy Leonida Kuchmy na sessii Verkhovnoi Rady Ukrainy 16 listopada 1994 r.," 2.

159. See Goldstein, "Understanding Nuclear Proliferation," 213–55.

160. Top-ranking Polish officials emphasized that their chief objective was to come "under the nuclear umbrella of the United States. . . . The interesting proposals put forward recently by France regarding a [French] nuclear umbrella cannot be regarded as an effective substitute. The same holds true of the British nuclear arsenal." See Ananicz *et al.*, "Polska-NATO," 3.

161. "Lawmakers Question Foreign Obligations," *The New York Times*, December 12, 1994, A-12.

162. U.S. Congress, Senate, Committee on Foreign Relations, *Hearings on The En-largement of NATO*, 105th Cong., 1st Sess., September-October 1997, 45, 49, 76–79.

163. Waltz, *The Spread of Nuclear Weapons*, 8.

164. Interviews by the author with Maciej Kozlowski, department chief in the Polish foreign ministry, in Cambridge, Mass., November 30, 1995, and with Geza Jeszensky, Hungarian foreign minister from 1990 to 1994, in Cambridge, Mass., January 30, 1998.

165. Frankel, "The Brooding Shadow," 37.

166. The concept of a "pluralistic security community" is explored at length in Karl W. Deutsch *et al.*, *Political Community and the North Atlantic Area: Interna-*

tional Organization in the Light of Historical Experience (Princeton: Princeton University Press, 1957). See also Karl W. Deutsch, "Security Communities," in James N. Rosenau, ed., *International Politics and Foreign Policy* (Cambridge: Harvard University Press, 1960), 98–105. Essentially, it refers to a group of interacting sovereign states that no longer prepare for, or have any expectation of ever fighting, a war with one another. All their interactions are peaceful, and the prospect of violent conflict among them is all but inconceivable.

167. Waltz, *Theory of International Politics*, esp. 116–28.

168. Walt, *The Origin of Alliances*, passim; Stephen M. Walt, "Alliance Formation and the Balance of World Power," *International Security* 9 (4) (Spring 1985): 3–43; Stephen M. Walt, "Testing Theories of Alliance Formation: The Case of Southwest Asia," *International Organization* 43 (2) (Spring 1988): 275–316; and Walt's contribution to a three-article forum on "Balancing vs. Bandwagoning: A Debate," *Security Studies* 1 (3) (Spring 1992): 383–482. In this last article ("Alliances, Threats, and U.S. Grand Strategy: A Reply to Kaufman and Labs," 448–82), Waltz acknowledged that his earlier discussions of bandwagoning were "ambiguous" and had led to "misunderstandings" (471).

169. Schweller, "Bandwagoning for Profit," 72–107.

170. See ibid.; Walt, *The Origins of Alliances*; Robert Jervis and Jack Snyder, eds., *Dominoes and Bandwagons: Strategic Beliefs and Great Power Competition in the Eurasian Rimland* (New York: Oxford University Press, 1991); Walt, "Alliance Formation and the Balance of World Power," 3–43; Walt, "Testing Theories of Alliance Formation," 275–316; and the three-article forum on "Balancing vs. Bandwagoning: A Debate" cited above. 1, No. 3 (Spring 1992): 383–482.

171. See, for example, the interview with the then-national defense minister of the Czech Republic, Antonin Baudys, in "Cim driv budeme v NATO, tim lepe," *Lidove noviny* (Prague), October 12, 1993, 8; and Andrzej Olechowski, "Lepsza historia kontynentu: Europa wedlug ministra spraw zagranicznych," *Polityka* (Warsaw), No. 50 (December 10, 1994): 1, 13.

172. Walt, *The Origins of Alliances*, 17, as well as Walt's clarifications in "Alliances, Threats, and U.S. Grand Strategy," 472–73. For a perceptive critique, see Schweller, "Bandwagoning for Profit," esp. 80–82.

173. By 1995, however, there was much evidence of growing impatience; see, for example, the interview with Polish deputy prime minister Aleksander Luczak in "Rzeczywistosc i sposobnosci Polski," *Polska zbrojna* (Warsaw), October 6–8, 1995, 1–2.

174. Detailed criteria for new members were laid out in NATO, *Study on NATO Enlargement*, esp. 23–24. Not surprisingly, this report was very closely studied by East-Central European officials; see, for example, "Rzeczywistosc i sposobnosci Polski," 2. It is worth emphasizing that that the criteria apply only to new

members, not existing members. Some existing NATO countries, especially Turkey, would have trouble in meeting the criteria. For country-by-country analyses of how well the East-Central European states fulfilled NATO's requirements, see U.S. Congress, Commission on Security and Cooperation in Europe, *Report on Human Rights and the Process of NATO Enlargement*, Washington, D.C., June 1997.

175. This point is covered in greater depth in Mark Kramer, *Soldier and State in Poland: Civil-Military Relations and Institutional Change After Communism* (Boulder, CO: Rowman & Littlefield, 1998).

176. Interview with Imre Mecs, chairman of the Hungarian parliament's defense committee, on Duna Television, Budapest, November 20, 1994.

177. Comments by Csaba Takacs, national executive chairman of the Hungarian Democratic Union of Romania, ibid.

178. Interview with Gyorgy Keleti, ibid. See also "Negyszemkozt Keleti Gyorgy," *Magyar Nemzet* (Budapest), December 12, 1994, 3. Similarly, in late 1994 the acting Slovak defense minister, Imrich Andrejcak, emphasized that "a prerequisite for NATO membership will be the dependability, security, and *neighborly cooperation* of the applicants." See "Zapadni orientace Slovenska je nezpochybnitelna," 4 (emphasis added).

179. Commission on Security and Cooperation in Europe, *Report on Human Rights and the Process of NATO Enlargement*, 30, 63–64, 75–76.

180. See, for example, "Horn: A kormany kesz azonnal targyalni Szlovakiaval Bosrol," *Nepszabadsag* (Budapest), September 30, 1997, 1; and "Ketezerot utan mar hivatasos hadseregunk lehet," Magyar Hirlap (Budapest), October 4, 1997, 9.

181. "Deutsch-Tschechische Erklarung uber die gegenseitigen Beziehungen und deren kunftige Entwicklung," January 21, 1997, in *Presse- und Informationsamt der Bundesregierung Bulletin* (Bonn), No. 7 (February 2, 1997), 111–15. In the Czech Republic, the most controversial part of the declaration was Article III, which affirmed that the Czech side "regrets that the forcible expulsion and forced resettlement of Sudeten Germans [in 1945–46] . . . inflicted great suffering and injustice on innocent people, and that guilt was attributed collectively. It particularly regrets the excesses that were contrary to basic humanitarian principles . . . "

182. In "The False Promise of International Institutions," John Mearsheimer treats regimes and institutions as synonyms. The relationship of the East-Central European states to NATO is one of many examples that could be cited to warrant keeping the terms distinct.

183. V. Mikhailov et al., "Minatom Rossii i obespechenie bezopasnosti yadernogo oruzhiya Rossiiskoi Federatsii," *Mezhdunarodnaya zhizn'* (Moscow), No. 6 (June 1996): 35–64; Batyakhar, "Problemy likvidatsii yaderno-raketnogo oru-

zhiya dislotsiruyushchego na territorii Ukrainy," 48–51; Ivan Sutyagin, "Problemy bezopasnosti rossiiskogo yadernogo oruzhiya," *Voennyi vestnik* (Moscow), No. 7 (1993): 62–76; and Office of Technology Assessment, *Dismantling the Bomb and Managing the Nuclear Materials*, OTA-O-572 (Washington, D.C.: U.S. Government Printing Office, November 1993), 137–47.

184. Interview with General Vadym Hrechaninov, Ukrainian deputy defense minister, in "Reformuvati armiyu vazhche, nizh buduvati ii zanovo," *Kievs'ki vidimosti* (Kiev), December 2, 1994, 4.

185. Oleksandr Honcharenko *et al.*, "Kontseptsiya natsional'noi bezpeky Ukrainy: Problemy i perspektyvy rozbudovy," *Viis'ko Ukrainy* (Kiev) No. 5 (March 1993): 9. On recent trends in Ukrainian defense spending and the effect on military capabilities, see A. Moshes, "Voennye reformy: Rossiya, Ukraina, Belorussiya," *Mirovaya ekonomika i mezhdunarodnye otnosheniya* (Moscow), No. 1 (January 1995): 142–51.

186. Mearsheimer, "The Case for a Ukrainian Nuclear Deterrent," 56.

187. Vladimir Skachko, "Iz mira vrazhdy—v mir problem: Kuchma v Budapeshte popytaetsya razblokirovat' pomoshch' Zapada Kievu," *Nezavisimaya gazeta* (Moscow), December 6, 1994, 3.

188. Cited in Nadiya Derkach, "Kholodnym mirom Evropu ne zlyakati: Vchora u Budapeshti zavershilas' zustrich glav derzhav-uchasnits' NBSE," *Za vilnu Ukrainu* (L'viv), December 7, 1994, 1.

189. "P'yat' derzhav garantuvali bezpeku Ukrainy," *Holos Ukrainy* (Kiev), December 8, 1994, 1.

190. Cohen, "Understanding Nuclear Proliferation," 254–55.

191. See, for example, Mearsheimer, "The Case for a Ukrainian Nuclear Deterrent," 50–51: "Ukraine cannot defend itself against a nuclear-armed Russia with conventional weapons, and no state, including the United States, is going to extend to it a meaningful security guarantee. Ukrainian nuclear weapons are the only reliable deterrent to Russian aggression."

192. "Prilozhenie k trekhstoronnemu zayavleniyu prezidentov Rossii, SShA i Ukrainy ot 14 yanvarya 1994 goda," *Diplomaticheskii vestnik* (Moscow), Nos. 3–4 (February 1994), 20.

193. Kuchma cited the EU's contribution of 85 million ecus during a press conference after his return from the CSCE summit; see "Ukraina mae stati mostom mizh Skhodom i zakhodom," *Holos Ukrainy* (Kiev), December 9, 1994, 2.

194. For a detailed survey of the twists in the debate, see Bohdan Nahaylo, "The Shaping of Ukrainian Attitudes Toward Nuclear Arms," *RFE/RL Research Report* 2 (8) (February 19, 1993): 21–45.

195. On the non-proliferation norm, see Roger K. Smith, "Explaining the Non-Proliferation Regime: Anomalies for Contemporary International Relations Theory," *International Organization* 41 (2) (Spring 1987): 252–81; Steven Lee,

"Nuclear Proliferation and Nuclear Entitlement," *Ethics & International Affairs*9 (1995): 101–31, esp. 123–31; and John Simpson, "Nuclear Non-Proliferation in the Post-Cold War Era," *International Affairs* 70 (1) (January 1994): 17–39, esp. 18, 36. For more general discussions of norms in world politics, see the essays in Volker Rittberger, ed., *Regime Theory and International Relations* (Oxford: Clarendon Press, 1993).

196. Mearsheimer, "The Case for a Ukrainian Nuclear Deterrent," 60.

197. For an overview, see the special section on "Ukrainian Security Issues" in *RFE/RL Research Report* 3 (4) (January 28, 1994): 1–32, esp. John W. R. Lepingwell, "Negotiations Over Nuclear Weapons: Past as Prologue?" 1–11.

198. Schroeder, "Historical Reality vs. Neo-Realist Theory," 117.

199. Waltz, *Theory of International Politics*, 72–74, 184–85. For a classic statement of this view, see Rothstein, *Alliances and Small Powers*, 26–27, 233–34.

200. Cooperation on this matter was greater than often realized, however. See Joseph S. Nye, Jr., "U.S.-Soviet Cooperation in a Nonproliferation Regime," in Alexander L. George, Philip J. Farley, and Alexander Dallin, eds., *U.S.-Soviet Security Cooperation: Achievements, Failures, Lessons* (New York: Oxford University Press, 1988), 336–52; William Potter, "Nuclear Proliferation: U.S.-Soviet Cooperation," *The Washington Quarterly* 8 (1) (Winter 1985): 37–49; and Peter R. Lavoy, "Learning and the Evolution of Cooperation in U.S. and Soviet Nuclear Nonproliferation Activities," in George W. Breslauer and Philip E. Tetlock, eds., *Learning in U.S. and Soviet Foreign Policy* (Boulder, CO: Westview Press, 1991), 735–83.

201. See, for example, Frankel, "The Brooding Shadow," 37–78; Thayer, "The Causes of Nuclear Proliferation and the Utility of the Nuclear Nonproliferation Regime," esp. 503–05; and Quester and Utgoff, "U.S. Arms Reductions and Nuclear Proliferation," 129–40.

202. Randall Schweller, as noted earlier, has convincingly argued that aggression, not bandwagoning, is the real opposite of balancing ("Bandwagoning for Profit," 72–107). The point here is somewhat different from Schweller's argument, which emphasizes the use of military bandwagoning by revisionist states, whether predators or scavengers. The point here is that bandwagoning can also be seen as a non-military activity.

203. Jack Snyder, "Averting Anarchy in the New Europe," *International Security* 14 (4) (Spring 1990): 5–41. It should be noted, however, that in Slovakia the impact of Western institutions was much less effective.

204. Waltz, *Theory of International Politics*, 105–12; Christopher Layne, "The Unipolar Illusion: Why New Great Powers Will Rise," *International Security* 17 (4) (Spring 1993): 10–11; Mearsheimer, "The False Promise of International Institutions," 10–11; and Mearsheimer, "Back to the Future," 12–13. For a critique, see Wendt, "Anarchy Is What States Make of It," 391–426.

205. It should be emphasized that the notion of a "democratic peace," to the extent it is well-founded, applies predominantly to *established* democracies. One recent study has suggested that for newly democratizing states, the risk of going to war may actually increase. See Edward D. Mansfield and Jack Snyder, "Democratization and the Danger of War," *International Security* 20 (1) (Summer 1995): 5–38. This view is not universally accepted, however. See, for example, William R. Thompson and Richard M. Tucker, "A Tale of Two Democratic Peace Critiques," *Journal of Conflict Resolution* 41 (2) (June 1997): 428–51; Michael D. Ward and Kristian S. Gleditsch, "Democratizing for Peace," *American Political Science Review* 92 (1) (March 1998): 51–61; and Andrew J. Enterline, "Driving While Democratizing: Correspondence," *International Security* 20 (1) (Summer 1996): 183–96.

206. The term "other-help" is used in Jonathan Mercer, "Anarchy and Identity," *International Organization* 49 (2) (Spring 1995): 229–52.

207. Glaser, "Realists as Optimists," 122–63.

12 Does Unipolarity Have a Future?

Ethan B. Kapstein

In a recent article I asked, Is Realism Dead?[1] It would seem so, given the pounding the paradigm has taken from a constant barrage of empirical evidence and theoretical arguments.[2] This has left, in the words of Bruce Russett, "a sinking hulk" instead of a disciplinary flagship.[3]

The chapters in this volume suggest that Russett's epitaph may have been premature. In analyzing the grand strategies of the great and middle-sized powers since the end of the Cold War, most of the authors find considerable merit in some variant of the realist paradigm, with its focus on anarchy, pervasive insecurity, and the primacy of state action. Even in such "hard" cases as the refusal of Eastern European countries to acquire nuclear weapons, we find a good realist response: the centrality of alliance relationships to the maintenance of their national security.[4]

Given that this book's chapters are situated mainly at the unit level, it is not surprising to find renewed interest among the authors in classical as opposed to structural or neorealism. Systemic forces, it seems, are too uncertain or indeterminate to say much of value about foreign policy decision-making in the post-Cold War era. Indeed, Kenneth Waltz himself explicitly stated that structural realism did not offer a theory of foreign policy.

This concluding chapter, however, relies on an important variant of modern realism—hegemonic stability theory—in analyzing the unipolar distribution of power. I argue that "hegemonic realism" provides powerful insights into the nature of contemporary politics, as states struggle to shape their domestic grand strategies in the face of the inescapable pressures generated by a dominant Washington. From economics to security to culture, it has become almost impossible for countries to hide from the long arm of the United States, or to pursue with any success strategies that are at odds with its preferences or interests.

Since there is little debate about the primacy of U.S. military power in today's world (although there is certainly debate about the *relevance* of those assets in influencing many international outcomes), my focus is on international economic relations, an arena that by some accounts is multi- rather than unipolar. Indeed, two decades after "the end of American hegemony" was proclaimed by many scholars, I seek to demonstrate that international outcomes in international trade, finance and investment still generally reflect Washington's preferences and interests, and are likely to do so for the foreseeable future.[5] My concerns in this essay are thus with the stability of the American-centered economic order, and with the potential challenges to it that appear on the horizon.

The politics of the world economy continue to provide a contested terrain for theorists. For many scholars (including some of the contributors to this volume), the future of the liberal international economy appears grim. As Samuel Huntington has written, "In the coming years, the principal conflicts of interests involving the United States and the major powers are likely to be over economic issues. U.S. economic primacy is now being challenged by Japan and is likely to be challenged in the future by Europe. . . . [T]he United States, Japan, and Europe . . . have deeply conflicting interests over the distribution of the benefits and costs of economic growth and the distribution of the costs of economic stagnation or decline."[6] This view is echoed by Randall Schweller, who writes in his contribution that "As economic might supplants military strength as the primary currency of national power and prestige, trade talks have replaced arms control as the most contentious form of diplomacy."[7]

Nor is this vision limited to political scientists. International economist Dominick Salvatore has asserted that "Trade relations among the world's major industrial nations have taken a turn for the worse during the past two decades and are now threatened by new and more dangerous forms of trade restrictions, collectively known as the 'new protectionism.' "[8] Of particular interest from the perspective of systemic stability are those cases in which not only distributional issues are in conflict, but fundamental values also, as when the United States insists on linking trade to human rights.

As a concrete sign of the alleged breakdown of the postwar multilateral trading order, some analysts would argue that we are witnessing the rise of a bloc-oriented international economy centered on the North American Free Trade Area (NAFTA), the European Union (EU), and the awkwardly named Asia-Pacific Economic Cooperation (APEC); these blocs, it is said, will replace multilateralism as the basis for economic decisionmaking. In 1994, regional arrangements already constituted 61 percent of world trade.[9] It remains an open question whether economic regionalism will lead to further liberalization of the international trading system as a whole (that is, whether these arrangements will be "trade creating"), or act as a brake on that process (that is, whether they will be "trade diverting," in that they divert trade away from the "world" and toward the bloc).

These developments seem to confirm what might be reflexively labeled as the realist vision of the international economy in the post-Cold War world. It is a world, like that of the 1930s, in which competitive geoeconomic blocs reappear, and the multilateral system of open trade and financial flows splinters. Building on this vision, Jonathan Kirshner makes a series of "realist predictions" for the future in his chapter, one of which is that "multilateral economic cooperation among the advanced industrial states will decline." Kirshner argues that, for realists, the economic order built after World War II by the western allies formed an integral part of their response to the Soviet threat; in essence, that threat was the glue that held the economic system, with its rules and regimes, together. With the passing of the Cold War, the glue has dissolved and concern over relative economic gains is again rising to the fore, leading to renewed struggle and conflict over global markets.[10]

Yet a number of counterindicators should give us pause before we accept this bleak assessment. After all, it is since the collapse of the Soviet Union that the Uruguay Round of trade talks has been completed and, in the process, the General Agreement on Tariffs and Trade (GATT) transformed into the more powerful World Trade Organization (WTO); that the Organization for Economic Cooperation and Development (OECD) has expanded its membership beyond its core group of industrial democracies (indeed, Russia has recently applied for membership); that the emergency support funds of the International Monetary Fund (IMF) have been bolstered, especially since the Mexican Peso Crisis of 1995 and Asian crisis of 1997–1998; that international regulation of the financial system has been strengthened by the Basle Committee of Banking Supervisors and the International Organization of Securities Commissions; and, most important, that a number of countries, including China and the former members of the Warsaw Pact, have entered the world economy as they liberalize at home and open their economies to foreign trade and direct investment. Thus, while some observers see a world ready to plunge into economic conflict, regionalism and renewed protectionism, others imagine an era of truly global trade and investment, with the growing insignificance of territorial boundaries for economic actors.[11]

One theoretical approach that may help to close the gap between these competing visions is provided by hegemonic stability theory.[12] That theory, it will be recalled, focuses on the role of a single dominant power in establishing and maintaining "the norms and rules of a liberal economic order." The hegemonic state lays down liberal rules, creates international organizations to monitor them, and acts as crisis manager, becoming a lender of last resort when needed and a market for distress goods in times of economic recession.[13] The system's openness is a function of the hegemon's capabilities, and when that powerful state suffers relative decline, "the liberal economic order is greatly weakened."[14]

The starting point for hegemonic stability by most accounts is found in the material capabilities of the would-be international leader. By this reading, it was America's tremendous military, economic, and political dominance after World War II that gave it the opportunity to shape the international economy in its own interest. By the 1970s, however, many observers believed that America's relative capabilities in such arenas as energy, trade, and finance had fallen greatly, raising questions about the durability of the postwar regimes. That such regimes remained relatively stable at all in the face of this decline was, according to Robert Keohane and several others, a function of the institutions that the United States had created in its heyday.[15] The more parsimonious but perhaps less obvious alternative, that the United States was still the dominant power across most issue-areas of international importance, was also argued, but by a smaller number of scholars.[16]

This essay reexamines the future of the international economy in hegemonic-realist perspective; that is, with a focus on the distribution of power at the systemic level. The issue at stake concerns the system-wide economic pressures being generated on states by the American-dominated order, and what scope governments have for erecting buffers against such pressures (should they want to), either internally or externally through balancing. As Bruce Russett has written, "the international system has been structurally transformed, largely by the United States."[17] It is the durability of that system that concerns me here.

Drawing on the essays in this volume and other contributions, I examine potential challenges to the "American century," and make some predictions about its future course. In brief, my argument is that states are facing an overwhelming set of American-generated economic forces (the word "globalization" is really a contemporary euphemism for American economic dominance) that they must adapt to if they wish to modernize and liberalize their economies. The United States, too, is subject to the pressures it unleashed, but it has a unique set of capabilities and "coping mechanisms" that keeps it relatively independent of them, including its production of the world's major reserve currency, its favored geopolitical setting, and its market size and thus market power. States that wish to counter this order and go their own way in economic policy will likely find the costs of doing so exceedingly high. I thus hypothesize that outcomes in international economic negotiations will closely resemble American preferences and interests.

Still, there is some systemic evidence that efforts are underway to balance against U.S. power. The introduction of a single currency within the context of the European Monetary Union could be analyzed as a challenge to the dollar's domination of international finance, and the increasing economic and military ties between Russia and China suggest that these countries are seeking to insulate themselves from American pressure. At the same time, in none of these cases can the regions or countries "go it alone" without the assistance of the United States in some critical arena.

Yet there might be another challenge to American leadership that, in the end, is the greatest of all, and that is the challenge coming from domestic politics. It may be that, absent the Cold War, Washington will find itself unable to define much less defend a "national interest" that transcends special-interest groups, and instead will find itself pulled-and-hauled in ways that undermine its ability to act. In this regard, the defeat of "fast-track" trade legislation in 1997 could be seen as a warning shot across the bow, a message that domestic interests will no longer permit themselves to be sacrificed on the altar of national security. Hegemonic stability theorists have long said that a dominant power needs domestic "willingness" to write and enforce the rules of the game, and it is here that the United States appears at its weakest.

MULTILATERALISM AND THE POSTWAR ORDER

As Dan Deudney and John Ikenberry observe in their chapter, the postwar American system of trade and financial liberalization represented a unique policy mixture that they label "structural liberalism." On the one hand, the ideas that animated the system were profoundly liberal, in that they focused on human liberty and its exercise in free markets; on the other, American leadership was profoundly influenced by fear of Soviet communism. The United States had to fashion a system that would prove the critics of its brand of democratic capitalism wrong; Washington thus had to be not just powerful, but generous and just in its dealings with its allies.

Multilateralism—the promotion of free trade and free investment flows on a multilateral rather than bilateral basis—was at the heart of the American approach toward reconciling these liberal and realist motive forces. It was an instrument designed not just to promote prosperity, but equally important, peace as well. As Michael Mastanduno has written, "the concept that best captures" America's postwar foreign policy goals is not containment but "multilateralism."[18] And that is the approach which has transcended the end of the Cold War.

Multilateralism and institution building have proved remarkable supple instruments of foreign and domestic policy. During the Cold War, these regimes, by promising greater prosperity than any alternative form of political economy, formed the economic bulwark against the external Soviet communist threat on the one hand and the domestic communist party threat on the other. Today, the external threat has vanished, and most countries around the world (East Asia is a notable exception) are reducing their defense expenditures. Yet the risk of domestic political disruption, not to mention peaceful changes in ruling parties, remains, making sustained economic growth a top priority for all political leaders, especially those who seek re-election to the offices they hold. In this sense, "membership" in the international economic order continues to provide governments with important domestic political benefits, to the extent that liberalization, openness and wealth creation are viewed as inextricably linked in the majority of voters' minds.

As hegemonic stability theory suggests, the United States was able to restructure the western economy according to its preferences after World War II because of its market size and its control over hard currency and critical resources, especially food and fuel. One influential report on foreign economic policy written in 1955 stated that "the American economy has a one-sided, or non-complementary, relationship to the international economy . . . The rest of the free world relies upon the American economy to a much greater extent than the American economy depends upon it. Indeed, the

rest of the free world could not live *without* the American economy."[19] While
the world has grown less dependent on America's natural resources (indeed,
the United States has become more dependent on petroleum and raw materials), entry to its domestic marketplace for goods and services still remains
essential for export-oriented nations. While often viewed as a weakness, the
United States remains by far the largest importing nation in the world, giving
it substantial market power.

In order to build a system of multilateral regimes for trade, finance, and
investment, the United States and its allies had to develop a set of operating
principles or rules of the game. For example, the basic principle of the
postwar trade regime, embodied in the GATT, is "most-favored nation"
(MFN) status. This means that members of the GATT (now the WTO)
must treat one another exactly as they treat their "most favored" trading
partner, thus leveling the playing field and putting an end to bilateral favor-
itism. As a result of this approach, member countries that previously had
few commercial dealings with one another now saw a new world of trade
opportunities available to them. In this light it is notable that debate over
China's continued MFN status is now at the heart of its bilateral relationship
with the United States, and that Russia is applying for membership in the
WTO. As Schweller observed, trade talks really have replaced arms control
negotiations in world politics.

One of the remarkable aspects of this regime has been the extent to which
it has implicated countries in each others' economic policies. Jock Finlayson
and Mark Zacher have written with respect to the international trade regime,
"Multilateralism signifies the willingness of governments to participate in
rulemaking conferences and to allow multilateral surveillance of, and even
a degree of control over, their trade policy. It symbolizes regime members'
acceptance of the proposition that they have a legitimate interest in each
other's policies and behavior."[20] International organizations like the GATT,
the IMF, and the OECD were given surveillance roles in their charters over
member countries' economic behavior, and they criticized domestic policies
that were at odds with established international practices. It is a surprising
fact that no state has ever left any of these international organizations (with
the exception of Peru, which briefly quit the IMF), and many have sought
to join.

Today, belief among the industrial countries in the continued benefits of
this international economic structure remains strong. As the leaders of the
Group of Seven (G-7) nations proclaimed at their 1996 summit in Lyons,
France, "Expanding trade and investment has led to marked increases in

global wealth and prosperity and should continue to play this role in the future. Growth in trade and investment will be sustainable and therefore most beneficial to all if conducted within a strong multilateral framework of rules." The G-7 leaders then went on to praise the work of the such organizations as the IMF, WTO, and OECD, which of course establish these rules.[21]

Given this history, one can only wonder why some scholars are so dismissive of the role that multilateral institutions have played in the postwar order.[22] They are part and parcel of the economic structure that the United States built and sustained. To say that they are epiphenomenal points to an important truth about American power, but to take the analysis no further is unsatisfactory. As Daniel Deudney and John Ikenberry point out, these multilateral institutions have played an instrumental role in legitimating that order worldwide, by giving member-states a voice, however small, in decisionmaking about its operations.[23] It is notable that many of these institutions, like the IMF, are not led by Americans at all.

Of course, self-styled realists have not been alone in raising doubts about the future of the postwar economic order. Reports of its demise have been widespread for years. Overwhelming pressures on the international economy were said to be coming from two directions: first, at the systemic level, some specialists argued that new challengers, such as Japan, were acting to undermine the postwar multilateral system or at least to modify it to suit particular national preferences. Second, at the unit level, other observers argued that protectionist forces within the United States were eroding domestic political support for the liberal economic regime. It is to these challenges that we now turn, beginning with systemic stresses.

UNIPOLARITY AND THE WORLD ECONOMY

In his *Theory of International Politics*, it is revealing that Kenneth Waltz opened the chapter on "Structural Causes and Economic Effects" with the sentence, "How should we count poles, and how can we measure power?"[24] He asked this, of course, because of his argument that international political structures varied according to the number of great powers in the system. His answer, not altogether scientific, was that states entered the "top rank" according to "how they score on *all* of the following items: size of population and territory, resource endowment, economic capability, military strength, political stability and competence."[25]

On this basis, it is accepted by many observers that today's international political structure is "unipolar," with America's unique set of material and cultural (or "soft") capabilities allowing it to achieve its preferred outcomes in the military and diplomatic if not economic spheres (though Schweller raises some interesting questions about the nature of polarity in his essay).[26] What remains disputed are the long-term consequences of this "unipolar moment" for world politics. Are we entering a prolonged period of peace and stability under American hegemony? Or are new challengers to American predominance on the rise?[27]

Here we find no common view. In a widely cited essay, Christopher Layne argues that America's unipolar moment must be ephemeral as smaller states inevitably balance against it, leading to a new multipolar era after 2000.[28] In a powerful rejoinder, however, Paul Schroeder warns us against assuming that historical patterns—like the alleged recurrence of balancing against hegemonic powers—will necessarily repeat themselves.[29] Still others, apparently including American policymakers, believe that at least the economic world is multipolar; for example, President Clinton proclaimed at the Tokyo summit in July 1993 that we now live in "a tripolar world, driven by the Americas, by Europe, and by Asia."[30]

But the President was unduly flattering to America's allies. The fact is that the United States remains by far the single largest and most influential actor in the international economy. Indeed, making this same point in 1985, after an alleged decade of hegemonic decline, Bruce Russett observed that the United States still had the world's largest gross national product, military expenditures, and manufacturing production.[31] That still remains the case. In 1993 the U.S. had a gross national product of $6.3 trillion; its closest competitor, Japan, had a GNP of $4.2 trillion. It is the largest exporter and importer; in fact, its share of world exports (12 percent) is the same today as it was during the early 1980s. American military expenditures of $280 billion represented nearly half of what the entire world spent on defense, and more than the European Union, Russia, and China put together. The United States invested a similar percentage of the global total on research and development, and its high technology industries continue to dominate in such areas as computer science and genetic engineering, not to mention in a wide array of military-related fields like stealth technology. Similarly, its industrial output has remained the world's largest, staying ahead of Japan's.

By other indices, the United States is also dominant. For example, its stock market capitalization in 1993 of $5.2 trillion was nearly twice the Japanese level, and more than ten times that of Germany![32] Further, the dollar remains the international reserve currency of choice, and in every single country with a currency board system (e.g. Hong Kong and Argentina) the dollar provides the monetary base.

The dominance of the American economy is all the more remarkable in light of the widespread judgment of only a few years ago that its performance was dismal and its decline irreversible; today, in contrast, the United States is generally regarded as resurgent. As Ernest Preeg points out, "the widespread pessimism of only two to three years ago about being surpassed by Japan is greatly muted. Leading-edge developments . . . are firmly concentrated in the United States." He argues that to the extent U.S. "hi-tech" firms face any serious competition (and it should be noted that several such firms hold near global monopoly positions in their sectors), "their rivals are American."[33] Between 1986 and 1992, Preeg observes, the U.S. trade balance in high technology more than doubled, and American exports during the 1990s have increased at an average rate of 13 percent per year.

Following hegemonic stability theory, we would expect these capabilities to serve the United States in advancing its agenda of what was once called "free multilateralism." From this perspective, it would be puzzling if the trade and financial systems evolved in a way that was clearly at odds with Washington's preferences; that is, toward closure rather than openness. This does not mean that the United States can or will dictate solutions to every problem; indeed, such a strategy might not be attractive to a liberal hegemon even if it were conceivable. It simply means that trade and financial relations will generally be consistent with the American view of how the international system ought to function.

Despite the growing scholarly attention devoted to regionalism, a few recent examples suggest that the global economy continues to evolve in an American-led direction. Perhaps of greatest prominence, the United States played a leading role in completing the Uruguay Round of trade talks, and the subsequent creation of the World Trade Organization (WTO) in 1994. The transformation of the GATT into the WTO—a topic still relatively unexplored by students of international political economy—is especially notable because of the strengthened dispute settlement mechanisms created in the new organization. This revised mechanism reflected American concerns about the former system. According to one report, "As the most frequent user of the dispute settlement mechanism, the United States often found the old system ineffective and slow. Despite reports in favor of the United States, other countries often refused to adopt panel decisions or to fully implement their obligations. The new mechanism, strongly supported by the United States, will enable more rapid and enforceable resolution of trade disputes."[34]

On other trade fronts, through its regional agreements in North America (NAFTA) and Asia-Pacific (APEC), the United States has sought to open markets long closed by protectionist forces. These developments suggest not a return to the bloc-oriented economies of the 1930s, as some have feared, but an unprecedented opening of the world to trade and investment—one that goes well beyond that achieved by Great Britain during its hegemonic period in the nineteenth century. And it should not be assumed that Washington is continuing to assume the leadership role of market-opening for path-dependent historical or liberal ideological reasons: it is also because American industries are as competitive today as at any time in recent memory.[35]

Another example of America's dominant role is provided by international finance, allegedly the most global and anational of economic realms. Yet the development of a more liberal financial regime during the 1980s was "the result of deliberate political decisions," in which the United States instigated liberalization by substantially deregulating its own domestic marketplace and then seeking market openings overseas. Far from creating a "borderless" world for finance, however, the United States insisted on the creation of a new *international* regulatory structure based on the concept of "home country control" of financial institutions, culminating in the 1988 Basle Accord on bank capital adequacy (the Basle Accord sets a single international capital adequacy standard for all major banking institutions). According to one recent study of the international financial regime, "the US Federal Reserve Board has been instrumental in developing initiatives in respect to (international) governance and regulation."[36]

With respect to crisis management, the United States also retains a unique position in systemic maintenance. The debt crisis of 1982 provides only the most obvious case where American resources were mobilized on behalf of the global financial structure. A more recent example is provided by the Mexican peso collapse of late 1994 and early 1995. As the U.S. Council on Economic Advisers wrote in a recent report, "The President responded swiftly to Mexico's crisis, leading a $50 billion multilateral effort to assist in Mexico's stabilization and making available $20 billion in U.S. credit. This effort helped attenuate the impact of the crisis on other emerging markets."[37]

Similar actions were taken by the United States and the International Monetary Fund during the Asian financial meltdown of 1997–98, which also prevented its global spread. In fact, while most Asian stock and bond markets fell to record lows during this period, the Dow Jones Industrial Average reached record highs, while long-term interest rates on U.S. treasury bonds reached their lowest levels in a generation. Incredibly, despite its immediate interest in the Asian crisis, given the exposure of its banks to such countries as Thailand and Indonesia, and its foreign investment and trade relations in the region, Japan acted like a deer caught in a car's headlights, seemingly incapable of action. Nor can it be argued that Japan lacked the resources to quell the crisis; despite its ongoing recession, it remains a wealthy country, holding among the largest foreign exchange reserves in the world. The Asian case shows clearly that, even where a potential "challenger" to its hegemony would seem to exist, crisis management remains the un-contested domain of the United States.

Given this American economic juggernaut, the important question for scholars is not why Washington is continuing to promote free trade and global finance, but how the rest of the world is responding. Are states trying to balance against that overwhelming force, or are they bandwagoning with it? Are any visible challengers to the United States yet visible on the horizon?

New Challenges?

It has been said of the British Empire that it was like a Model T Ford; easy to build and cheap to run. Perhaps this is what the postwar leaders had in mind as they designed the new, American-led international economy. Yet the British Empire ultimately collapsed. What threats now exist to the American order?

The most popular challenger in recent years, of course, has allegedly been Japan. While now somewhat passe in light of that country's severe financial difficulties (certainly not aided by American exchange rate and banking regulation policies), it is still instructive to consider this case for the theoretical illumination it provides. Indeed, it provides an excellent example of unit and systemic-level analyses becoming confounded, for even if Japan had *wanted* to overturn or disrupt the American-dominated order, the distribution of power would stand in the way of its domestic desires and actual international outcomes.

A good example of such exaggeration of Japanese power is found in an essay by Samuel Huntington. Huntington argues that Japan "has been and is, constantly, operating in classic realist fashion to increase its power, but only in the economic area. In the new world environment, however, economic power is what counts."[38] And speaking at Princeton University, he asserted that "America and Japan are engaged in an economic cold war . . . [and] Japan has been doing better than we in that war."[39] He calls Japan an "economic power-maximizing state."

Japan, however, lacks at least two essential ingredients for a potential economic power-maximizer; first, the ability to link economic and military power to advance national interests; second, a sufficiently large internal market to shape the behavior of its principal trading partners. To the extent that a state wishes to shape international economic outcomes, it may have to rely implicitly or explicitly on a variety of instruments, military power among them. Protection of trade routes and oil flows come to mind in this respect.[40]

Second, in contrast to the United States, Japan does not control a sufficiently large or dynamic domestic market for goods and services to give it monopsonistic power in world trade. Time and again the United States has successfully threatened closure of its marketplace in an effort to advance special or national interests in international economic negotiations. So long as the United States remains the world's biggest market for traded goods and services, it will have substantial leverage over its commercial partners (but here, watch out for China).[41] Ironically, Japan's alleged strategy of generating trade surpluses only undermines its international power in terms of its ability to exercise market leverage. Yet the Japanese-American relationship points to the strengths of the postwar order as much as its weaknesses. Despite their unbalanced trade relationship, and occasional periods of acrimony, U.S.-Japan bilateral disputes have never spilled over to the wider trading arena. Further, the U.S.-Japan security relationship has not only remained shielded, but it has actually retained its primacy, even with the collapse of the Soviet Union.

In contrast to Huntington, I would argue that, far from losing an "economic cold war" with Japan, the United States remains by far the world's largest and most powerful economy, where power is defined in terms of the ability to shape international outcomes.[42] Japan, in contrast, is struggling; the *Wall Street Journal* is close to the mark when its editorial page writes, "Today's Japan is not the economic powerhouse that gripped the conventional wisdom five years ago. Instead, it is the most fragile major member of an interdependent world economy."[43]

Ironically, what is missing from many accounts of Japan's economic strategy is the fundamental insight of structural realism: that the structure of world politics, with its given distribution of power, intervenes between national policies and international outcomes. This means that we need to examine not only the stated goals of Japanese economic policy, but also the results of the country's international interactions.

From a systemic perspective, I would suggest that the end of the Cold War has placed Japan in a delicate position, for it is now more vulnerable to U.S. economic pressure than it was in the past. At the same time, the United States is more likely to use such pressure against its allies. Further, new regional powers—chiefly China—threaten Japan's economic and security position in East Asia. All told, Japan faces an increasingly inhospitable international environment. Japan's contemporary challenge is hardly the achievement of regional hegemony, but rather the maintenance of its status as a relatively prosperous and secure nation-state.

As noted above, Huntington and other scholars assert that Japan has adopted a power-oriented or neomercantilist trade policy. Perhaps the most prominent regional expert associated with this view is Chalmers Johnson, whose work has been widely influential. In a recent article, Johnson argued that Japan is "a mercantilist trading state . . . Japan assuredly has a grand strategy . . . The essence of the strategy is to build in the Asia-Pacific region a new version of the Greater East Asia Co-Prosperity Sphere."[44] While he does not explicitly address the question of how the Japanese have implemented this strategy, or what they hope to gain from it, presumably he believes that Tokyo sees long-term economic and political benefits from becoming a regional hegemon. Unfortunately, he fails to tell us why a country which has allegedly been so successful at "free-riding" would wish to change places and assume hegemonic burdens.[45]

In the event, the essays in this volume by Eric Heginbotham and Richard Samuels, and by Joseph Grieco, provide a contending perspective. Heginbotham and Samuels report that, with respect to the internal Japanese debate over "the economic and political organization of East Asia, the America-first camp has prevailed."[46] Grieco similarly tells us that since 1991 every Japanese prime minister has refused to support any East Asian economic initiative that excluded the United States. He writes that "Japan was highly disinclined to pursue regionalist policies during the Cold War, and this has not changed since 1989." He suggests this is largely because "since the late 1980s, Japan has faced a . . . serious array of security challenges" in the region.[47]

Again, since Japan is sometimes viewed as a potential regional hegemon, we ought to remind ourselves of what this role entails before dismissing it as a possibility. For Gilpin, hegemony requires control over the "three sources of power in the modern world: nuclear weapons, monetary reserves, and petroleum."[48] Similarly, Robert Keohane has suggested that in order to play the hegemon a state must control, in addition to military power, a "preponderance of material resources. Four sets of resources are especially important. Hegemonic powers must have control over raw materials, control over sources of capital, control over markets, and competitive advantages in the production of highly valued goods."[49]

These analyses suggest that Japan lacks several of the crucial ingredients required to play the hegemon. In terms of military power, although Japan has by far the largest defense budget in Asia, it currently lacks the power projection capabilities required to maintain the sea lanes and freedom of navigation; and of course (unlike China and India) it does not possess nuclear weapons. Second, Japan is dependent on imports for nearly all its energy, food (it is the world's largest importer of foodstuffs), and raw materials—and its last attempt to seize control over these resources ultimately met with military disaster.

What is still open to question is whether Japan "controls" a large enough market to exercise anything like hegemonic power, if only at the regional level. Grieco argues that "Japan enjoys a much more pronounced overall hegemonic power in East Asia than does Germany in Western Europe," but this analysis only reflects trade flows. Here it must be recalled that an important source of German economic power in Europe flows from the position of the Bundesbank as the arbiter of monetary policy, a position that the Bank of Japan has not achieved (or even sought) in East Asia (again, hegemonic stability theory emphasizes the importance of monetary resources). If anything, the inability of Japan to respond to the financial crisis in its very backyard reminds us of Tokyo's international weakness.

Far from challenging the United States, Japan has worked hard to maintain and strengthen its bilateral alliance. As Michael Mastanduno emphasizes in his contribution to this volume, there is no evidence that it has engaged in a strategy of external balancing, and there is no indication that it is preparing to do so. This is not only because the United States remains a necessary ally in a dangerous neighborhood, but also because the U.S. market remains the single most important to that now fragile economy.

If Japan has any fear, it is of a renewed trade dispute with the United States as its external surplus again hits record levels in the face of a prolonged domestic recession. As *The Economist* has written: "Japan's . . . diplomats worry that trade friction will undermine America's commitment to defend Japan. This anxiety has only increased in the aftermath of the Cold War."[50]

It appears that analysts are now recognizing Japanese weakness in the international system, and fears of a Japanese challenge to American hegemony have largely receded in recent years. But they have been replaced by the supposed "threat" now emanating from China. China is a continental county with the world's largest population and fastest-growing economy. It is, in Samuel Huntington's phrase, a unique "civilization." It is investing in its military power and intimidating its neighbors. It has an abysmal human rights record. Isn't China priming to establish its own sphere of influence in Asia, and one that could be hostile to the United States?[51]

Such an evolution is unlikely. For as China continues to grow, it is also becoming increasingly dependent on the world economy for needed inputs. As James Shinn of the Council on Foreign Relations writes, "the Chinese economy depends on international markets for two of the essential factors for economic growth, capital and technology, as well as two critical commodities, petroleum and food grains. This external market dependence is increasing at a remarkable rate."[52]

Shinn argues that the "tyranny of markets" will force China to adopt more moderate political behavior. Capital markets, for example, "are not eager to deal with belligerent states, and firms that would otherwise be eager to invest in China and transfer their technology can get cold feet." And from a domestic political perspective, "the tyranny of markets is unleashing a host of forces within China that bolster the market access principle."[53] The source of that global "tyranny"? The American-designed liberal economy, with the pressure it is placing on trade and financial policies. If a country as large as China now finds that it must play by the rules of the game if it is to succeed economically, what other challengers to the United States could possibly exist?

If it is true that China has powerful incentives to respect the international economic system in order to maintain access to needed inputs, the big question then revolves around the United States and whether it will allow China to become a player on equal terms. Political forces within the United States wish to deny that country its MFN status as punishment for its human rights record and for its proliferation of military technology. The Clinton Administration, however, has remained in favor of MFN for China, recently approving renewal of that status.

This trade debate is consequential. As Dale Copeland argues, it is a country's expectation of *future* trade opportunities that plays a vital role in its calculation of whether to maintain peaceful relations with its partners and neighbors or seek military solutions to its economic requirements. He writes that "for any expected value of war, we can predict that the lower the expectations of future trade, the lower the expected value of trade, and therefore the more likely it is that war will be chosen."[54] In short, the liberalization policy is prudent in the Chinese context.

What about Russia? By all accounts, the honeymoon between Moscow and Washington has ended, despite President Clinton's active support of Boris Yeltsin's re-election. Russia has not only waged a brutal war in Chechnya, it has increasingly thrown its weight around in the near abroad. Indeed, with the proposed confederation between Russian and Belarus, parts of the Soviet empire appear to be reemerging.

Yet Russia is far from providing the sort of global challenge to the United States that the Soviet Union once did. As Neil MacFarlane writes, "Although the economic performance of the Soviet Union . . . left much to be desired . . . the USSR nonetheless was the center of one of two competing economic systems in the global economy. . . . The position collapsed in 1991 with the implosion of the Soviet state. . . . Russia is now substantially dependent on Western financial resources to stabilize its budget, and resuscitate its economic base."[55] Further, those states that once constituted the Council for Mutual Economic Assistance (CMEA) are even more dependent on western capital, technology and markets than Russia is. This makes it impossible for Russia to exercise anything like economic hegemony over its former empire.

This leaves, then, the European Union as perhaps the greatest potential — if not actual — challenger to the American economic order. The EU boasts a greater population and than the United States and similar level of GNP, and it is a major trading power which will soon have a single currency. While not a federal state, the EU does negotiate as a single actor in many economic settings, such as the trade rounds. Indeed, EU opposition to proposed agricultural liberalization doomed that initiative in the Uruguay Round.

Yet the EU also has glaring weaknesses that prevent it from challenging the United States as leader or even co-director of the world economy. Most obviously, Michael Loriaux reminds us that from a realist perspective, it does not have a unified foreign or defense policy, missions that remain under national jurisdiction. It is incapable of protecting its trading routes and oil supplies, as demonstrated during the Gulf War, much less maintaining the peace in its own backyard, as in the former Yugoslavia. In fact, neither the EU as a whole nor any of its constituent states have any independent power projection capability. To the extent that the global economic system still needs a military foundation, the EU certainly is not in a position to provide it.

In sum, the United States has no international challengers to its position as the leader of the international economy it built after World War II, and which it still maintains through its contributions to the major international institutions, and through the openness of its marketplace. Countries that need balance-of-payments support must go to the IMF, and those that wish to become full members of the trading system must seek membership in the WTO. Companies that seek to become world-class must enter the American marketplace, which continues to serve as the testbed for almost every good and service imaginable. Further, the dynamic American financial system provides most of the world's venture capital to those start-up companies that will become the future leaders in their respective sectors. Any country or group of countries that would challenge this American-dominated order face enormous systemic pressures, and there is little evidence that balancing against the United States is in fact emerging anywhere in the world. To the contrary, the global economy has become an enormous bandwagon, as more and more countries seek to join the international marketplace.

GLOBALIZATION AND AMERICAN POWER

How are these same economic forces affecting the United States? Students of hegemonic stability theory have traditionally been pessimistic about the hegemon's ability to maintain its relative position. As Robert Gilpin has written, "The unleashing of market forces transforms the political framework itself, undermines the hegemonic power, and creates a new political environment to which the world must eventually adjust. With the inevitable shift in the international distribution of economic and military power from the core to rising nations in the periphery and elsewhere, the capacity of the hegemon to maintain the system decreases. Capitalism and the market system thus tend to destroy the political foundations on which they must ultimately depend."[56]

Economic theory would seem to provide some support for the view that unfettered international market development—globalization—will itself undermine the unipolar structure of the world economy. If we accept that the economies of the great powers are becoming increasingly interdependent in trade and finance, then there are a number of "convergence hypotheses" that we must take seriously. Taken to their logical extreme, these could mean that economic integration itself will lead to a change in the international distribution of power, from unipolarity to multipolarity. These include hypotheses about the effects of trade and the spread of technology on productivity and domestic wage rates, and the effects of capital market integration on monetary policy and interest rates. Paul Samuelson's theory of "factor price equalization," for example, suggests that trade between countries A and B will lead the wages in each country toward convergence. In short, as integration proceeds, we should expect to see such economic variables as productivity levels, wages, interest rates, and ultimately growth rates converging toward some common values.[57]

For a structural realist like Waltz, in which systemic stability is a function of polarity, this growing equality would not be a good thing for the existing distribution of power and thus the chances for world peace. As he has written, "extreme equality is associated with instability. . . . The inequality of states, though it provides no guarantee, at least makes peace and stability possible."[58] Of course, convergence in economic performance would not in itself make all states equal, since most of them would not possess the other capabilities (e.g. population, military forces, "competence") needed to reach the "top rank" of great powers. However, to the extent that economic power provides the foundation for military power, it would mean that a growing number of states could conceivably acquire sophisticated conventional and nonconventional weapons, including weapons of mass destruction.

In a truly global economy we would also have to question the inherent advantages of national "size" that Waltz discussed. He observed, for example, that the size of the American domestic marketplace gave its producers the capacity to "operate on a large scale and to generate resources that can be used abroad to compete with or to overwhelm native industries. . . . The disadvantages of foreign firms relate directly to the smaller scale of their national economies."[59] On this basis he suggested that only such continental countries as Russia and China (one could add India and a truly unified Europe to the list), with their large domestic markets, could ever pose an economic challenge to the United States.

The question is whether this size advantage would still be consequential in a truly global economy, a world that was borderless from the transactions perspective. After all, if enterprises had equally open access to all markets, the distinction between "domestic" and "foreign" would be limited to a matter of differing cultures (in terms of language and tastes) rather than governments. To be sure, culture could constitute an important barrier to trade, but presumably another element of globalization—and one that is particularly threatening to many countries from France to Iran—is the increasing uniformity of tastes, as generated in Hollywood, on Madison Avenue, and at McDonald's *Hamburger University*.

In the event, we remain far from such a world, and the evidence points to the continuing importance of the domestic marketplace for even the largest firms.[60] A recent study of the activities of multinational corporations (MNCs), for example, concludes that they "still rely upon their 'home base' as the center of their economic activities, despite all the speculation about globalization."[61] This, incidentally, is as true of European-based firms as it is for those based in the United States and Japan. Even in finance, the penetration of foreigners into domestic markets is slight. For example, for the eleven largest members of the Organization of Economic Co-operation and Development (OECD), only 15 percent of outstanding domestic bonds were held by foreigners.[62]

A study of the data would suggest that American economic performance since 1945 appears to refute the grim predictions of hegemonic stability theory, which in its traditional variants did not admit the possibility of hegemonic regeneration. But alternative theories offer more optimistic prospects. Raymond Vernon's "product cycle theory," for example, suggests that firms can remain ahead of their competitors so long as they continue to invest in leading-edge research and development. The theory posits that every new technology goes through a three-stage development: (1) introduction of the technology or new product; (2) maturation and domestic market saturation; (3) product and process standardization. In each of these phases, different economies will possess differing comparative advantages. A country that has an advantage in initial innovation, for example, may not keep it when the product and process become standardized.[63] Vernon's lesson was that firms should keep investing in R&D and continually generate new technologies if they wish to stay ahead.

By way of analogy, this theory suggests the possibility for states to avoid inevitable decline by promoting those investments that provide the underlying conditions for ongoing national innovation. Investing in education, research, and infrastructure would seem to be among the most useful targets for national policy. While the United States clearly has a mixed record in this regard, in several areas it remains well ahead of any challengers. The American research university, for example, has no serious global competitors, and I have already noted that U.S. spending on research and development is about half the world total. The point is that hegemonic stability theory may have been unduly pessimistic, confounding a natural degree of relative decline (e.g. American decline between 1945—when the rest of the world was in ruins—and 1970) with a trend toward collapse.

Still, when we focus on the *domestic* conditions necessary for international leadership, there are plenty of reasons for pause in the American case. After all, pressures on a system can also come from the inside. As the leaders of the G-7 said at Lyon, "the development of a more global economy and advances in information technology are engines of economic growth and prosperity. But they also may be seen by some as a source of dislocation and insecurity."[64] The domestic concern of these elected officials is to ensure that the political voice of the "haves" continues to dominate the debate over liberalization.

Decreasing support for globalization and the policies it requires for support is as evident in the United States as in any other industrial country. As Michael Mastanduno writes, "How long domestic constraints will permit U.S. officials to pursue a comprehensive strategy is an open question."[65] James Kurth concurs, suggesting that it is unlikely that the United States can continue to act as the world's leader in the absence of a credible threat to its national security.[66]

Indeed, in countries around the world there is a rising risk of backlash by voters against the process of economic globalization. Double-digit unemployment in Europe and rising income inequality and job insecurity in the United States are hardly conducive to sustained political support for trade and financial liberalization, while in East Asia, once the poster child of globalization, whole populations now face a return to poverty. But in the context of shrinking government budgets everywhere, a phenomenon that is also a product of the global pressures unleashed by mobile capital, it is difficult to launch new programs that might help working people cope with economic change.[67]

Domestic politics is thus the global economy's achilles heel, for should voters turn against globalization—as may be happening in many places around the globe, including the United States—the postwar liberalization project could be in for a jolt. After all, the "foundation for American leadership in the Bretton Woods system . . . was the most productive and competitive industrial economy in the world, and the high employment, economic prosperity, and social cohesion that were the result. Without these, there would not have been the political consensus necessary to sustain American leadership."[68] That consensus may be breaking down, since there are increasing doubts about the distribution of globalization's benefits. If liberalization only makes the rich richer and the poor poorer, it will inevitably produce rising social strains everywhere it is advanced.

Yet despite these tensions, social disruption aimed at stopping globalization has thus far been minimal; nowhere in the world is there evidence of a profound "backlash" against liberalization. If anything, the multilateral structure of trade and finance built by the United States and its allies has not only endured but even prospered in the post-Soviet era, as the formerly communist states seek to join it as "members," and as China and East Asia continue to focus on an export orientation in their economic policy. There are certainly stresses in that system, but we must ask whether these are profound and destabilizing, or episodic. For now we can conclude the latter, since there is really no alternative available to the American-dominated multilateral system. And in the absence of alternatives, it is difficult to overturn the status quo.

CONCLUSIONS

Realism, it is said, presents an essentially pessimistic view of world politics. Security is scarce in the anarchic international environment, leading states to engage in economic and military competitions that must inevitably lead to conflict and war. With the collapse of the stable bipolar system, the world has entered a new, uncertain era, one that could prove more dangerous than anything we have known since World War II.

This essay presents a contending vision, drawn from insights generated by hegemonic stability theory. By focusing on the distribution of power at the systemic level, I have tried to show that there really are no obvious alternatives to the American-dominated economic structure that now governs international trade, finance and investment. Japan has shown no interest in rebuilding an Asian co-prosperity sphere, while China is becoming increasingly dependent on world markets. Russia is an economic pygmy that needs capital, technology, and food from the West, while it must export its energy and raw materials to earn desperately needed hard currency. The EU is not a unified actor in foreign or security policy and lacks military capability.

Why is this vision of the world economy seemingly so different from that presented by other self-defined realists? I would offer two answers. First, by focusing on the role of the external Soviet threat in building and maintaining the postwar economic order, they overlook the transcendent importance of the multilateral institutions established after World War II. These were designed not solely to promote Western military security, but Western prosperity as well. So long as they contribute to that process better than any alternative arrangement, they will endure.

Second, by devaluing American power, they fail to appreciate the unique position the country still holds in the international system; a focus on the outcomes of international economic interactions remains illuminating in this regard. The United States is far from a normal state; no country in modern history has ever held such overwhelming power across so many dimensions. It not only possesses the single largest, wealthiest, and most dynamic market for every good and service imaginable, but is also home to the world's strongest military forces. Its culture is incredibly dynamic, as it opens its doors to the best and brightest from every continent. In short, despite growing domestic doubts about the role, it remains the hegemonic power.

This state of affairs should be welcomed by those countries that seek to play by the rules of the game and liberalize their economies, but it's certainly bad for any would-be challengers. Those countries that seek to protect their domestic marketplace, perhaps for extremely valid political or cultural reasons, will find the pursuit of such policies extremely costly. Yet balancing against the United States is not a likely outcome, since in economic terms there is no good alternative to the American order, while in military terms it spends as much on defense as the rest of the world combined.

From all this, one can only conclude that the American century has just begun. How long it endures will be a function of whether an alternative form of political economy emerges that is capable of mobilizing widespread support. Policymakers would do well to pay greater attention to that distant possibility, by ensuring that the benefits that come with "free multilateralism" are widely distributed.

NOTES

1. Kapstein, "Is Realism Dead? The Domestic Sources of International Politics," *International Organization* 49 (Autumn 1995): 751–774.
2. See, for example, the essays in Richard Ned Lebow and Thomas Riss-Kappen,

eds., *International Relations Theory and the End of the Cold War* (New York: Columbia University Press, 1995).

3. Russett, "Processes of Dyadic Choice for War and Peace," *World Politics* 47 (January 1995), p. 269.

4. See Mark Kramer, "Realism, Nuclear Proliferation, and East-Central European Strategies," this volume.

5. For an earlier essay with a similar perspective, see Bruce Russett, "The Mysterious Case of Vanishing Hegemony; or, is Mark Twain Really Dead?" *International Organization* 39 (Spring 1985): 207–231.

6. Huntington, "Why International Primacy Matters," in Sean Lynn-Jones and Steven Miller, eds., *The Cold War and After: Prospects for Peace* (Cambridge, Ma.: MIT Press, 1993), 310–311.

7. Schweller, "Realism and the Present Great-Power System: Growth and Positional Conflict over Scarce Resources," this volume.

8. Salvatore, "Protectionism and World Welfare," in Salvatore, ed., *Protectionism and World Welfare* (New York: Cambridge University Press, 1993), 1.

9. C. Fred Bergsten, "Globalizing Free Trade," *Foreign Affairs* 75 (May/June 1996): 106.

10. Kirshner, "The Political Economy of Realism."

11. See, for example, Kenichi Ohmae, *The End of the Nation-State* (New York: Free Press, 1995).

12. I thank Michael Mastanduno for emphasizing this point.

13. See Charles P. Kindleberger, *The World in Depression* (Berkele: University of California Press, 1973).

14. Robert Gilpin, *The Political Economy of International Relations* (Princeton: Princeton University Press, 1987), 72.

15. Robert Keohane, *After Hegemony* (Princeton: Princeton University Press, 1984).

16. See, for example, Russett, "The Mysterious Case," and Susan Strange, "Still an Extraordinary Power: America's Role in a Global Monetary System," in Raymond Lombra and William Witte, eds., *Political Economy of International and Domestic Monetary Relations* (Ames, Iowa: Iowa State University Press, 1982), cited in Russett, "The Mysterious Case."

17. Russett, "The Mysterious Case," 208.

18. Mastanduno, *Economic Containment* (Ithaca: Cornell University Press, 1992), 89.

19. Woodrow Wilson Foundation and National Planning Association, *The Political Economy of American Foreign Policy* (New York: Greenwood, 1968; orig. 1955), 47.

20. Finlayson and Zacher, "The GATT and the Regulation of Trade Barriers," in Stephen D. Krasner, ed., *International Regimes* (Ithaca: Cornell University Press, 1983), 298.

21. "Economic Communique," G-7 Summit, Lyons, France, 28 June, 1996.

22. See, most prominently, John Mearsheimer, "The False Promise of International Institutions," in Michael Brown, Sean Lynn-Jones, and Steven Miller, eds., *The Perils of Anarchy* (Cambridge: MIT Press, 1995), 332–76.

23. Deudney and Ikenberry, "Realism, Structural Liberalism, and the Western Order," this volume.

24. Waltz, *Theory of International Politics* (New York: Random House, 1979), 129.

25. Waltz, *Theory of International Politics*, 131.

26. On America's "soft power," see Joseph Nye, *Bound to Lead* (New York: Basic Books, 1992).

27. For the debate over unipolarity, see Sean Lynn-Jones and Steven Miller, eds., *The Cold War and After: Prospects for Peace* (Cambridge: MIT Press, 1993).

28. Layne, "The Unipolar Illusion: Why New Great Powers Will Rise," in Lynn-Jones and Miller, *The Cold War and After*: 244–90.

29. Schroeder, "Historical Reality vs. Neo-realist Theory," *International Security* 19 (Summer 1994): 108–148.

30. Cited by Schweller, this volume.

31. Russett, "The Mysterious Case," 212.

32. See *Statistical Abstracts of the United States: 1995* (Washington, DC: Government Printing Office, 1995).

33. Preeg, "Who's Benefiting Whom? A Trade Agenda for High-Technology Industries," in Brad Roberts, *New Forces in the World Economy* (Cambridge: MIT Press, 1996), 147.

34. Jim Sanford," World Trade Organization Opens Global Markets, Protects U.S. Rights," *Business America* (January 1995): 5.

35. For a review of these developments, see Ernest Preeg, "The Post-Uruguay Round Free Trade Debate," in Roberts, *New Forces in the World Economy*, 79–91.

36. Hirst and Thompson, *Globalization in Question*, 131; see also Kapstein, *Governing the Global Economy: International Finance and the State* (Cambridge: Harvard University Press, 1994).

37. U.S. Council of Economic Advisers, *Economic Report to the President: 1996*, box 8–5.

38. Huntington, "Economic Renewal," p. 16.

39. Huntington, "Economic Power in International Relations," (Princeton Center for International Studies, Research Program in International Security, Monograph Series No. 1, 1993), p. 12. See also Huntington, "Why International Primacy Matters," *International Security* 17 (4) (Spring 1993): 68–83.

40. Quoted in Ethan B. Kapstein, *The Insecure Alliance: Energy Crises and Western Politics since 1944* (New York: Oxford University Press, 1990), 174.

41. On U.S. threats to close its domestic banking market to foreign competitors, see Ethan B. Kapstein, *Governing the Global Economy: International Finance and the State* (Cambridge: Harvard University Press, 1994).

42. For a comparative analysis of international competitiveness, based on several different statistical measures, see The Economist, "Survey: The Global Economy," p. 46, October 1, 1994.

43. "Japan, Eek," *The Wall Street Journal Europe*, June 1, 1995, 6.

44. Chalmers Johnson, "The State and Japanese Grand Strategy," in Richard Rosecrance and Arthur Stein, eds., *The Domestic Bases of Grand Strategy* (Ithaca, NY: Cornell Univ. Press, 1993), 216.

45. See, for example, Peter Katzenstein's discussion of Japan in "Conclusion: Domestic Structures and Strategies of Foreign Economic Policy," in Katzenstein, ed., *Between Power and Plenty* (Madison: University of Wisconsin Press, 1978), 313 ff.

46. Heginbotham and Samuels, "Mercantile Realism and Japanese Foreign Policy," this volume.

47. Grieco, "Realism and Regionalism: American Power and German and Japanese Institutional Strategies During and After the Cold War," this volume.

48. Robert Gilpin, *U.S. Power and the Multinational Corporation* (New York: Basic Books, 1975),103–4.

49. Keohane, *After Hegemony.*

50. The Economist, "Japan Gives Its Answer," May 13, 1995, 63.

51. James Kurth raises interesting questions about U.S. policy toward regional spheres of influence in his article, "American Grand Strategy."

52. Shinn, "Conditional Engagement with China," in Shinn, ed., *Weaving the Net: Conditional Engagement with China* (New York: Council on Foreign Relations, 1996), 35.

53. Shinn, "Conditional Engagement," 37–38.

54. Copeland, "Economic Interdependence and War: A Theory of Trade Expectations, *International Security* 20 (Spring 1996): 19.

55. MacFarlane, "Realism and Russian Strategy after the Collapse of the USSR," this volume.

56. Gilpin, *Political Economy*, 77–78.

57. On these convergence hypotheses, see James R. Golden, "Economics and National Strategy," in Brad Roberts, ed., *New Forces in the World Economy* (Cambridge: MIT Press, 1996), 15–37.

58. Waltz, *Theory of International Politics*, 132.

59. Waltz, *Theory of International Politics*, 149.

60. For further elaboration of this point, see Ethan B. Kapstein, "We are US!: The Myth of the Multinational," *The National Interest* (Winter 1991/92): 55–62.

Kenneth Waltz made a similar argument years earlier in "The Myth of National Interdependence," in Charles P. Kindleberger, ed., *The International Corporation* (Cambridge: MIT Press, 1974).

61. Paul Hirst and Grahame Thompson, *Globalization in Question* (Cambridge: Polity Press, 1996), 95.

62. Hirst and Thompson, *Globalization in Question*, 42.

63. Raymond Vernon, "International Investment and International Trade in the Product Cycle," *Quarterly Journal of Economics* 80 (1966): 190–207.

64. G-7, "Economic Communique."

65. Mastanduno, "Security Engagement," this volume.

66. Kurth, "America's Grand Strategy."

67. For an elaboration of this point, see Ethan B. Kapstein, "Workers and the World Economy," *Foreign Affairs* (May/June 1995).

68. James Kurth, "America's Grand Strategy: A Pattern of History," *The National Interest* (Spring 1996), 18.

Index

Index by Alan Greenberg

economic regionalism and, 343; expansion of, 163; global trade and, 474; prospects for, 466; U.S. debate on, 18
North Asia, 145
North Atlantic Cooperation Council, 413, 422
North Atlantic Treaty (1949), 336
North Atlantic Treaty Organization: Andrejcak on, 460n178; Central Europe and, 251; Chinese-Russian relations and, 245; consultative arrangements in, 111; creation of, 17, 357; Eastern Europe and (*see under* Eastern Europe); European Defense Community and, 337; European integration and, 22, 378; France and, 16, 358, 365, 370, 373; German-Western relations and, 338, 351n55; Germany and (*see under* Germany); nuclear issue and, 393, 404–5; Posen-Ross study on, 177n72; prospects for, 103, 143; purposes of, 107, 153; reaffirmation of, 125–26; realist predictions on, 124; Russia and (*see under* Russia); Russian-Western relations and, 9, 21, 249–50; Soviet threat and, 392; *Study on NATO Enlargement*, 404, 459–60n174; Ukraine and, 418, 421, 422, 432, 437, 458n154; WEU and, 153, 176n63, 383n43; Yugoslavian conflict and, 154–55, 241–42, 243, 258n64, 368, 369; *see also* Partnership for Peace
North Atlantic Treaty Organization Council, 111
North Atlantic Treaty Organization Nuclear Planning Group, 404
North Caucasia, 227, 232
Northeast Asia, 143, 193

Northern Abyssinia, 50
Northern Territories (Kurile Islands), 246
North Korea: Chinese relations with, 273; Japanese relations with, 189; nonproliferation deal with, 19, 153, 160; nuclear aspirations of, 335–36, 431, 435; Russian balancing with, 229; U.S.-Japanese cooperation and, 193–94, 329
North Sea, 356
Norway, 360
Novorossiisk, 237, 239
Nuclear deterrence, 32, 173n25, 308n46, 426
Nuclear guarantees: credibility of, 392–93; neorealism on, 391; Poland and, 458n160; popularity of, 436; semisovereign states and, 150; Ukraine and, 434
Nuclear nonproliferation, 10, 13; Chinese-U.S. relations and, 156, 273; East-Central Europe and, 15, 385–463; semisovereign states and, 115; *see also* Non-Proliferation Treaty (1968)
Nuclear power stations, 416, 434
Nuclear Suppliers' Group, 401
Nuclear weapons: economic capabilities and, 158; international relations and, 36–37; Japanese security and, 153, 188, 193, 204–5; polarity and, 38; structural realism on, 423, 424–25, 435; war costs and, 11, 40; *see also under* China; Russia; United States
Nye, Joseph, 152, 155–56, 329
"Nye Report," 213n43

Ob River Basin, 257n58
Oder-Neisse border, 372